The

CURSE OF IGNORANCE

A History of Mankind

The

CURSE OF IGNORANCE

A History of Mankind

From primitive times to the end of the
Second World War

BY

ARTHUR FINDLAY

IN TWO VOLUMES

"Ignorance is the curse of God.   Knowledge is the wing wherewith
we fly to heaven."—Shakespeare

VOLUME ONE

THE HEADQUARTERS PUBLISHING CO. LTD.
5 Alexandria Road, West Ealing,
London, W13 ONP.

First Impression	1947
Second Impression	1947
Third Impression	1948
Fourth Impression	1948
Fifth Impression	1956
Sixth Impression	1963
Seventh Impression	1993

Arthur Findlay was the first to give a scientific explanation of death and the hereafter. This he did in his famous book On the Edge of the Etheric, and translated into 18 foreign languages. He was the first to make the etheric world comprehensible in terms of vibrations, and this he did in The Rock of Truth and The Unfolding Universe. He was the first to trace the origin of all world religions to psychic phenomena, and show that all religious beliefs, rituals and ceremonials had a psychic origin. This he did in The Psychic Stream. In The Curse of Ignorance he is the first to write world history from the psychic angle of thought, and this presents the past from a completely new and different aspect.

THE SPIRITUALISTS' NATIONAL UNION was left the copyright to all of Arthur Findlay's books, with the request to keep the titles in print. The SNU is the largest Spiritualist Church organisation in the UK. The SNU also owns the Arthur Findlay College at Stansted Hall.

The SNU is based at Redwoods, Stansted Hall, Stansted Mountfitchet, Essex, CM24 8UD.

All of the Arthur Findlay books are now published by one of the foremost publishers in the psychic sphere:-
THE HEADQUARTERS PUBLISHING COMPANY LIMITED.
Booksellers, publishers of books and two Spiritualists' monthly magazines "TWO WORLDS" and "HERE AND THERE".
5 Alexandria Road, West Ealing, London, W13 0NP.

THE ANN THOMPSON FUND The publishers are indebted to the Ann Thompson Fund for providing an interest free loan that enabled us to bring these two important volumes back into print. Hylton Thompson established the Ann Thompson fund in memory of his first wife, for the advancement of psychic science.

THE SERIES ISBN 0 947823 32 8
VOLUME 1 ISBN 0 947823 33 6

Printed and bound in Great Britain

ARTHUR FINDLAY'S BOOKS

THE CURSE OF IGNORANCE Arthur Findlay took seven years to finish this two volume work. It covers troubles that have beset mankind in the past and present. Past follies and achievements are recorded, acting as a guide and signpost to present and future generations. Only after reading these volumes will you realise the revolution in thought this work stands for.
VOL 1 ISBN 0 947828 33 6   VOL 2 ISBN 0 947828 34 4

THE PSYCHIC STREAM This book traces the origin of all world religions to psychic phenomena, and shows that all religious beliefs, rituals and ceremonials had a psychic origin.
ISBN 0 947828 31 X

ON THE EDGE OF THE ETHERIC Is the spirit world real and tangible? Do its inhabitants retain their individuality? Is it true that spirit people eat? What is the afterlife like? Do animals survive? All these questions are answered.   ISBN 0 9723 05 0

THE UNFOLDING UNIVERSE Arthur Findlay writes of a new era 'The days of faith are passing and the day of knowledge has arrived. Creeds, dogmas, ceremonials and rites must fade away in the light of the new knowledge.'   ISBN 0 947828 13 1

THE ROCK OF TRUTH It is not the social side of the Church's work that this book attacks, but orthodox Christianity as preached from nearly every pulpit in Christendom, and it is this which affects the great majority of the people.   ISBN 0 947823 04 1

LOOKING BACK Is Arthur Findlay's story. A truly remarkable, important and absorbing volume detailing the life, times and beliefs of one of the world's finest ever Spiritualists. ISBN 0 847823 17 4

THE WAY OF LIFE 'If I could only describe to you the lovely walks we have sometimes. There is no waste and no decay. The flowers just fade away. You never see them decay, and then fresh ones come in their place.' So said a woman who died and returned to tell of her continued existence.   ISBN 0 947823 06 9

WHERE TWO WORLDS MEET This book tells of nineteen seances Arthur Findlay attended with famous Glasgow direct voice medium John Sloan. All these literally hundreds of spirit communicators spoke. An expert stenographer took down everything said by the so-called dead.   ISBN 0 947823 07 7

THE HEADQUARTERS PUBLISHING CO.LTD.
5 ALEXANDRIA ROAD, WEST EALING,
LONDON W13 0NP

DEDICATED
TO ALL WHO HAVE DIED OR SUFFERED IN
THE CAUSE OF HUMAN FREEDOM
AND LIBERTY

CONTENTS

First Volume

Contents

*The Contents of Volume Two will be found at the end of this book,
and the Index to both volumes at the end of Volume Two.*

The dates given against the names of Emperors, Kings, Popes and Presidents refer to the year they commenced to rule and the year they gave up office, either by death, resignation, or because their term of office expired. The dates given after the names of Prime Ministers refer to their period of office. All other dates following personal names relate to the year of birth and the year of death. The dates below the heading of each chapter refer to the earliest and latest dates mentioned so far as they relate to the period under review.

FOREWORD.

The aim of this book is to increase knowledge, as only by education, along the path of what we know to be true, can ethical conduct the world over rise to a level which will bring to everyone security, peace, contentment, and happiness. Most of our troubles come from ignorance, and from lack of knowledge of how we all should live together wisely, happily and contented, free from sickness, poverty and war. As ignorance is the root of most of the misfortunes which beset us, nothing is more important than the increase of knowledge, because this leads to wisdom, the source of happiness.

Ignorance has been the curse of the human race, from the time our primitive ancestors evolved into the creature which we call man. Away back in the far distant past, the mind which controlled sub-man, then the most advanced of the animal species, decided that it would strike out along a path of its own, and leave the jungle for the open spaces, there to find sustenance for its physical habitation. By so doing it entered an uncharted sea, abounding with rocks and shoals on which it was for ever foundering, but, by leaving safety behind, and seeking danger, it developed until it reached the stage of civilised man. Had this urge for change and exploration been lacking, man would never have risen above the beast.

The course set by early man led him against repeated dangers which had to be overcome if he were to survive, and if he had not developed memory, which to him was his compass, he would have foundered and been destroyed. Fortunately, by remembering his past mistakes, he did not always repeat them, and thus mind developed and reasoned thought took the place of instinct. From the time of primitive man to the present day, millions upon millions of causes and effects have evolved the human mind to its present standard, countless millions of thoughts remembered having raised us to the position we now occupy in the realm of life this earth supports.

Beginning in the darkness of ignorance, mind has gradually won its way, to some degree, into the light of knowledge. Forever cursed by ignorance, the struggle has been slow and uncertain, and only by finally remembering repeated mistakes did the blackness of ignorance give place to the light of knowledge. There is, however, still a long road to travel before the goal is reached, as many past mistakes have not yet been sufficiently remembered to prevent their repetition. Much knowledge must yet be accumulated, and greater wisdom must still be acquired, before man can secure the state of harmony and happiness he longs to attain. His life is still surrounded by hidden rocks into which he continually blunders, as he cannot yet remember sufficiently well the wounds and bruises they have already caused him. His compass of memory is still far from perfect, and much greater knowledge and experience must yet come his way before the curse of ignorance is finally removed.

This book has been written to help, in some small degree, the further removal of this sinister failing which brings so much sorrow and trouble in its train. Its subject is the long, long story of man's upward climb from ignorance to knowledge, and its object is still further to increase knowledge, so that past mistakes may be remembered and not repeated. No better way can be found to remove our present troubles than by learning about the mistakes of our ancestors, of how many were remembered and not repeated, and of how those continually forgotten involved them in sorrow, suffering and disappointment.

Though experience has taught mankind much, and much has been remembered, one past evil experience is still being constantly forgotten, to his sorrow and impoverishment. Instead of learning that misery and poverty too often come from theft and the desire for domination, man still pursues the methods of his jungle ancestors who grabbed and fought to secure what they wanted. This human weakness is kept in check within each nation by the police and the law, but we have so far discovered no means to prevent one nation from using all its resources to conquer another which it wishes to subdue to its will and pleasure. Nevertheless there is a remedy, and it will be stressed in the pages which follow.

This age-old evil, which we call war, is still with us today, and never before has greater destruction, misery and suffering followed in its wake. Nearly a thousand separate wars have been fought in Europe over the past 2500 years, and within the last 4000 years the world has enjoyed peace for only 268 years. Within the lifetime of some people living today twenty-three major wars have been waged, with the accompanying waste of wealth and energy, misery and suffering to all concerned. Besides these major wars numerous minor wars have been fought against native communities, such as Zulus, Matabele, Kaffirs, Sudanese, and on the frontier of India. Considering only the important wars since 1864, we find that during these last eighty-two years war was raging somewhere on earth for forty-six years, from which followed destruction of property, great misery and suffering, and the loss of valuable lives.[1]

This is an impressive example of human combativeness, cruelty and stupidity, and should give cause for serious thought. The suffering which the human family has endured from war over the past eighty years is but a small fraction of the misery it has caused since the time of primitive man, and, as we study the story of the past, we have cause to think deeply of the meaning of it all. Is war an infliction which the human race must bear, or, as with the plague, is it possible to find a remedy so that the great majority of mankind who love peace and hate war may be able to live in peaceful security? That is one of the problems this book sets out to solve.

Every war in the past can be traced to selfishness, greed, fear, or intolerance; in fact, in the ultimate analysis, the cause of war can be resolved into ignorance. If we think out the remedy for this curse of ignorance which afflicts mankind, we shall arrive at the conclusion that by education future generations could

---

[1] Prussian-Danish war 1864, Prussian-Austrian war 1866, Prussian-French war 1870-71, Serbian-Turkish war 1876, Russian-Turkish war 1877-8, First Boer war 1881, Serbian-Bulgarian war 1885-6, Italian-Abyssinian war 1887, Chinese-Japanese war 1894, Italian-Abyssinian war 1896, Grecian-Turkish war 1897, Spanish-American war 1898, Second Boer war 1899-1902, Russian-Japanese war 1904-5, Italian-Turkish war 1911-12, First and Second Balkan wars 1912-13, First World War 1914-18, Russian Civil war 1919-20, Paraguayan-Bolivian war 1932-4, Italian-Abyssinian war 1935-6, Spanish Civil war 1936-8, Chinese-Japanese war 1937-45, Second World War 1939-45.

prevent a repetition of all these past tragedies, if taught the wisdom and importance of unselfishness and compromise, besides being given a thorough grounding in history for the purpose of emphasising the follies and mistakes of our ancestors. Only by education along these lines will it be possible to build up a stable organisation; to which all nations will loyally contribute, for the purpose of ensuring the future peace of the world. Peace within the nation can only be maintained by force, and likewise international peace can only be so upheld until the ethical development of the race rises to such a level that force becomes unnecessary.

If there were no power within the nation to maintain peace there would be chaos, as boundaries would be for ever overrun by those who are always ready to take what does not belong to them. What applies to the nation likewise applies to the world community of nations. We have solved the problem of national peace, and we have now to set to work to solve the problem of international peace, but before this is possible the minds of the people must rise to a higher level. This can only come about by increased knowledge, and an advance in our ethical standards.

Until the human family can find a way to live together in peace we are little better than civilised animals. We may accomplish much in other spheres of activity, but, if we cannot find the means to live at peace one with another, all our other conquests of the forces of nature are relatively of little importance. Only wisdom and knowledge can bring to us the peace and happiness we all desire, and it should therefore be the aim of everyone to increase in wisdom and accumulate greater knowledge.

This, then, is the conclusion reached in the pages which follow, and the next question to be answered is how to bring home to everyone throughout the world this knowledge, from which will come increased wisdom. Surely the best way is to tell every child, in every school, in every land, honestly and simply, the story of the past achievements and mistakes of their ancestors, so that they may learn to emulate all that was good and avoid all that was evil. We have a record of the past experiences of the race from which to profit, and, if this is put forward for all to read in an attractive form, the lessons it has to teach will some day be learned, to the lasting happiness of all mankind.

That is what this book attempts to do. If it also succeeds in throwing further light on the cause of, and the remedy for, the greatest curse which afflicts the human race, its purpose will be served, and the labour of writing this book will not have been expended in vain. A knowledge of history, and the great latent power behind education, are the two forces which will finally destroy the dragon of war. History, however, must be honestly taught, and education must also include ethical instruction if these two influences are to have the desired effect, as, if misused, they can be equally employed for evil purposes. The future historian must write as a world citizen, as one who belongs to no country, professes no creed and has no party politics, and this is the policy I have tried to follow throughout this book.

What has been omitted, or glossed over, in other

history books is here included, as only the truth can make us free, free from ignorance and all that it entails, namely, war, cruelty, poverty, suffering and misery. Both politicians and priests have misled the people in the past, and will continue to do so until knowledge increases. A prominent British politician, a member of the Cabinet, for instance, broadcast over the radio on Empire Day (1942) a fulsome story of the rise of the British Empire, which he was at great pains to emphasise was not won by conquest! Leading ecclesiastics likewise, during the Second World War, were permitted to use the radio to give listeners a glowing account of the benefits which Christian civilisation had brought to Christendom. The motive behind all these misrepresentations of facts was to create a favourable effect, and not for the purpose of instruction in what is true.

As, however, most people accept what they hear without much knowledge, or reasoned thought to guide them, they carry through life many misconceptions which bias their judgment and affect their comprehension. To counteract these misunderstandings, and to increase knowledge, I have written my various books, the idea of writing for gain being entirely absent. This fact enables me always to express myself freely on all subjects, because I am not restricted by the feeling that unpopular opinions will retard their circulation. Fortunately I am able to give the necessary time and thought to this effort, no other reason influencing me than the advancement of understanding so as to bring about an increase in the happiness of mankind.

Much of my time during the past six years has

been occupied writing this book, *The Curse of Ignorance.*
It, and its immediate predecessor, *The Psychic Stream*,
embrace the religious, political and social history of
mankind from primitive times to the present day.
The compilation of both these books has been a long
and arduous undertaking, to which I have given much
time and thought during the past ten years, when I
could find the necessary leisure from my many other
duties. My labour, however, will be amply rewarded
if, by a study of their contents, my aim of greater
mental enlightenment is accomplished.

The pages which follow comprise the history of
mankind from the age when our ancestors, the sub-
men, pelted their enemies with stones from the tree-
tops, to the time when their descendants climbed into
the heavens on wings and dropped high-explosive
bombs on helpless men, women and children. Indeed
some of its earlier chapters were written when these
latter conditions prevailed in close proximity to my
home.

The war, to my wife and myself, as it did to others,
brought unexpected changes. When it began we
offered our home, Stansted Hall, as a gift to the Red
Cross for the duration of the war, if they would use it
as a Convalescent Home. This offer was accepted
in December 1940, and from then until the close of
hostilities over 5500 soldiers, recovering from acci-
dents, wounds and illness, recuperated within its
walls and enjoyed the beauties and pleasures of its
surroundings.

As the Red Cross required the entire house
we had to seek a war-time home, and I had to
give up my duties as Chief Warden for North-West

Essex, there being then no other house available in the neighbourhood because so many people from London had sought refuge in the country from the nightly air raids. We were, however, fortunate to be able to rent part of Rockingham Castle in Northamptonshire for the duration of the war, and there I wrote most of this book, having by then come to the definite conclusion that war would never cease to recur until the mental level of the people everywhere was raised to a higher standard, by means of greater knowledge and a much improved system of ethical education.

No more suitable place could have been found to write a history of the past, as this historic edifice has sheltered many who have been famous in our island's history. Doomsday Book mentions that it was originally a Saxon stronghold, and William the Conqueror transformed it into a castle. There, in 1095, his son William II, surrounded by his leading churchmen and nobles, in the Great Hall, disputed for two days with Anselm, the recently appointed Archbishop of Canterbury, who insisted on receiving his robe of office from a Pope whom the King had not yet recognised, there being then two claimants to the Holy See.

Until 1485 the castle was a royal residence, "The Windsor Castle of the Midlands", to become in after years the home of men prominent in British history. On its walls hang portraits of some of Britain's famous rulers, while, in the Great Hall, still stands an iron trunk said to have been left there by King John before he set out to cross the Wash, where disaster, caused by the rising tide, overtook what remained of his baggage. An iron chest, which is said to have belonged to Henry

V, stands nearby. In the room where part of this book was written, Charles Dickens, in 1849–50, wrote *David Copperfield*, and about the castle he weaved the setting of another of his stories.

Throughout the years of peace and war, the Wars of the Roses, and the Civil War, when the Roundheads took possession of the castle, its ancient walls have stood, and still give shelter to a descendant of the family which obtained possession of the property from King James I. What better setting could the historian desire to stimulate his thoughts when recording the deeds of the past, as from my study window I surveyed the ancient keep and battlements which remind us of the days when men, clad in armour or leather jerkins, with battle-axes, cross bows, pikes and staves drove off their enemies, and left the scars of conflict on the weather-beaten stones.

As the centuries passed, and war gave place to peace, Britain became an example of what the world at large may some day be—a peaceful, happy dwelling-place for all mankind. When that time comes ignorance will have been replaced by knowledge, unbridled passions tamed by self-control, and man have raised himself above the beasts. Until this longed-for era comes, let us all help to flood the world with intellectual light, as this alone will end the misery and suffering which comes from ignorance.

I know not what the mind of man may still imagine and then construct; I cannot tell to what heights his thoughts may soar; but this I know: that nothing is more desired than liberty, peace, security, happiness, comfort, good health, and prosperity, all of which can be attained by reasoned thought. Just as mental development has brought peace and happiness to our own once-disordered land, so in time will peaceful conditions spread until they embrace all the nations of earth. Then will have passed the worst of mankind's many afflictions, the curse of ignorance.

My wife, my most candid critic, patiently and willingly helped me at all times, and in various ways, especially in checking the proof sheets; my secretary, Mrs. Goodes, who has typed all my books, did her work again with her usual perseverance and cheerfulness; and Mr. F. S. Cook, M.A., kindly read over, and thoroughly checked, the completed manuscripts and printer's proofs. Here I acknowledge the help they have given to me, and I take this opportunity to express to them my warmest thanks.

ARTHUR FINDLAY.

Stansted Hall,
Essex.

CHAPTER I.

HAPPINESS OR MISERY?

Introduction. (1) *Education, the Hope of the Human Race.* (2) *Knowledge is Essential to Ethical Progress.*

HAPPINESS is the desire of the entire human race, and yet how few there be who know how it can be obtained. Ignorance is the cause of most of the world's troubles, many of which could be overcome by increased knowledge and greater wisdom. Unfortunately the mentality of the race has not yet risen sufficiently to make this possible. Mankind is still under the curse of ignorance. There is no darkness like ignorance, and the only way to enlighten this darkness is by increased knowledge.

Whatsoever causes happiness is good, provided no sentient being suffers, and whatever produces unhappiness is evil. The good, or righteous, man is the one who causes happiness; the evil, or unrighteous, man being the one who creates unhappiness. Happiness or unhappiness, apart from causes over which we have no control, are therefore determined by good or evil deeds, done by good or bad people, the former creating the conditions which make for mental harmony and contentment, while the latter create those which produce misery or mental disharmony. He who uses power wisely and with moderation is himself happy, whereas the reverse is equally true.

Happiness is caused by the mind being in harmony with its environment, and whatever causes disharmony causes unhappiness and misery. Many causes affect the harmony of the mind, such as fear, pain, discomfort, unkindness, the loss of money, and the loss of friends by separation and death. Fear is one of the chief causes of our unhappiness, and this is nourished by ignorance. Fear of want, fear of suffering, and fear of death are the three chief fears which have played havoc with the happiness of mankind down the ages. What a load of misery fear has caused the race; what unhappiness pain has caused, and yet, as we now see, when turning back the pages of the story of the human family, much of this could have been avoided if our ancestors had known more, if they had been more intelligent, and had had greater wisdom.

Much of mankind's past misery and suffering could have been avoided by wisdom and knowledge. Because these were lacking, the race has suffered from poverty, disease, famine and war. By increased knowledge both disease and famine have been largely conquered. By mechanical invention, combined with scientific treatment, the earth can easily be made to produce all that the human family requires, and, under proper direction, there need be no want of those things which add to our comfort and enjoyment. The last and greatest enemy of everyone, war, must now be fought and finally conquered if the human race is to attain its full measure of happiness.

Because of ignorance, the past history of mankind is the story of war, destruction, conquest, slavery, injustice, intolerance and depravity. The people have been the sport and prey of priest and king, of superstition and autocratic might. The people, being ignorant, were just like children who obeyed those they looked upon as their superiors. The king governed by instilling into his subjects respect for his divine majesty, and making the people fear his power to punish all who disobeyed him. The priest has governed by making the people afraid of what awaited them after death if they disobeyed the representatives of the gods on earth, but he has not taught righteousness for the good of the human race.

Kings and priests in the past have worked together to keep the people obedient to their wills. Tyranny and superstition, like two birds of prey, have fed on the ignorance of man. Liberty and education, as a rule, were alike distasteful to those in authority, and mental development was seldom encouraged. Both the throne and the altar were against liberty and progress, as these meant the end of servile obedience and the offerings to the priesthood. So kings have always tried to prevent the masses from becoming too independent, and the priests have proclaimed that the people must not think for themselves. These two facts run through the story of the human race, as the following pages will reveal.

An interesting relic of this effort to keep the mind in chains is to be found in the old story told in *Genesis*, of how the gods[1] were angry with Adam and Eve because they ate of the tree of knowledge of good and evil, thus bringing to the race all the afflictions it has had to bear. The Greeks, and other nations, had similar stories produced by the priests, who considered that knowledge was sinful and ignorance a virtue, and

[1] This is the correct translation from the Hebrew.

the people, being even more ignorant than their masters, accepted this as the will of the gods.

Until recent years this story kept Christendom in ignorance, knowledge being looked upon as sinful. A terrible fate, the people were told, overcame the race because Eve ate of "a tree to be desired to make one wise", and, as this was devoutly believed up to the end of last century, we can better understand why education was denounced by the Church, which directed its efforts towards keeping the people ignorant. The terrible results which followed from this wicked policy will be revealed as we proceed, because ignorance is at the source of all that is evil, and from it has flowed the past and present miseries of the human race.

Man, himself, is to blame for all his past and present troubles and miseries, because if he had had more intelligence he would never have allowed others slightly more clever than himself to domineer over him. This is still evident to all thinking people in our own time, as the masses, though now partially educated in civilised countries, can still be swayed this way and that by a politician or a priest who is clever and plausible enough to play upon their ignorance. The wise are astonished at such foolishness, just as the foolish are astonished at wisdom.

Most of the past and present religious and political systems have failed to bring happiness to the people, because they have given too little thought to ethical principles. These vitally affect the welfare of humanity, and their rejection by those in authority has brought upon the people both unhappiness and misery. Those who protested against injustice were termed traitors, and killed or imprisoned, while those who objected to the superstitions preached and practised by the priests were called infidels, and shared the same fate.

Little wonder that man's climb to liberty and greater knowledge has been slow and uncertain, and that, even now, the average of intelligence in matters affecting the welfare of the race is so backward that quite unnecessary suffering is caused by ignorance of the right way to live. Because of this, ethical principles have received scant attention in the past, as they are the last subject to receive respect from tyrants. Force and fear have been the two weapons used up to now by the rulers of State and Church to make their decisions obeyed. Only through complete liberty of thought can the tender ethical plant grow and flourish, but once it obtains a firm root everywhere on earth it will transform the life of mankind and bring happiness and contentment to all.

It is the purpose of this book to emphasise these ethical principles, in such a clear and concise way that future generations will realise plainly that, for the sake of their own happiness and well-being, they should be followed as a guide to human conduct. Besides this, there will be told the story of the past from this higher angle of thought, so that the younger generation may be introduced to history from a new line of vision. Thus, by means of greater wisdom and knowledge, we may expect that in time war, and other evils, will cease to curse mankind. A day will eventually dawn when the people will not only learn the facts, and the lessons history has to teach, but also profit by their knowledge. Knowledge is therefore essential to

ethical development, as, when we know about the
mistakes of our ancestors, we are less likely to repeat
them.

All that most people in Christendom know about
history, apart from that of their own country, is what
is contained in the Old Testament. From youth
upwards they have been taught at church and Sunday
school about a primitive tribe which had settled in
Egypt, and was led by Moses to the Promised Land,
of their exploits there, and eventual captivity in Babylon. Besides passages so obscene that no other book
would be allowed to print them, the most shocking
and revolting descriptions are given of the methods
pursued by these savages against their enemies, innocent men, women and children being treated in the
most inhuman and brutal manner. Christians have
been taught that God gave these savages, whom they
call "God's chosen people", instructions to carry
out these barbaric cruelties on their enemies, and on
all who did not accept the Hebrew form of religious
belief.

In the years of ignorance, which fortunately are
now passing away, the Bible gave comfort to millions
who considered themselves the elect, and who
believed that it contained the only way of salvation,
but few there be who realise the baneful effect it had
on Christendom throughout the Christian era. Likewise few appreciate the fact that Europe, in the 4th
century A.D., was faced with the choice of adopting the
high ethical philosophy of the Greeks, or the savagery
attributed to Jehovah, and that the former was cast
aside in favour of the latter. On that fateful decision
terrible consequences followed, one being that we are

still cursed by the ignorance which leads to war and its accompanying misery.

European history is a record of first one nation, and then another, adopting aggression towards its neighbour, and the map of Europe, over the past sixteen hundred years, is like a kaleidoscope, constant changes having occurred in the national frontiers, because one nation after another has devastated, pillaged, and occupied the lands of those unable to resist. Last century Britain and France were the chief world aggressors, whereas this century they have been the victims of aggression—Germany, Italy and Japan having put on the cloak of conquest.

The curse of ignorance is at the root of all the troubles that afflict the world, and only when the people have knowledge can they criticise and refute their priests and politicians if they tell them what is not the truth. Until then they must suffer, but the remedy is in their own hands if they will only make the effort. Unfortunately the great majority prefer to experience some ephemeral pleasure to acquiring real knowledge and wisdom, the consequence being that everyone, wise and foolish, intelligent and ignorant, suffers alike. Ignorance is behind all the miseries the world has recently suffered from the German, Italian and Japanese people following the evil path laid out by unscrupulous politicians intent on their own glorification and domination. No people with knowledge and wisdom would have been deceived as they were, and yet the consequence of ignorance came not only upon them, but upon many millions who were quite innocent of the crimes and wickedness practised by these dupes of political gangsters.

This may not always be so, and the last war may have raised the mental level everywhere to a higher range of thought. Great upheavals produce a new outlook, sometimes for the better and at other times for the worse, but if the last great disaster in human affairs is to be the prelude to a wiser and saner order in international relations this book may be appreciated, and its conclusions accepted, in a way never before possible.

Two changes are essential to ensure this result. The first is that all on earth must rise to a higher ethical level of thought, helped by the study of ethical science, which is devoted to the promotion of human happiness by the development of that which causes happiness, and the elimination from our conduct of all that creates unhappiness. The second essential is that all must acquire greater knowledge, which, in turn, will bring wisdom in its train. These two factors will be stressed and amplified as we proceed. Because ethical principles have been largely ignored in all past international relationships, humanity today finds itself in many respects poor, miserable, battered, and bruised. If only we, the people of earth, could learn that righteousness is always the best policy for everyone, how different our lives would be.

If all the labour and thought, which were devoted to produce weapons of destruction in the last two world wars, had been spent on constructive work, and improved methods of production and distribution, we today would be obtaining all our requirements, and enjoying much greater comfort, from half the number of hours of labour now required to maintain our present standard of livelihood. Man, by his stupidity and ignorance, has wasted on destructive purposes this earth's valuable assets, which should have been devoted to his increased comfort and the reduction of his toil.

Moreover, he has been guilty of a further folly. From childhood to manhood the individual is a burden to the community, as he must be fed, clothed and educated. Before he returns, by his work, what has been expended upon him, he becomes a soldier, to be, perhaps, killed or incapacitated. If the former, the expenditure on his upbringing has been lost, and, if the latter, it is not only lost but he remains a burden on the nation for the rest of his life. It is much wiser for men to live for their country than to die for it. There is no reason in this senseless cutting short of young lives with all their productive years ahead of them. These men did not die glorious deaths, their tragic end only displaying how great is human folly and wickedness, the entire community suffering from their untimely end.

The people who fought against German, Italian and Japanese aggression believe that their sailors and soldiers died, or were incapacitated, so that they might live in freedom. This is true, but it is equally true that the German, Italian, and Japanese fought just as bravely for what they had been taught was the object of the war. However much they were mistaken, the fact remains that men can be trained to think that, aggression is right and justified. All the so-called holy wars of the past have been caused by the aggressors believing that they were fighting for a cause which all should share. Consequently both sides in a conflict believed that their soldiers met glorious deaths.

Nevertheless the truth is that their death and mutilation were caused by ignorance of the right way to live, and this brought about the inevitable suffering, destruction and misery. Brave and gallant as men may be in warfare, conflict has always been, and always will be, misdirected effort. The art of wise living is to pursue a course from which we all derive the greatest amount of happiness out of life, and this can only come from mutual co-operation between individuals and nations, but never by injustice, intolerance and aggression.

The tragedy is that war is something which is unnecessary, and yet it and its accompanying misery and destruction are the most prominent features in history. During the past 4000 years there have been more than 8000 peace treaties signed between nations, but, in spite of this evident desire for peace, man has devoted himself as much to destruction and the creation of misery, as to construction and the production of happiness. By intolerance, selfishness, and the ignoring of ethical principles, the race has reduced its comforts and happiness, and increased its burdens, which could have been greatly lightened by intelligence and wisdom. Nations, in their dealings one with another, have no high moral conceptions, and what interests the individual nation takes first place over the affairs of its neighbours, a short-sighted view which in the end brings trouble to all concerned.

All the people of this earth must therefore rise to a higher mental level, and discard the old ideas and low ethical values of the past, when plundering one's neighbour was considered more advantageous than honest trade and commerce. Everyone, everywhere, must adopt, as a result of past experience, ethical principles which are simple to understand and practise if correctly taught to all when young. If this were done they would in time be accepted and practised naturally as a habit. These principles come from the accumulated wisdom of the human race, and belong to no particular nation, to no special religion or sect, and to no single political organisation. A right or wrong understanding of these principles vitally affects every one of us, and only when they are rightly understood and practised will humanity reach the realm of wisdom. Then will follow greater comfort, increased happiness, reduced toil and enlarged security.

This can only come about by increased knowledge, as only through knowledge is wisdom attainable. Knowledge leads to wisdom, and wisdom to a higher level of ethical conduct. Ethical conduct leads to harmony one with another, and so the good are those who create harmony and the evil those who create disharmony. No one can be wise if ignorant, and to increase in wisdom means first of all to increase in knowledge. Then will come wisdom and the practice of the virtues, from which will follow the harmony that brings peace and happiness.

(1) EDUCATION, THE HOPE OF THE HUMAN RACE.

The people in general are woefully backward in their knowledge of those things which make life worth living, and, because of this, we are losing much of the happiness we might otherwise enjoy. Recently much progress has been made in the improvement of the social conditions of the people in many lands, but this has only taken them part of the distance along the road leading to human happiness. War, the greatest curse of mankind, and the cause of so much misery and suffering, must now be abolished, and this can be done if we approach the problem with intelligence.

What is required is mental development, and from this all else will follow, as mind is king and we all live under its direction. A well-developed mind is more to be desired than honours, titles, and riches. Mind is man, and honours nothing great; the only thing that counts in life is mind, all else being but some tinsel stuff which falls away at death, to leave the mind unclothed of earthly ware, to build by thought its new domain within the etheric realm.

As it thought on earth, so will it think there. Character and mental wealth, being super-physical qualities, are more enduring than things material, and to their cultivation and increase the wise direct their main attention. As we build up our character and develop our mind here, so shall we be there. As the boy and girl make the man and woman on earth, so the man and woman make the etheric man and woman in the after life. What we sow here we reap hereafter, as the character we develop here does not die. If everyone realised the vital fact that we are laying here the foundation of our life hereafter, war would cease, and our way of life would change for the good of everyone.

Mind determines the individual's private life, just as the mass mind of the people determines the life of the individual nation, or the community of nations. Raise everywhere the individual mentality, and the national and international mentality will follow in consequence. Everything hinges on mental development. It is because of this evolution that our social conditions have improved of late, and, if this continues, most of the evils from which we suffer will vanish.

To attain this end many present-day ideas must change, and certain well-attested facts, not generally known, must be learned. We shall come across these as we proceed, but the following are amongst the most obvious.

All religions are based on psychic phenomena, but are encrusted with theological error, which sooner or later must be dismissed as the drapings of an age of ignorance.

Politics should only be concerned with matters which have to do with the prosperity, comfort and happiness of the greatest number. Whatever increases these blessings deserves support, so long as individual liberty and freedom are preserved, and justice always prevails.

The ethical conduct required by individuals and civilised communities must be extended to all nations by all nations. Only when this is done will war cease, but, so long as ethical conduct is confined to home use, and not practised towards neighbouring nations, aggression and conquest will continue to curse the race.

Every human being, so far as conditions permit, should have the same opportunity to receive a good education made up of facts, and be taught the lessons drawn from human experience. This must be divorced from all organised religious or political influences, and each one must have the chance to develop his mind on the lines for which it is best suited.

The ideas embraced within these four short paragraphs comprise much of what comes within our daily

lives, and, as we read on, we shall find how our
ancestors misdirected their energies, and lessened their
comforts and happiness, by not knowing the right
way to live. So the purpose of this book is to tell the
history of the past, as a guide to present and future
generations, so that they may avoid the mistakes of
their ancestors in a way we have not yet learned to do.
By examining past history, and the consequences of
the mistakes made in ignorance, as the result of an
undeveloped ethical standard, we shall better realise
how these errors can be avoided in the future. This
involves our reviewing the story of man's upward
climb from the time of sub-man to the present day,
just as it entails the consideration of the outstanding
crimes committed on humanity by the domination
and lust of autocrats, and the simple acceptance
of their rule by the people who blindly followed
them.

Never more than now does humanity need sound
guidance in the way to live together in peace and
happiness. With the increase of knowledge, and the
decay of the old political and religious systems, it is
groping for something new to take their place.
Ecclesiastical authority, where education exists, is
breaking down, but, on the other hand, we have, of
late years, experienced abroad the return to tyrannical
government, and the enslavement of large numbers
of people who, within the past hundred years, had
partially won their freedom.

Can the human race ever attain to a sane religious
and political outlook, and live as sensible intelligent
people should live? Yes, most certainly, but before
this happens the education of the young must be

radically altered. Education (Latin, *e*=out, *duco*=I lead) in future must not only mean teaching children certain facts, but be applied in the correct meaning of the word. This means providing intellectual and moral training for the mind, for the purpose of leading it out of the darkness of ignorance into the light of a true understanding of all things, and the development of each individual's personality.

Much of what children are now taught must be abandoned as error, and much new must be taught which is not yet included in a school curriculum. This change must be world-wide if we are to attain the peace and happiness everyone desires, but, because of the different mental levels prevailing amongst the various races, we can only expect the new order in education to come into being very slowly, and to suffer setbacks before the goal is reached.

Education for everyone is still so young, so new and novel an endeavour, that the majority have not yet passed the first elementary stage. Some day, when we have progressed further, everyone must be grounded in many subjects now omitted, one especially important study being anthropology (Greek *anthropos*, a man: *logos*, reason), the entire science of man from every angle, his origin, destiny, character and mental development. This subject embraces man both physiologically and psychologically, his physical body, his etheric body, and his mind. Everything that has to do with these should be studied for the purpose of developing aright both body and mind, in order to produce what Plato called "the good man".

Science does not create, it only discovers what

already exists, and the more we know of what exists
the better our mind is furnished to enable us to live
aright and make the best and most of life. Everything we learn should be a means to an end, which is
the increase of human comfort, harmony and happiness, this being only possible when, by mental
development, all learn a world-wide humanitarianism,
and the difficult but important art of world citizen-
ship, which will come when all are tolerant, just,
merciful, true and kind to every living creature.

What is taught to a child is not easily forgotten.
If error, instead of truth, be taught, the child is
handicapped throughout its life. On the other hand,
if truth, instead of error, be taught, it is unlikely that
the child in after life will adopt the wrong way of
thinking. There is a right and a wrong way to think,
and, because of ignorance, we have, in many instances,
been taught the wrong way.

Religion has been taught by a specially privileged
class, in every country, from the point of view favoured
by that class. It was, and is still, in the interests of
this class to propagate certain religious beliefs without
any regard as to whether they are true or not. These
have been handed down over the centuries, and are
accepted because of their age and not because of their
veracity. The young are encouraged to accept these
ancient beliefs, and not to think out for themselves
whether they are true or false. Orthodox religion is
rarely a subject open to debate, it is a closed formula
which each one is taught to accept. To try and
examine its mysteries for oneself has, from early
times, been looked upon as a sin against the unseen
higher powers. To question, or to doubt, the

orthodox faith of the times has always been represented by the religious authorities as stepping on to the broad path which leads to destruction.

Political education has been likewise bound up by similar restrictions. Those in authority expected obedience from the masses, whom they looked upon as serfs or slaves. The vast majority of the people received no education, and spent their lives working in the fields. Those who disliked this monotonous work became soldiers, and, under a leader, lived their lives killing their neighbours across arbitrary frontiers, and looting their property. They were members of a robber gang, led by a master robber, who, if he plundered successfully, became a historical character. If he were a really super-gangster, the historians gave him the title of "Great", and so we have been taught to admire these outstanding criminals, such as Alexander the Great, Napoleon the Great, and others about whom we shall hear as we go on.

The people, over whom these criminals ruled, supported them in the hope that their masters would have some scraps left over for them to enjoy, but these plunderers never increased the happiness nor the prosperity of the great majority, whilst incalculable sufferings were experienced by the victims as well as by many of the aggressors. Aggression and conquest, victors and vanquished, appear before us on nearly every page of world history, the people experiencing the effort and misery, while only the leaders, who won the glory and the booty, benefited from all the suffering they caused.

There is no darkness like that of ignorance, and, in the story of the past, one finds difficulty in dis-

covering much light of reason and sanity. This folly
will go on from generation to generation, until it is
stopped by the rays of intelligence and reason breaking
through man's cloudy mind. This last catastrophe
to the human race, from which we have emerged
maimed and poor, is not necessarily the last war;
it has not been a war which must end war. Sooner
or later another war will again come upon the race,
unless a radical improvement takes place in the mental
development of every nation. With the present low
level of human intelligence it will take many years to
educate the people, composing the different nations,
out of the lust for plunder and the grabbing of other
people's territory, into a way of all enjoying all that
the earth produces, irrespective of arbitrary boundaries,
which now denote different nationalities who wish
to keep to themselves, and retain what they have for
themselves.

Education of the people has just commenced in
some countries, as only towards the end of last
century did most of the people in so-called civilised
lands learn how to read and write. Elsewhere
millions are still illiterate and intensely ignorant.
Nearly everyone a hundred years ago was illiterate, to
be treated by those who knew slightly more as
children who were expected to do as they were told.
Most people today are little more than children in their
outlook on life, and we cannot expect a better and
happier world to come quickly while this is so.
Further mental development must occur, and will
occur wherever liberty reigns, in fact when we consider how much the human race has already accomplished there seems to be no limit to mental evolution.

The human race, since it left its primitive jungle abode, has discovered that the new life it set out to live has been far from pleasant. Pain and suffering, plague and disease, hunger and want, cold and discomfort, war and conflict, have been the constant companions of mankind on his road from his early abode to his present conditions. Just as his intelligence increased, so did his conditions improve, and the more he used his reason, and the more he thought, the less he suffered and the happier he became. By intelligent thought, by remembering past mistakes, we have arrived at our present-day state of existence, one which is greatly superior to that from which our ancestors originally developed.

Only in one instance have we made no development, and are still in the jungle state of existence. In this one case we are still brutes and beasts, wild animals of the forest life, snarling, fighting, grabbing and tearing one another to pieces. We have advanced far in many directions, we have discovered much, but one thing we have not yet found is how to stop war, how to end these continual international differences which cause war and produce destruction, misery and suffering. Once this is discovered we can say farewell to our original jungle home, and part company for ever from our bestial ancestors, but, until we do so, we are still brute beasts with all their cruelty and cunning, supplemented by a power for destruction and the causing of misery far beyond their understanding.

How ashamed we should be of ourselves! The animals have puny brains and little rational thought, and their conflicts are spontaneous, carried out in the heat of passion through jealousy, fear, or hunger. They quarrel, they snarl at one another, they grab and steal, they scratch, fight and kill, but they do not spend their peaceful hours, as we do, in thinking and planning the destruction of their fellow creatures. They steal and kill to live, and the strongest survives, but, with our present means of production, we need not kill one another to live, as nowadays there is enough for all. The human race has risen in many respects far above the animal stage, but, so far as killing and savagery are concerned, we have not advanced one step; in fact no animal has ever descended to such depths of cruelty, cunning and brutality as has been practised by man to man.

Some day, and in some way, we must break this chain which still binds us to the beasts, and this can only come about by developing mind, as it alone can set us on a plane far above their level. Education, on right lines, is the only hope of the human race, but it must be on right lines if our purpose is to succeed. We must educate ourselves out of this idea of war, of this glorifying of war, of this hero-worship of those aggressors who killed and plundered their fellow men Such creatures were not the benefactors of the race and, instead of being glorified and lauded, they should be denounced so vehemently by historians that future generations everywhere would shun all aspirants to this role as they would a deadly poison.

Those who were most skilful in the art of using weapons of destruction, the greatest soldiers, the greatest authorities in the game of "beggar my neighbour", are the ones who are honoured and exalted in world history. On the other hand, those who did their best to raise the people to a higher level of thought, to a higher, nobler and happier state of existence, those real heroes of the race, have seldom appealed to public imagination. When the time comes that this position is reversed, when the benefactors become the heroes, we shall be civilised, and at long last have cut the worst link which binds us to our animal ancestors.

Before we set about considering how to abolish war, it is important that we should first of all know the causes which bring it about. Thousands of wars have been waged since man left the jungle to become a human being, but, in the last analysis, they can all be set down to hate, greed and need. A hungry man will fight for food more readily than one who has plenty. Those who have little will fight for more, while those who have plenty are generally contented, and prefer to live comfortably at peace.

The needs of the body have been one of the principal reasons to account for man being a fighting creature, and they in turn have engendered hate and malice. Besides need there is also greed, as those who envy others fight for more than they already possess. Man is a greedy, selfish creature, and covets his neighbour's possessions. Besides this he is intolerant, and hates those who think differently from himself. Some therefore have fought to change the political and religious opinions of others, because they considered they were wrong and must be altered. To the hatred of the opinion of others, and the desire to possess what others have, can be traced the origin of most, if not all, of the wars of the past.

So history records wars for plunder, for the obtaining from others of food, clothing, land, houses and thrones, or other material possessions, on the one hand, and, on the other, for the purpose of changing ideas held by some which were disliked by others. The reason for war today is much the same as it was in the time of primitive man, the only change that has taken place being the growing conviction amongst increasing numbers of people that this method of obtaining desires should be avoided, because it is both cruel and wasteful, causing suffering, poverty, and misery to everyone, and lasting benefits only to the few.

Slowly, over thousands of years, the idea has developed that it is wrong to steal, because only the few are the gainers and the many are the sufferers. Slowly the belief has developed that the general happiness of the race is increased by everyone observing a certain measure of self-restraint in his conduct towards his neighbour, and, just as this self-restraint has developed, so has individual happiness increased. Man has painfully, and by degrees, discovered that by thinking more of others, and less of himself, he himself is the gainer, but, until this vital truth becomes the fixed idea of all, the benefit it confers on the human race is strictly limited.

However much the more intelligent may realise the remedy for our suffering and misery, so long as some do not do so we have no method to prevent the recurrence of war except by the use of force, and, so far, the race has been unable to organise this force against aggressors except by war. We have only been able to meet force by force, which means war, but we must now set about planning the means to use force to prevent war, until the time comes when the people, as a whole, rise mentally to realise that there are better ways of obtaining their desires than by aggression.

War, then, is caused by wrong thinking due to ignorance. By changing wrong thinking into right thinking, by replacing ignorance by knowledge, and folly by wisdom, we find the remedy for war. We now know the cause of war and the remedy, but this knowledge, possessed by some, will not stop war because it is not possessed by all. That is the real difficulty with which we are faced, and, if war is to cease, it must be overcome and removed. In the pages which follow, the plan to be adopted is set out, and here it is summarised under three headings.

(1) By education, future generations everywhere must be taught the observance of the virtues in their dealings one with another, both nationally and internationally.

(2) By education, future generations must be taught to tolerate other people's religious and political opinions, and the importance of compromise in dealing one with another.

(3) By education, future generations must learn the past history of the race, especially the mistakes, the follies, and the cruelties of the past, so that they may be avoided in the future. Based on this knowledge they must plan a system which will preserve peace and security for all mankind.

This book is consequently a history of the past, and a plea for a higher ethical standard of conduct everywhere for the future. Its story will make clear the mistakes of our ancestors, so that they may be avoided in the future, as only through knowledge, and the wisdom that comes therefrom, can the human race hope to enter upon an era of peace, happiness and general contentment.

The time was when family life consisted of snarling, bickering and blows. That was when men and women had just emerged from the animal stage, and had not yet learned the art of living in harmony one with another. The club was the only argument, and it was used on every occasion. Since those days great progress has been made in our family relationships. Likewise the same progress has been made amongst those communities which make up the different nations. The conduct of most people towards one another is guided by the golden rule, and only a small percentage would be happy acting otherwise. The time was, however, when families fought against families, and there were constant blood feuds.

Experience certainly has taught us that practising self-control leads to individual happiness, and that the more unselfish each one is the happier is the family and the community. Unfortunately we have not yet learned that the self-restraint which we adopt towards each other nationally must likewise be adopted internationally. Language, frontier barriers, and the absence of adequate ethical teaching have been largely the cause of the want of progress in this direction. Nations, living apart, do not understand each other as do people who live together and speak the same tongue. This difficulty must be overcome if the happiness which we have gained nationally is to reach world-wide proportions.

Because people who live in different countries cannot know each other as do people living in the same country, their rulers have often misrepresented the inhabitants of a country they wish to attack. In spite of present-day improved travel facilities this can now be done more easily than ever before. The radio and the press are powerful weapons in the hands of unscrupulous people. Bitter feelings are first of all engendered in the aggressor country against the intended victim, who is then pounced upon by the country whose inhabitants have been united by this false propaganda.

This method of preparing for an attack is as old as war itself. Hitler was not the first to invent it, Napoleon adopted it, Charlemagne used it, and many of the conquerors of the past have thus prepared the ground before they set out on their conquests, their people always being duped into believing that they were fighting for a righteous cause against those who were their enemies. Nothing can prevail against this form of propaganda, if the people are ignorant and unable to weigh up the case with complete knowledge of all sides of the question, but, where war is concerned, rational thought is absent and unbridled passion dominates the human being.

Here again it is all a matter of mental development, and when this comes about a better understanding between the inhabitants of earth will be established. Improved travel facilities will help, but, so long as the people of a nation agree to the dictates of its rulers that they must not listen to broadcasting from any transmitting station outside their own country, the value of the radio as an educator is limited. In fact it can do more harm than good, because the people are given one point of view only and never hear the other side. We seem to be up against an insoluble problem, and yet increased intelligence will slowly solve it, just as it has smoothed out other perplexing questions, which, at the time, must have seemed equally baffling.

Until the problem of how to make the different nations understand one another is solved, the most enlightened countries must come together and find some means of compelling a would-be aggressor nation to keep within its own frontiers. This was tried by means of a League of Nations, but it failed because the League had no power to stop an aggressor, and it will fail again under similar conditions.

The desire of every individual is liberty of action and freedom of thought, which craving increases as the mind develops. Just as the individual mind loves freedom, and abhors repression, so does the mass mind of a nation composed of intelligent people. National freedom appeals as much to the mass mind as does freedom to the individual. The individual has always endeavoured to obtain, and will always struggle for, freedom in thought and action, as the desire for liberty is the inherent characteristic of the human mind. As with the individual, so will the nation composed of individuals always struggle for freedom, it being the only soil in which happiness and contentment can flourish.

History is in part the story of this struggle for individual independence, either on the part of individuals or communities of individuals called nations. History contains the story of the struggle of the mass mind of communities of like ideas, of the same race, with the same traditions, against the mass minds of other communities which wished to impose upon them their will and purpose. The mind of man, as an individual or as a nation, revolts against this tyranny; it loves freedom and hates slavery, and will never rest until it is free to think and express its individual and national thoughts.

In spite of this ardent love of individual liberty, time and time again the majority, and sometimes a minority in a nation, has tried to impose its will upon others, always with disastrous results. Persecution, civil war, disease and misery have always followed. Likewise, over and over again, a more powerful nation has tried to dominate a less powerful community, with always the same tragic results, namely, war, destruction, suffering, misery, famine, plague and disease, the three latter following every war, and often causing more deaths than the actual warfare. Edmund Burke compressed a very vital truth into the following few words.

The use of force alone is but temporary. It may subdue for a moment; but it does not remove the necessity of subduing again; and a nation is not governed which is perpetually to be conquered.

Though the pages of history are crammed with the tragedies following this attempt at domination, the race never learns the lesson that all men and nations will never be content unless they are free. Consequently, as we turn over these pages of the past, century by century, we find first one nation and then another attempting to impose its will on its neighbours, with the inevitable tragic results. Will mankind never learn from the lessons of the past, that happiness, which all desire, can only come from liberty, which is the soil in which the mind grows and develops?

The soil may be polluted by tyrants, but it never loses its power to produce the plant which for ever reaches upwards towards the sun of freedom. It will never lose this urge, and, just as tyrants arise, so will come resistance, as the only people who will submit to oppression are those who are endowed with the slave mentality. Why does nature produce this overbearing type of mind which loves domination and aggression? Because man, by nature, is a selfish creature, and he wishes to gain either as an individual, or as a nation, something he desires and does not possess.

He is so ignorant that he only considers everything from his own individual or national point of view, not looking over the wide horizon and realising that his own happiness can be equally well attained by thinking of the happiness and wishes of others. Happiness can only be secured by all individuals and nations thinking one of another, and, until the race as a whole comes to realise this vital fact, misery, suffering and destruction will be the lot of mankind. There is no darkness like ignorance, and in this darkness we are all groping for something we all desire, namely, happiness, peace and prosperity, but we cannot find it for want of the light of intelligent understanding one of another.

(2) KNOWLEDGE IS ESSENTIAL TO ETHICAL PROGRESS.

Each reader of this book has doubtless come to the definite conclusion, which nothing will change, that what each one desires for himself must also be allowed to others. Each one of us is so firmly convinced of this that no argument, nothing and nobody, will ever make us change this opinion, because it is fixed in each mind as firmly as a diamond is embedded in a rock. This decision is so obviously rational and just that it is strange that so many are not loyal to it. They may give it lip service, but refuse to practise it, and it is just those people who are the enemies of the race.

We, who are prepared to give to all everything we claim for ourselves, have in consequence to endure the misery brought upon everyone by those undeveloped selfish minds which think only of their own interests, and try by all means in their power to force their will on others. Is there, then, any remedy for this state of affairs? Are the just and righteous to be for-ever the play-ball of evil-doers, to be kicked here and there as they desire? The only remedy is the raising of the mental level, and this can only come about by rational education, which must include a systematic instruction in ethical science.

The righteous meantime must for ever strive against the evil-doer. It is a continuation of the age-old war of good against evil, which started when man developed the sense to distinguish right from wrong, about which we shall learn more in Chapter III, and it has gone on ever since. It is a never-ending conflict between tyranny and liberty, between justice and injustice, and it will end only when there are sufficient individuals in every land, of a sufficiently high level of intelligence, to overpower completely those whose minds still wallow in the slime in which our ancestors sprawled and groped.

Even when the great majority of the citizens of one country have the intelligence to know how to live decently one with another, there is always a small percentage who take advantage of the weak to frighten, rob, or kill them. Against these outcasts of society we have the police, the gallows and prison. Disputes will always occur, but our remedy is the Law Court. Duelling, which was a common method of settling disputes one hundred years ago, is not now generally practised, and, instead of always carrying a sword, men now carry walking-sticks and umbrellas. The race has not degenerated because it has become more sane in these respects, and it will not degenerate if it never again experiences high explosives, incendiary bombs, and other deadly devices which destroy all and sundry, young and old, men and women alike.

Some people say that war is good for strengthening character, and that, if there were no war, we would all become weak and flabby. If this be true, why not make war part of our daily life, why not keep up constant warfare in the home, within the nation, and between nations *ad infinitum*, while all the time giving constant thought to the discovery of new atrocities for maiming and killing one another? By discovering how to release atomic energy we now have something immensely more violent than R.D.X. or T.N.T., and a much more deadly poison gas may be the next destructive discovery. How can anyone think that breathing in poison gas strengthens the character? How are our characters made stronger by our homes coming down on the top of us, or taking fire from incendiary bombs? If this sort of thing makes us better men and women, why not keep it up until we have no homes left, and we all return to the woods and jungles?

If all these devilish devices had never been invented would our characters be weaker than they now are, and were our forefathers more feeble because they knew them not? Has the discovery of gunpowder strengthened our characters, and was man a weaker individual when he fought in single combat without all the hideous inventions of modern science? Modern weapons have turned combat into mass murder and carnage, making it an evil, such as the plague, which we must destroy if the race is not to live in misery and fear of eventual destruction. Either we must go forward or backward, forward into a brighter, happier state of existence, or backwards into the jungle of misery and destruction.

Those who think that a long period of peace is bad for the race, and that to forget the art of war would weaken the character, would never advocate anyone, who has enjoyed a long life of good health, being inoculated with some deadly disease. Good health never weakens character, and we do not put our house on fire because we find it is becoming too comfortable. Since we have had a police force to protect us from attack, our characters have not degenerated, and no one would go back to the bad old days when it was unsafe to travel unarmed on a lonely road.

Our children's characters are no weaker today

because bullying does not now take place at school, as it did last century, when the bully was the terror of all but the strongest. The aim of everyone should be peace and happiness, as only thus can the mind be free to develop, and, if war some day vanishes from this earth, so much the better for us all. If this does happen, our descendants will no more wish to see it revived than we wish to return to the days of the highwayman.

Some say that war keeps the population from increasing too rapidly. If we must keep the population in check, let us do so in a rational way by the wise limitation of births, a simple remedy for over-population, but one which appeals only to intelligent people. Everyone, everywhere, should be educated into the methods of birth control, and every nation must learn to keep its population within the bounds of its resources. It is much more sensible and humane to have fewer children than to have an unwanted surplus to be destroyed in war.

This is one of mankind's greatest and most difficult problems, because of the danger of the most advanced people being overwhelmed by those more backward. The least intelligent are always the most prolific, and the right results can only be obtained by everyone everywhere working for the desired end. If this is not done the Asiatic races may eventually spread themselves over all the earth, when the most advanced and cultured people will be submerged by hordes of prolific breeders intent on their destruction, so as to obtain more, and still more, living space.

It is quite wrong to believe that without war the people would degenerate. Survival of the fittest is probably one reason for man's development from primeval protoplasm, but war in our time does nothing to destroy the weak and preserve the strong. It does quite the opposite, as it is the strong and virile who die and the weak who survive. France has never recovered from the Napoleonic wars, when it lost its best and bravest. Again, it is not always the fittest, the best, nor the most advanced nations which survive in war, as it is sometimes the other way about. Victory can be secured by the nation with the largest population, the greatest supply of coal and iron ore, the largest blast furnaces, the greatest number of factories, the greatest supply of oil fuel, and the thousand and one substances which are needed for a modern army.

A nation today which is well supplied with oil, coal, iron, and steel can secure victory over an enemy which is superior to it physically, mentally, and morally, if the latter lacks the necessary minerals and metals to produce weapons. In mechanical warfare it is not the survival of the fittest, but the survival of the country or combination of nations best provided with modern weapons.

A nation of low moral character, made up of men less physically strong than its enemy, and in other ways backward, could rule the world if only it could secure control of the necessary supplies, to produce and move a relatively larger and better number of tanks, guns, and planes. So the best and the fittest are not by any means the specially favoured, and, as things now are in the modern world, the most degenerate nation can survive and the most advanced succumb, if the former has been sufficiently fortunate to have settled on that part of the earth's surface under which is placed those raw materials required for modern aggression, and the other has not.

If the human race is to progress, and not return to barbarism, some new method must now be attempted to stop the terrible danger which mechanical invention has put into the hands of the aggressor. The moral weapon must be developed, and our only hope now lies in the ethical progress of the people, without which there is only the prospect of a setback to civilisation. This would entail the loss of all the comforts and pleasures now enjoyed by the most advanced of the human race.

The future of civilisation now depends on the more rapid development of mental evolution, but this must come about in every land, as otherwise the more developed nations will always have to be on their guard against those who are less developed. General education, which is only some seventy years old in the most advanced countries, should gradually solve the problem, and meantime let us lose no opportunity to tell our children the true story of mankind, for the purpose of preventing them repeating the follies, mistakes and wicked deeds of those who have lived before us. As often as we put what is right in place of what is wrong, and displace a falsehood by that which is true, we make progress and add to the welfare of the world. Ignorance being darkness, we thus increase intellectual light.

Dwelling only on the heroic deeds of the past is not enough, and too little attention has been given to the mistakes of the past, and their consequences. Children are given glowing accounts of episodes which were cruel and wicked, and men have been glorified because they won battles, but could not conquer their own passions of greed, lust and cruelty. The past has been quite misrepresented to everyone; the ignorance, misery, filth, and squalor in which our ancestors lived have not been emphasised, but only those deeds which appeal to the imagination, and men have been turned into heroes who in reality were debased and repulsive creatures.

All should be taught the philosophy of history, of the causes which brought about the events. Then will be discovered the reason for those great changes which have come about in the affairs of men. Herein lies the value of history, and it is because this book treats history from this aspect that a clearer picture of the past, it is hoped, is presented than is to be found in most other histories. We all wish to avoid the mistakes of our ancestors, and in history, honestly and intelligently understood, there is a vast field of experience from which to learn those things we should avoid and those we should never neglect.

As we proceed we shall discover how most of the suffering and misery which came upon our ancestors was due to their neglect of the virtues. Consequently we shall realise the great importance of teaching children from an early age the necessity of truth, justice and honesty, the need of toleration and understanding of the other person's point of view, the value of compromise in disputes, that glory and chivalry are to be found in protecting and succouring the weak, and that everyone, in all circumstances, should always be treated with compassion. The man and woman with strength of character always displays self-control, and only weak men and women give way to passion. If the virtues are taught to a child from the time it commences to reason and think, they will never be forgotten, and the time will come, after a few generations have received this teaching, when they will become part of each one and be carried into practice quite naturally.

One of the most monstrous characteristics of Nazi Germany was the deliberate perversion of the minds of the German children. A new generation was educated on ideas which, in the past, have brought about only hatred, misery, and suffering. They were taught to look upon themselves as superior to the rest of mankind, and to treat with contempt those of other nations. Hatred, malice, and all uncharitableness, intrigue, spying on their neighbours, and other revolting ideas were driven into the minds of the young by a gang of the most unscrupulous scoundrels who ever made it their business to rule a country. War, the children were taught, was the most heroic act of a nation, to be a soldier was to be a hero, and to treat foreigners with disdain, and as inferiors, was their birthright. This systematic form of education succeeded in producing a nation of intolerable selfish young fanatics, and we all now know the result to our cost.

Every schoolmaster in Germany was committed to this perversion of the mind of the German youth, as each took the following oath:—

Adolf Hitler, We swear that we will train the youth of Germany, that they grow up in your ideology, for your aims and purposes, in the direction set by your will. This is pledged to you by the whole German system of education, from the primary school through to the university.

What a depraved creature the Hitler ideology produced,[1] but it follows that if children, by debased education, become evil-doers, they can likewise become good and virtuous if they are taught righteousness. How the mind will develop, and what the ethical outlook on life will be when the child becomes a man or a woman, is largely a question of good or evil teaching when it is young and the mind is impressionable.

When we remember that children throughout the world have, for all practical purposes, never received any systematic training in ethical conduct, we need not be surprised at the moral depravity to be found in so many lands. Only one hundred years ago slavery was considered right, and Christians who persecuted non-Christians were considered honourable. Only fifty years ago there was little toleration either in religion or politics, and the children of the poor, from a tender age, had to work in coal pits and factories for a mere pittance. General education only came into being towards the end of last century, before which cruelty to man, woman, child and animal was part of everyday life. So we need not wonder that when the Nazi gang in Germany undertook the training of their youth, in a systematic way, they found virgin soil into which to plant their polluted doctrines.

The Christian Church, which had a dominant

---

[1] When the German army was forced back into German territory in 1944, after devastating and plundering most of Europe, the utter selfishness of the Hitler ideology was well expressed by the following order issued by Field Marshal Model to his troops: "All habits to which you have been accustomed in occupied countries are to be dropped. Smashing of window panes, damaging of furniture in billets, and stealing are strictly forbidden. Whoever trespasses on the property of the German population will be severely punished. Remember, you are back in the Reich."

position in most of Europe up to last century, neglected
not only the teaching of knowledge to the young, but
also to elevate the moral code to its right status.   Its
teachings consist principally of doctrines and dogmas,
and the importance of accepting the creeds of the
faith.   Europe only began to make ethical progress
over the past seventy years when education took the
place of theology, on which everyone before then
had been nurtured.   Unfortunately, in Germany and
Italy, education was used by evil men to help forward
their own wicked designs, and we have witnessed
the melancholy spectacle of young people being
degraded, instead of elevated, by this powerful force
which, if used aright, can bring such good in its
train.

Since the dawn, following a black night of ignorance, we discover a vast improvement in our treatment
of the poor and needy, the weak and the down-
trodden.   Social work then commenced for the betterment and well-being of the people, more being done
for the needs of the poor and of suffering humanity.
A new word, "humanitarianism", came into use, to
cover this new endeavour to create a heaven here on
earth.   What has already been accomplished in this,
and other countries, by the help given to the weak
and needy, should give us encouragement to continue
the effort, and extend the acceptance and practice of
the virtues amongst all nations in their dealings one
with another.

The great success made by Nazi Germany and
Fascist Italy, in the wrong direction, should point
the way to what can be done everywhere in the right
direction.   The child's mind is as impressionable as

molten lava, which, as it grows older, hardens into the strength of a rock. If we put diamonds into the lava it will be difficult to take them out when it becomes a rock. Thus can the mind in early days be moulded for good and not for evil, and it is on the children of the race that the future of civilisation depends.

Knowledge and wisdom are priceless assets. The first has to be acquired and the second cultivated Knowledge comes from effort, and wisdom from experience, but once the effort has been made, and the experience gained, we are endowed with something of greater value than can be measured in earthly terms. With knowledge comes wisdom, and wisdom ranks first of all the gifts with which man is endowed. To attain wisdom, knowledge is essential, but it must be knowledge based on facts. Otherwise the effort in its acquisition is misspent and worthless. It is therefore obvious that all must be trained in the art of weighing up of evidence and of forming sound opinions, as only by the development of the critical faculty can the truth be separated from the false, and herein lies the difficulty we must face.

Every mind thinks differently, because people born in China have another outlook from those born in England; the German aspect is quite dissimilar from the Polish, and the French from the Russian. The western American looks on life differently from the eastern American. Our mental vista is determined by such things as our birthplace, our neighbours, and our proximity to the sea or the mountains. The Tibetan, living in isolation on the slopes of the Himalaya, with few roads and little communication with other lands, has a quite different view of life from that of the people living on an island such as New Zealand.

How is it possible for all these people to form correct opinions, and thus acquire the knowledge which will lead them to wisdom? The world, as the result of the airplane and radio, has become a small place, and it should be possible for the more advanced nations to teach systematically those that are more backward. It will be a long and slow process, but we must remember that education everywhere is only just beginning. If we think of the time man has been a human being as twenty-four hours, then the time some have been only indifferently educated can be considered as the last two minutes of this time. So there is no cause for despair, but rather for much hope that by education he will acquire knowledge, and thus attain to wisdom, which, when reached, will bring peace and goodwill among mankind.

Some day fear will vanish from the earth—fear of disease, fear of death, fear of war, fear of want—but this will only come slowly as man increases in intelligence and wisdom. Meantime, all that each one of us can do should be directed towards helping forward the coming of a better and wiser way of life. This being so, let those who think, who use their reason, and have the welfare of humanity at heart, do their utmost, from this time onwards, to lay the foundation of this better world which will some day come.

CHAPTER II.

RELIGION OR ETHICS?

Introduction. (1) *Righteousness and Wisdom come from Mental Development.* (2) *First Place must be given to the Virtues.* (3) *The Key to the Correct Understanding of History.*

PROBABLY most people, if asked the cause of the evils which afflict the world, would reply by saying that they come from the lack of religion, and that increased religious teaching would put right much of what is wrong. Some of those who think like this have doubtless in mind such sayings as "Love your enemies" and "Love one another", but these ethical precepts have no more to do with religion than has astrology to do with astronomy.

Religion concerns our destiny after death, whereas ethics refer to our conduct one towards another here on earth. So, when we think of these things, let us keep a clear distinction in our minds between religion and ethics, which latter comes from the Greek word *ethikos*, meaning moral. Ethics, or morality, is the outcome of practical experience, and has developed slowly as the race has evolved from the sub-man to what we are today. Ethics, Morality and Law have developed as man has become more and more intelligent, because he has discovered, by experience, that, by practising restraint, or self-control, he has increased in happiness. Theft was the earliest of crimes, to be followed by murder, and then gradually, on this basis, was built up what we today call the moral code.

Morality and Religion, however, have been always associated though never related, and the reason is obvious. The belief in survival after death naturally included the idea that there was another world in which the dead lived, and, as morality developed, the idea arose that the hereafter was divided into two sections, the one where lived the good, and the other which was inhabited by those who had lived evil lives on earth. History has been profoundly influenced by this idea, and to a far greater extent than most people think. The beliefs concerning another world which would be reached after death, and its inhabitants, have deeply affected human thought and action from primitive times, and, as we proceed, we shall find them running like a thread through our story.

Every religion, from the time man developed a moral code, contained the belief about a place in the other world which is commonly called heaven, where live those termed good, and a place for the evil which is called hell. Besides this, the belief in survival, which primarily came from the seeing of apparitions, brought about the belief in the gods, which is just an old name for spirits, who were believed to be responsible for all natural phenomena, growth and decay, besides the creation of the earth and the stars.

Thus we find that every religion includes these beliefs, and from them have grown, like the branches from the parent stem, all the various and innumerable religious creeds of the past and present. As religion developed, the principal gods became known as angels or devils, Christianity arranging the former into archangels and saints, to whom were attributed minor powers, the supreme power resting in one divine Trinity, the creator of the universe and. all mankind. On the other hand, Satan, the god of evil, had a host of devils to do his bidding. Few religions have believed in only one God, the Jewish and Moslem faiths being the two outstanding exceptions of the present time, and it can be said that the vast majority of religions, from early times, have worshipped the gods and attributed to them the creation and sustaining of the universe.

Ethics cannot be termed religion, as a materialist, who has no belief in anything outside of physical matter, may practise, just as much as the believer in one or more gods, all the virtues enjoined by the moral code. He practises the virtues because he believes that it is right that he should do so, and not to please the gods, or for fear of punishment, or hope of reward hereafter. The moral man should need no bribe or threat to help him to lead a good life, as the golden rule of doing to others as he wishes to have done to himself should appeal to everyone, whatever he may think about another life after death. The shining example of this fact is to be found in that high-minded genial philosopher and martyr of the Renaissance, Giordano Bruno, who believed in neither heaven nor hell, and about whom we shall read more later on.

Religion is a very personal affair, and can easily produce selfishness and intolerance in the minds of the ignorant, who become more concerned with the salvation of their own souls, by belief, than with their

duty towards their neighbours. Theological beliefs
have generally been considered more important than
conduct, and this explains why so many religious
people have lived wicked lives. They have been
brought up to think that belief in theological dogmas
and doctrines ensures salvation, and have left aside the
primitive religious belief that one's actions, not one's
beliefs, determines one's place hereafter. This is
just one instance of how ignorance is the curse of
mankind. Many more examples of how ignorance
has adversely affected the happiness of the human
race will be given as we proceed, in the hope that
when the disease is correctly diagnosed future generations will then apply the only known cure to remedy
our present misfortunes.

Religion in future must embrace truth and accept
facts, and it needs no name. Men and women can be
religious without labelling themselves by a name, just
as they may have constructive and sound political
ideas without being connected with any political
party. Union makes for strength, but it does not
always make for righteousness, and the orthodox
of most religious creeds, besides the adherents to most
political formulas, have much to regret in the past and
present for the mistakes of the Church and the Party
to which they gave their support.

How much better it would be if everyone were
independent enough to think for himself, and not as
his Church or Political Party instructed him. If we
could all become sufficiently independent to be
guided by truth and facts, and not by priests and
politicians, how many of the world's troubles would
vanish. Alas, the people are still too ignorant to

think for themselves, and consequently they accept without intelligent thought or criticism what is told them by those they call their leaders. So we must expect that the evils connected with the world's present political and religious systems will remain for some generations to come.

If this book, however, succeeds in its purpose, a foundation will be laid for a better and more intelligent mental outlook which, some day, may gather sufficient force to sweep away the ignorance now destroying what otherwise would be a happy existence on earth. Politics and religion enter largely into the lives of most people, and a proper understanding of each will enhance the happiness of everyone in a way beyond our comprehension.

Another misunderstanding comes from confusing Christianity with ethics, but here again there is no relationship, as the former is a religion composed of certain theological assertions, clearly set down for all to believe, so as to secure salvation hereafter. With few exceptions they are the same for Orthodox Greeks, Roman Catholics and Protestants, and are to be found positively stated in *The Thirty-Nine Articles of Religion* of the Church of England and *The Confession of Faith* of the Church of Scotland. The differences between all the different Christian sects mostly refer to the method of worship and Church government, but, so far as the dogmas and doctrines are concerned, there is little difference of opinion.

In these declarations of the Faith, ethics find no place, in fact they are discouraged, as only believers in the Christian creeds, doctrines, and dogmas are acceptable before God in their practice of what is called "works". The words in the Church of England Prayer Book read:—"Works . . . are not pleasant to God . . . we doubt not but they have the nature of sin". The Roman Catholic Church has quite recently made the same declaration.

This means that the Christian Church teaches that God considers anyone who does acts of kindness, charity, mercy and pity is a sinner for so doing, if the doer is not a believer in the dogmas and doctrines contained in *The Thirty-Nine Articles of Religion*. If the reader will turn to Volume 2, Chapter XII, where these articles are summarised in the section entitled "The Effect of the Apostolic Church on the Reformation", he will better realise what this means. The Church discouraged works of mercy, and elevated faith, because, if the people thought that they could secure salvation by doing good deeds, then its influence would go, and its treasury would become empty.

This all makes clear that religion has nothing to do with conduct, but everything to do with belief. So the clergy are chosen, not because of their character, but because they either honestly believe, or say that they believe, the assertions contained in the articles of religion. These they swear before God to believe, and this act enables them to be ordained into the ministry of the Church. Belief, not conduct, is the standard of the Church, which fact accounts for the wickedness and evil about which we shall be reading in some of the pages which follow.

The Christian religion has given comfort to millions, but it has also been the cause of great misery and suffering. Those who have accepted its creed have felt relief in the belief that the consequence of their sins and wickedness have been taken from them by the death of another, who came to earth to suffer and die so that all believers, good and bad, kind and cruel, saints and evil-doers, victims and aggressors, would be certain óf reaching heaven. Faith came first and conduct last, as, with the punishment taken by another, there was nothing further to worry about if the rites of the Church were duly observed. Baptism, and the partaking of the Eucharist, ensured membership of the Church, and this secured salvation, because the Christian Church claimed to be the only door through which one could pass into heaven.

The terrible condition of Europe throughout the Christian era followed from the acceptance of this immoral teaching, as will be made clear in later chapters. All that need be said here is that the history of this era is a most damning indictment of Christian teaching. Salvation was always possible on the death-bed, provided the one dying partook of the Eucharist, while soldiers did likewise before battle, so as to be relieved and saved from their past sins and wickedness. For the same reason toreadors always receive the Eucharist before a bull-fight. Christianity has been tried and found wanting, and its doctrine of the salvation of all believers, no matter how wickedly and disgracefully they have lived, has made the Christian era a time of hypocrisy, intolerance and evil-doing for which there is no other parallel in history.

Wrong-doing is selfishness, and only the individual can make himself unselfish and rectify his past errors. We are our own saviours, and cannot pass the responsibility on to someone else, as everyone must reap what he sows. Slowly this vital lesson is being learned, and, as this happens, we become less selfish and more righteous. Just as man has gained more control over himself has .he been happier. Just as primitive man preferred the peace and harmony of a summer day, when the sun-god was reigning, to stormy, thundery weather, when the gods of thunder, storm and rain were in power, so he came to see that for his own peace of mind, for his own greater happiness, it was wiser to be less selfish, and to think of himself less and of others more. He found that when he ceased beating his wife he received, in exchange for giving up this pleasure, her love and sympathy and the same with his children.

Though he lost the satisfaction of clubbing his enemy, he gained in exchange a greater tranquillity of mind, because he was not so fearful of being clubbed by someone who considered him an enemy. Though he lost the gratification of letting loose his unbridled rage he did not suffer from the rage of others. He also found that it was not wise to interfere with his neighbour's property, and so he obtained greater security for his own. He thus exchanged a turbulent life for one of greater peace and security. The evolution of mind, from that revealed by a savage to mind as expressed by the righteous man, has been slow, but, as this development took place, man found it more expedient to control his passions, and thus increase his happiness and security.

This explains how morality developed. It has nothing whatever to do with religion, as it came about by learning from experience. Every individual is by nature selfish, and, if happiness could have come about better by constant fighting, quarrelling, cruelty, and persecution, this would have become the order of the day. The race would consequently have been obliterated, and the strongest or most cunning would have been the last to survive. Because man is a selfish individual he thinks of himself first, but, as he grew in intelligence, he realised that to think of others, and their feelings, was the height of wisdom, and that the more he thought of others the happier he was.

This policy is called unselfishness, but it is really due to intelligent selfishness. It is due to his own wish for happiness, and the happiness of those he likes and loves, whom he wishes, because of this affection, to be happy like himself. He thinks of the happiness of others because he has found that by making others happy he increases his own happiness. Love is the greatest force in the world, comprising as it does this thought for the feelings of others. It means that one's mind is telepathically in touch with the minds of others, and that to upset another mind reacts on the mind responsible, which is in turn upset. In other words, as our minds become more developed and refined, as they become less influenced by their physical habitation, they reach out and blend with the minds of others. Anything done or said which creates disharmony in one mind reacts on those with which it comes in contact, thus upsetting the mental harmony of all.

Ethical conduct has developed just as the human mind has become more refined. It has no more to do with religion than has marriage. Marriage is a social contract, and the moral law is a social law which has grown up and developed through the experience of thousands of years. Right and wrong, having nothing to do with religion, are in quite a different category from sin, which is a contravention of the religious code, and not of the social code.

The sinner is the one who, by his beliefs or deeds, is considered to have displeased one or more gods. A sinner is one who does not conform to the orthodox or prevailing religious opinions of his time. So we have the sin of unbelief, the sin of blasphemy, the sin of disobedience to the divine will as expressed by the priests, the sin of not keeping the religious taboos, the sin of communicating with the departed, and the unforgivable sin against the Holy Ghost, which we now know from *The Teaching of the Twelve Apostles*, an early 2nd century Christian document recently discovered, to be nothing more than doubting the fact that an honest medium is the mouthpiece of a communicating spirit.

Throughout religious history it has been a sin to do other than respect the priests, who were the representatives of the gods on earth. Anyone who ridiculed them, or doubted the claims they made, was one of the worst sinners, because he was undermining the standing of this class in the minds of the people. We remember the terrible punishment inflicted on forty-two little children, when they called out to Elisha, "Go up, thou bald head". Humour was evidently not one of the strong points of this representative of Jehovah on earth, as he cursed them, and then two bears came along and devoured them all. This story served as a warning to everybody that the priests must be respected, and that if they were not the gods would be angry.

One who denied the existence of the gods was a sinner. One who did not perform the sacrifices to the gods was likewise a sinner. He who scoffed at the waste involved in sacrifice, or in the religious beliefs of the time, was a· sinner. In other words, anyone who in any way did anything, or said anything, which could affect the social status of the priests, or endanger the regular supply of offerings to the gods, which were reserved for the priests, was a sinner.

The word "sin" is often used when the word "evil" or "wrong-doing" should be used. We talk of the seven deadly sins, namely pride, covetousness, lust, anger, gluttony, envy, and sloth, just as we talk of the sin of breaking the Ten Commandments. It is foolish to be proud, but not sinful. One can covet something, but so long as one does not steal it no wrong is done. Lust and anger are not sins in themselves but they often lead to unhappiness and wrong-doing. Gluttony is no sin, but it is unwise if one wishes to keep healthy. To envy your neighbour often acts as a spur to harder work. Certainly it is not a sin any more than is slothfulness or indolence.

Only two of the Ten Commandments refer to sin. It is sinful to take the name of the Lord thy God in vain, just as it is sinful not to keep holy the Sabbath day. Anyone who works on the Sabbath, or causes anyone to work, is a sinner if he is a Christian or a Jew, but not if he is a Hindu. If, on the other hand, a Christian, Jew, or Hindu steals he violates the moral law and becomes a wrong-doer, transgressor or evil-doer. This makes clear the point. The moral law is

world-wide, but the religious law relates only to the
religion professed.

To sin is to break the religious law, but to commit
a crime is to contravene the moral law. As to the
Commandment about honouring one's father and
mother, it depends on whether they deserve it or not.
If they do not deserve to be honoured, it is neither
sinful nor wrong not to honour them. Is it possible
for a child to honour a father who is a drunkard and a
criminal, and a mother who is vindictive and spiteful?
To commit a murder is a crime. To commit adultery
is the breaking of a contract, and comes under wrong-
doing. Theft is a crime just as is perjury or bearing
false witness, and the last Commandment forbids
covetousness, which we have already considered.

These Ten Commandments are interesting as
showing a stage in the development of the race, but
it is strange that they are still repeated in most churches
throughout the year, as if they contained the entire
moral code. If the Hebrews had been more developed
they would have attributed the following to Jehovah:
"Thou shalt not be cruel to animals", "Thou shalt
not hunt them nor cause them painful deaths", "Thou
shalt not be cruel to children and make them suffer",
"Thou shalt not permit poverty amidst plenty, and
those who have must give something to those who
have not", "Thou shalt not go to war against thy
neighbour", "Thou shalt not permit mediums to be
burned, as it is through them man's destiny is revealed",
"Thou shalt permit free speech and free thought,
as only through them is progress possible", "Thou
shalt acquire knowledge which is vital for thy health,
comfort and happiness", "Thou shalt always be kind

and considerate, showing mercy, kindness and toleration to all, irrespective of race or religion".

All these things, and many others, were omitted, because the Hebrews had not risen enough in intelligence and wisdom to incorporate them in their rules of life. They had only reached the position of realising that murder, theft, and perjury were crimes against the community. They were no further on than the savage of today, whose moral and social codes also recognise these as crimes. So long as savages do not murder, steal, or bear false witness against their neighbours, so long as they keep the taboos of the tribe, and believe in the tribe's priest-magician, they are good tribesmen, just as were those who kept Jehovah's Ten Commandments amongst the tribe of semi-savages Moses led out of Egypt.

A man might be an exemplary husband and father, fair and straight in his dealings with all men, generous and kind, have lived a pure and unspotted life, and yet, if he rejected the religious beliefs of his time, and was clever enough to realise the frauds and mistakes of the priests, or scoffed at the powers attributed to the gods, he was one of the blackest of sinners. On the other hand, belief in what the priests told the people were the wishes of the gods ensured happiness hereafter, no matter how one lived on earth.

To believe that the gods and goddesses were just discarnate men and women like ourselves made the order of the priesthood unnecessary, as it claimed to be the intermediary between those powers which ruled the universe and mankind. One who made such a suggestion was a sinner. Heaven and hell have always been the special preserves of the priests, and, from early times to the present day, they have opposed to the utmost of their power any attempt to solve the mystery of death by experimental methods or rational thinking. To find, as some have now discovered, that the other world is a natural one, that its order of existence resembles this one, that its inhabitants are men and women like ourselves, and that to enter it requires no special passport, is, in the eyes of the priests and the orthodox, nothing less than giving up religion.

When the discovery of the few becomes accepted by the many it will certainly change the religious outlook, and make the profession of the priesthood unnecessary, but it will never abolish the religious instinct in man, or deter people coming together in a church or elsewhere to commune on the deeper problems of existence. The religious instinct in man comes from his mind, related to what we call the divine. It is sustained by his psychic structure, and it can function apart from churches, temples, or priests. Just as a child grows up and can discard the use of a nurse, so the human race is gradually growing in intelligence and throwing off the priests, who are becoming unnecessary to the community. In their place teachers have arisen to lead the people along the path of truth and righteousness.

When man becomes intelligent enough to realise that sin, in its correct meaning, has no more existence than has a nightmare, he will be able to order his own life without ecclesiastical help. Sin and hell, both priestly inventions, without substance or reality as presented in the past, are the basis of all organised religion. On the wealth the clergy of Christendom have received from the faithful and the fearful, who mortgaged their lands and gave large endowments to the Church in the days gone by, on the labours of these men, who extracted this vast wealth from the people by expounding volubly on sin and hell, the present occupiers of all the state churches now live, quite independent of the small collections contributed by their meagre congregations.

Sin, Hell and Priestcraft are a trinity which has thrived on ignorance. When knowledge takes the place of ignorance the ecclesiastical organisation will become a skeleton without public support, and only kept in being by its accumulated wealth. Not until religion is purged of the priesthood will it occupy the place it should in the minds of an intelligent community, as religion, rightly understood, concerns man's relation to the etheric order of existence, and is entirely a personal matter, requiring no priestly intermediary. The medium will some day replace the priest, and churches will become places where contact is made with the etheric world, as happened in the Apostolic Church before the priest overthrew the medium and usurped his place.

Each saviour-god religion, as it developed, adopted the view that there was a heaven and a hell, one place for those who believed its creed, and another for unbelievers. Hell came to be looked upon as the destination of those who did not accept its Saviour, and heaven as the future abode of those who did. Little did these ancient people realise that as one sows so one reaps, and that punishment comes from mental remorse, just as happiness comes from mental contentment. We make our own heaven or hell, both in this world and the next. That, however, was beyond the grasp of our ancestors, and, in consequence, they imagined the misery of the unbeliever, just as they thought of the blissful happiness of the believer.

The sinner's misery hereafter reached its height when they pictured the damned in a never-dying fire, for ever suffering the torture of burning. Their ideas about heaven were just as extravagant as were their ideas about hell. Those living in towns imagined that it was a place with streets paved with gold; others, who enjoyed music, as one continual praising of the gods, while, to those living in the country, it was a happy hunting-ground where they could hunt and kill to their heart's content.

So religion will not stop war; in fact religion was the cause of many of the wars in Europe up to the 18th century, each side believing that God was its ally. Religion has its place in our lives, but each one must be at liberty to interpret its meaning as he thinks right. It is quite a personal matter, as the origin of the word makes clear. Our word comes from the Latin *re-ligare*, meaning "to bind again", and it relates to our psychic structure and its relation to that which we call divine.

Leaving mystical thought aside let us say, in terms which should be understood by all with a knowledge of physical science, that religion relates to the other order of life inhabiting a world of finer substance surrounding and interpenetrating this earth, the vibrations of which have a greater frequency than those which constitute the earth. To these vibrations of greater frequency our duplicate etheric bodies are related, as to that other order of life they pass at death, quite naturally, because survival of the mind and the etheric body conform to natural law.[1]

Orthodox religion, made up of mystical beliefs, ceremonials, doctrines and dogma, never has done anything, and never·can help, to bring mankind to a realization of the evil and folly of war. On the other hand, religion, in its right meaning, makes clear that this earth is a place of preparation for the next life, and that nothing should be done to interfere with the natural ordering of our lives. That marks the limit of religion so far as our ethical conduct is concerned. Here on earth we have our own problems to face, and concentrating our thoughts unduly on the next order of existence will never improve the lot of mankind on earth. It never has in the past, and never will in the future.

Religion has comforted untold millions, but those who only lay up their treasure in heaven cannot also give proper attention to the affairs of this earth.

---

[1] The etheric duplicate body, which has been seen on countless occasions down the ages, is the structure which interpenetrates the cells of the physical body and holds them together. At death, when it withdraws, accompanied by mind, the physical body decomposes as the frame which held it together has gone to function in another range of vibrations with which the etheric body is in tune.

Physical vibrations then become unreal and unsensed, and the etheric vibrations become real and tangible. This constitutes a new world to the released etheric individual, who continues to live in much the same space as formerly, but in a different range of vibrations. Consequently what was not seen and felt when in the physical body is now sensed, and what was real in the physical becomes unreal and unsensed.

The word "etheric" was used by the ancient Greeks to denote what they called the subtle invisible substance permeating space and filling the intervening space between the particles of air and matter. Now it is applied to the ranges of vibrations beyond the physical, beyond those we term ultra violet. Here on earth we perceive so limited a range of vibrations that what appeals to us can be compared to an inch in a mile. This vitally important subject is fully and simply explained in *On the Edge of the Etheric.*

Religion has also caused untold misery and cruelty, as it has bred intolerance, and the sense of superiority amongst large numbers who considered themselves amongst the saved and the elect. This has generated their hatred and dislike for all who did not worship the same god in the same way as they did.

Their religion has not made them kind, tolerant, merciful, just and honest, but often the reverse, and history records that the orthodox, as a rule, have often lacked the ethical sense, and all feeling of kindness, mercy and honesty when their religion became involved. Consequently war, torture, imprisonment, murder and loss of individual liberty are associated with religion down the ages. So let us pass religion by as of no help to us in solving our problem of bringing peace and goodwill to mankind.

(1) Righteousness and Wisdom come from Mental Development.

A study of the past makes clear that greater righteousness, and increased wisdom, always came from the development of the mind. For long periods the mind of man seemed to be stagnant, wickedness flourished, and follies abounded. Then a bright spot appeared, knowledge was encouraged, wisdom increased, and evil decreased. Then the spot-light of intelligence moved to some other land, but its illuminating influence was never wholly lost, the result being that gradually the mind of man has slowly developed, and this has happened in some places much more quickly than in others.

Looking back over past ages we have a long

period from which to draw our lessons to guide us in the years to come. The knowledge of the past experiences of the race, and the instruction to be gained therefrom, can be of practical help to us, because this knowledge can be applied to a code of ethics which will be found to be the most advantageous to follow. Expediency is the solution of the problem, as man, being a selfish creature, is always willing to follow the course from which he profits the most. Only ignorance has prevented him from doing this in the past, and thus attaining the comfort, prosperity and happiness which all desire.

How then should we act and speak one towards another, and how should each one live so as to secure his own, and the general happiness of everyone? Most people will admit that there is only one way to achieve this end, and that is by each one of us making and keeping the following personal resolve:

My conduct must be guided by the golden rule of only doing and saying what I would like to have done or said to me, and never of doing or saying anything which I would not like to have done or said to me.

The above sentence expresses a very vital fact. Though it contains few words, yet these words are of superlative importance to mankind. Who it was who first thought of this great idea we do not know. All we know is that it can first be traced to Confucius, the Chinese philosopher, who, in the 5th century B.C., was revered for his wisdom, and is today looked upon with respect and veneration by a third of the human race. If only the people of this world had been able to adapt themselves to this golden rule, how very different would have been the story of the race, and it is just because they have not been able to do so that history is a record of much unnecessary unhappiness and human misery.

Some, of course, will say that to live in accordance with this rule is impossible. This, however, is not the case, as the happiest families in the land are those who practise it in their daily lives. If it can be adopted in the family it can equally well be followed by the nation and internationally. The fact that it can be practised in the family is proof that it can be adopted universally, and that it is not an impracticable platitude. It just means consideration for others, and all should be taught this from childhood upwards.

Consideration for others is a state of mind which can be developed and cultivated. It has taken thousands of years for the most developed amongst mankind to discover that in this one word, "consideration", rests the cure for most of the world's troubles. How simple it seems, but how difficult it is to practise.

We frail creatures generally think the wrong way round, and are continually deceived by appearances, one of the greatest deceptions from which we suffer being that we think happiness can be attained by thinking only of ourselves. We all realise that this earth is no paradise, and that human frailty is the cause of much of our unhappiness, but how few try always to practise everywhere the only known cure, consideration for others. The happiness of the people of this earth rests with each individual, and only when each one does to others what he would like to have done to himself will this be fully attained.

The history of the human race reveals not only how little consideration our ancestors have shown

towards one another, but how lightly they have regarded the value of life. Life is the most sacred and
cherished possession of everyone, the highest expression of nature, and yet so many in the past and present
have treated it as of no account. Life cannot be
destroyed, but how easily it can be separated from its
contact with matter. Children are created on the
impulse of the moment, just as men, women and
children are murdered ruthlessly, as if life were something of no value, to be treated casually according to
the passing mood. So the accounts of mass massacres,
which have come about from war and other causes,
run through all the pages of history as if they pertained to everyday affairs.

Our ancestors took this mass slaughter as something natural; war and destruction, massacres and over-
population, being to them just part of their everyday
life, and nothing was ever done to raise life to a
height of sanctity, and have such deeds considered so
revolting that they never would be permitted. To kill
anyone is the most terrible crime anyone can commit,
and whether it is called war or murder the effect is the
same, the severing of a life from its body by violence.
No one can restore life to a body, and what we cannot
do we should never undo, as to break the life cord,
which none can mend, is to become involved in an act
of which we on earth, with our limited power of
comprehension, cannot see the end.

Only by a complete change of outlook on the
value of life will the human race cease to suffer from
all the heart-rending experiences which our own and
past generations have had to go through. Because
of collective human indifference, soldiers, under the

instructions of tyrants, intent on glory, plunder and power, have treated individual lives as if they were of no importance, the slaughter of battle being accepted as necessary so that the desire of the leader be satisfied. Solely by impressing on children everywhere the sanctity of life will all this wickedness cease, as only when everyone realises how terrible it is to force life out of the body will violence cease to be used to settle disputes, or to gain greater wealth or power for the individual or the nation.

Let us train up the children everywhere on these lines, and then they in turn will train their children. So on it will go like a snowball, until some day the great-grandchildren will look back on those who went before them as not only wicked but as utterly stupid and unpractical people, who wasted valuable lives, besides their energies and resources, in grabbing and quarrelling, a state of affairs which led only to destruction, suffering, and misery for everyone. Only the gangsters at the top secured anything, if they were successful, the people, who were their dupes or victims, gaining nothing.

If children, and their children, are taught aright, it will become in time second nature to future generations to think along right lines. If they think aright they will act aright, but the training must be systematic, the government of each nation making itself responsible for their ethical education. To begin with, some nations will stand out against this proposal, others will continue the old methods, but some day all must come into line as the mind of man develops.

The child must have drilled into his mind that it is wiser to be just than to be unjust, and likewise with all the other virtues. If this is done from childhood upwards it will be discovered in time, when the child becomes a man or a woman, that it will be mental agony to do what is wrong and wicked. The harmony of the mind is very easily upset, and, as we develop mentally, this psychic link which we have one with another becomes more pronounced. Thus we hate to hurt one we love; in fact we would rather be hurt ourselves than cause pain and suffering to our nearest and dearest.

It only requires increased mental development for the psychic connection to be strengthened to include all our fellow men and women, so that in time what we feel towards those we hold most dear will be felt towards everyone. To act unkindly towards any one will pain our descendants, if their minds are rightly developed, just as we today would feel if we committed an unjust act to our neighbour. Our neighbour means more than those we know and meet each day. Our neighbour must mean the people of other lands, and of all races and creeds. Our neighbour means the natives of Africa, the Chinese, the black, the white, the yellow races, and all mankind, and we must go even further and extend our sympathy to embrace all animals, both wild and tame.

If we read in our newspapers one day that the Pope had purchased some slaves, both Protestants and Roman Catholics alike would feel deep resentment at this outrage, and yet Pope Gregory I was the owner of a thousand slaves. Mental development has brought about this change of outlook. If the King today insulted a famous historian by treating him with disdain, and terming him a mere scribbler, he would lose our respect, but this is how the autocratic George III scorned the famous Gibbon, who wrote one of the greatest histories of all times, and Shakespeare was treated with the same disdainful contempt by Queen Elizabeth.

If a Bill were now before the House of Lords for the prevention of cruelty to animals, and we learned that no bishop supported it, we would express our feeling of disgust with considerable heat, and yet this is what happened in 1809 when the Bill for the prevention of cruelty to animals was voted upon in the House of Lords. If we heard today that a Bill for the abolition of the British trade in capturing and selling slaves had been introduced into the House of Lords, and had received the support of only two bishops, we would consider that those who opposed it, or did not support it, were entirely lacking in all feeling of human justice, and yet this is what happened in 1807 when this Bill was before the House of Lords.

Likewise we would be furious if we read in our newspapers that a Government Bill for the education of the people had been thrown out by the House of Lords, but this is what happened to the first Education Bill in 1807, against which the bishops raised so much opposition that nothing came of this attempt at education for another sixty-three years. Moreover,. only two bishops supported the various Bills introduced into the House of Lords to reduce the terrible drunkenness of those days.

The tale of opposition pursued by the Anglican bishops last century to all humanitarian reforms is recorded in Chapter XV, and yet, in those bad old days, when theology reigned supreme and education hardly existed, the people accepted it all as a matter of course, just as they countenanced drunkenness in all grades of society as part of their everyday life. Now education has largely cured drunkenness, and for the same reason we are more humane, and would be shocked if today Parliament was petitioned to continue the use of torture, as happened last century.

We would not now permit little boys to go up our chimneys to clean them, as happened up to 1875, or children of from five years of age upwards to work in our coal pits and factories, as happened up to 1890, but to our grandfathers this seemed to be what was right and proper. It was only after Lord Shaftesbury had fought for years against these evils, and endured untold abuse, that an effort was made to have them abolished, though fifty years had to pass before the worst were swept away. This came about as the result of developing intelligence, due to increased education, and less belief in orthodox religion which taught that God had placed everyone in the place intended, and all must accept conditions, good or bad, as they found them.

We would also revolt against the death sentence for petty theft, flogging criminals to death, debtors being put in prison, the press gang, children in rags begging and sleeping on the streets, labourers, artisans, and their families, living in filthy slums, and numerous other evils of less than a hundred years ago. At the beginning of the 19th century the insane were kept chained to walls in dark cells with only straw to lie on, while the village "natural" was chained up like a dog and slept in a kind of kennel, being often nearly naked or in rags.

These mentally unbalanced people were dropped into "surprise baths", bound to revolving chairs, confined in iron cages, and frequently flogged and starved, the purpose being to drive the devil out of them. If one were found dead, the jury at the inquest would return the verdict, "Death by the visitation of God". Today there are 8700 district nurses on duty in our towns and villages, and the insane, the poor, and the needy are treated with compassion and kindness at the expense of the nation, because we would rather have less to spend on ourselves than know that others suffered from want of proper care and nourishment.

We would be shocked beyond measure if we went to church one Sunday, and heard the parson say that "the majority of human beings are destined to eternal torture in hell fire in full view of Almighty God", and yet our grandfathers and grandmothers listened to this blasphemy without twitching an eyelid, and also gave their children books of sermons to read in which these abominable sentiments were expressed. They accepted the belief that all were eternally damned who did not believe as they did, just as they approved of sermons denouncing the use of chloroform, which was vividly described by one parson as "a decoy of Satan, robbing God of the deep earnest cries of pain that should arise to him in time of trouble".

Our ancestors were cruel, intolerant, ignorant, and stupid because of the fact that their minds had not developed beyond that stage. Consequently they accepted a social system, and religious beliefs, which today are repugnant, because our minds, through education, have developed and become more refined, making us all less self-centred, our individual happiness being now more dependent on all being happy and contented.

One hundred years ago there was much less liberty and freedom in Britain than there is now, and thousands suffered banishment and imprisonment for saying then what we today would consider they had every right to say. Bad as things were a hundred years ago, Britain was then a paradise to live in compared with what it was in the 17th century, when torture, imprisonment and death were inflicted on any one differing in any way from the authorities of Church and State.

There would be little sale today for books supporting slavery, and yet eighty years ago they circulated freely, especially in America. Today we would be shocked to hear the clergy of all denominations upholding slavery as a divine institution, just as our feelings would be revolted if we heard that a ship had set sail from Bristol for the west coast of Africa to take on board a cargo of negroes for transportation to Jamaica, where they were to work as slaves on the plantations. It would be no satisfaction to be told that this cheap labour would mean increased dividends to the shareholders in that country's sugar plantations. Still, the fact remains that only a little over one hundred years ago our ancestors regularly perpetrated this crime, and thought that it was the right and proper thing to do.

The cruelty and suffering inflicted on these poor wretches is past description. Husbands were separated from wives, and parents from children, and yet the slave-catchers, the slave-transporters, and those who bought the slaves from the fiends who caught them, were mostly all devout Christians, this state of affairs having gone on throughout the entire Christian era. When, however, the mentality of many of the people rose last century above the level of their inspired holy book to realise the wickedness of slavery, we find that from nearly every Christian pulpit there was an outcry against this departure from the Word of God. So it is evident that the Church authorities did not approve of the abolition of this ghastly traffic in human souls, though they now falsely state that it was their religion which brought it to an end!

Why, then, was all this cruelty stopped when it meant such a valuable addition to our national wealth? The reason is because we had developed mentally to a point when we would rather be poorer than obtain wealth made in such a way. The abolition of slavery in the British colonies marks a step forward, and is just one of many the race has taken from the time our primitive ancestors, the sub-men, gave thought to nothing beyond what concerned themselves. The abolition of slavery was only one step of many which developing mind brought about, and the same cause will force our descendants to take many more steps upwards, one of which will be the abolition of war as a means of settling international disputes.

If slavery could be abolished, with its accompanying loss to industry, because it revolted the human mind, war can likewise be abolished for the same reason, and it is only a matter of time until mental development makes this possible. Then a nation which wants something belonging to its neighbour will strive for it by every peaceful method, because its inhabitants would be horrified at the idea of killing their neighbours so as to get some of their territory. Mind is king, and this king is growing up from being a child, and is becoming a thinking rational man, leaving behind him the follies of youth. We must not be impatient, because evolution is a slow process. Though we may not see the realisation of our aspirations, our children may, and their children will perhaps some day realise that our dream has come true.

Everyone living in Christian countries has been morally retarded by the complete lack of ethical teaching each received when young, and it is now our duty to make certain that future generations do not suffer from the same mistakes. It does not help one morally to be living in a country which reveres a book containing the following instructions:—

Thus saith the Lord of hosts [to King Saul]. . . . Now go and smite Amalek, and utterly destroy all that they have, and spare them not; but slay both man and woman, infant and suckling, ox and sheep, camel and ass. (I *Samuel* xv, ·2–3.)

Because Saul spared Amalek and the cattle, which latter he reserved for a sacrifice to the Lord, the Philistines were sent by the Lord to attack Israel. The book inappropriately called *The Holy Bible*, which contains this story, and the record of many other ghastly atrocities, which were claimed to be approved by God, is also called by Christians "The Word of God", and was termed by Queen Victoria "the source of Britain's greatness".

At the coronation of each British king and queen the Archbishop of Canterbury hands this book to the newly crowned king or queen with the remark,

"This book contains the oracles of God", because it is believed that both the Old and New Testaments contain the only way of salvation, as revealed solely to Christians by God from heaven. They are read from in church each Sunday, the reader beginning with the exclamation "Here beginneth the Word of God" or "Here beginneth God's Holy Word", and, when he finishes the reading, he closes the book with another exclamation "Here endeth the Word of God".

In some Christian churches the clergy vary the exclamation, and the reader states that he is about to read the lesson for the day. "Here beginneth the first lesson" he says, and finishes by the statement "Here endeth the first lesson". So everyone is made fully aware that they have been listening to something to be remembered. The dictionary tells us that the word "lesson" means systematic instruction, and when we remember that from the Bible both young and old have in the past received their moral instruction, we can better appreciate the reason for the lack of ethical conduct throughout Christendom up to our own times.

The pronouncement, "When thou goest out to battle against thine enemies . . . the Lord your God is he that goeth with you, to fight for you against your enemies" (*Deuteronomy* xx, 1-4) has been a great inspiration to Christians throughout the Christian era in their wars one with another, each Christian nation believing that the same God which they all worship is fighting on its side. Every inter-Christian war reveals this extraordinary fact, and the last war was no exception, the same deity being appealed to for victory by both sides in the conflict. But one of the worst features of Christianity in the past has been its generation of hatred. "If any man come to me, and hate not his father, and mother, and wife, and children, and brethren, and sisters . . . he cannot be my disciple." (*Luke* xiv, 26.)

These words were put into the mouth of Jesus by some fanatical early Christian priest, and they have fomented the intolerance which has been such a feature during the Christian era. How these words came to be attributed to Jesus, and their evil consequences, will be made clear as we proceed.

When, therefore, we read in the coming chapters, of the wars and cruelty of the Christian era, let us remember that the people concerned had been trained from childhood in the idea that cruelty, injustice, and slaughter were approved by their god, who inspired David to write:—

Break their teeth, O God, in their mouth . . . let them be as cut in pieces. (*Psalm* lviii, 6.)

The righteous shall rejoice when he seeth the vengeance: he shall wash his feet in the blood of the wicked. (*Psalm* lviii, 10.)

Happy shall he be that taketh and dasheth thy little ones against the stones. (*Psalm* cxxxvii, 9.)

That thy foot may be dipped in the blood of thine enemies. (*Psalm* lxviii, 23.)

Let his days be few . . . Let his children be fatherless, and his wife a widow. Let his children be continually vagabonds, and beg: let them seek their bread also out of their desolate places. (*Psalm* cix, 8.)

Much more in the same strain could be quoted, but this should suffice. What a contrast to the beautiful and noble sentiments uttered by Marcus Aurelius, Seneca, and other Pagan philosophers, whom stupid and intolerant Christians have always

classed amongst the damned heathen! If Christians
must have ancient literature read to them in their
churches, if they prefer to hear the opinions of the
past instead of the greater wisdom of the present,
why do they not have read to them, in place of *The
Holy Bible*, passages from Seneca's *Epistulae Morales*
or the *Meditations* of Marcus Aurelius? Therein will
be found quite sufficient passages to provide two
fresh lessons each Sunday, and they would certainly
be more elevating than the stories about the exploits
of a savage warrior called Joshua, or the cut-throat
bandit who became King David.

Mental development has turned all intelligent
people in our own time against these savage ideas,
but our grandparents saw nothing wrong in them,
and considered it blasphemy to question the justice
of all the barbarities contained in the Bible. In the
18th century a schoolmaster named Peter Annet
criticised some of the blood-thirsty passages in the
Psalms, and the terrible punishment he received will be
told in Chapter XV, which deals with that period.
So, when we read almost daily of the lamentations of
the clergy at the falling off in church attendance, let us
remember that they stand for a discredited idea of God,
one which the people have outgrown, the prevalent
belief amongst the majority being that religion is an
aspect of thought, higher and nobler than the one
presented to us in Christian churches.

Nevertheless the ministers of religion persist in
preaching their threadbare theology, as they have
nothing else to put in its place. By means of the
B.B.C. Religious Committee, composed of churchmen and presided over by a priest, the clergy have

secured a monopoly of broadcasting, so far as religion is concerned, as only they and all who think the orthodox way are allowed near the microphone. Consequently both adults and children hear the same old theology which so degraded our ancestors. Not so long ago a panegyric was given to the children, during the "Children's Hour", about David, the reputed author of the foregoing and many other barbarous sentiments. One would think that this man, who is presented to us in Hebrew history as a cut-throat, bandit, plunderer, blackmailer, traitor, murderer, adulterer, and a savage towards his enemies, was the last person on earth to hold up to children as an example, especially at a time when we were fighting a war against imperialist aggression.

David, the unscrupulous Hebrew empire builder, and other barbarians of his race, who perpetrated crimes as black as any done by the Nazi gang of criminals, were the inspiration of our grandparents, and the Christians who preceded them, their lives being taken as a pattern for all to follow. This being so, there is little wonder that the Christian era is the most cruel and debased period in history. Need we be surprised that in this epoch more wars have been fought, and more persecution has been inflicted, than in any other period of history? Still, the people are so ignorant that they believe our priests, and certain politicians, when they say that the Second World War was fought by Britain to preserve Christian civilisation. Every lie is a welcome guest to the unscrupulous mind when to tell the truth presents difficulties.

This misleading of the people was a regular feature of the B.B.C. during the war, as its Religious

Committee made it their special duty to represent the Christian era as an age of righteousness, to which we must now return. Never would it allow those who knew better, or were more honest, to put forward the truth, and it faithfully followed the German method of propaganda by spreading false ideas while at the same time banning that which is true.

History contains numerous instances of the people being misled by their political and religious leaders, but never has there been a more glaring example of misrepresentation on the part of both politicians and priests, and placid acceptance by the majority of the people. The people were repeatedly told during the war, and are still being told from the pulpit, the platform, and by means of the radio, that we fought the last war to save Christian civilisation, to uphold the Christian tradition, to secure Christian democracy, Christian ideals, and to keep Christian morality from being banished off the face of this earth.

This downright falsehood is watered and fed by all those whose interests lie within the Christian religion, but their claims are like a tinsel fire which may sparkle but never can give heat. The priests know that if the people discover the true history of the Christian faith they will be abandoned, and that they will then have to earn their living as honest men, while the politicians know that most of their constituents are prejudiced towards the State religion, and they speak accordingly.

We fought the last war to prevent the return of Christian civilisation, and those who read this book to the end will agree that this is so. They will also agree that Viscount Halifax, when Foreign Secretary,

Dr. Cosmo Gordon Lang, when Archbishop of Canterbury, and numerous other outstanding politicians and priests, misled the people when they said over the radio, and in their public speeches, that we were fighting for Christian civilisation and a Christian way of life. This is just another example of public ignorance, as the newspapers took up the tale and the people believed it. Dr. Lang also proposed (*The Times*, 12th May, 1941) "A Christian Order for Britain". Surely everyone experienced more than enough of the Christian Order for Europe, including Britain, from the 4th to the 19th centuries, without wishing to have it back again.

This misleading of the people is possible because the vast majority know nothing about history. The only ancient history they know is contained in the Old Testament, about an insignificant tribe of barbarians who believed that their tribal deity approved, or disapproved, of what they did in their politics and religion. Their self-conceit was colossal, their ignorance profound, and in consequence they called themselves "God's chosen people". Their tribal deity was taken over by the Christian religion, and Christians in every land have been taught ever since to revere and follow the teachings contained in their holy book as God-inspired. Is there any wonder that Christendom is in its present tragic condition?

Another falsehood set about by both our priests and certain devout politicians is that the Germans are Pagans, and that we fought the last war against Paganism, whatever that might mean. The word Pagan in Latin means "country district", and came into use in the early days of Christianity because the country people accepted the new religion more slowly than did the town people. The German people are more Christian than the British, if church attendance is any guide, and a German Protestant bishop recently claimed that ninety-five per cent. of Germans were Christians. About one half are Roman Catholics, and the other half are Protestants, under the name of Lutherans, and one has only to visit Germany to see their well-attended churches every Sunday. Family worship is more common in Germany than in Great Britain, and from every point of view the Germans are Christians.

The last war was therefore a war between Christian nations, if we exclude the Japanese, a fact well known to every educated person. Why, therefore, did the British clergy and politicians spread the falsehood that the Germans are Pagans? The answer is doubtless because they were ashamed that a nation which has always taken such a prominent part in Christian Europe, the seat of the Holy Roman Empire, of many Church councils, and the land of the Reformation, should be guilty of such diabolical wickedness. So these crafty priests and unscrupulous politicians lied to the British people, and to all who heard them on the radio throughout the world, their object being to enhance Christianity at the expense of Paganism.

As we proceed we shall better realise how much our present-day civilisation owes to what we call Paganism, and how unfair it is thus to sneer at the Greeks, who gave the world the first democratic state, complete liberty of expression, schools, hospitals, doctors, social services, philosophy, national games, art, and the drama, the Romans leaving to posterity their famous legal codes on which all the laws of the civilised world are based. The Greek and Roman moralists, moreover, advocated a high ethical standard of conduct which Christendom has never been able to live up to, so much so that the pre-Christian Pagan age can compare favourably with much the greater part of the Christian era.

This being so, it is astonishing that no protest, challenge, or contradiction was made in any of the leading British newspapers to this often repeated and widespread falsehood; in fact it was passed on and accepted as meekly as the Germans accepted what their leaders thought they should know. Where ignorance reigns it is easy to deceive, and, although no harm will come from this particular deception, it acts as a pointer to the danger of ignorance, and shows how unscrupulous leaders can influence the simple-minded multitude by false propaganda.

If they can mislead them with such blatant falsehood as the foregoing, they can do so equally easily in other ways, and, in days gone by, when nearly everyone was illiterate, the people were just as clay in the hands of the potter, to be moulded as their leaders thought best. There is no darkness like ignorance, and the dire effect it has had, and still has, on the human race will become clear in the following pages. Under such circumstances, to start a war is not so difficult, and only by ignorance being replaced by knowledge and wisdom is there any hope of peace and security for our own time and for generations yet unborn.

Few politicians know much about economics or political economy, and their knowledge of history is generally hazy. Most of them before an election memorise the facts given them by the headquarters of the party to which they belong. These relate to the achievements of their party over the past fifty years or so, and are set out to make it appear that it was the only party to bring in legislation for the good of the people, its opponents having done little or nothing. This biased information is memorised by the would-be politician, to be passed on to those who will decide his fate.

The range of intelligence amongst priests is much worse, because they are trained in ignorance. From the time they enter the Theological College they are discouraged from acquiring knowledge apart from their special brand of religion, which they are taught has come direct from God. The clergy, as a rule, know little or nothing about other religions, about mythology, or psychic science. The great majority are quite ignorant about the origin of religion and the course of its evolution. They are, as a rule, as ignorant of ancient religious beliefs as they are of the beliefs of other present-day religions, their knowledge consisting only of the traditions concerning their own faith.

The clergy are never taught anything about the origin of their own religion, how it came into being, how a man came to be considered a god, how the Trinity, Eucharist, and belief in the Holy Spirit originated, how the Bible came into being, or the source of all their dogmas, doctrines, and ceremonials. They are blankly ignorant about their faith beyond what the Christian priests themselves invented in the 3rd, 4th, and 5th centuries. Few know anything about survival after death, or the enormous weight of evidence that now exists in support of this fact.

They are in fact nothing more than the repeaters of an ancient formula of theological dogmas, adapted by the priests in those early centuries from the other prevailing and surrounding religions, and yet it is to these men the radio is exclusively reserved for the propagation of religion. How can the people increase in religious knowledge when those who claim to be its interpreters know so little about religion, as it should be presented, while others, who have studied the subject intelligently, are excluded from expressing their opinions?

If a new order is to come into being as the result of the last war, the dictators of all kinds everywhere must be dethroned, and this also means those who monopolise the greatest instrument we have for disseminating knowledge. Only by increased knowledge can the people save themselves from what they have endured in the past at the hands of those who have governed the State and Church, and only thus will they make impossible a continuation of the deceptions practised by both politicians and priests.

The present generation, in most lands, is thinking differently from the last, and is coming to realise that changes must come about to prevent the recurrence of the terrible times the world has passed through during their lifetime. The greatest contribution the people can make to the future is to see that the children are better educated, that truth comes before tradition, and that their education is uninfluenced by political or religious creeds.

The importance of thinking and speaking only what is true should be instilled into a child's mind from an early age. He should be encouraged to accept and believe only what is true, and learn to know the value of evidence on which to base his beliefs. He must be told that in their own interests some people will always be telling him that this is true and that is true, but he must be taught to believe nothing without the evidence necessary to support their statements.

For instance, when a parson said recently on the radio that Christianity abolished slavery, most listeners doubtless believed this to be true. Most of them were ignorant of the fact that it existed in Christendom throughout the entire Christian era until last century, and still exists in one Christian country at the present time, but when the people know more, those who make such false statements will be brought to account. He then went on to tell another falsehood, namely that it was because of the help the Christian Church had given to Lord Shaftesbury he was able to get through his measures to improve the life of the poor. When we come to this period in British history we shall realise how untrue such a statement is, and we shall appreciate, as we proceed, the falsity of those remarks so systematically broadcast that Christianity was responsible for hospitals, education, and all the blessings we now enjoy from our social and medical services.

Doubtless many who listened to all these lies believed them, and those who made them gained their aim of enhancing the prestige of the Christian Church, by adopting the same methods as used by the Nazis of telling any falsehood which suited their purpose. There is no darkness like ignorance, and only when the people become enlightened will the British

Broadcasting Corporation take greater care that its speakers tell the people the truth, but, as it never permits any reply to its many misleading statements, this greater enlightenment can only come about by means of books written by authors who put truth before all else.

(2) First Place must be given to the Virtues.

Many instances could be given of how the people are misled, both as regards religion and politics, but here our aim is to increase knowledge by honestly relating the story of the past. In this way many misconceptions will be cleared away, and the past envisaged as it really was. Mental development, greater individuality, and more knowledge will give truth and honesty a higher place in the years to come. This means that the child will receive a better education and be given the necessary instruction to fit him to think for himself, and not as others would wish him to think. Independence in thought is most important for the development of character, and if we expect the truth to be told to us we must be equally careful always to speak the truth to others.

An honest education is the friend of all that is good and true. When the time comes that everyone is really educated the crafty priest, the zealous churchman, and the glib politician will have a less fertile soil in which to plant their seeds of lies and half-truths which today bring them in such an abundant harvest. Both political and religious propaganda will then have to conform to facts honestly stated, because the people will not otherwise believe them. "Seek truth and pursue it" should be the motto each child is urged to follow. Be honest with yourself, and honest in everything you think, never believing or passing on a statement unless you know it to be true.

Tell the child never to think a dishonest thought, and then he will never perform a dishonest deed. Infidelity consists of not being true to oneself. A dishonest person is like a slimy serpent wriggling unseen through the grass, always ready to strike down a victim on any favourable opportunity. Be straight, honest, and above-board, and in the end it will always be found to have been the wisest course to pursue. Do what is right, not to please God, but to satisfy yourself, because righteousness brings happiness to the individual and all with whom he comes in contact. The honest person is trusted and respected by everyone, and that is the foundation on which to build up a successful career. The dishonest individual sometimes seems to flourish for a time, but never for long, and, at the end of his life, if he looks back, he will realise that he would have been happier if he had lived straight and always done what was right and honest.

The ignorant cannot maintain self-control, whereas one who has been correctly educated can. The former is the slave of his passions, but the latter makes them his servant. The uneducated act without considered thought, but the educated think first and then act. Thinking first before acting is known as self-control, one of the most important virtues we can have. To do all the good we can, to attain as near perfection as possible in all we set our minds on, is the height of wisdom, as it makes life real, and gives to everyone an object for which to live. The one who achieves this aim lives a full and useful life, and leaves the world a better place than he found it.

Another virtue the child should be taught is tolerance, and this in turn leads to compromise. Be tolerant in all things. Speak and write your honest thoughts by all means—that is your birthright—but always allow others the same privilege. Remember how Voltaire, during a discussion with a friend, remarked that he entirely disagreed with everything his friend had said. But, he went on, "Though I disagree with you I would fight anyone who dared to take from you the right to speak your own thoughts." That is tolerance, which does not mean agreeing with everything you hear, but agreeing that everyone has the right to think and say what he thinks, so long as no one suffers from an untruth being uttered.

Intolerance in religion and politics has caused untold suffering and misery in the past. It has been the cause of countless wars, and has roused the bitterest of feelings. Families have been broken up by this vice, and much unhappiness has followed in its evil train. Be tolerant of other people's opinions. Listen attentively, and then give your own equally candidly, but always try to see the other person's point of view. His mind is different from your mind his outlook, his knowledge, his intelligence, are all different, and his heredity and environment have been quite different. So he cannot think as you do, and we should never expect this to be possible, but that is no reason why he should not express his opinions, or why we should not listen to them with courtesy.

When a dispute arises, compromise where possible, as it is always the wisest course in the long run. There are two sides to nearly every dispute, and one side only need not always be right and the other wrong. Compromise leads to feelings of friendship, whereas to hold out for the last ounce breeds bitterness which is often never lived down. Many friendships have been broken which would never have been severed if a little wisdom, and give and take, had taken the place of hard bargaining. Compromise must come from both sides, but, as the race grows in wisdom, this method of settling disputes will increase to the benefit of our private, national, and international relationships. If all the nations would only develop the spirit of compromise, one with another, war might vanish from off the face of the earth.

Every child should be taught to be merciful and compassionate, to help the helpless and raise the fallen, as kindness is the sunshine in which the virtues grow. Mercy and compassion are outstanding virtues which increase as the mind develops, as is shown by the growth of our social services. Mercy and compassion are now extended by all truly civilised nations to their enemies in war, as compared with what took place not so many hundred years ago, when all prisoners were either killed or made slaves. Think of our compassion to the wounded on both sides, who are now tended, cared for, and nursed back to health and strength, instead of being left on the battlefield to suffer and die.

Two hundred years ago little thought was given to those who were sick and suffering from infirmities and disease, but now there is a keen desire to make well those who are thus afflicted. Much is done today to prevent unnecessary suffering to tame

animals, but so far nothing is done to stop unnecessary
vivisection, and brutal blood sports, such as hunting
the fox, the stag, the otter, and coursing the hare.
These sports are degrading and some day will be
stopped, because our mental development is rising to
include in our thoughts the feelings of animals who
suffer just as we do, and have the same right to live as
we have, provided they do no harm.

If they must be reduced in number, let it be done
humanely by shooting, or by some other means, to
bring about sudden death without suffering. In
meat-eating countries one animal for about every
three people is killed each year to provide them with
food, and perhaps some day the idea of taking life so
that we may be fed on meat will be repugnant to our
descendants. Then they will live instead on a different
diet, but that Utopian dream is so far off that we need
not consider it when we have first of all to abolish the
slaughter of human beings.

So let us teach our children to be always kind,
merciful, and compassionate, but that does not mean
that they should be feeble and irresolute. Courage,
fortitude, and temperance are qualities which everyone
should be encouraged to develop. Too much courage
often leads to disaster, just as too much prudence
will take us nowhere. A wise combination of both
achieves the best results, and is to be found in those
men and women who have lived the most satisfactory
of lives. Never do anything in excess, and always
live a well-balanced life. Be temperate in all things,
and always maintain self-control, not giving way
to anger, which so upsets the harmony of the
mind.

All the foregoing virtues can be resolved into one word, namely, unselfishness. The truly unselfish person is an outstanding example of the victory of mind over matter, and is more to be admired than all the selfish so-called great men who have held the world's stage, and have lived to satisfy their ambitions and lusts on weak humanity. Selfishness is the only wickedness. If all were unselfish there would be no wrong-doers on earth. If everyone thought before speaking and acting as to whether he himself would like to hear, or experience, what he is about to say or do, and carried this into practice, a new era would dawn on earth. If we practise unselfishness we increase our own happiness by making others happy, because our happiness depends on others, and their happiness increases our happiness. When it is remembered that man is a social being, it follows that harmony one with another is essential for happiness, but harmony is only possible when each considers the feelings of others, and it is because so many people consider themselves first and others last that there is so much unhappiness on earth.

What brings satisfaction to one may bring unhappiness to others, and what may benefit one may hurt another. The sum of unhappiness is increased by selfishness, whereas unselfishness increases the total of human happiness. A vital truth everyone must remember is that we reap what we sow; if we sow happiness we shall reap it, if we sow kindness we shall reap it, and if we sow the seeds of righteousness they will be returned to us in full measure, it being equally true that if we do the opposite we shall reap the opposite.

When the virtues are systematically taught to children from an early age a new era will dawn for humanity, but only if we follow the advice of the Greek philosophers, who insisted that only by the practice of the virtues could virtue be obtained. Their repetition is not enough, but when they are practised happiness will take the place of misery, and friendship will displace disputes and quarrels. Besides this, knowledge is essential before we can attain to wisdom, which can best be defined as right thinking. To be able to think aright the child must be correctly educated, not by being taught religious and political falsehoods, but only that which is true. An honest education is essential before the race can reach knowledge and wisdom.

Socrates, when he went to the temple at Delphi, saw the inscription "Man know thyself", and this so impressed him that he set about his search for truth by making a study of his fellow men. An ardent desire for truth made him the wisest man of his time. To know ourselves embraces knowledge of others, and the only way to know about the ideas and doings of mankind is to know the history of the race, and how it has climbed and stumbled upwards out of primeval mud. Then we can admire its achievements and avoid its past follies.

The story which is now to be told is one of special interest to us in these times of disruption and stupendous changes. It is the story of man and how, little by little, he eventually learned to live peacefully and happily in the small family community. Then he learned to live happily when the families became tribes, and villages became towns, and lastly he found the means, after many failures, of forming a nation which lived together as a contented community. Here the harmony ends, because most of history, since writing was discovered, is given up to war and struggle between these nations. Nations have not yet learned to live at peace one with another, though our story will relate how attempt after attempt has been made by empire-builders to control groups of nations so as to secure obedience under one single rule.

So far all these attempts have failed, because they suffered from the employment of force for the purpose of subduing different nations who wished to live their own lives of liberty and freedom. Whenever the central authority weakened they broke away to resume their own independent existence. Force has dismally failed to secure unity, because force universally used means the suppression of liberty, for which mankind is always ready to fight to preserve, as it is his most priceless possession.

This, then, is the position of affairs in our own times, but with the coming of aviation, which has brought all nations more closely together and in more deadly danger from attack, the possibility of a world federation looms ahead, a combination which will be sustained by a central force all will mutually obey. Experience, however, teaches us that, though peace may be sustained by force, this federation must not be built upon force, or the curtailment of national and individual liberty, and any attempt at a form of world unity will only succeed if this is kept in mind.

The chapters which follow will relate how our

ancestors have climbed out of the jungle of disharmony and quarrelling to the peace prevailing within
individual nations. They will tell how all efforts to
consolidate different nations under one single rule
have finally failed, and how we must now attempt to
secure world peace by new and better methods than
those our forefathers tried without success. This
book tells the story of the human family in outline,
it being a record of what it has accomplished, and how,
through numerous and repeated mistakes, it has missed
reaching the happiness all have desired. It is a story
of success and failure, here and there interspersed by
the thoughts and actions of wise men who told the
people that righteousness led to happiness and wrong-
doing to misery.

In the pages which follow we shall read how
theology, for thousands of years, was man's only
means to explain growth and movement, how it
misinterpreted natural phenomena, and how, within
its boundaries, the gods were made responsible for
all that we experience. We shall discover how the
priesthood performed all the functions of ruler and
administrator, the people being too often considered
in the light of slaves and serfs. Out of the priesthood
developed the priest-monarch when greater progress
followed, but, until within the last hundred years,
intellectual progress was stifled in every land by the
people's fear of offending one or more gods, much of
their time being spent in prayer and sacrifice, or
making offerings to them, and observing taboos.
From the good gods, it was believed, came that which
brought happiness, the devils being blamed for sickness and misfortune, the former permitting the latter

to work their evil deeds on all who did not conform to the prevailing orthodox faith.

Under this blight of theological ignorance the people laboured on the land, there being taboos on nearly everything they did, and only by slow degrees did trade and industry make their appearance. Very gradually, as the mind of man developed, what we today call Science made its timid halting appearance, the few who began to think and reason being in ever increasing conflict with the priesthood, always ready to defend its theological explanation of the universe. One country after another added to the sum of human understanding: Babylonia, Egypt, Greece, and then Rome, carrying on the torch of knowledge, which was taken up by the Arabs, who passed it on to Europe where the fiercest fight of all developed between the Church and the thinkers. Only within the last hundred years has the bankruptcy of theology become generally recognised, when science took its place, and the scientist and the schoolmaster replaced the priest in public estimation.

Theology is responsible for our present-day backwardness, and our lack of ethical conduct, nationally and internationally, as it considered that all knowledge, as interpreted by the priests, centred round the gods, and that on a god rested our salvation quite irrespective of our conduct. It proved itself a good nurse when all had childish minds, but a bad schoolmaster, as it never wanted its children to grow up. Only recently has the scientific outlook taken the place of theological ignorance, and only now are we emerging into the light, from the valley of mental darkness in which theology has kept the race wandering since the time when the priest first became responsible for man's intellectual nourishment.

After reading these two introductory chapters the story which follows will be more interesting and instructive, as events will be considered from a new angle of thought hitherto absent in books on history. We shall now be reading history for a purpose, which is not only to increase our knowledge but also our wisdom, and this will add to the mental wealth of the race for its future upliftment. This increased knowledge and wisdom, it is hoped, will be a help and guide to us in these times in which we now live, and, if only everyone could profit by what the following pages will unfold, what a different world those who come after us would have in which to live.

(3) THE KEY TO THE CORRECT UNDERSTANDING OF HISTORY.

Before we commence to read the next chapter, which opens our study of the thoughts and deeds of mankind, certain facts should always be kept in mind if history is to be correctly understood. These will be found of great help in understanding the story which follows, and the conclusions to be drawn from our study of the experiences of those who have lived on earth in the years gone by.

History is a record of the thoughts and deeds of men and women who have lived before us. Consequently, to understand why they thought and acted as they did we must know something about the being we call man, *homo sapiens*, or man regarded as a group distinct from other life on earth. His thoughts govern his actions, and, if we analyse the ideas which are continually being created in his mind, we find that three of these in particular caused those actions which make up history. These we call

FEAR, DESIRE, LUST.

Fear and desire produced Religion and Politics, around which history revolves. Desire brought into being our comforts, as well as orderly government so that the legal and moral codes could be better enjoyed. Lust caused war, and all the destruction and suffering with which it is associated. Thus these three human emotions were the causes which made history, as without them the story of the human race would be a very tame affair. They appear before us on every page of history and fall into two groups:

RELIGION, POLITICS.

Religion is associated with four great fears which have had a tremendous influence on man's beliefs and conduct. These are the fear of

DEATH, BEREAVEMENT, WANT, ILLNESS.

Man feared the unknown, the mysterious, and the forces about him which he could neither understand nor control. He saw death and decay all around him, and he wondered and feared at the meaning of it all. A friend, a loved one, alive and conscious yesterday and dead today. He feared for his daily needs, his food being uncertain, he feared the cold, the storm, the thunder and lightning, and he feared sickness and disease. How it was that he attributed to the gods everything he could not understand we shall discover as we read on, but so it was, and this brought into being what we call religion, which greatly consoled him, as mentally he was just a child and needed comfort from his fears. Religion was also the cause of much misery, as it produced three vices which have adversely affected the happiness of mankind from early times:

INTOLERANCE, CRUELTY, INDOLENCE.

Intolerance and bigotry are associated with religion, and were the cause of war and much cruelty. Indolence came from man relying entirely on the gods for help and not exerting himself, he being dulled into complacency by two beliefs: (1) that novelty and progress were sinful, and (2) that improved conduct was unnecessary because sacrifice had been made on his behalf.

Politics is the other group into which history is divided by the emotions, fear, desire, and lust. Politics relate to man's social life, to the grouping of the people together into communities, and to their form of government. Fear of attack caused them to join together in self-defence. Desire made man dissatisfied with his conditions, something better being wanted, and this brought about progress. Desire also caused war when political zealots tried to force their ideas upon others, but the main cause of war is lust, or the ardent desire by one community or nation for something possessed by others.

Politics produced ordered government and greater safety for the community, but it also brought about

TYRANNY, INJUSTICE, SUPPRESSION,

which man more and more resented as he developed mentally. Many conflicts followed between tyrants and those desiring greater freedom and justice. The lust of some for domination, and for a unified belief in both politics and religion, have caused many wars, much suffering, and great misery. So, when reading history, it is always wise to remember the three principal causes behind most historical events, and the reason which brought them into being:—

(1) FEAR of death, of illness and disease, of poverty, of loss of possessions, and of bereavement.

(2) DESIRE for greater security, greater freedom, greater happiness, improved living conditions; more and better food and clothing.

(3) LUST for domination and power to make all obey and think alike, and craving for other people's possessions.

Desire for something better has often been thwarted by fear and lust, and these three emotions have continually pulled against one another, both fears and passions so often spoiling the desire for greater security, improved conditions, and increased happiness.

This book is divided into two volumes.

VOLUME I relates how man cringed and bowed before nature, which to him was represented by the gods and of the time when he was her slave.

VOLUME II tells how he learned to stand erect by discovering nature's laws, of the way he made nature his slave, and how this transformed civilisation.

Both volumes tell how man has always been the slave of his passions, and how, through lust, greed and ignorance, his desire for greater happiness and increased comforts was always being obstructed. Likewise they relate how mental development caused some wise men to declare that if he would calm his fears by greater knowledge, subdue his lusts by learning self-control, his desires could be met, and more happiness and additional comforts would be the result.

Material progress has come about by the greater security which has followed from this advice being acted upon to an ever-increasing degree, and also by man obtaining greater control over the forces of nature.

(1) Man without tools is no better than an animal.

(2) Man without instruments is an ignoramus.

Volume I relates how the discovery of the way to make and use tools civilised man. Volume II tells how instruments made him aware of himself and his surroundings, thus enlarging his mind and making it possible for him to cure and control disease, and employ the forces of nature for his greater comfort. Tools secured improved conditions, but when used as weapons of war they increased destruction and human suffering. Instruments removed the fear of the unknown, and opened up both earth and sky to man's inspection and comprehension, thus displacing the idea that the world was the centre of the universe and the stars were lamps set in the firmament for his benefit.

Volume I relates to the Supernatural Age, when theology darkened man's outlook on life, and the gods were believed to be the cause of all that happened. Volume II tells of the gradual overthrow of theology, and the birth and development of Science, with all the blessings it has brought to mankind, though it is still too often used for evil purposes. It removed his fear of the supernatural, and made him realise that all that happens is natural and can be largely controlled by enlightened thought.

Man lived in the Supernatural Age until, by mental development, he discovered how to make the instruments to prove that the universe is governed by law. This discovery ushered in the Natural Age in which we now live. When ignorance passes away everything becomes natural, even the most mysterious event of all experience, namely death. Psychic science not only reveals man's bodily construction, but also makes clear that ghosts are natural beings, men and women, who once lived on earth, and are not gods who govern the universe as was thought by our ancestors. This science also reveals that all the hitherto mysterious phenomena which occur in the presence of one we term a medium is natural and subject to universal laws. Thus we have found that these psychic experiences, which brought every religion into being, need not be feared, and that death is as natural as birth. Consequently the origin and evolution of religion, which was one of the principal causes in producing history, are now under-stood.

Ignorance produced fear, and when we know more we shall realise that it was also the cause of lust and all the misery this entailed. This will be made clear as we proceed. Desire will continue to bring about progress, and, when the curse of ignorance is lifted, fear and lust will vanish from this earth. That is the lesson history has to teach us, and, if we learn it correctly, and profit by this knowledge, the happiness which all desire will come to mankind.

CHAPTER III.

PRIMITIVE MAN.

Introduction. (1) *Man's Place in the Universe.* (2) *From the Prehistoric Age to the Beginning of Civilisation.*

BEFORE we commence to read the story of the past, and consider one by one the links in the endless chain of cause and effect, which produced the men and women of today, and the world in which we live, it would be wise to set down what we know about ourselves and our surroundings. All ancient historians have been influenced by their ignorance of these two subjects, the Hebrews believing that Jerusalem was the centre of a very limited universe, comprising what we today call the Middle East, round which circled the sun, moon and the stars; set in the heavens for the purpose of giving light to their small flat world by day and night. All other nations have had similar circumscribed ideas of their position in the universe, their capital city being the centre round which everything revolved.

Our ancestors' knowledge about themselves was as limited as it was about their environment, their belief being that man was a special creation of a few thousand years earlier, the animals being created for his use and benefit. The people of each tribe or nation divided the human race into two distinct divisions, those who called themselves the Children of God, or the Children of the gods, or the Chosen

People, and those who were the outcasts. Each individual and nation considered himself, and itself, the elect of God, and all who accepted a different religion were placed amongst those cast off by heaven. During the Christian era the human race was divided by the Christians into Christians, Jews and heathen, whereas the Jews, Moslems, and those of all the other world religions, made an equally distinctive demarcation between themselves and the believers in other religions.

The growth of knowledge over the past century has greatly widened the outlook of all educated people, and we now have a completely different idea of our surroundings and ourselves. We find that instead of being the lords of creation we are individually very insignificant beings, in a universe so vast that it passes comprehension. This knowledge has obliterated the outlook of our ancestors on their own importance in a very small universe, but we have not been humbled by our discoveries, in fact we are proud of them, as here on earth we contemplate the universe, this vast machine which moves with precision, never faltering and never getting out of step. We can think of it, and reason about it, but it cannot think and reason about us. Consequently, the vaster we discover space to be, our knowledge and imagination are correspondingly enlarged.

Because we think, we falter, and every human being is out of step with the other, as each one thinks differently from the other, the reason being that the individual is guided by mind, and the universe by fixed rigid laws of attraction and repulsion, the same cause always producing the same effect. If we drop

something it will always fall exactly in the same .
direction, at the same speed, and the same explosive
substance when released will always have the same
effect. On the other hand, no one can tell in what
direction a bird will fly, and it rises and falls at will.
A stone falls according to law, but a bird flies as its
mind desires. Here, then, is the great dividing line
in the universe, not one between the chosen of God
and the outcasts, but between the thinkers and unthinking matter, and to this important question some
serious thought will not be out of place.

(1) Man's Place in the Universe.

Mind and substance make up the universe, physical
matter being this substance within the range of our
physical experience, but space equally contains substance though it does not directly impinge upon our
senses. So far as we know, substance and mind have
been from all eternity and will remain to all eternity,
both time and space, as they appear to us, being conditioned by our mind, which is limited on earth to the
range of vibrations we call physical. To the universe
there seems to be no beginning and no end, no
creation, no destruction, only change of form, nebula
vibrations speeding up to become unseen, or slowing
down, to become visible to us as stars, as happened to
produce our earth. Its constituents existed before it
took shape and form, and for ever will exist, even
if it some day explodes and disappears from physical
sight and touch.

Mind is the active, and substance the passive, the
plus and the minus, the one the contemplator and the

other the contemplated, the one the thinker and the other that which is thought about. The one cannot exist without the other, no mind no matter, no matter no mind. Without mind, substance would not exist, its existence being determined by thought, and without substance mind could not exist, as there would be nothing to stimulate it into activity, action being as inseparable to mind as is motion to a cinematograph film.

Therefore we divide the universe into two compartments, the first being devoted to all that grows and moves and thinks, to that which is not determined by fixed physical law, and the other, which is regulated by fixed laws, to which astronomy, physics, and chemistry are devoted for the purpose of discovering their scope and range. Just as physical science is divided into different sections, so is biology, the science of plant, animal and human life, which last group is again subdivided, one being called history, or the story of the past, so far as it relates to the human family.

Astronomy tells us the story of the universe, geology that of the earth and early life, archaeology records the period before the story of the race was written down, and history relates to the time since writing was discovered, thus making possible the chronological recording of events. This is the branch of knowledge comprised within the covers of this book, but, as we wish to avoid the mistakes of earlier historians, let us be sure first of all that we truly know exactly what we are, and exactly where we live, thus avoiding their errors when comprehending the universe and man's place in it.

When we have our minds in harmony with truth,

and when we discard appearances to get down to
reality, we are then in a position to go back in thought
to the days of primitive man, and follow the course of
history through to the present day. Then we can
correctly understand the reason for the thoughts and
deeds of those who went before us, and better appreciate how ignorance was the cause of their many failures
and mistakes. They were always trying to solve the
riddle of the universe, but they lacked the necessary
instruments, which ingenuity and invention developed,
no human eye having the power to convey to the mind
that which can be seen through the telescope, the
microscope, and the instruments perfected to determine the constituents of matter.

What, then, is the universe? What is this earth
which forms such an insignificant part of this vast
machine? If we get down to reality, and away from
appearances, the answer is that the universe, including
the earth, is no more and no less than one gigantic
scale of vibrations. Only a small part of this range
of vibrations impinges on our mind, and much the
greater part passes by unnoticed. Within our own
lifetime we have discovered the way to make use of
some hitherto unsensed waves to carry the human
voice and music, by means of various transformers,
all over the world. The mechanism of the radio
transmitting machine transforms the atmospheric
vibrations, produced by a voice, into etheric vibrations, which are retransformed by our receiving sets
into atmospheric vibrations that vibrate our ear drums.
By this invention we make use of ether waves which
are beyond the physical range, and consequently
unperceived by our physical sense organs.

Only physical vibrations appeal to us, because our physical bodies are in tune with them. Thus we see physical things, and pass by everything above and below the physical range. These vibrations are caused by electrons which, along with protons, make up the atom, of which matter is composed. Matter, which appears to be solid, is in reality not solid at all, as what we see when we look at a table or chair, for instance, are the vibrations of a certain number of electrons which are revolving at immense speed around a centre known as the nucleus. Matter is made up of atoms, and these atoms are in turn composed of minute electric charges of negative and positive electricity, to which we give the name of electrons and protons. According to the number of electrons in an atom so is the substance and its chemical properties, but the weight is conditioned by the number of protons.

Physical matter is in reality an open network of electrons and protons, and the distance between them in an individual atom, in relation to its size, is immense. The protons, or positive units, form the nucleus of the atom, and, if we consider the nucleus as commanding the same position in an atom as the sun does in our solar system, then the relative distance the electrons are apart from one another, and from the protons, might be taken as equivalent to the distance the planets are from one another, and from the sun.

To put it another way, if we consider an atom as the size of a village church, then a pinhead would represent the relative size of one of the electrons of which it is composed. These protons and electrons in the atom are far asunder, moving at enormous speed, and are linked together by the invisible ether which occupies much the greater space within the atom. Nevertheless, by the activity of this comparatively small number of electrons, we sense all the range of colour, each colour being determined by the speed of the electrons in the object we are observing at the moment. On the other hand, the proton gives us the sense of solidity and weight, it being nearly two thousand times heavier than the electron.

So the electrons produce the colour, and the protons the weight of material substance, both of which appeal to us because of the vibrations they set up in the invisible ether, which is now believed to be the basic substance of the universe. We live in an ocean of ether vibrations, which encompass all space, and interpenetrate all matter, their undulations, or wave-like motion, moulding our mind into pictures, to which we give such names as ideas, emotions, sensations, experiences, all of which make up what we call life.

We see something, and determine its colour because ether vibrations, either from the sun or any other light, which undulate through space at the rate of 186,000 miles a second, strike the object after being diffused by the particles composing the atmosphere. Those light waves which are in tune with the electrons in the object at which we are looking, are reflected to our eyes. Thence by means of a series of nerves which conduct the waves, as a wire conducts electric vibrations, these etheric light waves are carried to our brain, where mind transforms them into pictures of the object seen. This picture is formed in the front portion of the head, just behind the forehead, but, as the mind which forms the picture is of a range of vibrations beyond the physical, it occupies the same space as is used by the physical brain.

When we think, we form a series of pictures which we call ideas, and if these are correctly assorted we think rationally. Our plastic mind is for ever in motion making pictures of what it sees, feels, hears, smells, or tastes. When awake we relate these rationally one to the other, but in sleep our mind recalls past pictures irrationally. This we call dreaming, and it is caused by our reasoning power being dormant and at rest. Thus we are refreshed, but our mind is never still, though the pictures it makes during sleep are generally forgotten.

What we call "seeing" consists of the pictures made by the mind, the colour of what we see being the colour produced by the mind. We see something, and our mind produces the object in colour, according to the frequency of the object's vibrations, which cause the mind to become what we call coloured   An object's size and colour are therefore the picture formed by the mind by vibrations, and, if we look at an object which we call blue, the picture formed by the mind is of the nature we call blue. Thus we think blue, but, as most objects seen are a variety of colour, the mind-picture consists of all the colours produced by the different frequency of movements of the vibrations reflected by the electrons in the atoms which make up an object. If we saw the mind at work it would be like looking at a technicolor film, the colours and objects continually changing, as our eyes roam from place to place.

Reality is centred in the mind, as without mind,

the picture-maker, nothing would exist. Our head can be compared with a cine-camera, the eyes being the lens, and the mind the film which is always picturing what takes place within its orbit, the only difference being that mind-pictures are also formed by hearing, touch, smell, and taste. This state of awareness to our surroundings, this mental film for ever picturing our environment, we term "living", which is agreeable or disagreeable according to the way our mind reacts. The mind has developed according to a certain mould, which we call normal, anything abnormal, or different from what has been its custom, being more or less resented to be called pain, discomfort, or annoyance.

The foregoing represents the process which we call thinking, as thinking consists of making pictures of present events or scenes, and recalling past pictures in a sequence, just as seeing or hearing consists of making pictures of what we at the moment see or hear. The vibrations of a noise, carried by atmospheric waves, affect the mind in such a' way that, when we hear the sound of an airplane overhead, we are reminded of an airplane by associating it with a particular noise, and so the mind moulds itself into the picture of one, the same being the case with what we feel, taste, or smell.

When we see a house, our mind becomes a picture of a house. It is the picture that is real to us, not the house, as if we shut our eyes the house vanishes because the picture has vanished, the vibrations which produced it having been interrupted. Only when the picture exists does the house exist to us, but once the picture is seen it can be recalled at will. That is what we mean by memory, as the picture once made can be re-made at will. The house is made up of all colours, the electrons in the red bricks, for instance, reflecting the red vibrations from the sun's rays to our eyes, and thence they travel to the mind, via the brain, to become pictured as red bricks, the name we give to that particular patch in the picture. Likewise, with all the other different coloured objects making up a house seen by the eye, every one of which goes to make a picture in our head of what we call a house.

So much for sight. The sense of solidity and weight comes from the protons in the atom, their number in an atom constituting its weight, the heaviest and most solid object having the most protons. These affect the mind by means of our nerves, touching an object once seen being sufficient to recall it to mind, which makes a picture of it. Because our body is made up of molecules, or groups of atoms composed of electrons and protons, we cannot go through another body likewise composed. Both are of equal density, but the molecules of water, gas, and of the atmosphere, can be pushed apart because they are not rigidly connected, as they are, for instance, in a stone wall.

If we get down to reality, and away from appearance, each one of us is made up of three different ranges of vibrations: (1) the mind, which pictures all we see, and (2) our etheric body, composed of vibrations of greater frequency than those which constitute (3) our physical body. This latter is within the range of physical vibrations, and so we appreciate, or sense, the earth and things material, but the fact that our mind and etheric body are the real and enduring part of each body, means that the physical body is no more than a temporary habitation which is discarded at death.[1]

The interlocking of these two bodies on earth, and their reaction on our mind, makes up life, and life makes history. The physical body is related to physical things, and consequently our food, clothing, and comforts are most important. They, and our carnal emotional impulses, direct our life along one line of thought, but our unseen etheric body, which is not related to carnal things, and has quite a different destiny from the physical body, influences our mind along another line of thought, it being responsible for our religious emotions, and all that follows from them.

So, when reading history, we must never forget that it has been influenced as much by the etheric as by the physical world. These two worlds, interpenetrating and revolving together in space, are indivisible and inseparable, the unseen influencing the imagination to produce the numerous and varied ideas which are embraced within the comprehensive word "religion." Only by means of instruments has all this now been brought home to us, in a way that our ancestors could never have imagined, and consequently they floundered in theological speculations. They realised vividly that they were more than mere flesh and blood, and that there was some place they were making for beyond the range of physical sight and hearing, but they had not the knowledge to enable them to grasp reality, the consequence being that their theology

[1] Many who have lost arms and legs feel that they are still there, and that they can move their hands and toes. What they feel is the etheric duplicate, which is no use to them on earth but which still remains as part of the etheric body, in which the individual, the mind, will function after death.

reflected not only their aspirations, but also their ignorance.

History reveals that mankind has given as much thought to things unseen as to things seen, and this explains why the story of man is as much devoted to religion as to politics, to the after life as to this one, and, as we proceed, we shall realise that the duality of our make-up has been the cause of thoughts and deeds which were, and are, quite apart from our present everyday life. Ignorance of how best to live on earth, and ignorance of our make-up and destiny, have produced all the folly, the cruelty, the misery, and the suffering which fill the pages of history, and, just as this ignorance has given place to knowledge, has happiness increased, suffering lessened, and our way of life improved.

Man's make-up, his environment and destiny, have determined history, and we find this fact even in pre-history, when we consider the feelings and ideas of primitive man. Why did he place food in the graves of the dead, and why did he sacrifice to the gods? Who indeed were the gods? Why did he build cairns and Stonehenges, and, when civilisation commenced, temples and churches, some of great size, beauty and variety? Why did he have religious taboos? Why did he worship and spend his time and money maintaining priests? All these questions, and many others, cannot be answered by the reply generally given in our materialistic age—that it was all due to fear of the unknown and to imagination.

Religion runs through history from primitive times, and, as it cannot be ignored, it must be rationally explained. The only way to explain it is to find

the cause of these religious ideas, and, because enquirers could not find it in the past, does not mean
that some in our own day have not made the discovery,
the author of this book, for instance, having spent
half a lifetime studying the question, and he has experimental proof for all he says. Psychic science, by
means of observation and experiment,' has now
accumulated a vast amount of information relating to
the supernormal phenomena which so frightened and
intrigued past generations. Now we know much
more about the duplicate etheric body and the mind,
both subjects about which our ancestors were quite
ignorant. Some believed that thought originated
in the heart, others imagined that the liver, or the
kidneys or the bowels, were its source,[1] while materi-
alists today declare, without a vestige of evidence,
that it is caused by some secretion of the brain.

Because official science is not concerned with
psychic research does not mean that it is not worthy
of examination. In reality, it is one of the most
important branches of knowledge, and many of our
scientists ignore it because they have never taken the
trouble to get the experience upon which psychic
knowledge is built.

Psychic phenomena have had a profound bearing
on man's outlook on life, and the universe. Consequently the historian should recognise this fact,
and not pass it by unnoticed, as has happened in the

---

[1] Consequently we read in the Bible "Create in me a clean heart", "The
heart of the foolish doeth not so", "A merry heart maketh a cheerful
countenance", "Refresh my bowels in the Lord", "Bowels of compassion",
"Lord, try my reins (kidneys)", "My reins also instruct me", to quote only
a few of many. We still speak of the heart as the centre of thought when we
say "Learn by heart", "With all my heart", "My sweetheart", and make many
other similar remarks.

past. Psychic phenomena brought every religion into being, and, as religion has influenced half the activities of mankind up to our own times, psychic phenomena has to a large extent determined history. Psychic phenomena comprise many separate phenomena, such as Trance, Clairaudience, Clairvoyance, Telekinesis, or the movement of objects without physical force, the Direct Voice, and the observation of apparitions, commonly called ghosts, which have been seen down the ages.

We are strange, illogical beings, because we believe in microbes, and ether waves, which we have never seen, but most people disbelieve in ghosts, which have been recorded as seen since the art of writing began, down to our own times. To test this fact the Society for Psychical Research of London sent out a questionnaire in 1894 to people in all walks of life. From 32,000 replies received, 9 per cent. men and 12 per cent. women declared that they had seen one or more ghosts in their lifetime, and the American Society for Psychical Research, which did likewise in the United States, received replies in much the same proportion to the same effect. All history testifies to the reality of these etheric visitors coming on rare occasions within our range of vibrations, the Bible, for instance, containing many instances, and these would have been even more numerous if its translation had been more accurate. Greek, Roman, Egyptian, Assyrian, Indian, and Chinese literature recognise their existence; in fact it is just as rational to believe that ghosts have been seen, on countless occasions, as to believe in the different events recorded in history.

When the scientific age came into being, all belief
in another order of substance and life was discarded
as belonging to the age of faith, because the early
scientists, lacking our present-day instruments and
knowledge, considered matter to be solid, and space
to be empty, nothing existing but matter which is
seen. That belief is now known to be wrong, the
present-day scientists having demonstrated that matter
is neither solid nor the sole substance which makes
up the universe. We now know that matter is sensed
by us because of its vibrations, and that vibrations of a
higher and lower frequency can function in the same
space as do physical vibrations.

This was demonstrated by Professor Röntgen in
1895. Then he discovered that when a highly exhausted glass tube produced a vivid green phos-
phorescence on the glass, from certain positive gas-
formed rays, called cathode, a nearby plate covered
with potassium began to glow. If a thick piece of
metal were placed between the tube and the plate, it
cast a sharp shadow, but if thin aluminium, or a piece
of wood, or a book, took the place of the metal no
shadow was cast. He thus made one of the greatest
of all scientific discoveries, which overthrew the age-
old belief that matter is solid. He had found a ray,
or short wave vibration, which passed through
matter, and by so doing opened the way for future
discoveries, which resolved the universe into different
ranges of vibrations that could pass through one
another and occupy the same space. .

Thus modern science discovered the etheric
world interpenetrating the physical world, and also
found a place for the etheric body, a duplicate of the

physical body, which interpenetrates the physical on earth, to become the real and tangible body after it separates from the carnal body at death. Science, instead of proving the earlier materialistic outlook on life to be true, has done the opposite, and found a place for what is called heaven, and for what the Apostle Paul termed the spiritual body. Thus science has made religion comprehensible, and, instead of dividing the universe into matter and empty space as heretofore, the universe was found to be indivisible, one mighty network of visible and invisible vibrations threading in and out like shuttles. Now can be understood the possibility of another world surrounding, interpenetrating, and revolving with this one, a larger world, somewhat similar to this earth, to which we pass when we make the change called death. There the vibrations of our etheric body respond to etheric substance, as do those of our physical body to earth substance, and, this being so, the etheric world will be as real to us after death as is this earth to us now.

The etheric body, after death, when it enters the vibrations to which it is attuned, is just as solid, substantial and tangible as are our bodies on earth, because solidity and tangibility are determined by our relationship to surrounding vibrations. Consequently the inhabitants of the etheric world are men, women, and children, with the same shaped bodies as on earth, less any physical defects, but when the theologians from early times turned them into gods, saints, angels and devils, they made what is probably the greatest mistake ever made by man, and one which has had a profound and retrograde effect on mankind's outlook and deeds. History overflows with the effect of this momentous blunder, which divided the two worlds into the natural and the supernatural.

The experience of death does not change us from natural into supernatural beings, in fact death can rightly be compared with moving from one room to another in a house. The change means that the one who passes out ceases to be seen, but he is still living under similar natural conditions as before, and surrounded by the same kind of people. This assertion is no flight of the author's imagination, as, over the past twenty-five years, he has himself conversed personally, or heard others do so, on hundreds of occasions, with different men, women and children who are considered to be dead, but are no more dead than is the reader of this book. He has, moreover, not only heard them speak, but also sing and laugh, cry, sneeze, cough, and be serious and amusing, grave and gay. He has talked with them on philosophy, religion, science, healing, the make-up and working of the mind, and its relationship to the brain, besides many other subjects, such as the way they live, what they do, and the nature of their surroundings.

He found them still interested in earth affairs, their memories of past events not having been destroyed by the change they had made, their love and affection for their friends on earth being unimpaired. Those who were doctors and nurses on earth were just as interested in healing as when here, the scientists being eager for greater knowledge, greater experience, and a better understanding of man and the universe.

In fact they are human beings like ourselves, who entered their new abode naked, just as does a new-born baby on earth. Having been accustomed to clothes on earth they consequently wear them there, they having the same habits, gifts, and failings as they had here on earth, but their capacity and outlook has increased, many having a wider and wiser vision of life in its different aspects. To call such people spirits is ridiculous, especially as the English language has the same word for whisky. Consequently, as this book is concerned only with facts, they will be always referred to in the pages which follow, when the occasion arises, as other-world men and women.

How foolish it was to translate such people into supernatural gods, angels and devils, and, if a true perception of the other world had been possible to our ancestors, how differently they would have thought and acted. To change what is natural into something unnatural has brought about all the waste, folly and misery which follows from the curse of ignorance, such as the countless millions of sacrificed victims, who have been offered up as food to these other-world men and women, who were supposed to relish the etheric bodies of those slain creatures. From fear of, or in order to get favours from, these other-world people, who were regarded as supernatural gods, man has been guilty of countless murders in the name of religion, of cruel intolerance, wars, persecution, the breaking-up of families, besides absurd taboos, and an enormous waste of time and wealth supporting the clergy and their numerous religious observances.

From fear of offending these other-world men and women, man has prostrated himself, denied himself, mutilated himself, and made his life miserable. For the same reason knowledge has been considered sinful, ignorance raised to a virtue, a dirty cell has been preferred to a comfortable home, and social welfare neglected. In place of practical useful knowledge, the theologians erected a vast mountain of speculative nonsense, which benefits only themselves, the consequence being that their interest has always lain in keeping the people ignorant.

The ignorance, folly, wickedness and crafty dealings of these theologians appear before us in every period of history, and the mis-spent effort of their dupes has helped to make the history of the race a sordid story, a tragedy to anyone who has emerged from the slough of theological ignorance into the light of psychic knowledge. Such a one is amazed and horrified at the folly and cruelty of the past, and, as our history unfolds, let it be always remembered that the gods, goddesses, spirits, angels and devils, who have shaped the course of earth events, were just men and women like ourselves. On them omnipotent powers were conferred by ignorant theologians, thus to change the inhabitants of the other world into supernatural beings, their abode likewise being imagined as something fantastic, a quite unnatural place, and not as it really is, a world subject to natural law.

If these momentous facts are remembered, history will become a different affair from what has been presented to us by the historians of the past, but, before we proceed with our story, we should have a correct and clear idea about some other facts that emerge, about which there is so much doubt, ignorance, and mystery. Man is certainly a trinity, made up of physical body, etheric duplicate body, and mind. On earth they live together as one body, the etheric body interpenetrating the physical body and maintaining its structure, but at death they separate, the etheric body, still guided by mind, functioning in an etheric range of vibrations of a higher frequency than the physical. Here it finds itelf in another world much like this one, to which it can return at will, to see and hear what is going on, but to be unseen except by a favoured few whose more developed sight enables them to catch its vibrations.

To understand why some can see apparitions, or ghosts, as we call them, and others cannot, let us sit down in front of a piano and press down a note about the middle of the keyboard. All the notes on either side of this one we cover up with a black cloth. Thus we see only one note, which represents the entire range of physical vibrations that appeal to our sight. The notes we have covered up on the left of our finger represent the different ranges of vibrations which do not appeal to our sight, because their frequency is too slow, those on the right representing the vibrations unseen because their frequency is too fast for us to sense. To these higher and lower ranges we give the name space, which seems to us to be empty, but in reality it is not, as, if we were tuned in to them, our mind would picture them just as it does the physical range to which the physical body is related.

The visible waves, represented by the note we have touched, have a wave-length of from 34,000 to 64,000 waves to the inch. Beyond the former is the infrared range and beyond the latter is the range known as the ultra-violet. The physical waves have a frequency of from 400 to 750 billion waves a second, waves of lesser frequency being known as dark heat waves and long electric waves. Several outstanding men have contributed to our greater knowledge of the constitution of matter. Clerk-Maxwell, Helmholtz, Hertz, Thomson, Rutherford, Einstein, Eddington, Millikan, Richards, Soddy, Aston, Ramsay, Rayleigh, Moseley, Langmuir, and last, but by no means least, the famous woman scientist Marie Curie and her equally famous husband. These, and others, were responsible for a complete revolution in the hitherto accepted idea of the constitution of the universe, and they have found a place for other worlds, and orders of life, beyond the range of what we term physical matter.

This may be quite new and strange to some, but nowadays we must think in terms of vibrations if we are to be able to follow the discoveries of physical and psychic science. The knowledge which these two sciences bring to us is closely related to our history, as it is because of these vibrations that all religion came into being. Man is an etheric being, functioning for a time within the physical range of vibrations. He is in this world, but not of it, and because of that he has the religious instinct which relates him to another order of life while still in this one.

Because man is an etheric being, some have the gift of sensing vibrations beyond the physical. Such people are termed mediums, because they act as intermediaries between this and the other world vibrating beyond the physical range of sight, just as the radio is the intermediary between the long electric waves and ourselves. Mediums are clairvoyant and clairaudient, because they can see and hear just beyond the physical range of vibrations, as if, for instance, they could sense the next note of the piano to the one we pressed down. This is due to some abnormal construction of their eyes and ear-drums, which enables them to catch vibrations of a greater frequency than those we normal people can sense, their etheric bodies being less deeply embedded in physical matter.

Because there have always been such people, we have the belief in ghosts and other psychic phenomena, a belief which prevails today just as it has done down the ages. Because of their psychic gifts we have the belief in another life after death, and all the different beliefs which have surrounded religion since early times. This is all quite natural, rational, and scientific, but because man, in his ignorance, has been unable to explain the phenomena, much folly, emotionalism, nonsense and humbug have been attached by religion to death, which is a biological affair, and just as simple and natural as is birth. Death is no more unnatural than birth, but, because of the ignorance and the uncertainty which surrounds it, we have all the accumulated religious beliefs which have influenced mankind since he became a thinking being.

These many and various religious ideas are all grouped together under the name of Theology, or the knowledge of the gods or spirits. Our ancestors considered knowledge pertaining to the etheric order of life so important that they elevated theology to the rank of the Queen of Science. To it they went to find an explanation for everything they could not understand, the gods being made the cause of creation, growth, movement, decay and death. From early times it was realised that a reason had to be given for the existence and movement of the sun, the moon and the planets, for the growth, movement and death of vegetation, animals and human beings, and they turned to the other order of life to find an explanation. Our present-day increased knowledge has entirely discredited the claims and explanations made by theology, but the cause behind these false claims still remains, and the etheric order in the universe must be recognised in its true perspective if we are to have a correct comprehension of the universe in all its aspects.

Life, then, is made up of the pictures, or ideas, made by our mind as the result of vibrations, and death means that we experience a change in the range of vibrations. After death we picture, or experience, through our etheric body a range of greater frequency, the physical body having been cast aside to rot away. We need not change our location at death to experience this higher range, as it exists about us now, though we sense it not, the other world being all about us here, interpenetrating this world of physical matter. Death means that we cease to picture the physical, because the etheric body and mind have withdrawn from the physical body. By death they become in tune with a higher range of vibrations, which we call etheric, and the mind pictures these instead of the physical, the etheric becoming the real and the physical the unreal.[1]

So death is only a change of the mind, and the

[1] *On the Edge of the Etheric, The Rock of Truth,* and *The Unfolding Universe* give consideration to the vast subject embraced by vibrations, so far as they relate to the etheric world, charts and diagrams being used to make the subject clearly understood.

etheric duplicate body, to a new environment, made up of vibrations of a higher frequency, to which they respond when apart from the physical body. Because memory pertains to the mind, we remember after death our past experiences on earth, as the mental pictures we made there can be recalled. By means of memory we develop both here on earth and hereafter, and, if we have no regrets, and are in harmony with our environment, we are happy wherever we are. Here on earth we do not always appreciate our failings and past mistakes, but hereafter we have a wider vision and in consequence bitter regrets may become mental anguish. This mental hell, produced by the memory of past failings, is a transient phase, as there is no impassable gulf fixed between the good and the evil. All can forget the mistakes of the past, and become good citizens of their new abode by striving after righteousness.

Righteousness relates to our attitude towards ourselves and all sentient beings with whom we come in contact. Consequently it must be developed on earth for the sake of our own and other people's happiness, and not for the sake of reward or fear of punishment hereafter. Religion has devoted itself to the consequences hereafter of our theological beliefs on earth, but has laid little stress on our conduct here, it being more concerned with the problem of saving the sinner from punishment hereafter, of wiping out the stain of guilt, than of improving the way of life. No religious belief can overcome natural law, which clearly reveals that as we sow we reap. Righteousness is essential, not to please God, or to attain happiness hereafter, but for the sake of our fellow men and women here on earth, and for the purpose of developing our mind, which is ourselves. What we term life consists of experiences, and the memory of past experiences. These are recorded by the mind, which makes pictures as does a cinematograph film, and, because the mind does not die, our life should be directed towards experiences which create happy memories. Knowledge comes from experience, and ignorance from lack of experience. The more we learn by elevating reading, or observation and experience, the less we suffer from the curse of ignorance, if only we remember and apply our knowledge to our everyday life. Unfortunately so many people concentrate on the unessentials of life, and pass by those things which bring happiness and contentment to themselves and those with whom they come in contact.

Memory constitutes a great part of life. If we remembered nothing of the past, and only experienced the present, life would be shorn of most of its reality. Memory enables us to live as rational beings and makes life full and varied. Our knowledge of right and wrong, of good and evil, and of all that comes within the range of the past, is the result of memory. Without memory our past would be blotted out, and we would be like a ship without a compass, drifting here and there, not knowing how to act, a helpless mass of living flesh, conscious only of the immediate present and nothing more. Memory, moreover, gives us the power to recognise and imitate, it makes us curious to know the why and wherefore of everything, it is the driving power behind the evolution of the race, and without it life would never have advanced beyond inhabiting a speck of matter floating in the ocean.

This mental process of recalling past pictures made by the mind produces what we call character, which comes from the strength or weakness of these images. Some minds fix each image more clearly, and hold it more resolutely, than do others, thus constituting what we term strong characters, while weak characters, vacillating characters, and so on, are unable to fix the image with such purpose. What we think and do being determined by this image-making process, our thoughts and actions are the result of our mental construction, so that every one thinks and acts as he must.

The reaction of the mind to what it experiences is always the same, it being like a mirror which always reflects what is before it in exactly the same way. If the mirror is dirty its reflection will not be perfect, if it is convex or concave the image it reflects will be distorted. By polishing, or levelling, the mirror its faulty reflecting power can be corrected, and so also with the mind. If we always remember that the mind reacts according to its construction, we can better appreciate all phases of thought and action, each one coming from the plastic images made by the mind in the forepart of our head, every image being the result of heredity and environment.

Education, mental development, and ethical training, about which much will be said in the pages which follow, are for the purpose of cultivating, or polishing, the mind into the way of rational and wise image-making. Though all do as they must, the great majority can be trained to do what is right and not what is wrong, if taken in hand young enough, provided the heredity is not too bad. Memory recalls past mistakes and failures, and, if this memory of the past is wisely cultivated, the mind will be moulded into making good, wise, and just images, instead of the reverse. So the mind can be trained to think the right way instead of the wrong way, and, the more rational each mind is, so will be the minds of the children which come from the union of two minds, each, the male and the female, contributing part of his and her mind substance to the mind of the child.

Likewise the parents pass on good or bad health, two strong healthy minds producing a strong healthy child, but, if one of the parents has a mental weakness, it will be passed on to the child unless it is neutralised by the strength of the other. Our bodily functions are kept working by the mind, the heart beats from its impulse, and so on with all the separate functions of the body, the nerves from all parts of the body being connected with the mind, the consequence being that when a part of the body is damaged we feel pain. This pain is not at the part affected, but in the mind, the pain being in the head because the mind has ceased to function harmoniously. Pain and sorrow, just as do joy and happiness, come from the mind, the physical body, composed of flesh and bones, having of itself no power of sensation. Moreover, the mind, which cannot be compared with anything material, draws its power and sustenance from unseen mind substance, its vehicle for action on the body being through the duplicate etheric brain which contacts the physical brain and makes the body respond to what the mind images.

We, the people of earth, are like an audience in a cinema, who experience second by second the story the picture has to tell. We remember much of what we have experienced, and imagine what is to come, but the future becomes the present, and the present instantly becomes the past. The picture is called "The Unfolding Universe", and, as we realise its unfolding, some notice details which are passed over by others, but all experience the picture as a whole. What we have experienced we call history, and we term life what we experience at the moment. This is either agreeable or disagreeable according to our reaction to these experiences. The picture is at times sad and tragic, and this causes us unhappiness, but at other times it is joyful and gay, and this gives us pleasure.

Here, in this book, we are concerned with the story the picture has already told, and it is related for the purpose of helping future generations who will be the audience. The picture, the film of life, goes on indefinitely, but for each one of us it will stop some day, and the curtain will be drawn for a moment. This event we call death, but, with only a momentary break, a fresh picture will commence in another range of vibrations around and interpenetrating this earth. The audience knows that the picture they are experiencing will some day stop, but only a few know anything about the other which will follow on. Consequently what interests them is what they are experiencing at the moment, but the more thoughtful reflect on the future as well as on the past.

The audience can influence coming events to some extent, as, by their thoughts, much colour and charm can be added to the scene. Those whose minds are undeveloped appreciate the picture differently from those whose minds are developed, but as, unfortunately, the majority have undeveloped minds, they often, by approving of what is disagreeable, spoil the picture for those who wish to concentrate on what is good, agreeable, and pleasant. This desire for what is good comes from mental development, as, by remembering the past, the wise try to avoid previous mistakes, and devote their thoughts and deeds to bringing about that which produces happiness.

The story this book has to tell is just the picture as seen by past audiences. It is being unrolled once again, so that we can pick out the mistakes, and remark on the achievements, of those who have gone before, in order that we may benefit from their experiences. Apart from natural forces, over which we have no control, that which our minds unanimously concentrate upon will happen. If they concentrate upon what is good, this will come about, and if they focus upon evil, this will occur, to the accompaniment of misery and suffering. By appreciating the unhappiness which evil thoughts have brought to our ancestors, let us learn not to repeat them, and so, by right thinking, flood the world with ideas which will bring only happiness and contentment.

History is largely made up of wars, and what has followed from war. It is the story of aggression and defence, but the sum of misery and suffering caused thereby is never told. In this both man and nature are at one, because if we turn to the science of geology we find a long record of earthquakes cracking the crust of the earth, destroying property, and causing death and misery. The earthquake of Messina in 1908 brought instant death to 140,000 people, and the destruction of towns and villages.[1] Storms, tempests and floods have destroyed countless ships, houses and other property, and likewise caused untold loss, misery and suffering. Plague and disease have swept away millions, and left millions in misery and sorrow.

This earth is certainly not a safe and peaceful place on which to live, and its story since life first took hold on its surface is made up of natural forces making existence difficult or impossible. Life on earth is one constant battle between the forces of nature and the products of the mind. Mind and natural forces are always at war, and this conflict is responsible for mental development, without which there would be no evolution and no progress.

Since mind developed into what we call man, all that he has produced has been destroyed, or is in process of being destroyed. Nothing material which he produces is permanent, everything is transient, the only permanence being mind and its etheric body which does not die. We are told at Christian funeral services that we take nothing with us into the next world, but this uninspiring doctrine is untrue, because our character and memory survive death, a fact which has only to be realised to act as an urge for improved conduct and increased mental development.

[1] The countryside around the prolific slopes of Mount Etna in Sicily is the most densely populated district on earth, and it is estimated that by its eruptions and earthquakes 1,500,000 people have perished down the ages.

(2) FROM THE PREHISTORIC AGE TO THE BEGINNING OF CIVILISATION.

Going back down the ages, we can trace the upward course of life from the time of the first simple blob of living matter, the amoeba, onwards through the early sea plants, the algae, to the seaweeds, worms, shell fish, to the fishes, and the more complicated forms of ocean life. Thence to life on land, as it creeps up from the sea in the form of plants, then to amphibian life that moved in and out of the sea to remain finally on land, through the invertebrates to the vertebrates, through the innumerable forms of fish, birds, insects, animals, and on to man. When we survey this immense panorama of life and thought, we discover that physical change and decay are the earthly heritage of every living thing.

The animal can do little to make life secure, but man, with his greater intelligence and reasoning power, has done much to make it happier and safer from the forces of nature. Increased knowledge of the human frame has reduced the danger of plague. Disease is being conquered by medical and surgical means, and, in consequence, life on earth is now longer and happier than it was. Stronger houses now better resist the earthquake, storm and flood, and larger, sounder-built ships make for safer passage against the storm, which in the past destroyed so many frailer craft. By intelligence, by thought, foresight and making better use of our reasoning powers, we are fortifying ourselves each year against the attacks nature makes upon us.

If these attacks had never been made would we have ever reached the position we now occupy? Would mind, in temporary contact with matter, ever have advanced beyond the amoeba and trilobite stage? Is struggle with adversity not our portion for the purpose of developing the mind which is the individual? Evolution is only a name for the results of a long unending struggle of the mind against the forces of nature, and the story of the ascent of man is the record of the development of mind in consequence of the difficulties and dangers it has had to overcome.

The power of sight is doubtless due to our primitive sightless ancestors, while swimming or floating in the sea, bumping a part of their bodies against rocks and the bottom of the ocean. In time they developed a mental connection between the surface of their bodies and their minds, which enabled them to anticipate danger by what we call sight. The mind developed a wonderful nerve mechanism, which enabled it to respond to and picture what exists outside of what had hitherto been a windowless prison. That was a great step forward, and it all came about through suffering and the experience gained therefrom.

Pain, which causes suffering, is disharmony of the mind. Mind is upset, and this we term pain at the part of the body affected, due to this mechanism of nerves, developed by the mind, which enables it to feel and sense its bodily covering and surroundings. When part of the body is out of harmony with the mind, pain follows as a warning that all is not right. When the mechanism of the body goes so far wrong as to make it impossible for it to support life, the mind, which is the seat of life, departs and leaves the physical body to decompose.

Pain, suffering, and experience have brought about the development of mind, and made us what we are both physically and mentally. As the mind developed, as intelligence increased, we discovered ways and means of making life easier. Better homes have made life more comfortable, just as our increased knowledge of the make-up of the body has reduced the number of diseases to which it was the victim.

Mental development has thus made life fuller, happier and easier, but we cannot stand still, as, without care and foresight, the forces of nature without, and the weaknesses of the body within, are always present, awaiting any slackening on our part to take advantage of every sign of feebleness. It is a hard and relentless process, but nature is quite devoid of pity, a quality which pertains to the mind when it attains a high state of development. If we discover how to surmount our difficulties and weaknesses, nature will not prevent us from using the means she provides, but the initiative must always come from us, as we have to think out our own problems so as to make life easier and safer. If we do not, suffering inevitably follows.

Besides the forces of nature which arise against us, including the weakness of the flesh, mind has always had one overpowering passion—to remain as long as possible in contact with matter. Mind is something permanent, something more enduring than matter. Within the limits of our present knowledge we would say that it does not decay like matter, and, if it obtains sustenance, this comes from something which is not physical. Mind is what we might term a super-etheric substance, housed in the etheric body, a duplicate of our physical body, and, in consequence, we are etheric beings inhabiting temporarily a framework of matter.

Because of this permanency of mind, which is ourselves, as the individual is mind and only mind, we survive death. This comes about by means of the duplicate etheric body which each one of us has from birth, as it and our mind come from our parents, they being able to pass on not only that which is the basis of our physical body, but also that which forms our etheric body and mind. This trinity, which we call man, grows and develops, to separate at death, the physical body to decompose and the etheric body and mind to function elsewhere, but with the ability to return to earth vibrations and be seen and heard under suitable conditions.

So long, however, as the mind is making use of the physical as its habitation, it uses every endeavour to keep it nourished. The physical body is constantly wasting away and being renewed on the permanent structure of the etheric body. This wastage must be replaced if the mind is to be able to remain with the body, and, from the time life first came to earth, its foremost occupation has been the sustenance and nourishment of its physical habitation.

This need of bodily renewal, this urge for nourishment, has been another cause of our evolution, just as it has been the cause of one mind disregarding the needs of other minds. Self-interest has been the guiding power of each mind, from the time that life first made its appearance in some Palaeozoic ocean. Man, by nature, is a selfish being, but this natural urge to gratify his bodily needs has been a contributing cause to his development. The satisfaction attained has, however, been counterbalanced by much misery and suffering. To secure the needs of the flesh has, moreover, brought into being an aggressiveness, which would have been wanting had he lived in a paradise where everything was obtained without effort.

If everyone in the past had been possessed with everything desired without effort, life would have been easy, but there would have been no urge for change. Evolution, in such an environment, is difficult to imagine. Mental development would have been lacking, because of the absence of any need for effort, and mental development is the purpose of life both here and hereafter.

After a slow and painful evolutionary process, mind brought into being what we now call primitive man. Directing mind, through millions and millions of years (estimated at five hundred million years), shaped this being, after moulding his ancestors from the simplest of forms, through numerous stages of life, until it finally completed the being we now call man. His immediate ancestors, who probably lived in all parts of the world, as far back as some five hundred thousand years ago, we now term sub-men, the remains of one having been discovered at Heidelberg in Germany, and a later specimen at Piltdown in Sussex not now being considered as genuine.

Then, by the discovery at Neanderthal, near Dusseldorf, of a skull and bones, we have the remains of a creature which resembles a human being, a rather grotesque man who lived some fifty thousand years ago in a cave. He may not have been able to speak, and it is thought that he did not walk quite erect. He shuffled rather than walked, with his head protruding in front of him. To begin with he was one of a species which was few in number, a wandering creature in search of food, often hungry and tired, but for ever on the prowl for something to eat.

There is some doubt as to whether this super-animal, and his contemporaries, produced the human race, but others like him were the ancestors of the first *Homo Sapiens*, the name given to the human species. These creatures, the parents of the men and women of the past and present, found themselves in a world very unlike the one we know today. In places there were long periods of cold and heat, as on three or four occasions a huge ice-field moved slowly down from the north, both Neanderthal and primitive man experiencing the last of these. Slowly it came and slowly it went, only to return and again cover Europe as far south as the English Channel, and stretch eastwards over Germany and part of Russia. Britain was at one time part of Europe, and much of the North Sea was dry land, over which flowed the Thames and the Rhine. Spain, it is believed, was then joined to Africa, the Mediterranean consisted of two smaller separate seas, the Red Sea hardly existed, the Caspian and Black Seas were one and of much greater size, and the Gobi desert was one great sea. India and Ceylon probably formed one complete island, detached from Asia by a sea which covered what is now the valleys of the rivers Indus and Ganges.

Such, then, was the land of our ancestors, and, as

the climate changed, and the configuration of the earth altered, they changed with them. Climatic changes, which in turn brought about changes in animal life, caused alterations in the lives and habits of these primitive men and women. Only by wearing skins could the most northerly inhabitants live, and so they learned the art of making and wearing clothes. To obtain food and clothes they hunted and killed their prey, they lived in caves to protect themselves from the rain and storm, and to cross rivers they used fallen trees. Slowly, as the sub-man became man, his needs increased, and the greater he grew in numbers and intelligence the more he required in the way of food, clothing and other necessary comforts.

To obtain these he had to labour with his hands, as little comes to those who stand by idly doing nothing. It meant either going back to the jungle or working to keep out of it, and early man decided that the balance was in favour of work. Better food, and warmer clothing, were to be preferred to the uncertainties of life in the forests. Thus the human mind developed as the result of the struggle for existence, and, as this happened under circumstances, and in surroundings, different from those experienced by his ape-like ancestors, man began to wonder and to think differently from the animals who were satisfied with their lot in life.

By learning to employ his right hand to wield a club, and then a tool, probably accounts for the beginning of the mental development which raised our species above that of the animal. Labour turned the sub-man into a human being. We are what we are because of our thumb and forefinger, as, by employing them to hold an instrument, we can not only protect ourselves from other and stronger animals but also mould matter into the shapes we desire. The thumb and forefinger enabled the human race to survive, increase in numbers, and also to construct. They developed the mind, and the more it developed the more primitive man used his hands for intelligent work, to be helped by the discovery of fire when two stones came sharply together, or when two sticks were rubbed together to produce a spark which set alight some nearby dry grass, a discovery which made possible all other inventions.

Because man was not entirely satisfied with his lot in life, he has developed farther and farther away from his jungle ancestors, and this urge for something better has been stimulated by his ability to use his hands for useful and productive purposes. The more he thought, the more he could produce, and the more he could produce, the more he thought. His mind, in consequence, developed a reasoning quality which is absent in the animal. This was helped by language, as, by learning to talk and understand what others said, new ideas were exchanged. By slow degrees he began to think intelligently, and to wonder why and how things happened. By so doing he discovered how to make tools, a hammer and a chisel, out of stone, and with these he fashioned wooden objects which he used as furniture or on his hunting expeditions. These he greatly valued, he was proud of his handicraft, and it gave him pleasure to show them to his wife, children and neighbours.

Thus labour, which consists of moving things, produced what we today call wealth. That part of his wealth which he used to produce more wealth, such as his hammer and chisel, we today term capital, it being of prime importance in producing more wealth, as without capital little can be obtained from the earth's storehouse. Capital is necessary to form the earth's substance into the shape conforming to our needs. At times a neighbour borrowed the hammer and chisel, and, if this happened once or twice, the owner perhaps did no more than growl, but if the neighbour took it without asking, the response was either a snarl or a blow.

To obviate this unpleasantness, the neighbour, when he next requested the hammer and chisel, brought with him a gift, perhaps some food, or a piece of clothing, which was increased in quantity the longer the capital was withdrawn from the original owner. This bringing of a gift in exchange for the capital became a regular custom, and so the capitalist, instead of growling or snarling when a neighbour desired to borrow a tool, was pleased and satisfied.

This gift we now call interest, which the capitalist obtains in exchange for his capital. So, in time, men made hammers, chisels, and other implements, which they either bartered or lent to their neighbours in return for interest. Those who had most to lend were richer than those who were always borrowing, because they had the capital, and, besides this, they received the interest in the form of gifts. Thus some had more than others, but, though this was so, they were more fearful, as they were always afraid that their neighbours, instead of bartering or borrowing, would take their capital and wealth and not return them.

The accumulation of capital and wealth thus led to constant feuds between the rich and the poor, and life, in those far-off days, must have been far from serene. Here we are at the beginning of what is now called war, when some desired to preserve their possessions, their hunting-grounds and caves against others who wanted them. Instead of being rational and wise, these primitive people were ignorant and foolish, and wasted their substance and lives fighting to settle a question which could equally well have been decided by negotiation and arrangement. Instead of dividing up the land equally, so that all would have their share, the strongest took all they could and drove out those they had conquered. Here we are at the cause of war, namely possessions, which primitive man not only fought to retain but also to take from others. Wealth, or that which we possess, has been the cause, not only of much of the happiness, but also of much of the misery, the race has endured, and this will become clear as we proceed.

To begin with, the capitalist probably enlisted the help of his sons, who were joined by others who worked and hunted with them for greater safety. By thus joining forces a tribe was in time formed for mutual protection. The larger the tribe, whose interest it was to protect the wealth they all secured and produced, the greater was the safety of that community. All worked with a common aim, the production, or securing, of food and wealth by means of capital, and so we arrive at the three foundations necessary to produce wealth, namely capital, labour and intelligence. Without these three pillars the production of wealth is impossible.

Another source of wealth was in animals, as
gradually primitive man tamed certain wild animals
for their flesh and skins. Some he tamed for their
milk. In his search for fish he was carried down the
river on a dug-out tree-trunk, to discover the sea,
which gave him food in ever greater abundance.
Gradually his fishing methods improved, and, when
he discovered the use of a sail, he was able to reach
farther out from land. So he sailed the sea, and
roamed over wide stretches of country, to find food
for himself and fodder for his beasts, to return in
time to some previous squatting-ground, to discover
a crop growing on what had been bare earth. The
seeds of the fodder he had previously used to feed his
herds had brought another crop into being. This
discovery was the beginning of agriculture, to change
entirely his habits and way of life. He ceased his
nomadic life in search of food, to settle down and
build a shelter which in time became a house, then a
cluster of dwellings, to eventually become a village or
a town.

The momentous discovery that crops grew from
their own seeds was a notable achievement. Now
he knew that, by sowing the seed of the fodder eaten
by his cattle, he could obtain crops without moving
about. He came to understand nature's method of
producing herbage, and, after he learned this lesson, he
also discovered that he, like his cattle, could also eat
this seed as food. From a comparatively small
amount of seed he was able to secure a sufficiently
large crop to sustain his cattle and family, because the
former ate the stalks and they the seeds. As this
crop grew each year, they learned in time that all that

was necessary for them to do was to keep some of the seed for sowing, and to store part of the crop to meet the needs of the tribe, the herds, and the flocks throughout the winter. So it came about that some tribes ceased being nomads, and settled down on the land that grew the best crops. This was the beginning of civilisation, which developed in river valleys and deltas where the rich alluvial soil produced the largest crops.

Looking back, we now realise that primitive human society then went through as great a change as has happened in our own time with the coming of the machine, and all the great discoveries of science. Our lives today are lived under completely different conditions from those of our great-grandparents, and so it was in the far-off days of primitive man, when agriculture superseded hunting, and civilisation took the place of wandering from place to place with flocks and herds in search of pasture. As science has made it possible for a much greater population to live from the produce of the land, and all that the earth contains, so the discovery of agriculture likewise made possible the support of larger numbers. Thus, by sowing seeds, the earth was made to give forth more food than it did when man just took what it gave to feed his animals, or relied on what he could kill when out hunting.

Though the wealth of our ancestors increased they remained selfish, and envied those who had greater possessions. This envy was often accompanied by hatred and all uncharitableness. The bodily needs of primitive man came first, and he gave little thought to those of his brother man. What he wanted he took,

and, if resisted, he killed if necessary to achieve his end. Self always came first, and his desires were always satisfied by any means within his power.

Those who settled down in the valleys and river deltas lived in companies, or tribes, because they discovered that union made for strength. The tribe pooled its requirements, and, as others likewise banded themselves together, robbery and pillage between neighbouring tribes became the common order. It was much easier to let others obtain the food and skins, and then rob them of their enterprise and skill. There was then no law and order, might was right, and the strongest overcame the weakest, in the belief that it was the only thing to do. Why work or hunt if others could be found to do it for you?

Naturally this robbery was resented and resisted. What we work for we desire to keep. The love of personal possessions is apparent even in an infant. It cries if something it is holding is taken away, and, as it grows up, it naturally resists any such attempt. So the desire to retain what we have is a primitive instinct, and is as strong in some animals as it is in man. So we resist aggression and robbery, the taking of what we call our own. This resistance, which doubtless began by single combat, when adopted by the tribe we term war. War is caused by aggression and resistance to the aggression. This action and reaction runs through the pages of history, it largely makes up history, and it forms a considerable part of the story of the life of mankind.

The aggressive character of the male of the species has made him determine the history of the race, the female playing a quite unspectacular part. Primitive woman pursued a line of evolution peculiarly her own. She was the common property of the males of the tribe, to become the slave of one man when ownership came into being. While he hunted and secured the food, she cooked it, hewed the wood, fetched the water, and produced and looked after the children. Neither men nor women in these early times knew about the part taken by the male in procreation. Like the present-day aborigine of Australia, they thought that child-birth was caused by spirit children entering women's bodies to take on flesh, an idea which probably gave rise to the ancient religious belief in reincarnation. When civilisation began, with the discovery of agriculture, the women sowed and gathered the crops, and did all the drudgery until slaves were captured, when their position changed, to rise ultimately to that of mistress of the house.

Primitive woman was a coarse, ugly, shrill-voiced, ill-mannered creature, her hair was short and her movement awkward. Then the men, not the women, of the tribe decorated their bodies with dyes and ornaments, the women being seized by the strongest men for their usefulness and not because of their beauty. So long as strength of body determined everything, woman, because of her inferiority in strength, was the serf of the man, but, amongst those who employed slaves, her position improved, she had time and opportunity to care for her looks and she became man's plaything.

Her influence tamed her lord's manners and customs, and he increased her intelligence, which developed her into a being taking pride in the adornment of her body because this gave him pleasure. She found that her looks improved by cultivating and fashioning her hair, and that she obtained by persuasion what she had not the force to secure. So she became long-haired, low-voiced, modest, graceful, and refined, her more delicate form and features making their appeal to her master. When civilisation came, her interests centred in her home and children, her husband and sons being those who determined the course of history. The mental development of each age has always established the position of women, and this being so it was no better than that of a slave in the time of primitive man, and for many centuries to come.

The story of man, as *Homo Sapiens*, probably starts some fifty thousand years ago, but chronological history takes us back only some three thousand years. Pre-history is, however, rich in warlike relics, such as flint spear-heads, axe-heads and arrow-heads. Prehistoric battlefields, where numerous bones and stone weapons have been uncovered, point to battles in the Stone Age when stone weapons had replaced wooden clubs and staves. The wooden handles have perished, but the stone remains to testify that man has always been an aggressive animal, and warfare part of his daily life.

If primitive man had been a really intelligent being, he would have found better means of obtaining his needs than by robbery and plunder. He would not have resorted to war, but confined his energies to trade by exchange of goods. If he had been sensible, instead of stupid, he would have devoted his time and effort to making the things his neighbours required, and they, in turn, would have made the articles their neighbours needed. So an exchange of goods would have developed, and the wealth, comfort and happiness of the people would have increased.

Instead of adopting this sensible way of living, prehistoric men spent much of their time making clubs, spears, bows, arrows and other warlike equipment, for the purpose of aggression or resistance to attack. They never felt secure, nor free from attack, and had to be perpetually on guard. If they could only have agreed between themselves to share the hunting-grounds and the rivers, they could have obtained their needs in animals and fish, and lived happy and peaceful lives free from the fear of sudden death, wounds, and all the misery which comes from war.

Unfortunately, instead of being wise, they were foolish, they were under the curse of ignorance, and pursued the path, adopted by their jungle ancestors, of conflict against their neighbours. Stealing seemed so much the easiest method, but the thief can be just as hard worked, and just as worried to secure his existence, as the honest man, because he requires to be continually on his guard against attack. He uses up his energy in an unproductive enterprise, and he lives as a parasite on the labour of others, because he neither produces wealth, nor does he do anything to increase the happiness and contentment of the community. Honesty is much the best policy for everyone, and only when everyone is educated sufficiently to realise that this is a fundamental truth will the world have peace and real prosperity.

We do not know when religion developed, as it must have come about slowly, but primitive man evidently believed in a life after death, because his body was buried with food to sustain him.[1] The beginning of religion, as we now understand its meaning, certainly came from early man seeing apparitions, or ghosts, a word which comes from the German *geist*, a spirit. Quite possibly, living then so close to nature, he was more psychically developed than we are now, and from reading ancient literature we are entitled to think that the spirits of the dead were seen and heard more often than they now are. These he recognised as those of his friends and relations. Out of this evolved Ancestor Worship, which was the only religion in these primitive times, prevailing as it did everywhere over the then inhabited world.

Primitive man undoubtedly saw occasionally the men and women of the other world, and accepted them naturally as beings who had lived on earth. The return to earth of those we call dead certainly gave rise much later to the numerous polytheistic religions. Monotheism was a much later development, based, not on observed facts, as was polytheism, but on speculation, when the belief in a unified universe led some to concentrate all creation within the jurisdiction of one all-powerful unseen creator and sustainer. What is today called Spiritualism is the modern form of the oldest of all religions, Ancestor Worship, the principal difference being that today the dead are not worshipped, or prayed to, but treated as

---

[1] Slowly this custom changed to that of laying food on the grave for the departed spirit to eat, until finally it ended by laying flowers, which, in our time, are neatly placed together to form a wreath.

men and women who have passed into another and
higher order of life, surrounding and interpenetrating
this earth, from which, under certain conditions, they
can again communicate and make their presence felt.

Out of all the supernormal phenomena that
develop in the presence of psychically endowed
people, which are the same today as in early times,
primitive man created his religion, now called Ancestor Worship, the parent of every religion. From
this natural and observed basis the people of earth,
as the result of mystical speculation and contemplation,
have evolved all the different so-called revealed religions which have comforted the human race for the
past five thousand years or more. The etheric men and
women, seen and heard, gradually came to be looked
upon as gods and goddesses, who controlled growth
and movement, but it was long before the unity of
nature was realised, to develop into the contemplation
of one supreme God, the gods then becoming known
as saints and angels.[1]

Whether ethics or religion came first we know not,
but, though they are often confused, there is only an
indirect connection. Morality, or ethics, as we have
already discovered, is the outcome of experience.
Property owners within the tribe realised in time that
if they were to remain secure with their possessions
they must allow others the same privilege. In exchange for not stealing from their neighbours they
expected their neighbours not to steal from them.

---

[1] *The Psychic Stream* commences with the study of religion from these
early times, when first the dead were worshipped, and all the phenomena of
nature received the reverence of primitive man. The further evolution of
religion is then recorded down the ages, to the time when many of the old
beliefs were brought together to produce what is now known as Christianity.

This mutual desire for security led to the belief that it was wrong to steal, and theft became a crime within the tribe, for which punishment was inflicted.

Theft, quite possibly, was the first act to which developing mind took sufficient exception to bring about amongst fellow tribesmen the conviction that it should not take place. Theft, we can say, was probably the first accepted crime. Man thus began to recognise right from wrong. It became wrong to steal and right to be honest, but, as in every community some are born who prefer being dishonest, the majority, who realised the wisdom of honesty, agreed to punish the wrong-doers. This decision became part of the tradition of the tribe, and formed the basis of what in time developed into a code of regulations governing the life of the community. Gradually other crimes and offences were added as they were found to be needed, the next probably being the crime of murder. In this way the laws governing the tribe were built up, but, as in these days there was no knowledge of writing, they were handed down from father to son until they became part of the accepted tradition of the community.

Likewise what are also known as taboos came to be accepted. It was wrong to do this or that. It was wrong to use an iron plough because iron attracted the devils, the idea probably originating when iron was an innovation and only wood was used to plough. It was wrong to eat certain parts of animals because they were not considered suitable as human food; it was wrong to eat meat cooked in a particular way, and it was wrong for women to dress their hair in a certain style. Taboos became so numerous that to enumerate them all would require a volume, but they entered largely into the lives of our ancestors, and, although it is difficult to understand the reason for every taboo, there is little doubt that each one originated from the objection to change from traditional usage, or from some practical reason which at a later date became unnecessary and in time was forgotten.

The connection between ethics and religion came about when the sense of right and wrong developed sufficiently to enable the imagination to transcend this life. As there were good and bad people on earth, it was assumed that these distinctions continued in the other world. As natural phenomena were either good or bad for man, it followed that the gods responsible were benign or wicked. Then came the belief that those who were wrong-doers on earth kept company after death with the bad gods or devils, while the good went into the presence of the good gods. Separate places were imagined in the next world, heaven where the good gods lived, and hell the abode of the bad gods. Later on, when priests took charge of the tribe's religion, the good were those who not only conformed to the tribe's traditions, but also accepted its religious beliefs. They, after death, it was believed, lived in heaven, but the unbelievers, the sinners, occupied hell.

Thus the idea of sin came into the world, the believers being the righteous and the unbelievers the sinners. This priestly dogma, which is of later origin than the distinction between right and wrong, was used by the priests to keep the people in order and obtain their offerings. To tell the people that the tenth of their produce was reserved for the gods, and that it was sinful to withhold it from the priests, who had been appointed by them to receive it, was much the simplest way to secure the sacred revenue. Likewise the crops would not grow, and children would not be born, if the people angered the gods by being disobedient to the dictates of the priests. Sin, which was related to something contrary to the wishes of the priesthood, was an idea which helped to preserve order and the functioning of the tribe or nation.

It had a powerful influence on government, largely doing away with the necessity for force, hitherto the only way to keep the unruly in order. The threat of the anger of the gods appealed to the childish minds of the people so effectively, that until our own times they have been ruled as much by religion as by the civil law. In the tribal state the god most feared was the dead chief, who, it was thought, still lived amongst them, and was regarded as the real ruler of the clan. He was ever present with his people, "nearer than hands or feet", both in peace and in war. Victories were won by him, crops grew, and everything prospered if the tribe carried out his wishes.

So the dead chief ruled the tribe through the tribe's medium, "he being dead yet speaketh", his words being sacred and only for the ear of the reigning chief. One tribal chief swore an oath in the name of his tribe's god to another chief, who swore in the name of his god, and this had more effect in keeping an agreement than armed might, as to break such an oath was to dishonour the tribe's god. This old custom is still in practice in our present-day Law Courts, but few realise the powerful effect it had on our ancestors from primitive times to within our own day, and how promises were kept through fear of dishonouring the national god. This effort to secure a good reputation in heaven, and to be on friendly terms with the gods, has mightily strengthened the structure of society during the childhood of the race.

In our day, when one of the family dies, a photograph recalls him or her to our memory. It is placed where all can see, and is looked upon with certain feelings of emotion. When there were no photographs, idols took their place, crude images of wood or stone, carved by simple people to remind them of the one who had gone. During the age of Ancestor Worship, the idol representing the father, or grandfather, was asked for the things required, until the family believed that his spirit actually inhabited his image. The image became sacred, and, if something considered to be wrong was about to be done, it was put in a corner so that it would not see and be angry. The image was talked to and argued with, washed and fondled, and if requests were not granted it was beaten and had pins stuck into it. Our childish ancestors treated the family image just as a little girl does her doll, until the time came when the priests made it an aid to devotion, and it was prayed to. Thus we find the origin of prayer. Images assumed all sorts of shapes and sizes, the Greeks, with their love of the beautiful, carving noble statues to represent the gods, but the more crude the people's minds, so were the images of their gods.

The gods, or spirits, came much into the lives of our ancestors, as it was believed that behind each phenomenon was a god. It was the only way they could explain movement. How did the sun move, the plants grow, or the wind blow? Because a god was the cause. Thunder was the voice of a god, and the lightning that split the tree was his axe. If the gods were well and duly fed the crops would flourish, and life would be comfortable, but, if their desires were neglected, then the thunder would roll, the sun and moon would eclipse, and the lightning would strike.

Because the gods, who were seen from time to time, looked like men, it was thought that they had human desires and passions. Consequently they ate and enjoyed food, especially the etheric bodies of men and animals, and to this belief can be traced the reason for sacrifice. Sacrifice was a gift to the gods of the immaterial body of the victim. Whether the sacrifice was a man, or an animal, the idea behind it was always the same, the return for something received, or hoped for, such as a good harvest or rain.

It was not the flesh that the gods were believed to desire, but the etheric duplicate, the part of man which is akin to the gods. All that the gods could receive and appreciate was the spirit freed from the flesh. Only through death could the spirits of humans, animals, and vegetation be set free. The material body meant nothing to the gods, but they greatly relished the spirit. As man ate the flesh of humans and animals, and the material part of vegetation, he imagined that the gods needed the spirit in each for their sustenance, as it was on this that they fed. As primitive man gave slaves, captives and animals as presents to his friends, so he presented their spirits as a thank-offering to the gods. The sacrifice of an animal, however, produced more succulent spirit-food than came from vegetation, and so we read that the Lord preferred the sacrifice of Abel, the shepherd, to that of Cain, the gardener.

In the Old Testament there are thirty-nine separate references to the "sweet savour", or savoury dish, which the priests offered to Jehovah. These palatable dishes he relished so much, that we are told he decided not to curse the earth any more, nor to act again as universal slaughterer, because Noah's enormous meal, consisting of the spirits from every clean beast and every clean fowl, smelled so appetising (*Genesis* viii, 21). Jehovah was very particular as to how his food was to be cooked, and the way it was to be served up. He was most fastidious about the seasoning, pickling, and sauces (*Leviticus* ii, 1).

Everything in connection with his meal was sacred and holy. The Chief Priest, or principal butcher, was a holy man, and everything he touched was holy, such as the table off which the Lord dined, the oil and gravy in the cooking process, and the knife the priest used to cut off the joints exactly as the Lord directed (*Leviticus*, Chapters i–iv). Priests have always surrounded themselves with this atmosphere of holiness, to increase the mystery of their calling, even the vast territories which were owned by the Christian Church being termed "spiritual land", and the more they elevated the importance of their god the greater became their own influence and power.

Truly the gods were to be feared, as they had the life and well-being of mankind in their hands. They constituted the science, religion, and philosophy of primitive man, and they still form the basis of the religious beliefs of a large part of the human race. All past, and present-day, sacrificial religions owe their origin to the simple ideas formed by primitive man about his relationship to the gods. As they were responsible for all the phenomena of nature, he prayed and sacrificed to them so as to obtain their favours for his daily needs, and, as we proceed, we shall see how this belief moulded the course of history.

Some ten thousand years ago primitive man had reached a much higher level of thought than had his Neanderthal predecessor, who was a creature living on what he could catch or kill, much as an animal does, but, in spite of the advance he had made, he was still very ignorant and superstitious. He knew little of the world and the universe of which he was part, and accepted his conditions much as he found them. This period is known as the Neolithic Age, when polished stone implements, axe-heads, pottery, necklaces of teeth and shells, besides domestic animals, were man's principal possessions.

His art consisted of outlines of animals, he employed magic rites to promote growth, and he sacrificed the first animal killed on his hunting expeditions to the god he believed had guided him. Some of the race by now had passed through the Steppe period, the time when they were nomads wandering in search of fodder for their animals. Some had settled down as cultivators of the soil, to become farmers, and, besides having traditional laws and taboos, they worshipped their ancestors, and believed in an after life in their company. So we have now reached the age of civilisation, which began in the Neolithic Age, and it continued through the Bronze and Iron Ages to the present time.

The thousand years from 4000 to 3000 B.C. was a period prolific in discoveries and inventions, as then it was that those things were discovered and invented by civilised man which are now in everyday use. At no period before or after this time, until we come to our own scientific age, was there such an output of new articles, because then it was that the metals (except iron, which was not much used before 1000 B.C.) came into everyday use in those lands we now call the Middle East. Copper, bronze, lead, tin, gold and silver were turned into weapons, implements and ornaments. Kilns were invented to harden the clay which the potter's wheel moulded into pots, jugs and vases of all descriptions. Bread was made from the flour which came from the grinding-stone. Beer was brewed, cotton and flax were spun, and the land gave forth abundant crops, by being watered by canals and ditches.

Then it was that the wheel was invented, two and four-wheeled carts and wagons coming into use. Harness was put on oxen, which were trained to pull the plough, horses being likewise used for tractor purposes, while camels and asses bore the burdens hitherto placed on human backs. Houses were built of bricks, their furniture consisting of seats, tables and beds, such useful articles as tongs, nails and other necessities being in everyday use. On the rivers and canals boats with sails carried the crops, while on the sea sailing-ships traded along the coast. Here we find the blessings which came from civilisation, when man discovered that by intelligent thought nature could be a friend as well as an enemy. The more he has combined his intelligence with his labour the more he has progressed, the more comforts he has had, and the more he has produced with the minimum of toil.

Unfortunately the intelligent of this world have always been harried and worried by those who pre-ferred to use their muscles instead of their brains. From the beginning of civilisation, some six thousand years ago, onwards to the 16th century of the Christian era, much of history is given over to the fight for supremacy between the nomads and those we term the civilised, a word which originally meant those who lived in towns. The nomads hated civilised life and preferred to live in tents, and roam over wide spaces. They were fierce, ignorant, greedy for loot, and so intolerant that their attempt to force everyone to live the same kind of open-air life as they did brought about widespread devastation everywhere, a state of affairs which came to an end in Europe only some four hundred years ago.

Those who lived settled lives in houses were always being raided by these wanderers, which the Greeks and Romans called barbarians, and whoever was unable to obtain protection was quickly plundered. In consequence nations, for self-protection, came into being, and the next chapter will tell of these earliest communities, which, in self-defence, formed them-selves together under the control of a priest-king.

Agriculture is the foundation of civilisation. If there had been no agriculture the people would have remained nomads, and cities, towns and villages would never have come into being. In this chapter, how-ever, we are at the stage when man was ruled by nature, and he had just a glimmering that nature could be made to do his bidding. He prayed and made his offerings to the gods of wind, thunder, lightning, rain, and all the other forces of nature, but the time came when he turned stone and wood to his service, the herbs into medicines and poisons, and fire into heat to create what he desired. He discovered the metals, and used the forces of nature to his own advantage. Here we are considering him when he is at the entrance to his kingdom, to become, thousands of years later, lord of nature, and use her forces, which he once feared and worshipped, for his own benefit.

As mind developed, as needs increased, as inventions and discoveries were made, life became more and more complicated. The more developed the nation the more comforts and conveniences are desired, and so roads, railways, telephones, drainage, water systems, social services, and all that makes up a civilised community eventually came into being. Laws for the regulation of life became more numerous and involved. Communication between nations improved, and now by steamship, railroad, radio, telephone, and airplane the world's family is knit together in a way never before experienced. Our comforts have increased, but our happiness has not advanced in the same degree, because our ethical conduct has not kept pace with our material progress.

Because early man was very ignorant, he did and thought many things which we now know to be wrong. He did not then think that it was wrong to steal from a neighbouring tribe, if this benefited his own tribe. Though he had developed a tribal morality he had not evolved what we might call a human morality, one that applied to the entire human race. His tribe, and its interests, came first, and all other tribes were his enemies, to be plundered and slaughtered when possible.

Though man, in many directions, has developed morally since those far-off days, it is unfortunately also true that his descendants have made little progress in their ethical attitude towards the human race as a whole, and it is this remarkable break in the moral development of the race that will be stressed in the pages which follow. Until this want in our ethical outlook is made good, the peace and happiness we have reached in our national life will not be secured internationally. By recording the outstanding deeds of our ancestors, many of which were not only morally wrong but also stupid, it is hoped to show that the future happiness of the race rests on the development of an enlarged ethical standard, which will break the bounds of frontiers and become world-wide. Thus, and thus only, will the worst effect of ignorance be removed, to the lasting happiness of all mankind.

How essential it is that a fresh page be started will be better realised when we study the history of the past. History is made up not only of the great achievements, but also of the folly, of humanity, which latter has been too little stressed by historians, because only within recent times have our minds developed sufficiently to realise it. Now let us hope that by educating the young to look upon the past in a new light, they will not repeat when they grow up the terrible mistakes of those who have gone before them.

CHAPTER IV.

THE OLDEST CIVILISATIONS.

Introduction. (1) *Sumerian, Babylonian, and Assyrian Civilisations* (3500–330 B.C.). (2) *Egyptian Civilisation* (3000–332 B.C.). (3) *Indian Civilisation* (2500–126 B.C.). (4) *Chinese Civilisation* (2356 B.C.–A.D. 384).

In the last chapter we brought the story of man down to about six thousand years ago, by which time the human species had become more numerous than that of any other similar creature. He had, moreover, become a being taking thought for the future, saving some of his food for the winter, and looking ahead in a way no other animal had ever done before. So life emerged from the Stone Age and passed into the Bronze Age, and this brings us to the period considered in this chapter.

Man had by now made one of his greatest discoveries—how to produce fire—and this had opened the way for him to make use of various metals. Agriculture was flourishing in the plains and valleys, wheat, barley and millet being grown. Bread, without yeast, was eaten and unfermented ale was drunk. Wealth was increasing, and cows, oxen, goats, sheep and pigs comprised the livestock. Houses, mostly constructed of wood, but also of baked clay and stone where it was available, were springing up and becoming villages. By the discovery of the art of weaving, cloth was taking the place of skins. Network was also in use. Household furnishings, such as tables and stools, were slowly making their appearance, as were musical instruments made of stretched skins, strings and bone. Ornaments for the house and personal wear had increased, and these were made of gold, jet and amber. Copper was also fashioned into pots and pans, and put to other useful purposes. In other words civilisation had commenced, as some had emerged from the nomad state to what we today call civilised life.

With the discovery of tin and copper, articles composed of a new metal made their appearance, as the way was found to smelt these two metals together and produce the alloy bronze, which is a much harder substance. By smelting zinc and copper together brass was discovered, and finally, some three to four thousand years ago, our ancestors found how to make iron implements from iron ore, by placing the ore in a charcoal fire and hammering it into shape when glowing hot.

Trade between the villages had become established, but, as there was no money, it was carried on by barter. Capitalists had increased in number, and the different branches of industry were sorting themselves out. Some owned tracts of land on which roamed great herds of animals, others produced the wooden and metal requirements of the community, while some owned the caravans which carried the merchandise from one centre to another.

Since the time of Neanderthal man, the surface of the earth had been changing, so much so that in the time we are now considering it was very like what it is today. The ice cap had receded into the Arctic regions and the two seas, which occupied the Mediterranean basin, had become one. The Straits of Gibraltar had come into being; the Red Sea, the Caspian Sea and the Black Sea were as we now know them. India had become a peninsula, and Ceylon an island. The mountain ranges, though higher, were like what they are today. These changes of the earth's surface had altered the climate, and made the northern regions fit for human habitation.

The melting of the ice cap in the north had released a great volume of pent-up water which raised the sea level, and geologists imagine that this raising of the ocean level brought it above the surface of the earth where is now the Straits of Gibraltar. The sea poured in through this gap and filled all the low-lying land, so much so that one great sea was formed, the Mediterranean as we now know it. This may have happened some ten or twenty thousand years ago, but it is considered possible that before this occurred primitive man had settled round the two smaller seas, then occupying what we now term the Mediterranean basin, these being supplied by the Nile and other rivers.

What a catastrophe this must have been, if geologists are correct in their surmise! What we today call lake dwellings would be engulfed by the torrents which swept in from the Atlantic Ocean, to the accompaniment of loss of life and property. Early man, from this experience and many others, found that this earth is no bed of roses, and that man is born to toil and suffer throughout his earthly pilgrimage.

All this was, however, unknown to the people of six thousand years ago. It had happened thousands of years earlier and been forgotten. It was perhaps the greatest of all the floods which have engulfed part of the human race, though others were to follow, and we have a record of one, which is found recorded on bricks by the Sumerians at a later date, when the Euphrates and Tigris burst their banks. This story the Jews learned when in captivity in these parts, and their account of Noah and his ark is known to everyone.

In spite of floods and earthquakes, life managed to keep its grip on the earth, the population grew, and the most civilised communities were living fairly comfortably in those parts which were most suitable for agriculture and husbandry. We ,do not know much of the thoughts and beliefs of the people of these early days. Relics discovered indicate that they had a religion which accepted the belief in a life after death. They believed in spirits, and worshipped the sun and other heavenly bodies. Some of their places of worship, such as Stonehenge, and also their burial places, still exist. Human sacrifice was general. The people were cannibals, and, so long as they remained so, they imagined their gods to be likewise. After ceasing to be cannibals some, however, continued, even up to our own times, to sacrifice animals and vegetation to the gods in the belief that they relished the etheric counterpart.

Such, then, was early civilisation some six thousand years ago. About mankind in general we know little, but of life and thought in Egypt and Mesopotamia we now know a great amount, as will be discovered as we read on. What has been told in this chapter, so far, relates only to those people who settled down to a more or less peaceful existence, and lived by farming and trade. Elsewhere there were these roving bands of nomadic tribes, hardy and brave, who lived their lives on horseback, of which our present-day gipsies are the last remnant in Europe. Wandering from place to place to find pasturage for their herds, and envious of the prosperity of the agriculturalists, they were always upsetting the lives of the settled communities, and never lost a chance to plunder those too weak to resist.

By seeking safety in numbers, by gathering together into settled communities, mankind gained greater safety and all the benefits which come from civilisation. On the other hand the common people lost their freedom and liberty. Over the nation arose a dictator, looked upon as a divine monarch, who was surrounded by a priesthood and the nobility. Under them, from the beginning of civilisation until our own times (except for a break when some of the cities of Greece adopted democratic government), were the people, who were either serfs or slaves, all the wealth produced being concentrated principally in the hands of the king, the priesthood, and the nobles. The nomadic craftsman had his simple tools, and found for himself his materials, but for centuries the civilised skilled artisan was the servant of a king, priest, or noble. When the arts and science developed, the musician, artist, scientist, skilled thinker, or worker was dependent on a patron, whose liberality enabled one who was often mentally his superior to express himself. The patron was the financier of these days, as money was not widespread, and joint-stock company enterprise had still to be evolved.

Much talent, under such circumstances, must have never come to light, and many a thinker passed his life performing menial tasks. . The merchant and trading class were similarly handicapped for centuries, and had little scope for development under the totalitarian regime of Egypt, about which we shall be reading in this chapter. In Mesopotamia trade was in the hands of the monarch, the priests, and the city governors. In their hands was the wealth, and all the knowledge then possessed. The illiterate mostly barter, and when the art of writing was discovered, when weights and measures were introduced, the nobles and the priests kept these mysteries to themselves. Until the Iron Age, when tools became more plentiful, bronze was too expensive for the common man, and he had to learn his trade and exploit his skill with his master's tools.

Only under democratic civilisation, with education and civilised comforts available for everyone, and with money wages from which the artisan can procure his working capital, has a higher standard of existence been secured by the toiling masses. Here, in this chapter, and for much the greater period embraced by this book, the story which will be unfolded of the human race relates mostly to the deeds and thoughts of the privileged classes. The vast majority toiled their way through life, living on what their overlords gave them, saving nothing, fighting their king's or lord's battles, suffering, and then being cast aside when their usefulness was over. Such was civilisation up to recent times, a state of affairs which was the outcome of ignorance, and only as the mind developed did the ordinary man, after many conflicts and much struggle, secure for himself that which had been so long denied him. Agriculture made man a serf, it being science, industry, and money that made him free.

The cradle of Western civilisation lay in Mesopotamia and Egypt. Here was born the culture which had a direct bearing on European civilisation in the years which followed. Six thousand years ago civilisation was beginning in Mesopotamia, when the Western world was still in a state of barbarism. Here small communities of nomads were beginning to settle down to farm and build houses, their example, as the centuries passed, being copied by others, until gradually a large and settled population occupied the deltas and valleys of the rivers Euphrates, Tigris and Nile.

We have now come to the time when we can sort out the people into different races. The Semites were amongst the first settlers in these river valleys, and to them we owe our present-day civilisation. They learned their arts and crafts from the early Sumerians, and then found their way into Assyria, Syria, and Palestine. At a later date Europe was overrun by the Aryans, who were to be civilised by Semite influence. These Aryan people came from the north and east, and reached as far west as Spain, France, and Britain, down south into Italy, the Balkans, and round the shores of the Mediterranean, into Asia Minor and along the shores of the Black and Caspian seas.

The Aryans are not a race, but a group of people whose language is derived from a common source. This parent tongue, spoken by a long-forgotten people, is now extinct, but it gave rise to Sanskrit, the ancient language of the Hindus, who called themselves Aryans, a word which means noble. This form of speech is allied to Persian, Greek, Latin, and the languages spoken by the Germanic, Celtic, and Slavonic races, in much the same way as Italian is related to Spanish, French, and Portuguese. Consequently all who speak those languages, derived from the now extinct parent tongue, are called Aryans, but they are not a race, rather a group of people whose language had a common source, a fact which makes ridiculous the German claim to represent the Aryan race which does not exist.

In these days, just as now, destruction came to those who could not defend their possessions. The surrounding roaming tribes, coveting the fertile lands and possessions, swept down upon them and occupied the towns and villages. Those who were not killed became slaves. The invaders then settled down to a new form of life, becoming in turn agriculturalists and traders. After a time a fresh nomadic invasion took place, and those who had been the conquerors became the conquered. Then might was everything, and the hardier nomadic races proved their superiority in battle, which has always been the final arbiter in disputes between tribes and nations.

What the nomads did was the accepted method in those days. Negotiations did not precede the battles, and no one expected such a procedure from tribes out for plunder. It was the only way they knew of obtaining ready-made houses, cattle and land, and plundering has been humorously styled "the oldest known labour-saving device ever invented". These robbers, like the highwayman, pounced upon their victims and took all they possessed. The question of it being right or wrong was never considered, as this idea had not yet developed in human minds. When the opportunity presented itself they rushed in and settled down in possession, adopting the methods still practised by aggressor nations.

In those far-off days, when the aggressors had no moral code, apart from the traditions relating only to the tribe, nothing different was to be expected. They acted just as we would expect a dog to act if it sees another dog with a bone it wishes to have. A fight ensues, the strongest and most cunning getting the bone, while the loser limps off to do the same to some smaller dog it discovers enjoying a similar delicacy.

So, in the days of early civilisation, men were like animals in their relationship with one another, just as on occasions they still are. Like wolves, they had learned to live in packs for greater protection, but this did not prevent another larger, or more cunning, pack destroying those who could not defend themselves. Animals know no better, because they cannot think and reason as man can. Is man, however, any more capable than an animal of reasoning wisely on this question of aggression? Six thousand years ago he was not, and it is tragic to think that only now is he just beginning to do so. So far, we still know of no way, which practice has proved practicable, to prevent a repetition of what the dwellers in the plains and valleys experienced from their nomadic enemies.

It is well that we should all clearly understand this unending story of aggression and defence. Most of us have experienced two tremendous bouts of it, something more terrible than many generations of the past have had to suffer, but, though we have been less fortunate, our experience has been that of mankind from the time our species began to hunt in companies. Aggression is the same today as it was ten thousand years ago, only its weapons having changed. The mentality is still the same, namely the determination on the part of the aggressor to obtain something he has not got, and the resolve of those who have this something to resist it being taken from them by every possible means in their power.

Organised theft on a large scale by one side, and organised resistance on the other, constitute war. Little do we realise how this action and reaction has gone on down the ages, and now that we are setting out to try to find the cure for a grievous sore in the body politic it is well that we all should make ourselves acquainted with the past history of this chronic disease.

In order that we may better understand human experience, let us start from the time civilisation began, away back some six thousand years ago in the fertile delta of the rivers Euphrates and Tigris, the effect of which has run through history from that time onwards. It influenced Egypt, and closely affected the manners, customs and literature of the Hebrews, the Phoenicians, the Greeks, the Romans, and the Aryan and Semitic people everywhere in the west, on to the present day. So let us now go back in thought to the cradle of civilisation, and learn about the people to whom we owe so much.

(1) Sumerian, Babylonian, and Assyrian Civilisations.
(3500–330 b.c.)

Mesopotamia, now called Iraq, is the dividing line between Western and Eastern civilisation, between the wheat-eaters and the rice-eaters of the human race. Here we find two great rivers, the Euphrates, 1700 miles, and the Tigris, 1150 miles long, heavily loaded with silt, flowing through fertile soil which, during the ages, has been brought down from the northern uplands. In this country, seven thousand years ago, some wandering tribes settled down to agriculture, built mud huts, grew crops, and used crude pottery, flint weapons and implements. Here they multiplied, and supplied the basis of what, centuries later, became a great nation.

Amongst the earliest settlers in the delta regions of these two rivers were the Sumerians, who may have come from the upper Indus valley or thereabouts, but this is uncertain. They established themselves in lower Mesopotamia some six thousand years ago on what seems to have been Neolithic settlements, and there founded the earliest known civilisation. This stretch of marshy ground made up of river silt was no larger than Holland, a land formed in like manner. They called their country Sumer, and on the islands of the delta they built their towns.

Then came a disastrous flood which swept away the mud huts of the primitive Neolithic people, but the better built towns withstood it sufficiently to remain in being after it subsided, though it laid down a silt eight feet in depth. The Sumerians then took possession of all the land previously occupied by the original inhabitants, extending their territory 200 miles inland from the head of the Persian Gulf. Since those far-off days the sea has receded about a hundred miles, having been pushed back by the silt brought down by the rivers, and what remains of cities which were then near to the sea is now a considerable distance inland.

The Sumerians were a remarkable race, and the towns and houses they built are the first about which we have any knowledge. They claim in their history, written on baked bricks, to have come to their new home already civilised, with knowledge of the arts, of agriculture, writing, the construction of houses and the knowledge of metal work. Besides being town dwellers they were farmers with herds of cattle, asses, goats and sheep. By skilful irrigation they carried the water from the two rivers over the adjoining land. It is believed that they were the first to sow wheat; in fact it still grows there in its wild state.

The land was very prolific when well watered, and this fact greatly impressed the Greek agriculturalist Theophrastus, of the 4th century B.C., who tells us that it grew two crops of wheat each year, yielding one hundred to one under careful tillage. This remarkable fertility will be better understood when we remember that wheat land in our climate in the west seldom yields more than fifteen times the amount sown.

As time went on a high culture developed, one instance of this being a library of more then 30,000 tablets, arranged in shelves, dating from 2700 B.C., which was found on the site of what was once the town of Tello. By means of these, and numerous other tablets, which were written upon when soft by a wedge-shaped cuneiform style, we can now read the political, social, and religious history of this great race which gave civilisation to the world.

We learned their language in the middle of the last century, largely owing to the untiring efforts of Sir Henry Rawlinson (1810–1895), who transcribed as much as he was able of the remarkable cuneiform inscription in the Persian language, 300 ft. high, on the precipitous Behistun Rock, near Kermanshah, in Iran. This valuable discovery, dating from 516 B.C., turned out to be an account of the victories of Darius I, two other inscriptions alongside being in Greek and Arabic. By continuous excavations he finally discovered sufficient material to enable him to decipher the cuneiform characters, and thus unlock for our times the history of Mesopotamian civilisation, as recorded on the numerous baked tiles and tablets which have been discovered.

The remains of great temples, numerous graves, houses, and implements have now been unearthed. What once were imposing cities have now come to light, some of which must go back some six thousand years. Their houses were well built, with the rooms arranged round an inner courtyard, from which a stair led to the floor above, and the average house had from twelve to fourteen rooms, all being well furnished. The abundant clay, when dried in the sun, made good building material, so much so that they were able to erect these houses for themselves and imposing temples to their gods.

The towns became the centre of city states, which were always fighting against one another. This blot on civilisation, of town fighting against town, has now passed away, which gives encouragement to the hope that in time, as civilisation develops further, nations will live peacefully together. Civilisation is still young, at the most not much more than six thousand years old. Education is younger still, as the mass of the people even in the most advanced countries have been able to read and write for not more than some sixty or seventy years. Civilisation is, therefore, still in the nursery stage. Man has only emerged from the being called sub-man within the past fifty thousand years, and it has taken five hundred thousand years for him to develop from the ape-man stage to what he is today. Nature never moves fast, and evolution is a slow-moving process, but, if past history is any guide, there is something better ahead of the human race than we, with our limited vision, can imagine.

Mesopotamia in these early days was divided in half by the domination of two cities, Eridu and Nippur, the former being the capital of Sumer in the south, and the latter of Akkad in the north, which was inhabited by a Semitic race. From these two cities flowed two streams of culture and religious belief. Ea, the god of light and beneficence, was the god of Eridu, and En-lil, the ruler of the spirit world, was the god of Nippur. From the latter came the Arabian word "Allah" and the Hebrew word "El", both meaning God. El was the god of Abraham, whereas Jehovah was the god of Moses, two distinctly different conceptions, as we shall discover later on.

The curse of ignorance, of intolerance, of greed,

of selfishness, malice and all uncharitableness was the cause which kept in being the constant inter-city wars which sapped the vitality of the Sumerian race, just as it did that of the Greeks at a later date. Eventually it decayed and withered away, to be forgotten for four thousand years, and then rediscovered by chance, to have its history rewritten from the records they had left behind. From under the dust of ages we now discover how much we owe to these remarkable people who, with all their faults and failings, were the first, so far as we know, to lay down the foundations of a civilised society, though it is probable that there were still earlier civilisations which are not yet known.

Sir Leonard Woolley, Director of the Joint Expedition of the British Museum and the Museum of the University of Pennsylvania to Mesopotamia, in his book *Ur of the Chaldees* considers that Sumerian civilisation is older than that of Egypt because, as he says :—

Our tombs date, as has already been said, between 3500 and 3200 B.C. and, as the nature of the civilisation would lead one to expect, and, as has been demonstrated by the discoveries in the rubbish below the tombs described in the last chapter, by 3500 B.C. this civilisation was already many centuries old. Until recently it was thought that the Egyptian civilisation was the oldest in the world, and that it was the fountain head wherefrom the later civilisations of other western countries drew, at any rate, the inspiration which informed them. But, in 3500 B.C. Egypt was still barbarous, divided into petty kingdoms not yet united by Menes, the founder of the first Dynasty, into a single state.

When Egypt does make a start, the beginnings of a new age are marked by the introduction of models and ideas which derive from that older civilisation, which, as we know now, had long been developing and flourishing in the Euphrates valley, and to the Sumerians we can trace much that is at the root, not only of Egyptian, but also of Babylonian, Assyrian, Hebrew and Phoenician art and thought, and so see that the Greeks also were in debt to this ancient and for long forgotten people, the pioneers of the progress of western man.

Accepting the opinion of this recognised authority as correct, it then follows that the Sumerians first brought civilisation to the Western world, and that to them we are indebted for the foundation of law, education, culture and religion on which those who followed them built the structure. They first of all influenced Egypt and the Semitic tribes in Mesopotamia, it being from these two lands that our present-day religious and cultural ideas came. Both these countries influenced Greece, which in turn influenced Rome, and so the structure of modern civilisation was erected over the centuries.

The Hebrews drew their inspiration from both Mesopotamia and Egypt, to come down to us as Judaism, Mahomedanism, and Christianity, three religions whose roots are to be found in these two lands. The Sumerians gave us the Sabbath, which, to many of the present-day older generation, cannot be looked back upon with happy recollections, and also the story of the creation, the fall of man, the flood, which was a local disaster, and the laws attributed to Moses. From them came the arts of sculpture, pottery and painting, the method of communication by writing, our architecture, they being the first to construct the arch, the dome, and the vault, and the manufacture of metal implements and cloth. To them we owe this and much more which makes up modern civilisation. Their culture lit up a world then accustomed only to primitive barbarism. They were the first cause of civilisation and culture, so far as our present knowledge goes, and whatever we owe to Greece and Rome we must remember that what these two countries passed on to us was first of all the conception of the Sumerians.

It is unfortunate that this great people died out, to be forgotten until our own time, but what they did and thought was imperishable. Though the origin of what they handed down to us was forgotten, their influence remained with the Babylonians and the Assyrians, to be passed on to the generations which followed. Gradually the Semites became the predominant population in Akkad, and the Sumerian language slowly gave place to the Semitic tongue.

We can also trace the close relationship between the Hebrews and the Sumerians, by the discovery of a Sumerian hymn describing the tree of life from which man was forbidden by the gods to eat. It grew in the garden of Edinnu, which means a plain, and therein walked the god Ea. Like all these ancient stories of the gods, this belief probably originated in one or more apparitions being seen. The return of etheric beings through mediums, or as apparitions and materialisations, without doubt is the cause of the belief of the ancients in the gods, who today are called by various names, such as angels, saints, or spirits. From psychic phenomena can be traced the creeds, ceremonies, rituals, doctrines and dogmas of every world religion.

Just as interesting is the discovery of a tablet recording the trial, death, and resurrection of Bel

(meaning The Son of God[1]), the Saviour-God of
Babylon, called by the Hebrews Baal, who was the
Christ, Redeemer and Mediator of the Babylonians.
They believed that he, a god-man, had died and risen
again for their salvation.   Its translation reads as
follows:—

> (1) BEL IS TAKEN PRISONER.
>
> (2) BEL IS TRIED IN THE HALL OF JUSTICE.
>
> (3) BEL IS SMITTEN.
>
> (4) BEL IS LED AWAY TO THE MOUNT.
>
> (5) WITH BEL ARE TAKEN TWO MALEFACTORS, ONE OF
>   WHOM IS RELEASED.
>
> (6) AFTER BEL HAS GONE TO THE MOUNT, THE CITY
>   BREAKS OUT INTO TUMULT.
>
> (7) BEL'S CLOTHES ARE CARRIED AWAY.
>
> (8) BEL GOES DOWN INTO THE MOUNT AND DISAPPEARS
>   FROM LIFE.
>
> (9) A WEEPING WOMAN SEEKS HIM AT THE GATE OF
>   BURIAL.
>
> (10) BEL IS BROUGHT BACK TO LIFE.

The foregoing is the programme of the Passion
Drama which was performed in Babylon, to keep the
people in remembrance of the death and resurrection
of their Saviour, the triumphant risen Christ of
Babylonia, and, at intervals during the performance,
the people sang hymns which are hardly distinguish-
able from the psalms and hymns sung by Christians.
The prayers offered up are equally similar, but, as this
very interesting event is carefully and fully considered in *The Psychic Stream*, a book devoted to the

[1] Bel was also adored and worshipped as The Lord, The Mighty Lord,
The Lord of the Covenant, The Lord Most High, and The Lord of Heaven.

study of the evolution of all religious beliefs since the time of primitive man, no more need here be said.

Bel took second place in the Babylonian trinity of gods, who were Ea, the Father; Bel, the Son; and Anu, the Holy Spirit, and, when the people sacrificed, they did so by offering up a lamb, because, as a tablet tells us, "The Lamb is the substitute for humanity", or, as it has come down to us in Christianity, "the lamb of God which taketh away the sin of the world" (*John* i, 29). A statue of a lamb caught in the thicket has also been discovered. This is believed to be an emblem of the saviour entangled in the world's wickedness, and there may be a connection between this and the story of Abraham discovering a lamb in a thicket, which he was told by his god to sacrifice in place of his son Isaac. A communion service of gold and silver chalices, patens, and small tumblers has also been discovered, as the Eucharist was celebrated in remembrance of Bel.

A story, similar to the one relating to the infancy of Moses, is found recorded on a tablet about Sargon, King of the Semites, of how he was hidden by his mother on the bank of the Euphrates in a basket made of bulrushes. Whether there is any connection between these two stories we know not, but we do know that their accounts of the Garden of Eden, the creation and the flood were brought back to Judea by the Jews after their time of captivity in Babylon.

These people, living on the banks of the two great rivers, were deeply religious, and, like their Egyptian neighbours, obtained their comfort and consolation by giving much time to the worship of their numerous gods and the thought of the life to come. Each city had its god, and the king was the god's representative. Nothing was done without prayer, and in war and peace the city god always took the first place. There was a temple in every city, and each temple had its Holy of Holies, where the priest consulted the god of the city, or, as we would say today, the medium's spirit control. Nearby lived the holy women, whom we would today term mediums, and these consisted of all classes of the people, from the highest to the lowest, provided they had psychic power. During the Christian era such gifted people were called witches, who were tortured and drowned, and in our day British law describes them as "rogues and vagabonds", anyone exercising psychic gifts being a criminal and liable to be imprisoned or heavily fined.

Where once was the city of Erech are ruins of successive settlements for 60 feet below the surface. The topmost structures reveal what was once a great city with its imposing temple, 245 feet long by 100 broad. Behind it is an artificial mud and brick structure 35 feet high known as a Ziggurat. A flight of steps leads to the summit, where there is an asphalt platform, on which are the remains of a temple 73 by 57 feet, containing the room where the gods communed with the people of earth. In lands where there were hills or mountains these Holy of Holies were placed above the level of the plains, so as to be nearer to heaven. Thus we find most of the principal temples of old, including St. Peter's in Rome, which is built on the site of a Pagan temple, situated on heights, but in the flat land of Sumer the people had to erect their mount to achieve their object.

Tablets and remains have been discovered in Mesopotamia, which make it abundantly clear that mediumship was a highly honoured profession, and that in the lands making up the Middle East, just as in Greece and Rome centuries later, contact was made through mediums with the etheric world, to which we pass at death. Other tablets found in Sumer give a full account of the Sumerian conception of the creation of the universe, the story given in *Genesis* being, in all essential features, a copy.

Social life, at the height of Sumerian civilisation, had reached a high level. Medicine and surgery were recognised arts, and for every disease there was the appropriate drug. Women were considered in law as equal to men, and could carry on business on their own account. They could inherit and bequeath property, hold civil offices and plead in a Court of Justice, in strange contrast to the position up to our own time. Polygamy was rare, and slaves were protected by law. They could acquire property of their own, under conditions, appear as witnesses at court, and the use of torture for extorting confessions was unknown.

The oldest surviving collections of tablets reveal the considerable knowledge these people had of mathematics. Weights' and measures were standardised by agreement. Measurement began by taking the length of a finger, a palm, a foot, a forearm, and an arm, but, as everyone is of different size, this method was abandoned in favour of one standard half-thumb length, an inch, a standard footlength, a foot, and a standard forearm, a cubit. So they produced standardised wooden rods with notches to indicate the different measurements, just as they moulded standard jugs which, when filled, represented different weights according to their size.

Next they invented a weighing machine by balancing a beam at its centre, and attaching to one end the jug filled with grain, and to the other end the thing to be weighed. They measured time by dividing the day and night into twelve hours each, and devised sundials and water clocks to record this division of time. The year was divided into twelve months, each month corresponding with the moon's passage round the earth, and, to adjust the difference between their calendar and the seasons, they added on an extra month from time to time.

The nightly spectacle of the orderly movement of the stars and planets aroused the emotion of the Babylonians, just as it did that of the Egyptians, and later the Greeks. This immense panoramic procession profoundly influenced their religion, and caused numerous weird explanations down the ages, a controversy which ended when the telescope revealed that the universe is governed by fixed laws.

Sumerian civilisation developed in spite of internal strife, foreign conquests and inter-city wars, as there were long periods during which the people lived in peace. The city of Ur was founded about 3500 B.C., and, for 1500 years, in spite of devastations caused by war, it enjoyed great prosperity. Joined to the sea by a canal, its harbours were filled with ships which traded along the shores of the Persian Gulf and as far as India. Its wall enclosed an area of two square miles, and its population probably exceeded 50,000. From here, according to Hebrew tradition, Abraham set out on his wanderings to the west. He was a citizen of a great city, whose inhabitants were cultured, educated, and living in such comfort that it might even be termed luxury.

For some three thousand years these civilised people lived and died, worshipped and rejoiced, were happy and miserable, and now the record of their history is being unearthed from beneath the mud brought down by the Euphrates and Tigris in the intervening centuries. Surely we have no better example of the transitory nature of our earthly pilgrimage, of the folly of quarrelling, fighting, plundering, and of making life miserable without reason, when, by greater wisdom, it could be made happy and comfortable. Everything physical, which the mind of man constructs, some day returns to its natural state, and only the mind, the immaterial part of us, the imperishable architect and builder, continues elsewhere its activities.

Long as was the comfortable existence of this ancient race free from foreign invasion, inter-city wars so weakened the Sumerians that the Semites, under the famous King Sargon (2418–2364 B.C.), conquered them, and his sons who succeeded him extended their conquests to the Persian Gulf on the east and the Mediterranean in the west. This invasion was followed some centuries later by another. The Elamites, whose origin is doubtful, descended from the east on to these fertile plains, and devastated the great city of Ur, thus ending for ever the independence of these exceptionally gifted Sumerians who had exhausted their vitality in fratricidal wars. Nevertheless the city again prospered, and at no time in its long history was it more important than during the years 2300 to 2180 B.C. when it was the capital of Sumer.

Then a tragedy occurred, when the Euphrates altered its course to ten miles east of the city, and thus rendered useless the canals and system of irrigation. Agriculture in consequence became impossible, the land became a wilderness, its towns heaps of ruins, and so they have remained from that day to this. The people emigrated further north, and centred their activities round the small river town of Babylon, which, in the following centuries, was to become a famous city.

The Amorites, another Semitic race from the west, of which the Hebrews are a branch, then invaded Mesopotamia and occupied Babylon. Within one hundred years they dominated the entire country, and welded Sumer and Akkad into one kingdom to become known as Babylonia. Their famous king Hammurabi (1792–1750 B.C.) consolidated the new kingdom by establishing a civil service, composed of governors, judges and other officials, and codifying the traditional laws hitherto observed in each city. Babylon now took the place of Ur, and Babylonia succeeded Sumer, while the Sumerians and the Semites coalesced into one great nation.

Hammurabi was one of the great monarchs of history, not because of his military conquests, which were substantial, but because he was the first man to establish national law and justice. Mighty warrior and eminent administrator, his fame rests upon the fact that he codified all the ancient laws, traditions and customs into one Code of Laws which were a pattern for all later civilisations. On them were based Hebrew,

Greek and Roman law, which forms the basis of present-day civilisation.

The first thirty years of his long reign were occupied in subduing his enemies, and in building up a powerful empire along the length of the Euphrates and Tigris to the Persian Gulf. His deeds were written on tablets of clay, and very proud indeed he was of them, because, after making secure his frontiers, his empire entered the time known as the Golden Age of Hammurabi, when he built, extended and restored the wonderful temples, palaces and canals. He made the land prosperous and wealthy, filling its plains with grain, sheep and cattle.

The Sabatu, or seventh day, was prescribed as the day of rest from work, which law the Jews continued to respect after they returned from their captivity in Babylon. Under Hammurabi the Empire was so peaceful that, as one tablet tells us, a boy could travel throughout its length and breadth in perfect safety. The administration of the law was taken away from the priests, and the judges were paid by the State, the consequence being that justice was meted out in greater measure than ever before.

The judges were thus able to weigh up impartially the evidence brought before them. Counsel pleaded in court for the prosecution and the defence, and all guilty of perjury were punished. Until the laws were codified under Hammurabi, the judges made their decisions as they do in England today, on precedent, which necessitated a careful registration and the dating of all former verdicts. Education was widespread, and both men and women could read and write, letters passing freely between all classes of the community. A careful study was given to mathematics, and the eclipses of the sun and moon could be foretold; in fact these observations existed in Babylon for twice the length of time they have been carried out in England.

Babylonia was above all else an industrial and commercial state, even the Royal Family acting as merchants, through agents, and much interesting information has been discovered of late throwing light on the traders' methods of book-keeping and business correspondence. The very ledgers themselves, and their entries, have been preserved to us in these clay tablets, on which was written, when in a soft condition, the cuneiform characters by means of a style. Contract tablets have been discovered, together with tablets giving business correspondence, receipts for money and goods, accounts, bills of lading and letters of credit. Money-lending was a very profitable profession, the lender receiving as much as from 20 per cent. to 33 per cent. per annum, and the currency consisted of stamped rings, or bars of gold, silver and copper. As there was no coinage, smaller values were recorded in barley, but gold and silver were also used according to weight.

Babylon, which means "The Gate of the Gods", was laid out artfully and artistically within a wall 56 miles long, 335 feet high, and 85 feet wide, enclosing an area of about 200 square miles. Within this space were beautiful gardens (one being on the flat roof of a great tower and called "The Hanging Gardens") and also parks, fields and orchards studded with houses three and four storeys high. Date-palm trees grew in abundance. There were universities and several great libraries. The cemeteries adjoined the city, and were laid out in streets along which flowed small streams. The tombs were surrounded with gardens, and there were special places reserved for the offerings to the dead. The Euphrates ran through the centre of the city, being crossed by a stone bridge and a tunnel underneath the river. Roads radiated in all directions and joined up with those leading into the country, the city, moreover, being connected with the Persian Gulf by small ships which sailed up and down the river.

It was only in December 1901 that a pillar of black diorite was discovered at Susa, in Persia, which, on being translated, was found to contain a code of laws relating to life and conduct in Babylonia, with a long inscription to the effect that these laws were given to Hammurabi by the god Bel and that the people must obey them. This pillar is now in the Louvre at Paris, but a very fine reproduction of it can be seen in the British Museum. Hammurabi laid the foundation of Babylon's military power. He had a genius for administrative detail, and records have been discovered which mention that he personally investigated quite trivial complaints and disputes amongst the humbler classes of his subjects, even sending back a case for re-trial and further information.

Hammurabi, as we have read, will always be remembered as the great law-giver, and his elaborate laws form the basis of present-day civilisation. They deal in detail with every class of the population, from the noble to the slave, but they can hardly be attributed exclusively to Hammurabi himself, as they were the outcome of precedent and established custom, derived directly from the earlier Sumerian civilisation. His great achievement was the codification of this mass of legal enactments, and the rigid enforcement of them on the people. It is impossible to give here more than just a glimpse of what these laws contain. They number 272, but the following, dealing with different aspects of life, are typical examples of the all-embracing nature of the Code. The number against each refers to its number in the Code.

Theft (22). If a man has perpetrated brigandage, and has been caught; that man shall be slain. (23). If the brigand has not been taken, the man plundered shall claim before God what he has lost: and the city and sheriff, in whose land and boundary the theft has taken place, shall restore to him all that he has lost. (25). If a fire break out in a man's house, and another man has gone to extinguish it, and has lifted his eyes upon the goods of the householder, and has taken the goods of the householder; that man shall be thrown into the same fire.

Agriculture (42). If a man take a field to farm, and grows no corn on the field, he shall be accused of neglecting to work the field; and he shall give to the lord of the field an amount of corn according to the yield in the district.

Irrigation (53). If a man has been too lazy to strengthen his dyke, and has not strengthened the dyke, and a breach has opened in the dyke, and the ground has been flooded with water, the man whose dyke the breach has opened shall reimburse the corn he has destroyed.

Horticulture (59). If a man, unknown to the lord of the orchard, has cut down a tree in another man's orchard, he shall pay half a mina of silver (£3 7s. 6d.).

Trade (104). If a trader has entrusted corn, wool, oil, or any other goods to a retailer to trade with, the retailer shall write down the value and give it to the trader. Then shall the retailer take a sealed receipt for the silver given to the trader in settlement.

Banking (122). If a man desires to deposit with another man silver, gold, or anything else, he shall exhibit all before the elders, draw up a contract, and then make the deposit.

Libel (127). If a man point the finger against a holy sister or a man's wife unjustifiably, that man shall be thrown before the judge, and his brow shall be branded.

Adultery (129). If the wife of a man is found lying with another male, they shall be bound and thrown into the water; unless the husband lets his wife live, and the king lets his servant live. (131). If a man's wife is accused by her husband, but has not been found lying with another male, she shall swear by the name of God and return to her house.

Divorce (141). If a man's wife, dwelling in a man's house, has set her face to leave, has been guilty of dissipation, has wasted her house, and has neglected her husband, then she shall be prosecuted. If her husband says "she is divorced," he shall let her go her way; he shall give her nothing for divorce. If her husband says "she is not divorced," her husband may espouse another woman, and that woman shall remain a slave in the house of her husband.

Separation (142). If a woman hate her husband, and say "Thou shalt not possess me," the reason for her dislike shall be inquired into. If she is careful, and has no fault, but her husband takes himself away and neglects her, then that woman is not to blame. She shall take her dowry and go back to her father's house. (148). If a man has a married wife, and sickness has seized her, and he has set his face to marry another, he may marry—but his wife whom the sickness has seized he shall not divorce. She shall dwell in the house he has built, and he shall support her while she lives. (149). If that woman is not content to dwell in the house of her husband, he shall return to her the dowry she brought from her father's house, and she shall go.

Marriage settlement (171). The spouse shall take her dowry, and the settlement which her husband made her and wrote in a tablet for her, and she shall dwell in the domicile of her husband. While she lives she shall enjoy it; she may not sell it for silver, but after her it belongs to her children.

Slavery (175). If either a slave of a great house, or the slave of a plebeian, marry the daughter of a free man, and she bears children, the owner of the slave has no claim for service upon the children of the free man's daughter.

Inheritance (181). If the father has dedicated a priestess, a consecrated woman, or temple maiden, to God, and has not given her a dowry; after the father has gone to his fate she shall take out of the possessions of the paternal house one-third of the portion of a son. She shall enjoy it during her life. What she leaves behind is to her brothers. (191). If a man has adopted an infant as a son, and brought him up, and has founded a household, and afterwards has had children, and if he has set his face to disown the adopted son, then that child shall not go his way. His foster-father shall give him out of his possessions one-third of the portion of a son, and then he shall go. Of field, or orchard, or house he shall not give him.

Surgery (215). If a doctor has treated a free man with a metal knife for a severe wound, and has cured the free man, or has opened a free man's tumour with a metal knife, and cured a free man's eye, then he shall receive ten shekels of silver (£1 2s. 6d.). (216). If the son of a plebeian, he shall receive five shekels of silver (11s. 3d.). (217). If a man's slave, the owner of the slave shall give two shekels of silver to the doctor (4s. 6d.). (221). If a doctor has healed a free man's broken bone, or has restored diseased flesh, the patient shall give the doctor five shekels of silver.

Bad workmanship (235). If a boat-builder has built a boat for a man, and his work is not firm, and in that same year that boat is disabled in use, then the boat-builder shall overhaul that boat and strengthen it with his own material, and he shall return the strengthened boat to the boat-owner.

Compensation (236). If a man has given his boat on hire to a boatman, and the boatman is careless, and the boat is sunk and lost, then the boatman shall replace the boat to the boat-owner. (251). If a man's ox is known to be addicted to goring, and he has not blunted his horns nor fastened up his ox, then if the ox has gored a free man and killed him he shall give half a mina of silver.

The foregoing give at least an idea of what justice meant to the people of Babylon four thousand years ago. It was a very rough and ready form of justice, and crimes, which today would justify prison, then brought death to the criminal. Considering, however, that the death penalty was inflicted in Great Britain up to last century for 223 offences, including petty theft, and that numerous people were then imprisoned and kept in foul cells without trial and ignorant of their offences, it will be realised that in the 19th century of the Christian era we were no further forward than the Babylonians four thousand years ago.

Our laws last century relating to the rights of women were likewise far from just, and slaves, up to the middle of the century, had no legal rights. Though slavery in British colonies was abolished a hundred years ago, the wages paid to manual workers in Britain were so small, their standard of living so low, their lack of privileges and say in government so pronounced, that they just managed to exist above the border line of bondage.

Slavery existed in the British colonies and North America up to last century, and it was only after a very great effort by the reformers that it was abolished. Christian priests, both Roman Catholic and Protestant, stoutly resisted its abolition, believing that it was instituted by God. Their opinions, like the laws of Christendom, were based on the laws of Moses, which were copied from Babylon and were believed to have been given by God. In past times everything was attributed to God, or to the gods, and nothing could be done without invoking their aid and protection. To them the people ascribed their laws, to them they sacrificed, and to them they built temples, which were the houses where the people and the gods came together to eat the sacrifice. The Christian Eucharist is just a development of this idea, as the eating of the body of the sacrificed victim, and the drinking of his blood, originated in the days of cannibalism, when it was believed that partaking of the sacrificed victim gave added strength to the communicant.

The history of Mesopotamia, which has been revealed by the discovery of these tablets, is now so voluminous that one hardly knows where to stop. Enough, however, has been said to give an idea of the life, the laws and customs of an advanced race of people who lived in what we today call the Middle East, when Europe was in a state of nomadic barbarism. As with us today, they had gradually found a way of living together as a community in peace, but their ethical code did not carry them beyond their own borders, and what was considered right or wrong at home was not considered to be so when dealing with neighbouring nations.

Most civilised countries today are only about a century in advance of the Babylonians, so far as their ethical outlook is concerned. This being so, we can hardly be surprised if each nation still limits the moral law to itself, mental development the world over not yet having reached the point when a way can be found to establish a code of laws to which every nation will adhere or suffer the consequences. When we can solve this problem, and find a way to punish the guilty, peace will take the place of war.

About 1700 B.C. the Kassites invaded Babylonia, swept away the Empire, and laid the foundation for a new order in Mesopotamia. Under this foreign domination, Babylonia lost control over western Asia,

Syria, and Palestine. Babylon then became more and more a priestly city, just as Rome did after the fall of the Roman Empire, living on its ancient prestige, and merging its ruler into a pontiff. From then onwards, until the Persian conquest, this great city, where stood the temple of Bel, remained the religious head of the civilised east.

Assyria, whose capital was Nineveh on the Tigris, three hundred miles farther north, then conquered Babylonia about 1280 B.C. and removed the treasures from the temple at Babylon. Thus began the Assyrian Empire, which in 1100 B.C. extended to the Mediterranean. When we come to the year 747 B.C. we find this empire in the throes of a revolution. Civil war and pestilence were devastating the kingdom, and it had lost its northern provinces. Tiglath-Pileser III, however, two years later, inaugurated a fresh and vigorous policy, and, under him and his successors, the Empire revived to include finally the entire civilised world of that time. Sennacherib became king in 705 B.C., but, because he was not crowned in Babylon, the province of Babylonia revolted, to be finally crushed a few years later, when its houses and temples were utterly destroyed. The images of its gods were broken in pieces, a catastrophe which aroused horror and indignation throughout western Asia.

Babylon, however, soon rose again phoenix-like from its ashes, the temple of Bel was restored, and the city became the second capital of the Empire. Assyria, with peace at home, then invaded Egypt, and, after two campaigns, completed its conquest in 670 B.C. Revolt at home, which shook the Assyrian Empire to its foundations, robbed it of the fruits of its conquest,

and soon afterwards Egypt recovered her independence. The long struggle against Egypt had so drained
Assyria of her manpower and wealth that the country
was maimed and exhausted. In this condition she
was called upon to face the hostile Babylonians and
the Medes, who began to encroach on her frontiers, to
penetrate finally the entire country as far as the
borders of Egypt. Nineveh was captured and
destroyed, and the Assyrian Empire came to an end.

The buildings of Nineveh, when the Assyrian
Empire was at its height, were unrivalled for size and
grandeur. Then the palaces throughout the land
glittered with precious metals, and were adorned with
the richest sculpture. The library at Nineveh far
surpassed any that had ever previously existed, and
learned men from neighbouring lands were attracted
to the Court. This great display of grandeur was,
however, marred by the cruelty practised by Assyrian
monarchs towards all who rebelled against their rule,
they taking a particular delight in carrying out wholesale massacres, which engendered such hatred that
eventually their oppressed subjects revolted, a disruption which hastened the end of the Empire.

Numerous sacrifices and much prayer were offered
up to the gods to induce them to preserve the Empire,
but they would not respond. Never can the mind of
man get away from the idea that one god, or many
gods, are always waiting to do his bidding, and that
he has only to ask to receive. This folly has gone on
from the time the first other-world man or woman was
seen and asked for help, down to the present time.
Frail humanity has always believed that his gods were
always working in partnership with him, individually,

or with his nation, and, although it would be wearisome to be continually referring to his constant prayers, sacrifices, and eucharists, it should be remembered that nothing of importance has ever happened in history without some imagined divine being, or beings, being associated with the event.

So, in spite of all the prayers and wailings of the Court, the great Assyrian Empire came to an end by being overrun by the Chaldean armies, the seat of the Empire being now transferred to Babylon. The long reign of Nebuchadnezzar (604–561 B.C.), who ruled for forty-three years, marks the highest point in the greatness of the Chaldean Empire. In 586 he invaded Egypt, and, as Judea was allied to Egypt, this unfortunate country, which lay so dangerously in the path of all the conquerors of the past, fell also a victim to his aggression. Many Jews were taken as captives to Babylon, where they learned a more civilised way of life. They left their home barbarians, and, when they returned, they were more or less a civilised people.

The end of the Chaldean Empire came when Cyrus, King of Persia (559–530 B.C.), the founder of the Persian Empire, conquered Babylonia in 539 B.C., and took as prisoner Nabonidus, the good but rather impractical successor to Nebuchadnezzar. The Jews, then captives in Babylon, hailed these wild hardy Persian mountaineers as sent by Jehovah to deliver them, and, although the Persians had never before seen a civilised community, and knew only how to ride a horse and hurl a javelin, they were ardent monotheists, a fact which appealed to the Jewish religious outlook.

Before setting out on his conquest, Cyrus, who

started life as a brigand, set in being a scurrilous propaganda campaign against Nabonidus, after which a swift attack brought the Babylonians to submission, Belshazzar, the son of Nabonidus, who was acting as regent, being slain. Thus these marauding barbarians overthrew an ancient civilisation, and took possession of an empire which stretched from the Mediterranean to the Persian Gulf, a tragic story which is graphically, but inaccurately, told in *The Book of Daniel.*

The conquest of Babylonia was simplified by the Jews aiding the conqueror, doubtless in the hope of their release, and, because of this, they were allowed to return to Judea, carrying with them their treasures and sacred vessels. Darius I (521–486 B.C.), King of Persia, after the death of Cambyses, the son of Cyrus, became King of Babylon, and brought with him the monotheistic Zoroastrian religion and Aryan customs, but the time was coming when the greatness of this famous city on the banks of the Euphrates was finally to end. In the 3rd century B.C. a new city called Seleucia became the capital, and this so diverted the population that within a few years the ruins of the old city became a quarry for the builders of the new seat of government.

The Persian Empire by 500 B.C. extended from the Nile to the borders of India. The political unification which followed promoted increased intercourse and the advance of knowledge. This came about by the building of the famous "Royal Road", equipped with inns and relays of horses, its length extending from Sardis, near the Ægean Sea, to Susa, near the head of the Persian Gulf, a distance of 1500 miles, thus enabling the journey to be accomplished within two months. This great enterprise, built primarily for the purpose of gathering tribute, enabled Herodotus, and other Greeks seeking greater knowledge, to visit Babylon and wonder at the marvels which there lay before them. Natives of India likewise found their way along this famous highway, to mix with Greeks and Syrians at the other end. Thus the people of the world began to get to know each other, opinions were exchanged and knowledge increased. Different religious and political ideas fused, the orient particularly influencing religion in the west, an event which became ever more noticeable as time passed.

We shall read in Chapter VI how the Persian Empire was to meet the fate of all empires based on force, though its system of administration was the best so far attempted. In 330 B.C. the feeble, incapable Darius III, and his empire, fell before the onslaught of Alexander the Great, who established a new empire to last only for a few years. Dictators appear before us in every age. Empires come and go, and cities arise to crumble into dust. In our own time bombs turned noble buildings and humble homes into ruins. Only the ever-abiding ideas formed by the mind are the lasting possession of mankind, to whom stone and brick are but passing impressions.

(2) EGYPTIAN CIVILISATION.
(3000–332 B.C.)

Civilisation in Egypt[1] probably commenced some time later than it did in Mesopotamia. The cradle of

---

[1] The name Egypt means "black land", because of the colour of the soil.

Western civilisation was the fertile lands at the delta of the Euphrates and the Tigris, but, at some later date, this cradle was enlarged to embrace the rich strip of land watered and nourished by the Nile.

Here we discover from the history of Egypt, written on monuments, and on walls, in their hieroglyphic writing, that on each side of this great river people had been settling from early times. The geographical situation of Egypt helped to protect its inhabitants from the danger of invasion, because they were shielded on the west by a waterless desert and on the east by both sea and desert. In the south there were unorganised bands of negroids who could be kept at bay.

We now know much about the history of this ancient race, through learning how to read their hieroglyphic writing. This came about by the discovery, at the mouth of the Nile near Rosetta, of what is called the Rosetta stone, when Napoleon invaded Egypt in 1798. It contains a decree in honour of Ptolemy, and is written in Hieroglyphic, Demotic, and Greek. As the Greek was known, Champollion, the famous French Egyptologist, learned how to read the other two languages, and this discovery has shed a new light on a long-forgotten past, one which we now know greatly influenced Western civilisation. From what is called *The Book of the Dead*, the title given to a great collection of funerary texts, which go back to 2800 B.C., we learn of the wondrous doings of their gods. This Egyptian Bible consists of spells, incantations, hymns, litanies, and prayers, all of which were designed to assure the well-being of the departed spirit, and they are found cut or painted on the walls of the pyramids and tombs, or painted on sarcophagi and rolls of papyrus.

Over five thousand years ago the Egyptian people, members of the Hamitic or African races, settled down to possess this fertile strip of country. They built their houses of wood and brick, and they could also hew stone to their requirements. They had decorated pottery, stone vessels, many bone and ivory utensils, and had mastered the art of spinning and weaving linen cloth. They could record the passing of the years and had some knowledge of astronomy. They could also record their thoughts by pictorial signs, and these they painted on monuments, walls, and papyrus, a reed which grew plentifully along the river bank. Egyptologists think it is possible that in the early days another race from Arabia filtered into Egypt by way of Upper Egypt, but little is known of these early times.

The early settlements are deeply buried in mud brought down by the Nile. In swamps, covered with a jungle of papyrus, the early Egyptians, by draining the land and devoting it to the production of grain, laid the foundation of what was to become a great nation. They secured flint for their knives and axes in the neighbouring desert, and with these they fashioned the abundant papyrus into dwellings, using their tools also as weapons to protect themselves from the roaming wild beasts, and the river crocodiles and hippopotami. They built boats of papyrus, which they used for fishing, hunting and transport, and on the meadows grazed their herds. Household articles consisted of jugs and articles of toilet. These have been preserved in graves, where they were placed for the use of the departed spirits, but doubtless they had their other home comforts made of papyrus, all of which have long since perished.

Time passed, the people multiplied, villages became towns, and an upper, middle, and lower class developed to bring about cultural and political differences which divided the people of the delta from those of the south. One of the earliest of their records (about 3000 B.C.) relates to a long and bitter war between Lower and Upper Egypt, which, by the victory of the latter, united the nation under Menes, the first Pharaoh (= great house), who established a line of dynasties over a period of twenty-seven centuries.

The pharaohs ruled with despotic power by means of a gestapo of picked men, a method which has been in use from these early days to our own times, as no dictator is safe unless all opposition is effectively nipped in the bud. He surrounds himself with "Yes Men", who always think as he thinks, and anyone who shows outstanding character and intelligence is liquidated, because no potential rival is tolerated. Dictators consequently live lives apart, and are out of touch with the thought of their times, no one daring to express ideas which might offend the imperial will.

In our own times, only amongst those who still have the slave mentality is this form of government possible, but in Egypt, in those far-off days, the people's outlook was simple and submissive, they obeying their rulers as does a child his parents. All the land was the property of the Crown or the priests, and was worked on their behalf by the people as serfs, or bestowed as a favour on officials the Pharaoh wished to reward. There was no freedom and liberty of expression, the entire state organisation revolving round one man, whom all worshipped as a god, and did his bidding, he having the power of life or death in his keeping.

The pharaohs established successive dynasties, and it was by these dynasties that a chronological order of events was kept. Unfortunately we have nothing to fix the beginning of the Ist dynasty, neither do we know how long it and the other dynasties lasted. Consequently this method of calculating time is very uncertain, and is largely a matter of guessing. Until recently Egyptian civilisation was considered to be the oldest in the world, but today the Ist dynasty is not placed so far back into the distant past. No one knows exactly when it began, and it is wiser to say that the Ist, IInd, IIIrd, and IVth dynasties go back to sometime before and about 3000 B.C.

In the IVth dynasty Egypt entered a period of great wealth and splendour, when expeditions went to Sinai to obtain copper, and to Byblus to bring home cedar wood, while her ships, 100 feet in length, sailed the sea. It was a time of exceptional brilliance, during which the pharaohs showed a passion for erecting gigantic stone mausoleums, now called pyramids, to preserve their embalmed earthly bodies until they again became united with their etheric bodies on the Resurrection Day. Fearing that their earth bodies would be stolen, or destroyed, they erected these burglar-proof and fire-proof safes for their protection, little realising that their efforts were in vain because they would never again return to their earth bodies and rule, along with their Christ Osiris, the people on earth.

In this dynasty reigned Khufu, called Cheops by Herodotus, the pharaoh who built the Great Pyramid and rebuilt the Temple of Isis. The incalculable amount of wealth and labour spent in the erection of these royal residences for the earth body, extending for sixty miles up the Nile, so impoverished the country that it took generations before it recovered.

From the Vth to the XVth dynasty (3000–1800 B.C.) Egypt's internal history is one of religious conflicts, of recurring wars between different towns, of separation into different kingdoms, and then their reunion, to be followed by wars of aggression. Ptah-hotep, of the Vth dynasty (3000–2800 B.C.), is, however, noted for his moral treatises, which are, on the whole, the best fruit of Egyptian thought of the times, and here we may note the high value placed on righteousness, as the following quotations, taken from Egyptian monuments, make clear:

Established is the man whose standard is righteousness, who walketh according to its way (2700 B.C.).

More acceptable is the virtue of the upright man than the ox of him that doeth iniquity (2300 B.C.).

Righteousness is for eternity. It descendeth with him that doeth it into the grave . . . his name is not effaced on earth, but he is remembered because of right (2300 B.C.).

A man's virtue is his monument, but forgotten is the man of evil repute (2200 B.C.).

The people of his time shall rejoice, the son of man shall make his name for ever and ever. . . .   Righteousness shall return to its place, unrighteousness shall be cast out. . . .   (2200 B.C.).

The VIth dynasty (2800–2600 B.C.) is noteworthy because of the long reign of Pepi I (2795–2742 B.C.), but the next nine dynasties call for no special remark. So we shall pass these by, and come to the XVth, which ended about 1800 B.C. with Egypt conquered by the Semites, who came from the east and established a new dynasty. This, the XVIth dynasty, is known as that of the Hyksos, or "Shepherd Kings", who were Bedouins and quite contemptuous of civilisation, they being only interested in the taxes they received from their more civilised subjects. They kept the Egyptians in servitude for about two hundred years, until 1600 B.C., the end of the XVIIth dynasty, and the fact that they were Bedouins, like the Israelites, probably accounts for the latter being allowed to settle in Egypt, there to become the nucleus of what later on became a nation. This event had its repercussions on Western civilisation, but that will become evident as we proceed, and more will be said about it in Chapter V.

This time of Bedouin domination of Egypt was a period of national suffering, which so united the Egyptians that they became sufficiently strong to drive out the invaders and liberate their country. After this followed a period of great prosperity, the country was united and powerful, so much so that its rulers cast covetous eyes across the Red Sea to the rich plains of Mesopotamia. So began the long struggle between Egypt, Assyria, and Babylon, when wealth and lives were sacrificed to satisfy the greed of ambitious rulers, who put their own lust for riches and greater power before the welfare of their people.

By the time of the XVIIIth dynasty (1600–1350 B.C.), a united Egypt, prosperous, and at the height of her power and splendour, ruled from the

Euphrates to Ethiopia, but the government was corrupt. The needs of the fighting forces took precedence over the needs of the people, priests and officials intrigued one with another, and all honest work was considered to be beneath a gentleman. Society was by now divided up into five different grades, the god-king, the priests and nobles, the merchants, the craftsmen, and the labourers, the two latter being dependent on their overlords, as even skilled craftsmen had to look to them for their tools or the materials they fashioned.

The two great monarchs of the XVIIIth dynasty were Thothmes III and Amenophis III, who left behind them great monuments and many inscriptions. During the reign of Thothmes III (1505–1450 B.C.) the town of Luxor was founded, and Karnak was greatly enlarged. The most unique character of this dynasty was Amenophis IV, who changed his name to Khu-n-aten, abolished the national religion, and abandoned Thebes as the capital, founding a new city in Middle Egypt. Under him the people worshipped Aten, the name they gave to the sun god, a religion marked by its simplicity, as idols and polytheism were abolished, but his successors re-established the old religion, and the name of this heretical monarch was expunged from the records of the land.

After a brief conquest of Egypt by Syria came the XIXth dynasty (1350–1200 B.C.), its two most outstanding monarchs being Setee I and his son Ramses II (1295–1228 B.C.), their legacy to their country being the numerous temples they built. Ramses II is considered to be the greatest of all the pharaohs, his country's master architect, and he left his name inscribed on almost every ancient shrine. The rich gold mines of Nubia made him probably the richest man who ever lived. He is vaguely supposed to be the pharaoh of the time of Moses, and reigned for sixty-seven years.

From now onwards both medicine and surgery reached a high level of perfection, as is proved by the many surgical instruments which have been discovered, besides treatises on surgical treatment and healing. Then it was that the first pharmacopoeia was compiled, and the signs invented which are still used in our present-day prescriptions. Special attention was given to eye and ear defects, and mummies have been found with well-set fractures and artificial teeth. Figures of patients bandaged and undergoing operations are to be seen on the walls of the temples, a fact to remember, because the first surgeon in Christendom was driven out of Europe in the 16th century by the Christian Church, to die of starvation on an island. The practice of healing must have continued to develop in Egypt as the centuries passed, because Herodotus (484–424 B.C.) tells us that in his day the country was full of medical practitioners who were all specialists in the art of healing, the Egyptian ophthalmic surgeons being particularly famous.

Life to these sun-tanned Egyptians passed pleasantly, when gaily decked barges with painted sails glided up and down the Nile, stopping to pick up or set down passengers or cargo at each village on its banks. Phoenician ships came up-river carrying their wares from distant lands, and bringing news of the outside world. Tournaments, archery, wrestling matches, bouts with single-sticks, ball games, and other athletic sports attracted the people out of doors, their pleasures indoors being draughts, dice, and other games. The girls played with their dolls, the boys at pitch-and-toss, while the mother dressed her hair with care and bedecked herself with armlets, gold ear-rings, and gold and porcelain necklaces.

The houses of the rich were luxuriously furnished, those of the middle classes being comfortable. The culture prevailing is noticeable by their elegant and costly cabinets, tables, and chairs, beautifully carved from rare wood, which was brought from Ethiopia and India. The internal decorations were equally lavish, the walls and ceilings being painted in exquisite patterns. Their one-storeyed houses had flat roofs, sometimes covered by awnings, where the family assembled to enjoy the cool of the evening. Outside the towns, the houses were surrounded by walled gardens, interplanted with trees, palms and shrubs, enclosing a vineyard and an artificial fishpond on which floated the blue flowers of the lotus.

After a day's sport, the gentry, who had been out hunting or shooting wild duck, or harpooning hippopotami in the Nile, would entertain their guests. The dinner service was elegant, there being everything that made for refinement, and musicians played during the meal, which was never started without a prayer of gratitude being first offered up by the head of the house. In England, three thousand years later, up to the 16th Christian century, everyone ate from a common pot, there were no knives, forks, or spoons, and no tablecloths or napkins to dry the greasy fingers and mouths. The clergy then denounced from the pulpits of England the use of table cutlery as contrivances of the devil, and poured out their eloquence against any improvement in the sordid way the people were then living. Throughout the Christian era, Christians have been under the delusion that only through Christianity has culture come to mankind, and that all who lived outside of Christian influence were damned heathen, an opinion which was held by many up to within our own times.

The market stalls of Egypt abounded with venison, joints of beef, geese, chickens, fish, cakes, sweetmeats, milk, cheese, beer, wines, and vegetables of all·kinds. Slaves from the interior did the hard manual work, and, on their labour, all but the poorest amongst the Egyptians enjoyed a carefree life, so long as the Nile annually overflowed its banks and covered the soil with its black silt. This acted as a top dressing of manure, and so fertilised the rich alluvial soil that it gave forth its abundant crops, to supply all their needs in exchange for a few days of toil. No other country in the ancient world secured its staple food so easily and at such small cost, but there is no certainty on earth, as some years the river did not flood the land, a drought having occurred in the Abyssinian highlands where rises the Blue Nile. In other years the reverse occurred, houses and cattle were swept away, and the flooded land did not dry up in time for seeding.

Prosperity, famine, and pestilence followed from the quantity of rain which fell in the interior, and the people accepted the good and bad years as they came, believing that these were willed by the gods. For centuries they remained too ignorant to appreciate the fact that nature's laws care nothing for mankind, and that only by mental development does man learn to use them for his benefit, and secure himself against their devastations. Our happiness lies within the framework of these laws, and the Egyptians came to realise this vital fact when necessity forced them to think out a system of dykes, reservoirs, and canals with locks, by means of which the excessive waters were stored in years of over-flood, and used in years of under-flood. The Egyptian engineers, moreover, extended their artificial waterways to land hitherto beyond the reach of the river, and thus increased the acreage under cultivation.

Then some discovered that the water always rose when the stars in the heavens were in certain positions, always in the same place, never a variation. Each year they measured the height of the flood, and over a period of fifty years discovered that the average interval between one high-water mark and the next was 365 days. By these, and other observations, the science of Astronomy was born, which divided time into the solar year, and the year into months and days, to be of great practical help in guiding the people when to start their annual sowing. So the needs of agriculture produced Astronomy, and a new class of men arose in Egypt, the scientists, who devoted their lives to thinking and wondering, to experimenting and discovering. The iron laws of nature in consequence began to give up their secrets to enquiring mind, and man, instead of being the slave of an unthinking master, began timidly but slowly to become the master and make nature his servant, agriculture being the first to feel the effect.

Next came industry, when the inventors produced

looms, and Egypt became celebrated for her linen goods, which were exported all over the Middle East. Laboratories were built, and many important chemical discoveries were made. Engineers found the way to overcome the pull of gravity, and were so successful that today we gaze in astonishment at the huge blocks of stone they were able to pile one on top of another. This mental advance made necessary others which were to play an important part in man's upward crawl. As happened in Mesopotamia, signs and symbols were employed as an aid to memory, and so began the science of writing and mathematics, art likewise developing by being used to plan the buildings and record in picture form events from everyday life.

Here we are at a very important period of man's development, one when some were trying to lift the dark curtain of ignorance to find what there was behind it. Here we are at the birth of science, which, for the next four thousand years, was to wage an uphill fight against the pseudo-science of theology. Only very slowly did man discover that the phenomena of nature were the result of natural law, and that cause and effect had pursued each other relentlessly down the ages, and would do so to all eternity. The Babylonians, Egyptians, Greeks, Romans, and Arabs all played their part in laying the foundation of that great discovery, but it was not until the 17th century of the Christian era, as the result of the accumulation and classification of knowledge, that the gods were displaced by the scientists from all part in the ordering of the universe, since when theology has been a dying superstition.

During much the greater part of her history,

Egypt was ruled by a single monarch, under whom were the nobles, the army, and the priesthood, the latter comprising all who controlled the religious, medical, scientific, legal, administrative, and clerical life of the community. On being elected by the military caste to the rank of pharaoh, the newly elected king was initiated into the mysteries of the state religion, to become the priest-king and a god in the eyes of his people.

He was the supreme law-giver, who received his authority from the gods, and, as chief commander of the army, he led his troops into battle, but tradition greatly limited his range of action, as he was hemmed in on all sides by law, custom and taboo. He was not permitted to do anything to excess, and thus in any way prejudice the opinion of the people in his divinity, his wisdom and his justice. The judges, moreover, on being sworn in to office, declared that they would only carry out his instructions if they were in accordance with the law of the land.

Striving after righteousness, during this era of national splendour, played a large part in the lives of this interesting and advanced people, and the cruelty and abominations, then so common in some of the surrounding lands, were conspicuous by their absence. A slave had his legal rights, and, if murdered, his murderer was put to death, in striking contrast to the status of slaves during the Christian era to as late as the 19th century, when a slave in the United States and Brazil could be murdered, and the murderer go unpunished, because there a slave had no legal rights whatever.

Women were also treated with due respect, and

husband and wife sat together at table, their guests at dinner parties consisting of the two sexes. Husband and wife went together to the temple to sacrifice and worship, and together they enjoyed the family life surrounded by their children. In the law courts, men and women, rich and poor, freemen and bondmen, had their rights, and the judges received high salaries so that they would never be tempted by money to disgrace the image of Truth which they wore round their necks suspended by a golden chain.

So punctilious were the Egyptians with regard to living righteous lives, that before each burial the corpse could only be placed in consecrated ground if no evil were found against the deceased. This enquiry was known as the Trial of the Dead, and it was conducted by forty-two judges, who heard all there was to be said for and against the departed, who was then committed to the keeping of the god Osiris, the Egyptian glorious arisen Christ, the final judge of the living and the dead, to whom only the righteous were acceptable, all others being committed by him to Set, the god of evil.

This thirst after righteousness and progress was in the end quenched by theology, to poison instead of refresh the people, and the Egyptians, under its influence, slumbered into oblivion. The creative period passed away, righteous living giving place to belief in creeds and a saviour who had died to save believers. Osiris, the Saviour and Redeemer, took the place of individual endeavour, the past became sacred, both the good and the evil it produced being equally worshipped. The priests sold indulgencies to secure salvation hereafter, just as happened during the

Christian era, the consequences in both cases being the same—a great deterioration in the ethical standard of the people. As happened during much the greater part of the Christian era, when the mental outlook was the same, progress came to be looked upon as a sin, inventions and novelties being regarded as the handiwork of the devil. Theology took the place of science, and Egypt lost the vitality which had made her great, because mental development was looked upon as contrary to the will of the gods.

The XXth dynasty (1200–1100 B.C.) saw the fullness, but also the decay, of the Empire. It was a period of priestly rule, abundant monuments, and many papyri rich in the records of the history, manners and religion of Egypt. Time passed, dynasties came and went, until the XXVth dynasty (716–685 B.C.) came into being, when Egypt was conquered by Ethiopia, to succumb later to the Assyrians, when, for the first time, the inhabitants of the Tigris dominated the people of the Nile.

This did not last for long, and Egypt was again under her own kings when the XXVIth dynasty (664–525 B.C.) was established, during which period Syria[1] was conquered by Neku II (611–595 B.C.), but a few years later he was forced by Nebuchadnezzar to abandon his gains. Three very important events occurred during the reign of the energetic Neku, all of which greatly contributed to future history, the first being that the Jews were taken as captives to Babylon because they became the allies of Egypt against the Babylonians. The other two

[1] Syria is merely an abbreviation of Assyria, a name which covered the subject lands of the once powerful Assyrian Empire, whose inhabitants were called Syrians.

great episodes were the forerunners of much that was to follow many centuries later, as this enterprising monarch attempted to build a canal between the Nile delta and the Red Sea, thus to join the Mediterranean with the Indian Ocean. Though this venture proved unsuccessful, the expedition he organised of Phoenician seamen succeeded in circumnavigating Africa, by going down the east coast and back by the west coast and the Mediterranean, thus anticipating the Portuguese by twenty-one centuries.

Egypt was not, however, to retain her independence for long, as by the next century the Persians were her overlords, only to be turned out two centuries later when in 332 Alexander the Great occupied the land. From that time onwards she was under the domination of successive foreign rulers, the Greeks, the Romans, the Arabs, the Turks, the French, and finally the British, from whom she obtained her present independence. In her early days, when communication was difficult, Egypt was left alone, but, as travel improved between her and her neighbours, the lust for her rich possessions attracted neighbouring states, who deprived her from time to time of her independent existence.

Most of Egypt's early history is of peaceful pursuits, the rich passing their time either in state affairs, or managing their vineyards, gardens and estates, or in superintending the handicraft of the people, such as weaving linen and making pottery. As in Europe, at a later date, the priests, apart from the Crown, were the largest landowners, receiving a tenth of the produce of all the land. In their spare time the upper classes gave and attended sumptuous

banquets or musical performances. Much thought
was given to the family tomb, and married life consisted of a man having only one wife, who was called
the lady of the house. The ordinary people were poor,
but from the recovered records they seem to have lived
a generally happy carefree life. Education extended
to the poor, who could rise to the highest posts in
the land, but the lowest classes were uneducated.

The Egyptians were deeply religious, and, as often
follows, very superstitious. In the time of the earlier
dynasties the pharaoh was the god-king, whose tomb
was the first care of the people, but, as time went on,
temples became of greater importance, and religion
entered into every phase of their life. The temples
were magnificent buildings, and even today they
excite the wonder and admiration of visitors. Some
of them were of vast size, the one at Karnak, to the
god Amen, which took two thousand years to finish,
occupying over sixty-one acres. It required a host
of stewards, treasurers, overseers and scribes, who
were almost as numerous as those employed by the
Crown.

In the early days, Egypt had two religious systems,
one centred at Memphis, where they worshipped Rā,
the sun god, and various other divinities, and the
other at Thebes where the god Amen received the
people's worship. Later these two gods became one
god, the Father god, who was known as Amen Rā,
and to the Egyptians he represented the Supreme
Being, just as Zeus did to the Greeks, Jupiter to the
Romans, and Jehovah to the Jews. After all procla-
mations and prayers the people said "Amen", just as
the Germans said "Heil Hitler" to all their dictator-

god said. This exclamation of "Amen" has come down, through Judaism, into Christian worship, though few Christians realise that they end their prayers by adding the name of one they would term a heathen deity to that of Jesus the Christ.

Besides these two outstanding gods, Rā and Amen, the much beloved Saviour-god of the Egyptians, Osiris (called by the Greeks Chrestos, and also Seraphis), was believed to have come to earth to suffer for them, and was waiting to judge them after death to decide their fate, the good going to heaven and the bad to hell. He was called by many different names for the purpose of heightening his glory, such as the Lord of Eternity, the Judge and Saviour of mankind, the Resurrection and the Life, the Bread of Life, the Redeemer and Mediator who gave his body to be broken so that believers might live. The centre of his worship was at Abydos, and, when remembering their dead, the people always prayed to Osiris, whom they termed the Saviour.

His worshippers believed about him much the same as Christians believe about their Christ, and showered on him the same phrases of gratitude and affection that Christians have lavished on their Saviour. The Egyptians were firm believers in various trinities of gods, the most popular being Osiris the father, Isis the mother, and Horus the son, who is depicted nestling on his mother's knee. From this conception Christians obtained the idea of the Madonna and child. Their god of evil was Set, who was adopted by Christianity under the name of Satan. This god, like Satan, was expelled from heaven, and was at constant war with Osiris for the souls of humanity.

The Egyptians believed intensely in a life after death. They embalmed their dead for two reasons, one being because the materially minded anticipated a physical resurrection of the body when the Ka, their name for the etheric duplicate body, would return to it, and the other was because they thought that the Ka desired the company of its physical body as long as possible. Consequently the Ka had to be provided with good accommodation, besides food, of which it partook of the essence, and also amusement, which accounts for the walls of the tomb being decorated with pictures of musicians, actors, and other subjects likely to interest the discarnate spirit.

The Book of the Dead has much to say about the other world, which the Egyptians called the Field of the Reeds, because they learned through the mediums attached to the temples how like it is to this earth. So heaven to them was a glorified Egypt, with harvests from fields intersected by ditches and canals, and watered by a noble river, on which floated ships, boats and canoes. There lived the men and women who had died on earth, death being but an entrance to a life which can hardly be distinguished from the one lived here on earth.

The Egyptian temples, from which the Hebrews copied the design of the Temple at Jerusalem, had each a Holy of Holies, or Sanctuary, and, from what took place there, such sacred places were what we today would call séance rooms, where the medium sat quietly and became entranced. In those days, only the priests were privileged to hear the voice of the other-world man, who controlled his earthly medium, as to them it was none other than the voice of a god. Mediumship, we now realise, is the foundation of all religious beliefs, and, from what occurred when early man communed with the departed through the tribe's medium, can be traced the design of all temples and churches, as all were, and most still are, provided with a sacred place where "the real presence" of the god made contact with the people on earth.

Today, with mediumship ignored by orthodox religion, the Sanctuary has become no more than the traditional abiding-place of the god the people worship, but everything is now so vague and nebulous that "the real presence" has become a flight of the imagination. No practical attempt is made to contact the etheric world, as was done in by-gone times, and consequently theology now rests only on past tradition, and lacks the source from which religious inspiration originally came. Today it lives on the husk and discards the kernel; in fact, to change the metaphor, the living stream, which nourished every religion at its birth, is now no more than a stagnant pool, filled with the putrid weeds of theological dogma and doctrine.

The influence of Egypt on Western religious beliefs is not yet generally realised. Prior to the Christian era she greatly influenced the Greek Mystery religions, which, in turn, were the foundation of Christianity. In Egypt the cross was a symbol of life for thousands of years, and, in an ancient triple fresco on the wall of the temple at Luxor, we see, in the first, the annunciation to the Virgin Mother, and, in the second, the Holy Spirit, or spirit control of the medium, holding a cross before her mouth, thus impregnating her. In consequence of this she is seen in the last scene as having given birth to a god-child, and being surrounded by figures in adoration. More-over, the Egyptians celebrated the festival of Easter, the day Horus died and descended to Hades, to rise again from the dead, when "he ascended to the Father" and became one with the Father.

Many of the stories told about Jesus were taken from those told about Horus and Osiris. The beliefs surrounding the death and resurrection of Osiris, and the Eucharist celebration partaken in memory of his death, resemble in all essentials those held by the Babylonians about their god Bel, both of whom were responsible for the production of the Christian Passion Drama and the ceremonies which followed.

The Christian story of the trial, death and resur-rection of Jesus is a copy of a Passion Drama performed to depict the passion of Bel, the Babylonian programme being given in the previous section. Unfortunately the Egyptian one has not been found, though we know that such a drama was performed, as Herodotus tells us that in his time the Egyptians staged a passion drama to Osiris. The religious beliefs of Babylon, Egypt and Greece laid the founda-tion of the Christian faith, its ceremonies and ritual, just as their social and political ideas were the basis of Western civilisation.

From the foregoing brief résumé of the life, customs and beliefs of the Egyptian people, we get a glimpse of early civilisation during the two thousand years before our era. They had the qualities, the faults and failings, which have made up mankind to our own times. Their geographical situation enabled them for a long period to live peaceful, industrious lives, free from outside interference, though they quarrelled amongst themselves because of differences about religion and politics. They suffered at times from invasion, and made other people suffer by their conquests; whereas, if they and their neighbours had just kept within their own frontiers, much suffering and material loss would have been avoided. Like the rest of mankind, they were like children who quarrel and snatch away each other's toys, and, in the end, everyone is the loser, no one being the gainer. Only by increased mental development shall we grow out of the nursery stage, and live together like sensible people.

When we turn from the various groups of communities in the Middle East, which were becoming established as nations, with a history and a culture of their own, to those lands further east, we find a different but distinct civilisation pertaining to each. India and China were developing a way of life peculiarly their own, a civilisation which was evolving from its own roots, quite independent of what was taking place farther west.

(3) INDIAN CIVILISATION.
(2500–126 B.C.)

Civilisation in India commenced somewhat later than in the Middle East. There, in the Punjab, before 2500 B.C., villages grew into towns, and towns into cities, containing large populations employed in highly skilled industries, and engaged in extensive commerce. There, on the banks of the Indus and its five tributaries, the fertile soil supported a community of mixed origin and diverse racial types. There these people cleared the jungle, invented picture-writing, loved and hated, traded and quarrelled, but today only the remains of their labours are left to tell us that in these far-off days they had an imposing civilisation, which created the foundation of Indian culture in the years that followed.

The ancient city of Mohenjo-daro covered an area of at least a square mile, and Harappa was about the same size. The inhabitants of these, and other towns, were supported by the same kind of grains and cattle as kept in being the city-dwellers of Sumer and Egypt. Probably the peasant also grew rice and kept poultry. Their industries likewise resembled those of the craftsmen of the Nile and Euphrates, the Punjab potters employing the same methods, and the smiths alloyed copper with tin to make bronze. Weavers produced cotton articles, glaziers glassware, and potters glazed jugs and pots. Carts on wheels trundled down the city streets and along the country roads, carrying the produce of the fields, while boats on the rivers transported it to villages along their banks. An extensive long-distance river trade existed, wood, gold, copper and tin being imported, in exchange for local manufactured goods which found their way to Mesopotamia, the Sumerians in turn exporting their specialities to the Punjab.

The best houses of these Punjab cities were commodious, two-storeyed brick buildings, each being provided with a bathroom, but the majority were only two-roomed dwellings. The houses of the rich were well furnished, and lavishly filled with gold, copper and bronze ornaments. The city streets were well planned, and the extensive drainage system makes clear that considerable attention was given to the hygiene of the people, who must have been surprisingly intelligent for these times. Their weights and measures were calculated on the decimal basis, and they evidently understood something of geometry and astronomy.

The Indian climate unfortunately makes preservation difficult, and little is known beyond what the remains of the cities have to tell. Not much of their picture-writing has survived, and what has cannot be read, but it seems likely that their religious beliefs were the forerunners of what is now Hinduism. Neither do we know why this imposing civilisation utterly perished, in fact it has been disinterred from complete oblivion only within the last twenty years. Yet, though it has passed away, to leave only a trace behind it, much of present-day Indian civilisation can be traced back to this ancient people who lived and died on the banks of the Indus river.

That is all we know about these far-off prehistoric days, and, at the best, it relates to only a small part of that great continent. Now we come to historical times, when our information is more reliable. India, by its geographical position, was cut off from the civilisations of the east and west by huge mountain barriers, and vast regions of desert, but this did not prevent her from being also the goal of northern nomads on the prowl for rich valleys and alluvial plains. The earlier primitive Dravidian civilisation of India was, in consequence, about 1500 B.C., overlaid by an invasion of Aryan tribes which came round the foothills of the Himalaya and penetrated the entire peninsula. These invaders in time lost touch with their wilder and less civilised brethren beyond the mountain ranges, and settled down to enjoy their valuable new-found possessions. The flat-nosed Dravidian aborigines became the outcasts, and now form the multitudes of the lower class of India today, the untouchables, whose treatment forms such a stain on Hindu civilisation.

Just as the Aryan tribes, which invaded Greece, changed its civilisation, so also did these fair-complexioned nomads change that of India from its more primitive Neolithic character to one of a more advanced type. From living in the cold northern uplands they now enjoyed the warm Indian climate. From having to roam from place to place in search of food, they now settled down to an easy form of existence on the fertile banks of the great rivers. The prolific soil gave them all the food they required, and there was enough for all. In this setting a new culture arose, one far removed from the one to which the newcomers had been for so long accustomed.

Instead of wandering, they became a settled agricultural people, fond of peaceful pursuits and enjoyment. They had few needs, and they made little effort to trade one with another. Numerous villages sprang up all over the country, over each of which ruled a chief. In time villages joined together to form a kind of republic, which again developed into a state over which ruled a rajah, under whom was a powerful priesthood. Under them were the people, whose position depended on their religion and social position. In this way the ruling caste of India arose, to become such a feature of their social life. While the villagers lived simply the nobles hunted, and life went on much as it did elsewhere, though here it had the protection of the northern mountain barrier which was so difficult for enemies to penetrate.

Compared with their Aryan brethren, who went farther west and settled in Europe, the Indian settlers enjoyed a much easier and more peaceful form of existence. For many centuries their lives were a dream-like form of existence, during which mystical thought developed, and much time was given over to religion and philosophy. India, then as now, was the garden of religions, as there they grew in profusion while the struggle for existence elsewhere made the rest of mankind much more practical and aggressive.

In this more peaceful atmosphere, the mind of India developed a mystical form of religious thought which in time penetrated both east and west, influencing China, on the east, and all the lands extending to the west. This has been India's great contribution to world affairs. Except among the northern states its people have not been warlike by nature, preferring more to think of the destiny of the mind than the needs of the physical body. This nation of contemplators never set out to be world conquerors, or great traders, taking little interest in traffic by sea, but they did export something of vital interest to mankind, which was the product of the accumulated thought of its people.

Here was developed an ethical code, which, if mankind followed it as intensely as he has followed the idea that might is right, would have made the world a better and happier place for the human race. Cruelty prevailed in India, as elsewhere, as man by nature is cruel, but there the thinkers moulded a code of ethics which, at the time, was far in advance of any prevailing elsewhere, with the exception of China. Here we are at the source of these moralisings which all thinking people today would like to see lived up to, if only it were possible. Here we are at the source of a philosophy of life, utterly at variance and opposed to that advocated in our own time by Nazi Germany.

How we would like to calm the tempest, and prevent all the damage it does to life and property. An inventor of an antidote to nature's aggressive actions would be hailed as a world's benefactor, and the people would not refuse it for fear of weakening their characters. Nevertheless they have turned away from the advice these Indian sages have given to mankind, which would have subdued the tempest of the mind. The human race has preferred to hate instead of to love, to steal instead of being honest, and to fight instead of living at peace.

The Aryan people, who came from central Asia, supplied the stock from which has sprung, amongst others, the British, German, French, Italian and Greek nations of Europe, as well as the Persians (called Iranians, meaning Aryans), and the Brahmans of India. Those who built the great cities of India came from the same cradle as did the builders of Rome, London, Paris, Berlin and Athens, each and all asserting their superiority over the earlier people they found in possession of the soil.

The history and evolution of India is just the story of the development of the eastern offshoots of the Aryan people who settled in that land. Aryan speech is the basis of most European languages, and the Aryan religions of Brahmanism and Buddhism have become the faiths of a quarter of the human race, they having spread Aryan thought and culture throughout all Asia. On the other hand, the Aryans in the west have been the cause of more wars, misery and suffering than any other. They made Europe a cockpit of conflicts, and wherever they obtained the power they dominated over every other race. Much of the story we have to tell, in the following chapters, is the history of this aggression against all the other weaker races, and their constant quarrels amongst themselves.

Brave, intelligent, cruel and ruthless sums up in four words the character of the western Aryan people, as history records it over the past three thousand years. Though they gained possession of the most favoured places of the earth, this bulldog breed has often lost its way by thinking that happiness comes only from great possessions. They have added largely to their wealth, but not always to their happiness, as their international life has been one of grab, quarrelling, and snarling. Besides this they have looked on other races with disdain, but, though these are relatively poorer, their past record of happiness is probably greater, and they have fewer crimes against humanity on their conscience.

Only within the past hundred years have the rights of man received consideration from these Aryan people, but, so far, they have made no progress in their international relationships. No sooner did one part of the Aryan family settle down to live a more decent life, than it was considered as weak by one of its more backward brothers. Over the past eighty years the most backward member of the family, from the moral standpoint, the Germans, have been responsible for five wars of aggression so as to enlarge their possessions at the expense of the other members of the Aryan family. This number might have been seven had they not been thwarted on two other occasions, but if we go back over the past two thousand years we find that the Germans have crossed their frontier over thirty times to ravage neighbouring lands.

Probably the climate has had much to do with the difference in temperament, character, and outlook on life between the Aryan Indian and his European brothers. The climate of India does not engender an active form of life. Contemplation, rather than action, is much more desired in a hot climate, where the few needs can be met without much exertion. The colder, more difficult life of the west stimulated the energies of the European Aryans, and made them of a harder temper, more aggressive and resolute of character, it invigorating their minds, and making them more active than those of their more dreamy contemplative brethren in the east.

In words preserved in the Aryan languages of the east and west we find many resemblances. The names for father, mother, brother, sister, and widow are similar in most of the Aryan languages, whether spoken on the banks of the Ganges, the Tiber, or the Thames. The word "daughter", for instance, which is similar throughout them all, is derived from two Sanskrit roots of the Aryan tongue, and means "to draw milk", the daughter being from early times the milkmaid of the Aryan household.

The ancient religions of Europe and India, made up of sacred stories and myths, had a similar common origin. Some of the Indian Vedic gods were also the gods of Greece and Rome, and God, to this day, is adored by names derived from the same old Aryan root, by both Christians and Brahmans, which latter name means The Born Again. Devata (literally "the Shining One")[1] means the same in Sanskrit as Dies-piter (or Jupiter, the Father god) and as Deus did to the Romans, Zeus to the Greeks, Duus to the Germans, Déité and Dusius to the French, and Deity and Deuce to the English, which latter has now become a slang word.

The Hindu father-god is Brahma, a trinity of three persons in one, Krishna is the Christ of the Hindu religion, and some think that both Krishna and Christ are names derived from the Sanskrit root meaning " the anointed one." Krishna is the Hindu saviour-god, and to him is attributed wise and ethical sayings which became associated with other World-saviours. Like the others he was once a man on earth, a priestly victim, but became, in the eyes of his worshippers, a god in heaven because he appeared in his etheric body after

---

[1] It is interesting to note how often in ancient literature a god is referred to as a shining being. Doubtless this comes about because the ancients believed that an apparition was a god; in fact, the seeing of apparitions is closely linked up with man's belief in a god and the gods. The German word for an apparition is "eine Erscheinung", or a Shining One, which is much more expressive than the English word, and conveys exactly what a German wishes his hearer or reader to understand was seen, namely a shining being. We are well aware of the accounts given about Paul, who claimed to have seen the apparition of Jesus. From that time onwards he refers to Jesus as a glorified and radiant being. His entire life was changed as the result, because Jesus was now to him a shining, glorified spirit, just as Jehovah was to Moses, as we are told that the "sight of the glory of the Lord was like devouring fire" (*Exodus* xxiv, 17). From numerous accounts by people who have seen apparitions in the days gone by, and in our own time, this brightness which surrounds them is often the subject of special comment. So it is hardly surprising that to the ancients the reappearing of the dead in bright array made them look upon these beings as gods. Now we can explain the fact as being due to the higher range of vibrations which constitute the etheric body, and their effect on light radiation.

his death. He is looked upon as the Saviour, Mediator, and Redeemer, and round the funeral pyres of the dead the mourners still sing hymns to the Saviour which are much like those Christians sing today.

He is believed to have lived some three thousand years ago, but it would be unwise to accept all the sayings attributed to him as having been said by him. Rather, they represent the stock of wisdom of the Indian sages, which his worshippers attributed to him out of love and respect, just as, at a later date, similar sayings were attributed to Gautama the Buddha, Jesus the Christ, and others whom circumstances raised to the level of gods in the eyes of their worshippers.

Around Krishna gathered much mystical lore, which corresponds to that which came to be believed about the saviour gods who followed after him, but what interests us here are the moral teachings he is believed to have uttered. They are many in number, but the following are some of the hundreds which are to be found in Indian sacred literature.

Those who do not control their passions cannot act properly towards others.

The evils we inflict upon others follow us as our shadows follow our bodies.

Virtue sustains the spirit as the muscles sustain the body.

Let your hand be always open to the unfortunate.

Avoid envy, covetousness, falsehood, imposture, slander and sexual desires.

Above all things cultivate love for your neighbour.

When you die you leave your worldly wealth behind you, but your virtues and vices go with you.

Kill not, steal not, lie not, swear not, revenge not, avoid all impure words and never testify falsely.

Shew mercy and sympathy to all living things and avoid all cruelty to men and animals.

Do good for its own sake, and expect not your reward for it on earth.

The mind is immortal, but must be pure and free from all evil and stain before it can return to Him who gave it.

Cultivate that inner knowledge which teaches what is right and what is wrong.

Never take delight in another's misfortunes.

It is better to forgive an injury than to avenge it.

You can accomplish by kindness what you cannot do by force.

A noble spirit finds a cure for injustice by forgetting it.

Pardon the offences of others but not your own.

What you blame in others do not practise yourself.

Do right from hatred of evil, and not from fear of punishment.

A wise man corrects his own errors by observing those of others.

He who rules his temper conquers his greatest enemy.

The wise man governs his passions, but the fool obeys them.

Be at war with men's vices, but at peace with their persons.

There should be no disagreement between your lives and your beliefs.

Spend every day as though it is your last on earth.

Lead not one life in public and another in private.

We must master our evil propensities, or they will master us.

He who conquers his passions rules over a kingdom.

Protect, love and assist others if you would serve God.

He who gives to the needy loses nothing himself.

The wounds of the mind are more important than those of the body. The wounds of conscience leave a scar.

The virtuous woman will have but one husband, and the right-minded man but one wife.

It is the highest crime to take advantage of the weakness of a woman.

Women should be loved, respected and protected by husbands, fathers and brothers.

Wise men can only advise the people how to live, but cannot force them to accept and practise their advice. As most people have always been foolish and ignorant, the small minority have had to stand by and regret the stupidity of their contemporaries, which brought unhappiness and misery to the wise and senseless alike. All human life intermingles, and the innocent suffer from the mistakes made by the backward. The evil-doer is a curse, not only to himself but to all his neighbours, and, if he cannot reform his ways, he is set apart from those who can live decently. What applies to the individual should also apply to the nation. We can confine the individual transgressor of the moral law, but we have yet to find a way to prevent the individual nation, set on the evil path, from injuring its neighbours. That is the problem which lies before us, and it is one we must solve if the curse of evil is to be wiped from off this earth.

Five hundred years after the time of Krishna another distinguished Indian Aryan reformer, Siddhartha Gautama, set out to try and reform mankind. He became famous by that set of circumstances which follow some, and leave others unknown to history. As Jesus became a world-wide figure by the action of an autocrat, the Emperor Constantine, so did Gautama by the influence of the powerful King Asoka. Now he is known throughout the world as Gautama the Buddha, which means Gautama the Enlightened, just as Jesus is known as Jesus the Christ, or Jesus the Anointed, though it must be remembered that the lives of both are so surrounded by legend that it is difficult to discover much about either of them which is in any way historical.

Everywhere Gautama is called Buddha, and so we shall continue the usual practice. He was born in India about 560 B.C. We are told that he was a good-looking energetic young prince, his father being a rajah in the Punjab, and up to the age of twenty-nine he lived a life of ease, comfort and luxury. He had a beautiful wife, and everything that he could possibly desire.

Amidst plenty and beauty he passed from gratification to gratification, and yet he was not satisfied. He felt that there was something real which he had not yet found, and that all he had grasped so far was but the shadow. One day, when out driving, he encountered a poor, bent, miserable creature. His driver remarked, "Such is the way of life, and to that we must all come." Next he came upon a man suffering from some horrible disease, about whom his driver passed the same remark, and lastly he saw the unburied body of a man which had been mauled by an animal. Again his driver made the same remark.

The insecurity of life, which is always followed by bodily decay, its passing pleasures on the one hand, and its miseries on the other, struck the sensitive mind of this young aristocrat so forcibly, that the idea came to him that if happiness could be obtained with poverty, then there would be nothing to lose. Was it not a question of mental exercise, which, when correctly carried out, obviated the need of material things to produce happiness? In other words, Buddha argued that by contemplation, and the ignoring of what this earth has to offer, one can obtain happiness. He was one of many who have formed the same opinion, but he turned his thoughts into a philosophy which he preached to those who became his disciples.

On his return from the drive, Buddha heard that his first son was born, and now he made his momentous decision. His life was either to be spent with his wife and son amidst his lavish surroundings, or apart from them all, devoid of every comfort and luxury. He chose the latter and, amid the great rejoicings aroused by his son's birth, he called his servant and told him to prepare his horse. Taking a passing look at his wife and child, he resisted a last embrace in case he awoke her, and she prevented him from carrying out his decision. He thus turned his back on everything he loved, on all his possessions, and went off into the night alone, changing his costly clothes for the rags of the first poor man he met. Again and again he was tempted to return, but never yielded, and pursued the path he had so deliberately chosen, gathering round him pupils to whom he taught his philosophy.

All the misery of life he traced to selfishness. Unhappiness, he said, is due to the craving for individuality and the torment of greed. Man must overcome every sort of personal craving, and, until he does so, trouble and sorrow will follow humanity. Craving is noticeable in three different ways: the first through sensuality, the desire to gratify the senses; secondly, by the desire to penetrate beyond death; and thirdly, by the wish for prosperity, the accumulation of wealth, and the love of the things of this world. These desires must be abolished before life can become serene, but, when they are overcome and man has conquered desire, he has then reached the highest state of wisdom, Nirvana, the mental state in which the mind is at peace.

Nirvana may not quite mean the extinction of individuality, but the extinction of desires, though it is difficult to imagine individuality without desire and aspiration. This way of conquering, or rather destroying, what the Buddhists call our Karma, this seed of a new existence, is no less than a policy of defeatism. This self-extinction is practised for the purpose of bringing to an end the weary round of ever-recurring reincarnation into a possible lower form of life, an idea which has always been to so many easterners a constant nightmare. The wise control of our desires and passions seems much more to be desired than this policy of destroying them, as our personality cannot be extinguished, and, moreover, no one has ever brought forward a vestige of evidence in support of reincarnation.

Buddha practised what he preached. He, like all monks and nuns, withdrew himself from the world, and to those who followed him he taught that there was something greater than earth's pleasures, something beyond earth's desires, and that, by renouncing these, reality could be found in contemplation. Though he was doubtless influenced by Brahmanic philosophy, he comes down to us as one of the world's greatest philosophic pioneers. We may not agree with all his esoteric ideas, and these can be passed by, but his exoteric teaching was rational and practical, and the code of ethics attributed to him is of as high an order as any before or after his time. He is credited with more ethical wisdom than any other moral teacher, and his influence for righteousness has been beyond all comprehension.

He produced, for the benefit of humanity, his eight-fold way of right thinking and right acting, known as the Aryan path, which is much more practical and sensible than his scheme for destroying Karma. First and foremost he insisted on truth, and the abandonment of all superstitions. Next came the holding of right views and of right aspirations. As base cravings are to be expelled, love of service to others, and desire to do and to secure justice must take their place. From this it is evident that Buddha also taught a change of desire, and not the annihilation of desire. Then came devotion to knowledge, to right speech, right conduct, right living, right effort (because no one must be lazy), and, lastly, right rapture, which is aimed against the ecstasies of the devout.

He was the first to declare the universal brotherhood of man, and his followers, though they have degraded much of his teaching, and turned it into creeds and dogmas, have at least on many occasions made an attempt to follow his precepts of peace and love to all men. He insisted that reasoned thinking, based on evidence, is our only guide to truth, and that only when greed, covetousness, and all selfish desires are annihilated will justice, mercy, and goodness remain. Then human happiness will naturally follow. Buddhism, which is accepted by 150,000,000 people, can proudly claim that it has seldom been the cause of war and strife, and that its founder was one of the first to proclaim, so far as we know, that knowledge and wisdom are the only two levers capable of raising mankind.

Buddha taught that all men and women should enjoy equal rights. He denounced the priests of his day, and fortunately escaped their wrath. He put forward an altruistic system of conduct, advocating kindness and love towards all men, and the return of good for evil. If mankind could only live up to his teachings, to his principles of peace and love, oppression and tryanny would be no more. He taught no cruel doctrine of sacrifice, he believed in no angry God, nor in that most immoral of all religious doctrines—that a saviour took the punishment for the transgressions of believers. His was a purely materialistic atheistic philosophy, of passive conduct and service, not a religion of sacrifice, worship and observance. He propounded no creeds or dogmas, and advocated no rites and ceremonies, right conduct to him being everything.

As happened with all outstanding men in those days, legends grew round his name after his death. He came to be looked upon as having been a godman, who had performed numerous miracles, and it was believed that his mother at the time of his birth was a virgin. It is said that when he was born the celestial choir sang, "This day is born for the good of men, Buddha, to dispel the darkness of ignorance, and to give joy and peace to the world." To him at birth came wise men with rich gifts to proclaim him the Saviour of the World.

This, and much more in the same strain, was told of him, and is similar to the legends surrounding all those who, after death, came to be looked upon as the saviours of the world. He lived to be an old man and continued his teaching to the last. Though he was rich, yet, for the sake of others, he became poor, so that they, through his poverty, might reach

Nirvana. His teachings made rapid headway, and, by the 3rd century B.C., the new cult was gaining wealth and power, the teaching of the master now having been consolidated into dogmas and doctrines. One of the greatest and noblest monarchs of history, King Asoka (264–227 B.C.), still revered by millions, whose kingdom extended from Afghanistan to Madras, adopted the faith, and, influenced by the teachings of Buddha, gave up his contemplated conquest of the Indian peninsula. Instead of continuing to conquer by force, he set out to conquer by love, sending missionaries everywhere to spread the teachings of Buddha. He erected monuments all over his kingdom, on which were inscribed Buddha's simple precepts. His missionaries found their way to Alexandria, where they influenced the west, their principal contribution to Christianity being the Monastic system, with its orders of monks and nuns. In turn, the Buddhists were influenced by some of the beliefs and teachings surrounding Osiris, which found their way into the religion of Buddha. They copied what is now known as the Madonna and child from Isis with Horus in her arms, and so we find Buddha pictured in the arms of the goddess Hariti.

As we shall discover later on, Christianity became an international religion for much the same reason as did Buddhism. What Constantine did for Christianity at the Council of Nicaea, in the year A.D. 325, Asoka did for Buddhism. Both these potentates consolidated simple teaching into creeds and dogmas. In both cases the words of the master were transformed into definite and fixed doctrines, and conferences and councils followed each other for the purpose of bringing unanimity amongst the priests and people. Just as numerous gospels were written, reporting what Jesus said and did, likewise many documents appeared recording the sayings and deeds of Buddha. These are known as the Buddhist *Suttas,* and they have the same place in that religion as have the Gospels in Christianity.

Krishna and Buddha are the two outstanding god-men of India. Krishna still receives the veneration of millions of pious Hindus, whereas Buddhism is now accepted more by those countries surrounding India, Brahmanism, the name given to the Hindu priestly caste, having proved itself too strong a rival to permit that which took shape within its orbit to survive. Moreover, the Brahman priesthood had behind it a long tradition as the intermediaries between the gods and mankind, going back to the days when the priests were the caretakers of the tribe's mediums, to the time before they abolished the medium and assumed for themselves the duties of interpreting the will of the gods. The Buddhist period in India lasted from the 6th century B.C. to the 8th century A.D., but from this time onwards Brahmanism became the ruling religion, with the accompanying persecution common to all saviour-god religions, to end in Buddhism being banished from its native home.

Exiled from India, it has won greater triumphs than it could ever have achieved in the land of its birth, and has created a literature and a faith for more than a third of the human race, while profoundly affecting the beliefs of the rest. Today it has more followers than any other form of belief, while in India, where it exerted an influence on Hinduism, it still survives in the teaching it left behind. Stressing, as it has always done, the brotherhood of man, Buddhism has been more a philosophy for humanity than a religion of salvation by faith. By its record of peaceful conquest, it stands out as a shining example of toleration, because, unlike both the Moslems and the Christians, it has gained its converts by persuasion and without recourse to the use of force.

The external history of India commences with the Greek invasion in 327 B.C., though Greek historians mention the country two centuries earlier. The Greeks found the Punjab divided into petty kingdoms, jealous of one another, and each ready to join the invader to help pay off the grievances they had one against the other. After Alexander's death, this part of his empire was taken over by his general Seleucus, who founded the Syrian monarchy, but, while he was winning his way to this position, Chandra Gupta (316–292 B.C.) seized Patna and established himself firmly in the Ganges valley. Here he built up an empire in northern India, expelled the Greeks, and, after a successful war with Seleucus, was recognised by them as the King of Patna.

This was the dynasty from which came the great Asoka who established Buddhism throughout India, and spread its doctrines from Afghanistan to China, and from Central Asia to Ceylon. Greek influence continued to affect Indian science and sculpture, but, from the time of their withdrawal, for the next twelve centuries until the Moslem conquest, the Indian historian is dependent on a mass of conflicting evidence derived from inscriptions, legends and tradition. In the midst of this confusion we see dim masses moving southwards from Central Asia into India, when Tartar and Scythian hordes began (126 B.C.) to expunge all that the Greeks had left behind them. These invaders poured into India in such masses that they supplanted the previous population.

Here we must leave India in the fog following the Tartar and Scythian invasions. We shall, however, again take up her history in the chapter devoted to Moslem civilisation, when this new power made its influence felt on this great continent where so much has happened, but where, owing to the climate, paper or parchment does not long survive to tell the tale. Now we shall pass on to consider a civilisation farther east, one which has lasted as long as any other.

(4) CHINESE CIVILISATION.
(2356 B.C.–A.D. 384.)

As civilisation was developing in Egypt, India and Mesopotamia, so also was it progressing in China, where philosophical and mystical thought was reaching a high level. Here again we find a civilisation quite distinct and apart from the others. Here a separate race was developing alone, and quite apart from what was taking place in the rest of the world.

In the valleys of the two great rivers, the Hwang-ho (or Yellow River, 2600 miles in length) and the Yang-tse-Kiang (3400 miles in length), people from some unknown source had gathered together in increasing numbers, separated from the rest of the world by the desolate Gobi desert in the north, mountains in the west, and the sea on the east. They lived in villages, used primitive stone implements, and domes-

ticated animals such as the wild boar. They knew
how to spin and make pottery. This incipient civilisation was, for long, uninfluenced by the nomadic
tribes which were then reaching the sea elsewhere
from the northern regions. Not until some two
thousand eight hundred years ago were these settlers
made aware of certain roving people called Heung-
noos, or Huns, as we call them, who entered China
bringing with them the knowledge of iron and its
uses.

Neolithic culture, which was world-wide, affected
China, as it did other countries, but there ends the
connection between Chinese civilisation and that
farther west. Its roots are thus known, but what
became a separate civilisation can be traced to the
intermingling of people, separated from the rest of
the world by sea, mountain and desert, who worked
out a way of life all on their own.

These village people settled on the banks of the
two great rivers, which brought them annually the
rich alluvial soil from the mountains to nourish their
land. Government was bad as a rule, because seldom
were they blessed by good rulers. Inter-state wars
were frequent, and the ethical life of the nobility was
at a low level, but probably no worse than it was elsewhere in these times. Trade nevertheless developed,
and fairs were held at different centres in each district;
in fact, some four thousand years ago there were the
elements of an intellectual culture, including the
knowledge of writing and astronomy. Development
continued, so much so that from the 7th to the 5th
century B.C. there was a much more advanced literary
culture than was to be found in Europe up to the 17th

century of the Christian era. The same applies to many of the arts which flourished in China some three thousand years ago, and were unknown in Europe until within the past three hundred years. The Chinese grew flax, which they wove into garments, and they moreover knew the value of the silk-worm, from which they obtained silk.

The early history of China is enveloped in the mist of legend, which contained stories of the creation of both the earth and the life which came to live upon it. Like the Hebrews, the Chinese started their legendary history from the creation of man and woman, who were settled on its soil by the gods. From these primitive beings sprang a long line of dynastic rulers who lived incredibly long lives. The events connected with most of these are purely fabulous, but the nearer they come to historical times the more rational they appear, until at last we read of a ruler who directed the people how to live and fight. He taught them how to make huts from the boughs of trees, and produce fire by rubbing two sticks together. He, moreover, taught them to look upon Teen as their creator and preserver. Then the people, living in separate tribes, invented the plough, produced silk from the silk-worm, and observed certain days for worship and the making of offerings to the gods.

From now onwards we feel that we are treading more on facts and less on fiction, and from the time the plough was discovered Chinese civilisation proceeds by rapid and progressive steps. With the reign of Yaou (2356 B.C.) we emerge to some extent from the mist which hangs over the earlier records of the land. He, and his successor, Shun, set the people such a good example that virtue, we are told, pervaded the land, crime was unknown, the nation increased in size and prosperity, markets and fairs being established in all the towns, and the flood-lands were drained.

Both the bane and blessing of China has been the overflowing of the Hwang-ho, as it brings disaster and prosperity by the flooding of its banks and the changing of its course. Its receding waters leave behind them rich alluvial soil, eminently suitable for cultivation, and one of the early heroes was the great Yu, who freed large tracts of country of flood-land after nine years of labour, for which service his grateful countrymen made him king on the death of Shun. Then followed a number of bad rulers until, under Kee (1818 B.C.), the people arose in rebellion and swept away all traces of him and his bloody house. So ended the dynasty of Yu, the engineer monarch, who had brought such prosperity to China.

Tang, who had replaced the deposed king, became the first emperor (1766 B.C.) of the Shang dynasty, and, with the aid of wise counsellors, restored the country to some measure of prosperity. His descendants, however, brought misery and privation to the people, until they again arose in rebellion, dethroned the emperor, and put Woo-Wang in his place. He was the first of the Chow dynasty, brave, talented, and virtuous, but made the mistake of dividing his empire into seventy-two feudal states, in order to bestow principalities on his relations and friends. This error soon became apparent, as jealousies developed between the princes, civil war commenced, and the power of the Emperor rapidly dwindled. Other enemies now appeared outside the Empire's borders, when the Mongolian Tartars in 936 B.C. made their appearance for the first time, and, taking advantage of the confusion, raided the land, thus adding to the prevailing misery.

For centuries China was distracted by internal wars, besides being harassed by the attacks of a foreign foe, and this was the position when Confucius, the greatest of her sons, was born. Confucius (551–475 B.C.), the founder of Confucianism, was poor in worldly goods but of good birth, as he could trace his ancestry through the sovereigns of the Shang dynasty. The name Confucius is the Latinised form of K'ung Fu-tze, meaning the Master K'ung. His life coincided with a time in China which can be compared with the one world affairs have been passing through in our own time, and he set out to find the way of solving his country's difficulty of self-government, only to discover that his fellow countrymen were too ignorant, and their rulers too selfish and stupid, to take heed of his advice.

His poverty made it necessary for him to start life at twenty-two years of age as a schoolmaster. Like Plato, he set up an Academy to teach boys the principles of good government and right conduct. His wisdom and knowledge soon attracted disciples, who aided him financially with his work, so much so that by the time he was thirty he was well known and respected for his sound and constructive ideas. Chaotic conditions ruled in his state, and he was asked by the ruler how to put matters right. His advice was refused, and he, in consequence, declined to take any remuneration for his help.

For another fifteen years he pursued his teaching and studies, and only relinquished them to take up the position of chief magistrate of the city of Chungtoo. A marvellous reformation, we are told, forthwith ensued in the manners of the people, which so pleased the Marquis ruler of the state that he made Confucius Minister of Crime. His biographers relate that this appointment also surpassed all expectation, as crime at once came to an end. A transformation came about, evil-doers hid their heads, the men became loyal and the women docile, so much so that "He was the idol of the people and flew in songs through their mouths". In spite of this success, we are surprised to read that he could find no other ruler to give him charge of affairs of state, though he travelled for thirteen years from state to state, hoping that someone would accept him as their counsellor, and initiate a government that would become the centre of a universal reformation.

One of his precepts was that all rule should be righteous and benevolent, and that if the ruler were good and virtuous the people would be likewise. He stressed greatly the power of example. Another maxim was that by education almost anything could be achieved. One of his reported remarks tells us that:—

If any ruler would submit to me as his director for twelve months I should accomplish something considerable, and in three years I could attain the realisation of my hopes.

When advised by the recluses of his time to withdraw from worldly aaffirs, and leave the people to their fate, he replied:—

It is impossible to withdraw from the world, and associate with birds and fishes which have no affinity with us. With whom should I associate but with suffering men? The disorder that prevails is what requires my efforts. If right principles ruled throughout the kingdom there would be no necessity for me to change its condition.

Confucius would not abandon the cause of the people, and held on his way to the end, even though the princes of China spurned his advice. His life, in consequence, was one of disappointment, notwithstanding the success he achieved at Chung-too, the report of which is doubtless a panegyric composed by his disciples after his death. He passed away an old man with the feeling that his life had not fulfilled its mission, and it was only when he had gone that the Chinese discovered his wisdom.

The man, who had been neglected when alive, seemed to become all at once the object of unbounded admiration. The tide then began to flow, and during twenty-three centuries it has never ebbed. His body was given an imposing tomb at K'iuh-fow, the approach of which is reached through a magnificent gate and an avenue lined with cypress trees. All around his tomb are imperial tablets, of different dynasties, with glowing tributes to the one man whom China delights to honour. A marble statue stands guard over the grave, bearing the inscription, "The most sagely ancient teacher, the all accomplished, all informed K'ung."

Such are the heights to which time and tradition can raise a human being, by those whose imagination discerns genius in the past but only mediocrity in the present. The three thousand disciples who delighted to honour him in life grew in numbers after his death, encouraged by the record of his life as presented in *The Great Learning* by Tsang Sin, the most profound of his disciples, and *The Doctrine of the Mean* by his grandson, which gives us the greatest amount of information about the sage, and contains many of his sayings. Confucius himself left no writings detailing the principles of his moral and social system, an unfortunate omission, as disciples are so apt to gloss over faults and failures, and dwell on those aspects most favourable to their master.

Confucius was not a religious man, and died with no hope of a hereafter. His work, he said, was for the betterment of the people on earth, which, if followed, would make the world a place worthy in which to live. The principles he set down dwelt on the importance of the development of individual character, and the manner in which each one can contribute to the raising of morality and the social order of society to a higher level.

Foremost amongst his principles for the proper order of society is the one which has come to be known throughout the world as the golden rule. Several times he gave that rule definitely and distinctly in these words: "What you do not like when done to yourself do not do to others." He gave it not only in negative form but also insisted on its positive application, deploring that he had not always been able to take the initiative in doing to others as he would that they should do to him. This principle of conduct forms the foundation of the new order of peace, prosperity and happiness which this book envisages, and it is consequently appropriate that we should have learned something of the sage who first tried to apply it to the ordering of human conduct.

Confucius was an ardent social reformer. His teaching was pure Secularism, combined with a code of ethics. He had faith in his fellow men, and believed that each individual had within himself the power to achieve a well-ordered society. He was interested in conduct on earth, and the effect it had on the welfare of the people. He was not interested in their fate after death. Heaven, to him, would come on earth to the good, just as the evil-doer could make his hell on earth. The reward of good was good, and of evil evil, which came about by the law of cause and effect, if not directly to the individual, then to his descendants. Over all he believed there was a Supreme Being ordering all and determining everything.

Such then was the founder of Secularism, who, all these centuries, has been so much revered by a third of mankind, but whose advice has been so persistently rejected. Reverence for wisdom is so easy but its practice is so difficult. Still, the fact should be noted that the Chinese have been greatly helped and comforted in our own times by his precepts during the terrible experiences they went through between the years 1937 and 1945, when the Japanese were devastating their country and bringing death and misery into so many homes. To the precepts of Confucius, which are to be found inscribed everywhere in China, they turned for the mental nourishment which gave them the strength to carry on during these years of sorrow and affliction.

Here we have a well-attested illustration of how

the mind can be trained to rise above its surroundings. As a rule, however, wise counsels are swept aside, the consequence being that the story of the race, from the time of Confucius to the present day, is one of much misery and unhappiness, brought about by the selfishness and stupidity inherent in humanity. The great warriors of this world, by their spectacular deeds, influence the people because ignorance cannot appreciate wisdom. So Confucius, like many a wise man after him, died a neglected and disappointed man. Hitler, and all his prototypes who preceded him, received honour and glory by appealing to the lower instincts of mankind, their lack of knowledge and wisdom being no barrier amongst nations quite devoid of these attainments.

The Chinese not only spurned the advice of Confucius, but also that of Lao-tsze, who was a few years his senior, and of Mencius who succeeded him in the century which followed. The human race has either murdered or ignored its really great men, and then, after their death, worshipped at their graves.

Lao-tsze was the founder of Taoism, which occupies a place close to Buddhism, and his teachings, like those of Buddha, have been debased by his followers. He was a contemporary of Confucius, but very different in his outlook, he being a mystic, whereas Confucius was philosophical and practical. For many years Lao-tsze was in charge of the Imperial Library. He preached a stoical indifference to the pleasures and powers of this world, and advocated simplicity, modesty, unselfishness, returning good for evil, and the subjection of all desires. Like most mystics, his meanings are very obscure, and, because of this indefiniteness, his teaching was overlaid, as time went on, with legends, and had grafted upon it complex and extraordinary observances.

Between the 8th and 4th centuries B.C. the valleys of the Hwang-ho and the Yang-tse-Kiang supported some ten to fifteen million people, divided into many small states, and subject to the overlordship of about a dozen larger states. In the 6th century B.C. the northern states of the Hwang-ho valley, and the southern states of the Yang-tse-Kiang valley were at war, which ended in a league of both the northern and southern states. This brought about disarmament, and more peaceful and prosperous times, but it was only temporary, as the people soon forgot the misery and suffering which war had caused.

After the collapse of the Chow dynasty in 255 B.C., Che Hwang-ti (246–210 B.C.) ascended the throne as "The First Universal Emperor", and with him passed also the old feudal system. He was one of the greatest rulers China has ever had, and, under him, the country became united as never before. It was he who started the building of the Great Wall in 214 B.C., 1500 miles long, and one of mankind's greatest enterprises, as a protection against the Huns, who were a constant worry to the Chinese. He built a magnificent palace, constructed roads throughout the Empire, and built canals and numerous handsome public buildings. Under him the Empire reached to the limit of what is today known as China.

As the reign of this outstanding monarch came to a close, civil war again broke out because many of the nobles thought he was too progressive. They quoted from past history in support of their conservative policy, only to find that their emperor destroyed their books, which was certainly not a wise act as it made the intelligentsia very bitter against him. After his death in 210 B.C. came the establishment of the Han dynasty, which was a period of literary activity and general prosperity. During this dynasty the Huns were so restrained, that instead of looking eastwards for loot and plunder they began to turn their eyes westwards, a change of policy which was a misfortune for Europe.

Two thousand years ago China was much as it was at the end of the last century. Education and learning were in the hands of the Mandarins, who were the scholars and leaders of thought. Their knowledge consisted only of the classical literature of China, which to them contained everything there was to know, and, in consequence, their influence was always against change or progress. It took each one many years to learn how to read and write, as their writing consists of signs for every idea, each of which has to be separately learned. Chinese writing is both peculiar and complex, a very great number of signs having to be learned, and by the time these are all remembered the Mandarins have passed into middle age, when thought of change becomes rather repugnant to the individual. To this form of education, more than anything else, must be attributed the conservative nature of the Chinese mind.

The Western world, by adopting an alphabet, was enabled to communicate its thoughts much more simply by writing. A schoolboy today, who knows our alphabet, can learn to read and write at an early age, whereas a Mandarin spent half his life in acquiring the art. How could a country progress in such a fashion, and we need not wonder that to their system of writing is attributed the lack of progress made by the Chinese people, whose fate rested on the Mandarin class, as only they could read and write.

Backward as they were in their method of conveying their thoughts one to another, they were advanced in methods of production. It was from China that we obtained the knowledge of making paper from the wool of the cotton plant, an idea which was to be the means of liberating the mind of Europe. Prior to the discovery of how to make paper, everything had to be written on papyrus, the supply of which was limited, but in China paper was being used, on which to print their books, in the 2nd century A.D. They also knew how to print their signs from block type.

The art of making paper, however, did not come to Europe until the beginning of the 8th century A.D., when Europeans learned the secret from the Arabs, who had acquired it from the Chinese by way of Central Asia. Damascus, under Arab rule, was for a time the chief place of manufacture. Thence the art was passed to the Moors in Spain, as the Arab conquest of Egypt had cut off from Europe the source of the supply of papyrus. A substitute had to be found, and paper took the place of papyrus. Then it was possible to produce books as we now know them, but only in small numbers, as printing was not yet known in Europe. Not until the 15th century, when it was discovered how to print by moveable type, did paper come into its own, and since then books have become part of our everyday life.

Kaou-te, who founded the Han dynasty in 206 B.C., after defeating his enemies, and dethroning the grandson of the great Che Hwang-ti, repealed all oppressive laws, with the exception of the one relating to the destruction of all books, which remained until the next emperor withdrew the ban. Then literature was encouraged, the banned books were republished, and this ushered in an era of great literary activity. This progressive period added to the general prosperity of the Empire, as peace reigned, the Huns suffering bitter defeats whenever they attempted to cross the frontier. Then it was that they began to move westwards to Turkestan and the shores of the Caspian Sea. The Emperor followed this up by sending to the ruler of these parts an ambassador to attempt the formation of an alliance against these marauders, but he was unsuccessful in his mission, though it had the effect of introducing silk into Europe, because this envoy brought with him the precious silk-worm.

By A.D. 93 the Huns, after suffering severe defeats, were driven out of Eastern Asia, and what remained of them settled in a district to the north-east of the Caspian Sea. Thus was China freed for some centuries from this constant menace, but, if her borders were now secure, internal strife remained, finally to overthrow the Han dynasty.

At the beginning of the Christian era Wang Mang, in A.D. 9, set himself up as emperor, but, after fourteen years, he was dethroned by Lew Sew, who in turn was murdered by his soldiers. Kwang-woo-te now became emperor, and the first of the Eastern Han dynasty. Within this period are embraced some of the most remarkable events in the history of China, the most notable being the introduction of Buddhism in A.D. 65 during the reign of Ming-te.

This new dynasty lasted no longer than the others, as within two hundred years it was blotted out by three aspirants to·the throne, each of whom was so equal in strength that they agreed to divide the Empire between them. This time is known as the period of the Three Kingdoms, when China was a house divided against itself. Wars became chronic, until all the power passed from the rulers into the hands of the generals. Finally Sze-ma-Yen, the strongest of all the generals, proclaimed himself emperor (A.D. 265) and started the Western Tsin dynasty with the title of Woo-te.

For the first time in Chinese history we now find contact made with Europe, by the arrival in the capital (A.D. 384) of ambassadors from the Roman Emperor Theodosius, curious to learn more of this land from which none came, and into which no European hitherto had entered. From this time onwards, for the next thousand years, only slight European contact was made with China, but we shall discover more about this mysterious country later on in Chapter X.

It was not in the East, but in the West, that history was made, the people of the Western hemisphere having largely shaped the destiny of mankind. So let us now begin the tale of Western civilisation by telling of a virile people, small in numbers, living between the east and west, who have exerted a great influence on the entire Western world.

CHAPTER V.

HEBREW CIVILISATION.
(1800 B.C.–A.D. 614.)

Introduction. (1) *Early tradition of the Children of Israel.* (2) *The rise and fall of the Kingdom of Israel.* (3) *The Jews, from the captivity to their final dispersal.*

ABOUT the time Hammurabi was flourishing in Babylon, in the 18th century B.C., an event occurred which was destined to have profound historical consequences. Then the famous city of Ur fell on evil days. For fifteen centuries this town had acted as the port of Mesopotamia, from which ships sailed down the Persian Gulf to India and the east coast of Africa, but now the entire scene changed. The Euphrates altered its course, and so made useless the wonderful system of canals by which the ships reached the sea, the entire irrigation system becoming sun-baked ditches and the land a desert.

In consequence of this disaster, the people of Sumer emigrated farther inland, and centred their activities around the river town of Babylon. In *Genesis,* Amraphel, King of Shinar, is mentioned as contemporary with Abraham, and this king has been considered by some to be Hammurabi, though the tendency of modern scholarship is opposed to this opinion. So far as we can tell, Hammurabi lived in the 18th century B.C., and the disaster to Sumer probably occurred about that time. We cannot be sure of our dates, but, if we assume that Abraham was forced to seek fresh land for his herds because of the catastrophe, we find that we are dealing with a period in history round about the 18th century B.C.

We are to a great extent in the realm of legend and tradition when dealing with Abraham and all the other early Old Testament characters, as historically they rank very much as King Arthur does in English history. When there were no written records, tradition took the place of facts, but the setting relates to the times, and, so far as Abraham is concerned, we find ourselves back in these far-off days of Hammurabi. Then the city of Ur was a place and not just a name, then the Amorites, over whom he ruled, were a great power, and places which have come to light as the result of recent excavations were inhabited.

(1) EARLY TRADITION OF THE CHILDREN OF ISRAEL.

Hebrew tradition commences with Abraham leaving the city of Ur. He was then an elderly man, and his old father and nephew, together with their wives, families and slaves, accompanied him. Such a removal, with all their possessions, for two men advanced in years, could only have been brought about by some unusual cause, and perhaps we are not far wrong in thinking that the disaster to Ur, which we know took place about then, was the cause of them being forced by circumstances to try their fortunes elsewhere. Soon the old father died, and Abraham journeyed on with Lot, his nephew. Eventually, after a long and weary trek of about 800 miles, they found themselves on the shores of the Mediterranean. Doubtless, on their wandering westward, they kept as near as possible to the course of the Euphrates, as only there would food and drink be found for themselves and their animals.

We are told in the Hebrew scriptures that they then settled in a part of Syria, to which the Hebrews afterwards gave the name of Canaan, meaning lowlands, and this name was later applied to all the land they conquered lying west of the Jordan. Here they found wide pastoral regions suitable for their flocks and herds, the natives of the country being farmers and vine-growers in the fertile regions which sloped towards the sea. Here also were walled cities, and on the coast were ports whence sailed ships along the shores of the Mediterranean. In these products of civilisation, nomadic shepherds were not interested, as to them tents were sufficient protection, and so these strangers from Ur wandered south, intent only on securing sufficient nourishment for their animals. At certain seasons of the year they would encamp close to the walls of the cities, and there exchange their wool for flour, oil and wine, but that represented the limit of their contact with civilisation.

As they travelled south the vegetation became less plentiful, so much so that they were forced by famine to enter Egypt, where Sarai, Abraham's wife, was placed in the royal harem, but later restored to her husband in consequence of what was believed to be divine chastisements inflicted upon Pharaoh. Thus the ruler of Egypt discovered that she was the wife of Abraham, and not his sister, as he had been led to believe. Consequently he asked him to leave the country, but there seems to have been no bad feeling between them, because he allowed him to take with him his great possessions. The manifold wisdom of the Egyptians evidently greatly impressed Abraham, and he departed both a wiser and richer man, as during his stay he acquired a great substance in flocks and herds, besides a large number of male and female slaves.

Abraham, on his return to Canaan, established friendly relations with the native chiefs, and, with his 318 armed slaves, he helped one side or the other in their constant inter-city wars. As his herds grew and multiplied he became a wealthy and influential man, to be honoured by the native kings, or chiefs, as a prince. He occupied the Great Tent, which also served as the centre for judgment, and here also the food rations were served out. In fact it was the head-quarters of the tribe, as from it came all the orders and instructions relating to the life of the small community.

As the flocks and herds grew and multiplied, Abraham and Lot separated because of disputes between their herdsmen, there not being sufficient pasture for all. After this separation, the possession of Canaan was again assured to Abraham and his seed by divine promise. Then Hagar, his wife's handmaid, gave him Ishmael, and later Isaac was born to Sarai. Circumcision, about which he had learned in Egypt, was now introduced, the object being to make this a mark of distinction between the worshippers of the true God and the Canaanites, the idea evidently being that it placed the former within a magic circle where no evil could follow them.

When Sarai died her body was buried in the Cave of Machpelah, which Abraham purchased along with an adjoining field, and there also later was placed his own body. Isaac now took his father's place as the head of the family. His twin sons, Esau and Jacob, like their father and grandfather before them, were also rich and influential sheiks, and lived much as do the Arab nomads of our own times. If this had continued there would probably have been little Hebrew history to relate, but an event happened which separated the children of Jacob from their cousins, the children of Esau, and brought them under the influence of Egyptian culture, to change them from being Arab Bedouins into a settled community.

The story is that Jacob had twelve sons, one being called Joseph, whom his brothers, through jealousy, sold to a company of travelling desert merchants, who took him to Egypt, where he became a house slave. Finally he rose to be the favourite of the Pharaoh. Thus it was that the house of Jacob, about the 17th century B.C., separated from their brethren, to have a destiny far different from the rest of the descendants of Abraham, because of the events which followed from the rise to power of Joseph, the Arab slave.

Famine drove ten of the sons of Jacob to Egypt, there to seek food, and then it was that they were recognised by Joseph, who now occupied the position of Prime Minister and Minister of Food. From this meeting, the children of Israel (= El does battle), the name by which Jacob came to be known, ceased being Bedouins, because Jacob, his family, his slaves, and his herds moved into the fertile land of Goshen, which is situated within the easternmost part of Lower Egypt. As they were of the same race as the Hyksos, "the Shepherd Kings", who were hated by the Egyptians for their oppressive rule, it is unlikely that they were welcome visitors to the natives, then under the domination of these Bedouin pharaohs.

It must seem strange, to all who read intelligently the story of this migration of these Arab Israelites into Egypt, why they were given a large tract of fertile land. It is quite contrary to human nature for a nation, with an established culture such as then prevailed in Egypt, to welcome people in their midst who were looked upon as barbarians. The reason, we now know, was because the Egyptians were then under Bedouin rule, and had no say in the management of their own affairs. Consequently this was one reason why the Pharaoh of the time of Joseph (perhaps Apophis) elevated this Arab youth to be his Prime Minister. Both were of the same race, and he welcomed the Israelites into the land, favouring them as no Egyptian ever would have done.

Joseph married the daughter of a priest of On (Heliopolis), but when he died the connection between the Israelites and the Court ceased, as his two sons Manasseh and Ephraim decided to dwell with their brethren in the land which the Pharaoh had given them as their own possession. In course of time the twelve families of the sons of Jacob expanded into twelve tribes, to become eventually, after the lapse of some four hundred and thirty years, a nation, much to the alarm of the Egyptians, whose hatred of the shepherds increased as their numbers multiplied. So long as the Bedouins ruled Egypt (1800–1600 B.C.) the Israelites were secure, but, when these intruders were expelled, their position changed from freedom to servitude, as, in fear that the Bedouins would again invade Egypt, and that the Israelites would side with them, certain precautionary measures were taken to secure the safety of the land.

The Israelites were placed under supervision, disarmed, and employed in public works, but, as they continued to grow in numbers, it was decreed that all the male children be murdered, the girls being spared to become the wives or concubines of the Egyptians. Thus it was hoped to exterminate eventually the children of Israel, but it so happened that from their midst arose a powerful leader who freed them from their oppressors, and, after many dangers and privations, led them back to the land of Canaan by the road their forefathers had come many years earlier.

We are told that Moses (about the 13th century B.C.), their liberator, was brought up by the daughter of the Pharaoh as her son, and, if this be so, he was probably trained as a priest at the University of Heliopolis, but, in spite of his Egyptian upbringing, he never forgot his people. Because he killed an Egyptian for ill-treating an Israelite, he fled to the peninsula of Sinai, where he entered the family of an Arab priest, whose daughter he married. In this mountainous wilderness, wherein lie patches of vegetation on which feed the Bedouin flocks, Moses dwelt in a tent close to nature, surrounded by the awful silence of these deserted stony regions, whence five granite peaks point upwards to the sky. Here he was amongst another branch of the children of Abraham, and his thoughts went out to his own people in bondage, never forgetting the land whence they came, and their illustrious forefather, whose tomb in Canaan acted as a magnet to his constant thoughts for their deliverance.

In Sinai he learned of Allah, pronounced by the Hebrews and the Phoenicians as El, originally the sun god, the outcome of desert silence ruled over by the ever-present sun, and there also he heard voices, saw visions, and dreamed dreams. So he abandoned the trinitarian Egyptian religious beliefs, worshipped Allah as his god, and, when the Pharaoh died, returned to Egypt to put his plans into practice. There he told his people that Allah, the god of Abraham, had appeared to him in Sinai, and revealed the name by which he was to be known by his chosen people, the children of Israel. From now onwards Allah was to be known to the Israelites as Yhvh, pronounced Yaweh, and now called Jehovah, meaning Rain Cloud, an appropriate name for a god in a parched and waterless land.

From a careful reading of the original text relating the contact Jehovah had with Moses, it would appear that Moses was a medium and Rain Cloud was the other-world man who controlled him in trance and was seen by him clairvoyantly. Who Rain Cloud was in the flesh no one knows, but probably he had been a priest on earth, as in those days only the priests were educated.

Whoever this other-world man was he must have been a powerful personality, to have been able, during his control of his medium in trance, to make such an impression on the people who adopted him as their tribal god. Once this happened, then for some centuries to come, the spirit controls of different Hebrew mediums were considered to be Jehovah, and thus the "forever-living god" was continually with them, in both peace and war, guiding them, praising them, scolding them, and making promises which were never realised. Later, as intelligence increased, and the Hebrews became less isolationist, when they learned that the earth was something more than that which comprised their own abode, prophets (the Greek name for mediums) arose who claimed to be guided by a more universal god.[1] Some, in fact, claimed to be guided by a spirit sent from God, which new designation of their control corresponds to what happened in Greece, whose mediums first claimed to be controlled by Zeus, or Apollo, but later by Mercury, the messenger of Zeus.

Moses is represented as a medium, priest and magician. Mixed with his magic we find stories which may have a psychic origin, but here we are dealing with legend and not with history. His intercourse with Jehovah on Mount Sinai makes us think of the stories of Zeus on Mount Olympus, and the story of the burning bush reminds us of one relating to Apollo. The tale of Moses and Aaron outwitting Pharaoh's magicians is typical of this magic age, and brings to our recollection similar incidents in mythology. Moses, like Jesus, was transfigured, as was also Krishna, the Hindu god-man, and, like all the mediums of old, he imagined that the voice of his spirit control

---

[1] He (the Lord) spake by the mouth of his holy prophets (mediums) which have been since the world began. (*L.uke* i, 70.)

was the voice of God.[1] All this, however, is quite unhistorical, and can be placed in the same category as all ancient mythology, which is the outcome of psychic stories handed down orally for generations, to be finally set down in writing somewhat after the fashion we now have them.

A pharaoh who knew not Joseph now reigned over Egypt, and to him Moses went, to say that Jehovah had informed him that the Children of Israel had now come under special divine protection, and that they must leave Egypt and return to the land of their forefather Abraham. To this request Pharaoh agreed, and the Israelites took their leave, removing with them the mummy of Joseph and all they could carry, including the jewellery, gold, silver, and clothes of their former masters. The route Moses led them was by Suez into Asia, and thence along the shore of the Red Sea to the wilderness of Sinai, where, amidst much ceremony and many imposing rites, he delivered to them certain tribal laws, which he claimed to have received from Jehovah in the clouds of the Holy Mountain. The same route was followed, centuries later, by Napoleon I and his army on their way from Egypt to Syria, and in both cases the high prevailing wind kept back the tide, and so secured for them a dry passage across the mile-wide sand bar.

Moses belonged to the tribe of Levi, and to the men of his tribe he gave the privilege of forming the priesthood, his brother Aaron becoming the High Priest. From Egypt, Moses took the idea of taxing the produce of the land ten per cent. to keep the priests in comfort. In Egypt, as already mentioned,

[1] This subject is considered at length in *The Psychic Stream.*

circumcision was practised, and from them the Israelities copied this unnatural operation. Likewise the form of worship adopted came from Egypt, the Ark of the Covenant being of Egyptian design. The priests adopted the vestments worn by the Egyptian priests, the only difference in their make-up being the fact that they wore their hair long, and did not shave their heads as did the priests of Egypt. A dried skin tent formed their temple, in which rested the Ark, the symbol of Jehovah's continued presence with his chosen people, its practical use being explained a few pages farther on.

Thus the Israelites, a rabble of field slaves, started on their journey to Canaan, which they called the Promised Land, the Ark always being carried in front of this great motley throng when on the march. Over a stony waterless desert they wearily plodded on, suffering much privation, and being dependent on manna, a sticky substance which exudes from a desert shrub. Quite defenceless, as they were entirely lacking in the use of weapons, they arrived at the borders of Canaan, to find a well-armed people living in walled cities ready to resist their further approach. This was something quite unforeseen, as their zealous devout leader had given them no warning of resistance, having led them to expect a vacant land awaiting their occupation.

So both Moses and Jehovah received much abuse, and some suggested returning to Egypt, but, before a decision was reached, the Canaanites drove them back into the wilderness, where they wandered as Bedouins for forty years. There they grew out of their slave mentality, and, under hardship, became fierce warriors.

Massacre and theft became part of their everyday life, the conquest of Canaan being the object for which every man was trained. Moses meantime had died, and, in his place, arose Joshua, a man of war, both fierce and cruel, whose savagery and barbarities were quite in keeping with the instructions Moses declared he had received from Jehovah, on the method his chosen people were to employ in their conquest of Canaan.

It is quite clear that to the Israelites, Jehovah was no more than an invisible super-man, and this explains why throughout the Hebrew scriptures he is endowed with human characteristics. Therein we read that he had arms, hands, feet, ears, nose, mouth, and behaved in quite a human fashion. The reason for this anthropomorphic conception was because clair-voyants saw the etheric bodies of those who had passed on, to whom they gave the name of gods. Most nations worshipped these beings, over whom some believed a supreme being reigned, but the Hebrews in time directed their worship to one god only, who, to them, was the only god as he had taken them under his direct protection. So Jehovah took the place occupied by the gods worshipped by the surrounding nations, though he retained his human attributes, and in all the expressions and deeds attributed to him he was very much a man.

Doubtless the Hebrews also associated him with nature, as in those days each god had his place in the natural economy, but the tribal gods were more than producers of rain, wind and all the other functions of nature. They went with their chosen people into battle, and received the praise or blame according to its outcome. The Hebrews believed that Jehovah

travelled with them and lived in the sacred tent, that
he walked about the camp at night, and was particular
about it being kept clean and tidy. If properly fed,
and all went well, he was pleased with his people,
but defeat, pestilence and famine were his
punishments.

He had all the failings of mankind, and flew into
violent and sudden rage, ordering the murder and
massacre of those he called his enemies. He was
subject to all the vices of the Bedouin, such as petty
theft, and he even employed angels to tell lies. On the
other hand he had the Bedouin's virtues, hating
adultery, being hospitable to strangers, and charitable
to the poor. In Jehovah we find the reflection of the
character of the Hebrew people, and the utterances of
the tribe's oracle, or medium, were transformed by the
priests, as was the practice everywhere in these days,
into the language the people could understand. The
priests, very naturally, made certain that their interpretation of what the god said was in accordance with their
own policy and desires.

The Philistines lived on the coast, the Arabs
wandered over the upland pasture lands of the interior, and in between dwelt a race of farmers and
traders, whose towns and villages were placed on the
top of rising ground, from which sloped rich valleys
planted with vines. These the Israelites called
Canaanites, or lowlanders, their army being composed
of cavalry and iron chariots. Against them, and the
Philistines, who were probably an Aryan people, the
Israelites could make little headway, because they had
neither horses nor chariots. But Joshua succeeded in
expelling the Arab shepherds from the entire central

plateau, and took their land, upon which the Chosen People settled down to become a nation.

This region became known as Palestine, the Israelites becoming a pastoral and agricultural people, each tribe being ruled by a sheik. They were still very primitive, as they had as yet no knowledge of the use of metals, stone knives being used for their circumcision operations, and for killing their sacrifices. At Shiloh they erected their sacred tent, or House of God, where dwelt Jehovah, and there came all the tribes each year to sacrifice, and, by dance and prayer, give thanks for their deliverance from Egyptian bondage. In the Holy of Holies of this simple temple sat the tribe's medium on special occasions, the High Priest only having access to this sacred séance room, where it was believed Jehovah controlled the medium and spoke through him when in trance. At times supernormal voices spoke, a phenomenon which is today called the Direct Voice, and the Ark of the Covenant, a specially constructed box, copied from Egypt, was probably the cabinet in which the psychic power given off by the medium concentrated, a similar erection being in use in séance rooms of the present day.[1]

Mediums, or prophets, are natural products. At times they are plentiful and at others scarce. Mediumship is both a biological and psychological condition, entirely dependent on the make-up of the human body. In one way mediums are oddities of nature, their etheric bodies not being normally connected with their

[1] The author's experience of the Direct Voice, and a scientific explanation of how voices speak apparently from the void, is to be found in his book *On the Edge of the Etheric.*

physical bodies. Consequently they relapse into trance, which is the effect on their consciousness of a further loosening of this contact. This permits certain psychic phenomena to occur, one being that a temporary control can be taken of their physical vocal organs by those who have passed over from this earth into the etheric order surrounding and interpenetrating our world. This fact has had its influence on history to a much greater extent· than is generally thought, but, so far as the Israelites were concerned, the effect was to displace Jehovah from time to time in the affections of his people.

When mediums were not to be found, the other-world man, who was called Jehovah, could not communicate with his priests on earth, and so the people forsook him and worshipped Baal, the god of the Canaanites, the giver of corn, wine and oil. The Babylonians called this god Bel, meaning the Son of God, the Greeks naming him Dionysus,[1] and, as the Israelites increased their control over the land, the worship of Baal became merged into that of Jehovah. Hence arose a certain syncretism between Baal and Jehovah which had not been overcome up to the time of Hosea, but, whenever mediums increased in number, Jehovah's position was re-established, so much so that the time came when the priesthood became so powerful that they could dispense altogether with mediumship. Later developed the conflict between the priests and the prophets (mediums), the same development as took place in early Christian

---

[1] When we come to Chapter VII we shall discover that the beliefs surrounding Dionysus contributed to a considerable degree in producing the Christian religion.

times, as we shall later discover. Psychic phenomena, produced through mediums, have been the cause of every religion, to be abandoned later in favour of ceremonial, rites and beliefs when the religion became established on tradition.

(2) THE RISE AND FALL OF THE KINGDOM OF ISRAEL.

A thousand years have passed since Abraham arrived in the land of Canaan from his home in Ur of the Chaldees, and now we find a branch of his family fully blossomed into a young nation, with a destiny which few other communities were to experience. Its choice of location was unfortunate, as it placed itself right in the middle of the highway between Europe and Africa. Its situation was just as dangerous as is that of Belgium, the battlefield of Europe, and in the centuries to come Palestine was to bear the full brunt of contending armies, either intent on its conquest or on a passage through from both north and south.

If we are to understand world history aright, let us always keep in mind, not only the geographical situation of Palestine, but also the situation of those lands we now call the Middle East, the door for Europe to India and the Far East. Here countless battles have been fought, because the nation which dominated the Middle East held a powerful strategic position. This we clearly realise today, and Britain, which has held the key for the last two hundred years, because of her naval supremacy, fears Russian penetration by way of Turkey and Persia. Consequently

in years gone by she bolstered up the tottering Otto-
man Empire, and was involved in the tragic Crimean
War. To prevent France holding the door she fought
Napoleon in Egypt, and resented her building the
Suez Canal, though Britain's bolder policy eventually
secured its control and the retiral of France from
Egypt. Truly the Middle East has played a vital
part in history, and this should be remembered.

The implicit faith of the Israelites in Jehovah, and
that he was guiding them through their national
oracle, or medium, preserved them as a nation, the
Levitical priesthood, who travelled throughout the
land like mendicant friars, acting as a strong bond of
union between the different tribes. This, however,
did not prevent inter-tribal conflicts, of which their
enemies took full advantage, to conquer them at
times, until a leader arose to restore to them again
their independence.

After Moses, the name of Joshua stands out as
that of their greatest hero, others being Barak and
that brave woman Deborah, the Joan of Arc of the
Israelites, who, guided by a voice, finally conquered
the Canaanites. Then comes Gideon, who conquered the Midianites, and now we come to the time,
about 1150 B.C., when another leader arose, to become
the undisputed authority throughout the land.

Samuel secured the office of High Priest, and combined it with that of Judge, his claim to these two
offices being that it was the will of Jehovah. Here
again a careful reading of this story in the original
language of the Hebrew scriptures reveals that
Samuel was a medium, and doubtless his psychic
powers increased his authority and the respect in

which he was held by the people. He wielded power equal to that of the Pope in the Middle Ages, and this authority he would have handed down to his sons had they not been so disreputable. The Israelites were then a vassal state, the Philistines being their overlords, and to Samuel is due the distinction of uniting the nation, and lighting the fire of liberty which burned so fiercely that the people demanded a king to lead them to national independence.

By the combined will of the people, Saul (1095–1055 B.C.) was elected king, an appointment which was much against the wish of Samuel, who resented having to relinquish his temporal power. He however anointed the young soldier, believing that he would still retain his authority, because of the fact that he was the accepted mouthpiece of Jehovah. Saul, however, also proved himself to be a god-inspired man, and, when in trance, to be as much in contact with the other-world man, who was known by the name of Jehovah, as was Samuel. Consequently he displaced Samuel, and took over the office of High Priest, Samuel being forced to retire into private life. Saul raised the tribe of Judah to the position it ever afterwards occupied, as the leading force in Israel, to become eventually the sole representative of the Children of Israel.

Saul conquered the Philistines, and regained for the nation its independence, but an equally brilliant soldier remained his rival throughout the remainder of his reign. David, of the tribe of Judah, was privately anointed King in Saul's lifetime, but, because he was the hero of the people, Saul's hatred and persecution increased against him. To secure his own safety David took refuge in the wilderness of Judea, where he lived the life of a bandit, in company with all the scoundrels and brigands of the land. From the cave of Adullam he, and his fellow criminals, sallied forth to rob the Hebrew farmers and secure their possessions by means of blackmail, cutting the throats of all who would not pay. None who resisted was spared alive—men, women, and children being massacred wholesale.

Just as the Arabs never commit a crime without first praying to Allah for help and guidance, so David, a deeply devout man, always asked the help of Jehovah before setting out on his plundering expeditions. Finally, he and his robber band were forced out of their stronghold, when they transferred their services to the Philistines, the enemies of their country. By them they were well received, the town of Ziglag being given to them as their residence. Here David continued his pillaging expeditions, blackmailing and murdering all who would not pay the price demanded. With the Philistines he marched against Judah, and, when Saul and his three sons fell in the Battle of Mount Gilboa, David began war against Ishbosheth, the remaining son of Saul, who had been declared king.

Though the other eleven tribes accepted the new king, David defied the nation, and, with the support of his robber band, commenced civil war. Ishbosheth was murdered, and then the elders of Israel offered the crown to David (1055–1015 B.C.), who quelled all rebellious elements, and set about the conquest of his past friends, the Philistines. What Saul began David successfully completed. Jerusalem, which had retained its independence for four hundred years, was the first city to be conquered, and then came the submission of the Philistines everywhere. Next followed the defeat of the Canaanites, who lived in the lowlands. Then the Syrians, and the prosperous city of Damascus, were his next victims, and this was followed by the conquest of the Bedouin tribes who roamed the desert. Finally he subdued northern Arabia, and this made him ruler of all the land from the Euphrates to the Red Sea, a population, numbering three millions, being his subjects.

Thus did David establish an Israelite Empire, under the leadership of the house of Judah, but before he died he had to quell a rising led by his son Absalom. All his conquests were followed by the most savage ferocity. His cruelties were terrible, his prisoners being either burned to death, or hacked or sawn in pieces alive. It is difficult for us to believe, but it is nevertheless true, that up to last century fines and imprisonment were inflicted on people in Britain, and other Christian countries, who criticised the deeds of David, and the other Old Testament heroes, all of whom were considered to be examples of righteousness and amongst the elect of God.

Besides the foregoing, David was guilty of other crimes, the most noteworthy being the way he obtained his favourite wife by murdering her husband. Many obscene details are given in the Bible about David's private life, his well-stocked harem giving his chroniclers ample material to discourse on subjects which nowadays would not be permitted to be published in any other book.

One has only to read the Old Testament from start to finish, to discover how debased was the mentality of our ancestors up to the time of our parents and grandparents, to whom this interesting, but in places quite sordid, literature was their religious meat and drink. *The Holy Bible* to them was the direct message of God to man, delivered by him to holy men for the guidance of mankind on his pilgrimage from the cradle to the grave. This holy book was always touched with reverent fingers, and seldom opened without a prayer for guidance in its perusal. To them Jehovah was their idea of God, because they had the Jehovah mentality, but, when education began at the end of the 19th century, the minds of the people developed, until finally Jehovah was abandoned by all intelligent people. Still, the unswerving belief and devotion of our ancestors towards him reveals their mentality in a way nothing else can do, and explains why the Christian era was an age of crime and bloodshed such as has not been equalled since civilisation began.

When David died, Solomon (1015–984 B.C.), his son, succeeded to the throne, and commenced his reign by murdering his elder brother, who was the elect of the people, and should have been the King. Next he threatened the life of the High Priest, deposed him from office, and then murdered his Commander-in-Chief. He was a typical oriental despot, murdering all who differed from him, but such was the position to which David, by his conquests, had raised the nation, that Solomon was able to make an alliance with Egypt and marry a daughter of the Pharaoh. He lived luxuriously and in magnificent state, Jerusalem, his capital, being surrounded by a great wall, within which arose new and costly buildings which overshadowed the filthy squalid dwellings of the poor. His palaces were built of ivory and cedar wood, and, as a lasting memorial to himself, he built a great temple to house Jehovah.

"And Solomon loved the Lord, and walked in the statutes of David his father", the consequence being that he built unto the Lord a great house with the cedar and fir trees he received as a gift from the King of Tyre. This place of worship and sacrifice was nothing more than an immense slaughter-house, as from its altars were sent each day to heaven, to gratify Jehovah's appetite, the spirits of droves of bulls, oxen, heifers, goats, sheep and lambs. This butcher's shop was presided over by the High Priest, who was Butcher-in-Chief to the Lord, and, while he performed his holy duties, he was arrayed in rich linen robes, embroidered in blue, purple and scarlet, over which was a breastplate studded with precious stones, and on his head was a golden mitre. Under him were 30,000 priests, or assistant butchers, who kept alight the fire of the altar, burned incense to satisfy Jehovah's sense of smell,[1] and performed the ceremonies, besides carrying out the bloody work of butchering the victims whose spirits were offered to the Lord.

The central theme in supernatural religion is the belief that the shedding of blood, which was believed to contain the life, propitiated the gods, who partook of its essence. Consequently we read of an offering "of a sweet savour unto the Lord" (*Leviticus* ii, 2,) and "the Lord smelled a sweet savour" (*Genesis* viii, 21)

---

[1] The use of incense in religious worship comes from it being first used to induce trance, to enable the men and women of the other world to make contact with earth through a medium.

and expressed his gratitude and satisfaction. Originally this read "the gods", to be changed to read "the Lord" when the Israelites became monotheists, but whether the belief prevailed in one god, or in many gods, everyone was unanimous that the appetites of the powers in heaven had to be satisfied first before they would confer their favours on mankind.

When, however, we rationalise this sacrificial ceremony, which went on everywhere throughout the world, what do we find? Believing, as did our ancestors, that the gods ate the etheric duplicate bodies of the victims, and, in return for these gifts, ordered affairs to the wishes of their worshippers, the matter was an elaborate business transaction, involving the handing over of food for services rendered by the gods. The truth, however, is far otherwise. The gods, either singly or plurally, are not supernatural beings with the powers ascribed to them, but men and women who once lived here on earth, and at death took up another order of life surrounding and interpenetrating this earth. There, because their etheric bodies are in tune with its vibrations, everything is just as solid and substantial as were their surroundings on earth. They did not need to be fed by the people of earth, their wants being supplied to them from etheric substance, as are ours here from physical matter, and they no more control the affairs of earth than we do.

Surely, in this fundamental religious rite of sacrifice, we are at the top of the pinnacle of ignorance, and one which has involved tremendous waste and suffering. Poor, stupid, hardworking humanity has given the tenth of its produce to a chimera, and supported an army of priests to no purposes whatever.

A great multitude of indolent clerics were thus fed and maintained on the labour of the people, and, if we except the waste which comes from war, there is surely no other folly more patent to the discerning eye than this waste of time, this waste of effort, and this waste of life and wealth. Besides all this must be added the suffering which has come from the belief that the men and women of the other world are supernatural gods, who require to be fed on the food produced from human and animal victims before they will answer our prayers and give us our needs and desires.

If we could get back to the mentality of those days we would understand so much better the meaning of it all. Theology, to everyone up to within the past hundred years or so, was the name given to what we now call Science. When we want a field to become more fertile we give it a dressing of manure, when we want good crops we plough deeper, keep the fields free of weeds, and kill off insects and wire-worms by chemicals. We also rotate our crops, because we now know that to grow always the same crop every year on the same land takes out of it the chemical ingredients needed for worthwhile growth.

Our ancestors, however, knew nothing about such things, which have been learned only recently as the result of observation and experience, but in past times it was far otherwise, as then one or more gods were considered to be responsible for everything that happened. It was the only way mankind could explain growth and production. So covenants were made with the gods. The Jews made a bargain with Jehovah, for instance, that he would look after them, and give them his undivided attention. Consequently it was believed that he promised to make the women prolific, send rain, make the crops grow, and generally take care of his chosen people to the best of his ability. In exchange for this attention, the Israelites, who believed that he was fond of the etheric counterparts of their animals, and the essence of their crops, promised to give him a tenth of all they produced.

It was a form of insurance premium, the priests being the agents who got as their commission the roasted carcases to eat, but, as they had to burn the vegetation to secure the essence, they did not encourage this form of offering. Consequently Jehovah was represented as preferring the spirits of animals to the essence of the vegetation. This explains why it was that "the Lord had respect unto Abel, and his offering, but unto Cain, and to his offering, he had not respect" (*Genesis* iv, 4), because Abel brought sheep to be slaughtered and Cain the fruits of the ground.

Religion was quite a materialistic affair with our ancestors, who, by supporting the Church, Temple, Mosque, Pagoda, or whatever name they used for their House of God, and making their offerings to the gods through the priests, expected to have rain when needed, fruitful wives, cattle and fields, and get back their divine insurance premiums in ever greater measure by increased production. Hence every country in the world is dotted about with buildings dedicated to one or more gods, each being the office where the people made their offerings, or paid their premium, in exchange for the benefits they expected in return.

Jerusalem, into which flowed so much of the

wealth of the country, was certainly prosperous. It was thronged with pilgrims who came to sacrifice their offerings, and with travellers intent on trade. Here came and went the tax-gatherers and the administrators, because Solomon took much greater pains than either of his predecessors in matters of internal administration. Disregarding the tribal system, he divided the kingdom into twelve provinces, over each of which he placed a governor, thus establishing a vigorous and orderly administration. He devoted himself to architecture, maintained a gorgeous court, and set up his harem as a rival to that of his father-in-law, the Pharaoh of Egypt. He achieved his architectural ambitions by the use of slave labour and tribute from vassal states, and with this he made Jerusalem an outstanding capital, his temple being his crowning achievement.

During his reign the Canaanites were completely absorbed into the kingdom, but the borders of the Empire broke away. Without resistance he allowed a new Syrian kingdom to arise in Damascus, and Edom also regained her independence. He imported into the worship of Jehovah both Phoenician and Egyptian beliefs, and greater intercourse followed with neighbouring kingdoms. So long as he lived he kept the people in subjection, but immediately on his death the Empire revolted and dissolved, as his innovations were deeply resented by the people who hated his form of government. Damascus had already gained its independence, Egypt broke her alliance, and Pharaoh destroyed Jerusalem and rifled the Temple. The Arabs again became free, and ten of the tribes of Israel, hating the tyranny of Judah, seceded, thus to establish another distinct Israelitish kingdom. Such was the result of the oppressive rule of Solomon, and the folly of his son Rehoboam, who refused justice to the ten tribes and threatened them with even greater oppression.

The ten seceding tribes, under the kingship of Jeroboam, some time about the 10th century B.C., occupied the northern lands of Samaria and Galilee, Shechem being their capital. The tribes of Judah and Benjamin, ruled by Rehoboam, remained in the highlands of Judea, Jerusalem being their capital, the Temple their place of sacrifice, and the Levites their priests. Neither state was larger than an average English county, and the history of the Israelites, as the northern race was now called, and the Jews, as the southern people of Judea came to be known, would not have deserved a special chapter, had their religion not been married to Paganism to produce Christianity, and profoundly influence the laws, religious beliefs and customs of Christendom.

The history of Israel, from now onwards, principally concerns the struggle for supremacy of the religion of Jehovah over that of Baal. Ahab, the King, some time about 850 B.C., erected in Samaria a richly endowed temple to the worship of Baal, though he still looked upon Jehovah as the national god. A hundred years earlier the gay-living Solomon, influenced by his many foreign lady-loves, had followed the same course, but Ahab found in Elijah a strong opponent, though the prophet had not the people behind him. It was, however, left to Elisha to bring into practice the threats which the fanatical Elijah had hurled at the head of his king, and, by subtlety and cunning, the entire royal house was destroyed. All the followers of Baal in Samaria fared likewise, waverers were soundly cursed and upbraided, and from that date no worship of foreign gods was permitted in the land. So the priests of Jehovah secured a decisive victory over the priests of Baal.

Jehu founded the second and last dynasty of Samaria, in the 9th century B.C., and, to guard his kingdom against invasion, he invoked the help of the Assyrians. These were evil times for Israel, because a frontier war, involving terrible barbarities, followed, and only with difficulty could Samaria retain her independence. Finally, under the guidance of Elisha, victory came and the frontiers of Samaria were made secure. Then it was that under Jeroboam II the kingdom reached its greatest height. A new Israel now arose under the direction of the prophets, when Hebrew literature flourished. Laws were put into writing and named the laws of Moses, the legends about the patriarchs and primitive times being written down and preserved.

Neither Elijah nor Elisha left any written work, and only when we come to the time of the prophet Amos, a hundred years later, does writing become usual. Still, in spite of this development in culture, the country was directed by savage customs. Women were just chattels, and treated as men treat their dogs, to be played with or beaten at pleasure. They could be bought and sold, and handed down, on the death of their husbands, along with his cattle. Incest was commonly practised, and parents could do what they pleased with their children—sell them, sacrifice them, or cruelly ill-treat them. Slavery was the general

custom. Art and industry were unknown, agriculture, gardening and the tending of flocks being
the only means of livelihood.

The influence of the Canaanites eventually encouraged trade and industry, that of Phoenicia having
introduced writing. Towns increased in number,
ports developed on the coast, money began to circulate, and all the denunciations of the priests were
unable to halt a certain measure of progress. Stone,
to some extent, replaced wood for houses, luxury
increased, and horses and chariots came into use.

Israel was now struck with the realisation that all
was not well, that a powerful enemy was about to
strike, and that there was danger ahead. At Bethel,
the greatest and most conspicuous sanctuary of
Jehovah in Israel, a multitude was assembled to partake in a great festival when a grim and serious-
looking man stepped forward to interrupt the joy of
the feast. Amos, a shepherd, now declared that the
Lord had informed him of the impending downfall of
the kingdom, as the cruel and blood-stained Assyrians
would soon be upon them to swallow them up.
This he knew, because Jehovah himself was going to
lead the hosts against his own people, who had not
walked in his ways.

This was something new and strange to the
Israelites, because in the past they had imagined that
Jehovah had always been on their side no matter what
they had done. To them no other nation counted.
They only were to inherit the earth, and all other
nations were some day to bow before them, but Amos
saw farther ahead than his isolationist contemporaries,
and the event which he feared was not slow in coming.

In 745 B.C. civil war commenced, and twenty-four years later the Israelites were easily conquered by the Assyrians, who made them their vassals. Thus began the disintegration of the northern ten tribes of Israel, to be continued by the Babylonians, Persians, Greeks, and completed by the Romans.

The prophets, beginning with Amos, kindled neither enthusiasm nor fanaticism. They swam not with the mainstream of public opinion, but against it. They were not patriotic, as to them Jehovah was now the god of the righteous only and, that being so, he could not only be Israel's god but the God of all creation. The ethics of the prophets somewhat destroyed nationalism, isolationism, and a narrow conception of God, and their writings help to raise the Old Testament above that of an ancient history of a primitive people.

Amos and Hosea resented the priesthood being an exclusive and national affair, and its purpose being only to serve the tribal god. Though the prophets were neither learned nor profound, yet, like the priests who broke away from the Catholic Church, to bring about the Reformation, they were in advance of the majority, and helped to lead the minority to an outlook of greater toleration and a wider aspect on life. Thus they helped to weaken the curse of priestcraft, an ever-running sore, which always festers on the poor and ignorant. The prophets tried to break the illusion about Jehovah, by putting before the people a more noble conception of God; the prophet Micah, for instance, expressing his philosophy in these simple words: "What doth the Lord require of thee, but to do justly and to love mercy, and to walk humbly with

thy God." Had religion been confined to this alone,
what a happier story history would have had to tell.

As just recorded, the prophetical warnings materialised when Sargon III, the King of Assyria, conquered
Samaria in 721 B.C. All the leading inhabitants were
carried off into captivity, and many of those who remained were absorbed by the surrounding people.
Thus ended the history of the ten tribes of Israel as
a nation, but Judea, being more mountainous, was
more difficult to conquer, and though Jerusalem
was next besieged it held out and barred the way of
the Assyrians to Egypt. Moreover, it was more
united, and, from the time of Uzziah, had maintained a
stable dynasty. Successive kings, from his time, had
ruled tolerably well, the most conspicuous being
Hezekiah, about the end of the 8th century B.C., and
all had manifested a sincere interest in the Temple,
which was the hub round which turned the entire
wheel of national existence.

Step by step, with the decline of Israel, did Judah
rise in importance, the man who was the outstanding
force during this period being Isaiah, he also being the
means of obtaining for the latter kingdom a period of
respite. The record of his activities is the history of
Judah. Fearing a clash between Egypt and Assyria
on Judaic soil, he warned the King not to call in the
assistance of Assyria, but this conflict did not happen,
because Egypt stood by while Israel met her fate.
Judah became a vassal state to Assyria, during
which time she enjoyed considerable prosperity and
thirty years of peace, largely due to Isaiah's wisdom
in keeping his country from interfering in outside
affairs.

Against the advice of Isaiah, Hezekiah secured the independence of his country, and the prophet could only utter warnings against the folly of the King allying Judah with Egypt at a later date. This caused Sennacherib, King of Assyria, in 701 B.C., to strike at Judah, and, after he had captured various outlying cities, Hezekiah, in panic, so as to save Jerusalem, again became his vassal and paid a heavy indemnity. The Assyrians now passed through the land on their march against Egypt, but, fearing the disloyalty of the Jews, Sennacherib now demanded the surrender of the capital, which was refused on the advice of Isaiah. This advice proved to be wise, because the Egyptians annihilated the Assyrians and Jerusalem was spared. Isaiah's wisdom and foresight, over a long period of time, certainly entitles him to rank as one of the greatest statesmen of the Jewish race.

With the passing of Isaiah, the priests, during the long reign of Manasseh, returned to power, and Jehovah again occupied the place of honour. Consequently the universal God of the prophets vanished from the minds of the people. The old idolatrous furniture of the sanctuaries was reinstated, and many new religious ideas were imported from Babylon. The old cruel superstitious priestly practices were re-introduced, and human sacrifice was offered to Jehovah. When the abominations practised by the Jewish priesthood were at their height, Zephaniah and Jeremiah arose to warn the nation of its impending doom, and, when the Assyrians passed through the land, on their way to conquer Egypt, the people took heed and carried through the reforms advocated by the prophets. Jehovah was banished from the land except in Jerusalem, where the priests attained their greatest power, and the Temple its greatest importance. Their tyrannical rule aroused the indignation of Jeremiah, who foretold the destruction of the Temple and the holy city.

Now the Jews were to share the fate of their brethren, the Israelites, because of their alliance with Egypt, as Nebuchadnezzar, King of the Medes and Chaldeans, came upon them (602 B.C.) from Babylon, and compelled their submission. When they refused to pay further tribute five years later, he captured Jerusalem, its most important citizens being taken captive, including the King. When those who remained behind revolted, much against the advice of Jeremiah, Jerusalem was again besieged, captured, and reduced to ruins, many being taken into captivity. Thus terminated, in 586 B.C., the Kingdom of Judah.

The exiled Jews were now scattered all over Chaldea, but retained their freedom, and were allowed to live together in families and clans. Though many adopted Bel as their god, Jehovah still continued to receive the devotion of many others. Then it was that these met together for worship on the Chaldean seventh day of rest, the Sabatu, which practice they continued on their return home, when the custom began of attending the synagogues to hear read aloud the prophetic writings. All the hopes and fears of the exiles were finally settled when Cyrus, the King of Persia, conquered Babylon (538 B.C.), and permitted them to return home, though not even the majority took advantage of the permission. Many had prospered in their new abode, and had no wish to return to the comparative poverty of their old home, which was by now filled by people from the neighbouring lands.

(3) THE JEWS, FROM THE CAPTIVITY TO THEIR FINAL DISPERSAL.

When the Jews first left their country, they looked upon their captivity as a punishment by Jehovah. When they returned, bringing with them the golden candlesticks, and other holy vessels taken to Babylon by Nebuchadnezzar, they expected the Messiah to appear to lead them to prosperity and happiness. Their expectations were not realised, as the Persian yoke pressed ever more heavily upon them, until their bondage was more severe than it had been under Chaldean domination. As the years passed conditions improved, and by 516 B.C. they were able to rebuild the Temple, a matter which was to them of supreme importance, it being their only bond, because they were no longer a nation, a Persian governor ruling the land.

Ezekiel, by his writings, opened the way for the monarchy of the High Priest, and the Jews ceased being a political community, to become a religious one, much as did the Western Roman Empire after the fall of Rome in A.D. 410. Farther east, in Babylon, the Jewish community were more happily placed, as there they were absorbing the traditions and customs of their adopted home. Thence came Ezra in 458 B.C., to arrive in Jerusalem with a large number of his compatriots, he being intent on reforming Jewish law, and its ancient traditions, in the light of the greater Babylonian wisdom.

This influence of Babylon on Jewish beliefs was further helped by the arrival in Jerusalem (445 B.C.) of a Jew, Nehemiah, the cupbearer and favourite of the Persian monarch, who was appointed governor of Judea. He and Ezra worked together with the common aim of reforming the *Book of the Law*, and reorganising the life of the community on a more civilised basis. This came into effect in 444 B.C., and Ezra's new *Book of the Law* can be looked upon as the Hammurabi Code of Judaism, though it still bore the name of Moses as its author. From that date to this, no great change has taken place in the text of this document.

The destruction of the Temple by Nebuchadnezzar evidently destroyed the old *Book of the Law*, which was deposited in the Holy of Holies, as we find in the Apocryphal *Book of Esdras* that the Lord instructed Ezra to rewrite it, to which he replied:—

For thy law is burnt, therefore no man knoweth the things that are done of thee—but, if I have found grace before thee, send the holy spirit into me and I shall write all that hath been done since the beginning. (2 *Esdras* xiv, 21.)

Ezra is just an abbreviation of Esdras, which means "help", and, after his stay in Babylon, he was well aware of the Chaldean stories of the creation, of the Tower of Babel (Babylon), of the Flood, and of the exploits of the Babylonian Noah. There also he learned their laws, and, with this knowledge at his disposal, he rewrote the *Book of the Law*. Consequently it does not astonish us that the laws he attributed to Moses were more or less copies of the laws of Babylon, the Jewish Sabbath, as already mentioned, which came into vogue in Judea after the captivity, being the Babylonian Sabatu, the Babylonians believing that on the seventh day after the creation the creator rested from his labours.

The captivity of the Jews in Babylon had the effect of civilising an otherwise semi-savage race. They went into Babylon a primitive people, and returned home tolerably civilised. A literary class now came into being, and Jerusalem became a city of some culture. Their laws became more civilised, and Jehovah evolved into a more merciful being. To find the level of culture and civilisation of any nation, discover the kind of god its people worship. From this mental creation judge the people, because man makes God in his own image. So we find that as the Jews became more civilised their tribal god likewise improved, so much so that some ceased to think of him as the god of the Jews alone, but as the creator of the universe and the God of all mankind. For this advance the Persian monotheism they had learned in Babylon was responsible.

Never again did the Jews desert Jehovah, however much their minds changed in their conception of him, and for this loyalty they suffered bitterly, to be finally dispersed by the Romans, because his instructions were that his people were never to bow the knee to a foreign monarch. Their fidelity to the law brought upon them all the curses the law had reserved for unbelievers. To them the captivity in Babylon had been Jehovah's punishment for their past disloyalty, and from that time onwards they resolved that their religion and their politics were one, a way of life which could not be divided into separate compartments.

Wherever Jews went, Jehovah went with them, and theological schools and synagogues arose in their midst. Soon Palestine was too small for this prolific race, and Jews were to be found in every city of the east. They were constantly rubbing shoulders with Greeks, likewise a nation whose country was too small for them, and by them they were called Hebrews, meaning "the people from the other side" of the Mediterranean.

As these dispersed Jews owned no land in the countries of their adoption, they became traders, travelling all over the east peddling out their wares. Uninterested in actual production, but very interested in the thing produced, and its value, they became experts in their knowledge of values and the purchasing power of the currencies of different countries. They became money-lenders, or, as we would say to-day, bankers or pawnbrokers, taking ample security in exchange for the money advanced. Their financial abilities, about which subject few knew much in those days, enabled them to become rich and influential, so much so that they were retained by kings as their treasurers and advisers.

No empire built upon force lasts for long, and the Persian despotism shared the fate of all which went before it. With its collapse, under the hammer-blows delivered by Alexander the Great, Palestine became part of his empire in 332 B.C. and, after his death, it had an ample share of the troubles arising from the partition of his conquests. In 320 B.C. it was seized by Ptolemy I, one of his generals, who captured

Jerusalem on the Sabbath because the Jews would not fight on this holy day. For a century the land was ruled by him and his successors from Egypt, through a priestly dynasty in Jerusalem, the most outstanding priest being Simon II (219–199 B.C.).

In the 3rd century B.C., a great dispersal movement amongst the Jews took place, an exodus which had very important historical consequences to themselves and the Gentiles amongst whom they now began to live. Hitherto the Jews had been isolationists, to whom only Judea existed. Their sojourn in Babylon first opened their eyes to their own ignorance and stupidity, and so the time came when they voluntarily emigrated to seek their fortunes in other lands. This event is known as the Diaspora, the time of the dispersion, and it was encouraged by the rulers of the neighbouring lands.

Consequently we now find the Jews everywhere in the Middle East—in Asia Minor, Syria, and Egypt, where a large community settled in Alexandria. Here the books, now contained in the Old Testament, including the Apocrypha, were translated into Greek about 270 B.C., to become known as *The Septuagint*, their translation being done by seventy men, and around this sprang up an extensive Jewish Greek literature. At the Egyptian court, and in the army, many Jews rose to prominent positions, and in consequence they earned the hatred of the indigenous population. As the Jews spread outwards, Greek influence spread inwards, so much so that the citizens of Jerusalem, for so many centuries fenced in by the Law, now broke down this barrier, and many welcomed Greek culture and literature, openly proclaiming their shame at their ignorance and isolationism, the High Priest even going so far as to advocate the complete Hellenisation of the Jews.

This remarkable historical event is well worth remembering. If the Jews had then embraced Greek thought, and abandoned the barbaric Jehovah in favour of the more cultured and kindly Zeus, the entire destiny of the Western world would have been different from now onwards. Why then did this pro-Greek movement fail? Here are the facts. Jason, the zealous advocate of the abandonment of Jehovah, and the adoption of Greek civilisation and her religion, had secured the position of High Priest by outbidding all rivals when this holy office, as was the custom, came up for auction. He overshadowed everyone else in his propagation of Greek culture, and it seemed for a time as if he, and his party, would completely succeed in raising the Jews to a higher and wiser outlook on life.

An event, however, unfortunately occurred to change the course of affairs. Menelaus, who wanted to turn out Jason, when the position of High Priest again came up for sale, robbed the Temple of its treasures to secure the cash, and with this he obtained nomination. Jason took this opportunity to raise the people against the priest who had desecrated the holy place, and this brought about an insurrection. Corruption and intrigue were open and unashamed, to end in Antiochus IV (175–164 B.C.), the King of Syria, then part of Alexander's old empire, falling upon Jerusalem, disarming the inhabitants with much bloodshed, and installing a garrison. Everything distinctly Judaic was abolished, and in the desecrated and partially destroyed temple, Pagan ceremonies were conducted, the great altar being now dedicated to Jove. In the country districts the altars to Jehovah were destroyed and Pagan ones took their place, every Jew on pain of death being made to renounce Jehovah publicly and worship the gods of Greece.

This wicked policy came from the advice given to Antiochus by the Hellenised Jews in Jerusalem, who believed that the peasants were ripe to adopt Paganism. When he found how ill-advised he had been, coercion followed—a hopeless method, as persecution produces resistance, so much so that his end could only be attained by making Judea one vast graveyard. Many made their escape to Egypt, or hid in the caves and rocks of the desert. A Jewish priest, named Mattathias, killed another Jew making sacrifice to Jove, and destroyed the altar. Thereupon he fled to the hill country, where he gathered round him a band determined to resist actively the persecution. From the time of his death, his son Judas Maccabaeus carried on the struggle, and after two years of bitter warfare (166–165 B.C.) he defeated the Syrians in four separate engagements.

Though the worship of Jehovah in Judea was now no longer in peril, much further fighting took place, Judas Maccabaeus winning every battle but the last, in which he was killed. For long Palestine was torn asunder in bloody strife, one side after the other gaining and then losing power, Jerusalem being the centre of the conflict, to be captured and lost more than once. We are well informed about this phase of history, because Josephus (A.D. 38–100), the Jewish historian, was at great pains to set down the facts about this long-drawn-out struggle in his work *The History of the Jewish Wars.*

Eventually the invaders were driven from the land, and Jehovah was reinstated in his temple in Jerusalem. Had wisdom prevailed, and the Jews been Hellenised by degrees, how the course of history would have been altered; in fact the story this book has now to tell would have been completely different. The belief in Jehovah has been a tremendous factor in history. So far it had been limited to a comparatively small number living in a petty state, but the time came when he was accepted as the father of the Christian saviour, and the one responsible for sacrificing his son to satisfy his wrath, because Adam and Eve had brought sin into the world.

Consequently the barbarous laws in the Old Testament were taken over by Christians as his divine decrees, and this very important decision accounts for much of the wickedness which has disgraced the Christian era. How unfortunate it was for the Jews themselves, and the Western world which suffered from their cruel laws and beliefs, that the opportunity was then missed to banish Jehovah once and for all, and replace this evil conception by Greek culture and its higher philosophical conception of life.

Disorder in Judea continued to increase, and this unrest forced the Romans to intervene (63 B.C.), to bring about a more ordered state of affairs. Jerusalem was besieged and finally captured, the Temple being the scene of the last fierce resistance. Judea was materially reduced in size and made a tributary state, the city being occupied by a Roman garrison. Henceforward Roman intervention forms a constant disturbing factor in Jewish history, as the struggle between two factions, the Pharisees and the Sadducees, continued. Neither side would agree upon a ruler who would be accepted by the nation. Finally Herod (40–4 B.C.), an Arab prince, one of the aspirants to the throne, was nominated by the Roman senate, and, after a protracted war, with the help of the legions of Caesar, he made himself master of Jerusalem in 37 B.C., his rival being beheaded.

Forty-five of the seventy-one members of the Sanhedrim, the highest court of justice and supreme council in Jerusalem, who had opposed him, were executed. He abolished the life tenure of the office of High Priest, and brought it under the control of the throne. Other important offices were filled by men from Babylon and Alexandria. By these and other means he broke the power of the Sadducees, his bitterest opponents, and drove them out of the political arena, to continue their old disputes with the Pharisees on theoretical and religious questions. Thus did Herod submerge the Sadducees, and elevate the Pharisees, his supporters, who enjoyed their greatest prosperity during his reign, but never did he wound the religious susceptibilities of the nation, though the people hated him, as he was the representative of a foreign power, and had overthrown the old priestly dynasty.

For some years he was threatened from both without and within, but after the death of Cleopatra, his dangerous enemy, he had the leisure to carry out some great works of peaceful construction. He founded cities and built harbours, he constructed roads, theatres, temples and works of public utility.

On his death in 4 B.C. all the old trouble started again. His kingdom was divided between his three sons, Judea being given to Archelaus, who, because of his cruelties, was deposed by the Romans. From this time onwards, for the next forty years, the country was ruled by means of procurators, the most famous of all being Pontius Pilatus (A.D. 26–36).

The Romans were much less oppressive to the Jews than were the rulers of the house of Herod, their principle being to interfere as little as possible with their religious liberty. Consequently when their nominee, Agrippa I (A.D. 38–44), became king there was peace and contentment, the country already having enjoyed under the procurators a period of considerable prosperity. On his death, government by procurators again commenced, this time to cause much discontent, which found violent expression under the lead of a new party, called Zealots, composed of both the good and the bad elements of the population. The unwise policy of the governor Felix (A.D. 52–60) now reduced the country to such a state of anarchy, that his successor Festus (A.D. 60–62) could do nothing to restore law and order.

Resentment by the Jews against the Romans deepened as each year passed, and when the governor Florus laid hands on the Temple treasure, to follow this up by fresh insults, their patience was exhausted and they drove the procurator out of Jerusalem. Agrippa II then became king, but the Zealots, flushed by their success, formed a war party which defied authority, and opened their campaign by murdering the High Priest Ananias. Matters reached their height in A.D. 67, when the Roman general Vespasian commenced the subjugation of the country, but before his task was completed he became emperor after the death of Nero, and to Titus was entrusted the work of capturing Jerusalem.

In the year A.D. 70 the siege began, and gradually, bit by bit, the city was occupied, though only at the cost of a terrible slaughter of the inhabitants. Those who survived were carried off as slaves, the city was levelled to the ground, and animal sacrifice came to an end because the Law forbade it outside the Temple, which had been destroyed. Titus took back with him to Rome the leaders and 700 prisoners, together with much sacred booty from the Temple, including the golden candlesticks and the golden table. From that time onwards the Jews have been without a national home, king, or temple, but no one could destroy the mental image each Jewish mind made of Jehovah. Mentally, Jehovah went with every Jew, to comfort and support him in all his troubles and adversities.

The Jews always regarded themselves as superior to all the other Israelites who sprang from Jacob's concubines, whereas they came from his wives Rachel and Leah. Later on they regarded the Gentiles as their enemies, and a people who were hostile to Jehovah. Moreover, they considered their brethren, who lived abroad, as outcasts, and that all Jews were sinners who spoke a foreign language or used foreign oil to anoint their bodies. The Jews of Judea only were Jehovah's chosen people, for them alone the world was created, and all others were but dirt and ashes in his sight. How the role has been reversed in our own times, the Gentile Germans considering that they had replaced the Jews as the chosen people, the Jews to them being the scum of humanity!

The Jews could not live peacefully under Roman rule, Jehovah to them was their only ruler, and this being so their pacification was impossible. All taxes were paid to the Romans under protest, and those who collected them were treated as thieves. Nevertheless the Romans permitted the Jews to administer their own laws, which were expounded by the Rabbis, or doctors of the law, and administered by the Scribes, but the death penalty had to oe approved by the Procurator or Governor.

The Sadducees were the strong supporters of the Mosaic law, and because nothing is said therein about heaven or hell they rejected the belief. Virtue to them was sufficient reward, and they held that its practice should not be dependent on the hope of bliss or fear of punishment. The Pharisees were the devotional section of the community, who spent much of their time in prayer, quoted texts, and observed the ceremonials of their religion, the Sabbath being to them a day of perpetual gloom. When they prayed they addressed Jehovah as "Our Father", and the best amongst them tried to follow the golden rule to do to others as they themselves would be done by, an adage which to them embraced the entire law.

The Israelites did not believe in a conscious after-life, Sheol, the land of the shades, being a state of gloom in which the dead lived unconscious of their personality. Only after the captivity did some Jews respond to the teaching of the Persian religion, of a conscious heaven for the righteous and a conscious hell for the wicked. Either from Egypt or Persia they received the idea of the resurrection of the body, the existence of a devil, the eventual destruction of evil, and a millennium of righteousness. From Persia they also received the idea of a Messiah, who would precede the conquest of evil to deliver his message of good tidings. Then would come great calamities, after which the earth would be regenerated, and the Jews, as the chosen people, would rule the earth in the name of Jehovah.

This idea of a millennium, preceded by a Messiah, was for long prevalent throughout the east, but, when it came to Jewish ears, they took it to mean that the Messiah would come to them, restore the Kingdom of David, rule in Jerusalem, eject the hated Romans, and set up the Jews as his chosen people who would carry out his will and pleasure. All the Jews would then become priests, and gather in the tithes from over the face of the earth, when Jehovah would become acknowledged as the God of all mankind. The Jewish dead would arise from their graves to participate in the pleasures of the new earth, and to the old heroes of Israel was allotted the important role of world government.

The unfortunate Gentiles were then to be the subjects of the Jews, and be allotted all the menial tasks; in fact the millennium to the Jews was very much what the Germans in our time believed was allotted to the Germanic race. When such a ridiculous belief could be entertained in the 20th century, it is possible to understand how these grotesque ideas could be accepted by the ignorant Jews of two thousand years ago, to whom Jehovah was just another Hitler who would lead his people into their inheritance.

So it was but natural that these absurd ideas would become embodied in their holy scriptures, and, later on, when some believed that the Messiah had actually come, these so-called prophecies would be used to support the belief. Consequently his followers concocted a pedigree of his descent from King David,[1] and envisaged him, on his return to earth, as sitting on the throne of his ancestors, a fantastic idea, which, to the great surprise of later generations, never came to pass. This belief that the Messiah had actually come was held by only a few of the Jews of Judea, it being those of the dispersion who were more influenced by the belief that the Messiah had come in the person of Jeshuah, called by the Greeks Jesus. These formed the nucleus of the new Jesuian sect, out of which grew Christianity, as we shall discover in Chapter VII.

So Jesus in no way disturbed the orthodox Jewish belief in the coming Messiah, and devout Jews to this day live in daily expectation of his arrival, when they will be recognised as the elect who had prepared the way for his reign of righteousness. Before the time of Jesus, men claiming to be Messiahs were accepted by some but not all of the Jews, and since his time others have been proclaimed, but the one their prophecies have envisaged has not yet appeared. With this hope for ever burning, the Jews have lived apart from the rest of mankind, maintaining the ceremonials which alone will fit them to be worthy of their responsibilities when the great day comes. Then they will be called upon to form the bodyguard

---

[1] This fraudulent family tree is clearly exposed in *The Psychic Stream*.

of him they term the Son of Man, the Son of God, the Messiah.

Once a year, as has been their age-old custom, the members of each family meet together to celebrate a sacred feast. A roasted lamb is eaten, and four cups of wine are drunk in remembrance of the institution of the Passover, the day when the angel of the Lord slew the first-born of the Egyptians, and the Israelites made their escape from bondage. This solemn ceremony, which ends with the singing of a hymn, has bound the Jews together everywhere over the past two thousand five hundred years. They have regularly intermarried, and thus maintained their race and their religion. Though they have lost their land, their temple and their holy city, they have never lost faith in Jehovah, their sorrows being but his punishment, and their joys and triumphs his reward.

The Roman emperor Hadrian (A.D. 117–138), who did so much to restore Athens, rebuilt Jerusalem but not the Temple. The city became a Pagan town, and only by the spread of Christianity did its fame return. After Constantine's emissaries faked the discovery of the Holy Sepulchre, pilgrims commenced to visit the city as the scene of the crucifixion and resurrection of Jesus, the erection of the magnificent Church of the Anastasis, dedicated in A.D. 336, again making Jerusalem a great religious centre. Under the Emperor Julian, an attempt was made to rebuild the Temple in A.D. 362, but an earthquake destroyed the foundations, and this was taken by the Christians as a sign from heaven that Jehovah was no longer the god of the Jews.[1] Consequently, on the death of Julian,

[1] Behold, your house is left unto you desolate. (*Matthew* xxiii, 38.)

the work of rebuilding was stopped, and the Christians laid God's curse on this exiled people, by putting into the mouths of the contemporaries of Jesus the words "His blood be on us and on our children" (*Matthew* xxvii, 25), a remark which was inserted in this gospel by some zealous anti-Semitic at a date much later than that of its first compilation.

It was unfortunate that Julian died when the Jews were planning their return to the home of their ancestors, as he had encouraged them in their efforts. The Emperor who followed him was a Christian, and he, influenced by the Christian priests, put an end to this last chance the Jews ever had of permanently recovering their national home. From now onwards this virile people have been wanderers over the face of the earth. Never have they forsaken Jehovah, though his promises have never been fulfilled. Instead of the Children of Israel covering the earth, and being the lords of creation for ever, as they believed he promised them, they have been harried from one country to another, persecuted, and hated by the people amongst whom they settled. If only they had abandoned their ridiculous policy of isolation, and intermarried with those amongst whom they lived, how different would have been their destiny.

Instead of this they have always maintained their reputation as a peculiar people by their right of circumcision, their customs with regard to food, their unswerving faith in Jehovah, and the annual observance of the Day of Atonement, when, by prayer and fasting, they believed that their past sins were forgiven. Believing themselves to be the Chosen People, they have assumed an air of superiority towards those they lived amongst, but with whom they never mixed because their religious beliefs, customs and habits kept them apart from the national life of the community.

Hatred and persecution have followed, especially as the Christians, in their own way, were likewise afflicted by the same feeling of superiority over all the other people of earth. The Jews, living as they do as a minority amongst those of a different race and faith, have, in consequence, always been the victims of Christian hatred, and until they abandon all feeling of superiority, and also their foolish religious prejudices, the future of the Jews will remain insecure and their happiness uncertain.

It is now abundantly clear that no homeland will be found to house the entire Jewish people, and that those living amongst the Gentiles must adapt themselves, even more than they have already done, to their present circumstances, by abandoning their hitherto rigid ban on marriage into Gentile families. They must cease to preserve their own nationality, and become absorbed amongst those with whom they live, until they cease to be a distinctive people. If they cannot do this because it means abandoning Jehovah, if to them religion and nationality are more than security, comfort and peace, then trouble will always be their lot, but surely increased knowledge will make evident the way of escape from an intolerable position. Jehovah must be overthrown, his false promises forgotten, while the consequent curses of the Jewish priesthood are ignored, and past tradition and customs are broken. When this is done, and the curse of ignorance is lifted, a gifted people will then become merged with Aryan stock to the benefit of all concerned.

In the 5th century, Palestine[1] ceased to occupy any place in the Jewish faith, and, with the elevation of Christianity in the preceding century to the position of the official religion of the Roman Empire, the position of Judaism everywhere changed for the worse. From then onwards Babylonia became its centre, as there, since the exile, a numerous and coherent body of Jews had continued to live. A native prince became the Patriarch, and under him flourished theological schools where the Law was taught. By now this centre of Judaism was quite detached from the Western world, though, for a short period in 614, the Jews again secured possession of Jerusalem, when their friends and allies, the Persians, were at war with the Byzantine Empire. Once more their hopes were disappointed, as, with the coming of Mahomet, Palestine in 656 fell under the control of the Moslems.

Jehovah, the god of Moses, was now finally displaced by Allah, the god of Abraham, in the land over which he had ruled for so long. Consequently what remained of the Children of Israel in these parts returned to the worship of the god of the shepherd patriarch, who, twenty-four centuries earlier, had left the neighbourhood of the city of Ur, to establish the people, who founded a nation, on the borders of the Mediterranean Sea.

---

[1] Called Palestine after Philistine, the tribe which occupied the land before it was conquered by David.

CHAPTER VI.

GREEK CIVILISATION.
(2500–146 B.C.)

Introduction. (1) *Aryan Nomads Become Known as Greeks.* (2) *The Political, Social, and Religious Life of Greece.* (3) *Greece Saves Europe from a Persian Invasion.* (4) *The Intellectual Life of Greece.* (5) *Greece is Devastated by Civil War.* (6) *Education Spreads from Greece Throughout the Roman Empire.* (7) *Alexander Conquers Much of the Civilised World.* (8) *The Decline and Conquest of Greece.* (9) *The Contribution Greece Made to the Christian Religion.*

LONG before the time of Abraham and Hammurabi, when civilisation was flourishing on the delta of the Tigris and Euphrates, and on the banks of the Indus in the Punjab, there thrived an equally advanced culture around the north-eastern shores of the Mediterranean Sea. This ancient civilisation, which can be traced back to the Stone Age, reached a high level as far back as 2500 B.C., seven centuries before Hammurabi ruled in Babylon. It was originally called Mycenaean, its remains having been first discovered at Mycenae, about sixty miles west of Athens, in 1876, but since then relics have been found in Sicily, Malta, Crete, Cyprus, and the islands of the Ægean Sea.

The remarkable ruins discovered last century show the high level to which the culture of these people reached, because they lived in cities decorated

with columns and sculpture, their temples and grave-
yards being adorned with sepulchres richer in gold
than any found elsewhere in the world. They were,
moreover, expert in weaving textiles, in sculpture
work, in the making of ornaments, in metal work, in
the production of pottery of all kinds and shapes, and
their ships are believed to have traded along the
Mediterranean coast as far as Egypt, in the east, and
Sicily in the west.

Their gold was worked up into heavy death-masks
and lighter breast-plates, diadems, pendants, armlets,
goblets, hairpins, rings, miniature balances, and an
immense number of circular plaques and buttons.
Bronze ornamented daggers, inlaid with gold, were
worn by the rich, whose houses were furnished with
articles of beautiful and costly design. Figures of
men, women and animals in gold, ornaments in
crystal and of amber, ivory mirrors and much pottery
also filled their houses. They worshipped a trinity
of gods, their religious symbol being a cross, and,
like all the people of the past, they placed many of their
most precious possessions in the graves of the dead
for their use in an after-life.

At Knossos, in Crete, the ruins have been found
of a great palace, which was originally constructed
before 2000 B.C., to be rebuilt at the acme of the
Mycenaean age. Stairways, galleries and fragments
of the upper storeys still remain, as do store galleries,
sunken baths, connected by pipes with reservoirs, and
a throne room. Much has been recovered of internal
decoration in fresco, painted plaster, relief work and
carved stone, together with a great variety of furniture
in all materials. Its size is so great that it is called the

Labyrinth, and it has revealed as advanced a state of existence as is to be found anywhere in the ancient world.

This Cretian-Mycenaean civilisation is known as Minoan, and was supported by the export of the articles manufactured by the island's craftsmen and its other resources, especially olive oil and timber. Wealth accumulated in the hands of merchant princes, who were also priest-kings, and they built for themselves these palaces, others having existed in other parts of the island. These great buildings were not only dwelling-houses but also factories, warehouses and offices, which accommodated specialised craftsmen, potters and glaziers, whose work went all over the Middle East, their accounts and records being kept on clay tablets. The people of the island dwelt in two-storeyed houses, used wheeled vehicles, which travelled over roads and bridges, and the ships which traded with the island were accommodated in specially built harbours.

Mycenaean civilisation was at its height around 2000 B.C. It dominated the Mediterranean, when there was an age of prosperity and peace unexampled in the ancient world. Doubtless these advanced people thought very much as did our ancestors during the Victorian age—that peace and prosperity were now their heritage, and that life would always pursue its placid course. They were the favoured ones of what we call the Bronze Age, when only the inhabitants of the rich plains and valleys could afford armour, the barbarian nomads in the northern regions being dependent on bows and arrows, spears, clubs, and their own bravery and skill. Nature, however, allows the human race little rest, and the cultured people living in cities were soon to find that life was no bed of roses, peace being always but an interlude between periods of violent upheavals.

Now we come to one of the great turning points of history, when the road on which man is travelling opens out to reveal fresh vistas ahead. Had he been wise instead of stupid, the increased command he now secured over nature would have been used only for the good of the race, but, as always happened, he found something he was not sufficiently advanced ethically to handle. Someone found the way to smelt iron ore, and this momentous discovery resounded right round the world.

Between the 14th and the 10th centuries B.C. the Bronze Age gave place to the Iron Age, an event which revolutionised trade and warfare, as did the Oil Age in which we now live, and as the Atomic Age will do in the years to come. The long rapiers of costly bronze, the huge bronze shields, and the bronze horse-drawn chariots were replaced by chariots and weapons of iron, thus democratising war. The nomad and the peasant could now afford the new armour, just as the craftsman could own his own tools. The comparative scarcity of copper and tin, which constitute bronze, had so far confined trade and weapons to the kings, princes, priests, and nobles, who made the common man their slave. Iron, on the other hand, is one of the most common of metals, and can be extracted from its ores by heat, combined with charcoal, as simply as the other metals.

Hitherto the lack of sufficient heat, the mechanical blast being unknown, had made smelting difficult, and iron implements scarce. A new process, however, was eventually discovered by a barbarian tribe living in the mountains of Armenia. For long they kept their secret to themselves, but, after their conquest by the Hittites, who rearmed their own forces with iron weapons, the secret of their manufacture became known. Efficient and cheap iron weapons and tools now became possible, to revolutionise warfare, crafts-manship, industry, and agriculture. Land could now be cleared by the peasants with iron axes, and then ploughed with iron ploughs, the artisan could have his own iron tools, and with iron armour and weapons the common man could meet the bronze-clad knight on equal terms. Barbarians, moreover, could arm themselves as efficiently as civilised states, which hither-to had been protected by their costly bronze armour.

At the beginning of the 14th century B.C. we are at a time of social and economic revolution when the barbarians threatened all civilisation with chaos. Instead of confining this new discovery only to productive purposes, stupid humanity employed it also for destructive purposes, just as in our day precious petroleum was wasted to destroy the labours of past generations. Plundering now became general, and tribute consisted of the removal of old wealth to new owners, new wealth becoming a secondary con-sideration. Poverty consequently increased, trade declined, and culture vanished.

By 1200 B.C. the lands of the Middle East were in the grip of a dark age as opaque as had ever befallen humanity since civilisation began, all progress having ceased, while culture and refinement were curtailed. When, at last, the midnight hour had passed, the

Mycenaean civilisation of Greece had been wiped out, the Hittite Empire, with Syria as its centre, had collapsed, the Assyrians had conquered Babylonia, the Nubians were the dominant power in Egypt, to be later driven out by the Assyrians, and the Phoenician cities had only retained enough of their old culture to be able to set to work to re-establish what they had lost. Fortunately the foundations of civilisation had been preserved, and when day replaced the night, the traditions of the past produced the new civilisation which arose out of barbaric ignorance.

By 1000 B.C. we find the beginning of a new age in which, during the next five hundred years, the losses caused by the nomadic devastations were more than recovered. The area of civilisation expanded, to reach dimensions greater than ever before. From Spain in the west to Central Asia and India in the east, from Arabia to the coasts of the Mediterranean and the Black Sea, Western civilisation had spread by 500 B.C. to such a degree that a world of comfort and culture four times the size of what had preceded it was open to humanity.

The story this chapter has to tell relates to the doings of one branch of the Aryan family, which found its way from Central Asia into the land we now call Greece. We shall read of how these Aryan nomads destroyed the ancient civilisation in the land they made their own, and how, from the ashes, they reared a better and greater culture which was to influence profoundly the most virile part of the human family up to the present day. They laid the foundation for democratic civilisation, established private enterprise, which led to an export trade of continental dimensions, increased the range of knowledge beyond anything hitherto imagined, and added priceless treasures to the world's store of wisdom. For these great achievements they deserve the eternal gratitude of mankind, but we must not forget that before they built up this new civilisation they destroyed an old one which contributed to what they eventually produced.

We have just read about the civilisation they discovered when they arrived on the shores of the Mediterranean. Here they found a way of life very different from what they had left behind in their cold northern arid steppes, but they mixed with these earlier gifted people whom they conquered, and those we now call ancient Greeks are no pure race, but the result of a blend of several racial stocks which together produced the more advanced Greek civilisation of a later date.

(1) Aryan Nomads Become Known as Greeks.

Greek history commences with the beginning of the Iron Age, when a plentiful supply of iron enabled the nomads to arm themselves as effectively as those who had settled down to manufacture and agriculture in the rich alluvial plains and river valleys. Everywhere nomads reached ever closer to the shores of the ocean in search of new lands for their herds, until finally the sea barred their further progress.

The people already living in the pleasant pastures, nourished by the great rivers, had always to be on their guard against those who coveted their possessions. Any slackness or weakness in their armour made them an immediate prey to some surrounding community not so favourably situated. War by now had developed into a conflict between nations, which had at their command considerable armed strength. Kings fought against kings for plunder, but, with the increased use of iron, their attention had now to be directed to preserving their kingdoms from barbarian devastation.

These barbarian nomads who invaded the west and Middle East became known as Aryans, and we have already read of their descent on India. Here we are concerned with those who reached south to the shores of the Mediterranean. Climatic changes probably accounted for this Aryan invasion, as it is now accepted that the climate of Central Europe and Asia, over the past ten thousand years, has gradually changed from being warm to cold, because of the shrinkage of what are now the Black and Caspian seas, which at one time covered much more ground than they now do.[1] As this happened the climate hardened, and the colder and drier it became, the vegetation was less able to support the roving nomads. What are now steppes and deserts in these parts are believed to have been once rich in growth, but, as this gave place to more arid conditions, the inhabitants had to find their food elsewhere. Consequently they thrust to the south and west.

Two groups of people have been responsible for

---

[1] Within a very recent geological period there was a vast fresh-water "Asiatic Mediterranean" of which the Black and Caspian seas, the Sea Azov, and the Sea of Aral, are all that now remain. The reason for this change is thought to be a break through by the sea at the neck of land now called the Bosphorus, which had hitherto held back this great inland sea.

the civilisation of half the world, the Aryans and the Semites. Many centuries before history begins those of Aryan speech were migrating into India and Europe. From the loins of these hardy shepherds came the British, Kelts, Germans, Norwegians, Swedes, Danes, Russians, Poles, Italians, Greeks, Persians and Hindus, whose ancestors originally inhabited the land just east of the Caspian Sea. They are quite distinct from the people who became the Assyrians, Arabs, Hebrews, Phoenicians and Carthaginians, now known as Semites, as these came originally from the land lying between the Black and Caspian seas.

Those who were to become known as Kelts first migrated west into Europe, to be followed by those who became known as Italians and Greeks, and then followed the tribes we know today as Germans and Slavs. The people who came to be called Persians and Hindus went south to occupy what is now Persia and India. All these people intermarried with the inhabitants already in the lands they invaded, and this explains the many different breeds. The Kelts and Slavs especially intermarried with the nomadic people they found in Europe, but the Germans, coming later, kept more to themselves, which accounts for the difference between the Nordic people and the other inhabitants of Europe.

One tribe of these wandering pastoral people, of Aryan speech, found their way down to the shores of Greece, and, because of their war-like qualities and abilities, they eventually impressed their culture and civilisation far and wide. Everyone should be well acquainted with the history of these people, as on their deeds and thoughts hinges so much of the story to be unfolded in the pages which follow. The great events of history are from now onwards largely determined by the Aryan people, who, at the time we have reached, were occupying most of Europe. This being so, the rest of our story, on to the present day, mostly concerns the deeds and thoughts of these outstanding people, who were brave and intelligent, but always aggressive.

These Aryans, as they penetrated west, and then south towards the sea, came up against the old inhabitants of the civilised Middle East, but, until ships were built, Crete was safe from invasion. Its peaceful prosperous form of existence was not, however, to last, as about 1400 B.C. Crete was conquered by the Mycenaens, and then, some centuries later, about 1000 B.C., the Labyrinth was destroyed, never to be rebuilt. Who was responsible for this vandalism? Either the Greeks, who were to be the builders of Athens, and those other Greek cities which were to become famous, or the Phoenicians, who were to be the founders of Carthage, which was to dispute the power of Rome some eight hundred years later, and finally fall before her repeated blows.

It is uncertain how this destruction came about, but we do know that from now onwards the Aryan Greeks, and the Semite Phoenicians, disputed the command of the Mediterranean, both having powerful fleets. From this time also dates the antagonism which remains to our day between the Aryans and the Semites, to flare up at intervals and be the cause of great conflicts and atrocities such as the Punic wars, the Crusades, the persecution by Moslems of Christians and of Moslems by Christians, and the long-drawn-out persecution of the Jews.

These Aryan tribes seem to have come south in successive waves to occupy the rich alluvial valleys of Greece, as, from their writings, three different varieties are noticeable, the Ionic, the Aeolic, and the Doric. They worshipped Zeus, and besides having a common religion their language was sufficiently alike to make them all known under the same name. Their poets wrote of the great deeds of their heroes, but this loosely knit ·mass of people did not solidify into a nation until as late as 338 B.C., when a foreign ruler, Philip of Macedonia, became master of Greece.

After destroying the older civilisation these Aryan tribes raised a new one, the influence of which was to reach to the ends of the earth. Undoubtedly the cause which brought this about was their proximity to the learning and culture of both Babylonia and Egypt. In consequence their history is the first chapter in the political and intellectual life of Europe. In our day we call them the Ancient Greeks, but they were also known as Hellenes, a name of sacred associations, connected with the Helloi, a name applied to the priesthood of Zeus at Dodona. So we speak of Hellenic culture and Hellenic literature.

Thus it came about that these Greek, or Hellenic tribes, settled down in the land we now call Greece, which the Romans called Graecia, and which the Greeks named Graikoi, meaning honourable, spreading out over the numerous islands which string out like a necklace in the Ægean sea. They settled on the coasts of Asia Minor, and sailed through the

Hellespont, their name for the Dardanelles, founding colonies all round the coast of the Black Sea. They also founded free, independent, and non-tributary colonies in North Africa (Cyrene), southern Italy, Sicily, Spain, and France, one being at Marseilles, which they established in 600 B.C. on the site of what was probably a Phoenician settlement.

Kindred races in the north had by now settled down in the lands we today call Yugoslavia, Bulgaria, and Turkey. Yugoslavia in those days was called Macedonia and its port was Thessalonica, now known as Salonika. Bulgaria was known as Thrace, and Turkey in Asia Minor as Phrygia. This, then, was the position in 800 B.C. after a various assortment of kindred Aryan tribes had migrated from the north into the Balkans, and taken possession of the lands of the previous inhabitants, who were too weak to resist. Just the same story as we read about China, Mesopotamia and Egypt was repeated in Europe. What happened in these lands, as the result of the invasion of other nomadic tribes, likewise took place in Europe, the only difference being that in Europe it all came about a thousand years later.

Thus arose ancient Greece, out of the ruins of a still older civilisation which is only today coming to light, and the story we have now to tell is both fascinating and enthralling. When simply told it reads like a tale, which is both dramatic and full of lively interest for those of us today who have just been fighting those evil things which wicked men bring from time to time upon humanity. The history of Greece is one of tyranny over the right of free people to live their own lives, just as it is the story of freedom becoming triumphant and good conquering evil. It is the story of how Democracy, Oligarchy, Autocracy, and Bureaucracy (all words which come from the Greek language) fought against each other, and how those men who were really great fought, at times to win and at others to lose, their battles for the rights of man. It is a story of a rising intellectual culture, never before enjoyed by mankind, which was to last for a thousand years, and be eventually obliterated by Christian civilisation, when Western culture withered under the blight of what historians term the Dark Ages.

(2) The Political, Social, and Religious Life of Greece.

Ancient Greece was not a nation as we today understand the meaning of the word, but a land made up of many separate states. Consequently there was a great variety in the forms of government, each state having the government it preferred. These can be classed under four general heads: (1) the rule of a constitutional king, (2) an oligarchy, or the rule of a small privileged class possessing the chief political rights, (3) a democracy, in which all the freemen of the state had equal rights and an equal say in the framing of the laws of the state, and (4) a despotism by one they called a tyrant, which meant a ruler who seized power and placed himself above the hitherto accepted constitution of the state.

The first form of government was the oldest, going back beyond the time of Homer. In this the king was assisted by a council of elders, and at times referred matters to a public assembly. Since historical times the king was replaced by a democracy or oligarchy, but, from the 6th century B.C. onwards, democratic government was the one which was most popular. Tyrannies were spasmodic and never lasted for long, the tyrants who secured power generally having the people behind them, following a time when an oligarchy had misused its power.

When we reach the time of written history, we are no longer dependent on relics and tradition to guide us about the past story of the human race. To Herodotus (484–424 B.C.), the "Father of History"; Thucydides (471–396 B.C.), and Xenophon (430–357 B.C.) we are indebted for much we know about Greece and neighbouring lands. The Greeks, by means of their alphabet, have left us a record which, if not quite correct in some details, is sufficiently so to enable us to know how the people lived in the lands bordering the Mediterranean, and also what they thought in the millennium prior to the Christian era.

After wrecking the old order the Greeks built a new one, quite different from any we have so far considered. Thus far civilised communities had centred round the god-king, the temple, and the priesthood, which, as time went on, grew into states and empires. In Greece there were no god-kings, as the temples and the priests performed their own independent functions, and, instead of these, the Greeks developed the City State.

There were in the early days three classes of society, the nobles, those without rank, and the slaves. The king, who was one of the nobles, was their leader and nothing more. The nobles, and all freemen, were the landowners and farmers, who engaged in trade, built and navigated the ships, and from them the official classes were drawn. Then came the other forms of government just mentioned. In the democratic states the freemen were the citizens of the state, and had the voting rights which were denied to the slaves.

Besides being of the same race, and having the same language, literature and religion, the Greeks had their common festivals, the Olympic (founded 776 B.C.) and three others, to which the freemen from every state could claim admission and partake in the sports, games and competitions. These created intense enthusiasm throughout every part of the country, and the man who won the coveted olive garland was famous for ever afterwards. His statue was erected in the public hall at Delphi, and he was received by his native city as a hero who had made it famous by his deeds. No honours could fit the triumph and for him the city gates were beneath his dignity, so part of the surrounding wall was taken down for him to enter as the conquering hero. For the next five years his native town basked in the sunshine of his glory, and its citizens were welcomed as honoured guests wherever they travelled.

So the gymnasiums of every city were crowded by eager naked young men training for the day when they too might bring honour to themselves, their kinsfolk, and their birthplace. As time passed the scope of the national competition widened, and national prizes were given to the man who wrote the best book, the most popular music, painted the finest picture, or carved the noblest statue. To encourage the zest for trade and the accumulation of wealth, the man who could turn out the best equipped carriage and retinue was likewise honoured. Dramatic entertainments, and the collection of works of art, were the pleasure of the rich, who spent little money on their wives, homes, or food, the market place being their club and business centre. There also the philosophers instructed their pupils, education in Greece being free up to eighteen years of age and available to all except slaves.

No people knew better than the democratic Greeks how to get the greatest happiness out of life. The way they rejoiced in life, and found the world beautiful and delightful, distinguishes them from most of their neighbours and those who had lived previously. Their minds were free to roam at will, no priests nor rulers, during her golden age, keeping the mind in chains. The democratic states made their own laws, and, if these were observed, no one was molested.

They were amongst the first people to live a rational life, their freedom from fear encouraging them to produce all manner of recreations and pleasures, they being the first to introduce national and inter-city games, sports and competitions. All over Greece every kind of game was played, horse races, boat races, torch races, chariot races, disc-throwing, so many, in fact, that they cannot all be mentioned. In freedom, strictly limited by self-control, obedient only to laws of their own making, these wonderful people stand out in a world of tyranny, injustice and ignorance, directing the human race to the road of happiness which only in our own days some nations are beginning to follow.

Besides the national games, which united the city states, the Greeks had a common language, and the people worshipped the same gods, the father of the household, as in China, being considered the family priest who offered thanks to the gods before and after meals, and laid aside for them the family offerings of food. The priests took no part in government, but were kept to their temples, where they conducted the sacrificial ceremonies. They were not a class distinct from the rest of the community, and were elected to perform their duties for a term of years just like the city officials. They continued in their ordinary occupations during the week, as did the ministers of the Apostolic Church before it became the Christian Church, its organisation being copied from Greece. They exercised no power as a united body, in the way they did in the east, and were to do again in the west when the Christian Church took over the role of governing Europe. Here, in Greece, we find the end of priostly rule, which, in Egypt and Mesopotamia, always took first place under the god-king.

The Greeks, on the other hand, developed a personal and not a state religion. Each one worshipped the gods as he thought right, and round them were woven myths, legends and superstitions. The most outstanding mediums, or oracles, as they were called, were maintained by the different Greek states, and they exercised a unifying effect throughout all the land. The gods were looked upon as beings with supernatural powers, and, when the people wished to make contact with a god, to ask for help and advice, they went to one of the two hundred oracles who lived in the temples and shrines throughout the land. Thus they discovered what they termed was the Will of God, just as the adherents of the Apostolic Church, at a later date, believed that the Holy Spirit controlled the mediums, who spoke in trance or passed on what they saw clairvoyantly, or heard clairaudiently, at their church services. The Pagans believed that those they called angels (Greek angelos, a messenger) were divine messengers, the chief of whom was Mercury, who was the principal of Apollo's messengers to earth, just as the Christians thought that the one they called the Holy Spirit was the messenger to earth of Christ in heaven.

To the Greeks the gods were very real and ever near to them. Originally they were their ancestors whom they worshipped, but later they deified important men and women who had lived on earth. Then came the belief that these gods had the control of nature in their hands, Zeus, their heavenly father-god, personifying the open sky in which he lived, "covering the earth as with a mantle", the sun being his chariot which carried him over his domains.[1] Demeter, the mother-goddess, personified the earth, the producer of life, Poseidon the sea, and so on. Their gods and goddesses were believed to live in the sky, much as men and women live on earth, with like desires and passions, and the same form of bodies, of etheric substance, as have the people on earth. Heaven, to the Greeks, we learn from their tomb-stones, was a very delightful place which they compared with Arcadia, the most beautiful part of Greece,

---

[1] All the world religions have their Father God who sustained the earth and his children. Jupiter, a corruption of Deus Pater, meant the same to the Romans as did El to the Mesopotamians, Amen to the Egyptians, Ormuzd to the Persians, and Jehovah to the Hebrews, to mention just a few.

and in this Elysium sorrows and partings were at an end.

All the phenomena of nature were believed to be under the control of divine beings, whom Homer in his *Iliad* and *Odyssey*, the oldest surviving specimens of European speech, made so real to the people that these epic poems were as beloved by the Greeks as nursery stories are by children. These poems, based on the accumulated traditions of past glories and valorous deeds, rich with the joy of life and the dignity of man, were the sacred writings of the Greeks, who believed that every word was true and inspired from heaven. Only when they began to travel did they find that they were false and the outcome of poetic imagination. Delphi, they discovered, was not the centre of a saucer-shaped earth, surrounded by a flowing sea, and the travels of Ulysses were imaginary.

No one knew what the stars and planets were, but the general impression in Greece was that they were divine and eternal animate beings, and, when a philosopher declared in the 5th century B.C. that they were separate worlds like this earth, the Athenians were both shocked and angry. Athens by then had lost her position as the champion of freedom, as, by her lust for power, and folly, she had degraded democracy in the minds of all lovers of justice. As freedom of speech was now considered dangerous, a law was passed that all who denied the commonly accepted religion were traitors to their city. Damon, the distinguished musician, and Anaxagoras, the gentle and dignified astronomer and mathematician, the originator of the idea that matter consists of atoms, were banished, and the noble woman Aspasia was impeached for blasphemy, to be saved only by the entreaty of Pericles. Socrates, however, was made to drink the hemlock, but, when Plato returned from his travels abroad, toleration, after its brief eclipse, had been re-established, and he was able to propound his opinions in peace.

In Greece, as in Christendom, it required a brave and outstanding man to lead the people away from the theological myths and legends into the realm of reality. In Greece, Xenophanes was the pioneer in the 6th century B.C., and he attacked Homer and all his works. As the writings of Homer were to the Greeks what the Bible has always been to the Christians, Xenophanes had to remove from his Ionian home to Sicily, where he founded what is known as the Eleatic school of philosophy.

This philosophy taught : (1) That there is only one God. (2) God is not a person but the mind which orders the universe. (3) God is the mental creation of each individual, as the people of each race and nation imagine God as like unto themselves, black, yellow, or white. If horses, lions, or cattle had a god they would imagine one like themselves. (4) God is beyond human comprehension. (5) There is a unity in nature, "the All is One and the One is God", and (6) no God came to earth to suffer, die, and rise again for the sins of humanity. If Serapis (Osiris) was once a man they should not worship him as their Saviour, Redeemer, or Mediator, but, on the other hand, if he be a god they need not lament his sufferings.

A very interesting parallel to this attempt by Xenophanes to raise the people out of superstition occurred in the 18th Christian century, when Voltaire followed in the steps of this famous Greek philo-sopher. Twenty-four centuries separated these two great men, but, in the interval, through lack of education, the people had made no advance in their mental outlook on religion. Voltaire emphasised the unity of nature and of God, and scoffed at Christian mythology, to be in consequence expelled from Paris and forced to find refuge abroad.

In the 4th century B.C. religious people of the Greek and Roman world were again roused to in-dignation by the publication of a book in 316 B.C. by another Greek philosopher. He created con-sternation and bewilderment by asserting that the gods and goddesses were none other than men and women who had once lived on earth. The author of this heretical book, called *Sacred History,* was Euhe-merus, his birthplace being the Greek town of Messina in Sicily. He made a scientific study of mythology, a subject which comprises all the stories told about the gods and goddesses, who came to earth and frater-nised with mankind, and he accounted for them all in quite a natural way.

There have been mediums since early times, quite sane individuals, on whose eyes and ear-drums im-pinged vibrations too fast to influence the picture-producing process of the normal mind. Con-sequently clairaudience and clairvoyance have long been known as psychic gifts, possessed by some who could hear and see more than others, they being able to catch vibrations beyond the physical range. In early times everywhere the people took these abnormal gifts for granted, and believed that those who died had the power to return to earth to be occasionally seen and heard. This was the foundation of Ancestor Worship, but, as time went on, these etheric beings came to be looked upon as gods, each phenomenon of nature being explained as due to the action of one or more gods.

This was the mental attitude of the people when Euhemerus told them that the gods and goddesses were none other than men and women who had once lived on earth, and that to sacrifice to them and maintain a priesthood was quite unnecessary and wasteful. Though he was termed an atheist, he is the first man recorded in history to find a natural explanation of psychic phenomena. His interpretation of this rare, though world-wide and age-old, natural manifestation is the one adopted by Spiritualists of the present day, who likewise have been cursed by the clergy just as he was. He, however, opened up a new vista of thought, as from his time to our own day there have been two aspects of opinion on the universe, the theological one that one or more gods order the heavens and the earth, and the other that the universe is governed by fixed natural law, the same cause always producing the same effect.

The priests, as well as the great unthinking majority, have always supported the theologians, and only within our own times has the scientific aspect become generally accepted. This is due to increased education, which is playing such havoc with all the old theological beliefs. Psychic science has made clear the origin of all the theology and mythology of the past. Every religion came into being as the result of the observance of different forms of psychic phenomena. Every religious belief, rite and ceremony, is based on the phenomena. Their origin was forgotten long ago, and only the effects remembered, but a knowledge of psychic science and ancient literature makes quite evident the cause which produced all the different world religions.

Freed from fear of the anger of a god or many gods, Euhemerus, and his followers, accepted a philosophy having the attainment of happiness as its chief aim. Intellectual cultivation, self-control, a calm and tranquil mind, cheerfulness, the avoidance of evil, and the striving after that which is good, they claimed, produced happiness which was the outcome of right living. This great and wise philosopher commenced an era of rational religious thought, which, but for the coming of Christianity, might have developed into a world-wide philosophy to the lasting good of all mankind. The Christian Church, as we shall discover, obliterated this sensible outlook on life, and clamped the gods as firmly as ever on the minds of its faithful followers. It produced a hierarchy in heaven consisting of three principal gods and one chief goddess, besides a great array of lesser male and female gods, called saints, to whom the people prayed, believing, as did the Pagans, that these beings ordered the universe and would make it conform to their desires.

Nevertheless, in the 4th century B.C., we are at the time when a few wise men made the great discovery that the universe is governed by law, and not by the dictates of the gods. We are at the birthday of the scientific age, which was to be suppressed by the Christian Church, but kept alive by the Arabs until some in Europe developed mentally to be able to throw off the blight of superstition, and again resume the work commenced by Euhemerus. This time we now call the Renaissance, or new birth, the rebirth of that to which Euhemerus first gave life, the rebirth of that which the Christian Church did its utmost to destroy, the re-birth of that which in our own time is known as Science, whose guiding principle is that the universe is governed by law and not by the gods.

The opinions of Euhemerus reacted on Greek mythology, in much the same way as the writings of two outstanding heretics affected Christian mythology many centuries later. Thomas Paine, at the end of the 18th century, and Robert Ingersoll, a century later, startled Christendom, just as much as Euhemerus excited the Pagan world, when they proclaimed that Jesus was not a god, but a man like other men, who had been transformed into a god in the same way as other men had been evolved into the gods of other religions. Euhemerus ushered in the age of scepticism to Pagan mythology, just as these two more modern sceptics did to Christian theology. His ideas put such an effective check on god-making, that from his day onwards only two new gods, Apollonius and Christ, the name Jesus received when he was elevated to be a god, were produced, both being evolved in the 1st century of the Christian era.

The freedom of thought and action, which generally prevailed everywhere in Greece in those days, were two of the principal contributions she gave to the world, and they also showed themselves in their form of government. The Greeks never coalesced into a kingdom, or a nation, as happened elsewhere. They were so individualistic, so independent in their political outlook, that each city preferred to have its own rule as a separate little state, which comprised the immediate country-side, and this continued until the time when Greece was dominated by Macedonia.

In everything pertaining to knowledge, art, literature and religion the Greeks were one nation, but, when it came to politics, the jealousy of one city state for another knew no bounds. This vice so weakened them that the Ionian cities were enslaved from time to time by Asiatic despots, because they could not unite against a common foe. They never trusted one another, as honesty in those days did not extend beyond the city boundaries. An oath, or treaty, with a neighbouring state meant nothing, and most Greeks could be bought with money, as corruption and intrigue were rife in every city. In our days we have reached the stage when people can live harmoniously as a nation, and this gives us hope that the next step will be a world federation of nations, trusting one another, because honesty and fair dealing will then have become part of the life of mankind.

Only in the time of great national danger did the Greek city states combine to fight a common enemy. When there was no danger they passed much of their time quarrelling and fighting amongst themselves. Great indeed as is the history of the Greeks, great as was their contribution in raising the mind of man to a higher level of thought, this blemish in their character must be remembered. Their Aryan heritage, which gave them so many other fine qualities, produced this aggressiveness, and brought in its train great material loss and sacrifice of life. To what heights might the

Greeks not have risen had they been only able to live at peace amongst themselves, and with their neighbours!

In the days of democratic Athens (507–404 B.C.), which name includes all Attica, all the free men in industry, commerce and agriculture had an equal standing. Property qualifications for magistrates were abolished, and most public offices were filled by election, every citizen being expected to vote, attend political meetings, take his turn on juries, and prove himself worthy of his freedom. Members of the City Assembly, magistrates, councillors, and jurors were paid for the time they gave to public affairs, and this meant that landowners, farmers, traders, and craftsmen met on equal terms, no preference being given to those who aspired to hold the higher offices of state. Marriage was a legal agreement, and not a religious bond, but women had no say in public affairs, their lives being quite secluded. At law they were at a greater disadvantage than the women of Mesopotamia, who, we remember, were more emancipated than the women of 19th century Christian Europe.

City republics in time replaced city kingdoms in some cities, while in others the King gave place to a form of government which bestowed power on the few, to an oligarchy, in which the strongest and ablest man took the lead. At times he was known as a tyrant, or turannos, a ruler who was more like the modern dictator, and claimed to represent the wishes of the majority of the people. Aristotle was in favour of kingship and against the rule of tyrants, but he was doubtless influenced by his loyalty to the King of Macedonia, by whom he was retained as the tutor of his son, who became Alexander the Great.

Democracy, however, became the popular form of government in most states in the 6th and 5th centuries B.C. In these days democracy did not mean government by all the people for all the people as it means today, but rule by the citizens of each state for the citizens of that state. All strangers, even if born in another Greek city, were excluded from having a vote. Some cities required that all voters must be property owners. Only freemen born within the city state could vote, the slaves had no vote, in fact the position was much the same as it was in England before the passing of the Reform Bills last century. These acts enfranchised the working classes, who, before then, were quite unable to influence in any way the government of their own country.

Nevertheless, the Greeks made a great advance in the idea of government of the people by the people, as they were the first to recognise that at least the freemen should and could govern themselves. If they had only carried their democratic ideas further, abolished slavery, and put all men and women on an equal footing, they would have been as advanced in their form of government as all democratic countries are today. Only this century has Great Britain been a truly democratic country, when women obtained the right to vote. So we must not criticise the Greeks, who were so much in advance of their times that they laid the foundation of the ideal form of government.

With the coming of democratic government to Greece the rich were taxed, and the poor citizen was maintained if in need. Only the citizen had any standing in court, and the disfranchised had to employ a citizen to plead for him. Every citizen between eighteen and sixty had to undergo military service, but in exchange for this they had their freedom. All had the right to speak and vote in the popular assembly, but this was only possible because of the limited number of citizens in each state. Each political party had its leader, but there was no government in power, and no opposition, as we now understand this to mean. Their method was to ostracise the least popular leaders, and leave the government in the hands of those the people liked best. To ostracise them meant writing the name of the least popular leaders on a tile, the Greek word for which was ostrakon, and these retired into private life for ten years.

What we have read so far gives a background to the political, social and religious life of the Greek people. The insular form of government, each separate state governing itself and going its own way quite independently of the others, has already been noted, and this disunity remained the weak link in the chain of Greek independence to the last. The reason was because Greece is so mountainous that communication between the different cities was difficult. Many of their cities were on islands great distances apart, others were in Asia Minor, Italy, and Sicily, and at no time do we come across one with a large population. Athens, the largest, had never a population greater than some 300,000, few others exceeded 50,000, and the rest had varying smaller populations down to a few thousand inhabitants.

The Greeks were only bound together by their

common language, religion, tradition and culture, and not by political reasons. These were not strong enough links when those states, far removed from Athens, found themselves threatened by their neighbours. In consequence we find these outlying Greek states falling one by one to enemies stronger than themselves, and the first to do so were the Ionian states in Asia Minor and the outlying islands.

So that the position may be better understood, it is necessary to know something about these foreign lands which were always a menace to the independence of one or more Greek states. Greece was surrounded by Aryan tribes which had also come from the north. The Macedonians and Thracians lived where is now Yugoslavia and Bulgaria. The Phrygians were in what we would now call eastern Turkey, and farther east were the Persians, all of whom looked longingly at the Greek mainland and islands because of their fertility and proximity to the sea. What is now western Turkey, bordering the Ægean Sea, then comprised the Kingdom of Lydia, whose people were a pre-Aryan race, its capital being Sardis.

The Greeks, Macedonians, Thracians, and Phrygians all spoke a similar language, but both in language and religion the Lydians were different. When the Greeks first arrived from the north they drove the Lydians inland from the coast, occupying places such as Troy, whose legendary heroes Paris, Hector, and others are so well known, but later on they were conquered, and the Greek cities held in subjection by Lydia. Lydia was then invaded by other Aryans coming from the north, and on two occasions Sardis was captured and destroyed by these barbarians.

Lydia was rich in metals, particularly in gold, and she is believed to have been the first to mint a coinage. Her kings were bankers and financiers, one of them, Croesus, being especially noted for his wealth, the saying "as rich as Croesus" having come down to us from that time.

The invention of what we today call money, or the production of coins to represent values, changed the entire economic condition of mankind. Before this idea developed man was literally chained to the land, and his only means of exchange was by barter. He could sell his cattle for land and his land for cattle. If he had neither he sold himself and his family in exchange for food, clothing and shelter, to become a slave for the rest of his life. With money came wages, and with wages came freedom, freedom to decide with whom to work, freedom to change his employment, and ability to save and make himself independent. Where money circulates freely there need be no slavery, but without it there is no alternative.

Unfortunately the development of the use of currency was very slow, and the Greeks and Romans were too ignorant of its value to encourage its circulation to the extent which would have made slavery unnecessary. Slavery continued throughout the Christian era, and it is to the lasting shame of Christians that it remained in Christendom up to the end of last century when money was circulating freely, thus making this form of labour, with its accompanying loss of liberty and cruelty, both unjustified and unnecessary.

Besides being pioneers in trade, the Greeks produced, by means of their alphabet, a highly developed speech and writing which influenced the uncouth speech of all the surrounding nations, especially the Latin tongue. Moreover, they used it to perfection when putting on record their thoughts, some of which have come down to us in their mythology that tells us, in so many highly imaginative stories, of the doings of their gods. Greek historians also wrote about the exploits of their countrymen in peace and at war. Their astronomers foretold eclipses and measured the distances of space. Their scientists were the pioneers in chemistry, physics, mathematics, biology, psychology and botany. Their doctors freed themselves from the age-old idea that illness and disease came from devils within the body, and laid the basis for modern medicine and surgery. Philosophy gave mankind a new and truer conception of man's place in the universe, and the poets and dramatists reproduced in words the thoughts and aspirations of the people.

All this became possible by the discovery of the way to write ideas simply and clearly on papyrus. We have already read of the means adopted by the Sumerians and Babylonians to record their thoughts. Their cuneiform writing spread all over the Middle East, but about 1500 B.C. some priests and traders selected twenty-nine of these characters, and agreed to assign to each a single phonetic value. Thus the alphabet was born, to be copied by the Phoenicians, from whom the Greeks, in the 9th century B.C., obtained the idea, which they improved upon by adding vowels, thus enabling them more clearly and harmoniously to express themselves. This they called the alphabet, which word comes from the Greek Alpha, their name for the letter A, and Beta, their name for the letter B. Likewise from the Greeks we get our word Bible, which means book, as at the town of Byblus, on the coast of Syria, the first book was produced in an alphabet invented by the Egyptians, the Greeks calling this novel production a biblion, a name taken from this town in which it first saw the light.

The invention of an alphabet was a great step forward in man's endeavour to remove the curse of ignorance. Step by step, as he applied his mind to his surroundings, he overcame his difficulties and improved his lot on earth. Reading and writing now became simple and available for everyone. Unlike the Chinese, who were so handicapped by their picture-writing, the people of the Middle East now could express their thoughts on papyrus with ease, and were consequently no longer dependent on the clerks of the priesthood, who hitherto had been the only people trained in the mystery of reading and writing. The new learning quickly took root, the Greeks, Etruscans, Romans, Phoenicians, and Arabs each producing an alphabet to conform to their speech, to such effect that by the 7th century B.C. some of the humblest Greeks and Phoenicians could read and write, an accomplishment that did not come to the masses of Christian Europe for another twenty-five centuries.

The discovery of the practical use of iron, and the invention of a simple alphabet, which greatly encouraged trade, as did the circulation of coined money, mark the division between the old Egyptian and

Mesopotamian civilisations and those which followed. Because industry by the 8th century B.C. had sufficiently adjusted itself to the new conditions, skilled craftsmen became so numerous that work could not be found for all, the mass production of good and cheap articles having satisfied the demand. These cheap utensils of daily use found their way into the centre of Russia, along the Mediterranean, and into Germany and France. They came principally from Greece in exchange for other articles, and thus we find the beginning of trade of continental dimensions.

Greece became an important export centre made up mostly of independent craftsmen, her cities becoming dependent for their foodstuffs and luxuries from abroad. In consequence her towns became cities, to increase in size at the expense of her agriculture. She therefore became dependent on her shipping, her ships grew in size, some being several hundred feet long, with three decks, and having considerable carrying capacity. Like Britain, since the beginning of her industrial age, she was able to support by her export trade four times the population she could have fed if she had been wholly dependent on her own agriculture. So her cities grew in wealth, harbours and lighthouses were built, not only in the homeland proper but on all her numerous islands, and in her colonies on the coasts of the Mediterranean and Black seas.

Thus did industry provide the citizens of Greece with many new comforts and refinements, including sufficient money and leisure to enable some to devote their talents to learning, to such effect that she became the recognised authority on all that pertained to knowledge. First iron, and then coined money, emancipated the mind, which produced philosophy, the forerunner of present-day science. Wealth and leisure are prerequisites to the accumulation and dissemination of knowledge, and, as they increase, so likewise do learning, the arts and culture.

As the Greek cities grew rich from trade and industry, slavery increased, the former craftsman relying on slave labour instead of on his own, thus bringing down to a low level the wages and standard of living of the free artisans. Slavery also reduced the purchasing power of the community, because the free artisans had less money to spend and the slaves none at all. Wealth thus became concentrated in fewer hands, and manual labour became degraded because it was looked upon as only fit for slaves.

During the Bronze Age of civilisation, the monarchs received the surplus wealth of the community who were their slaves. This they wasted in wars instead of applying it to create new wealth. Likewise in the Iron Age, which had brought private enterprise into being, the surplus wealth was frittered away in senseless conflicts. The Greeks thus wasted their substance in inter-city wars to such an extent that eventually their economic and social structure collapsed, and they became subservient to a greater power, which grew rich and powerful by adopting the wicked but age-old method of plundering its neighbours. Several centuries were, however, to pass before that happened, and meantime we have reached a chapter in their history which is rich in heroism and valour, and one which greatly influenced world events.

(3) Greece Saves Europe from a Persian Invasion.

Before telling this epic story, let us first of all turn our thoughts to that small country situated on the east coast of the Ægean Sea, called Lydia. East of Lydia lay the land, now called Iran, which, a thousand years B.C., was invaded by nomadic Aryans who grew and multiplied, to become known as Persians. By the 7th century B.C. they had over-run the neighbouring lands of Assyria, and a century later Babylonia. Part of the story is vividly told in the *Book of Daniel,* of how Belshazzar, the Regent, at a great feast, heard from Daniel of his approaching fate.

Other races, such as the Elamites, the Scythians, and the Medes, settled between the Euphrates and the shores of the Caspian and Black seas. For some hundreds of years they were all fighting for domination, to end in the supremacy of Persia when Cyrus I (558–529 B.C.) became king. He ruled over an empire which stretched from the frontiers of Lydia, in the west, to the Indus river on the east, and this became ever greater as time went on. We can well understand how uncomfortable Croesus, King of Lydia, felt with this expanding empire on his doorstep. He, therefore, determined to attack the Persians before they made ready to attack him. The Persians gained the first victory at Pteria (546 B.C.), and this was followed by another which was decisive.

Herodotus tells us the story in his usual graphic style, of how, after the first Persian victory, when they had followed up the retreating Lydians, Cyrus placed:—

all the camels which were in the train of his army . . . and set men upon them provided with the equipment of cavalry . . . and appointed them to go in front of the rest of the army towards the horsemen of Croesus, and, after the camel troop, he ordered the infantry to follow, and behind the infantry he placed the whole force of cavalry . . . because the horse has a fear of the camel, and cannot endure either to see his form or scent his smell. For this reason the trick had been devised, in order that the cavalry of Croesus might be useless. . . . And, as they were coming together to battle, so soon as the horses scented the camels, and saw them, they turned back away, and the hopes of Croesus were at once brought to nought.

Thus was Lydia defeated by a new device, just as France was in 1940 by the new method of warfare introduced by the Germans utilising tanks and dive bombers. So Croesus was captured, Lydia was subdued, the Greek Ionian and Aeolian cities of Asia Minor were freed from her domination, to pass under that of Persia, and then Cyrus turned his attention to Babylon which capitulated in 539 B.C. Conquest breeds the lust for more conquest, and, when Cambyses (528–521 B.C.) succeeded his father Cyrus, he marched into Egypt in 525 B.C., where he became insane and died a few years later. He was succeeded by Darius I (521–486 B.C.), whose empire now contained Egypt and Syria, besides all the lands eastwards to the frontier of India, and, in the west, Lydia and Thrace, the largest and best organised empire so far ever established, with good roads and an efficient transport system, much of which was due to his organising and administrative abilities.

Darius, after this great task was completed, next turned his eyes westwards, and the Greeks felt that their time had now come to lose their independence. After crossing the Bosphorus he, however, turned north instead of south, and, passing through Thrace, crossed over the Danube into Russia. His plan was to capture Ukrainia and Kuban, districts famous for their crops, and then surround the Black and Caspian seas with Persian territory. Hitler had a similar scheme for Germany, but could not realise it, as the Russians, after they were driven into the heart of the vast plain, turned and there defeated him. Darius was met by a Scythian army which, instead of fighting, retreated, with Darius in pursuit, adopting the same tactics as did the Russians when Napoleon made his famous march on Moscow. The further Darius went the more precarious became his position, as everything was destroyed by the retreating Scythians, whose horsemen harried the invaders on every occasion.

Fatigue and want of provisions at last made Darius decide to return, only to find his bridge across the Danube destroyed by the Greeks, who were very much in the position of some neutral countries in Europe in 1940 and 1941, when Germany was triumphant. They wanted to see the Persian Empire swept away, but were too afraid to make any move to help this to materialise. They destroyed the bridge, but retained sufficient boats on their side of the river to enable them to say to Darius, if he came back with his army unbeaten, that they had broken the bridge to keep the Scythians from crossing it, but had kept their boats ready to take his army across.

They hoped that the Persians would be so closely pursued by the Scythians that they would be destroyed before returning to the river. The Persians, however, slipped through the ring the Scythians had made round them, and were met by the Greeks with their boats and ferried across to safety. Thus ended the first great invasion of Russia by a would-be world conqueror, and the Greeks, by their cunning, staved off for a time the threat of invasion, because Darius went home with the remnants of his army, leaving the Greeks in peace.

This insane way of living can only be put down to the stupidity of humanity. Why are people so simple as to follow in the footsteps of one with the criminal type of mind of a Darius, or a Hitler? There have been dozens of others between these two monstrosities, as we shall learn as we proceed, but still nations follow some individual who promises them great things. Can history not teach them that these never materialise for long? If anyone ever gets anything out of the mess these men make, it is the criminal gang who pull the strings, whereas the mob do the fighting.

Darius left all his sick and wounded behind him in Russia, with thousands of dead, and then went home with regrets at his want of success, but his people accepted the position and continued to supply him with more men, arms and money. Ignorant humanity has always been dragged along by the chariot of war. Darius then established an army in Thrace and Macedonia, which so angered the Macedonians that they set about preparing for revenge, and this ultimately brought about the downfall of Persia. Other great events were, however, to take place before this happened.

Darius, undaunted by his failure in Russia, now decided to attack Greece, and this time he did not turn north after crossing the Bosphorus. Between his return home from Russia and his attack on Greece, conflicts on land and sea had occurred between the Greeks and the Persians, but these were just the prelude to the main invasion which took place in 490 B.C., to end in the notable Greek victory at Marathon under the leadership of Miltiades. After destroying Miletus, and slaying its population, the Persians commenced their attack on Athens from the sea. Everything had been carefully prepared, and a landing was successfully made near Marathon, some miles to the north, the enemy being guided ashore by a Greek, the exiled tyrant Hippias, who was promised the governorship of Athens when the city was captured.

Athens was in such danger that a runner was sent to Sparta, away down in the south of Greece, requesting aid against the common enemy, and he ran well over a hundred miles in under forty-eight hours. Before the Spartans could arrive, they being delayed because religious scruples prevented them from starting before the time of full moon, the battle was fought and won. The Athenian army of 9000 men attacked, and before their onslaught the Persians gave way, first on the flanks and then in the centre. Those of the enemy who could do so fled to their ships, some of which were captured by the Athenian fleet, while the rest, on being headed off from reaching Athens, returned to their home base.

Athens was now the centre of Greek resistance to

the Persian menace, as, though the other city states contributed their money, they provided few men to do the fighting. Consequently the citizens of Athens had to bear most of the burden which should have been spread over all the states, and yet they stood out against the greatest empire the world had so far known, and won.

Marathon was not the end, because the real testing time was yet to come. Egypt rebelled, and this distracted the attention of Darius, who soon afterwards died, to be succeeded by his son Xerxes (486–464 B.C.), he likewise possessing the criminal mind of all would-be world conquerors. For four years he made careful preparations, as this time he must succeed in an enterprise in which his father had so ingloriously failed. Herodotus tells us that he sucked the Empire dry so as to have a sufficient host to make success a certainty, and yet, like his father, he failed just as ignominiously.

Xerxes, in the year 480 B.C., with his army of about a million men, crossed the Dardanelles at Abydos by means of 3000 transport ships. There, on a hill, prior to the crossing, this arch-criminal seated himself upon a marble throne so as better to survey the scene, and gorge his insatiable desire for power and splendour at the expense of his stupid rabble of mixed breeds, comprising forty-six nations, who either preferred the excitement of war to the humdrum existence of honest toil, or were there under compulsion. He could see his army on land, his navy on the sea, and we are told that he then expressed himself as happy, happy at being at the head of this motley plundering gang, just as Hitler was happy when he surveyed his hordes of murderers before they ravaged Poland, Norway, Belgium, Holland and France.

What did anyone gain from the Persian campaign against Greece, or the German attacks on their neighbours? Nothing; only misery, suffering, and loss; and yet it will all happen again and again if the young of every nation are not taught history as it should be taught, and the practice of the virtues as part of their daily education.

Then Xerxes gave the order to cross the Dardanelles, and, when his army arrived on Greek soil, the Persian fleet of 1200 ships accompanied the invaders southwards, only to suffer heavily, as did the Spanish Armada, from a great gale. The Greeks retreated until they came to Thermopylae, a hundred miles north-west of Athens, where they made their stand, as there stood a high cliff rising from the shore, leaving a passage only sufficient to allow a few chariots to pass through. To reach Athens the Persians had to force this gap, and this was their undoing, because they could not employ either their cavalry or chariots in sufficient numbers.

This battle might have been a decisive victory, as the Greeks, with small loss to themselves, held the enemy at bay. A traitor, however, guided the Persians over the mountains, and they were thus able to come upon the rear of the Greeks. Fourteen hundred Greeks, under the leadership of Leonidas, were detailed to hold the pass while the rest of the army withdrew. For a day the gallant band held their ground, attacked on both sides by the enemy, but this was long enough for the main Greek army to retire to new positions. Preponderance in numbers, how-

ever, won the day, and eventually the Persians poured
through the gap and marched towards Athens, sweeping the Greeks before them.[1]

Athens was quickly evacuated, the people going to
the neighbouring islands and to Salamis. When the
Persians were finished with their fiendish work,
Athens, and all it contained, was a heap of burning
ruins. Xerxes then went to the Acropolis and was
again happy. Like all conquerors, he thanked God
for his guidance and help, as he, a Persian, was a
zealous monotheist. God has always been a god of
battles to the scoundrels who make their god in their
own image, and are sustained by the thought that
they are doing his holy will. Such is the superstitious ignorance in which live all cursed with a
mind bent on conquest. In our own times we have
witnessed this peculiar psychological fact in the War-
Lord Kaiser William II, in Mussolini, and in Hitler,
all of whom suffered from megalomania, the insanity
of self-exaltation and passion for great things, and the
belief that they walked in step with God.

Xerxes, however, offered up his thanks too soon,
as the Greek fleet was lying off the coast of Salamis,
an island opposite Athens. These ships, under the
inspiring guidance of Themistocles and Aristides,
fought the Persian navy and gained a great victory
over an enemy three times its size. This came about
by the knowledge the Greeks had of their own waters,

---

[1] This interesting old epic in Greek history was repeated in April, 1941,
when British and Imperial troops, largely outnumbered by the Germans,
held this pass long enough to enable the main British army to be successfully
evacuated from Greece. The pass itself is more difficult to defend today
than in 480 B.C., for whereas it was then a passage of 165 feet between the
precipice and the sea, there now extends a flat, and partly marshy, plain, from
1½ to 3 miles wide.

and because their ships were manned by freemen fighting for their own land and liberty.

Xerxes again sat upon his throne to watch the battle, and this time he was not so happy. One by one he saw 200 of his galleys rammed, sunk or captured. Most of the crews were drowned, and those ships still seaworthy either made for the shore to secure the protection of the Persian army, or sailed off in flight, pursued by the victorious Greeks. As the disaster unfolded itself before the Persian monarch his misery increased. His God had deserted him who had so recently offered up thanks, and sacrifices on the High Altar. He remained for some days undecided what to do, and then he removed himself and his army to the north, fearful lest he might not be able to cross the sea to reach his home.

Plundering as they went, this multitude of thieves, devastators, and murderers left Athens, to meet their doom a year later. Until then a Persian army remained in Thessaly in the north, in constant battle with the Greeks. Then at Plataea (479 B.C.), thirty miles north-west of Athens, the conflict ended with the defeat of the invaders, who had great difficulty in returning to Asia because the Greeks severed their sea communications. The goddess Athena, it was devoutly believed by the Athenians, had delivered the enemy into their hands, as the Persians, after the sea battle of the previous year at Salamis, were now afraid to put to sea, and drew their ships on shore at Mycale in Lydia. There they built a wall round them, but the Greeks landed and succeeded in destroying the remainder of the Persian navy.

Revolts against Persia by the former Greek cities

in Asia Minor now followed, and sporadic fighting continued for another thirty years, during which time they regained their freedom. Xerxes was murdered in his palace in 464 B.C., and never again was Greece invaded by Persia. Instead, the idea gradually grew up in Greece that an invasion of Persia was possible, Athens having grown wealthy by the discovery of a rich silver mine, but this aggression did not materialise until a hundred years later, when the Macedonians, led by Alexander the Great, brought about the downfall of this mighty empire. Until then its rottenness became more and more apparent, and, under Artaxerxes I, Darius II, Artaxerxes II, and Cyrus II we read of rebellions, intrigues, bloody crimes and moral depravity. This bloodstained confederation was ripe for a fall, and it only awaited nature producing a clever enough individual, who was sufficiently callous of human suffering, and had the means, together with the lust for plunder sufficiently developed, to bring it about.

It was not to find food to sustain them, or new homes, that caused this Persian invasion of Greece, as had been the reason for the Aryan nomads coming south. These nomads were no more than savage barbarians, wheieas the Persians were by now a civilised people who needed no new lands for their sustenance. The lust for loot and the fear of starvation caused the nomadic invasions, but for a civilised country, having all it needs, to invade another country just for the sake of plunder, and to increase its empire, is robbery combined with murder. We must, therefore, make a distinction between the early nomadic invasions, and the conquests of weaker

people by stronger nations who already had all they
required. Here mention is made of this difference
because it relates to the early days of man's struggle for
existence, and should have come to an end when
there was enough for all without the need of conquest.

These Greek victories over Persia are regarded by
historians as amongst the many turning points in
history, those times when mankind came to a fork in
the road on which he is for ever travelling. By some
seeming chance he takes one way and not the other,
a decision which has momentous consequences, and
yet everything that has happened, or ever will happen,
is the result of a cause producing an effect which in
turn produces a cause, and so on. Cause and effect
rule our destiny, but we are not quite helpless. Individually we can direct our lives aright if we think
the right and not the wrong way. Nationally this is
more difficult, because, if the mass mind thinks the
wrong way, the individual has to accept the consequences, the only remedy being right thinking by
everyone and not by the few.

The student of history is always coming across
those turning points in the story of the race, and can
realise how often the wrong road was taken, and the
right way was passed by, to the detriment of the
happiness of everyone. The value of history lies in
the fact that it makes clear mankind's past mistakes,
and points us to the right road to take in the future.
History is a sign-post, but such an aid is useless to one
who is blind through ignorance, and, unless history
is systematically taught the right way to everyone, and
remembered, the people grope along life's highway

without seeing the sign-post to point them in the right direction. It is to be hoped that education will some day so enlarge the outlook of future generations everywhere throughout the world, that the sign-posts of history will be followed, and the mistakes of past generations averted.

The Persian domination of Greece might have led to a Persian supremacy over Europe, and, if that had happened, what a different story history would have had to tell! The Greek victory, and the Persian defeat, altered the centre of gravity of human affairs, which moved west to the Mediterranean and beyond. Athens became the intellectual centre of the then known world, and, if Europe had then been ready, this city would have lit a torch of learning never to be extinguished. Nevertheless this important victory enabled Greece to leave an indelible mark on history, and erect a sign-post which lasted long enough to show mankind the right road to take. For a time it seemed that her efforts would succeed, but unfortunately they failed, and, from that time onwards, Europe, sunk in ignorance, floundered and groped for what the Greeks had discovered, only to succeed in finding it within recent years.

The position then in Greece was in some respects very similar to what we have recently experienced in Europe. Athens was politically democratic, and can be likened to the British Commonwealth and the United States in the war against Nazi dictatorship. Persia was ruled by a dictator who wished to have complete domination over the then known civilised world. Many Greeks, outside of Athens, then believed that a dictatorship was the only possible way to secure stable government, and so we find that Thessaly, a Greek autocratic state, and Thebes, which hated Athens and all it stood for, supported the Persian invasion of Greece, believing that a Persian victory would kill democratic rule in Greece for ever.

Wherever Democracy had enemies Persia had friends. Sparta, however, and the other southern Greek states, who at first were inclined to let Athens and the northern cities fight Persia alone, realised before it was too late that a Persian victory meant their enslavement, and so changed their policy. To the wise statesmanship of Themistocles (514–449 B.C.) this united front was largely due. He.it was more than anyone who saved democracy in these days. He was the Winston Churchill of Greece, and, foreseeing the danger, he prepared the Athenians, leading them victoriously through a hell similar to what Britain experienced in her fight against dictatorship.

All democratic Greece thus rallied to fight against autocracy, and their victory over a host greatly superior in numbers was the first instance we have in history of a free people conquering an empire of slaves. The democratic Greeks fought better, and with more intelligence, than the Persians, who, brought up to obey, and not to think for themselves, scattered at the first reverse. The Persians, like the Germans and Italians, could not understand their enemy's psychology, and, by their blundering methods, such as the destruction of the Greek temples, united all democratic Greece against them, just as the Germans united all the freedom-loving people against them by their barbarous methods of warfare. A Persian victory would have meant the end of democracy in Greece, just as a German victory would have meant the end of democracy in Europe, and perhaps the world, until the people at some future date arose to secure their rights. A Persian victory would certainly have retarded, if not destroyed, the intellectual life which at this time was developing in Greece. That indeed would have been a disaster, as it is the mental wealth which Greece has contributed to the world that has made this little country so famous. Her wars, her courage, her aggression are an oft-told tale, and while many lands can sing praises to their war-like heroes, the Greeks alone, of all the people of the ancient world, produced a mental revolution, which, in spite of a sharp set-back during the Christian era, is still the basis of our intellectual life today. The Greek classics, which, for a time, were smothered under a heap of Christian superstition, again came to light in Europe in the 16th century of our era, to bring about the Renaissance, and kindle once again the love of freedom and knowledge.

(4) The Intellectual Life of Greece.

The feeling of freedom from the danger of invasion which followed the Persian defeat gave the intellectuals of Greece the opportunity which war always denies. Great thoughts cannot be produced when men are always thinking of danger, of battles, and the atmosphere is loaded with hatred. True, the intervals of peace were short, but long enough for Greece to produce her immortal literature, studded with those deep thoughts which influence us to this day.

In the years between 600 and 300 B.C., in the in-intervals of peace, Greece made her greatest contribution to the mental wealth of the world, and if only she 'had put her knowledge to practical use in the form of inventions, as happened some two thousand years later, what might we not be today in our control of the forces of nature ? The plentiful supply of slaves made labour-saving inventions unnecessary, and so robbed the next twenty centuries of many of the comforts and luxuries we now enjoy.

During the harmony of peace, when the din of war had subsided, there sprang up a new type of literature such as the world had never before experienced. Greek scientists and philosophers then added new thoughts and ideas to the world's store of knowledge, and these became the foundation of our present-day science. Sculptors produced the statues which are still the wonder of the world, and architects erected those buildings whose ruins still compel our admiration. Every Greek city had its market square, which was used for public assemblies, its government offices, a theatre, a gymnasium, and a fountain which kept a great basin always full of fresh water. Her political writers and speakers laid the foundation of modern democratic society, and her philosophers taught men to think and reason, thus leading them away from the idea that every natural event is due to the action of a god.

In the days of ancient Greece, the land of Egypt was a live, active, pulsating centre, not a museum as it became in after-years. It was the university of Greece, being visited by all Greeks who wished to advance their knowledge. Tradition tells us that it was visited by Orpheus and Homer, and in Egypt Solon studied law and legislation. Pythagoras there first learned mathematics and Thales geometry. Plato went to Egypt for inspiration, and Herodotus for facts to add to his history of the then known world. In Egypt, the Greeks assimilated all there was to discover, to return home and ponder over what they had seen and heard. There in Greece these argumentative individualistic Greek scientists discussed everything they had learned, and, on the papyrus, imported into Greece from Egypt, they gave their own ideas to the world in better and wiser shape than ever before, because truth, and truth only, was their aim, and facts their only guide.

The historians of Greece told the story of the past from facts and not from myths and legends, while the poets wove it into rhapsodies which have immortalized her heroes and their deeds. Drama and tragedy reached the stage, and the people saw acted before their eyes human emotions, love, courage, hate, and fear, such as we experience each day. What we now call Science (Latin, scientia = knowledge), such as Physics, Chemistry, Astronomy, Geometry, Algebra, Mathematics, Engineering and Medicine, was born and nurtured in Greece. There men began to think, to doubt, to argue, to wonder and to reason as never before, and, as they did so, knowledge accumulated. At long last mankind began to discover something of his place in the universe.

Thales (640–546 B.C.) and Pythagoras (580–500 B.C.) were the first Greek scientists. The former was the founder of Greek geometry, astronomy and philosophy, and the first to attempt an explanation of the universe apart from theology, while the latter was the father of mathematics, besides introducing to the Greeks the use of weights and measures. Pythagoras, moreover, taught that the sun was the centre of the planetary world, and that the earth, which was a sphere, revolved round it, thus anticipating Copernicus, who confirmed the theory by hard incontestable arguments.

Pythagoras, besides being a pioneer in science, was the first man to place ethical conduct on a scientific basis, relating conduct to truth and error in mathematics, justice, for instance, being identified with the number four because it is the first square number, the product of equals, and so today we talk of a square deal. Thus he made conduct a question for study and investigation, and not one of mere platitudes as hitherto. Religion in his time had become corrupt in Greece, the ennobling influence of Orpheus having waned. Pythagoras was an ethical and religious reformer, and founded a system of ethical and esoteric philosophy. He was the connecting link between Orpheus, who, seven hundred years earlier, had founded the sacred mysteries, and Plato.

Pythagoras translated the thoughts of his predecessor into the intellectual requirements of his day. He taught purity of living, and the need of lofty aims and ideals. His philosophy was an appeal to the intellect. From his childhood he had a love of learning, and conferred freely from an early age with all who could satisfy his longings, always searching for unity so as to obtain a rational explanation of the universe. He visited Egypt and Babylon in his search, gleaned all he could from their wise men, and then returned to Greece to teach what he had learned. The Christian Church, throughout the era of its power, has so impressed Christendom with the idea that all the virtues centre in Christianity, Jesus being the first to teach love, kindness, gentleness, brotherhood and all the other virtues, that this falsehood has become generally accepted and taken for granted. The truth is far otherwise, and to Pythagoras is due the honour, not of speaking moralising platitudes, such as later generations attributed to Krishna, Buddha and Jesus, but of placing ethical conduct on a sound scientific basis, so much so that at the time of Jesus the teaching of the virtues was neither new nor strange.

Pythagoras was animated, not merely by the thirst for knowledge, but also by the enthusiasm for a much higher ethical standard of life, so much so that his biographers, centuries later, claimed that he was the son of Apollo, and had received his teaching direct from the god through the mouth of the oracle, or medium, at Delphi. A mythology grew round his name, not less varied than that which surrounded all the great religious teachers of the past.

Pythagoras became the centre of a great brotherhood, whose aim was the moral reformation of society by the people being educated in ethical principles. These were not to be taught as mere platitudes, but as natural law which must be observed for the purpose of increasing their comfort, prosperity and happiness. His arguments on justice, honesty and truth are unanswerable, and so also are those in favour of every other virtue, each of which was subject to a strict scientific examination to show that if the way of righteousness was not taken misery naturally followed.

Another common delusion amongst Christians is that their religion was responsible for all the hospitals, healing centres and organisations of mercy and charity now in our midst. The clergy from the pulpit have been the instructors of the people for so many centuries, that their false teaching will take several generations to extinguish, and only by education will their pernicious influence be overcome. The Greeks, for hundreds of years prior to the Christian era, devoted themselves to healing the sick, relieving the poor and raising the fallen. Pergamon, where a great temple was built, and known as the Temple of Æsculapius, was the centre of healing in Greece, Delphi being the centre of religion where lived the chief oracle, or medium, of the gods, Apollo being the god who was believed to be her principal control.

Besides Pergamon, healing centres existed at Epidauros and Cos; in fact we know of two hundred places in Greece, which we would now term hospitals and sanatoria, where the sick were healed. The numerous tablets on which they recorded their thanks to Æsculapius, the god of healing, testifies to the efficiency of the doctors of these days, herbal remedies being used in many cases, but the Greeks also claimed many cures to be due to psychic causes. Livy, who was writing his history of Rome and her greatness a generation before the Christian era commenced, gives particulars in his various books of many noteworthy psychic cures, and, when these were all gathered together in the 3rd century A.D., they formed a ponderous volume.

The hospital at Pergamon, dedicated in the 4th century B.C. to Æsculapius, must have been a remarkable place, and we are indebted to Ælius Aristides (A.D. 117–189) for our knowledge of what there took place. According to him no medicines were used, the patients, while undergoing treatment, being encouraged in all forms of bodily exercise. During the day they were expected to run a certain distance, or ride or hunt. Music was played at regular intervals, and there were constant theatrical performances. This famous healing centre has been unearthed within the past fifteen years, and the remains still exist of the theatre which seated 350 people, the library, the temple and the hospital. Attached to these were dormitories, a swimming-bath and other amenities. From a recent analysis, the water there has been discovered to be radio-active, and this doubtless was the reason for the spot being chosen as a healing centre.

The first man we would call by the name of 'doctor' was the celebrated Hippocrates (460–370 B.C.), who approached the cure of disease in the truly scientific manner, realising as he did that the doctor's duty was to help nature to effect its own cures. He is known as "the Father of Medicine", and was one of the first to discard the idea that illness was a punishment for sin, or caused by devils. By the 3rd century B.C. anatomy had revealed something of the internal workings of the human body, and, under the direction of two famous anatomists, Herophilus and Erasistratus, surgery was becoming a science. However, the Christian belief in the resurrection of the body brought investigation to an end until the 17th century, because to tamper with a corpse would mean that a mutilated body would arise on the resurrection day.

When Christianity rose to power in the 4th century, Pergamon and all the other Greek and Roman hospitals and sanatoria were destroyed by Christian fanatics, their doctors and healers being massacred or exiled. From that time onwards Christians paid their priests to pray the devils out of them, and teach them falsehoods about the wonders Christianity had done for humanity. It only, they claimed, had brought light to a world living in heathen darkness and wickedness, but now we know that this religion destroyed all that was good in Paganism and gave in exchange nothing new of any value.

Long before the Persian invasion of Greece, about the 10th or 11h century B.C.—no one knows exactly when, lived Homer. He is the reputed author of the legend about Troy, and his writings also tell of the early political and social life of the Greeks. He was followed by Hesiod and Archilochus, both poets of distinction. Sappho, who lived about the 6th century B.C. and is acknowledged as the greatest of all poetesses, wrote hymns, elegies and odes of great beauty. After her lived Simonides, Anacreon, Pindar, Aristophanes and Callimachus, all of whom were outstanding men for their poetry and lyrics. Pittacus, Antisthenes and Theophrastus are renowned for their wisdom, and Aristarchus, with rare fore-knowledge, believed that the earth was not the centre of the universe but revolved round the sun.

Two most illustrious moral philosophers deserve special mention. Epicurus (341–270 B.C.) emphasised the need of improved ethical conduct, and taught that only through right living could happiness be attained. Zeno (340–264 B.C.), the founder of Stoic philosophy, placed virtue and right conduct before all else. No closer approach has since been made to a more rational acceptable system of human conduct than that which these two noble men advocated. Life to them was an active conscious evolution towards greater wisdom, greater perfection, increased harmony and enlarged happiness, and they advocated a philosophic calm and courage towards death, pain and all the difficulties and sorrows of life. Righteousness, they taught, was the remedy for most of the world's troubles, and to do one's duty on every occasion produced character, which is more precious than wealth.

Both these great moralists freed men from the burden of fear produced by supernatural religion; happiness, they taught, coming from unselfishness, friendship, kindness and service to others. Their wide humanitarianism advocated the recognition of the brotherhood of man, that justice and equal opportunity should be given to everyone, and that slavery was the most intolerable of all the wrongs man ever committed against man. Some of the greatest and best of the Pagans were their followers from the 4th century B.C. until their teaching was overthrown by Christianity, and the lives lived by their numerous disciples could well be a pattern for anyone to follow.

The most peculiar and extreme of all the philosophers was Diogenes, the greatest of all the Cynics.

He despised everything of value in life except goodness, and lived with no more comforts than has an animal, freed from every social and family care. He wielded considerable influence for long after his time, and, much as we may disagree with his distorted monkish outlook, we should not forget that it was largely due to the influence of his later followers that the cruel Roman gladiatorial contests came to an end.

Solon, the celebrated Athenian legislator, one of the greatest figures in Greek history, is famous for his wise and just laws. He repealed the harsh laws of his predecessor Draco, and put all citizens on an equality in law, making the legal code of Athens the pattern for the world. Bias is noted for his skill as an advocate and his love of justice. Æschylus wrote 70 tragedies besides numerous dramas, and after him came Sophocles, Euripides, Menander and Posidippus, all of whom were famous for their dramatic art. Æsop is well known for his clever fables. Eratosthenes was the first to make Geography a science. Herodotus, Hecataeus, Thucydides and Xenophon were the world's first historians. Their writings, when they came to light at the Renaissance, revealed the pre-Christian world in its true light, and not as it had been so grotesquely portrayed by the Christian Church.

Much the most advanced and revolutionary school of thought were the physicists, those who sought for the basic substance of the universe, because, in their speculations on the composition of matter, and the laws which govern it, they found no place for the gods. This was a momentous break with past tradition, but it came naturally when law and order were discovered to rule the universe, each cause producing an effect, which in turn became a cause, one following the other in remorseless regularity. Consequently three men, Anaximander, Anaximenes and Heraclitus stand out in the 6th century B.C. as the founders of physical science, they establishing what is called the Ionian school of thought, and in their day they were regarded as atheists.

These wonderful men were followed by others of the same school, such as Anaxagoras, Leucippus, Parmenides, Empedocles and, lastly but by no means least, by Democritus, who, working on ideas propounded by Leucippus, anticipated the famous John Dalton (1766–1844) by propounding the theory that matter is composed of atoms. This brilliant hypothesis of two thousand four hundred years ago, which was revived by Dalton and accepted by modern science, was crowned in our time by the method being found to release atomic energy. This epoch-making and revolutionary discovery came about by means of instruments, but what marvellous penetration both Leucippus and Democritus had into one of nature's best-kept secrets, especially when we remember that they lacked the modern instruments on which present-day scientists rely to make their discoveries. Charles Darwin's theory of the evolution of the species was likewise anticipated by Anaximander, and Xenophanes was the first to explain correctly the fossils found in rocks.

Just as Greece was rich in scientists, philosophers, poets and play-writers, so was she also rich in orators, men such as Lysias, Isocrates, Aeschines and Demosthenes being outstanding for their power of speech.

It was Demosthenes, by his oratory, who roused the Greeks to the menace of Philip of Macedonia, arming steadily while the Greek city states, divided amongst themselves, looked on in consternation. One extract from his speeches (341 B.C.) can be so well applied to recent European history:

They look on while this man (Philip of Macedonia) grows more powerful, each resolved to use for his own advantage the time during which another nation is being destroyed, instead of considering and acting to preserve the common cause of Hellas. Every dictator is an enemy of freedom, and opponent of law.

Archimedes was the father of inventions and practical scientific discoveries, being the discoverer of the law of specific gravity, and the greatest mathematician of his age. Euclid taught men to think, calculate and reason. Ictinus, one of the greatest architects, built the Parthenon (the Temple of Athena) at Athens, which Phidias adorned with the most perfect statues ever carved. They were so beautiful that they were worshipped as heaven-made things. The Greeks were passionately fond of everything beautiful, especially the perfect human figure, the women having a statue of Apollo or Narcissus in their bedrooms, to whom they prayed for children as handsome. Beauty exhibitions were held, when prizes were given for the most beautiful creation. Athens became the centre of Greek art, and to it came every young man with talent and ambition, as at the Academy, situated amidst wide-spreading plane trees and olive groves, was taught everything in those days there was to know.

Many Greeks knew that the dead lived on in a

world contacting this world, and the wording on their tombstones reveals how to them death was no Christian "Rest in Peace", but the entrance to a fuller and more abundant life. They knew this because they had mediums in their temples. From this knowledge developed their mythology, in which they fashioned the men and women, who had left this world for what they called the Etheric World, into divine beings—the gods, as they called them. Each one of them originally had lived on earth, a hero, a chief, or a gifted woman, who, in her day, had exercised distinct charm. All had attributed to them supernatural power, but the Greeks knew enough about the gods to realise that they had bodies like human beings, which they called astral bodies, and that they were human in their behaviour, so much so that they were more friends to be loved than supernatural beings to be feared and dreaded.

Polygnotas, in the middle of the 5th century B.C., was one of the first portrait-painters of distinction, but what was more enduring was the work of the sculptors who fashioned the gods into beautiful marble images, to keep them in remembrance, just as photographs or portraits today are reminders to us of those who have lived on earth and passed into the beyond.

Besides all these men of talent and wisdom already mentioned, three men stand out in brilliance above them all, Socrates, Plato and Aristotle, a trio whose influence down the centuries has been world-wide. Socrates (470–399 B.C.) was a martyr, and suffered because he was courageous enough to advocate the speaking of one's honest thoughts, which in his day did not always appeal to the state authorities. He received the ordinary education common to a son of an Athenian freeman. He grew up short and sturdy in figure, his movement was ungainly and he lived and dressed quite simply. His brow was a dome of intellect, below which was an ugly nose above his two thick lips. After starting life as a sculptor, like his father, he soon abandoned his chisel and devoted himself to the study of philosophy.

He did not travel much, but once at Delphi he saw inscribed on one of the doors of the temple the words "Know Thyself". From that time onwards he set about the great task of learning to know himself, and this he did by dissecting the minds of others through questioning. By the same method he set about finding out the qualities that made for goodness, kindness, sympathy, honesty, truth, happiness, bravery and justice. To him the greatest virtue was pure knowledge, and he would accept nothing that would not pass the acid test of reason.

He fought as a common soldier during the Peloponnesian war, which lasted almost a generation. One of the greatest philosophers of that age thus fought side by side with the ordinary man and the slave, because service was the debt he owed to his beloved Athens. When the war was over he set about seriously instructing his fellow citizens. For some years he spent his days in the market place, at the street corners, and wherever he could challenge the people to give heed to his thoughts. Then all the young men were eager for knowledge, and wherever he went he was surrounded by groups of enquirers craving for instruction. His theme was the attainment of righteousness, justice and wisdom, and he was

rigid in extracting absolute truth and applying it to all
that concerns life.   Virtue is wisdom, he taught, and
when men know how to think aright they will do what
is right.   When men know how to think justly they
will act justly, as "all virtues are summed up in
wisdom or knowledge of good".

We only know Socrates through the writings of his
two devoted disciples, Xenophon and Plato, the latter
pouring all his marvellous genius into his account
of the conversations which he records.   Socrates was
a medium, and, during trance, he spoke under the
control of other-world people.   He was clairaudient,
and, like others so constituted, was guided by the
voices of his etheric friends who, he said, never
misled him.   He was the first eminent Spiritualist,
the first to explain scientifically the mystery of
death, the first to penetrate scientifically beyond the
physical into the etheric realm, our future home, and
the first to teach in a rational way that our duty on
earth is to live so as to fit ourselves for the life
beyond.

Here on earth, he said, we are like frogs at the
bottom of a pool, but, when we emerge from it, we
shall find reality, our true place, where we shall more
fully understand the mysteries of existence.   Around
this earth "are many mansions for the soul" where
dwell, as human beings, not as supernatural gods,
those who lived on earth.   Such opinions shocked the
priests, who decided that such teaching was heretical.

During the Christian era countless mediums were
burned and drowned as witches.   Today they are put
in prison, and Socrates was the first of these priestly
victims mentioned in history.   He was accused of

introducing new ideas, and thus corrupting the youth of Athens. The penalty was death, but before drinking the poison he was asked by his friend Crito, "How shall we bury you?", to which he answered:

Wherever you will, if only you can catch me. Is it not strange that, after all I have said to convince you that I am going to the society of the happy, you still think this body to be Socrates? To die and be released is better for me.

When Crito later recounted the sublime death of this noble man he said, "Such was the end of our friend, concerning whom I may truly say that of all the men of his time whom I have known, he was the wisest, the justest and the best." If he had been seen after death as a ghost in his etheric body, he would doubtless have been transformed into a saviour-god, an arisen Christ, who had reappeared to show that he had broken the curse of death. Otherwise all the conditions favoured this transformation, and were similar to those which encompassed others, before and after his time, who became saviours during the Theological Age in the eyes of their worshippers, and the reputed founders of a new religion. Then, as with them, the mythology which accompanied all saviour-gods would have been draped round his life, but fortunately we know Socrates as the man he was, and superstitious priests took no part in producing his biography.

Considering the liberty the freemen of Athens had previously enjoyed, freedom of speech, freedom in religion and in politics, the trial and condemnation of Socrates strikes a discordant note, but we should remember that the Athenians had recently suffered a severe military defeat, and were off their balance. Nevertheless the fact remains that all his life he was allowed to speak his own thoughts, and not until he was an elderly man did his enemies prevail. At his trial he was convicted by only a small majority, but he was not forced to meet a cruel death as the Greeks were a kindly people. They had no figure like Torquemada, the Christian priest, who spent his leisure thinking out new methods of torture to inflict on Jews and heretics brought before the Inquisition. Socrates alone amongst the Greek philosophers met an unnatural death, and only three others were exiled.

When we remember that in Persia, the neighbouring land, the king struck down whom he pleased, no one, not even the greatest, daring to express his honest thoughts, and that at his whim and pleasure the people, without a murmur, accepted death and mutilation to themselves and their families, we better realise the height to which Athens rose in its championship of the rights of man. The Athenians, on this occasion, lapsed from their high ideals, and made the noble Socrates the exception to the prevailing custom, as Plato, on his return from his travels abroad, continued, without molestation, the work of mental development which his famous teacher had so earnestly pursued.

Plato (427–347 B.C.) was a king of thought, and the age in which he lived was unique for outstanding men. He was born just after the death of Pericles, the eminent soldier and statesman who lifted Athens to the pinnacle of her fame. In his day lived Sophocles, known as the best of all the Greek tragic poets; Euripides, the great Greek dramatist; Thucydides, the most celebrated historian of antiquity, and Isocrates, the orator, one of the most remarkable men in the literary history of Greece. Socrates taught Plato, who in turn taught Aristotle, and when the dawn came to Europe in the 16th century A.D., after a black night of ignorance, men turned to the thoughts expressed by these three wise philosophers, seeking from them guidance in their efforts to create a new and better world.

Plato served as a soldier, as did all Athenians, and fortunately escaped capture and death when the Spartans over-ran Athens, and razed the city walls to the ground. His intercourse with Socrates moulded his thoughts, and taught him to think clearly, his lasting memorial to his teacher being *Phaedo*, containing an account of the last conversations between Socrates and his friends before his death. Throughout he depicts his hero as the conductor of the discussions, and the world's cleverest and wittiest cross-examiner. His description of the last talk, and the last scene, before Socrates drank the poison, is one of the most moving dramas to be found in world literature.

Broken by the tragedy of his teacher's death, Plato, while men were flocking to Athens to learn from him, went forth abroad to study philosophy, a subject which he defines as the attempt by reasoned thought to find reality behind the appearance of things. From Egypt he went to Palestine, and returned home by way of Italy and Sicily. Wherever he went he discoursed on philosophy, emphasising the need of virtue, fortitude and justice. He denounced tyranny as cowardice, and taught that happiness could only come through justice. While speaking thus before Dionysius, the tyrant king of Sicily, he was arrested and sold as a slave. Happily this was to an admirer, who restored his liberty, and so he returned safely to Athens.

With his accumulated experiences he started to write and teach. He opened a school of philosophy, called the Academy after the name of the garden in which it was situated, and it was from here that intellectual light penetrated a dark world of ignorance. Demosthenes, the great orator, was amongst his pupils, as was also Aristotle who worked with his master for twenty years. In this school Plato taught for forty years, and, after that, he spent the remainder of his life amidst his friends and pupils at Athens, teaching and writing the philosophy which has influenced mankind for two thousand three hundred years, he being the first to make men understand that things were not always what they seemed to be.

He propounded a philosophy to prove that ideas are imperishable, whereas material things pass away, and in his greatest book, *Republic*, he set justice, goodness and social righteousness first and foremost. Virtue, he taught, followed from knowledge and wisdom, and, when these are mastered, good naturally takes the place of evil. He envisaged a Republic embracing the utopias imagined by idealists, and, in this flight of imagination, he expressed superb thoughts. He was the first outstanding Socialist, the first schoolmaster, one of the first to emphasise the need of knowledge to raise humanity and bring about human progress.

He was one of the first to tell his fellow men to rely on themselves and not on the gods, and he always advocated the supremacy of reason and logical thinking. He loved everything that was beautiful, and whatever he wrote was full of rich and noble thoughts, which were taken up by his successor Aristotle. If only his elevating ideas had been made the pattern for human conduct, what a different world we would be living in today, but, when the Christian Church obtained power, its priests burned and banned his writings, putting in their place the debased teaching to be found in many parts of what is still called *The Holy Bible.*

If humanity had taken Plato as its guide, instead of superstitious priests, two thousand three hundred years would not have had to pass before education for the people came into being. If mankind, in these bygone days, had only been sufficiently developed to put philosophy before superstition, and make it their guide through life, what a different story this history would have to tell. This, of all the opportunities passed over by man, is the most outstanding—in fact it is the greatest tragedy revealed by history—as the consequence, which the following pages record, brought destruction, misery and suffering to half the human race.

Fortunately for us, Greek philosophy, in spite of Christian opposition, eventually found its way into Europe, to produce the Renaissance, and Aristotle (384–322 B.C.), more than any other, influenced the thinking mind of Europe away from superstition into the way of reasoned thought. He was the supreme thinker of his time, being sane and luminous in all he wrote. His influence brought about the foundation of the University of Alexandria, and, while this lasted, he, though dead, yet spoke through the mouths of the philosophers who attended that first great seat of learning. Unfortunately, in the 2nd Christian century, the University became a Theological College, and priests took the place of teachers, when the light of knowledge was extinguished by the darkness of superstition, because theology hates facts and dare not look truth in the face.

A thousand years after Aristotle's death his writings stimulated the Arabs and Persians to pursue their scientific investigations, which research laid the foundation of the European Renaissance. He was the last of the immortal three—Socrates, Plato and Aristotle—and his influence on European thought was greater than that of Socrates and Plato, because his line of approach appealed more to the practical men who brought intellectual light to Europe. Plato was too much of a metaphysician, as he argued that what seems real in time and space is not real, but only the reflection of the real, and, because of this, he took a place in science which was quite his own up to within recent times.

Plato was therefore the pioneer of one aspect of scientific thought, that which today is comprised within psychic science, while the other more materialistic Greek scientists advocated what is today accepted by orthodox science. Then, as now, orthodox science did not admit the possibility of the individual mind functioning apart from the physical body. Plato believed that it did, and he doubtless formed this opinion as the result of his observations of the mediumship of Socrates and others likewise endowed with psychic gifts.

Today, those who have made the investigation, know that the individual mind can function apart from the physical body, its vehicle being the etheric body which separates from the physical body at death. That, however, was a subject the other Greek scientists did not investigate, and it is one which has also been neglected by orthodox science in our own time. Socrates was the first Spiritualist, and Plato was the first psychic philosopher, and some day science will comprise both the psychic and the physical aspects of thought. Both in their own way are true, and neither one nor the other can be neglected if we wish to have a balanced opinion of man and the universe. When that time comes natural religion will be accepted by science, which never will, and never can, countenance the error, stupidity and folly associated with supernatural religion.

Aristotle, unlike Plato, was a realist, and, while respecting the aspect of truth behind his master's teaching, he taught that reality is that which appears to us as actual in space and time. The sun, the earth, the planets, the passage of time, all are real, and the thought which registers them is transient. Aristotle was a natural philosopher, and anticipated Francis Bacon and modern science, by ordering and classifying the knowledge of his time. He collected and arranged plants and animals, being the first biologist, groping for the idea of evolution. With the wealth of Alexander behind him, he had at one time a thousand men in different parts of the known world collecting material for his natural history.

His writings found their way to Alexandria, and thence, seven hundred years later, to Constantinople. Fortunately, before this city was captured by the Turks in 1453, they reached Venice. Their translation into Italian determined the whole course of European mediaeval and modern culture. Though the theologians, led by Thomas Aquinas, Erasmus and Thomas More, distorted Aristotle's teaching, they at least recovered his words from the oblivion into which they had been cast by the Christian Church. Thus they prepared the way for others, at a later date, to expound his ideas as he meant them to be understood.

Like Plato, Aristotle had his own school, known as the Lyceum. Here he expounded his own philosophic system, and it is said that his pupils discussed everything in heaven and earth. His method of teaching was similar to the one adopted by Socrates and Plato, as he did not dogmatise but instructed in the form of question and answer, a method which was greatly preferred to continuous exposition. He, and his students under him, made an encyclopedia of philosophy, which was the first attempt to bring all knowledge within two covers.

Aristotle was the first to lay down the principles of logic, and was the outstanding chemist, physicist, biologist, mathematician, astronomer, botanist, anatomist and psychologist of his time, whilst always admitting that further research would yield increased knowledge. He also wrote on ethics, rhetoric, politics and history, but we must remember his limitations and also those of Plato, Socrates and the other Greek scientists. They were all pioneers, and suffered from the limited knowledge then available.

Consequently they condoned slavery as part of the natural order, it being the duty of the slave to work and the master to think, just as the head rules the body, and they also accepted many other ideas now abandoned as false. Nevertheless they laid the basis for present-day scientific thought, and Aristotle will always stand out as a tremendous intellectual force. Unfortunately for him, he had so identified himself with the domination of Greece by Macedonia, that he had to leave Athens on the death of Alexander, and died a year later.

For forty years, after the Persians withdrew from Greece, comparative peace reigned, during which time Pericles (490–429 B.C.), her greatest ruler, and one of the most remarkable men of antiquity, set to work to expand the trade of Athens, and make it the most beautiful city in the world. Under him Athens, and her empire of scattered city states, reached their highest point in prosperity and splendour, many men who became famous in later years being her citizens.

Pericles was an outstanding statesman, and, for a time, the Athenians gladly followed his lead. He remained in power for over thirty years, greatly helped by a woman he could not make his wife because she was not an Athenian, such being the stupid narrow outlook of one Greek city towards another. Aspasia lived with him as his wife, and no woman ever did more to help the man she loved. She gathered in her home all the men of renown of her time, several of whom praised her wisdom.

Believing that Greece was now safe from invasion, Pericles lavished on Athens the money which all the states had deposited at Delos, to provide for mutual defence against Persia. Architects and sculptors were set to work, and the Parthenon arose to crown their labours. Pericles represented all that was best in Athens, but the Athenians were not generous towards their leaders. He received much hard criticism in his later years, though it was felt that they could not get on without him. In spite of it all he went his way, always working for what he believed was the good of Athens. He worked for peace and prosperity, directing the people to live for all that is beautiful. Painting, music, the drama, sculpture and architecture had each its place in his scheme. His public and private life stands out as pure and honest. Plutarch accuses him of bringing about the Peloponnesian war, to unite the Athenians behind him, but this is not supported by evidence, and there is little doubt that the war was caused by Sparta's hatred, jealousy and fear of the growing power of Athens, which city always considered itself first and the rest of Greece last. In 429 B.C. Pericles died a poor man, and in the same year died also Herodotus.

Sparta was a notable exception to the rest of Greece, as its citizens carved out for themselves a way of life quite different from the other city states. They enjoyed a high reputation for their steadfastness and simplicity of living, life to them being one unending round of military discipline, based on the entire abnegation of the individual. Private luxury was forbidden, intercourse with other city states discouraged, delicate infants were exposed in the open until they died, and every heroic virtue and martial quality elevated. Women were emancipated, and underwent disciplinary training, participating in games and gymnastics. The entire state was ordered as a military barracks, no account being taken of private tastes and inclinations.

To the Spartans, war was the main object of life, and being solely organised for war they made no contribution to the upliftment or the increased comfort and the happiness of mankind, becoming a harsh and unsympathetic people to be disliked by everyone. What a contrast there was between Spartan austerity, and the culture, art, philosophy and civilisation of Miletus, situated on the eastern shore of the Ægean Sea, where science was born, and whence flowed all that is best in life, to produce the ideas, the customs and the culture for which Athens, and so many other Greek cities and colonies, became famous.

War and peace, storm and calm, good and evil run like a thread through history, and now once again we are at a black page in the story of the human race, ignorance of the way to secure happiness being the cause of a long tale of misery. It has not been possible to record the various inter-city conflicts, the quarrels, intrigues and all the achievements of each city, but we now come to the time when all Greece, for more than a generation, was ablaze, and this sad tale will now be told.

(5) Greece is Devastated by Civil War.

The Peloponnesian war, Peloponnesus being the name given to the most southern part of Greece, went on for twenty-seven years, after which Greece was bankrupt. Thucydides, in lucid and dignified words, tells the story of this terrible fratricidal war between

Athens and Sparta, which reveals the deadly hatred and narrow rivalries between the different Greek cities. Athens, during the years of peace, had become supreme and the greatest of all the Greek states. A league of states, for mutual defence, was formed in 477 B.C., with Athens at the head, and this Delian League, as it was called, developed into the Athenian Empire, to which all the states contributed in money, ships and men. This led to quarrels, because the Athenians spent the money on beautifying Athens, and neglected to protect the Ægean Sea against the feared inroads of the Persians.

The year before the death of Pericles, Athens and Sparta were sparring for a fight. Athens was a democracy, and Sparta had become an oligarchy, with its government in the hands of a small number of men. All Greece was then divided between these two methods of government, the different city states grouping themselves round Athens and Sparta according to their political outlook. The position was not unlike that in Europe between the two world wars, when dictator states were ranged against democratic communities. In Greece the democracies, under the lead of Athens, were anxious to see democratic government adopted by all, but the dictator-governed states hated all shades of democracy, being jealous of the position it had attained, and wished to see it broken for ever.

The trouble began in Epidamnus (Durazzo), a colony of Corcyra (Corfu), which expelled its oligarchs and set up a democracy. Corinth and Corcyra came to blows and the latter persuaded Athens that, as war with Corinth and Sparta was certain, she would do well to accept the alliance of Corcyra. The Athenians blockaded Potidæa, a Corinthian colony which had revolted from Athens, and, as time passed, intrigue, dishonesty, treachery and cunning increased, so much so that Athens eventually found herself alone, feared and distrusted.

Thus came about the disastrous Peloponnesian war, which began in 432 B.C. when the Corinthians induced Sparta, and her satellite states, to join together to crush the Athenians, a project which had the active help of Cyrus II, the Persian monarch, who was also anxious to humiliate proud Athens. Fear doubtless brought all the pent-up feelings to a head, fear that Athens would become too strong and dominate all Greece, just as fear that Germany would dominate Europe brought about the two world wars.

To follow the victories and defeats on sea and land, which each side inflicted on the other in this long-drawn-out struggle, is here impossible, though one interesting event occurred which makes clear Athenian imperialistic ambitions. For long she had coveted Sicily, and now she decided on the island's conquest on the first opportunity. This came in 416 B.C., when the different towns on the island were at one another's throats. A year later 134 ships left Athens, amidst the prayers of the people, who feared the worst because it was rumoured that Alcibiades, the most prominent amongst her military leaders, whom Socrates had done his utmost to lead into the path of virtue, had been guilty of a shocking sacrilege. He was accused of holding a mock celebration of the Eleusinian mysteries (equivalent to the Christian eucharist) in his own house, and of mutilating the statue of the god Hermes.

He was allowed to proceed with the fleet, but, before the conquest began, he was recalled, the incompetent Nicias being left in command. The absence of Alcibiades was a serious loss to the expedition, as everything depended on his plans being correctly executed. The Athenian troops landed at Catania, where they were attacked by the army of Syracuse, during which battle the Athenians also landed at Syracuse, to be driven back in disorder. Then began its siege, which must have ended with its capitulation had not Sparta joined in against Athens, landed a force on the north of Sicily, marched across the island, defeated the investing army and entered Syracuse.

Corinth next joined in, and battles raged on land, and at sea off Syracuse, until the Athenians both on shore and at sea were defeated. On land the victors did not terminate the struggle until every Athenian was killed or made a slave, while on sea those ships which remained were either destroyed or captured. Such was the end of the attempt by Athens to capture Sicily, but, though this enterprise was a failure, the war against Sparta in Greece continued, to end in the complete defeat of Athens, as her allies now deserted her and Persia entered the war on the side of Sparta.

In 404 B.C. Athens surrendered to her enemies, the twenty-seven years of conflict having bled her and all Greece white, some hundred thousand of the most gifted people on earth perishing in this disastrous war. Sparta now took the place of Athens as the leading Greek state, but the Athenians preserved their freedom though they lost their colonies and their fleet. The city walls were demolished, her citizens being too reduced by famine, disease and misery to resist. The humiliation was certainly lessened by the withdrawal of the victorious armies, but imperialistic democracy had received a severe defeat, and oligarchy had triumphed.

Democratic government returned, but, in the interval, political passions rose to fever heat, and then it was that Socrates arose to tell the people that happiness could only come from right thinking and right acting, misery always following evil deeds. The lesson he preached in favour of everyone living righteous lives was never learned by his countrymen, and unfortunately it has not been learned since then up to our own times, though nearly twenty-four centuries have passed to prove that what he said was true.

(6) Education Spreads from Greece throughout the Roman Empire.

Though the Greeks never learned all the lessons which come from knowledge, their philosophers and schoolmasters, in advocating the pursuit of learning, and the wisdom of ethical conduct, laid the only sound foundation on which the peace and happiness of mankind can be built. These men were comparatively few in number, amidst a multitude who were not sufficiently developed mentally to appreciate their wisdom, but the great misfortune to humanity is the fact that the tree of knowledge, which grew from the seed they planted, was cut down by the Christian

Church, and did not begin to grow again until the time we now call the Renaissance. If it had been allowed to develop and flourish over the thousand years known as the Dark Ages, what a different place the world would now have been in which to live. This thousand years of lost opportunity is the greatest tragedy suffered by mankind. If only the knowledge and wisdom propounded by the Greek philosophers, which the savants of Rome later embraced, had taken hold, instead of theological superstition, we might confidently say that by now we would have known how best to live to secure peace, prosperity and happiness without the continual interruption of war and social upheavals. A thousand years of lost opportunity is, however, an understatement, because it was not until the end of the 19th century that Europe partially returned to the Roman educational system which was destroyed by Christianity in the 5th century. Only last century a start was made, in the more advanced European countries, to rebuild that which was obliterated fourteen centuries earlier, and, as knowledge accumulates like a snowball, all these centuries, when its assembly should have been proceeding, have been wasted by neglect.

As this vital historical fact has been ignored by Christian historians, religious prejudice blinding them to what is obvious to others, it is well that we should now give some consideration to the educational work done by those who have been classed by Christendom as "the heathen". Christians, confined as they were within a narrow creed, which they considered contained the only divine revelation, never, until comparatively recently, acknowledged the possibility of knowledge and wisdom being found outside the covers of their sacred book *The Holy Bible*. The Greeks, on the other hand, freely admitted that their learning came from Egypt, and the Romans paid warm tribute to the fact that Greece was the source of their increased understanding of mankind and his environment.

For countless years, since primitive times, the only form of instruction was that obtained from family life, the child being taught by its parents the way to live and to interfere as little as possible with their convenience. Later, when the priesthood arose, the child was given some theological instruction appertaining to the gods, who were then believed to be the cause of every mystery, everything which could not be naturally explained being attributed to them. That constituted education for countless centuries, until the time came when the Babylonians and the Egyptians found a way to put down their thoughts on something that preserved them for their own guidance and future generations, this method finally culminating in the Egyptians and neighbouring people inventing what we now call the alphabet.

That vitally important invention was the beginning of the accumulation of knowledge, which, in Egypt, reached to great heights in the millennium prior to the Christian era, when no branch of science was neglected, progress being made in everything so far as observation and experience could guide. The Egyptian scientists were a source of enlightenment to all surrounding nations, the Greeks especially absorbing their accumulated wisdom. Few Greek philosophers

were satisfied until they themselves had visited this
great seat of learning, to return home and separate
much that was theological speculation from what was
undoubtedly proven facts, the consequence being
that learning in Greece was separated from theology,
to become secular and reliable.

This constitutes the great contribution Greece
gave to learning, as, until now, the gods were for ever
becoming mixed up with what we today call natural
law, and, until they were excluded, no one troubled
to find another explanation for observed phenomena.
So long as the sun was considered a divine chariot,
there was no place for the astronomer, and medicine
made no progress until devils ceased to be made
responsible for sickness and disease. The Greeks,
by eliminating the superstition, put the pursuit of
knowledge on a firm foundation, and for this they
have earned our eternal gratitude; the Romans, for
four centuries, until they became Christians, continuing the good work. Then, in the 5th century A.D.,
when the Church banned all knowledge as being of the
devil, and closed all the schools, the Arabs preserved
and advanced what was already known, but it was not
until the 16th century that this precious heritage
of mankind reached Christendom. Only then were
some brave enough to defy ecclesiastial authority
and put science before theology, to suffer persecution
and often violent deaths for their presumption.

The Greeks were the first to develop the science
of education as distinct from theological instruction.
By so doing they gave to the world secular education,
from which comes knowledge to produce wisdom.
They divided education into different departments,

the arts, the sciences and the care of health by bodily exercise, thus comprising in their curriculum an all-round study of mental and physical training. In the intervals, between instruction by means of questions and answers, gymnastic exercises followed, or the study of the arts and music, nothing being considered too insignificant to examine and explore, all that is good, beautiful and true receiving their veneration.

The teacher's object during instruction was to take up a subject and examine it from all angles of thought, and then train the pupil to express himself aptly on what he had learned, in dignified and elegant language, touching on every aspect of the subject. Every effort was made to stimulate the craving for knowledge, to rouse curiosity for the unknown, to develop the critical faculty and independent thinking, as generally accepted opinions received no reverence unless they were supported by facts.

Plato is the author of the first systematic treatise on education, he dealing with the subject in much detail in his book *Republic*, where he advocates that the duty of every state is to educate the young, both boys and girls, honestly in all things that relate to ourselves and the world in which we live, advice which was unfortunately ignored by Christendom until last century. He laid great stress on heredity, strong and intelligent children coming from parents who are healthy in body and mind. With these he foresaw a future race ready to make good use of everything nature supplies, their bodies well cared for, and their minds instructed in science and ethical conduct. Thus equipped they are best prepared to secure the happiness all desire, as wise and righteous living brings its own reward.

Plato's conception of education was to train the mind, so as to make his pupil "a good man" in every sense of the word, education to him being more than book-learning, character-building being as important as the accumulation of knowledge. How wise he was we realise today, as the knowledge acquired at schools and universities throughout the world is used for both good and evil purposes. With science solely confined to material things, the chemist learns to destroy what the architect is taught to build, there being nothing to balance the human mind in its recently acquired control of the forces of nature. Consequently our present-day achievements are as much a curse as a blessing to the human family, and will continue to be so until we learn to employ our knowledge only for good and never for evil purposes. Plato's idea of "the good man", trained to live a good life, embraced moral training as well as learning, because wisdom, self-control, tolerance, justice and mercy are just as important as knowledge, the elimination of the bestial heredity in the race being as necessary as the inculcation of facts.

Fifteen years of instruction he considered were necessary to produce the man fit to live peacefully and harmoniously with his neighbours, such a one thus trained being then endowed with those virtues which produce happiness and the knowledge which will bring wealth and comfort. From amongst the best should be chosen the men to lead and govern. None were to be irrational in their thoughts, loose thinking and loose living being to him something which must never be tolerated. All subjects must be open to discussion, and every opinion was welcome; intolerance, aggression, selfishness and domination being abhorrent to the cultured man who gives to all the freedom and liberty he claims for himself.

This method of training the young spread from Greece all over the Roman Empire, Quintilian (A.D. 35–96), a Roman citizen, born in Spain, continuing to lead the Roman world in education on the lines laid down by Plato. His high conception of conduct could hardly be surpassed, his wonderful work, devoted to the training and instruction of the young, being rewarded by the Emperor Vespasian appointing him to a professorship, and liberally endowing his schemes with public money, to enable him to extend education all over the Empire and earn for himself the sobriquet "the supreme controller of the restless youth". Today we would call him the Minister of Education, a government office which was not created in Britain until 1868, some eighteen hundred years later, and only then after much religious opposition. His life-long work for education was so much appreciated that the Emperor Domitian raised him to the rank of consul, and also entrusted his two grand-nephews to his care.

This refined, unassuming, kindly Roman, with his clear, intellectual vision and wide sympathies, one of the most attractive figures of the time, laid the foundation for the extensive system of Roman education. This most outstanding of all the Roman school-masters loved liberty, justice, truth and mercy, besides abhorring all forms of cruelty and oppression. He lived a noble life, instructing the young in all the knowledge of his time, his aim being to cultivate the young mind in the pursuit of wisdom and the development of righteous living, while injustice and oppression in every form always received his severe condemnation.

His life and work reveal the vast change which, within a few generations, had passed over Roman taste, feeling and society, for which the influence of Greece was largely due, Cicero (106–43 B.C.), the previous century, arguing that if learning was a noble art the teacher was indeed a noble man. So, within little more than one hundred years, the love for knowledge had so advanced that Quintilian's appointment as Minister of Education marked the beginning of the systematic instruction of the young, a movement which developed all over the Empire, to become a powerful force for good. During this period, educational development spread enormously, mental culture, self-control, and the correct expression of one's thoughts, being subjects which attracted wide attention, not only in Rome but throughout Italy, Gaul, Spain, Asia and North Africa, where important state schools abounded, Gaul and Spain responding most to the educational and cultural opportunities presented to the youth of the Empire.

The younger Pliny, a man who lived a highly virtuous life, kind, humane, forgiving, and generous with his great wealth, was one of Quintilian's pupils, and well represents the noble type of man who was cultivated in the imperial academies under the direction of this illustrious instructor of youth. In his book on education Quintilian advocated that everyone should attempt to attain the widest culture, there being no form of knowledge from which something may not be extracted to improve our understanding, strengthen our characters, and deepen our respect for justice, goodness, mercy and truth, no detail being too small to be neglected. To him the love of humanity was so strong that he wrote not as a Roman, but as a world citizen, the advancement of everything which would ennoble and advance the happiness of the human race having his encouragement. To him, ethics took the place of religion as the only safe guide to correct conduct. He was quite agnostic about those subjects on which theologians profess such confident knowledge, and his politics embraced a wide humanitarianism which comprised the world.

Such, then, was the man who spread education throughout the Roman Empire. He planted the tree of knowledge, which, if it had been allowed to live until our time, would have grown into the great protector against most of the evils from which Christendom suffered, and to which we are still the heirs. Unfortunately the Christian Church, believing that all learning outside Christian belief was sinful, cut down the young tree, and left Christendom under the protection of its crude theology, when faith and not reason became the guide of life. Much of what this book has still to tell is the terrible story which followed from this shocking tragedy, by far the greatest crime ever perpetrated against humanity, and, if the reader is sufficiently curious to know why it was that the Christian era was the most wicked time in history, he should turn forward to Volume II, Chapter XVI, and read Section 4 entitled "The Roman Catholic Church curses all progress and reform".

Here we find the Chief Priest of the Christian faith (eighteen hundred years after the foundation of

Roman education, and fifteen hundred years after the Christian Church had destroyed it by confiscating the schools, depriving them of support, and liquidating the teachers) denouncing everything that Quintilian had advocated. Here we find Christian civilisation laid bare, naked and unashamed. To the clergy of the Orthodox Greek Church, the Roman Catholic Church, or the Protestant Church, the only form of government was one administered by a divine priest or a divine monarch, the only form of instruction being theological, and only last century, after bitter controversy, did education take the place of theological dogma, when the school replaced the Church for the purpose of mental development.

During the age of Christian civilisation the clergy considered that all secular knowledge was sinful, and that theology contained everything there was to know. Progress, and the increase of knowledge, they never ceased to declare, were contrary to the will of God, and, as the Church was the custodian of, and solely responsible for, the mental welfare of Christendom during the Christian era, it dragged humanity down to the lowest depths of degradation. We shall not, however, anticipate, as this will become evident as we proceed, history making it crystal clear that the Christian Church has been the greatest enemy to human well-being and progress of which there is any record.

During the first four centuries of the Christian era there was a race between Christianity and education. Unfortunately the Romans did not make education compulsory for everyone, the consequence being that only the middle and upper classes took advantage of the facilities offered to acquire learning, the great majority remaining wedded to theological superstition. In Palestine education did not exist, only theological instruction, and because Paul was not educated along Greek, or secular, lines, his emotions carried him off the path of reason, the result being that he imagined Dionysus, the much-beloved Greek saviour-god, had returned to earth in the person of Jesus. One of the principal centres of worship of the Dionysian cult was Tarsus, Paul's home town, and there he learned all the mystical beliefs surrounding Dionysus, which he draped around Jesus, but more will be said on this subject in the next chapter.

This competition between education and Christianity went on during the first four Christian centuries, and, if Constantine had not made Christianity the state religion of Rome, and, if the Christian Church had not taken the place of the Roman emperor when the Empire collapsed, education would not have been obliterated as it was. If only it had survived there is no reason to doubt that it would have increased in power, until all the people of Europe had been raised mentally and morally by its influence. The tragedy is that it was swamped by theology, a catastrophe from which all Christendom suffered terribly, and is still suffering at the present time.

The noble and widespread educational organisation built up by Quintilian, and his loyal and able colleagues, did not long survive the blight of Christian theology, and, by the beginning of the 6th century, all the schoolmasters had been either murdered or exiled, and their schools confiscated, Simplicius being the last to be forced to leave his home and school in

Athens and seek protection abroad. This brought to an end Plato's famous Academy, which had for nine hundred years enlightened mankind without interruption. Simplicius, and six other schoolmasters, were exiled from Greece in A.D. 529, their property was confiscated, and they would have starved had they not been welcomed for their learning by Chosroes I, the King of Persia. Disestablished, disendowed, and silenced, the last schools to remain open in Christendom closed their doors in the very city in which learning had been nurtured, and from which it had spread over the vast Roman Empire.

From now onwards, for the next thousand years, the names of Plato, Aristotle, Socrates, and the other great Greek philosophers, were unknown in Christendom, the early Christians having consigned them all to everlasting torment in hell, and Europe consequently sank into the depths of ignorance so profound that this period is known as the Dark Ages. Only last century did education partially take the place in Europe planned for it by the Greek and Roman educationalists, but the effect still remains of these fourteen hundred wasted years, when the people were caught in the grip of theological superstition as firmly as ever were the Germans by Hitler and his gestapo. Here we have the explanation of the degradation to which civilisation fell during the Christian era, and of its plight in our own times, an outstanding fact which must never be forgotten when we read the remaining pages of this book.

(7) ALEXANDER CONQUERS MUCH OF THE CIVILISED WORLD.

We must now leave Greece for a time and consider what was taking place further north. Macedonia (now Yugoslavia), made up of Greek-speaking Aryans, under its able ruler Philip (359–336 B.C.), was becoming an ever more powerful kingdom and preparing for war against Persia. The discovery of a gold mine within its borders made it the richest state in Europe. Philip, however, did not live to see his plans put into effect, but he laid the foundation of the achievements of his son, commonly called Alexander the Great. Philip, a man of great ambition, was also a ruler of outstanding ability and foresight, as is revealed by his having Aristotle at his court as tutor to his son.

Philip built up a powerful army from amongst his war-loving people, and educated his son in all the arts of war. His influence was so great that after the fierce battle of Chaeronea (338 B.C.), which made him master of Greece, he succeeded in consolidating the Greek people into one confederacy with the support of Isocrates and the Pan-Hellenic party in Greece. Greece and Macedonia became united under one king, and Greece, for the first time in her history, was a nation under one ruler. Demosthenes stood out against this subjection to a foreign power, but no Greek state had now the vigour to resist, as the land had been bled white by war. After capturing Athens, and giving her generous peace terms, Philip was from that time onwards recognised by the Greek states as their sovereign leader. His ambition was to found a Macedonian-Hellenic-Persian confederation of Aryan people, and, though his army set out for Asia, he never lived to see his dream come true, as he was murdered in 336 B.C. on his way to a theatre.

His son Alexander (336–323 B.C.) became king at the age of twenty. He started his regal career as the most powerful monarch in Europe, educated to his great position with all the knowledge and training of the times lavished upon him. Unfortunately his heredity was bad, as his mother was an evil-minded superstitious creature whose influence on her son was deplorable. Under these circumstances we are better able to understand how vanity, passion, cruelty and folly centred in one individual.

Alexander lost no time, after the death of his father, in carrying out the plans already prepared for the invasion of Persia. First of all he protected his flank by occupying Thrace, thus putting the Danube between him and the Scythians. With that secure he attacked the city of Thebes, which he looted and destroyed. Its 30,000 inhabitants were either massacred or sold as slaves. This was the Hitler method, and it had the desired effect, as all the other Greek states were too stupefied to be in any way a danger to his communications.

Hitler obtained important military advantages by occupying Norway, Denmark, Holland and Belgium, but he lost the benefit of most of their shipping which was bringing produce and raw material into them as neutral countries, some of which in turn was passed on to Germany. In the case of Alexander his treatment of Thebes deprived him of the use of all Greek ships, as the Greeks refused to put them at his service. They remained in port, thus leaving the Persian ships in command of the Mediterranean, and at liberty to cut his communications in his march round the coast of Asia Minor. He overcame the difficulty by capturing port after port from the land, until eventually the Persians were without a base.

After crossing the Dardanelles, with 30,000 men and 4000 cavalry, made up of Macedonians, Greeks and barbarians from the lands lying north of Macedonia, he met and defeated the Persians under Darius III on the banks of the river Granicus in 334 B.C. This enabled him to push on and take Sardis and the ports of Ephesus and Miletus. His communications were still in danger, but his capture of the port of Halicarnassus somewhat relieved the position, as it deprived the enemy of a nearby sea base. The next year he marched on along the coast, only to find that the enemy had got behind him by taking an inland route. His only course now was to turn back, defeat the enemy, or perish. Without hesitation he turned his army round, and, with his superior cavalry, utterly defeated the Persians at the Battle of Issus (333 B.C.), a victory which opened his path into Syria and Egypt, and altered the entire course of history. Darius fled, and his badly organised army, including its camp-followers, made up of women of the harem, officers' families, musicians and dancers, scattered.

The victorious Macedonians continued round the coast, capturing Sidon without difficulty, and then Tyre, which was to the Persians what Portsmouth is to Britain. A siege of seven months was necessary before Tyre capitulated, and only then did it fall because of the help given by the Sidonese fleet, which decided that it was wiser to be on the winning side. This gave the Macedonians superiority at sea. Gaza then fell after a siege of two months, a victory which removed the last obstacle in his path. Alexander now pushed on, to arrive in Egypt in 332 B.C. without opposition, because the Egyptians had suffered from the harshness of Persian rule for two hundred years. Many of the inhabitants of the three captured ports were either massacred, or sold into slavery, by this plundering murderer, who was now to change his character for a time, while he devoted himself to religious exercises under the guidance of the Egyptian priests.

Mention has already been made of Alexander's mother, Olympias, and stress has also been laid on the fact that what is taught to a child is never forgotten. Olympias, a murderess, and a vile creature from every standpoint, was very religious, both priests and their mysteries having a great influence upon her. The religious teaching of her son had been her constant care, and Alexander had developed into a devout and pious man. He treated the religious feelings of the Egyptians with great respect, visiting their temples and shrines, and attending their services.

He also visited the shrine of Amen-Rā, where the priests convinced him that he was not a naturally born being, but that, as his mother had been overshadowed by the god Amen-Rā, he was the product of this divine intercourse. The miraculous birth of great men was then a general belief, the idea being that an other-world man, called a god, could impregnate a woman, when in trance, under his control. The belief in his divinity went to Alexander's head, he repudiated his father Philip, and announced publicly his miraculous origin.

There may have been some method in this madness, his idea being perhaps that before he replaced Darius as King of Kings he must likewise be considered of divine origin. Who can tell what he thought? When dealing with an Alexander, a Napoleon, or a Hitler, one is not studying a man with a normal brain. Today they are accepted as sane, but some day mankind will be wiser and treat such moral perverts as insane criminals, dangerous to the public welfare, and only safe when kept in custody.

One constructive deed which Alexander did while in Egypt was to establish a new city, Alexandria, on the site of an old trading centre, and then, in 331 B.C., he started off to liquidate Darius and seize his empire. When he came near to Nineveh he was met by a great host of Persians, but Darius seems to have learned nothing from the superior strategy and tactics of his enemy. Again the Macedonian cavalry broke through the Persian centre, whose flanks crumpled up, and soon this vast throng was a mass of fugitives with the Macedonians in close pursuit.

First of all Babylon was occupied, and when Susa, the Persian capital, was reached, the dream of Philip of Macedonia was realised. Alexander, his son, was now in command of the great Persian Empire, which included Egypt, Palestine, Syria, Asia Minor, Persia, Assyria and Babylonia, to which must also be added Greece, as none could now stand up to this mighty son of the god Amen-Rā. When he reached Persepolis he indulged in a drunken bout, during which he gave orders for the great palace of the King of Kings to be burned to the ground, an action he excused, when he became sober, by declaring that it was his revenge for the Persian destruction of Athens by Xerxes.

One would think that his ambitions would now be satisfied, but this was not so as he had other lands to conquer, and he was still a young man. He had the best of life before him, and the then known world was not so very large, but, first of all, he must dispose of Darius, who was still at large. This did not take long, as, after a short pursuit, he overtook his caravan, only to find the King of Kings stabbed and dead.

With his enemy liquidated he was now free to seek fresh adventures, and he turned his face towards India, eventually reaching its frontier, the Indus river, by way of Turkestan, Cabul and the Khyber Pass, fighting and plundering as he went along. His troops by now were tired out by this precarious marauding existence, and wanted to get home. Alexander wished to go on farther, and add the wealth of India to his possessions. Where he might have ended no one can say, but a mutiny settled the matter, and, after spending three days alone, torn by anger and disappointment, he decided to return to Persia.

He divided his army, one part being sent by sea in a fleet which he built on the banks of the Indus, but his main force returned by land along the coast to Susa, his capital, which was reached in 324 B.C. On the return journey his army suffered terrible hardships, and many died from want of water. His wandering in the East had occupied six years, and, when he returned home, with his army dispirited, tattered and torn, he was faced by an empire in disorder. His treasurer had decamped with all he could take away, Macedonia, which had been left in charge of his mother as regent, was in revolt, and throughout other parts of the Empire the provincial governors were raising their own armies.

During his six years of undisputed possession of the Persian Empire he did nothing towards its government. He left it to get along as best it could, and that it did hang together, and not dissolve completely, is doubtless due to the excellent organisation built up by Cyrus, who, whatever we may think of his plunderings and conquests, was a great administrator. Alexander, on the other hand, was a great soldier but no administrator, though he showed wisdom in giving to the lands he conquered their own local government, and making all his subjects of equal standing in his eyes.

He founded seventeen towns to which he gave his name, but, if these had been required, they would have grown up by themselves. This was no compensation for the massacres at Sidon, Tyre and Gaza, for the obliteration of Thebes, the annihilation of her inhabitants, the destruction of Tyre and the consequent ruination of her great Mediterranean trade. He therefore gave nothing to the world of any value, with two very important exceptions.

A small portion of his ill-gotten gains he handed over to Aristotle, who was able to employ a thousand men in scientific work. This enabled the eminent scientist to become the greatest accumulator of knowledge of any man up to his time, and attain a position never before reached in the intellectual world. By his conquests Alexander certainly hellenised the East, opened it to Greek trade, and made Greek the international language, but Greek influence had been steadily making itself felt all over the Eastern world before his time, and he only greatly hastened an inevitable process.

This event is called by historians the marriage of the East to the West, and it certainly brought about two hundred years of close collaboration between the scientists of Greece and Babylonia, the achievements of the Middle East, prior to the introduction of iron, being thus preserved and improved upon. Greek scientists, moreover, took the title "Chaldaean", to let it be known that they had studied in one or other of the Mesopotamian seats of learning. Thus the East and West got to know each other as never before, and Buddhism, besides the other Eastern religions, reached Alexandria, where a great pan-religious college was established.

One great event which emerged from this opening of the East to Europe was the establishment of Christianity as the state religion of the Roman Empire six centuries later. If there had been no Alexander it is very improbable that Christianity would ever have come into being, and it would be difficult to dispute the fact that he was the prime cause of its birth. By his opening up of the East, its mysticism, which hitherto had been absent in the West, found converts in Greece and Rome. From now onwards we find the influence of the worship of Osiris, Mithra, Bel (Dionysus) and Krishna, who were the saviour-gods of the East, and of Buddha, the Indian sage, pervading Western thought to an ever greater degree, while the beautiful young goddess, the Holy Mother Isis, with the infant Horus in her arms, after some four hundred years of adoration, developed into the Virgin Mary, around whom was draped what was believed concerning the Egyptian goddess.

Under this influence arose everywhere in the West those voluntary associations devoted to religious ceremonial and contemplation, known as the Mystery Cults, which constituted the Greek Church for the two hundred years prior to the commencement of the Christian era. This Church was the foundation stone on which the Christian Church was built, and the Greek Church of the present day is the direct descendant of this pre-Christian Greek Church, which had the same beliefs and ritual, the only difference being the change in the name of the god worshipped. The Greek Church still calls itself the Orthodox Church, and it has every right to this name.

In the next chapter we shall see how, and why, Paul of Tarsus transformed Jesus into a Greek Christ, and so established Christianity,[1] but what interests us at the moment is the fact that the beliefs surrounding the Eastern Christs came to Greece as the direct consequence of Alexander's conquest of the Middle East, because this event opened up Babylonia, Persia, Egypt and India to European thought. This momentous effect followed from the successful outcome of Alexander's Persian adventure, but it was

---

[1] It is interesting to note how closely the nomenclature connected with Christianity and the Christian Church is related to Greek. The names Christ and Christianity are Greek, as are Church (the Lord's house), Ecclesiastical (Ecclesia being the Greek Assembly or Parliament), Apostle (Missionary), Presbyter (an elder), from which came the word Priest; Baptism (immersion), and Eucharist (Thanksgiving), to mention only a few.

certainly never part of his scheme—power and rich booty being his aim in life.

His great empire hung together, supported only by his military reputation, and when he died it all fell apart. All his mass murders, conquests, and the suffering which he inflicted on humanity, brought no good to mankind. Nothing was gained by all this misdirected effort which finally went up in smoke. This all-powerful man left nothing constructive behind him, and nothing, apart from financing Aristotle, that succeeding generations could claim as his contribution to the raising of humanity.

For the two years prior to his death, history records deeds which would make it appear that he gloried in the pomp and circumstance appertaining to an Eastern potentate. He always appeared in public dressed in the robes and tiara of a Persian monarch, and demanded the prostrations of all, even of his friends. His new environment doubtless made this necessary, as he well knew that he could only govern his immense empire by securing the allegiance of the Persian nobles, who would never have respected him had he not surrounded himself with this atmosphere of divinity. To them he was either a god or an upstart, and, as they accepted him as the former, this obeisance before him was their duty, and one which the Macedonians had likewise to perform.

His vanity reached the stage of madness, and doubtless he did consider himself a god-man, as he never permitted anyone ever to question his words or deeds. He had no self-control, and when drunk his fits of ungovernable rage made him quite irresponsible. He was quite unbalanced, his good deeds being just as extravagant as his evil ones. Never did he do anything within reason, and, when he murdered Clitus, his closest friend, who had insulted him, his repentance was as violent as his wrath. After murdering his foster-brother, and behaving in one way and another like the scoundrel he was, he died in Babylon (323 B.C.) after a bout of heavy drinking at the early age of thirty-three years. A few years passed during which his wife, his two sons, his half-brother and his mother were all murdered in different ways, and his great empire lay in pieces, a shattered wreck.

Alexander died leaving no plans behind him for the better government of his empire, but, as he was a young man when his end came, this can be understood because to him his empire-building career was by no means finished, it having in fact only just begun. Some think that he intended to turn Greece into a Persian province, and thus bring her inter-city wars to an end. If this be so, what he failed to do Rome accomplished two hundred years later. His other plans are fairly obvious. Arabia was to be his next victim, and a thousand warships were being prepared for the project. He murdered Clitus because this courtier foolishly taunted him for first attacking "the chamber of the women", meaning Persia, and not being brave enough to go west and conquer "the chamber of the men". So we may be sure that the conquest of the West was in his mind.

He had already planned to conquer North Africa, a plan which was followed by the British in the Second World War—Carthage, in what is now Tunisia, being his goal. He would not have stopped there, as Sicily, and later all Italy, would next have fallen to his blows, because Rome, in his day, had not then built up her power. Had this young warrior not gone out in a boat amongst the marshes surrounding Babylon, and there contracted fever, which was aggravated by a night of drunkenness, what a difference it would have made to everyone throughout the world up to our own times. No Roman Empire, no Christianity; but why speculate, as Rome, some centuries later, and not Persia or Carthage, became the master of the Western world, and round her doings our history now centres.

When dead, Alexander's crimes and follies were forgotten. Babylon became a city of mourning, and the Macedonians could not overcome their grief. The Persians, whom he had conquered and treated kindly, felt that they had lost a merciful master, but the Greeks had other feelings. Into a magnificent coffin of gold his embalmed mortal remains were reverently placed, which, after remaining two years in Babylon, was removed to Alexandria, where it was housed in a specially built magnificent temple fit only for a god. There, later Roman emperors gazed upon the earthly remains of one who so easily might have altered the entire course of history, as by then the gold coffin had been sold and replaced by one of glass!

We today talk of Alexander the Great. He was certainly a brilliant soldier, though he was brought up from childhood to think of military matters, and he received from his father a ready-made, fully-trained army, besides all his father's expert knowledge. So his achievements were not remarkable. He behaved towards the Persians as a statesman, and not as a conqueror, but by then he had secured their submission, to obtain which he had robbed and massacred thousands of innocent people. As a man he was a weak creature in so far as he was a vicious drunkard, vain and unbalanced. Moreover he lacked self-control, and that sense of righteousness without which all else on earth falls into insignificance. So in reality he was not a great man, only a master criminal, who grew rich and powerful on what others had produced, his birth and training being responsible for the fact that his deeds occupy more pages of history than falls to the lot of most people.

Our sense of values is all wrong. The great men and women are those who control their passions, and show to others the same consideration as they like to receive themselves. All other greatness, without these primary qualities of decency, is hollow. It is not always great qualities which raise a man above his neighbours, but very often because he is callous, cunning, intriguing, and is prepared to do things a more honourable man would not do. True greatness consists of self-control and living an unselfish life. The remedy for most of humanity's troubles is consideration for one another, or doing to others as we would have them do to us, and all who practise this are wise because each one is thus helping to make a better and happier world. This is not only what is right and just, but it is also the wisest course for everyone to pursue, and we have only to read history from the correct angle to find this borne out.

The story of Alexander is one which reveals the effect on humanity of ignorance and folly. This is here emphasised, as these failings have been evident from his time to our own days, some section or other of humanity always following the lead of master criminals who lure them to ultimate destruction. Since those days of over two thousand years ago, has the race made such progress to enable us to say that the human family is today ethically in advance of those past times? Mass murder, cruelty, butchery, the destruction of towns and villages, and the deportation of populations into exile or serfdom, have all been enacted before our eyes in this 20th century of the Christian era.

Man has advanced in material knowledge, but in wisdom very little. Ethically, in many ways, we have stood still. The ethics attributed to Krishna, Buddha, Confucius and others still stand unchallenged, but internationally they are dismissed with contempt. The moralising of Seneca, Epictetus, Pythagoras and Epicurus still holds good, and cannot be refuted. Their followers trained themselves to practise what they taught, but what could a few do amongst so many who always put self first? The time has certainly now come to concentrate less on material and more on ethical progress, less on building gorgeous temples of stone, which bombs can so easily demolish, and more on the temple of the mind, which nothing can destroy. If we would only give the necessary time to cultivating, with the right seed, the garden of the mind, all else that we desire would follow, to the lasting happiness of the entire human race.

(8) THE DECLINE AND CONQUEST OF GREECE.

Again we take up the thread of our story. There will be other opportunities, as we go on, to force home the lesson history teaches to all who study it aright. With the death of Alexander his empire split up into four parts, which were taken over by former generals or administrators. They, and their successors, defended Greek culture for 150 years against the worst inroads of the barbarians, ever pressing south from their fens and forests of Central Europe and Asia, but the glory of Greece had already vanished with the loss of independence of the city states. Then Rome took up the task successfully for the next six centuries, only to end by being ultimately overwhelmed.

Seleucus, one of Alexander's generals, became master of Persia, Mesopotamia and southern Asia Minor. Macedonia and Greece fell to Cassander. Ptolemy became ruler of Egypt, Cyprus, the coast of Phoenicia and Asia Minor. Lysimachus took over Thrace (Bulgaria) and northern Asia Minor. The small Greek state of Pergamon, in Asia Minor, alone preserved its independence until it became a Roman province in 133 B.C. There, for two hundred years, civilisation reached its height. Its library was un-rivalled, and its museum, arts and sculptures had no equal. Alexandria, under the able and wise rule of Ptolemy I and Ptolemy II, developed and prospered, to become the greatest city of its time. Here Greek influence predominated, and so we find the Greeks, who could never form themselves into a nation, spreading out everywhere along the shores of the Mediterranean and towards the East, influencing with their culture and learning all with whom they came in contact, their language becoming the international speech of the Middle East.

The break-up of stable government was another

opportunity for the nomads in the north to penetrate south, and we now find new tribes, such as the Gauls, pushing into Macedonia, Greece and Asia Minor, to become known a few centuries later as the Galatians, to whom the Apostle Paul wrote several letters. Other tribal movements took place, but, as these do not come within the main-stream of our story relating to Greek civilisation, they can be passed by for the present.

The time from the death of Alexander until the conquest of Greece by the Romans was, for the Greeks, a period which swung between liberty and subjection. Greece became a bone of contention to the neighbouring potentates of Macedonia, Asia Minor, Syria and Egypt. Her different states, with the exception of Sparta, were dominated sometimes by one and sometimes by another of them. At times, when her different masters quarrelled amongst themselves, they secured a partial independence. At length the constant danger to which their liberties were exposed brought about the Achaean League in 280 B.C., which, for a time, revived the dying energies of the Greeks, and produced a lustre on their period of decline. Nevertheless the internal condition of the city states was rotten. Their manpower and wealth had been squandered on fruitless wars, agriculture was neglected, while slavery had reduced the free citizens to the level of slaves. They were unable to compete with the slave-manned factories, and glad to sell themselves as mercenaries to foreign powers, or to become pirates, robbery being preferable to starvation.

A new power, moreover, had now arisen in the Mediterranean, against which no Greek state could stand. The Achaean League eventually collapsed as the Roman tide of conquest advanced, and bit by bit Greece was swallowed up by her more powerful neighbour. The days of the Greek states ended with the capture, pillage and destruction of Corinth in 146 B.C., and, from this time onwards, Greece was ruled by Rome, her history merging with that of her conqueror for the next five centuries, until Rome herself was submerged by the northern barbarians.

From the date of the Roman occupation, Athens enjoyed good government and submitted peacefully to her conquerors. The Romans placed no garrison in the city, no tribute was paid, and the constitution remained unaltered. Athens, for the first time for many years, was safe, and had no need to fear her once powerful neighbour Macedonia. The Romans showed great respect for the national pride of the Athenians, and their attitude is exemplified by the warm expressions of admiration which fell from the pens of Cicero and Horace. A visit to Athens was regarded by the Romans as a pilgrimage and an education, and from what they wrote of their experiences we realise how delightful and beautiful the city was in those days. The munificence of the Romans left nothing more to be added to its embellishment, masterpieces in art were to be seen everywhere, visitors being particularly impressed by the city's great buildings, the Acropolis, the Academy, the arches, the streets and the spacious harbour.

Though Rome became her ruler politically, Greece ruled Rome intellectually. Though, from now onwards, until she won her freedom from Turkey in 1829, Greece has no separate history of her own, the thoughts of her sons have influenced the minds of thinking people everywhere over the past two thousand years. Most of what we have that is good in our present-day intellectual life can be traced back to Greece, the country which was responsible for writing the first chapter on justice, democracy, philosophy, ethics, toleration, humanitarianism and education in the world's book of knowledge. If we read our history aright, we shall, moreover, find that this small country did even more than that, as it established a vital principle which has not yet been everywhere learned.

The Greeks demonstrated that the love of freedom and liberty in a community is as strong as in an individual. The passionate desire which the individual Greek cities had for their freedom made union between them impossible, but it was that same love of liberty which made Greece intellectually great, and made possible the imperishable thoughts which she has given to the world. If the Greeks had only been politically intelligent enough to realise that unity made for greater strength and a wider freedom, their history would not have been smeared by inter-city wars, and no Philip, no Alexander, nor Darius, nor Xerxes might ever have sought their domination, as Greece, with its high mountains and deep valleys, is not difficult to defend.

Instead of uniting into one nation, the Athenians so feared and hated Sparta that they enlisted in the Persian army when Persia was at war with Sparta, and the Spartans joined the Persians when Persia was fighting Athens. When civil war commenced in Persia in 401 B.C., 10,000 Greeks were not ashamed to fight in the ranks of their bitterest enemy under the leadership of the Athenian Xenophon, who, in his *Anabasis*, describes their victories and their desperate retreat back to Greece.' Nothing was left undone by one city to score off a rival city, each one ever striving for domination. The curse of Hellenic politics, said Isocrates, was the desire for empire—Athens, Sparta, Thebes and others, all in turn, being set upon by the others when they became affluent and influential.

The history of the quarrels of Greece is but the story in miniature of Europe, to be recorded in the pages which follow. From now onwards the tale we have to tell is the continuation of the one already told, a story of fear and hatred, of pillage and grab by those who wished the property of others and cared nothing for human liberty. The great conquerors who will pass before us one by one as we proceed, preferred theft to honest toil, as to steal what others had produced was so much easier than a concentrated productive effort. They had neither the ability to create, nor the wisdom to realise that individual nations will never be content to be under foreign domination, and that an empire built on force must sooner or later collapse.

History is the record of one failure after another to establish an empire, made up of different nations who were determined to be free whenever opportunity offered. Every empire has been built up on tyranny, and has consequently ended in disruption, the only exception so far being the British Empire, which would have ended likewise had her statesmen not learned their lesson from the American War of Independence. World history, for the next two thousand years, demonstrates everywhere this inherent love of freedom and justice, thus proving conclusively that unless the virtues are practised between nations there can be no peace, security and happiness.

(9) THE CONTRIBUTION GREECE MADE TO THE CHRISTIAN RELIGION.

So Greece was conquered, and she lost all semblance of independence, but her virile people, living under Roman rule, continued to influence the religious, intellectual and ethical thought of their times, so much so that they largely contributed to the foundation of a new religion which came to be known as Christianity. Considering the potent influence this form of thought has had on the people of the Western hemisphere, it is necessary that we should be aware of the link which binds Christianity to the Greek religion, without which there would have been no Christianity, and no Christian Church, to mould the history of what became Christendom, as well as the lives of the people, throughout the Christian era.

Greece was the channel between the religions of Egypt, Babylonia, India and Christianity, as she adopted their saviour-gods and the religious beliefs surrounding them. She only changed their names, just as the Christians gave new names to their three gods when they in turn adopted the Greek religious beliefs. But let us first of all go back to earlier times.

Every supernatural religion is Spiritualism in masquerade, and different disguises of the original are to be found everywhere throughout the world, the drapings only being different, and the Greek religion was no exception. When the savage uncultured Greeks first appeared in Europe, the gods they brought with them from western Asia were as depraved as themselves, and their beliefs just "silly nonsense", to quote Herodotus, but, as time went on, and they discarded much of the more grotesque beliefs and customs of·supernatural religion, their religious outlook advanced to reach a level hitherto unattained.

Two aspects of Greek religious thought were largely responsible for the ideas which came to be collected under the name of Christianity, the oldest, which we shall consider first of all being the Olympian religion, whose gods' names were changed by Christianity, to become known as saints and angels, they performing the same role as was allotted to the Olympian gods. About the Christian hierarchy similar fantastic stories were told as were recorded about the Olympian deities. At the Reformation this side of Christian mythology was rejected by the Protestants, but the books relating to it still circulate amongst Roman Catholics and Orthodox Greeks, who evidently accept what they read.

It seems impossible for ignorant people to accept the fact that the life in the world we pass to at death is just as natural as is the one we live on earth, and that all who have died live there a rational well-ordered existence. Consequently the mentality of Homer, who spun the wonderful romances of the lives led by the gods and goddesses in heaven, still persists, and Christian mythology is no more than the Christian version of the same fairy tales.

Homer nationalised these divine beings when he gave them a Greek home on the top of Mount

Olympus, but, if we go back to earlier times, we find
that they originated as apparitions, seen during the age
of Ancestor Worship. Time and imagination evolved
them into divine Greek heroes and heroines, the
conquerors who had banished all the earlier gods worshipped by the people who had previously occupied
the land. Now, as the national gods, they fraternised
with men and women on earth when they found
opportunity to break away from their feasting, music
and love affairs in their world above the mountain
tops.

As Greek mentality developed, under the influence
of philosophy, so likewise did her gods, so much so
that during the 5th and 4th centuries B.C. the Olympian
religion reached sublime heights in the most civilised
parts of Greece, combining as it did much of natural
religion, besides philosophy and ethical instruction.
All mankind was embraced within its orbit, and human
endeavour was encouraged to pursue the path of
righteousness, toleration and purity of living.

Consequently it had a profound effect on Greek
character, as it encouraged progressive thought,
harmony and concord. The aim of life, it taught,
was the pursuit of truth, and, with certain few exceptions, everyone was allowed to speak and think as they
pleased. In those lands where many gods were
worshipped there was room for all shades of opinion,
it being amongst those who worshipped only one god
that there was no toleration.

This being so there was no religious persecution
in Greece, no torture or imprisonment for unbelievers,
no creeds to contradict knowledge, and no one was
expected to transgress, against his own conscience.

The conception of the gods likewise advanced, and they became symbols of nobility of character and a developed humanity, never before attained. This improved mental conception was registered in stone, from which was carved the most beautiful statues of their divine guardians, and presiding over Athens was the goddess Athena, the beautiful, the ideal of purity, wisdom and righteousness, whose love for mankind transcended that of any man or woman on earth.

Then Olympian religion came nearest to natural religion so far attained in Greece, and not to be again reached anywhere until last century, with the coming of Spiritualism devoid of theology. How unfortunate it was that the Olympian religion did not last to develop into natural religion, but the Western world was not ready. Even today supernatural religion captures the imagination, as ignorance prefers mystery to knowledge. For the same reason the Olympian religion was gradually engulfed by the importation from the East of the beliefs surrounding the saviour-gods, and the torch of knowledge, which the Greeks had lit, was in consequence extinguished when they came into the keeping of the all-powerful Christian Church.

The Greeks loved their Olympian gods, and obtained real and solid comfort from the belief that both nationally, and individually, they were being guided and protected by them, each Greek, moreover, obtaining satisfaction from the idea that one was his special protector, or guardian angel. Furthermore, their link between heaven and earth was strengthened by the fact that through the medium in the local temple, the gods gave help and guidance to the people on earth, and the words of cheerful hope on their tombstones make us realise how death to them was but a temporary incident in the unbroken melody of life. Not lost but gone before was the theme, as some day separation would end, and the joyful reunion in heaven would take place.

This outlook produced a tolerant and contented people, and it is unfortunate that it became over-shadowed by increasing attention being devoted to the imported oriental saviour-god religions which became increasingly popular. So we find that concurrently with the Olympian religion the different saviour-god religions flourished, all of which are grouped under the name of the Greek Mysteries. Ultimately these saviours fused into one only, the Christ, a theological conception which came under the protection of a powerful church that permitted no variation from its fixed creed. Then, instead of religious belief being fluid, and open to individual interpretation, intoler-ance and persecution followed, to cause much misery and suffering, besides the death of at least 25,000,000 innocent people whom the Christian Church authori-ties termed heretics.

In pre-Christian Greece no religious belief was challenged, and the Mysteries endeavoured to main-tain a high standard of conduct amongst their wor-shippers. A 4th century B.C. inscription over the temple at Lindus reads, "All who enter this sacred place must be pure in heart and not conscious of any crime". The churches were open to all, male and female, rich and poor, freeman and slave, and the initia-tion ceremony of new members was solemn though bloody.

After being washed in the precious blood of the

lamb, representing the slain Saviour,[1] the one initiated was allowed to handle and kiss the sacred objects laid on the altar, and, when this was done, he received the Holy Sacrament, the bread and wine representing the Saviour's body. Then it was that his religious experience reached its culmination, as he believed that the *mana*, meaning the vitality and virtue of his Mediator in heaven, had been absorbed by him to make him one of the saved and elect.

This ceremony, which the Greeks called *eukharistia* (meaning thanksgiving), was a ceremonial and ritual of remarkable magnificence. On special occasions sacred objects were exposed in a peculiarly impressive manner to the worshippers. Painting, sculpture, architecture, music and lighting were combined with lavish skill to form one grand impressive spectacle, and the priests, in their gorgeous robes, added to the magnificence of the sacred ceremony. Here centred all that wealth and art could do, to impress those partaking of the greatness and solemnity of the occasion, and, if we wish to experience what this meant to the pre-Christian Greeks, we have only to attend a similar service in a Roman or Greek church of the present day, as little change in the ritual or music has taken place.

By partaking of the Eucharist, the initiated believed that he had reached at-one-ment with God, and that

---

[1] The hymn sung by Christians, in which the following lines occur,

> "There is a fountain filled with blood,
> Drawn from Emmanuel's veins—
> And sinners plunged beneath that flood
> Lose all their guilty stains"

would have been equally appreciated by both Greeks and Romans if the name of their saviour-god had taken the place of Emmanuel.

through the rising of his Saviour from the dead all believers would share with him eternal glory hereafter. Nevertheless Greek life and character deteriorated under the influence of the megalomania produced by these rites and ceremonies, whose theme throughout cannot be better expressed than in the words attributed to Paul, "Without the shedding of blood" there "is no remission" of sins (*Hebrews* ix, 22), an idea which was taken up by Christianity to spread throughout the entire Western world.

The Mysteries certainly helped to strengthen and comfort believers entering the Valley of Death, as to be with their Lord in glory was something to be looked forward to with great joy. Though comforting, it was not an ethically elevating religion, as believers were taught that man is a fallen being, who could not raise himself without the saving power of the Saviour and Mediator, a belief which Paul later took up in his letter to the Romans, where he said, "We also joy in God, through our Lord Jesus Christ, by whom we have now received the atonement". Belief, to the Mystery worshippers, as to the Christians of a later date, secured salvation, whereas the Olympian faith was one which produced a stronger and finer character, as it taught that the gods were just and punished the evil-doer, while rewarding the righteous man, whose deeds, and not his beliefs, secured for him happiness hereafter.

To the believer in a saviour and mediator, at-onement came from outside oneself, and not by individual merit; an easy way of salvation, and one which inhibited any incentive to personal effort. By faith, by allowing the emotions to lift him to an exalted state of ecstasy, the believer found his satisfaction. His fear of death, his fear of punishment hereafter, were soothed by the emotional exercise produced by performing certain mysterious rites, which he thought brought him into union with God, and stamped on his soul the hall-mark reserved for the elect.

To see an apparition was the height of religious experience, as a ghost to the ancients, devoid of psychic knowledge, was no less a person than a god. The one who had this psychic experience believed that God had highly favoured him by this revelation, but to meet God, or a god, in this way, to see God face to face, was a rare experience and reserved only for those possessing the natural psychic gift of clairvoyance. Apart from such records in the Bible, the Koran, and other sacred books, secular literature also reports these strange experiences, and reliable prominent Greeks and Romans, such as Plotinus, Porphyry, Apuleius, and others, claim that on different occasions they were thus favoured.

The vast majority, those more deeply imbedded in the flesh, had to be satisfied with emotional ceremonial, in order to quench their craving for union with God, which became an obsession to many Pagans. By mystical rites, which were later carried on by the Christians, the aim was to produce a state of *Ekstasis*, in an endeavour to project the etheric body from the physical body, in order to produce *Enthousiasmos*, a condition which left a place for God to enter and dwell inside the worshipper. "To prepare thyself, as a bride to receive her bridegroom" became the life-aim of countless sincere mystically minded Greeks, as well as Romans who also became converted to the idea after their conquest of Greece. "I in Thee, and Thou in me" through the merits and mediation of the Saviour, who is both man and God, the Son of the Father, was the substance of their prayers, all of which produced a thoroughly unhealthy state of mind. If we read the epistles to the Colossians and Ephesians; we find the influence the Greek Mystery religions had on the mystical Paul; in fact his writings have as their background the beliefs of the Greek Mysteries. Much more than that developed in his emotional mind, because it was he who, after a psychic experience, was responsible for transforming Jesus into the Christ, and in the next chapter we shall read of the Greek saviour-god he took as his model for this theological conception. Here we are concerned only with the Greek doctrines which formed the foundation, on which Paul built up a new religion on old and widely accepted ideas.

As life dies within mother earth to bring forth new life, so the saviour-god-man died to bestow ever-lasting life to all believers. This idea was borrowed by Paul when he wrote "Like as Christ was raised from the dead . . . even so we also should walk in newness of life", and "in the likeness of his resurrection" body. (*Romans* vi, 4.) Just as the Gospels depict the miraculous lives, under the name of Jesus, of the Greek saviour-gods on earth, so Paul's epistles embrace the teaching and beliefs of the Mysteries, which emphasised, as he put it, that "The flesh lusteth against the Spirit, and the Spirit against the flesh". (*Galatians* v, 17.) Consequently regeneration by means of baptism, and the performance of mystical rites, ejected what Paul called "the old man, which is corrupt", and "put on the new man, which after God is created in righteousness and true holiness". (*Ephesians* iv, 22–24.)

One has only to read the *Liturgy of Mithra*, one of the saviour-gods, to discover where Paul found his material to enable him to write as he did to his different converts, whom he had persuaded that his theological conception of the saviour-god, whom he called Christ, now took the place of the Pagan saviour-gods then worshipped throughout the Roman Empire. How ignorant most Christians are of Greek religious history, as they still imagine Paul journeying and preaching through a heathen world, whose gods were idols and whose prayers were offered to images of wood and stone. In fact, the Pagans were an advanced and deeply religious people, and to think of them otherwise is a cardinal error.

From the Greek Mysteries Paul found the material for his teaching, and any Pagan who disagreed with his conclusions was to him a heathen, meaning an unenlightened person, an attitude which only an intolerant zealot would adopt. Many of the most illustrious Pagans, to whom religion and worship were a prime necessity of life, used the same religious expressions as have soothed and comforted Christian people, because they believed the same doctrines though their gods were called by different names. This being so, the continuity of the belief in a saviour-god persisted, by Christianity absorbing these age-old beliefs, to become eventually strong enough, with the help of the Emperor Constantine, to crush out all its rivals.

To end here the history of Greek religion would

consequently be wrong, as to make its record complete we must carry on throughout the Christian era. The Greek Orthodox Church of the present day can trace back its lineage to the Mystery religions of Ancient Greece, the only break that occurred being in the name of the god-man who was worshipped. Otherwise the foundation of Christian teaching is to be found in the beliefs held by the Greek Mysteries. Greece, by this mystical theology, made a tremendous contribution to the world, and though it is most unfortunate that it was chosen instead of Greek philosophy and Greek ethics, nevertheless Europe mentally was moulded by Greek religious thought in a way few imagine. Two small nations, Greece and Judea, determined the religious beliefs, the civilisation, the culture and the outlook of the people living in the Western world up to our own times.

The fusion of Greek and Jewish thought took place after the Temple of Jerusalem was destroyed and the priesthood scattered, an event which gave the Hellenised Jews, dispersed throughout the Roman Empire, the opportunity to adopt the Greek outlook, and merge their beliefs in the coming Messiah with those surrounding the Greek saviour-gods. These became the first converts to Christianity, which combined both Greek and Jewish theology, and they formed the nucleus around which the new religion grew. How all this happened will be explained as we proceed, and meantime we must concentrate our attention on another nation which was to leave its indelible mark on civilisation.

CHAPTER VII.

ROMAN CIVILISATION.
(753 B.C.–A.D. 410.)

Introduction. (1) *The Republic, from its Inception to its First Dictator.* (2) *Julius Caesar, and the Emperors to Marcus Aurelius.* (3) *Rome's Contribution to the World's Mental Wealth.* (4) *The Tragic History of the God Emperors.* (5) *The Origin and Growth of the Christian Church.* (6) *From Constantine to the Collapse of the Empire.*

ALL the political troubles from which Greece suffered were due to selfishness, intolerance, the want of understanding and consideration of the feelings of one towards another, and the entire absence of the spirit of compromise. Individually, the virtues were practised just as they are in our own times, but, in the mass, they were quite forgotten. The mass mind of Athens showed no tolerance towards the mass mind of Sparta, or that of Sparta towards that of Athens, and the same was the case with all the other states one to another.

Today the mass mind of London does not treat the mass mind of Edinburgh as Athens treated Sparta. Washington's mass mind does not treat New York's mass mind as Athens treated Naxos or Thasos, and the people of Milan, Florence, Genoa and Venice are not today perpetually at enmity and in conflict one with another, as they were during the Middle Ages, the reason being that cities are now incorporated within states whose people have a common political, commercial and cultural outlook. Though cities are not now in conflict, the states in which they are situated still are, the consequence being that international wars continue to convulse the face of the entire globe.

The thoughtful people in these past times, just as they now do, earnestly desired peace and hated war, but they were no more able to devise the means to prevent it than have those who followed them, because war is a psychological affair, and until the mass mind of the people everywhere changes, to oppose war, nothing can be done to stop it. Some have always been ready to take by force what others produced, considering themselves first and everyone else last. These forceful few have always been able to dominate the many, train them to fight, and thus carry on a campaign of violence against all who opposed them. The lack of intelligent independent thought in the average man is the cause of the trouble. In the old days cities destroyed and pillaged cities just as do nations today, and only the leaders obtained the power, the satisfaction, and the pick of the plunder, the common man who did their bidding always being left to lick his wounds, to suffer and die, and end his days in poverty.

Now we come to the time when, by the same process, another city arises by force of arms, the neglect of every virtue, and every economic law, to become eventually the centre of a great empire. Our story takes us to Italy, where an Aryan community has gathered together upon some of the fertile plains and valleys guarded by rugged and barren mountains.

Being quite ignorant of the right way to live, their unbridled carnal passions predominating over intelligent reasoned thought, and surrounded by other tribes cursed with the same mentality, these Aryans were at constant war with their neighbours, to arise eventually by superior talent, cunning, and good fortune above the rest and dominate the entire Mediterranean world.

Mention has already been made of the nomadic Aryan tribes which forced their way south and populated Greece, the coast of Asia Minor, the south of Italy, Sicily, and the Islands of the Ægean Sea. Other tribes of the same stock came south, and scattered over the land we now call Italy. By 1000 B.C. the centre of Italy was inhabited by these northern nomads, who had settled down and intermarried with the darker coloured Iberian tribes they found there on their arrival. A similar dusky race, the Kelt Iberians, occupied Spain, and what is today called France was peopled by the Gauls. They all spoke a Keltic language, and in Italy this in time fused with the Aryan tongue, to produce eventually the language known today as Latin.

The Aryans, who settled on the productive plains on either side of the river Tiber, became known as Latins, from Latium, the name they gave to their settlement. Great indeed was to be their contribution to civilisation, and, though their roads, bridges, aqueducts, temples and amphitheatres will some day perish, the mental wealth they left behind them never will.

Besides the Greeks in the south and the Latins in the centre, we find another race in the north of Italy, the Etruscans, a civilised people, believed to be

similar to those the Greeks found in Greece and
Crete. Other tribes occupied different parts of Italy.
Between the years 800 and 600 B.C. Italy was therefore
mainly populated in the north by the gifted Etruscans,
their land being called Etruria, now known as Tuscany.
In the centre were the semi-barbaric Latins, and in the
south the semi-civilised Greeks, all of whom had intermingled by marriage with the older Iberian races
which inhabited the country on their arrival.

On the other side of the Mediterranean a Semitic
race, the Phoenicians, had occupied the part of north
Africa now called Tunisia, where they built a town
which they named Carthage, meaning New City.
This town, which was older than Rome, was founded
about the middle of the 9th century B.C. It was
situated ten miles from what is now the town of
Tunis, at the head of a bay looking straight across the
Sicilian Straits to Sicily, a distance of 150 miles, which
area became well known during the Second World War.

Those Phoenicians, who built Carthage, now to be
called Carthaginians, were of the same race as the
Hebrews, Babylonians and Canaanites, which latter
we read much about in the Old Testament, as they
and the Hebrews were at constant war. The Carthaginians worshipped the god Bel, the saviour-god of
Babylon. They were a deeply religious people, both
children and adults being freely sacrificed, and, like
most Semites, active and keen traders. Carthage was
a republic, ruled by a Senate, with tributory states
situated in Sardinia, Corsica and Sicily, and she had
a powerful fleet of vessels trading throughout the
Mediterranean.

From the time the Aryans reached the Mediterranean there was a conflict of interests between them and the Semites. Both were clever traders, and this led to quarrels between the Greeks and the Phoenicians, and then later these developed into a long and bitter war between the Carthaginians and the Romans. Phoenicia, like Palestine, was situated on the borders of Egypt and Syria, to whom she paid tribute in turn, so as to be left in peace. Her ruination came about firstly when the Persians destroyed Tyre, her principal city and port, secondly when Alexander did the same again, and lastly when the new city of Alexandria took away her trade.

Before the Aryans arrived in Greece, the Phoenicians had outgrown their little strip of country just behind Tyre and Sidon, and taken to the sea. They invented the deep-sea fishing net, and with this they worked round the Mediterranean, trading with the natives. From Lebanon they had ample timber to build their boats, which they used to colonise Cyprus and Carthage. From being fishermen they became pirates and traders, ever searching for the shell-fish which produced the purple dye, the fashionable colour in the East.

Instead of bringing home large supplies of shells, they started factories along the coasts of the Mediterranean and Black Sea, to extract the dye where the shells were found. The dye was then brought home, and, with the wool obtained from the Arabs, they worked up a large trade with Egypt and Babylonia in manufactured coloured woven woollen goods. The articles they received in exchange were bartered for other things along the shore of the Mediterranean, and some were brave enough to go south along the coast of Morocco, others going north to Spain and Britain, and even penetrating the Baltiç Sea. Along with the Greeks, the Phoenicians were the pioneers of land and ocean trade of continental dimensions. They were brave and enterprising men, intent on making money, and their wanderings in search of new markets stimulated industry amongst the savages of the West, who now required to produce something if they were to get the luxuries from the East these merchants dangled before their eyes. Thus was spread throughout the West the culture of the East, and, by this means, was laid the foundation of Western civilisation.

From the 10th century B.C. onwards a variety of races, around the shores of the Mediterranean, some more civilised than others, were all playing for position, attacking, grabbing and fighting with each other. Sicily became half Greek and half Carthaginian; Italy was mostly a third Etruscan, a third Latin and a third Greek, while Tunisia was wholly Carthaginian, and they were all afraid of losing anything, though each wanted the trade and lands belonging to her neighbours. It was like a nursery full of children, with the floor spread out with toys. Each child wants what the other has, instead of being content with what he already has. So they grab from one another, and soon there is a howling row.

The people of those days had the minds of children, just like the mentality of many of the present day. They had never studied economic law or the laws of ethics; they were selfish, intolerant and inconsiderate of the rights and feelings of any nation but their own. Every nation put itself first and the other last. What each could not get peacefully was taken, if possible, by force. Consequently there was played the old game of snatch and resistance, of attack and defence, with the misery, suffering and unhappiness which always follow in their train. It never occurred to these stupid people that there was enough for all, and that, if they divided it up, they could live comfortably, happily and peacefully together on the proceeds. Instead, they fought and snarled at one another, and were miserable ever afterwards.. Nearly everyone always thinks of his own country, but seldom of the people of the world at large. How the lack of wisdom is the curse of the human race!

The Latins, in the 8th century B.C., were purely an agricultural community who grazed their cattle in the marsh and forest, of which the land was mostly composed. The Tiber divided them from the Etruscans in the north, and there, according to tradition, they established a trading centre in 753 B.C. which they named Roma, nearby which were seven hills, on one of which at a later date they built their temple. In these early days the Romans, as we can now call them, were ruled by kings, but their history is rather obscure. When we come to 474 B.C. we are on firmer ground, as we know that in that year the Greeks in Sicily fought a sea battle with the Etruscans, resulting in the destruction of the Etruscan fleet. Eighty years later the Gauls in the north flowed into the valley of the river Po, and the unfortunate Etruscans, who up to now had been the dominating race in Italy, were caught between the Gauls and the Romans. Taking advantage of their plight, the latter pushed north across the Tiber for several miles and captured one of their fortresses.

The Roman success was only temporary, as the Gauls, after defeating the Etruscans, pushed on south and sacked Rome in 390 B.C. The Gauls, suffering from disease, were induced after seven months to leave by the payment of a ransom, and they never troubled Rome again. From now onwards Rome became more powerful, having gradually extended her territory both north and south. In the north she reached the river Arno, on which Florence is now situated, a town which centuries later was to be the birthplace of Dante and the home of Michael Angelo. In the south her territory reached to what is now Naples, near which was to rise the towns of Pompeii and Herculaeneum.

Her northern neighbours were now the Gauls, as she had conquered the Etruscans, adopted their culture, and learned their arts, but, as the Gauls were now firmly held by the Roman garrison on the Arno, some of them turned their attention to Asia Minor to settle down as the Galatians in Galatia. Three centuries later they received letters from the Apostle Paul in which he termed them "O foolish Galatians, who hath bewitched you, that ye should not obey the truth", a rebuke which could be applied with equal force to the entire human race.

(1) THE REPUBLIC, FROM ITS INCEPTION TO ITS FIRST DICTATOR.

Rome became a Republic in 509 B.C., and though for a time the title of King was retained, it applied only to the Rex Sacrorum, later to be known as the Pontifex Maximus, and, in Christian times, as the

Pope, or Papa, the father of the people. Roman history, throughout the Republician period, is one succession of quarrels amongst the people. The patricians,[1] or nobles, tried to keep the government and the land in their own hands, while the plebeians steadily strove to attain their rights. Eventually they succeeded, and a plebeian was made consul in 356 B.C., when the people also gained control of the Assembly.

After battles, in which the fortunes of the Romans varied greatly, they, by stern discipline, hardihood and frugality, slowly but surely conquered the surrounding tribes, the chief of which was the Sabellian. Like Germany, in the centre of Europe, able in war to strike out in all directions, Rome enjoyed an equally good strategical position, but it required five hundred years of constant struggle before she obtained command of the entire Italian peninsula from the river Arno southwards. During this time of conquest the famous Via Appia was constructed, which gave the Romans quick access to Campania, and this enabled them to strike quickly and effectively at the last important stronghold of their nomadic enemies, but, before all Italy was subdued, the Greeks in the south had to be conquered.

The Greeks, in the 3rd century B.C., were still in southern Italy, with their city states dotted here and there. Syracuse in Sicily, and Tarentum were the two most important. The latter, as Taranto, was to become prominent in our times, as in its harbour the Italian fleet was attacked by British bombers in 1940

---

[1] The patricians were formerly known as the gentes, the name given to the leading families, from which word we get our words gentle, gentle-birth, gentlefolks, gentleman, gentry and gentile.

and badly damaged. Alarmed at the growing power of Rome, the Greeks implored the help of King Pyrrhus of Epirus, a small country now in part Greece and in part Albania. From this Royal House came Olympias, the wife of Philip of Macedonia and mother of Alexander. Consequently the sympathies of the King were towards the Greeks, and doubtless he also feared the growing power of Rome, always pressing south and nearer to his dominions.

Epirus, in 280 B.C., came to the help of the Greeks with a well-supplied and efficient army, and defeated the Romans who retreated on Rome. Epirus might have defeated them utterly, if the King had not been so anxious to secure Sicily, which he next invaded. After initial successes he was there conquered, to return to Italy and be defeated by the Romans (275 B.C.), who thus gained command of southern Italy. Rome was now the undisputed mistress of all Italy south of the Arno, and, from this time onwards, she built up the system of government by proconsuls and prefects, through whom she ruled as her empire expanded.

It is clear that the King of Epirus made a mistake in not following up his victory and utterly defeating the Romans, as his incursion into Sicily gave them time to rearm. Moreover, he angered Carthage, which owned the western half of Sicily. If Rome had then been defeated, Carthage might have had the place Rome was to occupy, but so it was, and this interference by Epirus only started the pot boiling until it boiled over into the three most terrible wars in ancient history, about which the story will now be told.

The King of Epirus, broken and disappointed,

withdrew his army from Italy across the Straits of Otranto, leaving behind him two powers which were bound sooner or later to fall out, or, as he put it, he left Sicily to be the battle-ground of Rome and Carthage. His foresight was fully justified by events. Carthage had enabled the Romans to win by giving them the support of her powerful fleet, but how bitterly in after years she must have regretted it, as Epirus could never have become such a deadly enemy as Rome was to be in the years which followed.

Carthage and Rome divided the spoils of victory, the Greeks were turned out of southern Italy and most of Sicily, the former being taken over by Rome, and the latter, except Syracuse, which still remained Greek, by Carthage, but this state of affairs was only to last for eleven years. To avoid the piracy which was rife off the coast of Sicily, Carthage put a garrison in Messina, just opposite the toe of Italy, a reasonable proceeding as Carthage was then the dominant sea power in the Mediterranean, having inherited the colonies and trade of Phoenicia, now in her decline. Consequently her trade routes required protection. Rome took this opportunity to help the pirates, and an expedition was despatched to Messina, which naturally started a conflict with the Carthaginians. Rome excused her aggressive action by explaining that the garrison at Messina endangered Roman interests on the mainland, and doubtless the Romans did genuinely fear the Carthaginians coming into such close contact with Italy.

This was the spark which lit up one of the great conflagrations in world history, to last, off and on, for one hundred and sixteen years, leaving Carthage in the end a heap of ruins and Rome bankrupt. Messina was captured by the Romans in 264 B.C., and the enemy driven to the western shore of the island, where he made a desperate resistance, so much so that Rome realised that victory would come only on the sea. Therefore she set to work to build a fleet, large and powerful enough to defeat her enemy, and in two months produced one hundred five-decked ships, and twenty three-decked ships, with oars on each deck.

Hitherto the means pursued to defeat enemy ships was to ram them and break their oars, but the Romans improved upon this method by adding to each ship grappling irons and a drawbridge, which, when it came alongside an enemy ship, were let down, thus enabling the crew to board the enemy vessel and attack its occupants. This new type of warship was called the Còrvus, from which term the British navy adopted the name Corvette for a new type of submarine destroyer. The crew of the Carthaginian vessels were seamen only, trained to ram and break the oars of enemy vessels, but the Romans also filled their ships with trained soldiers, who boarded the enemy vessels and killed or captured the crew. This new device worked in a way which surprised everyone, with the result that off Mylae in 260 B.C. the Carthaginians were completely defeated, the Romans capturing and destroying fifty of their ships.

The Carthaginians, like Darius in his war against Alexander, learned nothing from their defeat, with the result that when their ships again met the enemy, in the battle of Ecnomus four years later, the Romans, adopting the same tactics, again defeated them.

Seven hundred ships were engaged in this the greatest
sea battle so far ever fought, and when it was over
the Carthaginian fleet was reduced by ninety-four
vessels.   Rome then pursued the war in Africa, landing a force near Carthage, but this was defeated after
a successful start, as the Roman Senate recalled one of
the commanders, who was a consul, to conduct the
election then due, and also a large number of troops
who would not fight during the winter.

Carthage, on the verge of capitulation, took heart,
and, under the leadership of Hamilcar, in 255 B.C.,
routed the invaders just outside Carthage.   Only 2000
Romans escaped, to be picked up on the coast by the
Roman fleet which later suffered disaster.   A storm
wrecked 284 of her ships, and she had to start again to
build up a navy, a task which was accomplished in
three months.   This she had to do three times, as her
next fleet was lost in a storm, and the one that followed was defeated at Drepanum in 249 B.C., when
180 ships were lost to the enemy.   Finally, the third
fleet defeated the Carthaginians at the Battle of the
Ægates Isles in 241 B.C., when the vanquished enemy
sued for peace.   Carthage paid a large war indemnity
to the victor, handing over all she possessed of Sicily,
and, three years later, both Sardinia and Corsica.
Thus ended this disastrous war which lasted for
twenty-one years.

This was the first of three such wars which are
known as the Punic wars, Punicus being the Latin
name for Phoenician.   Twenty years later the trouble
all began again, this time the Ebro river in Spain,
which runs into the Mediterranean eighty miles
south of where Barcelona is now situated, being the

cause. The Romans, both fearful of Carthage and
greedy for her trade, considered her a dangerous
enemy and rival. To Rome, Carthage always stood
in her path of further expansion, and, when an excuse
arose, war between them was inevitable.

After the first Punic war, Carthage invaded Spain,
and, under Hamilcar and Hasdrubal, built up a colony.
Rome, fearing attack by land through France, demanded that the river Ebro be the boundary, and that
no Carthaginian troops cross the river. This the
Carthaginians in 219 disregarded, which meant a
fresh rupture with Rome. Hannibal (247–183 B.C.),
the son of Hamilcar, now comes into the story at the
age of twenty-six, to prove himself one of the most
outstanding military leaders of all time. He hated
Rome, and was bent on a war of revenge. War
breeds war, and the defeated always when possible
seek revenge, as did Germany in 1939. Hannibal
marched through France, along by the coast, and
crossed the Alps into Italy, one of the most spectacular and daring feats in all the annals of war,
elephants being used to carry some of his equipment.

Hannibal defeated the Romans in every battle, but,
if the Romans could not defeat him, they at least could
cut off his supplies from Spain. Cornelius Scipio
(233–183 B.C.), the outstanding Roman general, at
once saw this weak link in the enemy's armour, and, at
the outbreak of the war, started off with a force for
Spain. He arrived by sea in France too late to prevent Hannibal getting through to Italy, but he pressed
on to Spain, and there sat down on his line of supply.
For fifteen years Scipio continued this land blockade,
with the result that Hannibal, though he always won

his battles as the result of his superior generalship, could never get through sufficient supplies to enable him to follow up and secure a decisive victory. At Cannae he won an outstanding victory against the enemy, which he utterly destroyed, but he could not capture Rome because he lacked siege equipment. It was very like what happened in the Second World War, when the Germans won battle after battle but lost the war because they could not capture Britain.

Hannibal's great victories much embarrassed the Romans, because a large portion of southern Italy joined his standard, including the Macedonians from across the sea. Syracuse also supported the victorious general, but Rome would not admit defeat, and held on, refusing to seek peace with the enemy. Gradually the tide turned, but not before Hannibal reached to within three miles of the capital. Taranto, through which Hannibal was obtaining supplies from Carthage, was captured, and then followed Syracuse. Spain, during this time, was gradually slipping from the control of Carthage, and Hannibal at last found himself left in Italy high and dry without supplies.

The Romans then decided to cross over to Africa and capture Carthage, and Hannibal returned home to organise resistance. His army met the Romans at Zama, close to Carthage, in 202 B.C., where he was defeated for the first time in his great military career. The Roman forces greatly outnumbered the Carthaginian army, as the Numidians, a tribe which lived in the desert regions, joined forces with the Romans, and it was because of the cavalry they supplied that Scipio won his great victory. So, for the second time, Carthage was defeated and made to pay an indemnity

of (1) 10,000 talents, roughly £2,500,000 sterling,
(2) to hand over to the victor her fleet of warships,
except ten vessels, (3) to give over Spain to Rome,
(4) to agree never again to go to war without the
permission of Rome, and lastly, (5) to hand Hannibal
over to the Romans. This last condition never
materialised as he escaped to Asia, to be finally
captured, but he never reached Rome as he took
poison and died in 183 B.C., the same year as did
Scipio, his great antagonist.

Few Romans, after these conditions had been
accepted, expected a third Punic war, just as Great
Britain never expected a second war with Germany.
History always repeats itself, and its pages contain
other instances of the conquered, at some later day,
waging the struggle afresh. Fifty-three years had,
however, to elapse before Carthage was able to arise
from its ashes, and again be a rival to Rome, during
which time Rome went on adding to her dominions.
In the space of a little over eleven years (200–189 B.C.),
she had broken the power of the successors to Alexander's empire in the East, and established throughout
the eastern Mediterranean a Roman protectorate, but
at home the peasants were impoverished, as during
the Hannibal invasion many mortgaged their lands,
which they had finally to abandon.

Carthage made no further attempt to expand her
territory. She had given up all ambitions of becoming an empire; all she now asked was to be allowed to
trade and prosper once again. Rome was, however,
determined to have no rival in the Mediterranean.
It was to be her sea, and hers alone, and all trade and
commerce must be for her benefit only. Marcus Cato,

known as Cato the Censor, a conservative puritanical pedant, was sent to Carthage to spy out the land, to come back with the report that Carthage was again wealthy and prosperous, and must be finally destroyed. An excuse had, in consequence, to be found for a third war on Carthage, one that this time would wipe the hated Carthaginian Semites from off the face of the earth.

The method Rome adopted was subtle. She encouraged the Numidians to encroach nearer and nearer to Carthage, to a point which made resistance by its citizens a necessity. The diabolical plan worked out as was expected, and Rome then made the excuse that, by resisting, Carthage had broken the treaty concluded at the end of the last war, which laid down that never again would she raise an army and fight. Rome demanded hostages, the surrender of all implements of war and territorial concessions, to which the Carthaginians agreed, but their ready acceptance only made the Romans more than ever determined to ruin their enemy. Then followed a fresh demand that Carthage be abandoned, and its population moved ten miles inland.

To the Carthaginians this was nothing less than condemning them to starvation, as their substance was derived from their ships and the trade they carried on with other lands. To abandon their port was to abandon their trade, and without trade their population was doomed to destruction. In desperation Carthage refused to agree, preferring to fight and die rather than to succumb without a fight. In the hour of their greatest danger they preferred sudden death in battle rather than slow strangulation as the victims of a brutal enemy; to die standing erect rather than to live on their knees.

The Romans by no means obtained the quick success they expected, and their military effort was not equal to their threats. Their first attack on Carthage (149 B.C.) was a failure, due to incompetent leadership and poor equipment. Not until three years had passed was Carthage conquered, during which time its inhabitants suffered terribly from famine, as the Romans laid siege to the town and prevented the entry of all foodstuffs by either land or sea. When starvation had reduced the besieged citizens to a state of prostration, the Romans stormed the city, and for six days the slaughter went on, to end in the capitulation of those who remained alive.

A city, which had a population of over 500,000 before the war started, was thus reduced to one of 50,000, but even these were not allowed to remain at home. They were sold into slavery, the entire city was pulled down, and left without a house standing. With great ceremony the Romans then placed a curse upon the spot, and invoked the wrath of the gods on any one who would ever again build on the site where once this great city had so proudly stood. A new Carthage, however, arose when Julius Caesar built a city, bearing the same name, on a spot near to which the old one was covered over by rubble. This new city played a prominent role in the life of the Roman Empire, and became famous for its part in the early days of the Christian Church.

Our ancestors, who lived during the comparative peace of the latter half of the 19th century, doubtless thought and believed, when they read of such stories as the destruction of Carthage, that such atrocities could not happen now, as we had advanced since those days. These bad old days, they believed, belonged to a time when the world was in heathen darkness, before the light of Christianity had come to illumine mankind. Their school histories generally made little reference to the cruelties which have gone on throughout the Christian era, and so their ignorance can be excused. We, on the other hand, who have experienced what war means, realise now that it is the same today as in Roman days. It brings out everything that is bad and brutal in humanity, and takes us back to the time when our animal ancestors roamed the jungle destroying every living thing weaker than themselves.

What took place at Carthage was likewise perpetrated by the Christians in their attacks on Moslem cities during the Crusades. A new religion does not change man from being a brute into being kind and considerate. Something apart from his emotions, and beyond a selfish desire to secure salvation for his soul, is required to stop the barbarities which the strong practise on the weak. What is required is an entire change of outlook, a mental revolution of such a nature that every race on earth alters its outlook on life and sets a new course. This must be done all together, as war will not cease until the great majority, or a sufficient number, think alike to keep aggressors disarmed and incapable of causing trouble.

What happened to Carthage happened to Jericho, as we read "And they [the Israelites] utterly destroyed all that was in the city, both man and woman, young and old, and ox and sheep, and ass with the edge of the

sword." (*Joshua* vi, 21.) Joshua was just another of
that criminal class of aggressive warriors, who stole
the land of Canaan from the Canaanites to whom it
belonged. He laid a curse on Jericho in these
words, "Cursed be the man before the Lord, that
riseth up and buildeth this city Jericho . . . so the
Lord was with Joshua, and his fame was noised
throughout all the country." (*Joshua* vi, 26.) The
destruction of Carthage, and the curse laid upon it,
was just history repeating itself, as it has been doing
in our own day.

War brutalised the Romans, and the mentality of
the nation became coarse, intolerant and debased.
It made the distinction of the classes more obvious,
the ruling class becoming more objectionable, and their
treatment of everyone who was not a Roman citizen
more insufferable. As the power of Rome increased
her morality decreased. Increased territory enlarged
the authority of those in power, to the detriment of
her once free agricultural population, until the people
themselves were bound in the chains of the same
tyranny which they had shackled on those they had
conquered. At the end of the last Punic war the
Roman mentality was at its lowest, as low as its
exchequer. All they now lived for was more, and
still more, plunder, more lands to conquer and more
men to enslave.

Corinth was the next victim, as the same year
(146 B.C.), which witnessed the destruction of Carthage,
saw also the complete destruction of, and the massacre
of the inhabitants of, this prosperous historic Greek
city: A generation earlier the once mighty Macedonians, who, under Alexander, had been the terror

of the Middle East, were conquered by the Romans at the Battle of Pydna (168 B.C.), and from now onwards, for the next two hundred and fifty years, when the Empire reached its height, Rome was a nation of plunderers, its upper and middle classes living largely on the proceeds obtained from the rape of other nations. Her soldiers were paid, and the booty they looted was considered as a bonus which they either sold or brought home to Italy.

General education in Christendom is not yet a century old, and so far history has been taught according to the outlook of the Hebrews as contained in the Old Testament. By teaching history truthfully, and laying emphasis on the failings and mistakes of our ancestors, as well as on their good qualities, the children of the future will discover that there is little of hero-worship to be found in the past. The terrible mistakes made by our ancestors should serve as a guide to them to take the path of righteousness and avoid the way of evil, because, with all their conquests, the average Roman citizen would have been happier and better off if his country had remained at peace.

So far emphasis has been laid on the weakness of Roman rule, but, bad as it was, we must remember that it was in advance of anything so far attempted. Here was no nation of illiterate citizens, leaving all their destinies in the hands of a god-king. Neither was it a city state of limited outlook, thinking only of its own petty interests. If Greece wrote the first chapter in the story of man's attempt to govern, Rome certainly wrote the second. Like the Greeks before them, the Romans in their time were attempting, in their own blundering way, to construct a state which was better than had gone before, and gradually they produced a legal code which formed the basis of Western civilisation. They attempted, but did not succeed for long, to carry the Greek democratic principles far enough to cover a nation instead of a state, the want of efficient means of communication dooming such an experiment to failure.

Democratic government, as we understand it, only became possible after the arrival of the widely read newspapers and the railways, the first to inform, and the second to enable representatives to keep in touch with the opinions of their constituencies. Before that time arrived it was quite impossible for the country people to be sufficiently informed to enable them to be entrusted with a vote. When the world began to open up, under the influence of printing and the steam engine, the people became more intelligently interested in both national and world affairs, and consequently demanded a greater voice in the conduct of government. Slavery, as we have already noticed, was the outcome of the general absence of money, its circulation being limited to the wealthy. In the old days, before money circulated freely, there was not sufficient with which to pay the labourer or servant, and men and women had to work in exchange for their keep, clothes and shelter.

No other method of payment was possible, but there is no excuse for the cruelty inflicted on slaves, or for them being bought and sold like chattels. Many masters were kind to their slaves, who showed in return their gratitude and affection, but it was a degrading system, and only when the working classes obtained their emancipation last century did labour receive its right status in the community. So, when we compare the Roman Republic with our own times, the different conditions then prevailing must be remembered.

The Roman Senate, and the popular assemblies, cannot be looked upon as representative bodies, but they made a step forward, as they informed the people of their decisions. In 60 B.C. their proceedings were made public by being posted up on notice boards, and there were special copyists who copied these announcements and sent them to their patrons in the country upon an album, meaning a white board. This was the beginning of a news service, as all items of interest were also included. When Rome fell, and the Christian Church took over control, all intellectual life ceased, the consequence being that this, the earliest newspaper, ceased publication. Not until 1566 did a newspaper again appear in Europe, when a printed sheet was displayed in the streets of Venice, and anyone who paid a small coin, called a gazzetta, was allowed to read *Il Gazzetta*, as the paper came to be named.

The people of these Republican days were so ignorant that they knew little or nothing of the world at large; in fact the earth to the educated was in the form of an oval, with the Mediterranean in the centre, its extremities reaching to the Pillars of Hercules at the Strait of Gibraltar in the west, the Indus river in the east, the Danube in the north, and the Sahara desert in the south. Beyond these extremes they knew nothing, and were quite ignorant of how other people lived or what they thought. Economic science was quite unknown. Medicine was in its infancy, and the people knew little more than does an animal of the make-up of the human body. With such ignorance, representative government was impossible, but here we see it in embryo, embracing for the first time the country at large, and not only a city, which was the limit even the brilliant mind of Plato could foresee of community rule.

Communication by air brings all parts of the world together as never before, and makes it easier to travel 3000 miles than it was possible to traverse fifty miles a hundred years ago. This being so, is it not possible that representatives of all the inhabitants of this earth may some day be able to meet regularly at a selected spot, and there settle world disputes with the backing of an international air force? The steam engine made representative government possible a hundred years ago. Let us hope that the airplane will be able to make international government possible, and so put an end to these endless disputes which lead to war.

The airplane and the radio may make all this possible some day. Otherwise narrow national propaganda, which leads to war, is the only alternative. We must educate the children of the coming generation everywhere to make the right choice. Knowledge gives power for good or evil. Wisdom puts knowledge to its right use. So let it be our aim to develop wisdom and increase in knowledge.

Some Romans realised this, and Seneca wrote many inspiring lines on the subject, but his knowledge was limited. Then it was more restricted than in our own times, and so, when we read of their superstitions, their priests examining the heart or liver of

animals to discover the will of the gods,[1] or their crude
political ideas, let us remember that they had the minds
of children and that to them the world was much as
it is to a child in the nursery. They retained their
captives as slaves, but at least they did not make a
practice of sacrificing them to their gods, as was done
in an earlier age and continued until more recent times
in other lands. Their sports were crude and cruel,
but the blood-lust is strong in those who have not
risen beyond the animal in their pleasures, and the
inflicting of needless pain has always given satisfaction
to undeveloped minds.

Some slaves, captives and condemned criminals
were made to fight to the death before a multitude of
spectators. Cicero, Seneca, and others, protested
against all killing for sport, but only last century
boxers in England were regularly set against each
other to fight until one fell exhausted, at times to die.
Bear baiting and cock fighting have now passed away
in most civilised countries, but bull-fighting, hunting
the fox, the otter, the stag and the hare still persist.
We have made some progress but really not very
much. The Greeks, with all their love of quarrelling
and fighting, seldom descended to gladiatorial sport
and amusement, and they termed the Romans barbarians because they did so. Undoubtedly it was
through Greek, and not Christian, influence that
gladiatorial contests came to an end in Rome, because
they continued for one hundred years after the
Romans had adopted the Christian faith.

With Carthage destroyed, Rome was now com-

---

[1] Both the heart and liver were believed to be the seat of the mind and
used by the gods, by mysterious signs, to convey their wishes to the priests.

pletely mistress of the Mediterranean, and, with her fleet, all the other lands bordering this sea were at her mercy. From now onwards her history is a story of one conquest after another, so much so that by 50 B.C. her possessions comprised most of Spain, Gaul (France), the whole of Italy, Dalmatia, Macedonia, Greece, Asia Minor, Syria, Palestine, Lybia, Numidia and all the Mediterranean islands, including Corsica, Sardinia, Sicily, Crete and Cyprus. Egypt was an ally under her protection, and only Persia, Mesopotamia and Arabia in the world as known to her were outside her sway. How largely her appetite for conquest had increased will be better realised when we remember that after the third Punic war (146 B.C.) her possessions included only Numidia, Carthage, half of Spain, Dalmatia, Madedonia and Greece, and the islands of Corsica, Sardinia and Sicily.

Those who think that war accomplishes nothing are wrong. What they should say is that war accomplishes nothing of a permanent nature, but this is true of everything, as nothing on earth persists, everything being subject to change and decay. War does produce changes of a more or less enduring nature, and what the Romans succeeded in doing by force brought under their domination a great part of the world which was then known to them. They, moreover, retained these possessions, and continued to add to them for a further 150 years, when the Empire reached its limit in A.D. 100. Then it comprised every land touched by the Mediterranean Sea, besides most of Britain and Mesopotamia.

Such, then, is the outline of the rise of the Roman Empire, which, to its inhabitants, must have seemed as secure and firmly established as the rock of Gibraltar. Doubtless the various lands she conquered benefited from her strong rule. When her power wilted we know that Europe was left in a chaos which lasted for centuries. All this is accepted, and, in spite of her cruelties, it must be freely acknowledged that where she ruled there was, generally speaking, peace and prosperity, but it does not follow that all this would not have been the case had Rome never existed.

Carthage very nearly defeated Rome on several occasions during the Punic wars. If she had done so, and had treated Rome as she herself was treated, she would have had the place Rome had, and been the dominant power in the Mediterranean. If this had happened, and Carthage had continued her trading, leaving conquest aside, what then would have been the position? Numidia, the land surrounding Carthage, would have been prosperous. Egypt was getting along well and happily under the wise rule of the Ptolemy administration. Greece would doubtless have worked out her own salvation without the help of an overlord. Mesopotamia was civilised long before the Romans had been heard of, and, as for Gaul, Spain and Britain, civilisation was slowly but surely reaching these parts by way of the Mediterranean. On the other hand, the nomads, which the Romans kept in check, might have spread chaos everywhere and brought civilisation to ruin, and only a combination of the civilised nations could have kept them at bay.

The Carthaginians, before the time of Julius Caesar, were trading with Britain, Spain, and along the coast of Gaul, bringing with them their civilisation which might gradually have permeated all over Western Europe. The Roman destruction of Carthage stopped all this, and, instead of peaceful traders, all Western Europe resounded with the tramp of her legions bringing the sword, but not the trade by which the people improve their standard of living. Trade, and not conquest, has always been the best civilising influence, and the obliteration of Carthage was undoubtedly a shattering blow against this peaceful method of mental development.

The Roman Empire, though brought about by the inevitable laws of cause and effect, was not therefore a necessity. It just happened, as other things have happened which we accept and think of as necessary preludes to our present conditions. It would not be difficult to go back in history, and pick out many things that might easily have happened which, if they had, would have made world conditions better than they are today. We must, however, always take things as they are, and, on this basis, plan a better world with the help we can obtain from observing the mistakes of our ancestors.

The history of empire-building gives no justification for every small country being dominated by one which is more powerful. Why should any group of people be intimidated, and, if they do not yield, be conquered and deprived of liberty and independence? Every nation, however small, has the right to govern itself in the way it likes best, provided it does nothing to affect injuriously the well-being of its neighbours. What it claims for itself is equally claimed by its neighbours, and no country, great or small, should do to its neighbours that which it does not wish done to itself. On that basic principle nations must order their national policy, just as individuals are expected to do, and it is because they have never applied this fundamental law of right living that the people of this earth have wallowed through rivers of blood, seeing their possessions destroyed and their happiness impaired.

At this period of her history Rome, by her conquests and aggressive policy, added little to the happiness of humanity, and this should always be the touch-stone by which we judge success or failure. Taking this as our guiding compass, it follows that all wars of aggression, all keeping of people down under a rule they dislike, all interference with individual or national liberty, are wrong and contrary to the best interests of society. Only when there is national and individual liberty can progress take place, and the people be happy and contented. History is one long story of liberty being deprived to nations and individuals, and their fight for its return. No nation or individual will remain for ever in bondage, and sooner or later the tyrant is overthrown and freedom is recovered. What we want to avoid in the future is the repetition of this age-old mistake, which has been repeated time and time again to the accompaniment of loss of life, property and happiness. Only by increased knowledge, and by greater wisdom, is this possible, so let all who have the good of humanity at heart help to flood the world with intellectual light.

When Rome was a republic, those who steered the ship of the Roman Empire were for ever producing mental unrest amongst their neighbours, they were always seeking storms and tempests instead of keeping in calm and placid waters. Thus only can an empire be built up by force. We, in our time, have experienced all this with the coming of the modern empire-builders. Hitler and Mussolini gave no rest or peace to their own people or their neighbours. Harmonious conditions ceased with their arrival on the scene, and Europe for a generation was in a turmoil, to end in the terrible catastrophe of total war, bringing suffering and misery to millions of innocent men, women and children.

The conquered nations have .always been kept down and suppressed by the stronger power, but this does not add to the happiness and welfare of the dominant people. So we may well ask if the Roman people were happy and contented during the time their great empire was in the making. Were all the spoils of victory making the mass of its citizens more comfortable in better houses, and had they more and better food to eat? So far as one can tell from the records which have come down to us, the answer is in the negative. Between the end of the last Punic war and the coming of the Caesars, injustices were glaring and rousing to anger the people, who, densely ignorant of the meaning and effects of empire-building, constantly grumbled, and at times revolted, because they felt that they were being denied their rights as free citizens of a democratic state.

The system of voting was stupid, and did not represent the views of those who were entitled to vote. The government was vested in the hands of two elected rulers, called consuls, who originally appointed the senators. The Senate, like our House of Lords, was unelected and came to consist largely of ex-magistrates.

The Comita Tributa, one of the three main forms of the Popular Assembly, corresponding to the British House of Commons, was an elected body, but the method of election was crude and unrepresentative.

It was called together by proclamation, issued seventeen days before the date chosen for its assembly in Rome. The priests then examined the hearts and livers of certain sacrificial beasts the night before the chosen date, and, if they found therefrom that the gods were not agreeable, the meeting was called off. On the other hand, if all was well the horns were blown, and, after prayers were offered, business proceeded. Discussion then commenced, but no questions were permitted though private individuals were allowed to speak. Then came the voting by tribes, each member of a tribe going with all the other members of the same tribe into the voting pen. Each tribe had a vote, so that the measure under discussion was decided not by the majority present, but by the majority of the tribes which voted.

There were other voting methods adopted, but they were of the same character, all equally unjust as a minority present could carry measures against the majority. What would happen if our electoral system in Scotland worked in a like manner? Then we would have all the Campbells, the McPhersons and the McTavishes voting according to their clans, but, though the Campbells far outnumber the McTavishes, their votes would be no more effective than the smaller number cast by the McTavishes. Surely the inequality of it all should have been perceived and corrected, but this was never done.

As the number of citizens increased, it was

obviously impossible for them all to gather in Rome. Consequently the Popular Assembly became more and more unrepresentative of the mass of the Roman people, with the result that the power of the Senate increased. This compact body of from 300 to 900, made up of the most influential members of the community, some of whom were keen politicians, conducted the affairs of state but was held in check by the Popular Assembly. It had little executive power or control over the consuls and proconsuls, but, owing to its experience and prestige, its influence was great.

In 100 B.C. there were about 900,000 citizens scattered throughout Italy, many of whom had never seen Rome. The Popular Assembly was therefore, to all intents and purposes, elected by the votes of the citizens of the capital. Intrigue, political juggling and trickery were rife, and even the Roman citizen could hardly be said to cast a free vote for or against a motion. Only when matters reached a head, and popular opinion grew in volume, did the citizens from outlying districts come to the capital and make their wishes felt. This often meant riots, strikes and in-surrection, to be quelled by force. If they came to Rome unarmed they were easily dispersed and sent home, whereas if they came armed they were the enemies of the State and treated accordingly.

This applies to the citizen who was the freeman, either a patrician, one of the aristocracy, or a plebeian who had no blue blood in his veins, but the bondman had no say in the affairs of state. The people, how-ever, as can be well understood, felt that they had little or no say in the government of their own country, and so we read of revolutionary leaders coming on the scene from time to time. The poor received little consideration from the rich, who regarded them with contempt because of their ignorance. So the Romans in general obtained little happiness from their looting of other countries, any gain there was going mostly into the hands of those who already had sufficient for their needs.

The period between 146 and 49 B.C. was one of constant internal strife between the reformers, those who worked for the good of the people, and the reactionaries who looked on them as pawns to be used for the purpose of the State. Tiberius and Gaius Gracchus, two brothers, stand out as leading agrarian reformers and champions of the people, the former being the author of the remark attributed to Jesus, "The son of man hath not where to lay his head".

On the other side is Cornelius Sulla, the victor of the bloody conflict (87–84 B.C.) against Mithradates VI, King of Pontus, who attempted to free Greece and the Middle East from Roman domination, during which uprising 100,000 Italian residents in these parts were massacred. Within this period civil war raged in Rome, to end in Sulla succeeding Caius Marius, the proletarian leader and famous general, and becoming dictator in 82 B.C. He instituted some useful administrative reforms, but soon set about massacring, banishing, outlawing and confiscating the property of all his enemies. Here we find the gestapo in full swing, and the people in abject fear of the secret police and arrest, so much so that they became sullen under the terror. The legacy of hatred Sulla left behind him was long remembered, and for years remained a source of danger to the State.

Sulla was the Hitler and Mussolini of ancient Rome. All moderate men, such as Marius and Sulpicius, fled the country. Republican government ceased, and what we now call totalitarian government, under a dictator, took its place. Money was hoarded and not put into use, towns became desolate, land and property were confiscated and left to lie waste, all of which, following the past civil and social wars, left a long train of evils, hatred and discontent. The gestapo, or "Sulla men", as they were called, under the directions of Sulla, maintained this terror for nine years, to be finally overthrown by his friend Pompey, who, after subduing successfully all insurrection in Sicily, Africa, Spain and Italy, which was seriously interfering with Rome's food supplies, deserted his master and denounced his evil political methods.

How history is for ever repeating itself! What has happened in our own times happened in Rome two thousand years ago. A man was given complete power, and the people lost all control in their own affairs. He rose to power on false promises made to a confused and discontented people, who soon discovered that their lot under a dictator was worse than under the Senate. If the masses were only educated in the history of the past, they would avoid the mistakes of their ancestors, but, instead, they continue to repeat, time and time again, the old mistakes so often made before.

This is what the Romans did, as within a century they were again within the grip of emperor dictators, who deprived the people of all say in the affairs of state. It is so much easier to avoid the responsibility of government and allow some dictator to think for you, but as with an individual, so with a nation, the price of indolence must be paid, and this is what the Romans ultimately discovered. So we shall now commence the study of this new epoch in Roman history.

(2) JULIUS CAESAR, AND THE EMPERORS TO MARCUS AURELIUS

The Republic was not to last. The first attempt of a community to govern an area greater than a city ended in failure. Rome was a republic in name only, but it had worked, with many creaks, while it was a small state. The expanding Empire made a change necessary, as it brought into being something much greater than a democracy could manage in those days. An empire which was always quarrelling at the seat of government could not command the authority, or retain the respect, of its subject nations who were now looking for guidance to Rome as their capital and legislative centre.

Divine rulers in the East had kept their people in order, and Alexander, the first European monarch to reach the status of a god-man, had also found the idea to work well. So the Romans, anxious to end the ever occurring disturbances at home, came to realise that the time was ripe to make a change. Now that there was an empire to govern, why not adopt the Eastern idea of a god-emperor, and so abolish the hatred and confusion caused by rich ambitious men

dominating the Senate by bribery and intrigue?
Then wealth determined everything, and anyone
could have what he wanted if he were prepared to
pay the price. Gradually force of circumstance
forced a change in the constitution, and the bridge
between the Republic and the divine ruler came into
being when the right man arrived on the scene.

Julius Caesar (100–44 B.C.) was the man the
country was awaiting. He is looked upon as the
greatest man of the Roman world, but it all depends
on what we mean by great. He was certainly an
able administrator, an artful politician, a powerful
orator and an outstanding general. He had great
literary ability, and was a wise statesman with far-
seeing vision. So much for his good qualities, but,
on the basis of the new morality which we hope is
coming to enlighten mankind, he must also be
described as a super-murderer and a master-thief, one
who murdered people in battle for the purpose of
plunder, tribute and territory. The glamour of his
great success must not blind us to the facts which will
be noted in their right place. The riches of the
Empire which were now flowing into Rome increased
the desire for more, and, as he added to the loot, he
received his reward in the honours and dignity conferred upon him by a grateful people.

Rome, politically, in his day was morally bankrupt, however full her treasure chest may have been.
Her politicians were debased, and her unjust laws led
to violence and bloodshed. Internal rottenness was
sapping the Empire's strength, and, had the strong
man not appeared, the structure might easily have
collapsed from want of the guiding power which

Julius Caesar supplied. He was a patrician, the son of a noble house whose members had held high offices of state, and he entered political life at a time of great crisis in his country's history. Then lived men whose names have been handed down the centuries: Crassus, the vain purse-proud millionaire big business man, who paid off Caesar's youthful heavy debts, and became joint consul with Pompey, the famous incorruptible soldier-politician, who later spent five years subduing and governing the Middle East.

During Pompey's absence another Roman rose to power, whose wise moderation helped to guide the ship of state. He was Cicero, and both he and Caesar worked to undo the injustices which the tyrant Sulla had fastened on the people. Cicero was rewarded with the high position of consul, and Caesar received the propraetorship of Spain. There he remained for only a short time, and, on his return home, he became consul largely owing to the influence and wealth of his friend Crassus. The Senate was composed of men intent on climbing up the political ladder by fair means or foul, and the growing political power of Caesar caused his enemies considerable concern, to end in his being appointed to the command of the army in northern Italy. Anxious to win for himself the great military reputation held by his son-in-law Pompey, he was quick to see that his chance had come, and there he built up his army with which he ravaged and subdued Gaul during the next eight years.

It is interesting to think that Napoleon's all-powerful career started when he was given command of the French troops in northern Italy, and likewise there now opened up to Caesar a great military career, and eventual dictatorship, by his appointment to the command of the Roman legions in the same part of Italy. Dangerous as Caesar was to his opponents when he was a private citizen, he was immensely more dangerous in command of his well-trained legions. But first of all he must show his fellow countrymen what he could do.

The Gauls and German tribes resisted his onslaughts to their utmost, but, after defeats and victories, Caesar drove the Germans across the Rhine. The Gauls, who made a heroic resistance, were mercilessly slaughtered and the captives sold into slavery, but it required three bloody campaigns before they were brought to submission. He used new and cunning devices, combined with diabolical treachery, to defeat the people he had so inhumanly attacked without just cause. Then, after thus brutally bringing his enemies to subjection, he started off (55 B.C.) hoping to repeat the same performance in Britain. But he found the British tougher than the Gauls and, after two defeats, gave up the attempt. The Gauls, inspired by the resistance of the British, attempted to regain their freedom, but this was thwarted by terrible vengeance. Everywhere he caused devastation, suffering, misery and loss of life, and, after experiencing defeat which nearly drove him out of Gaul, he finally, with great effort, overcame the resistance. By the next year the country was pacified, to become the most subservient of all Rome's conquests, adopting her laws, language and civilisation.

Julius Caesar was a typical example of the Roman general who rose by military skill, and political ability, to the position of governor of a district with a well-trained army under him. These legions were composed of men who were just adventurers, those people who hate honest work and are always anxious for excitement and pillage, parasites who live on the labour of others. When these men were skilfully led their leader became powerful, as they were always willing to engage in any enterprise which brought adventure and loot. At times the leader became so powerful that he could defy the authority of the Senate, and rule as he pleased. After the 2nd century A.D. the army had generally the principal say in the election of the Emperor, which accounts for so many of them being adventurers and men of debased character.

Julius Caesar's career, though more outstanding, was just like that of so many who succeeded him, that of a man who, because of his past successes, had a large army behind him. After plundering and massacring a million inhabitants of Gaul—hundreds of thousands by the basest treachery—he, like other master murderers and thieves, used his immense fortune from stolen lands for his own advancement. Because he was successful he has been lauded by the historians, but no one with moral sense can look upon him as other than a master criminal who, when he secured the loot, settled down as a good and law-abiding citizen.

The excuse for all his butchery and pillage is that the Gauls were undisciplined tribes, but, however much past historians may praise him for his bloody work, the coming generations, if war is to cease, must view it all in a very different light. Civilising effort,

by means of educational propaganda, could in time
have performed the results Caesar obtained by force,
but these methods never occurred to our ancestors.
King Asoka, to whom reference is made in the chapter
dealing with Indian civilisation, adopted wise and
peaceful propaganda instead of conquest, with eminently satisfactory results, but he is the only ruler
in history who expanded his influence in this
way.

Because Asoka discarded force and adopted peaceful methods, he is unknown to most people in the
West, but this ignorance only emphasises how history
has been wrongly taught in the past, and how those
who were really great have been left in the shadow by
the dazzling light shone on the super-criminals who
appeal to the imagination.

On Caesar's return home from Gaul, disputes
arose in the Senate, which feared his growing power,
and he resigned his command, but retained the confidence of his legionaries. Fifteen months later he
put himself once again at their head and crossed the
Rubicon, the stream dividing his province from the
rest of Italy. He invaded his own country, and town
after town was captured. Pompey, who had been
invested by the Senate with extraordinary powers,
tried to stop the triumphant progress, but without
success. His troops were brushed aside, and
when the invader reached Rome he was the undisputed master of Italy—Pompey, and all his other
opponents, having fled. After subduing the civil
war then raging and showing leniency to all, Caesar
started off for Alexandria, where the attractions of
Cleopatra (Queen of Egypt jointly with her brother

Ptolemy) kept him a dangerously long time away from his fickle supporters at home, who were much shocked at this open display of immorality, she being a married woman. Then Caesar moved to Asia, where he placed affairs in the East on a secure basis. He was by now the absolute autocrat of the Roman world, the man who solidified and expanded the Roman Empire, and, after this was accomplished, he returned to Rome with Cleopatra to celebrate his triumphs.

Caesar was five times Consul, four times Dictator, the last time being for life. Coins were struck with his effigy upon them. He took over the office of Pontifex Maximus, thus becoming head of the State religion, and he was treated as a divine being. All these honours made his enemies hate him ever more fiercely, so much so that they murdered him on the Ides (= 15th) of March in the Senate in the year 44 B.C. This was the signal for the renewal of the civil war which Caesar's strong rule had quelled, but danger also threatened from the east, as Mark Antony prepared to invade Italy with seventeen legions. Cicero did his utmost to restore order and rally the country to meet the danger, but all in vain, and, though Antony did not carry out his threat, disorder continued until another strong man arose to take command of this seething mass of ignorant, stupid people.

Caesar was brilliantly succesful in all he did, but nevertheless he was the product of the idea, which two thousand years has done so little to alter, that the moral law does not apply to strangers outside our gates. As a statesman he tried to remove many of the injustices of his time, he reformed the law and the calendar, he made regulations for the better government of the provinces, and remedied the worst abuses, including bribery and corruption, but, in spite of it all, his hands were stained with the blood of a million Gauls whom he sacrificed in his lust for wealth and success.

In a book on the life of Julius Caesar, written by a mid-Victorian author of much repute, occur these words :—

In this sketch of Caesar's life we have found little to blame and have been able to add few shadows to the picture, while the dignity, sweetness and nobleness of his character cannot be concealed.   We have preferred rather to attempt to construct, from very imperfect materials, some faint resemblance of the marvellous personality of him whom the genius of Shakespeare rightly recognised as "the foremost man of all this world".

This panegyric to a man who on one occasion sold 53,000 white prisoners as slaves to the highest bidder, shows the low ethical standard of Christian civilisation last century.   Such an action was, however, quite in keeping with "God's Holy Word", to which the people always went for moral guidance. We must also remember that in Victorian times it was believed by all Christian people, and these comprised most of the population of Europe and America, that God was a god of war, the Lord of Hosts, the God of Battles, who instructed the Israelites to treat their enemies in just the same way as Caesar treated the Gauls. When we remember that to Christians "The Lord is a man of war" (*Exodus* xv, 3), the reason for the foregoing opinion of a mid-Victorian author will be better understood, as will also be appreciated why Christians, throughout the Christian era, always believed that they had divine authority for the numberless atrocities they committed.

This way of looking at the lives of all the great adventurers of history pervades the biographies of last century, as similar quotations about Cortez, Charlemagne, and other successful criminals of the past, could be given. If they were triumphant they were looked upon as great and wonderful men, no matter how many innocent people they had persecuted and slaughtered. Success was the standard of greatness to our ancestors, the keeping of the moral law, and ethical conduct, being quite secondary considerations.

When the next act in Roman history opens we find three men in charge of the affairs of the Empire— Octavius in command of the west, Mark Antony of the east, and Lepidus of Numidia, but it is around the first two that our story now centres. Octavius was a man of great capacity and breadth of vision, and showed little liking for the way Antony was conducting affairs in the east. He was evidently scheming a new eastern empire of his own making. In fact Antony seems to have fallen so deeply for the charms of Cleopatra that he gave her, and her affairs, more attention than the interests of Rome. Perhaps, because of this, or to get him out of the way, Octavius decided that Antony must be relieved of his command, and this the Senate endorsed. Cleopatra proved unfaithful in war, however faithful she may have been in love, and, by withdrawing her fleet of sixty ships, she left Antony to face those of Octavius alone. He was defeated and fled, leaving his sailors to get away as

best they could. Finally he committed suicide, and
some time later Cleopatra followed his example, when
Egypt became a province of the Empire.

Octavius (44 B.C.–A.D. 14) had now no rival, but
he refused to become a dictator. He was, however,
given such authority that he was one in all but name.
He was invested by the Senate with certain powers,
and became first magistrate with the title of Augustus.
These special prerogatives conferred upon him, in
substance, autocratic authority, which he used for the
reorganisation of the provincial governments, to
reform the finances of the State, and to bring order to
an empire worn out with twenty years of civil war and
anarchy. He set up the European boundaries of the
Empire along the Rhine and Danube, leaving Germany
outside Roman influence, in the backwood with the
other barbarians, and he made similar demarcations
in the east.

Germany in those days was composed of some
forty different farming tribes, and it is interesting to
see how alike they were to their descendants of the
present day. The German tribesman, like the rest of
mankind, had a dual nature, one being friendly and
the other unfriendly, or, as biologists call it, amity and
enmity complexes. He loved his home, his wife and
family, was devout, docile and loyal to his chief, but
towards those not of his own tribe the enmity side of
his conduct prevailed, and he sought the blood of
strangers without mercy. War was part of his
religion, and death in battle opened the gates of heaven.
To die fighting, he considered, was the most glorious
possible experience, and to follow his chief the sacred
duty of every tribesman.

Very nearly did Octavius succeed in bringing these brave fanatical German tribes within the circle of Roman civilisation. At one time the Romans reached the Elbe, and if they had been able to hold this line of defence European history would probably have been very different. It was a shorter and more easily held defence than the Rhine and the Danube, but unfortunately, after some twenty years, they lost it by the folly of Varus, the governor, who had succeeded the wiser Tiberius. Varus, by his tyranny, goaded the Germans into revolt, when they destroyed him and his army in A.D. 9, one of the most momentous events in history, and one which has had its repercussions right up to our own times.

Because of this disaster the Romans withdrew from Germany, the Germans lost their civilising influence, and the Romans had to be content with a longer and less secure line of defence which ultimately cracked, to bring down the Empire. Battles determine history, and this one fought at Teutoberg sealed the fate of the Roman Empire and of Europe, though four centuries were to pass before the barbarians engulfed civilisation, to destroy Pagan culture and put Christian civilisation in its place.

Augustus takes his place as the first of the Roman emperors. He received sole and supreme command of all the naval and military forces, and all the provincial governors were put directly under his control. He copied the efficient accountancy methods of Egypt, and constituted a sound bureaucracy fit to control the complexities of a wide-flung empire. He became Pontifex Maximus, and, in 28 B.C., was given the title of Princeps. With him the republican form of government definitely came to an end, and for thirty years his benign authority in the State was unquestioned. A monarch had at last arrived to occupy a throne, to whom the entire Roman world now looked in the hope that peace had come and party strife had ended.

During his reign another, who was to become a divine monarch to the greater part of the Western world, was born. We are told that he was born in humble circumstances, lived a short life of simplicity and service, and died the death of a criminal. This was Jesus of Nazareth, whose birthplace is uncertain, whose birthday is unknown, and of whose place and date of death we are likewise ignorant. All we know about him comes from writings attributed to some of his faithful followers, who, in their later years, gave a brief account of his life. Upon this, as the centuries passed, was laid stratum upon stratum of myth and legend, the effect being that the original story was so mutilated as to be of no historical value. What, at the time, was considered an ordinary everyday affair, became, as time passed, one of supreme importance to a large part of the human race, and, because this is so, the subject will be carefully considered further on in this chapter.

Tiberius (A.D. 14–37) followed Octavius, and reigned for twenty-three years. He was an able administrator but very unpopular in Rome, he being so inscrutable that he had no friends and few admirers. Nevertheless under him the Empire prospered. Then followed Caligula (A.D. 37–41), who was insane, to meet his end by being murdered by his own servants. Claudius (A.D. 41–54) then became Emperor, during which reign Rome annexed southern Britain. He was poisoned by Agrippina, the mother of Nero. For the next fourteen years Nero (A.D. 54–68) reigned, during which time we read of his various vices and cruelties. The general opinion is that he set fire to Rome and fiddled while it burned, but this is untrue as he was fifty miles away when the disaster occurred, and moreover, fiddles had not then been invented. He murdered his mother and his wife, but this, and his other atrocities, were overlooked by his subjects who, however, could never forgive him because his troops in Britain were defeated by the British under the command of Boadicea in the year 61. Then followed an insurrection in Spain, when the Roman legions rose in rebellion under Galba, who advanced on Rome, and Nero, with no public support behind him, committed suicide.

A scramble now ensued for the throne, and Galba, Otho, Vitellius and Vespasian followed each other in quick succession. Vespasian (A.D. 70–79) retained his grip longer than the others, remaining Emperor for over nine years. He founded the Flavian dynasty of god-emperors, and Caesar became a divine name, an event which appealed to the ignorant multitude. Much more impressive and important was the fact that during this reign Quintilian was appointed Minister of Education, to start schools all over the Empire, as was related in the previous chapter. Then it was that the influence of Plato and Aristotle spread to Rome, when an elaborate educational and cultural system was organised, which raised the mental level in many parts of the Empire. Had this young and fruitful tree of knowledge been allowed to grow and flourish from that time onwards to the present day, what a different world we would now be experiencing.

Instead of this happening the Christian Church obliterated all the good work done by the noble Quintilian and his army of teachers, thus throwing the world back into the age of barbaric savagery. Until this tragedy occurred education received imperial recognition, and to Vespasian is due the honour of having laid the foundation of an empire-wide scheme for the purpose of raising the mental level of the people. It was also during his reign that Jerusalem capitulated in A.D. 70 after a long and bitter struggle, when the Jews were dispersed, never again to have a home of their own. Titus, the adopted son of Vespasian, was in charge of this epoch-making event which was to have such far-reaching consequences. Jerusalem was destroyed, the Temple was burned and razed to the ground, and the Jewish priesthood scattered.

This catastrophe shook the faith of many provincial Jews in the protecting power of Jehovah, and many, especially those called Hellenised Jews, came over to the belief that the Messiah had come in the person of Jesus, the old order having now given place to a new one. The destruction of the Temple, and the dispersal of the priesthood, heightened the belief, found so clearly stated in the *Epistle to the Hebrews*, that the priesthood had come to an end—Jesus, who was gradually being evolved into the Christ, having taken over the priestly office of mediator between God and man. The demolition of the Temple had a profound influence on the spread of Christianity, as, had this event not occurred, it is unlikely that the Hellenised Jews would have abandoned their old faith in favour of the new. They it was who formed the nucleus outside of Palestine from which Christianity developed, and but for them it is improbable that it would ever have evolved into a new distinctive religion.

Jerusalem has had a tragic history, and Judea was certainly the last place for the Chosen People to have settled in to make their home. It was on the coast, and consequently coveted by the empires of Assyria, Babylonia and Persia, to come in turn under their domination. Its situation was also unfortunate, as it cut across the main thoroughfare of the Middle East. To squat in the middle of a main road, and build your house in the midst of a stream of traffic, could hardly be more dangerous than to establish yourself in the Land of Promise, and this the Hebrews found to their cost. Jerusalem was captured three times during the period it housed the Children of Israel, and the Temple was several times destroyed and rebuilt. On two occasions Jerusalem was captured because its defenders would not fight on the Sabbath. The destruction of the Temple by Titus was, however, its end, and never since has it been rebuilt. Over a million Jews perished in this bloody siege, and the Golden Table, the Golden Candlesticks, and the Book of the Law were carried off to Rome.

The Romans hated the Jews just as bitterly as do the Germans, and they were just as ruthless in their attempt at their utter destruction. From this time onwards Jewish history is one of recurring tragedies. They became wanderers over the face of the earth,

without a king or country, but never wavering in their
faith that Jehovah would still be mindful of his
promises. Their Semitic gift for trade enriched many
in their new homes, but this ability to succeed, where
the Aryan failed, only increased the bitterness between
two races, and the fact that they crucified him whom
Christians look upon as their Saviour made the bitterness all the more intense.

Logic is never present in religion, as, if it were, the
Christians could hardly have condemned the people
who committed this crime, as the Jews, by their action,
had brought salvation, according to the Christian
doctrines, to all who believed in the death of the
Saviour of mankind. The Jews had thus saved the
Christians from eternal damnation. It was the intolerance of the Christians which made them overlook
this obvious point, as they could not bear rubbing
shoulders with unbelievers. As the Jews were always
in the minority, and as zealous in their beliefs as were
the Christians, their presence in Europe throughout
the Christian era has been one long-drawn-out period
of misery and suffering, which, unfortunately in our
own times, we have had so many opportunities to
experience.

Titus (79–81) followed his foster-father Vespasian,
and reigned only two years. Domitian (81–96)
succeeded him and reigned for fifteen years, when he
was murdered, and this brought the Flavian dynasty
to an end. During this reign most of Britain
became a Roman province, and several other minor
territories were added to the Empire. A new dynasty
now commenced with Nerva (96–98), who was followed by Trajan (98–117), under whose rule Parthia

(now part of Persia), Armenia, Assyria and Mesopotamia came under the domination of the Roman
eagle. It was under his rule that the Empire reached
its utmost limit, to begin the crumbling process in the
reign of his successor.

The Roman Empire, at the height of its power,
comprised most of Britain, all Gaul, Spain and the
entire north African coast, including Egypt, Palestine,
Syria, Mesopotamia, Armenia, Asia Minor, Greece,
Macedonia, Thrace, Dacia, which lay north of the
Danube, Dalmatia, Italy, and all the islands of the
Mediterranean. All this extensive territory was controlled from Rome, and its inhabitants had the satisfaction of feeling that they were the citizens of the
greatest empire the world had ever known. This
had been secured at a great price, paid in money
and lives, and as the result of much suffering and
sacrifice. But it was not to last. Bit by bit this great
confederation of different nationalities slowly melted
away, and Rome itself, in A.D. 410, three hundred
years after reaching the zenith of her power, was
captured and sacked by the barbarians driving down
from the north.

After Trajan came Hadrian (117–138), one of the
most outstanding of all the Roman emperors, who
renounced all the conquests of Trajan, including
north Britain. His policy was to make the Empire
secure, and he felt that to retain these conquests
weakened it by its enormous extent. So, like the
Chinese, he started building walls against the barbarians, the one across Britain still bearing his name.
The Rhine and the Danube were themselves sufficient
defence, but, between the sources of these two rivers,

he built a palisade to protect the Empire from the German barbarians. In Africa, the desert was an adequate protection, while in the east he relied on the barrier of the Black Sea and the Caucasus mountains. He was wise enough, however, to see the red light of danger ahead, and this grew in brilliance in the reign of his successor. Empires, like the moon, wax and wane, and this great mass of conglomerate material was beginning to break up for want of sufficient cement, in the form of mental unity and lack of common interest. Force alone can never keep an empire together, and that was all upon which Rome could rely.

Hadrian, who did much to restore Athens, also rebuilt Jerusalem, but not the Temple. The city became a Pagan town under the name of Ælia Capitolina, and only by the spread of Christianity did its fame return. In place of the Temple he erected two temples, one to the goddess Aphrodite and the other to Jupiter. Thus the spot made holy by the presence of Jehovah passed under the domination of other gods, who, in turn, were to give place some centuries later to Allah, the god of Abraham. Jehovah, the god of Moses, never recovered his place of worship where so much slaughter had occurred to keep him well fed and in good humour. Names change, but not the desire of man for a place where he can worship one or more discarnate beings who, he believes, fights his battles, and whose protection and succour he feels he requires to help him on his earthly pilgrimage from the cradle to the grave.

Following the death of Hadrian, Titus Antoninus (A.D. 138–161) was enthusiastically welcomed to the throne, and for once the Roman people were not disappointed with their ruler, his reign constituting what was probably the happiest period in the annals of the Empire, a happy, tolerant, free and easy life generally prevailing everywhere. Its citizens were provided with amusements, public baths and other amenities on a cheap and lavish scale, and not until we come to our own times in the 20th century do we find the people again supplied with these in the same profusion.

Titus Antoninus had simple tastes, a kindly disposition, extensive experience, a well-trained intelligence and a sincere desire for the welfare of his subjects. He put a stop to the practice of despoiling the provinces, and used his private treasury for their benefit. Traitors were shown clemency, and religious toleration abounded. During his reign men of ability and integrity administered the law, education was encouraged, and the enactments passed were humane and just. In memory of his wife he founded an orphanage for girls, and his Stoical humanism raised the people to a higher ethical level than had ever before been reached.

He built a wall between the Clyde and the Forth, attempted no conquests, and his reign was peaceful. Here indeed was a really great emperor, but, as nothing spectacular took place during his reign of twenty-three years, he is little known and not much has been written about him. In this reign, and the one which followed, we find Roman civilisation and culture at its zenith, and, when we hear, as we do in our own time from dishonest ecclesiastics, that the last world war was a conflict between Christianity and Paganism, let us remember all the facts about Pagan

civilisation and compare them with those contained
in the following chapters relating to Christian civilisation.   We shall then realise how foolish it is to
disparage Paganism and elevate Christianity, when,
during the reign of the Christian Church, nearly everything good in Paganism was destroyed and that
which was evil predominated.

Marcus Aurelius Antoninus (A.D. 161–180), who
followed, was another of the good emperors who
ruled in Rome.   He devoted himself to the welfare
of the people, considering himself their servant, but
misfortune pursued him throughout his reign.   Famine,
plague, floods, barbaric invasions and revolts occupied
much of his thoughts, but, in spite of the disasters
which crowded on him one by one, he was able to
give time to philosophic discussion and literature, his
Meditations being well known to this day.   It comprises twelve chapters upholding the practice of the
virtues.   He was a Stoic and taught that virtue came
before all else, and one can readily believe how the
cares of the Empire, and the wickedness of human
nature, were a constant weariness to his mind.

His was certainly a troubled reign, which came at a
time when the Empire was beginning to feel the
pains of indigestion.   No further conquests were now
planned, and Aurelius and his successors were mainly
occupied in keeping together their far-flung dominions,
protecting them from further invasions of the German
barbarians in the north, and the Parthians in the east
who for long had been a terror to the Roman arms.
Here, indeed, were the two weak spots in the Empire's
armour, defects which were ultimately to bring it to
confusion.

So this peace-loving emperor had to defend his empire, both in the north and the east, but even on the battlefield he found time to write his *Meditations* and pour out his ardent mind in an attempt to show that benevolence, honesty, justice, self-control, the restraint of the passions and righteousness should be the aim of all who desire happiness and the good of their fellow men and women. He organised relief for his suffering subjects, stricken down by famine and plague, and, in the midst of it all, Cassius, one of his most trusted and ablest generals, revolted in Syria and attempted to overthrow his emperor, only to be killed by one of his own officers.

Here indeed is an example, if one is needed, of how good is always being pursued by evil, and how force must be retained, so long as the evil-doer is in wait for any weakness on the part of the followers after righteousness. The revolt of Cassius came about because he considered that the Emperor was too full of compassion and generosity to inspire the confidence of the army, qualities which never appeal to the undeveloped mind. Aurelius, on hearing of his enemy's death, expressed regret that he was deprived of the privilege of granting his personal forgiveness, and he carefully destroyed all documents which might implicate others. Thus, in all the trials of his life, philosophy inspired his actions, and he rightly deserves the honour of being ranked as "the noblest of the Pagans, the crown and flower of Stoicism". What a contrast is this noble life to the lives of the scoundrels who preceded and succeeded him on the imperial throne !

One blot only is to be discovered in all this record

of righteous conduct, and that is the martyrdom of
Polycarp, and the persecution of the Christians during his reign, but it is doubtful if he knew everything
that was taking place within his wide empire. No
cruel law has been discovered as having emanated
from him; in fact Tertullian says that during his reign
he made no laws against the Christians, and who
should know better than this outstanding Christian
who was twenty years of age when the Emperor died?
Most historians relieve the Emperor of blame, and
believe that the persecution, slight as it was, was
carried out by officials unknown to him.

In Roman law all who did not give the Emperor
divine honours were rebels, and the Christians, and
others, who refused to grant this suffered in consequence. The Romans were not intolerant about
their religious beliefs, and the comparatively slight
persecution suffered by the Christians was therefore
caused more from political reasons than because of
religious differences. When we read further on about
the wholesale massacres of the Pagans by the Christians, over a period extending for hundreds of years,
we will better realise the deception practised by
Christian historians, who have always given much
space to the sufferings of the Christian martyrs, and
passed over without notice the vast multitude of
Pagans, Jews and heretics who were slaughtered or
banished by the Christians when they obtained
power. After the Reformation the Protestants, who
set up divine monarchs in place of the Pope, put to
death, tortured or banished those who did not
accept the divinity claimed by the King, a host of
victims which exceeded one hundred times as many

as the number of Christians who were persecuted by the Romans.

Aurelius was quite ignorant of the beliefs of the new Christian sect, and, if he consented to its persecution, it was on political and. not on religious grounds, though this in no way excuses the action. It must, however, be remembered that the Christians were active bigots, often courting arrest, and quite intolerant, defacing the statues of the gods which meant so much to the Romans, displacing and destroying the statues of the Emperor, and insulting the gods and the Emperor on many occasions.

Justin, commonly called Justin Martyr, at this time was beheaded after trial because of his fierce attack on one named Crescens, who was a Cynic, a sect which set the attainment of right conduct as its sole aim. Justin termed him "a very vile member of his repulsive sect". When Christians adopted this aggressive attitude towards other people's opinions, there is small wonder that they received the hatred of their neighbours, who considered them to be atheists because they did not worship the gods of the Empire. We must not therefore be surprised that the Romans looked upon the Christians with suspicion, especially as they met in secret to perform their strange mystical rites.

The Emperor doubtless allowed the old law, that all must regard the Emperor as a divine being, to take its course, and we need not wonder that persecution followed the excesses of a minority, whose beliefs were not considered sufficiently important for the Romans to try to understand. Marcus Aurelius stands high above many of his predecessors, and there

are few Christian monarchs who have been his equal.
We have to go back to Asoka in India to find one who
could take this place. Worn out by anxiety and
fatigue, Aurelius died in A.D. 180, mourned with a
note of such true sorrow as never before nor again
was raised at the death of an emperor. He had the
satisfaction of knowing that he had raised public
morals, encouraged education, passed laws for the
welfare of children, improved the State finances,
developed the roads, set up magistrates who were
just and honest, and restricted gladiatorial displays.
In a few words, he left the Empire well and justly
governed, but all his work for the people was undone
by Commodus, his son and successor, who turned
order into chaos.

The death of Marcus Aurelius was followed by a
century of war and disorder, during which time only
the stern rule of the soldier-emperors saved the Empire
from dissolution. Time had brought a changed outlook, as in the old days of the Republic the frontiers
were safe but there was disorder at home. Now it
was just the opposite. The emperors had brought
internal peace which the Republic could not achieve,
but the frontiers were now in danger, as the Parthians
in the east, the Germans on the Rhine and the Goths
on the Danube had become more and more aggressive.
This state of affairs was aggravated during the 3rd
century by a series of desperate conflicts between rival
generals in their attempts to secure the imperial
purple. Within seventy-three years no fewer than
twenty-three emperors ruled in Rome, and of these all
but three died violent deaths at the hands of mutinous
legions, or by the orders of a successful rival.

So far we have been considering Roman political life, and now we shall leave politics for a little and turn our attention to the thoughts of those men who, by their writings, tried to lift the human mind above the sordid things of life into a realm more beautiful and more enduring. To Rome, as well as to Greece, we can go for intellectual refreshment, as her philosophers, besides her law-givers, have left their indelible mark on the mental life of Europe.

(3) ROME'S CONTRIBUTION TO THE WORLD'S MENTAL WEALTH.

It is perhaps opportune here to glance round the times we have been considering; and, for a short space, forget politics in order to consider those higher and nobler themes which Marcus Aurelius did so much to cultivate. What was Rome's contribution to the mental wealth of mankind? For two centuries peace had reigned within the Empire, however much the frontiers had been distracted by the wilder elements who were always anxious to get inside and share in the prosperity which peace always brings. Let us first of all glance at the capital of this great assembly of people of different races and religions. Rome was the jewel in the Empire's crown, one which was also studded with many minor gems, cities of size, beauty and distinction, all of which were built on the pattern of the capital.

Rome, at the beginning of the Christian era, was the centre of the civilised world. It was a magnificent city, adorned with the spoils of the many conquered lands comprising the Roman Empire, besides being enriched by many rare luxuries purchased from distant lands. To Rome came silks from India and China, grain from Egypt and North Africa, and her ships sailed to and from the ports of the then known world. For fifteen miles luxurious villas, and costly tombs, were dotted on either side of the road leading to the centre of the city, and on the neighbouring hills were public gardens watered by swiftly flowing brooks. These, when they reached the city, were conducted underground in pipes to private houses, public baths, and the fountains and grottoes everywhere to be seen.

Tall houses, displaying flowers on their roofs and balconies, were on each side of colonnaded streets lined with statues, the Via Sacra being the shopping centre where the silks and spices of the East were on sale; wool from Spain; glassware from Egypt; wine from Greece; cheese from what is now Switzerland; apples from Crete, and oysters from Britain. Here every language spoken, and costume worn, in the Empire was to be heard and seen. Philosophers pondered over the books gathered from every land, while rich and poor mingled together, as the street was too narrow for carriages to pass through, and all had to do their shopping on foot.

The rich found their privacy in the carefully laid-out gardens surrounding their luxurious and spacious homes. These well-appointed dwellings, fitted with central heating and hot baths, the theatres of tasteful design, the colonnaded temples, the stately museums, and the spacious public baths, mingled with the marble palaces placed in groves of trees. Travelling in those days was safe from robbers and pirates, whom the Romans everywhere had suppressed, and it was unhindered as no passports or visas were required. Not until the 19th century was it again so easy, Latin and Greek being the only two languages necessary, and anyone who could pay, or beg his way, was free to travel at will between Syene, 600 miles up the Nile in the south, and Carlisle in the north.

To Rome, the beautiful capital of the Empire, came all who could make the journey, by sea, or along the wonderful roads which united every city in the Empire. These roads were unrivalled up to last century, their grading was exact and their foundation was laid on natural cement so strong that it has been the envy and wonder of architects and builders ever since. Rome, the greatest city of its age, gave inspiration to the architects, sculptors, painters, scientists and literary men of her day, whose thoughts and deeds we shall now consider.

If we are to remember all the men of outstanding distinction, we must go back to the days before there was any Roman Empire, to the days when the learned Ennius (239–169 B.C.) wrote his tragedies, when Marcus Cato (234–149 B.C.) gave the impulse to the creation of oratory, history and literature, when Terence (185–159 B.C.), the celebrated poet, took up the role made famous by his illustrious Greek predecessors. Terence indeed holds a unique position amongst Roman writers, as he imparted culture and elegance to the language which in his day was so crude and uncouth. Greek influence was now bringing culture to the rough Romans. Athens was to become the seat of learning, the university city of the

Empire, and, from this time onwards, every Roman who wished to be considered as educated, learned the Greek language, and had Greek literature in his library.

Livius Andronicus, in the 3rd century B.C., was the first to make the old name of poet a title of honour instead of reproach, and, by familiarising the Romans with the forms of the Greek drama and epic, he determined the main line which Roman literature followed for more than a century afterwards. He was followed by Naevius and Plautus, who were the great comic and dramatic genii of their time, Lucilius (166–102 B.C.) being another great originating force in literature. Posidonius (130–50 B.C.), the distinguished Stoic philosopher, was the most learned man of his time, and spent many years seeking knowledge, travelling extensively throughout the Roman dominions.

The great intellectual ability and learning of Cicero (106–43 B.C.) raised him far above his contemporaries. He, a good citizen and a good man, is the outstanding figure of the Golden Age of Roman literature. Like Socrates he discovered through his experiences of psychic phenomena that we live on after death, and can come back to be both seen and heard. He was the most prominent Spiritualist of his time, and his psychic knowledge certainly influenced his life and philosophy. In his orations he displayed a profound knowledge of human nature, and, during the time he was consul, he showed outstanding rectitude, courage, ability and energy. As an orator, a statesman and a man of letters he became the most consummate specimen of the Roman character under the influence of Hellenic culture, contending that to settle disputes by force degraded man to the level of the beast. His ethical teaching was always of the highest order.

He wrote masterly treatises on philosophy and hundreds of letters, many of which have been preserved, and from these we learn much of Roman life and thought during the time when the Republic was coming to an end and the Empire was looming ahead. Roman life was completely wrapped up in politics, the country came first and the individual last, politicians became soldiers and soldiers politicians as a matter of course, and Cicero makes us realise everything that is both good and bad in human nature.

Wealth in his time was pouring into Rome, corruption was everywhere, politicians and judges were easily bought, morals were loose, though home life was held in high esteem, the Roman matron having greater freedom than ever before experienced. Her training in chastity, her education since girlhood that a wife's supreme duty is to be faithful to her lord, enabled her husband to trust her while he, enjoying what was called *Patria Potestas*, the "Father's Authority", had complete power in his own household and could live as he pleased. Cicero wrote freely and spoke freely—too freely, because he was assassinated after he expressed the opinion that the Emperor Augustus should be removed.

The first Roman to write history was Sallust (86–34 B.C.). He held several public offices, and in his later life devoted himself to literature. His career was blemished by immoral conduct, which brought about his removal from the Senate. Another historian was Julius Caesar, who, in *De Bello Gallico*, displayed his literary genius in his admirable and concise account of his wars in Gaul. Lucretius (99–55 B.C.) is noted for the grace and beauty of his language, which he used in some of the most powerful poetry ever written. In his book *On the Nature of the World* he advocated knowledge in place of the belief that death and the gods are to be feared, and showed a firm grasp of the scientific knowledge of his day.

Virgil (70–19 B.C.) was by far the greatest of the Roman epic poets, and *The Æneid*, which he wrote, has been classed as among the poems destined to receive immortal fame. His pre-eminence in poetry is as distinctly recognised as that of Cicero in prose. He stressed the need for greater righteousness everywhere, and longed for the time when war would be no more. Seneca (3 B.C.–A.D. 65), the eminent Stoic philosopher and teacher, the most brilliant figure of his time, devoted his life to philosophy, rhetoric and law, and he as much as anyone sowed the seed which has produced the social conscience of today. He was an eloquent and popular writer, with a clear, strong style, and his writings on moral and philosophical subjects, on kindness and justice, and on the curse of war, are so elevating that he stands out as one whose wisdom will echo down the ages, long after the follies and ignorance associated with supernatural religion have passed away.

The Odes of Horace (65–8 B.C.) and his epistles and satires are masterpieces of literary skill. No other ancient writer has been at once so familiarly known and so generally appreciated in modern times. He was a man of supreme good sense who, by his wise advice, shares with his reader his private tastes and pleasures, in a style so natural and lively that each new generation feels that here is a familiar friend who appreciates and understands its most inmost feelings.

Impersonal and charming in his conversation and behaviour, an epicure and dilettante, one who must always have a clean tablecloth and napkin at his meals, he was the darling of Roman society at a time when his contemporary Livy (59 B.C.–A.D. 17), the Herodotus of Rome, was writing a history of her greatness which made him famous. Livy's style is clear and bright, with wonderful powers of description. He was a consummate artist, but an unskilled and often careless investigator and critic. These faults are also attributed to Herodotus, but in those days accuracy was not considered so essential if the writer could produce a good story. The writings of Valerius Catullus (87–47 B.C.) are also noted for the ease and grace of his language.

The love of poetry led Ovid (43 B.C.–A.D. 17) to abandon his profession of law and become an author. In his *Metamorphoses* he tells many stories of gods and men in a delightfully easy style. He was the last, in order of time, of the poets of the Augustan age, whose works have given to it the distinction of ranking among the great eras in the history of human culture. He represents the last of the Golden Age of Roman literature, a period when the influence of Greece was able to combat the grossness of the times.

As the 1st century continues, Pliny, the elder (A.D. 23–79), stands out as a prominent writer of prose and lover of nature. His *Natural History* is an outstanding work of the times, as herein he attempted an encyclopaedia of knowledge, mainly based on the researches and speculations of the Greeks. Valerius Flaccus is the greatest poet of this time, and Quintilian (A.D. 35–95), the famous educationalist, to whom we have already referred, and Silius (A.D. 25–101) stand out as examples of conspicuous literary ability. The noble humane Plutarch (A.D. 50–120) recorded in his charming and kindly way the lives of the heroes of the past, and produced a vivid account of prominent historical figures.

Beyond dispute Tacitus (A.D. 54–119), the historian, takes a high place amongst men of letters of all ages, his descriptive annals revealing his gloomy opinion of the past record of the Empire. Lucian, an outstanding essayist and satirist, a brilliant and original writer, in his criticism of the times, as well as the satires of Persius and Juvenal, expressed the feelings of the age. Both Tacitus and Juvenal, with their scorn and fierce indignation at the moral depravity of their period, are the last powerful voices raised in Rome, the last expression of the freedom of an earlier age.

Human life is now shallower, the wealth and luxury of preceding generations, and the strong division between the classes, having produced an enervating effect on the mainspring of literary effort. Nevertheless the gross immorality of the times produced abundant material for the satirist, as it also evoked from Persius and Martial withering scorn, and, though we notice the beginning of literary decay, their writings show that the Empire is still capable of producing men of originality and talent.

Pliny, the younger (A.D. 65–115), a man of refined

tastes and high character, the nephew of the naturalist, usually known as Pliny the elder, while not contradicting this representation of Roman life, somewhat modified their sombre picture, but it was left to Suetonius (A.D. 75–160) to carry on the story told by Tacitus, he being the outstanding historian of his period. Apuleius (A.D. 125–185) was an original genius, his books revealing him to be a philosopher who tried to combat a materialistic outlook on life, doubtless due to the fact that he was endowed with psychic as well as literary gifts. Genial and enthusiastic for all that is beautiful and good, he, as a devoted disciple of Plato, was the leading exponent of Spiritualism in his time.

From now onwards literary effort is barren, so far as Rome is concerned. From Greece it had originally come, and to Greece it returned, as once again literature found its organ in the Greek language. Long after Roman literature had ceased to count, the Hellenic world was still producing a steady and rich supply. Rome, however, made a valuable contribution to its age. It gave to the world many great and profound thinkers, great poets and dramatists, in such contrast to the sordid array of greedy and place-seeking politicians and corrupt rulers. How brightly this galaxy of thinkers shines against the black background of political intrigue, insincerity and double dealing. On the one hand we have the thinkers, who brighten the lives of the people, and, on the other, those who are greedy for power and territory, bringing misery and suffering in contrast to the joy and happiness which literature, poetry, music and the drama shed all around.

For some two hundred years the Roman people had enjoyed peace, the upper classes wealth, the middle classes a comfortable existence, but the lower classes and the slaves found life hard and dreary. An extensive literature had come into existence, architecture flourished, helped by the knowledge of the manufacture of cement, and beautiful houses, artfully decorated with well-laid-out surroundings, were to be seen in every Roman town from Britain in the north to Numidia and Cyrenaica in the south. Wealth was in abundance and lavishly displayed. Trade increased within the Empire, and the rich grew richer while the poor remained poor. Life to the rich and well-to-do must have been easy, and yet they added little to the productive capacity of the world. When the Empire wilted away productive effort still pursued its age-old course, slaves doing the work which nowadays is done both quicker and better by machinery, the consequence being that the burden of toil was as heavy as ever before.

The ruins of beautiful temples, triumphal arches, amphitheatres, theatres, markets, colonnaded streets, squares, aqueducts, roads and bridges remain for us to wander over, but nothing of a scientific nature was passed down to succeeding generations to relieve the drudgery of life. The sciences were neglected, geography untouched, and general knowledge much as it was at the time Greece was at her zenith. No attempt was made to study economics or social science. Dictator-ruled lands are never free to discuss social and political problems, as this is always considered as treason to the powers that be. Nothing new was discovered about chemistry, biology, medi-

cine, surgery, physics, astronomy and the hundred
and one other subjects which now add to the comfort
and happiness of mankind.

The Romans, with all their remarkable constructive
abilities, their empire-wide schools, their wonderful
roads and buildings, never saw the need to follow up
and make useful the discoveries of the two great
inventors of the age. Heron of Alexandria, a century
before the Christian era, had discovered the use of
steam and compressed air, and made the first steam
engine. Archimedes (287–212 B.C.), the greatest mathematician and the most inventive genius of antiquity,
made many useful and warlike inventions. He was
killed by a Roman soldier, when at work on a mathematical problem during the massacre which followed
the capture of Syracuse in 212 B.C. Lucretius, of
whom mention has already been made for his talent in
poetic writing, showed in his work *De Rerum Natura*
extraordinary insight concerning the constitution of
matter and the history of primitive man, and yet no
one enquired more into these subjects. They did not
interest the Romans, who never investigated further.
The fields were well cultivated by slave labour, but it
never occurred to them that this type of service lowered
the dignity of man, and that, by increasing the use of
money, wages could be paid and labour could be
secured free from bondage.

The abundance of slaves destroyed all urge to
invent labour-saving machines, as the ruling classes
were well satisfied with existing conditions. Education was devoted to acquiring the knowledge of the
times, to correct speaking and writing, to the improvement of manners and customs, to the making of

a cultured gentleman, but, as the philosophers were enquiring ever more into the quality of everything, the time would undoubtedly have come when the secrets of nature would have been discovered. Unfortunately education and science were never allowed to develop, as the Christian Church liquidated everything relating to the acquisition of knowledge. Theology doomed Europe to mental isolation, while the Arabs pursued the quest for greater knowledge, Arabian scientists achieving discoveries which, but for Christianity, would doubtless have been made by Europeans.

In our day we have come to think of war as a terrible calamity, and, as we have become less orthodox, we have become kinder and juster, more tolerant and sympathetic. We try to be kind to animals, and humane in our thoughts and deeds, but this is just a return to the teaching of the Greek and Roman philosophers. The golden thread they spun was snapped by Christianity, and only in our time have we returned to their mental level, to continue the pattern of life they laboured to weave. Through their influence human sacrifice was abolished throughout the Roman Republic in 96 B.C., the priests who practised it being hanged, and the sacrifice of animals was discouraged because the philosophers taught that God needed not the shedding of blood but repentance and righteous lives. Gladiatorial combats eventually ceased because of philosophic influence, and the hardships of slavery were greatly mitigated by the legislation passed during the time when philosophy influenced Roman life, the reaction coming under the Christian emperors, to whom philosophy did not appeal.

With its decay, and the rise of Christianity to power, the 5th century witnessed a corrupt and rotten Church, and Salvian, the Presbyter of Marseilles, tells of the delight the Christians took in seeing their fellow men torn and devoured by wild beasts in the amphitheatres, "numberless thousands of Christians" being daily spectators of the obscenities of the theatres or the cruelties of the circus. If only philosophy had become accepted instead of Christianity, how different would have been the story this history has to tell, but, when the belief in God's vengeance towards his innocent only-begotten son took root, there was no place for philosophy, and injustice and cruelty, instead of justice and kindness, became the order of the day.

Christendom, by being clamped in mental chains, was denied the opportunity of carrying on the torch of knowledge, but, before this tragedy befell mankind, education had undoubtedly elevated Roman manners and customs to a remarkable degree. Trade increased, and Pagan civilisation had risen to as high a level as had prevailed in Athens when at the zenith of her glory.

Ships of considerable tonnage sailed the seas as far as India, and these brought to the West the wealth of the East. Beautiful clothes were worn, silk coming from China by way of India, and also much jewellery. Sumptuous banquets were given, and these were accompanied by music, dancing and acrobatic displays. Books and libraries were plentiful, and the Romans not only learned Greek but adopted Greek culture and manners. The coarseness of the republican period gave way to a time of greater refinement

in all directions.   There was a marked increase
in human kindness one towards another, much
less cruelty, slaves being treated more humanely,
and it was made illegal to neglect them, kill them,
torture them, or to sell them for gladiatorial displays ;
in fact more and more men and women of culture
expressed openly their disgust at the brutality of these
performances, while Plutarch led a campaign against
cruelty to animals and their being hunted for
sport.   Though Rome dominated Greece politically,
Greek culture and ideals were now dominating
Rome, and mind was proving itself superior to
force.

Epictetus, the Greek, who in early life was a slave,
had to leave Rome in A.D. 90 because of his opposition
to the tyrannical Emperor Domitian.   He represents
the best in Greek culture and thought of this period,
the practical ethical philosophy which he advocated
being so high, noble, pure and logical that his influence for good has been felt from his day to the
present time.   To him man's mind is supreme, and
he made or marred his character by his thoughts.
Each one, he taught, makes his own happiness or
misery, and, by mental development, heaven can be
found on earth.   Our body is not ourself, it is our
thoughts that are, and they, formed by the never dying
mind, are eternal.   The mind, he believed, incarnated
from a higher realm than physical matter, to which it
returns at death.   This being so, he considered that
the duty of everyone is to cultivate the mind to fit
it for its greater experiences after death, the world
being but a school in which we each can devote ourselves to either righteousness or evil, the choice being

with everyone alone, our eternal happiness coming only from doing what is right.

His mind being pure and elevated, he visualised God as absolute goodness, his attitude to life being one of thankfulness for all the blessings of Providence, and this was the burden of philosophic religious teaching whether it came from Epictetus, Seneca, Plutarch, Maximus of Tyre, or Porphyry, the out-spoken opponent of Christianity, and many others. "Love cannot be mingled with fear," writes Seneca, who deplored ritual, ceremonies, sacrifices, fastings and abnegation in the worship of God, the duty of everyone being to rise ethically and so reach harmony with the divine.

Justice, mercy, truth and righteousness were all that God required, and consequently it was wrong to try to propitiate the divine by means of religious observances, in which the evil-doer partook, thinking that by so doing he could influence heaven in his favour. This was the philosophic outlook on re-ligion in those days which appealed only to the educated, and so we find philosophers, not priests and confessors, attached to the courts of kings and noble-men to advise them and educate their children, their teaching being spread by missionaries who went from land to land endeavouring to promote virtue and oppose vice.

Though culture increased, as the result of the teaching of Epictetus and other Stoics, little real understanding developed to enable the Roman mind to grasp its responsibilities. The people took little intelligent interest in their vast domains, whence came their wealth. The Empire produced no explorers or travellers, and consequently the Romans were blankly ignorant of the people and lands bordering their frontiers. We discover no literature on the geography of the world and the lives of the people outside the Empire's boundaries. We find no Herodotus travelling far and wide picking up information, first in one country and then in another. The Chinese were much more enterprising, as they have their stories of what their travellers discovered in India and Siberia, but the Romans tell us nothing about Scotland, or about the people in other lands where they traded, such as Babylonia, Persia and Syria, whence came their carpets and damasks, or Arabia, or India to which country the silk they used was sent from China.

If they had only attempted to educate the barbarians into a civilised way of life, the Empire might have been the foundation for a structure of culture and civilisation which would have been for the lasting good of mankind. Instead of so doing, they ignored their neighbours, and treated them as barbarians who must be kept as far away as possible from the centre of civilisation. To Rome, force was the only expedient, as she had no more idea of psychology than the modern German. To her, might only was right, and she never progressed beyond the jungle law, the law of brute force. She hired foreign mercenaries from the provinces who obeyed, in exchange for money, and returned home to teach their fellow countrymen the art of war. So long as they were willing to fight for her without, on the frontiers, the pleasures of life went on within. But the time was to come when the weakness of it all was to become apparent, when, for the want of an ideal and the lack of conscious participation in the affairs of the State, the Empire would collapse with little attempt by anyone to keep it together.

We have already discovered that education was not neglected—Julius Caesar, Vespasian, Titus Antoninus, Marcus Aurelius and others encouraging it throughout the Empire, wealthy citizens endowing professorships, and building well-equipped schools and colleges, but, just as happened in our own times, it was inadequate and often misdirected. In Athens all were educated to share in the responsibility of governing the State, but in the Roman Empire only one man ruled, and the people never learned the art of government or how best to solve outstanding social problems. Education is such an all-embracing affair, relating as it does to every phase of life, that only by slow evolution is it possible for the mind to encompass all it has to learn, in order to produce a worthy citizen and a good neighbour in both a national and worldly sense.

Knowledge, moreover, must be based on facts, and not as it may be conceived by those having their own selfish interests to consider. The truth about everything in life will never be learned so long as it is constructed by authorities having their own ambitions to serve, be they politicians, churchmen or soldiers. The moral and social laws will always be twisted and thwarted in such hands. Honest, unprejudiced and factual education must therefore be directed only by those to whom facts and truth come first and all else last. Because our ancestors were too ignorant to pursue truth, and truth only, for the sake of its discovery, the story of mankind is one of suffering and misery, and will continue to be so until intellectual light takes the place of the darkness of ignorance.

This is only possible in the atmosphere of complete freedom. Just as a light will be extinguished if confined, and can only burn brightly when free to absorb the atmosphere around it, so the mind can only develop when it is free to receive everything nature has to give it, untrammelled by restraint from those who put their own prejudices before the goal of all education, which is truth and truth only, based on facts and evidence.

The Empire did not bring general happiness to the people, as restraint by the government, and domination by the rich, left underneath the surface of things an apathy which corresponded to conditions in Great Britain last century before social welfare activities raised the lives of the poor from their drab existence of misery and poverty. The Roman Empire was outwardly a splendid sepulchre containing a decaying corpse within. Apathy was widespread, as it must always be in dictator-run countries, because the people had no power to influence events, and so emperors came and went, leaving the masses quite indifferent.

Because of this, from the 2nd century B.C. onwards, the common people gave heed to the missionaries who came to Italy from the East bringing with them glad tidings of better days to come, if not in this world, then in the life hereafter. So it was that the saviour-god religions, Mithraism from Persia, the worship of Osiris, Horus and Isis, the three gods of the Egyptian trinity, and the Greek mystery religions found fresh virgin soil amongst the ignorant masses, where they grew and flourished, much to the regret of the philosophic minded, who beheld with sorrow the noble teachings of the philosophers being submerged by supernatural religion. But the Roman Pantheon was hospitable to every god, the cities were allowed self-government which permitted religious freedom, and every freeman could believe whatever religion he pleased, and win his way unhampered to wealth and influence.

The more the contact with the East increased, the more were the Romans influenced by the thousands of orientals who travelled westwards, bringing with them their wares for sale, and proselytising from place to place as they went. Missionaries came from Egypt, carrying with them the gospel tidings of the saving power of Osiris, just as they came from Persia with the good news that through the death and resurrection of Mithra all could now be born again to a life hereafter throughout eternity. These missionaries were encouraged by Roman law, which considered all races equal, and so they preached to everyone, and embraced everyone, in their scheme of salvation, both bond and free. This explains why it was Christianity adopted the comprehensiveness to include men of all races, both freemen and slaves, because it grew out of these Eastern saviour-god religions, the influence of Judaic isolationism having been broken by the destruction of the Temple at Jerusalem.

We have already read of the different appellations used by the Babylonians, Egyptians and Hindus, to heighten the glory of their saviour-gods. Mithra was likewise honoured by titles such as the Supreme God, the Logos, the Incarnate Word, the Mediator, the Saviour, the Redeemer, the Son of the Most High,

the Alpha and Omega, the Creator of all things, and
the Lamb of God who taketh away the sins of the
world.   Other terms of worship were the Lord, the
Lord of all, the Purity of the Eternal Light, the King
of Glory, the Good Shepherd, and the Lamb slain
for the sins of the world.

The saviour-god religions appealed to the slaves,
who in turn influenced their masters and mistresses.
All this occurred at a time of reaction from unbelief,
when the idea was gaining ground that the universe
was an ordered cosmos, and not a chaos at the mercy
of the caprices of the gods.   So trinitarian monotheism
made progress, and the universe became intimately
related with the saviour-god who was worshipped.

The creator of the Universe was termed the
Father of mankind, the Saviour and Redeemer was
termed the Son, both of whom were brought into
close relationship with mankind through the Holy
Spirit.   We read in the Liturgy of Mithra that the
devotee prayed, "Abide with me in my soul, leave me
not, that I may be initiated and that the Holy Spirit
may breathe within me.   So that I am thou and thou
art I."   God was believed to be the All in All, the
First and the Last.   Knowledge of him increased
through grace, which brought about at-one-ment
(atonement) by belief in the saving power of the Son.
This was the message these Persian and Egyptian
missionaries brought to the West.   They preached
the need of a saviour from sin, and followed this up
by telling the people of the death of their Christ,
who to them was both Saviour and Redeemer.
Along with them came Greeks to Rome, bringing
with them their mystery beliefs, and preaching that

everyone must be saved, that "everyone must be born again, and washed from sin in the blood of the lamb".

Religion then was the prevailing conversation in the home, in the street, in the shops, at the market, in fact everywhere. Going along the street one would be stopped by an enthusiast who enquired if he or she were saved; a purchaser in a shop was met with the same question, the shopkeeper expounding on the merits of his new-found belief in either Dionysus, Osiris or Mithra. Sin and salvation were the topics of the time, and in this atmosphere the Eastern saviour-god religions swept like a whirlwind through the western Roman Empire.

The Romans, during this religious revival, were evidently feeling their sins pressing heavily upon them, and, as they had no saviour-god of their own, were converted in large numbers to this new form of belief. They had no rich mythology, like the Greeks, to fall back upon, their own gods were falling into disrepute; in fact a pre-Christian Pope, the Pontifex Maximus, questioned their very existence. From Egypt, Persia and Greece the Romans obtained their religious comfort, the result being that the Eastern religions rapidly gained in prestige throughout the Roman Empire, and saviour-gods were worshipped wherever the Roman eagle flew—with only one exception, Judea.

The Pagan Church of Rome, in consequence, was similar in most respects to the Christian Church which grew out of it, a Roman Catholic, or Greek, Church service of today differing little in belief and ceremony from what was believed, and took place, in the Roman

saviour-god churches before the advent of Christianity. The names of the gods worshipped were the
only difference. Then the principal church in Rome,
dedicated to Mithra, was on the Vatican mount,
where St. Peter's now stands, a spot which for long
has been devoted to sacred shrines. Here, as elsewhere,
the devout of all classes in the community attended
Matins and Evensong, to receive the consolation
which supernatural religion brings to everyone lacking
philosophic minds. The thoughtful, on the other
hand, obtained mental satisfaction from the writings of
Plotinus (A.D. 205–270), the leading exponent of
Neo-platonic philosophy, a mode of thought which
aimed at uniting the wisdom of all the ages into one
great comprehensive system of thought, embracing
the belief in one supreme God, and that this life is a
preparation for the one to come.

Meantime, as this great religious and philosophic
revival proceeded, enemies were massing at the
Empire's portals, so far kept closed by the rivers
Rhine, Danube and Euphrates, and yet no arrangement was made for the swift transport of troops from
one side of the Empire to the other. The neglect of
the use of sea power was to be the undoing of the
whole structure two centuries later, but, before this
happened, there is still very much to tell, as momentous
events occurred which completely changed the entire
history of the Western world. First of all, however,
let us briefly review a phase of Roman history, sordid
indeed, but one to be remembered.

(4) The Tragic History of the God-Emperors.

The accession of the degenerate Commodus (180–192), who succeeded his father, the noble-minded Marcus Aurelius, was a great calamity. He was the unworthy son of a worthy father, but, as his mother was a wanton woman, he was fated to inherit her failings. He chose the society of profligates and gladiators, and gave himself up to unbounded licence. His unseemly conduct lowered the dignity of the throne, and, after various attempts on his life, he was poisoned when thirty-two years of age, having reigned for twelve years, during which time nothing of importance happened. He was succeeded by Pertinax, who reigned for only a few months. Then came Didius Julian, who had a similar short reign.

Lucius Severus (193–211), an African by birth, was a resolute cruel man with great organising ability. He was occupied, especially towards the end of his reign of eighteen years, with a war in the east. One called Niger proclaimed himself emperor of the eastern half of the Empire, but Severus finally conquered him and took Byzantium. Then he had to turn west to defeat Albinus, who had been proclaimed emperor by his soldiers. A great and bloody battle ensued, which was won by Severus as the result of his personal bravery. This victory made him secure, and he then exercised the utmost severity towards all his enemies. After his revenge was satisfied he started war on the Parthians, who now controlled the old Persian Empire, and when victory was

won, and Mesopotamia was definitely secured as a
Roman province, he devoted his time to reorganising
the Empire, after which he went to Britain, where he
was engaged in constant warfare against the Picts, to
die finally in York.

The son of Severus, Caracalla (211–217) was one
of the greatest scoundrels ever born. He had
attempted to murder his father, and later succeeded in
murdering his brother, after which he seized supreme
power. Then he butchered 20,000 subjects he sus-
pected of disloyalty. After this massacre he spent the
rest of his reign in the maddest acts of destruction and
bloodshed, plundering everywhere, and committing
the most atrocious crimes. In Alexandria he took
vengeance on the people for their contempt, by ordering a general massacre, and then laid waste Mesopotamia because the Parthian king would not give
him his daughter in marriage. Finally he was
murdered. Such are the products of an empire built
on force, regardless of the rights of man. He was
followed by Macrinus, his murderer, who reigned only
one year, and then came Elagabalus (218–222), called
after the god he devoutly worshipped, his term of
office lasting for only four years. The shameless
profligacy of his life shocked the Roman people, and
he was killed during a mutiny of his soldiers.

Alexander Severus (222–235) ascended the throne
as a lad of seventeen. He was amiable, well meaning,
but weak, and very much under the influence of his
mother, a woman of many virtues' who surrounded
him with wise counsellors. Mutinies became frequent in all parts of the Empire, and he had to meet
invasions from Persia and Gaul, in which latter country

he was killed along with his mother. His personal virtues should be noted, but he was a pliable man and quite unfitted to rule a military empire.

Now comes Maximinus I (235–238), a giant in build and strength, whose oppressive rule culminated in revolt, and he was followed by Gordianus (238–244), who reluctantly yielded to the popular clamour to assume the purple. He was a man of amiable character and good reputation, of great accomplishments and fond of literature, but too intellectual to be powerful enough for these troubled times. In a mutiny of the army which was started by a rival he was slain in 244. Philip (244–249), who led this rebellion, then became emperor, to perish five years later during a revolt of the army, leaving behind him a very evil reputation. During his reign the Goths crossed the Danube and overran Thrace and Macedonia. Decius (249–251), then became emperor, only to be killed two years later in Thrace fighting the Goths, who, by now, were ravaging the seaboard of Asia Minor with their ships sailing from the Black Sea.

Then came Gallus (251–253) who also reigned for two years, and he was followed by Valerian, who became emperor at seventy years of age, to be later captured in Persia in 260, his fate being unknown. During his reign affairs in the Empire went from bad to worse, and the whole of the west fell into disorder. Gallienus (253–268), the son of Valerian, reigned jointly with his father. He was a brave and able man, but made no effort to repel the Goths, who, with a fleet of 500 ships, sacked Athens, Corinth, Argos, Sparta and Epirus. He gave himself up to excess and debauchery, and his generals, in almost every province, rebelled against him. He was overthrown and finally killed, while the rebel generals governed as a body. This period is known as the reign of the Thirty Tyrants, although in reality the usurpers numbered only nineteen. Claudius (268–270), a man of considerable ability and strength of character, followed, but his imperial career lasted for only two years. He gained a great victory in Serbia over the Goths, who were driven across the Danube, and he then died of the plague.

This terrible tale of the soldier god-emperors might easily be passed over by an historian anxious to keep his reader's attention, but it would have been unwise to do so, as everyone should know the fate of empires, or countries, cursed by military dictatorships. So, let the sordid story run to its bitter end, and this will soon be reached. Aurelian (270–275) commenced the work of fortifying the Empire against internal sedition and foreign invasion, a task which went on year by year. He met his death by assassination. Claudius Tacitus then became emperor, but his reign lasted only seven months. He was a man of culture and literary attainment, immensely rich, and, in his short reign, he introduced some domestic reforms. He was proud to claim descent from the great historian who bore his name.

Probus (276–282), a distinguished soldier, continued the work of strengthening the Empire by his successful wars against the Germans and Franks. This was only a temporary relief from an ever growing danger, as, on the farther banks of the Rhine and Danube, was gathering a growing host of hostile people. Probus bore a high character, he was just and cared for his soldiers, but this did not prevent him sharing the fate of so many of his predecessors, as he was attacked and slain in a sudden mutiny, leaving behind him a reputation few of his predecessors could equal. His death was mourned by the Senate and the people. Even the soldiers who killed him raised a memorial in his honour. He was succeeded by Carus, who reigned for only one year, and then the Empire was divided between Carinus and Numerian, who also reigned for only about a year, the former being murdered, and the latter dying a natural death.

Diocletian (284–305), the emperor who followed, reigned for twenty-one years, and received the veneration of an oriental potentate. He was the last of the God-emperors and reigned as absolute monarch. His high military achievements made him the choice of the army, which always had the say in the election of the soldier emperors, the opinion of the people in general never being considered. He commenced his reign by murdering, with his own hand, one of his enemies, a prerogative enjoyed by all Roman emperors. He divided the Empire into four parts, each under a ruler who bore the title of Caesar, and each was given a separate capital. This constituted an entirely new organisation of the Empire, for the purpose of increasing its power of resistance against the growing menace of internal disruption and invasion from without. He abdicated his sovereignty in 305, and died eight years later.

His reign is memorable for the persecution of the Christians, but, to the Romans in his time, this was just an incident, as now the Empire was showing.

serious signs of decay. The peace of the previous
two centuries had vanished, and in its place were war,
plague and famine, which thinned the population and
reduced the Empire's resources. Everywhere land
was lying waste, cities and towns were decaying,
culture and civilisation had declined, and commerce
was paralysed. The world cannot have war and
prosperity, plenty and happiness, and the powerful
Roman Empire was discovering this only too well.

Three of the Caesars appointed by Diocletian,
namely Maximian, Galerius and Constantius, continued to rule after Diocletian's abdication, and during
this period the enormous expenditure caused by civil
war at home, and endless conflicts with the barbarians
without, strained the Empire's resources. Maximian,
who had a distinguished career in the army, finally
strangled himself in 310 rather than fall into the hands
of his enemies, and Galerius, who now planned for
sole sovereignty, found, on the unexpected death of
Constantius, that the army in Britain had elevated to
the rank of Caesar of the Western Empire the son of
Constantius. Constantius, the son of a noble Dalmatian family, had distinguished himself by his
military capacity and able gentle rule, and it was his
wife, Helena, the daughter of an innkeeper, now a
canonised Christian saint, who bore him the son who
was to become known in later years as Constantine
the Great, one of the most outstanding of all the
Roman emperors.

If ever we required a reason why nations should
shun dictatorships like poison, we have it in this
terrible catalogue of crime which we have just perused,
and it is only by knowing what has taken place in the

past that we can learn to avoid the distasteful experiences of our ancestors. The art of good government comes only from long and bitter experience, and, because the Romans gave over the reins of authority to a dictator, their political history, under the bad emperors, reveals a truly sordid state of affairs. Little wonder that they became apathetic, and quite indifferent to the kind of emperor they had. The dreadful tale is not yet finished, but we shall now break into the story of Roman life and tell of something quite different, a series of events which led to the greatest occurrence in history.

(5) The Origin and Growth of the Christian Church.

A correct understanding of the origin of this great, and once powerful, institution should be one of the first endeavours of every intelligent man and woman who wishes to have a right knowledge of the Christian era. Nothing in history has been more misrepresented, and consequently no other great historical event is so little understood. No other episode in history should be studied with greater care, free from all religious prejudices, in a rational, logical way, and yet how few opportunities the average person has of obtaining any information apart from the various orthodox religious associations which have been the cause of so much erroneous teaching.

To find the origin of the Christian faith, a subject to which *The Psychic Stream* is devoted, we have to go back to the time of primitive man and study the evolution of religion. This knowledge is of vital

importance, but equally important is a correct understanding of the origin of the Christian Church. Here
and now is the place to give this subject our thoughtful consideration, but first of all we must know
something about the beliefs which brought it into
being.

Those of us who lived through the years of
terror, when at times it seemed as if Germany
would conquer, and then dominate, all Europe, and
perhaps the greater part of the world, will better
appreciate the story now about to be told. All the
freedom-loving nations feared for the future of the
human race if Germany obtained the power to force
the Nazi creed on the victims of her brutal violence,
but, at the beginning of the Christian era, no one foresaw what was to be the fate of, first of all, the inhabitants of the Roman Empire, then of all Europe, and
finally of that part of the earth's surface still to be discovered. Here we are at that period of history which
culminated in the greatest event in the recorded story
of the human race, the decision reached at the Council
of Nicæa in 325, but before we can understand what
then happened we must go back several hundred
years.

The Council of Nicaea was held because it was
believed that about three hundred years earlier a
Jew, named Jeshuah (a very common name in
these days, the Greek translation being Jesus),
lived, and died a violent death, and also because a
man, who called himself Paul, likewise lived. Had
these two men not lived the foregoing greatest event
in history would not have occurred. They were the
cause of history taking the course it did from the 4th

century to the present day, and how important their influence was on the future will be discovered by all who read this book to the end. So that this interesting and vital story may be clearly understood, this section will be divided up into three parts, the first dealing with what was believed about Jesus by his early disciples, the second with the opinions formed by Paul, and the last with what followed from what Paul did and taught.

Jesus, as he was known to his disciples.

Everyone in Christian countries is aware of the story told about Jesus and Paul, and that it is to be found in *The New Testament,* that part of the Bible which was added to the Hebrew scriptures in the 6th century, but very few people know the true story. Our information is slender, and so much that is not true has been added, century after century, that it has required extensive knowledge, deep thought, and considerable time to arrive at the truth. The story of the life of Jesus, as set out in the gospels, is not accepted by scholars as historical; in fact it is the outcome of tradition, to which has been added stories and beliefs then current about other saviour-gods worshipped in those days by the people of the Roman Empire. Why these additions were made will become clear as we go on, but here we are considering how much of the story is historical, and to find this we must go to the books of the learned scholars who have spent most of their lives trying to solve this problem.

No historian of the time mentions Jesus, the only

brief reference by Josephus being now accepted as a much later interpolation. We do not know what Jesus taught; in fact we know nothing about him historically, everything being surmise. Eusebius (265–340), the early Church historian, who was born in Palestine, tells us that all his efforts to discover something definite about Jesus ended in failure. The story of his life, as given in the Gospels, is not history, and by historians is ranked as legend, interspersed with the same myths which surrounded the other saviour-gods of earlier times. Jesus is not an historical character, as he did nothing to make himself such, and it was what his followers thought and did after his death that made him famous.

Guignebert, the Professor of the History of Christianity at the Sorbonne, Paris, in his work entitled *Jesus*, which he published in 1935, remarks:—

All that can be legitimately sought for in the Gospels is the material of the earliest history of Christian dogma, not that of the life of Jesus. Of the latter they tell us absolutely nothing. . . . There is not the slightest doubt that Jesus never uttered the discourses attributed to him by the Gospels. They are artificial compositions. . . . Even The Sermon on the Mount is no exception to this rule.

Gibbon, in his *Decline and Fall of the Roman Empire*, stresses from yet another angle the obscurity from which the religion arose:—

The names of Seneca, of the elder and younger Pliny, of Tacitus, of Plutarch, of Galen, of the slave Epictetus, of the emperor Marcus Antoninus adorn the age in which they flourished and exalt the dignity of human nature. They filled with glory their respective stations, either in active or contemplative life. Their excellent understandings were improved by study. Philosophy had purified their minds from the prejudice of the popular superstition, and their days were spent in the pursuit of truth and the practice of virtue. Yet, all the sages overlooked, or rejected, the perfection of the Christian system. Their language, or their silence, equally discover their contempt for the growing sect, which in their time had diffused itself over the Roman Empire. Those among them who condescend to mention the Christians consider them only as obstinate and perverse enthusiasts, who exacted an implicit submission to their mysterious doctrines, without being able to produce a single argument that could engage the attention of men of sense and learning.

These two quotations, the first by one of the foremost scholars of our times, and the second by one of the world's greatest historians, are only two of many similar conclusions formed by men of profound learning, after long study and research, earnestly undertaken in their search for truth. It is impossible to give further quotations, as space does not permit, and we must pass on to see if any basis exists to enable us to discover some kind of foundation for all the stories which came to be told about Jesus. Numerous gospels were written about him, some much more interesting than the four incorporated in the Bible, this quartet being selected by an assembly of superstitious and uncritical priests at the Council of Carthage in 397. For so much interest to be taken in Jesus, elaborated as those writings undoubtedly are, makes it evident that he lived, and that either his life, or death, or his reappearance after death, was the cause of this spontaneous gospel literature which appeared in different countries in the Roman Empire during the two hundred years succeeding his death.

Professor Harnack, the famous German 19th-century scholar, one of the greatest authorities on the origin of The New Testament, set to work to try to solve the problem. First of all he discarded *The Gospel of John* as a late production, as quite unhistorical, and also because it contradicts in every essential the other three gospels, which are called the Synoptic gospels, they professing to give a general survey of the public life of Jesus. Professor Burkitt, the late Professor of Divinity at Cambridge, came to the same opinion, remarking, in his book *Jesus Christ, An Historical Outline,* that

the contents of *The Gospel of John* do not seem historical at all . . . and I greatly doubt whether we can distinguish often in that gospel what is derived from tradition and what is derived from imagination.

Harnack took the first three gospels as the basis for his enquiry, because they agree more or less in style and contents ; in fact Matthew and Luke are so much in general verbal agreement with Mark, that if you strike out from Mark every verse repeated in Matthew and Luke very little will be left of Mark. This means that Matthew and Luke independently copied from Mark, abridging and altering here and there, which was the common practice of those days. After eliminating all the matter Matthew and Luke copied from Mark there is much left over in these two gospels which is not included in Mark. Here again Matthew and Luke copied from another source to obtain their information, as they tell the same stories and repeat sayings in much the same words. They must therefore have obtained this information from a common source, which is unfortunately lost, but it was reconstructed by Harnack from what Matthew and Luke have preserved.

The name he gave to this reconstructed document is "Quelle", from the German, meaning "source", and its reconstruction will be found in full in *The Psychic Stream.* We therefore find that Matthew and Luke compiled their narratives from two sources, the one being Mark, which we know, and the other called "Quelle", which is lost. Mark and "Quelle" formed the basis of Matthew and Luke, and this takes us back a step to the original documents before they were tampered with by the Christian priests at a later date. As Mark is full of Aramaic phrases and idioms it is now accepted that the documents from which the writer of this gospel copied were translations into Greek of Aramaic originals. Mark is composed of different layers, and, like the other gospels, stratum was laid upon stratum.

First came the oral story, which eventually was written down. Then some scribe added another version of the same story, which in time was taken as a separate episode. New stories and ideas, as they came to be believed, were added, and this went on for three hundred years. Just as Matthew and Luke copied from an earlier source, so also did Mark. Scholars have deduced this from a careful study of the gospel, and the name they give to this source is "Urmarcus" which was a patchwork of traditions of varying authenticity. *The Gospel of Mark,* as we now know it, is no more reliable as history than the others, and all three gospels are copies of two or more earlier sources which have been lost.

These two sources were of doubtful value, but

it is better to have this described by Professor Guignebert in his own words:—

One important fact is certain, the synoptic tradition still presents Jesus as a living person. It does not translate him into the realms of divinity, as the Pauline writings go on to do. But, if it vouches for the actuality of his life, it does not reveal the truth of it. . . . We are confronted by the problem of distinguishing between genuine tradition and apologetic figments. . . . Optimistic conviction is based on the belief that Urmarcus and Quelle were originally trustworthy documents, which is precisely what we have endeavoured to show they were not. Even had they really been so, it would help us little, because they have been so mishandled by the gospel redactors.

Jesus is therefore not an historical character, and the nearest we can approach to his life and teachings is as they are recorded in the "Quelle", which, in a primitive form, may have come into circulation about the middle of the 1st century. What, then, was thought of Jesus in these early times? Was he considered a virgin-born god, one of a trinity of gods, who altered the laws of nature at will, was put to death as a sacrifice for the sins of mankind, arose in his physical body after death, and then soared up to heaven like a balloon? No, all that, and much more, was added later, as in this, the earliest known record, we have Jesus depicted as an ordinary individual, one who was a naturally born Jew, who lived as a Jew, and died a Jew, nothing miraculous being mentioned. Here he is pictured as a man who is dissatisfied with existing conditions, and anticipates what he calls the coming of the Kingdom of God. He teaches love and non-resistance, denounces hypocrites, and warns everyone that each reaps as he sows. Nothing is said about his birth, his death or his resurrection.

His gospel was the early coming of the Kingdom of God on earth, for which all should prepare, not by believing a creed but by forsaking wickedness and living righteous lives. His moralising, as recorded, was very simple, and confined to only a few short sentences, emphasis being laid on forsaking the things of this world and trusting God to feed, clothe and sustain every one. What we call the Lord's Prayer consisted only of a request for daily bread and forgiveness. Always in the "Quelle" he is referred to as Jesus, and never by the Pagan theological name of Christ, which was applied to him by Paul for the reason we shall soon discover. He condemned the Pharisees for their forms and ceremonies, as their lives were evil, goodness being much more acceptable to God than temple observances.

That the foregoing was the burden of his teaching is confirmed from the manuscript discovered in 1873, and known as *The Teaching of the Twelve Apostles*, which is thought to have been first published early in the 2nd century, its value resting on the fact that it is one of the few documents relating to Jesus which was not altered and embellished by the Christian priesthood at a later date. Herein Jesus is referred to as "Jesus thy servant" of the seed of David, the manuscript mostly containing moral teaching, as the Incarnation, the Sacrament, the Trinity, the Resurrection and Ascension, the Atonement, and other doctrines and ceremonies, are passed by unmentioned. Though we find nothing therein to support Christian doctrines and dogma, much is said about psychic gifts, which, during the period when the book was written, evidently continued to be greatly reverenced in the early Church, just as they were in the time of the apostles.

Tertullian (160–230), who was one of Rome's most eminent jurists, fortunately has left us a description of an early Jesuian service before the priests captured the Church. In his work *De Anima* he gives this account of a service in his church, in which a highly gifted medium played the leading part:—

For seeing that we acknowledge spiritual charismata, or gifts, we too have merited the attainment of the prophetic gift. We have now amongst us a sister whose lot it has been to be favoured with sundry gifts of revelation, which she experiences in the spirit by ecstatic vision amidst the sacred rites of the Lord's day in the church. She converses with the angels, and sometimes even with the Lord; she both sees and hears mysterious communications; some men's hearts she understands, and to them who are in need she distributes remedies. Whether it be in the reading of the Scriptures or in the chanting of psalms, or in the preaching of sermons, or in the offering up of prayers, in all these religious services, matter and opportunity are afforded her of seeing visions.

It may possibly have happened to us, whilst this sister of ours was rapt in the spirit (in trance), that we had discoursed in some ineffable way about the soul. After the people are dismissed at the conclusion of the sacred services, she is in the regular habit of reporting to us whatever things she may have seen in vision; for all her communications are examined with the most scrupulous care, in order that their truth may be probed. "Amongst other things," says she, "there has been shewn to me a soul in bodily shape, and a spirit has been in the habit of appearing to me; not, however, a void and empty illusion, but such as would offer itself to be even grasped by the hand, soft and transparent and of an ethereal colour, and in form resembling that of a human being in every respect. This was her vision, and for her witness there was God; and the Apostle Paul most assuredly foretold that there were to be spiritual gifts in the Church.

This description of what took place in the Apostolic Church, when the medium occupied a leading place in the church service, is in strange contrast to what followed from the 4th century onwards when the priests obtained control. We shall be reading later on how these gifted mediums, known to the early Church as "the oracles of God", came to be called "the servants of the Devil", but what is just as extraordinary is the fact that in Britain today, and elsewhere, they are legally termed "rogues and vagabonds". Moreover, they are not only regarded in our own times as outcasts, but heavily fined and given long terms of imprisonment for one reason only, namely, that they claim to possess "the spiritual gifts" praised by the Apostle Paul.

According to the Witchcraft Act of 1735, a piece of ignorant legislation brought into being by the Christian Church, to communicate with the departed is impossible, and all who claim to be the medium for this communication are *ipso facto* frauds and consequently criminals, the medium's honesty never being considered. How few there be who know that in Apostolic days "the unforgivable sin" was to doubt the fact that mediums were controlled by other-world people, but, as we proceed, we shall discover many other strange contrasts between the beliefs of the early Church and those considered orthodox from the 4th century onwards.

In those Apostolic days the people, moreover, often relied on what we today would call psychic healing, and in ancient literature hundreds of cases are recorded of the sick being healed by the touch of mediums who had this gift. The Greeks encouraged this method of healing, and we are told that Jesus also had this power, as we read of him thus healing the sick, the blind, the lame, the deaf and the lepers, and claiming, as do mediums today, that his power to heal came from a source beyond himself. For two hundred years before his birth the Essenes, or Therapeutae, meaning healers, a sect which was an offshoot of Buddhism, had dwelt in Palestine and Egypt. At the medical school of Alexandria they learned the art of healing, and it is quite possible that Jesus, a natural psychic, was influenced by them, as what he is said to have taught, they taught.

By his psychic gifts, and condemnation of the priests, he aroused their wrath. On one occasion we are told the law was invoked against him when he was doing his "good works" (*John* x, 31–33), and he nearly suffered from being stoned, this being the punishment prescribed for sorcerers, the name the priests gave to everyone endowed with psychic power. Quite possibly his mediumship was the cause of his arrest and death, but, as the Romans would not be influenced by the Jewish law, which condemned all mediums to death, the priests put forward charges of a political nature in so subtle a manner that his conviction followed as a matter of course. We do not know why Jesus became a priestly victim, but, knowing as we do the terrible fate which came to all mediums who fell into the power of the Jewish or Christian priesthood, it is reasonable to think that his psychic gifts were the cause which brought about his death.

The ethical teaching which we find in the gospels was in no way new to the Pagans and the Jews, as it formed part of the moral code of the time, Hillel (70 B.C.–A.D. 10), the famous Jewish rabbi, focussing the moral code within one short sentence, namely "What we dislike, do not do to others." Pythagoras in Greece, and Buddha and Krishna in India, then received the credit for laying down a code of morals much more extensive than is to be found in the gospels. Eusebius tells us that what was contained in the Essene literature, probably a translation of the Buddhist scriptures, was used to make up the Christian gospels, and, if this were so, the source of much attributed to Jesus can be traced to India. The substance of the Essene faith was the laying up of treasure in heaven and not on earth, and that the rich should give to the poor, but the similarity between what was attributed to Jesus, and what the Essenes taught, is so striking that the only conclusion we can reach is that Jesus was an Essene, or that those who compiled the original gospels were of that persuasion, Jesus being made the mouthpiece of the substance of the Essene teaching.

The followers of Jesus were Jews, as were the Essenes, and they continued their old form of worship after their master's death, but the destruction of Jerusalem (A.D. 70) by the Romans brought to an end the close relationship between the Jewish religion and the Jesuian sect, whose first church was the Temple in Jerusalem. (*Acts* ii, 46.) The destruction of this building altered everything, and, from now onwards, what later came to be known as the Christian Church pursued its separate existence. This important event marks the birthday of the Apostolic Church, and many Jews, having now lost faith in the promises of Jehovah, came over to the new belief that the Messiah had come in the person of Jesus.

To begin with, the Jesuians were a small offshoot of the Jewish faith, and had Paul of Tarsus not appeared on the scene they would probably have disappeared in time, as many other such sects had done before them, or again been merged into the faith of their fathers. It was not until the 4th century that most óf the different sects of Jesuians came to adopt a common belief and call themselves Christians, though some, for centuries thereafter, retained their own different beliefs and were classed as heretics.

The Apostolic Church, in the 1st and 2nd centuries, consisted of a community of Jesuians, or believers in Jesus as the Messiah, a name also given to others who had preached liberation from oppression. They were intent on living good and pure lives in anticipation of their Lord's return, the belief in his messiahship and early return being probably due to his being seen after death as an apparition.[1] Scholars believe that the story of his resurrection, as given in the gospels, is a late addition, and that this was superimposed on an earlier story of him being seen in his etheric body. Something must have occurred to bring courage and hope to the dispirited band who saw their master's hope of the coming Kingdom of God fade out on the cross,[2] and this psychic experience is the most probable

[1] The belief in the Second Coming is an ancient idea, and can be traced back to sun-worship, when the sun god was awaited each morning with prayer and thanksgiving.

[2] How Jesus met his death is as much a mystery as everything else about his life, as, in three separate places in the New Testament, it is stated that he was hanged on a tree.

explanation, especially so as the seeing of the ghost of a victim after death produced similar effects at the opening stages of other earlier religions.

Whatever was the cause, the fact remains that the Jesuians grew and multiplied wherever Jews were to be found, dividing in time into different sects which came to be known as Gnostics, Ebionites and Nazarenes, each of which held different opinions about Jesus. All, however, expected his early return to earth, and during the interval they were consoled by communications which they believed came from heaven through the mediums who became entranced at their meetings.

These mediums, who passed on what they saw clairvoyantly or heard clairaudiently, or what they were inspired to say when in trance, were believed to be the sacred link between heaven and earth. The early Jesuian literature makes clear how much they were respected, and they received such designations as "Organs of the Spirit" who were filled with the "Spirit of the Lord". They were also described as "vessels" and "vases" who were filled during trance with the divine or holy spirit, and passed on the "word of the Lord". Mediums were also likened to a harp, and the holy spirit to the plectrum, the ivory implement the player uses to pluck the strings, this divine spirit control being termed "The Comforter", "The Voice of God", and "the Spirit of the Lord". Mediums, when in trance, were said to be "filled with the spirit" and were regarded as "the oracles of God", all of these descriptions making clear that the Apostolic Church was based on what is today known as Spiritualism, it deriving its inspiration from the communications its members believed they had with the men and women of the other world.

If the priests had not banished the mediums from the churches, in the 4th century, and put their irrational mystical theology in place of these communications, Jesus, instead of becoming one of three gods in heaven, would have been recognised as the human medium he was, a man endowed with that rare capacity of acting as a channel between this world and the next. That his contemporaries accepted him as such is evident, because we are told of "the spirit, like a dove, descending upon him" (*Mark* i, 10) and then about a voice speaking, two phenomena which can be seen and heard today at any direct-voice séance.

A record of the author's personal experience of the bluish semi-circular light which descended on the medium, and the voices which followed, will be found in his book *On the Edge of the Etheric* where he clears up the age-old mystery of the holy spirit. Hundreds of books have been written by theologians on this puzzling doctrine, but not one of these so-called learnèd men has understood the first principles of his subject, and, lacking all psychic knowledge or experience, they have written round and round an imaginary mystery, displaying their profound ignorance by every sentence they wrote.

The holy spirit was no mystery to the worshippers in the Apostolic Church, a Spiritualist organisation which lasted until it was captured by the priesthood. Its first minister was Matthias, and we are also given the names of others, but these men were ministers only. They conducted the services, offered up prayer,

and read from what we now call *The Old Testament*,
continuing their ordinary occupation during the week.
The one endowed with charismata, the Greek name
for psychic gifts, was the one the people came to hear,
and the account given by Tertullian of an Apostolic
Church service in the 3rd century, with the medium
taking the leading part, more resembles one held
in a Spiritualist church of the present day than any
other.

How, then, did it come about that this simple faith
was turned into creeds, dogmas and doctrines, the
belief in which was necessary for salvation? How was
it that Jesus was transformed into a sacrificed victim,
slain for the sins of humanity, and then elevated to the
high position after death of Saviour, Judge, Mediator
and Redeemer, the second person of a trinity of gods?
To find the answer to this vital question we must
study the writings of one who called himself Paul,
as he was the cause of what became the greatest event
in history, the decision reached by the Council of
Nicaea, which made the Christian Church eventually
the dominant power in Europe, and later of the entire
Western hemisphere.

Paul founded Christianity, and transformed Jesus,
the Jew, into Christ the god. Paul, figuratively
speaking, lifted Jesus from his Jewish cradle and transported him to Greece, where he grew up as a Pagan
god. Paul introduced into Jesuism the Pagan beliefs
relating to their saviour-gods, who were believed to
have been miraculously born, to have lived amongst
men, to have suffered for their sins by violent deaths,
to have risen again for their salvation, and ascended to
heaven whence they had come, each being worshipped

by his followers on earth as Saviour, Redeemer and Mediator.

Paul was a man with great force of character, a mystic, a sincere zealous enthusiast for a cause he made his own, but he lacked knowledge and wisdom, being also quite devoid of logical or rational thought. However mistaken he was, it cannot be denied that he was an outstanding man ; in fact few men in history are more so when the effects of his actions are taken into account.

The coming of Paul on the scene opens the second phase of the evolution of Jesuism into Christianity. Now we enter an entirely new environment, having left behind the simple teaching of a simple man. Now we are in the realm of mysticism and theology, of sin and sacrifice, of gods and devils, of salvation or damnation, of heaven and hell, of all those mystical abstruse speculations so loved by the unpractical, illogical, priestly, mystical, theological mind. This being so, we leave a gap to emphasise the fact that we are now dealing with quite a new phase of thought, as

We now leave Jesus, the man, to consider Christ, the God.

We are first introduced to Paul when, as a Jew, he was persecuting these unorthodox Jesuians, but his entire life was changed by an event which, whatever it was, altered the whole course of history. He claims to have seen and heard Jesus as a spirit, and, because of this, he came to believe that Jesus was a god, a very common belief about the men and women of the other world who were seen on earth. In those days, these etheric beings were considered messengers from

Zeus, Jupiter, Jehovah or Brahma, according to the faith into which the clairvoyant was born.

The mind of Paul, saturated as it was with the theology and mysticism of the times, and with the speculations of his contemporaries Gamaliel and Philo, developed this idea much further. A careful reading of his writings in the original Greek makes it clear that he believed Jesus could influence him from the other world, an idea which made him feel that Jesus had a personal message for him alone. This gave him the courage, and the audacity, to defy the disciples who had known Jesus on earth, and to tell them that they had misunderstood their master's mission, its purport having been revealed to him only. (I *Galatians* ii.)

The Greeks based their mythology on the return to earth of those who had once lived here as men and women. Their revelation came as the result of psychic experiences, and the Babylonians, Egyptians, Persians and Hindus developed their saviour-god religions from the same source. It is therefore not surprising that the mediumistic, mystically minded Paul imagined from his psychic revelations much more than the belief that his etheric visitor was just another of God's messengers. His experience changed him from being a persecutor into an ardent enthusiast for the cause he cherished as his own, namely, that he had been appointed by God to proclaim that Jesus was the Christ, the anointed victim who had taken away the sins of the race by his death on the cross. Likewise he linked his ideas to the old rather ambiguous promise that "it [the serpent] shall bruise thy head, and thou shalt bruise his heel"

(*Genesis* iii, 15), and so bound the faith he produced to the Hebrew religion from which it is inseparable.

What Paul preached contained the same beliefs as had gone through earlier pre-Christian religions, which held that the one they considered to be the Christ had died to redeem all believers. Plato, in his *Republic*, writes of the ideal Righteous Man, scourged, tortured, bound, his eyes burned out, and finally, after suffering every misery, crucified. Of his own free will he came from heaven to earth to die to fulfil his Father's purpose to save mankind. Thus he conquered the devil and made him captive, to ascend triumphantly to heaven and sit beside his Father in glory. This is the central theme of the worship of the saviour-gods, the most outstanding being Bel, the Babylonian god; Mithra, the Persian god; Prometheus, and Dionysus, and other Greek gods; Osiris, the Egyptian god, and Krishna, the Hindu god. The moving passage in *Isaiah* (liii, 1–12), depicting the man of sorrows who was acquainted with grief, is just a reflection of the religious beliefs of the time, and certainly not a prophecy of the coming saviour, as Christians believe. This reference, in all probability, relates to the saviour Bel (Baal), who shared with Jehovah the affection of the Israelites.

Paul's momentous innovation consisted of draping round Jesus the beliefs which had accumulated about those other gods over the previous two thousand years, and by so doing he flatly contradicted him he called his Lord. Jesus is reported as saying that there is only one God, that the way of · salvation is by doing what was right, and that if one forgave he would be forgiven, whereas Paul made salvation a question of faith. Paul preached belief in the saving power of the glorified Christ, who, like one of the lambs continually being butchered in that slaughter-house called the Temple, had shed his blood on the cross to atone for the sins of the human race.

Paul, then, was the inventor and founder of the Christian faith. He was the first Christian, but it took many years before what he candidly admits is his own interpretation of the death of Jesus (*Galatians* i, 11) was accepted by all the followers of Jesus, who, as time went on, increased in numbers, to become known under different names, until eventually the majority came to be called Christians. How it was possible for an apparition to be the cause of the Christian creeds, doctrines and dogmas is too long and complicated a process to explain in this outline of world history. Likewise this is not the place to enquire into the reason why the reappearance after death of different priestly victims caused the people to transform them into gods, arisen from the dead, who had suffered and died to expiate the sins of believers. To understand this requires the study of ancient theological beliefs on sacrifice, and anyone sufficiently interested will find in *The Psychic Stream* a clear explanation of the process from its early inception to its final phase.

We remember the bargain the Jews made with Jehovah, that if they gave him the etheric counter-parts of a tenth of their animals and crops he would look after them, and see that their herds and fields were fruitful. That was the business side of religion everywhere in those days, but there was also the mystical aspect of sacrifice which led to the evolution of the saviour-god. When the people were cannibals they imagined that the gods relished especially the spirits of human beings, just as much as they, the people, enjoyed eating human flesh. So, on special occasions, the son of the King, or Chief, or other notable, became the victim to produce a meal of special delicacy, the idea being that this was the choicest food they could offer up to heaven, while they themselves were fortified by partaking of the aristocratic flesh.

When the knowledge of good and evil increased, sacrifice became a means of reconciling the angry gods by the offerings of the etheric bodies of the victims, in exchange for pardon after death for wrong-doing here on earth, the more important the victim the greater the pardon. Then followed the saviour-god religions, when a priestly victim, after sacrifice, was considered in the light of a god-man, who had died to save all believers, because after his death he was seen as an apparition. Thus he had conquered death, which was believed to be the punishment inflicted on mankind for human wickedness.

The return of a priestly victim after death always produced the same type of Saviour, Redeemer and Mediator, if the religious conditions of the time were ripe for such an event. Round him were woven similar beliefs as later came to surround Jesus, a priestly victim, who, because some declared they had seen him after death, came to be looked upon as a god-man who had suffered, died and risen again. By his death he had satisfied divine justice, and his etheric resurrection had proved that death had been conquered, all believers partaking of his physical body being likewise endowed with his power over death. Thus the ancient cannibalistic idea, that by eating part of the sacrificed victim the partaker was endowed with his power over death, was continued by Christianity, to become its principal rite.

This ceremony, known to the Greeks as Eukharistia, and much revered, was the central theme of Paganism, whose temples were slaughter-houses, and altars butchers' blocks, off which it was thought the gods ate the spirits of the sacrificed animals. The altar, or Lord's Table, has a bloody origin and a sanguinary history, but the priests were not only butchers but also purveyors, as they handed round to the worshippers pieces of bread and cups filled with wine. This they claimed to have changed into the Saviour's body and blood by some mystical magical process known only to themselves, a claim which was continued by the Christian priesthood.

This dual idea relating to sacrifice was continued by the Christian Church up to the time of the Reformation, when it was abandoned by some but not all of the Protestants. The Roman Catholic Mass is today the survival of the custom of offering an animal or herbage to the gods, as, until the 9th Christian century, this ceremony was devoted to the offering of the fruits of the earth to the three Christian gods, who were considered to be vegetarians, and we still have our harvest thanksgiving when the church is laden with grain, fruit and vegetables. From the 9th century onwards the offering of vegetation ceased, the ceremony becoming one solely of a cannibalistic nature, namely the eating and drinking of bread and wine changed into the body and blood of the Saviour.

All the ceremonials and expressions used by the Pagans were likewise continued by Christianity, an interesting papyrus of the 2nd century A.D. reading as follows:—

Chaeremon invites thee to dine at the Table of the Lord Serapis in the Serapeum tomorrow, the fifteenth, at nine o'clock.

Serapis was the Greek name for the Egyptian saviour-god Osiris, the Lord's Table was the table on which lay the consecrated elements, as they did in the early Christian Church and still do in Presbyterian and Non-conformist churches, and the Serapeum was the name of the magnificent temple dedicated to Serapis in Alexandria. Aristides (A.D. 117–189), the distinguished Greek sophist, moreover, tells us that the worshippers of Serapis enjoyed a real communion with him in his sacrifice for them, that he met them at the altar during the Communion service, where he partook with them of the sacrament.

We are told in *The Acts* (xi, 46) that the disciples of Jesus continued to worship in the Temple and to break bread from house to house, a purely Jewish custom which was quite devoid of Eucharistic meaning. Paul, or someone else, transformed this into the Pagan Eucharist, claiming to have received the idea from heaven, and the story of the Last Supper,[1] as told by him when writing to the Corinthians, was later incorporated almost verbally into the Gospels of Matthew, Mark and Luke, but not into John, which passes it by with the words "and the supper being

---

[1] It is thought by many scholars that the account of the Last Supper, as given in the Epistle to the Corinthians, is a later interpolation which was afterwards copied into the gospels.

ended". Paul, or some unknown person, was the originator of the Christian Eucharist, and his writings teem with the idea of Jesus as the sacrificed victim offered up for mankind, a fantasy which was quite strange and unbelievable to the disciples if we go back for our information to the oldest available documents.

Paul's writings so encompass what was believed about the Greek saviour-god Dionysus, that it is evident he came to believe Jesus to be none other than this god returned to earth a second time. Dionysus, like Jesus, was believed to have performed wonderful deeds when on earth—miracles, they were called—and, moreover, Dionysus was the god of Tarsus, Paul's home town. So we need not be surprised that Paul knew much about the beliefs surrounding this famous Greek god, and that he attached to Jesus all the mystical phraseology connected with the worship of Dionysus,[1] the heavenly being, born on earth to a virgin impregnated by Zeus, who suffered and died for mankind, a divine creation from all eternity who had humbled himself to save humanity. Dionysus was represented by his statues as radiant, triumphant and glorious, and above his head were the words "I am Life, Death and Resurrection, I hold the winged crown", the crown which Paul at the end of his career believed he would receive from him he called the Christ, who had become to him the symbol of the resurrection and the life.

[1] Dionysus, the Greek Christ, and second person in the Greek Trinity, was also known as Our Lord, the Vine, the Saviour, the Judge of the Dead, the Deliverer, the Born Again, the Only Begotten Son of God, and his followers believed that he said "I am one with my father in heaven", a eucharist service being celebrated by his worshippers in his memory. In Rome a temple was dedicated to the Greek Trinity, Demeter, Dionysus and Persephone, and called the Temple of the Trinity.

Only through Dionysus could one arrive at the fullness of knowledge, could one hear the inner voice, and some day become like unto this heavenly being of transcendental beauty, this divine model of humanity. "One day perhaps thou wilt resemble him" was told to believers. At the Festival of Eleusis, which surely Paul witnessed, the image of the child Dionysus was carried through the assembled crowds, and then was enacted his mysterious birth, life and resurrection on the stage of the amphitheatre, to conclude with the chorus chanting:—

You who have contemplated the holy mystery in which the gods and man have taken part, take with you its remembrance on earth. Let it console you during life, but keep it locked in your heart like a diamond in a rock. You can receive the truth in this Sanctuary and carry its rays in the world, but whosoever betrays its sublime origin will lose it for ever.

This concluded a moving drama, gorgeously staged, which the Greeks described as "the most beautiful sight in the world" and as "divine visions", Plato comparing it with the sights happy souls enjoy after death. Then followed clairvoyant demonstrations by the carefully tended mediums, who were specially chosen because of their psychic power, "when a window was opened showing the fullness of the living Light suffused with divine love". The emotional, mediumistic, mystical Paul knew about this wonderful spectacle, and all the devotional phrases used to glorify Dionysus, but to him Dionysus, the Greek Christ, had returned to earth as a god-man, as Jesus, to die again and suffer for mankind.

From his home in heaven he now used his servant

Paul as his medium, to bring the gospel message to all mankind, and so Paul declared: "Since ye seek a proof of Christ speaking in me" (2 *Corinthians* xiii, 3), "it pleased God . . . to reveal his son in me, that I might preach him" (*Galatians* i, 15), and "Christ liveth in me" (*Galatians* ii, 20). Great indeed did this "chosen vessel"[1] of the Lord (*Acts* ix, 15) feel his mission, and sincerely did he believe that his heavenly Christ had revealed himself through him to all mankind.

Mediums know the etheric men or women who act as their controls in trance, or during clairaudience, and in our day they recognise them as the men and women they are. In Paul's day it was far otherwise, as they were none other than gods and goddesses who came to earth to converse with and instruct mankind. Consquently Paul's emotions were so aroused that, when he saw an etheric man whom he took to be Jesus, and then felt that this being was acting as his control, he imagined that he too was being inspired from heaven for a purpose.

On earth, Jesus had been regarded by some as a god-man,[2] because of his remarkable psychic gifts, and, now that he had returned as a god, Paul argued that he could be none other than the long-awaited Christ, no less than Dionysus himself come back to earth as his worshippers had so long anticipated. To this heavenly being, this "Christ speaking in me", he consequently attached all the beliefs relating to Dionysus, to such effect that Plutarch, a generation later, caustically complained of the unscrupulous use

---

[1] The term used for a medium in those days.

[2] A medium in these days was called "a man of God", and frequently considered to be a god-man.

Christians made of the beliefs surrounding his saviour Dionysus. Never before, or since, did such world-wide repercussions follow from irrational emotion, and here indeed we have the supreme example of the effect on human history of the appearance of a god, or, as we would say today, of an other-world man, commonly called a ghost.

This being so, we are now in a completely different environment from the one experienced by Peter, and the other disciples, who knew the human Jesus, a man like unto themselves. Consequently a distinct separation of Jesus from Paul's heavenly Christ, a mystical theological heavenly creation, is absolutely essential, if what follows from now onwards up to our own times is to be understood. Because past historians have never made this distinction, and have considered Jesus as the founder of the Christian faith, there is so much misuse of the words Christian and Christianity, an example being the remark made by President Roosevelt during his sixtieth birthday speech (31–1–1942), that "Democracy stands for all the ideals of Christianity". What he perhaps meant was that democracy stood for what we imagine was the teaching of Jesus, which was as different from Christianity as night is from day. Field-Marshal Smuts made the same mistake, when he associated Christianity with the parable of the good Samaritan in his speech in the London Guildhall on 19th October, 1943.

During the time Paul was on the first of his four missionary travels, meeting his expenses by making tents, the disciples of Jesus remained in Palestine under the belief that the teaching of Jesus was for the Jews only, and not for the Gentiles. Paul, after a space of three years since his conversion, met Peter, and James, the brother of Jesus, for the first time, but could not succeed in making them see his point of view, and he did not return to Jerusalem again for fourteen years, where, as he tells the Galatians, he did not dare to preach his gospel because of the opposition of the disciples. Those who had known Jesus could not look upon him as other than "a man approved of God among you by miracles and wonders and signs" (*Acts* ii, 22), as is the recorded opinion of Peter, who, we are told, was his daily companion.

If Peter has been correctly reported, and if this old expression is given its modern meaning, then Jesus was a medium through whom the other-world doctors could heal diseases, in just the same way as they do through healing mediums in our own times. Paul, however, tells us that he treated the opinions of the disciples with contempt, and was quite rude to them, a strange attitude to adopt when we remember that he never knew Jesus on earth. This learned Pharisee had no use for the beliefs of simple fishermen. So Peter and Paul quarrelled, as Peter considered that the message Jesus had brought, of the early coming of the Kingdom of God on earth, was for the Jews only. Paul, however, with his knowledge of the Greek mystery religions, and his own psychic experiences, believed that Jesus was something far greater than a local Messiah, and none other than the glorified Christ, the World-Saviour who had come to redeem humanity.

From the beginning there were these two opinions about Jesus, known as the Pauline and Petrine, the former being taken up by the Greeks and the latter by the Hellenised Jews. For many years these differences split the early believers in Jesus into two camps, the Christians and the Jesuians, but, as the Christians belonged to much more important countries than did the despised Jews, who by then had no land of their own, the Christian Church gradually over-shadowed, and finally absorbed, the Jewish Apostolic Church, so much so that Jesuism gradually changed into Christianity. The Pagan priests, who became Christians, naturally introduced the ideas in which they had been nurtured, as the Jesuian beliefs meant little to them, the consequence being that Christianity became the new name for the old Pagan beliefs, ceremonies and customs.

The Pagan religion which was the strongest rival of Christianity was Mithraism. From Mithraism Christianity copied most of all; it absorbed Mithraism and Mithraism became Christianity. Almost everything Christians believe, the Mithraists believed long before the Christian era. Mithraism celebrated the 25th December (the beginning of Winter, from which date the days lengthen and the sun strengthens), this day being regarded by the Mithraists as the birth-day of their saviour Mithra. So this day was adopted as the birthday of Jesus. Likewise the Pagans, who became Christians, introduced the festival of Easter (the beginning of Spring and the return of life to the earth), when Mithra was believed to have risen from the dead, and also the other days now considered as Christian holy days. Sunday was the most important, as on that day (which the Mithraists called "The Lord's Day") Mithra came forth alive from his rock tomb after being buried for some days.

Infant baptism, the Eucharist, and then the

Trinity (the Father, the Son and Holy Spirit being Pagan designations), were borrowed from Egypt; the Virgin mother, and her bringing forth a god-child, being also taken from the Egyptian religion, and other Pagan beliefs, rituals and ceremonies were added as the centuries passed. The Pagan prayers were copied, in some cases verbatim, as were their hymns, until eventually Jesus was evolved into another Pagan Christ, his mother taking the place of the Roman Magna Mater, the Mother of God. Paul, and not Jesus, consequently became the authority of the Christian Church, until the time came when the original Jesuian, or Apostolic, beliefs were smothered under a heap of dogma and doctrine to which the name of Christianity was given.

The wide difference between Jesuism and Christianity is clearly noticeable in the first chapter of Matthew, which begins with the words "The book of the generation of Jesus Christ, the son of David, the son of Abraham", and then follows a quite inaccurate genealogy from Abraham to "Joseph the husband of Mary,[1] of whom was born Jesus". The fact that this family tree is a fake, as is likewise a completely different one given in Luke, is not specially important, but what is interesting is the certainty that when it was written Jesus was considered to be a human being, the son of Joseph and born in a natural way. When, however, Christianity came into being, and Jesus was elevated at the Council of Nicaea in 325, and the Council of Constantinople in 381, to the position of a saviour-god, and a member of

---

[1] This originally read "Joseph begat Jesus", and the oldest Greek and Syrian manuscripts have this wording, the Latin versions only having been altered.

a trinity of gods, it became obvious to the priests that something must be done to counteract this glaring admission that he was a human being like everyone else.

So they made the entire genealogy from Abraham, via David, to Joseph invalid by inserting immediately after this family tree the following words: "When, as his mother Mary was espoused to Joseph before they came together, she was found with child of the Holy Ghost . . . for that which is conceived in her is of the Holy Ghost". This momentous news came by means of a dream to Joseph, and on this nebulous foundation Christianity built up its theological and mystical dogmas based on the writings of Paul. Jesus being God, and the Holy Ghost being God, it logically follows that Jesus was his own father, because, as Euclid tells us, "Things that are equal to the same thing are equal to one another." Evidently this is still the orthodox opinion on the subject, as Dr. Temple, the Archbishop of Canterbury, declared in his Easter 1943 broadcast that "He who died on the Cross was Almighty God".

What an angel said in a dream to a Jewish carpenter, and what an angel told Mary, a Jewish maiden, does not here concern us, as this fable only gained currency many years later, and they themselves never mentioned the episode, always looking upon Jesus as their son born in a natural way. The interest to us lies in the fact that the earliest gospels portrayed Jesus as a human being, and it was only by means of later interpolations, and the rewriting of the original documents, that Jesus was transformed into the Christ, to give rise to Christianity, an assembly of beliefs

which are as different from the beliefs of the early
Jesuians as black is from white.

Those responsible for these alterations did their
work in a very slip-shod fashion, because they not
only allowed the original genealogy, tracing Jesus
back to Abraham, to remain, but they also left in
many of the older passages depicting him as very
much of a man. Likewise the original passages, which
related that Jesus taught that good deeds bring their
own reward here and hereafter, have been left, while
additions have been made to the effect that only by
belief in Christ as the Saviour can salvation be secured.
The most obvious of these additions is to the last
chapter of Mark, the verses from 9 to 20 having been
added at a later date, as they are not to be found in the
oldest extant copies. Herein is to be found a remark
attributed to Jesus, and made use of by the priests
throughout the Christian era to justify their torturing,
murdering and persecuting of unbelievers: "He that
believeth and is baptised shall be saved, but he that
believeth not shall be damned."

Everything relating to belief, baptism and the
Eucharist was emphasised by the Christian priests
during the Christian era, and all that Jesus is reported
to have said about good deeds bringing salvation was
ignored, because we can all be good without the help of
the clergy, but they are needed if the beliefs, rites and
ceremonies of the Christian Church are required for
salvation. Jesus had quite different views on the
question of God and salvation from those expressed so
boldly by men who falsely claim to be his representatives and mouthpieces on earth, as, when on the
cross he realised that his mission had been a failure,

he is reported to have cried out "My God, my God, why hast thou forsaken me"?[1]   On another occasion, when asked "Good master, what shall I do that I may inherit eternal life?", he replied, "Why callest thou me good?   There is none good but one, that is God," and then went on to say that salvation came from keeping the commandments (*Mark* x, 17).   In other words, how we live here determines our condition hereafter, and creeds, ceremonials, baptism, rites, and all that surrounds orthodox religion, had, in his opinion, nothing whatever to do with salvation.

Much of the history of the Christian era revolves round the wars and persecutions which followed from these contradictory passages in the gospels, the priests and the heretics both claiming authority for their opinions, but historians hitherto have always passed by the vital facts to which this section is devoted, the reason being that they do not come within the range of history.   True, the New Testament is not history, but the beliefs contained therein made history, and because historians have passed over the important facts recorded in this section, the history of the Christian era has never been correctly set out or understood.   This grave omission, due to ignorance, has not been repeated in this book, which places what happened in the first four Christian centuries in its right perspective, and so makes intelligible much of the history which follows.

Here a clear-cut distinction is made between Jesuism and Christianity, as only by so doing can the mists of misunderstanding be cleared away.   Here

[1] A reference to *Mark* xv, 34, will reveal the fact that the writer believed Jesus called on El, the Sumerian god of Abraham, and not on Jehovah, the god of Moses and of the Jews.

also is emphasised the close and indissoluble connection between Christianity and the Christian Church.
There cannot be one without the other, as the Church
is indispensable for the ceremonials, such as baptism,
the Eucharist and a Christian burial. Christianity
and the Church, of all denominations, are one and the
same, and cannot be separated.

The Christian era was dominated by the Church,
the interpreter of Christianity, and it was one of the
worst and cruellest ages in history. If it had been
dominated by Jesuism it is unlikely that this terrible
condemnation of an age could have been made, as
Jesuism is not Christianity and Christianity is not
Jesuism. It is just because people confuse the one
with the other that they attribute to Christianity that
which belongs to Jesuism, and consider that the
former stands for high ethical principles when in
reality it has no ethical basis whatever, its foundation
being evil and its teaching viciously immoral.

To confuse Jesus, the Jewish teacher and healer,
with Christ, the Pagan saviour-god, is a gross historical
blunder. If what we imagine Jesus taught had guided
the time we call the Christian era, how different we
would be today! Instead of this being so, the Christ
idea, and all the superstitious Paganism which surrounds it, obliterated the Jesus ideology, and when
that is remembered the story which the following
pages unfold will be understood. This vital fact is
the crux of much of what now follows in the story of
the most virile portion of the human race, from the
4th century onwards to our own time.

The virgin birth episode, the final drama of the
trial, the Last Supper, and the death and resurrection

of the Saviour were performed by the Pagans, in relation to their saviour-gods, as a dramatic performance
on the stage, much as takes place in our own time at
Oberammergau in Bavaria, and the gospel versions
are probably the Christian adaptations of these performances. The virgin birth narrative, as related of
the Egyptian god Horus and his virgin mother, has
been found displayed on the walls of a temple at Luxor,
and the passion drama of the Babylonian god Bel, as
already recorded in Chapter IV, has also been recently
discovered during excavations in Assyria. Both these
interesting discoveries make clear where the details
of the Christian stories came from, as in all essentials
they are the same, and we now know the basis of those
additions which were made to the early gospels when
Jesus was evolved into the Christ.

The beliefs, ritual and ceremonials of Christianity
thus became similar to those held and practised by the
different Pagan mystery religions, and there is nothing
new in Christianity that was not accepted before its
inception, except in the names given to its three gods,
and the different names given to the gods called
saints. Paul, who was responsible for starting the
movement away from the original Jesuian form of
worship, makes it quite clear by his writings that he
was not following in the footsteps of Jesus, whom he
had elevated to the rank of the Christ.

Paul believed, to his own satisfaction, that the
original disciples of Jesus had misunderstood the
mission of their master, and so he put forward what he
termed his own gospel, which eventually took the
place of the earlier sayings attributed to Jesus. A careful study of Paul's writings thus reveals the startling

fact that he contradicted Jesus on thirty-five fundamental points, and thus changed a movement which
may have been for the reform of the Jewish faith,
into one which became a combination of the theologies
pertaining to Judaism and Paganism.

Christianity and the Christian Church now become inseparable.

So much for the new religion produced by Paul,
and now we come to the organisation which arose for
its protection and propagation.   We have reached the
third and last stage in the evolution of the Christian
Church.   After Paul, many others took part in its
development, the most important being those now
called the Church Fathers, but their writings, which
are purely theological and unelevating, are a study
by themselves.   Dr. Davidson, the eminent Church
authority, described these men as "credulous and
blundering, passionate and one sided", but, as this
book is not a Church history, we must pass them by
and confine ourselves to the outstanding events
which produced the decisive results.

The Pagan priests, who entered the Apostolic
Church, brought with them the theology in which
they had been nurtured.   Likewise they brought
the Jesuian form of worship into line with that
prevailing in Greece, at the service of the Mysteries, as this religion was called, its form of service
being then much the same as still prevails in our own
time in the Roman Catholic and Greek Orthodox
churches.   Consequently under Greek influence the
Apostolic Church evolved into the Christian Church.

Elsewhere the change over did not take place without disruption, and where Jews predominated the Greek influence was fiercely resisted. Bitter was the fight in widely separated countries to retain the original Jesuian form of worship. One particularly heated account has come down to us from Tertullian, who for years fought a spirited battle against the once Pagan priests getting control. In his book *Adversus Praxean*, which he published in 213, he accuses a priest called Praxeas of influencing the Bishop of Rome against the Jesuians, in these words:—

For, when the then Bishop of Rome was now recognising the prophecies of Montanus, Prisca and Maximilla (three mediums) and . . . was seeking to introduce peace to the churches of Asia and Phrygia, it was he (Praxeas) who did, by making false statements about these very prophets and their churches . . . compel him (Victor, Bishop of Rome) both to recall the letters of peace that had already been despatched, and to give up his project of welcoming their gifts (of mediumship). So Praxeas managed two pieces of the devil's business at Rome, he drove out prophesy and brought in heresy, and he put the Comforter to flight. Praxeas's tares have borne fruit here, having been sown above the pure teaching.

How small events sometimes produce momentous results! From that time onwards the priests increased their power and influence, so much so that they changed the Jesuian, or Apostolic Spiritualist, Church into the Christian Church. The monotheistic Jesuians became polytheistic Christians, the doctrine of the Trinity being introduced in the 3rd century, before which time it had been applied only to the gods of the Pagans. What hitherto had been considered heresy became orthodoxy. What had been regarded

by the Jesuians as heathenism became Christianity, and
what had been looked upon as the true faith and pure
teaching was cast aside, those holding it being persecuted, tortured and murdered.

Cyprian (200–258) was another priestly zealot like
Praxeas. He became Bishop of Carthage, and was
the first to put forward what became the strongest
weapon of the Church—that there would be no forgiveness of sins or salvation outside its ranks, and that
the Christian priesthood had received from Christ the
keys of heaven and hell. He did as much as anyone
to raise the Christian priesthood to the position it now
occupies in the Church. Cyprian took advantage of
the upheaval, to which Tertullian refers, to produce
and push forward his ecclesiastical scheme, on which
the Church, both Roman and Anglican, is now built.
He was the father of the episcopacy, and his zeal
split in two his own congregation, the majority
preferring to retain the medium instead of introducing
the priest. They refused to accept the dogmas and
doctrines to which the priests had attached the name
of Jesus, declaring that they were contrary to his
teaching, and that the introduction of the priesthood
into the Apostolic Church was at variance with the
writings of the disciples.

Cyprian was an opportunist, and, like all who became dictators, struck when the opportunity was
favourable. He was an intolerant absolutist, believing
in the priesthood being the unquestioned masters of
the entire Church, and that only by the abolition of all
freedom of thought could sectarianism come to an
end. He was the first of a great multitude of Christian
"Nazis" who believed in totalitarian government, and

that the people, in their thinking, must have no independent opinions but accept without question what the priests told them. Likewise the priests were instructed, from youth upwards, in a unified form of belief, and taught to think only as the Church authorities decreed. To them the Church became the mouthpiece of God, just as the dictators in our day became divine oracles to those they trained to be their obedient servants.

The historical importance of the capture of the Apostolic Church by the priests cannot be overrated, in view of the power the Christian Church was to secure as the result of the Council of Nicaea in 325, an event which brought about its elevation to the position of the State Church of the Roman Empire. In the next section we shall read how all this came about, and why the Church was given a position it was quite unfitted to occupy. From now onwards, in the chapters which follow, the evil effect of this great event will become more and more apparent, as for the next fifteen hundred years the people of Christendom were confined within this bastion of ignorance, to the great deterioration of their mental and ethical qualities.

Instead of knowledge continuing to spread, as it had done over the preceding six hundred years, a black curtain of ignorance descended upon the most virile portion of the human race, all the efforts of the Greek philosophers to raise the people to a higher level becoming of no account, their teaching now being denounced as of the devil. Knowledge was now regarded as sinful, ignorance was elevated to rank as a virtue, and upon production was clamped the burden of supporting this factory of ignorance, the clergy taking the first ten per cent. of all that the land produced, thus making sure that whoever else starved they would not.

Here we are at the root of much of the misery about which the following chapters have to tell, as autocratic priestly rule, the most reactionary form of government it is possible to have, took the place of the absolute civil government then prevailing, which, whatever its other faults, allowed every variety of religious opinion and freedom of philosophic and scientific expression. Superstition took over the ship of state and reason was thrown overboard, all expressing philosophical opinions being rounded up, tortured, imprisoned, banished or put to death. The eminent Roman and Greek philosophers had attempted to find law and order in the universe, but now everything was again chaotic, the saints or angels being praised for what was good and the devils blamed for all that was evil.

It is no exaggeration to say that by Christianity becoming the State religion of the Roman Empire, after the Council of Nicaea, a blight settled on the Empire such as mankind had never before experienced, and this in time covered all Europe, to extend ultimately over the entire Western hemisphere. Church rule, and Bible worship, became the only guide to mankind in his pilgrimage from the cradle to the grave, and in consequence the course of progress was set back for more than a thousand years. A thousand years of progress lost! Verily we have now come to the beginning of the most important stage in human history, a period which was to affect a third of mankind up to our own times.

From this time onwards what the priesthood of
the Christian Church decreed gradually became the
religious belief, and mental outlook, of the entire
Empire, the people being taught to accept what the
priests ordered as the will of the three Christian gods,
all other gods worshipped being now classed as devils.
Never had Cyprian imagined the momentous consequences of his policy, which produced an organisation the Emperor Constantine decided was fit to
dominate the religious and intellectual life of the
Empire. The Christian priesthood put itself above the
law of every land, and, so long as it had the power to
maintain this privileged position, the clergy were free
from all taxation, and tried only by their own ecclesiastical courts. Gross wickedness and abuses were consequently passed over, and for centuries to come the
lives of many of the popes, cardinals, bishops and
priests were a scandal to Christian civilisation.

Young boys were made abbots if they were of
noble lineage, the fitness of the clergy for a position
being rarely considered, a disgrace which is still so
noticeable in our own times. Young men, with no
experience, and only the pseudo-knowledge of the
theological college, are still put in charge of parishes.
They are under little restraint, quite undisciplined,
childishly ignorant of men and affairs, their income
being certain for life even if they grossly neglect their
duties, provided they are not imprisoned or convicted of drunkenness or adultery. That is the
position today, and the results which follow are
known to most people living in the country districts
of Christendom. What the position must have been
like when the clergy were above the law of the land,

and could do just as they pleased, can easily be imagined.

From the 4th century onwards the word Priest in Christian literature is used to denote one previously termed Minister, and the bishops, who now claimed to be the true successors of the apostles, are termed the High Priests. This is quite contrary to original Apostolic teaching, which proclaimed that the priest was now abolished by the coming of Jesus, who alone communicated his wishes through the divine spirit, or, as we would say today, the medium's spirit control. The Church now became the only means of interpreting what it falsely claimed to be the instructions of the one it had elevated to be the Christ. The Bishop of Rome became the Pope, and claimed to be the Oracle of God in place of the medium.[1]

So he replaced the mediums supplied by nature, those who were the oracles of their controlling spirits. The Church's creeds, doctrines and dogmas now took the place of what the Jesuians termed "The Conversations of the Lord", which came through the "Oracles of God", or those "filled with the holy or divine spirit". What hitherto had been believed was now termed heresy, and, unlike the toleration of the Pagans to all forms of religion, a bitter feud developed between the Christians, now termed the orthodox, and the Jesuians, who were fanatically regarded as the agents of Satan, and destined for hell.

For such sinners there was only one form of treatment, namely persecution, to be carried on so effectively throughout most of the Christian era that only the

---

[1] This claim has also always been made, and still is, by all the high priests, patriarchs, cardinals, archbishops and bishops of the Orthodox, the Roman Catholic and Protestant branches of the Christian Church.

remnants remain today under the name of Unitarians. These Unitarians only secured complete liberty to worship in Christendom last century, though today in Britain they are not permitted to broadcast a service, as their beliefs "do not come within the mainstream of Christian tradition". This announcement by the B.B.C. makes clear how completely Christianity submerged Jesuism, and if such is the position today we can understand how it came about that all who held the beliefs of the early followers of Jesus were tortured, banished, imprisoned or put to death during the age of Christian domination when intolerance reigned supreme.

Thus it was that Christianity developed from birth to manhood, the first four centuries of the era witnessing the evolution of a system of mystical theology which has not a particle of evidence for its claims. Consequently the light of reason was extinguished so that its hollowness could not be probed, and the Church became the great enemy of truth, education and progress. In the Apostolic Church mediums had occupied a privileged position, being considered the instruments of the divine or holy spirit, but now they became outcasts, branded as "the Servants of the Devil" and burned, drowned or persecuted, which savagery accounts for the lack of psychic gifts throughout the Christian era, as they are hereditary.

The priests, moreover, had used a free hand in altering and manufacturing additions to the numerous gospels and epistles then in circulation, to meet the new doctrines as they came to be believed. Consequently, at the Council of Carthage (397), a decision was reached that the books, as now included in The

New Testament, be accepted as canonical, or those to which the Church had given approval for use in worship. Up to this date anyone had been free to alter and interpolate as he pleased, but from now onwards the canonical books were considered as inspired by God, and, after the 5th century, further alterations were not numerous. Prior to this time no one had authority to protect the text. No one could authoritatively challenge a deletion or an insertion, and, as the Jews had been for long dispersed from Palestine, no one knew what was true or untrue, no historical records having been made or kept of any of the deeds or sayings of Jesus, and those who came after him.

Fraud, forgery, intrigue, terror, persecution, imprisonment and wholesale murder combined to produce the Christian Church, which set itself up as the protector of the Eucharist, a Pagan ceremony to which it attached the name of Christ. Likewise it adopted the Pagan form of infant baptism and abolished the Jesuian form of adult baptism.[1] From the Pagans it acquired the form of Church service, their marriage and other ceremonies, their ritual, their holy days and vestments, in fact the entire Apostolic outlook was changed to conform to Pagan customs and beliefs. Even the new name it gave to Jesus came from

[1] False propaganda has always been a feature of the Christian Church, the clergy, in their zeal to present their religion as superior to all others, being quite indifferent to truth. The following pronouncement by Dr. Herbert Williams, Bishop of Carlisle, made in October 1944, and widely quoted in the newspapers, is an example: "We have now reached a stage in urban dioceses when it is literally true that large numbers of our fellow countrymen are Pagans. They are Pagan in the sense that they have not even been baptised." The truth is of course that the Pagans were so attached to the ceremony of infant baptism that the Christian Church had to adopt it in place of adult baptism.

Paganism, as the Egyptian god Osiris was known as Chrest, and to the Greeks as Chrestos.

That which is based on falsehood and intolerance produces evil, and the record of the Christian Church is in keeping with its origin. Righteousness was never its mission, but rather to protect and continue the Pagan beliefs, now called Christian. Its priests maintained the tradition for which the Pagan priesthood was notorious—of utter indifference to the moral code, their interest being only in their own theology, ceremonial and ritual. Like the dictators of our own times, the Church secured great power and wealth by every evil device, and, just as Hitler and Mussolini did for Germany and Italy, it brought Europe to the depths of degradation. Its pernicious influence, its antagonism to learning and all that stands for righteousness, is the cause of our present-day troubles, as Christendom is still suffering from the lack of education, and ethical teaching, denied to it up to last century because of its reactionary influence.

Few there be who realise the historical importance of the rise and development of the Christian Church. From the 4th century onwards it became ever more important, until, within two centuries, it completely dominated much of Europe and the lands surrounding the Mediterranean. Likewise few realise the abysmal ignorance of the men responsible for its foundation, or their stupidity and gross superstition as revealed by their writings. If they were living today they would be looked upon by a child as pitifully backward, and lacking in everything nice and refined. Nevertheless they were the men responsible for laying the foundation of an institution which was to be the exponent of "Christian culture" throughout a great part of the world for the next sixteen hundred years. They were quite ignorant of ethics, and of what is today looked upon as general knowledge. They knew nothing about astronomy, geography, geology, biology, physics, chemistry, sociology, and their knowledge of disease was as limited as their comprehension of the earth on which they lived.

To them Jerusalem was the centre of a flat earth, an idea which was a cardinal Christian belief up to the 16th century. Below the earth's surface was a place called hell, composed of hot molten substance which was shot up through volcanoes acting as chimneys. It reeked with the smell of roasting flesh, and echoed with the eternal shrieks of the agonised damned, its inhabitants being all the non-Christians, who were called devils, whereas the angels, who had been orthodox Christians when on earth, lived somewhere above the clouds with God in heaven. The Christians, still on earth, regarded themselves as do emigrants, awaiting a ship to carry them to some distant pleasant land. Many had lost interest in earthly affairs, and to them the question was whether they would go first, or be amongst the elect on earth who would welcome their Lord, who was daily expected to arrive to give each Christian his just reward.

This idea of heaven and hell dominated Christian civilisation up to our own times, a fact which must be remembered if we are to understand what follows, as from now onwards it made its mark on all thought and action. Those early Christians were quite ignorant of natural law, and considered that the earth, and the heavens, were ruled by decrees issued by God, who employed the saints and angels as his agents. These were at constant war with the devils, who, on behalf of their master Satan, were always trying to take the control of affairs into their own hands. It was also believed that disease was caused by these devils, and that by prayer God, or a saint, could be influenced to direct human and worldly affairs to the desire of the suppliant. This appeal had only a chance of success if made through the priesthood, which claimed to have direct access to the throne of God, an assertion which made the priesthood more powerful than any monarchy.

To Christians there was no law and order in the universe, as everything happened according to the will of God, who ordered this world only for their benefit. Moreover, the existing order was any day to be brought to an end by the second coming of Christ, who, for a thousand years, would rule on earth, when they would become the dominant people and rule the nations for him. Like the Jews, they claimed that when all accepted their way of thinking the millennium would come. Wrong-doing consisted of disbelieving the dogma and doctrines of the Christian Church, and the test of a good Christian was belief in the Trinity, both conduct and righteousness playing a small part in their lives. The priests were intolerant of, and pitilessly cruel to, all unbelievers in the orthodox interpretation of Christianity, and, when they secured complete power in the 4th century, only Christians could obtain preferment and employment in the administration of the countries which comprised the Roman Empire.

We all feared for the future when we were in

danger of Nazi domination, but few appreciate that in the 4th century something far more dreadful, and of much longer duration, was clamped on humanity, the evil effects of which continued up to our own times. If we ask ourselves the reason for much of the wickedness in Christendom today, and for the terrible record of the Christian era, the answer is plain. It comes largely from the omissions and commissions of the Christian Church, which obtained full authority over the minds of Christian people, and disgracefully misused it.

How it came into being, and its early history, has now been briefly told, but, in the pages which follow, its deeds will speak for themselves, when we shall realise that what is founded on error and fraud can never be otherwise than a drag on man's upward progress. To reform the Church is impossible, as, if the falsehood is withdrawn, the entire structure collapses. Only by education and knowledge can its influence be removed, and then it will perish from neglect. That will come some day, and then Christendom will be relieved of the annual expenditure of £300,000,000 now being spent on the propagation of the error and falsehood which was produced at the time we are now considering.

The period of history covered by this section contains events which laid the seeds for Christian civilisation, to which most of what remains of this book is devoted. The most important of these events were (1) Paul transforming Jesus into the Christ, and preaching and writing about him as the one whose death had saved believers from everlasting damnation; (2) Paul's journey to Rome, thus bringing his new

religion, Christianity, to the capital of the Empire;
(3) the capture of the Apostolic Church by the priesthood in the 3rd century, and (4) the decision reached
at the Council of Nicaea, about which we shall be
reading in the next section. Before this chapter
ends, we shall discover that after the Council
of Nicaea Constantine made Christianity the State
religion of Rome, and finally, when Rome was overrun by the Visigoths, the Christian Church took the
place of the Emperor, to rule first the Empire and then
extend its domination over all the Western world.

Paul is therefore a very important link in history,
in fact his misinterpretation of the teaching of Jesus
profoundly altered the course of history. What
follows, from now onwards to our own times, will
not be correctly understood unless it is first of all
clearly appreciated that Christianity is something altogether different from Jesuism, which comprised the
teaching attributed to Jesus. Jesuism is a way of
life, Christianity is a way of salvation, not by personal
effort but by ceremony and belief, and its terrible
history lies in this fact. Its central core, the hub
round which all else revolves, is the cannibalistic idea
of a sacrificed victim, whose body when eaten, and
whose blood when drunk, secures to the partaker
regeneration and salvation. This, combined with the
doctrine that baptism secured entry into a saved community, the Church, and that belief in its creeds, and
the partaking of the Eucharist, ensures forgiveness for
wickedness, destroyed the urge to live better lives,
there being no incentive to do so when forgiveness
had already been obtained.

On this vicious immoral basis the priests, who

claimed to have the power of salvation or damnation in their hands, obtained sovereign power over a larger number, for a longer period of time, than ever before happened in history. The Christian clergy have never been men chosen for their goodness, knowledge or wisdom, but for their readiness to conform to everything the Church authorities decreed. Naturally they could be none other than stupid or knavish, besides being superstitious and devoid of logic or the critical faculty. Being trained only in theology, they were an easy prey to the curse of ignorance, and did and taught that which was evil because they lacked the standard of righteousness which comes from knowledge.

These men were responsible for the moral education of our ancestors, and the effect they had on character and conduct up to the present day will be seen as we proceed. Priests, greedy for power but untrained to rule, reduced the Western world to barbarism, put out the torch of knowledge, and enslaved the people. That did not come from what we imagine was the teaching of Jesus, and to confuse this with Christianity is a gross historical blunder, as the two systems of thought are as opposite as the east is from the west.

Meantime we have arrived at the period when the Christian Church becomes the state Church of Rome, from which date it starts on its long career of suppression of knowledge, of intolerance, murder, violence and persecution. So we shall now return to Roman history, into which its power and influence threads ever more closely.

(6) From Constantine to the Collapse of the Empire.

We have now come to the end of the God-emperors, as from this time onwards the emperors refused to carry this distinction. Constantine I (312–337), surnamed "the Great", served with distinction under Diocletian and Galerius in Egypt and Persia. His majestic presence, personal courage and military ability made him a great favourite with the army, much to the annoyance of Galerius, who exposed him repeatedly to unusual hazards in the hope of getting him out of the way. Eventually Constantine joined his father in Britain. Soon afterwards his father died, and Constantine, in 306, was enthusiastically elected by the army as Caesar of the west, to become sole Emperor of both east and west seventeen years later. He repeatedly defeated the barbarians east of the Rhine, and built a line of forts to increase the security of the Empire, continuing his father's policy of toleration towards the Christians, who, from now onwards, ceased to be persecuted.

Here mention should be made of this often much exaggerated persecution. Gibbon, the historian, went carefully into the question, taking as his basis the figures given by Eusebius, the early Church historian, who certainly would not make the number less than it really was. Taking these figures, Gibbon concluded that the total number of Christians who suffered death, as the result of Roman persecution, did not greatly exceed 2000. This he contrasted with the 25,000,000 who died as the result of Christian intolerance and persecution. Origen, the Christian father, in the 3rd century, tells us that "There have been but a few now and again, easily counted, who have died for the Christian religion."

Before Constantine could obtain supreme power to carry out his policy of strengthening the fabric of the Empire he had to get rid of his rivals. The division of the Empire by Diocletian had resulted in those who should have co-operated treating each other as rivals, because no empire can have four dictators. Civil war consequently followed, and when Constantine became Caesar of the west he immediately set to work to finish off the other Caesars. One by one he defeated and murdered them, including some of their children and courtiers. It was at his great victory at Milvian Bridge, near Rome, where Eusebius tells us the Emperor saw a cross in the sky at noon with the motto "By this conquer". No historian believes this, but it has been a good fable which the Christian priests have made the most of during the Christian era.

Constantine, during his reign, was never a Christian. He remained half a Pagan and half a Christian all his life, only accepting baptism on his death-bed by a non-trinitarian bishop, but, for some reason or other, he looked upon the cross as his lucky emblem. He worshipped Apollo and Christ, and considered that the latter was a type of the former. He had impressed upon his coins the name of the one, and the figure of the other, while throughout his reign he remained Pontifex Maximus, the Chief Priest of Paganism.

His rule of twenty-five years was generally beneficial, and he instituted humane legal reforms while at the same time pursuing vigorously his measures against the barbarians, but he was cruel, treacherous and a murderer. He promised to spare the life of his last rival Licinius, whom he defeated in 324, but did not keep his word. He also murdered his own eldest son, his nephew, a number of his courtiers and his wife, but he did not indulge in a bloody massacre of the people, as did Theodosius the Great, the first outstanding Christian emperor.

Constantine's attitude towards all forms of religion was tolerant. Whatever were his other faults he was no bigot, and seemed to be genuinely interested at all times in discussing theology and religion with those of similar tastes. By his various edicts the Christian religion was given the same status as the other religions of the Empire. He showed his liking for Christianity by giving large donations to different Christian communities, and also for the building of churches. He liked having Christian bishops as his companions, and often they were his guests at the imperial palace. In the various disputes the bishops had with one another, Constantine adopted a moderate policy and tried to settle all differences amicably.

By an edict he withdrew the ban on the Church receiving legacies, a decision which had a very important effect on its accumulation of wealth, as there could now be no dispute on the question of money which had been left to it by the faithful. Here was the beginning of the enormous possessions the Church has gathered together from that date to this. Here we are at the time when the Christian Church first experiences power and prestige. Constantine recalled all Christian exiles, and decreed that those who had been deprived of public employment, because they professed the Christian faith, were to be reinstated. Any property left by martyrs was to be restored to their relatives, and, if the heirs could not be found, it was then to be given to the Church.

He seems to have had a special attachment to the hitherto despised faith, as he endeavoured to increase the number of converts by giving good positions and honours to all the upper-class Pagans who adopted the new religion. The poor were bribed to become Christians by liberal donations, all of which, as Eusebius says, produced an enormous amount of hypocrisy. Then he planned for sufficient churches to be built to accommodate the entire population, though, as Gibbon says, only one in twenty were then Christians. He did not interfere with the Pagans worshipping as of old, but he discontinued all state sacrificing to the gods.

Such, then, was the attitude of this semi-Christian, semi-Pagan, towards the religious opinions of his subjects. In politics he was equally revolutionary, as he decided that Byzantium was in future to be the capital of the Empire, a fact which ultimately split the Roman Empire in two, and left Rome vacant for the Pope to take the place of the Emperor. At great speed he built the new city, to which he gave the name of Constantinople. Here we find him favouring Christianity on the one hand, and Paganism on the other, by erecting numerous Christian churches, and lining the streets and squares with statues of the gods and famous men, taken from the temples and cities of Greece and Asia. Sacred Pagan relics and art adorned the imperial palace alongside a picture of the crucifixion of Jesus.

No gladiatorial performances were allowed in the new city, the reason being that they did not appeal to the more cultured people of these parts. In Rome they still continued, but so disgusted the Greeks that they called the Romans "Barbaroi", and there were riots when the Romans tried to introduce them into Corinth. The better-class Romans equally disliked these displays, and a hundred years later they died out when this distaste permeated the people, though combats for sport, which at times resulted in the death of one or both combatants, continued throughout Europe until last century.

Constantinople was the first city to have only Christian churches, as no Pagan temples were allowed. It was dedicated, in 330, to the Virgin Mary, and its inauguration was conducted exclusively by Christian priests. Here we find the consequence of the Council of Nicaea, as, after it was held, Christianity became the State religion of the Empire. Constantine kept his promise to the Christian priests, to the effect that if they produced and agreed upon a creed he would recognise their religion. How this all came about will be told a few pages further on.

On the subject of the doctrines and beliefs of the Christian faith he was very ignorant, and yet he seemed at times anxious to learn more, for he attended church services and listened to bishops preaching sermons. He even delivered religious discourses himself, in which he emphasised how he had been blessed through protecting the Christians, while his rivals, who had not, had been defeated by him. He seems to have been endowed with a very simple mind in religious matters, and, if he had not been an emperor, he might easily have been a Pagan or Christian priest. He caused himself to be represented on medals, coins and statues in the attitude of prayer, and, besides this, kept vigils and read the Scriptures.

The seeming duality of his nature is quite in keeping with what we know of others in religious history, as one may be devoutly religious and at the same time quite immoral. Morality, or ethics, and religion must never be confused, as piety has been too often associated with intolerance, injustice and cruelty. Religion is the outcome of man's psychic construction, whereas morality or ethics are conditioned by how unselfish he is, and how much he is prepared to put himself last and others first. The only wickedness is selfishness. The one who can live an unselfish life, without allowing the selfish to impose upon his unselfishness, has the truly balanced character and the one best fitted to produce the perfect life. Do to others as we would that they should do to us has often been emphasised by the sages since the time of Confucius, and this constitutes the best rule of life in the fewest possible words.

It seems doubtful whether Helena, the mother of Constantine, was responsible for his Christian leanings, or whether he converted her to the faith. In her later life she certainly devoted herself wholeheartedly to its propagation, and visited Palestine for the purpose of discovering those places which to Christians had become holy and sacred. The temple of Jupiter, built by Hadrian, was demolished by Constantine, and, as Eusebius naively remarks, his lavishness in supplying his mother with ample money soon enabled the people on the spot to discover the exact places where the Lord had been born, crucified and buried.   Even the place from which the ascension occurred was located.   On each of these a church was built. Equally astonishing is the information that after rotting for three centuries the three crosses were found, and also the superscription which was placed on the Saviour's cross.

Having learned something of the man who established the Christian Faith as the State religion of the Roman Empire, let us now consider the cause which made him take a decision that history proves to have been one of the most momentous ever made by man. It so happened that in the year 312 one called Arius, who was to become famous in the years which followed, aspired to become Bishop of Alexandria.   A man by name of Alexander was, however, elected, and with these two men starts the story of the reason why one third of the people of the world are today known as Christians.

Arius, a presbyter of Alexandria, denied the Saviour's godhead and contended that he could not be equal with Jehovah as he was the only begotten son.   A son, he argued, could not be equal to his father and could not be co-eternal with the father, as a time must have been when he was not.   Otherwise the son could not have been begotten.   This could mean only one thing, namely that the son came into existence after his father, and, in any case, Jehovah had always claimed that he alone was God.   Arius took the occasion, when Alexander was discoursing on the unity of the Holy Trinity, to question him on these points. This greatly perturbed the Christian bishop, as sides were taken for and against the unity of the Trinity, a problem which has not yet been solved. Alexander made this the reason for calling a conference so that both sides could express their opinions. He presided and decided against Arius. From that time onwards, and for very many years, this seemingly unimportant question was the burning topic of the Church, and the cause of terrible persecution directed against the unorthodox heretics.

Arius, who is described as one who lived a strict life and was of agreeable manner, found many sympathisers amongst the Jesuians and, as he was a determined man, he made certain that his side was kept well to the fore. He said, in fact, that the Christian Church must now decide this question once and for all, as three hundred years was quite long enough to leave it unsettled. He was, however, forced to leave Alexandria, though he knew that he had behind him two bishops, twelve presbyters and many deacons. He took refuge in Palestine, where Eusebius (270–340), who was Bishop of Caesarea, tried to settle the quarrel by mediation. Alexander, on the other hand, sent out notices to all Christian churches warning them of Arius and his hateful opinions. As a counter move, the Bishop of Nicomedia, a friend of Arius, called together in 319 a synod of priests at Bithynia, which passed a resolution that Arius was quite orthodox in his beliefs.

Constantine was much worried by the dispute, as it threatened the very existence of the Church he had so befriended, and it rendered impossible an idea which he had formed of making Christianity the faith of the Empire. He had, moreover, to withstand the jeers of the great majority of his subjects, who were delighted at the turn of events. The Pagan priests compared the unity of belief prevailing in the ranks of their followers with the dissension and wrangling which was for ever occurring amongst the Christians. Constantine was in a quandary, as he saw that he must either stop this quarrelling amongst his friends, once and for all, or throw them over and return wholeheartedly to the gods of his people.

His first move showed his wisdom and moderation, as he wrote a joint letter to Alexander and Arius, in which he expressed his opinion that the belief in Providence was the one essential religious belief, and that to continue quarrelling over imaginary differences was greatly damaging the prestige of their religion. Work for peace and concord, he continued, not for strife, and settle your differences in the dignified way adopted by the Pagans.

This letter was carried by the Bishop of Cordova to Alexandria, where a synod was called. Arius, however, would not give way. Constantine was now seriously alarmed, as he and the Christians were being openly ridiculed in the theatres, and his statues were being treated with abuse and contempt. So he called together a general council of the entire Church, and fixed the meeting-place at Nicaea in Bithynia. The first meeting took place in June 325, a date that was to fix the turning-point in the history of the Western world. For the first time in its history the Christian system of belief was dominated by a man who had the power to compel obedience. No Senate questioned his power, as he was the supreme autocrat of the far-flung Roman Empire.

Athanasius, made famous for a creed he never produced, tells us that there were present at Nicaea 318 bishops, and that these were accompanied by many of the minor clergy and some Pagan philosophers. Why the latter should have been present at a gathering which one writer of those times says "was not one which required any high intellectual qualifications" is difficult to understand, unless it was from natural curiosity.

The first Council was held before Constantine arrived, and was presided over by the Bishop of Cordova and others in turn. On this occasion Arius received the support of thirteen, seventeen, and twenty-two bishops, according to three different accounts of the proceedings. No agreement could be reached, and it was distinguished by the usual bitterness and bad feeling. It would have ended as it began, without agreement, but for the fact that within a fortnight of its opening Constantine arrived. The proceedings were then transferred to the imperial palace, and from that time onwards Constantine presided, arrayed in a wig of many colours and a silken robe. He told the bishops that it was now or never, and that they must decide once and for all what Christianity was to stand for in the years to come.

On his arrival at Nicaea, which is situated forty-four miles from Constantinople, on the other side of the Bosphorus, he was welcomed by all the bishops and presbyters. Eusebius was responsible for an address of welcome which, as we might expect from one who was more a courtier than a bishop, became an extravagant panegyrical oration, in spite of the fact that shortly before this conference the Emperor had murdered his wife and eldest son. Hardly a good beginning for one who was about to decide whether Jesus was a god or a man. Constantine then received a large deputation of bishops, who asked him to hear their individual opinions and grievances.

He commanded them to submit these in writing, and, when all were ready, he appointed a day for them to be considered. When the day arrived he took his seat on the imperial throne and received the pleadings one by one, placing them on a table before him. After the last was received he rose and told his suppliants that "lest the contentions of the priests should become known to any one" he had decided to burn all the documents before him without reading them, and that their quarrels were nothing less than scandalous. He then announced that the Council would proceed with the business for which it was called, and that a decision must be reached.

When business started, Eusebius, who beforehand had been in close conference with the Emperor, sat on his right hand and continued to do so at each meeting which followed. The proceedings opened by Eusebius producing a creed which he stated contained the substance of what he had been told was the Christian faith. It was accepted by Arius and his followers, but, just because of this, their opponents refused to do so. Then Alexander, the Bishop of Alexandria, put forward his creed, which Arius and his followers refused to accept.

A struggle then took place in which documents were torn to pieces and blows were delivered. The uproar was often so great that at times the assembly was a veritable pandemonium. In the end, by the inclusion of the Greek word *Homoousion*, which means "of the same substance", the majority proposed a creed similar to the one produced by Eusebius, but the Arians refused to accept it and protested vehemently. Constantine expressed his approval of the motion supported by the majority, as all he cared about was peace amongst those to whom he had given his patronage.

The Bishop of Cordova then rose and announced that the creed of Christianity had been finally defined and accepted by a majority of the bishops of the Church. It read as follows:

We believe in one God, the Father almighty, maker of all things, both visible and invisible; and in one Lord, Jesus Christ, the son of God, begotten of the Father, only begotten, that is to say, of the same substance of the Father, God of God and Light of Light, Very God of Very God, begotten, not made, being of one substance with the Father, by whom all things were made, both things in heaven and things on earth; who, for us men and for our salvation, came down and was made flesh, made man, suffered and rose again on the third day, went up into the heavens, and is to come again to-judge the quick and the dead; and in the Holy Ghost.

At Nicaea the Christian belief was at long last defined and put into words. New words were employed for old theological ideas, which for centuries had been used in Pagan theology. Christians now knew for what their faith stood in the opinion of the Emperor and the majority of the bishops. What came to be called Catholic Christianity was now formulated and definitely established as the State

Church of the Empire, the bishops becoming peers of the realm, and all who did not accept the Nicaean definition were banished or put to death.

Little did these men who gathered at this fateful council realise that they were deciding the fate of a great part of the human race for the next sixteen hundred years, and bringing to pass what a scribe of the times attributed to Jesus: "I came not to send peace but a sword." Every abomination practised in the name of religion, throughout what became Christendom, was the outcome of the Council of Nicaea, which reduced the Western world to a state of degradation impossible for the imagination to visualise. Whenever we think of the Christian Church we should remember Nicaea, as from this fateful place leads a bloodstained path to its very door.

The definition of the faith had, however, the effect of binding most of the one-time Apostolic churches into one Christian Church, but for centuries to come the fate of those who continued the original Unitarian Jesuian beliefs was persecution and banishment, by the hand of those who were now able to determine what Christians were to believe. Under Constantine the Christian Church was established to be consolidated under Theodosius fifty years later, and become, when the Empire collapsed, the dominant power in those lands for so long ruled by imperial edicts. When we consider the effect this was to have eventually on a third of the human race, it is reasonable to say that Constantine's decision to establish the Christian Church was the most momentous in history, and, for that reason only, he is entitled to be considered as the world's most outstanding sovereign.

The followers of the new religion, which from now onwards was known as Christianity, had at last discovered, three hundred years after the death of Jesus, who he was, how he was related to the Father God, why he had come to earth, and that the Holy Ghost, formerly the divine spirit who controlled the medium, was the third person in the Godhead. To make a comparison which can be better understood, let us suppose that Jesus had been crucified in 1649, the year Charles I was executed, and that only now, after some three hundred·years have elapsed, we are made acquainted, under the compulsion of the autocrat Hitler, as to who he was, why and how he had been born, and the reason for his execution.

The first to receive the holy curse of the Christian Church were the Arians, as, before the Council of Nicaea closed, the priests, who were much more interested in the Fatherhood of God than the Brotherhood of Man, performed what they considered was a very important duty, namely to curse Arius and all his followers. So they petitioned the Emperor to have them put to death, imprisoned or banished, and to punish by death all who read their writings. To this Constantine agreed, following it up with decrees against all other Jesuians who did not accept the new creed, and then he invited the bishops to a sumptuous banquet to celebrate the occasion. Again he took the opportunity to advise them to live together in peace, and, before they parted, he asked for their prayers.

Here we have the first account of Christians persecuting the unorthodox, this occasion inaugurating the reign of savagery which was to become such a feature of this religion throughout its history. From now onwards the Jesuians were known as Arians, until finally their fate was sealed at the bloody Battle of Vouillé in 507. When we come to this important event in history, as recorded in Chapter X, we shall find that their defeat completely liquidated Arianism as an organised and effective force. After the Reformation they became known as Unitarians, but whether as Arians or Unitarians they were the outcasts of Christendom. No one from now onwards could have God as his heavenly father without acknowledging the Church as his spiritual mother on earth, excommunication from which was equal to sentence of death. One who was excommunicated was outside the law, and could be murdered without his murderer being considered guilty, and hereafter his fate was eternal torment in hell.

The year 325 marks the beginning of Christian persecution, as thousands of Arians were murdered or banished. From now onwards for the next three hundred years Europe was drenched in a bloody theological war over the question of the definition of the Holy Trinity. What a time of woe and desolation came upon the Western world because theologians had not the mentality to keep to scientific facts, and instead indulged themselves in quite meaningless speculative fancy on the constitution of the creator of heaven and earth. For the same reason, likewise began fifteen hundred years of persecution, crime and violence, as was never before experienced, for the purpose of making everyone believe in the Nicene Creed and the doctrines on which it is based. Nevertheless, after some 25,000,000 have been tortured and murdered, and a countless number banished, to secure a uniform belief in Christianity, Christians today are so ignorant that they consider Christian civilisation has brought only good to mankind.

The peace that Constantine anticipated never came, and, instead of this, much bitterness continued to be expressed throughout Christendom over this question of the nature of the Godhead. Eusebius was the first to break the harmony, as he was sufficiently frank to declare in a pastoral letter, which he addressed to his flock, that the creed he had produced and signed at Nicaea was more creditable to his ingenuity than to his honesty. This man, who played such an important part in the production and establishment of the Christian faith, was as much a courtier as a priest, an opportunist to whom facts were not sacred. This is revealed in his history of the Christian Church, as in his preface he candidly states that he has suppressed everything that does not redound to its credit, a policy which Christian historians have continued to this day.

Constantine, who never seems to have cared much one way or the other as to whether Arius or Alexander won, over their definition of the Trinity, was persuaded by his sister, a few years after the Council of Nicaea, to recall Arius from exile. The Arian influence, in consequence, increased so much at court that all Catholic bishops were dismissed from the imperial palace and persecuted. Constantine then ordered the readmission of Arius into the communion of the Church, but, before this could be carried through, Arius died under mysterious circumstances, so mysterious that there is little doubt he was murdered, and a year later Constantine also passed away.

After the Council of Nicaea, Constantine decreed that the Christian religion was to be in future the religion of the Roman Empire, an edict which historians think was nothing more than an astute political move. In the reign of the previous Caesar, Maximian (285–305), the saviour-god Mithra had been raised to be the chief god and protector of the Roman Empire, an event which took place in 304, but, after Nicaea, Christ received his place and Mithra was deposed. If the Emperor Julian, who became emperor twenty-four years after the death of Constantine, had had a longer reign, Mithra would undoubtedly have returned to his former throne. Such is the power of autocrats, who can make gods great, just as they can make them small, and can determine the religion which is to be believed, not only in their own time, but by succeeding generations. A similar honour, as was conferred by Constantine on Christ, was performed by King Asoka on the Buddha.

From the religious point of view, the establishment of Christianity as the State religion of the Roman Empire was quite unnecessary, as Christians by now had the same freedom to worship as the Pagans had always enjoyed. Evidently the reason which prompted Constantine to take this step was for the purpose of binding together his scattered empire. Christianity had penetrated into every land ruled by Rome, whereas Mithraism was not so widespread and its priests had not been able to secure the Emperor's patronage.

One Emperor and one Faith appealed to Constantine as the right policy to pursue, if all the straggling elements of his empire were to be kept together.

So the conclusion that his decision was for political reasons seems to be correct, but it had the effect of raising the Christian Church to a status for which it was not suitable. It had to adapt itself to its new responsibilities, which, if for the better ordering of the State, was certainly not for the good of its morals. Instead of developing into a great organisation for the uplifting of humanity, the Church became one for the harnessing of the minds of the people into a rigid code of superstitious beliefs which all must observe as loyal citizens of the State, all unbelievers being liquidated as traitors.

The consciousness of power inspired the priests with the desire for its insignia, and they quickly adorned themselves in the official robes of the Empire's officers. Soon no provincial or municipal office was without its Christian priests arrayed in gorgeous robes. No function could take place without these Reverend Fathers in God being prominently present. Then, as now, they blessed warships when launched, said prayers over regimental flags, performed on all important occasions, and at every royal and official function.

The aggrandizement of the Church became the aim of the priesthood, and it translated what are called spiritual forces into physical equivalents. The very term Spiritual, which concerns the affections, the emotions, our thoughts and ideas, in fact our entire mental being, that part of us which is the individual and passes over to the etheric world at death, was, and is still, used to denote everything that belongs to the Church and its priests. Land becomes spiritual when it passes into the hands of the Church. Men

are spiritual servants of the Church if they are priests.
The bishops are spiritual princes and spiritual peers.
All Church property is termed spiritual, in fact everything the Church handles and the garments the priests
wear are spiritual.

The spiritually minded are those who are
orthodox Christians, but all that pertains to a
higher morality, and to a better understanding of
human personality and the etheric world, has always
been discouraged in the strife for wealth, worldly
power and position. Christians have brought the
word Spiritual into such disrepute and contempt that,
for this reason, it has not been used throughout this
book.

The Church has not recruited its clergy only
from men conspicuous because of their nobility of
character, but often from the unscrupulous and ambitious. Such men encouraged any kind of superstitious error that tended to bring them, or the
Church, increased power or wealth. In exchange for
money the priests relieved the people of all their shortcomings, by posing as the intermediaries between
God and man. They alone could settle the difference
between God and the individual, provided sufficient
payment was forthcoming, and, after Callistus,
Bishop of Rome (219–223), decreed that the Church
would absolve all fornicators and adulterers, converts
to the Christian religion flowed in, in ever increasing
numbers.

The contemporary Bishop Hippolytus tells us
that all that the Christian Church required of its
members was baptism, after which women could
"take to their beds any man they chose" and men

could do as they pleased. Thus the Christian Church gained a march on its rival, the Pagan Church, which refused to lower itself to such a debased level, and Christendom, in consequence, wallowed in crime, vice and licentious living during the next sixteen hundred years.

The priests, during the Christian era, have relieved the people of all need to live better lives, and of the trouble of taking serious thought of the deeper things of life. To the priests only has God revealed the mysteries, and it was not the divine will that these should be understood by the laity. Simple minds gladly accept this doctrine, and are soothed by having all their religious worries taken from them by a priest, just as a lawyer relieves his clients of legal worries. All that is necessary is to pay when asked, attend the Church services, employ a priest to baptise the infant, confirm the youth, perform the marriage ceremony and celebrate the Eucharist to the dying.

If these services and ceremonies are always remembered by the individual, then he or she is a good Christian, irrespective of the life led. As every wickedness can be absolved before death, there is no incentive to lead a good life or trouble about the deeper things of existence. Such was the religion preached everywhere throughout Christendom during the Christian era, and only now are some Protestants beginning to realise how immoral all this is, and have, in consequence, become unorthodox, the modern word for heretic.

A Church claiming and exercising such a power over the people has always been in constant use by rulers, who fawned upon the organisation which had the power to make or break them. At times it worked with these rulers and at others against them, according to where its interests lay. Always it was on the side of tyranny and oppression, and against education and the elevation of the people, its instruments in the past being murder, persecution, war, torture, banishment and prison. All that now remains is the bribe of heaven for those who support its claims, and the threat of hell for those who do not, but even this weapon has become blunt and useless amongst the educated.

It is important that the meaning and effect of Constantine's decision should be realised, because the consequences run through the history of the Western world to this day, as will be seen from the facts related in the chapters which follow. From now onwards a new tyranny and force come into European political life, namely Church rule, its aim being to found a European empire, based on the Nicene Creed, and ruled by the Pope of Rome. The history of the centuries between this time and the Reformation is largely a record of the rise and decline of this great ecclesiastical enterprise.

Perhaps it was because Constantine set this idea in motion that he is called "Great", but definitely he did not attain the title by any outstanding virtue. He was certainly fearless in both war and politics, he being endowed with great political sagacity and religious tolerance. The transfer of the capital of the Empire to Constantinople was a very astute move, as round this nearly impregnable city the old empire, in an attenuated form, survived for a further thousand years. The Empire was never so strong after his firm rule ceased, but, what was more enduring, and makes him an outstanding figure in history, was the legacy he left of the Christian Church, which was soon to become the dominant power in the Western world. Its omnipotence is still noticeably strong even to the present day, especially in those countries now called Roman Catholic and Orthodox Greek.

The death of Constantine was followed by an outbreak of quarrels between his three sons, who divided the Empire. The eldest, bearing the same name as his father, died in a war against his tyrannical and vicious brother Constans, who, in turn, was also killed in war, thus leaving the only surviving son Constantius to become sole emperor. Constantius (337–361) appointed his cousin Julian as Caesar, and placed him in charge of Gaul, because the inroads of the Franks were causing alarm. Here, as the result of his military successes, which checked the barbarian advance across the Rhine, the soldiers elected him as emperor, an action which, but for the timely death of Constantius, would have brought about civil war.

Constantius adopted the Arian form of belief, and during his reign many Catholics were murdered, persecuted or banished, the massacre being particularly severe in Alexandria, where the large Catholic population was nearly exterminated by the most revolting cruelties. So continued the persecution of Christians by Christians, which was to last for the next fourteen hundred years. In this reign alone ten times as many victims perished as died under the Pagan emperors because of their Christian faith, new and savage methods of torture being employed that the heathen Vandals had so far shrunk from adopting.

The tolerant kindly Julian (361–363) followed, and reigned for only two years. Lecky, in his *History of Rationalism*, describes him as "among the best men who ever sat upon a throne", as his standard of conduct was of the highest order. He was in early life brought up as a Christian, but, after he became emperor, he declared himself a Pagan. For that reason he is called Julian the Apostate. He was only six years old when his uncle Constantine died, and one of his earliest recollections was the massacre of his father and kinsfolk in order to protect the continuation of the line of Christian emperors. He, therefore, had no cause to love the Christian faith. Though trained to its profession, he became attracted in early life by the religion of his ancestors. He adopted a form of Hellenic philosophy which was popular in those days amongst the educated, and worshipped Mithra, who, he believed, had revealed the only true God.

He was tolerant to the Jews, and gave them permission to rebuild the Temple at Jerusalem. By this act he annulled the edict of Hadrian, and consequently the Jews had access once more to the Holy City. They were enthusiastic and vigorous in making their plans for the new Temple ; the foundations were laid, and building was about to commence, when they were destroyed by an earthquake. Julian died about the time of this catastrophe, and the attempt to rebuild the Temple was abandoned because of the hostility of the Christians, who looked upon the disaster as an act of God.

Looking back, we now see how unfortunate it was that religious hatred thwarted the Jews in this their last opportunity to recover their old sacred city, and again build up a home for their nation. What a difference it would have made to them if they had had a home, and been no longer strangers in foreign lands.! Christianity prevented this materialising, as Christians argued that it was contrary to the Scriptures that the Temple should be rebuilt, it having been foretold that it was to remain desolate. (*Matthew* xxiii, 38.) Instead, they built churches in Jerusalem, and it became a place of religious pilgrimages.

The Emperor Julian was no indifferent religious believer and held his opinions strongly. He announced his determination to restore the Pagan faith to the old position it occupied before the time of Constantine, and, in this endeavour, produced an elaborate exposition of the false claims made by the Christians. His reign was too short to show what precise form the Pagan revival was to take, and how far his antagonistic attitude towards Christianity would affect the new religion, but everything he did pointed to moderation and the reduction of cruelty and the suppression of immorality. He issued an edict of universal toleration, and then used his influence to restore the old faith and suppress the new. In no case was violence used, and he even allowed Christians to hold high office of state. If his reign had been longer the history of Europe would undoubtedly have been different, and probably less stained in blood and crime.

Julian was a brave general and ever at the front with his men. He was killed in a battle against the Persians in 363, a tragedy which was considered to be an omen in favour of Christianity, as Julian met his death in the home of Mithraism, the rival of the

Christian faith. He was a good emperor, temperate in all things, and always showed self-control and zeal for the public good. He was cultured and fond of literature. One of the most remarkable features of his public life was his perfect ease and mastery, in associating the cares of war and statesmanship with the assiduous cultivation of literature and philosophy. Nevertheless he was also devoted to the old superstitions which appealed to the masses, being noted for the number of sacrifices he offered to the gods.

With the death of Julian ended all hope the Pagans had of their religion being restored to its old position. On the day following his death, Jovian, who was a Christian, was chosen to be emperor, and, as the army's religious beliefs generally followed those of the emperor, the soldiers declared themselves in favour of the Christian faith. From that time onwards Christianity went ahead without a setback, though quarrelling still continued in its ranks between the Arians and the Catholics.

Jovian reigned only eight months, during which time the Empire lost its possessions east of the Tigris. Valentinian I (364–375) and Valens (364–378), both brothers, then divided the Empire between them, the former becoming emperor of the west and the latter of the east. The pressure by the barbarians from the north continued, to end finally in the Goths reaching the walls of Constantinople, burning and pillaging as they went. The defeated Valens died in the Battle of Adrianople (378) following the natural death of his brother three years previously.

Theodosius the Great (379–395), the son of the famous general who drove the Picts and Scots out of

Roman-occupied Britain, was now proclaimed emperor of the east. By his skill and tact he conciliated the Goths for a time, and large numbers entered the Roman army. Maximus (383–388) became Caesar of Gaul, Spain and Britain, but, when he attempted to depose Valentinian II (375–392) from Italy and Africa, Theodosius marched westward, crushed him and made Valentinian II emperor of the west.

Theodosius mercilessly crushed all his rivals, but, besides this, he exhibited his cruel nature to the people in general. In Thessalonica, in the year 390, some of the inhabitants murdered the Commander-in-Chief of the district and some of his soldiers. Theodosius promised the people pardon for this crime, and asked them to be present at a performance of games in the Circus. When they were all assembled, they were attacked by an overwhelming force of soldiers. None was spared, and every man, woman and child was slaughtered. No distinction was made between those who might have been guilty of the murder and those who were innocent. Guilty and innocent, citizen and stranger, met the same fate. For three hours this indiscriminate butchery was carried on, and, when the soldiers were tired of their ghastly work, 15,000 people lay dead in the Circus grounds.

Theodosius was the first outstanding Christian emperor, and this exhibition of merciless carnage was an unfortunate start for the new State religion of the Empire. If it were the only example of Christian cruelty, it might be explained away by the excuse that he had not been nurtured in the new religion, but the history of the next fifteen hundred years does not justify this explanation. Besides this ferocity, his

Christianity caused him to bring to an end the Olympic games, and cruelly stamp out the mystery religion of Eleusis, thus inaugurating the liquidation of everything Greek, as her education, her science, her culture, and her outlook on life had become hateful to the bigoted Christians.

Besides, this, Philosophy was attacked by the Christians, who destroyed every book of an elevating nature they could lay their hands upon, and those of philosophic mind were fortunate if they escaped with their lives. What literature remained was only a remnant of the vast store of reasoned knowledge which had existed over the previous thousand years. Thus commenced the greatest tragedy in all human history, the obliteration of Greek and Roman education and culture, which had raised the Roman Empire over the past three hundred years to a height never before attained by any great community of people. If only the philosophic way of life had been allowed to survive and develop, our world of today would undoubtedly be a better and happier place in which to live. Instead of this being so, both the Jesuians and the Pagans, who did not subscribe to the Nicene Creed, were exterminated or banished, and Christian civilisation replaced Greek and Roman culture, to the lasting detriment of the entire Western hemisphere.

Theodosius was an evil man, who, according to Zosimus, the historian of the time, gave himself up to gluttony and voluptuous living. He was succeeded by his two sons Arcadius and Honorious, who jointly shared the Empire, but, ten years later, the first wave of barbaric invasion swept over their dominions and for six days, in 410, Rome was sacked and pillaged by the Visigoths.

This deplorable event made a great impression everywhere, and those who had been forced to adopt the Christian faith were bitter in expressing their opinions, attributing the calamity as one sent by the gods in anger against the Christians. From the time of the foundation of Rome, for a thousand years, the people had believed that the gods they worshipped, and to whom they sacrificed, had protected and made great their empire, and now, immediately Rome becomes a Christian state, and Christian emperors rule, it collapses. Little wonder that both Pagans and Christians questioned the wisdom of the change. "The gods have been overthrown, and now they have deserted us. We are now without their help, and our empire has collapsed!" This was the cry that went up everywhere. Can we wonder at their deep despair and dismay?

Zosimus, moreover, tells us that the Pope, Innocent I (402–417), a strong and resolute opportunist, who had set himself up as the imperial ruler in place of the Emperor when Rome was captured, bowed to the popular panic and gave permission for sacrifices and prayers to be made to the gods. The priests themselves were equally puzzled to account for the disaster, the more so because these barbarians were also Christians, they having been converted to Christianity by missionaries sent from Constantinople. The Visigoths were amongst those who had come over to the new faith, and they were the first to break through the defences of the Empire to usher in the age of barbarism.

The frontiers of the Empire now gave way everywhere, and in poured Vandals, Goths and Franks, Britain likewise being invaded by the Jutes, Angles and Saxons. So began the collapse of the once mighty Roman Empire, built up by force, maintained by force and destroyed by force, the same methods of warfare as the barbarians had learned from the Romans being the cause of its destruction. Here indeed we are at one of the prominent turning-points in world history, one which set the waves of events rolling so high that we can hear them breaking on the shores of time all through the ages up to our own day.

What indeed would Jesus have thought if he could have foreseen that a priest, claiming to be his representative on earth, would sit upon the imperial throne and govern the western Roman Empire, an event which was to have tremendous historical repercussions down the centuries, every one of which can be traced back directly to Paul's misinterpretation of his own psychic experiences. This being so, who can doubt that the other order of existence, which is just beyond our normal sight and hearing, has had a profound effect on the course of human history, for good when correctly understood, and for evil when ignorance has brought about erroneous conclusions?

In Section 3 of the next chapter we shall consider the causes which were responsible for this great disaster to the Western world, this blow to the heart of the world, as Europe was then, and still is, that organ in the body politic. Imperfect as was this mighty imperial structure, it maintained peace within its borders, and, until the coming of Christianity, encouraged education, which had reached a standard that Britain did not attain until late in the 19th century. If something better had taken its place, its passing need not have been mourned, but, unfortunately for a third of the human race, ecclesiastical rule took the place of imperial rule, and the bigoted, intolerant, ignorant priest replaced the civil administration. Theological beliefs took the place of the pursuit of knowledge, as the schools were now closed and all education abolished.

The people, under the new Christian order, were not treated as grown-up men and women, but as children with childish minds. Doubtless the majority were childish and simple in their outlook, and they received the only mental food they could digest, but no attempt was made to raise the intellectual level, its low state being encouraged by the people being denied education. Securing the mercy of God by a form of superstitious belief was considered to be more important than the development of the mind. Belief was looked upon as more pleasing to God than conduct, and no attempt was ever made to raise the ethical standard of the people, who were told what to believe, failing which all kinds of dreadful things would happen.

Nothing was done to improve their standard of living, develop their minds and make them better men and women. Ecclesiastical government suits those who still remain children mentally, it works on their emotions, but it is not the form of administration which makes for greater righteousness. Certainly it is not suitable for men and women who have developed out of the nursery mentality, as the priest wishes his flock always to remain sheep and do his bidding.

Such, then, was the catastrophe which came upon Europe in the 5th Christian century, when the people exchanged imperial rule for Church rule. This new form of government spread quickly over the lands comprising the Roman Empire, to include later on those countries whose inhabitants were considered by the Romans as barbarians. This is the story which will now be told.

CHAPTER VIII.

CHRISTIAN CIVILISATION.
(376–642.)

Introduction. (1) *The Rise to Power of the Christian Church.* (2) *The Beginning of Christian Civilisation.* (3) *Europe Before and After the Fall of the Roman Empire.* (4) *The Middle East After the Collapse of the Roman Empire.*

WE must know about the past if we are to understand the present. The ideology of today can only be appreciated if we know something about the ideas of our ancestors, as we are the products of the past, and to a great extent think and act as we do because we are the effects of previous causes. We accept our conditions very much as we find them, but, when we realise that these are the outcome of previous thought and effort, which took place before our birth, our interest in what our ancestors thought and did should be greatly increased.

In whatever land we live, to whatever country we travel, we find that in each town or village the most outstanding building is usually a place of worship. Whether it is called a temple or a church, a pagoda or a mosque, its purpose is the same, but how few think of the long and interesting history attached to this sacred edifice. Away back, before history came to be recorded, tribes and nations erected these important structures which English-speaking people call churches,

The Greeks called a church *Kuriakon*, meaning the Lord's house, and that definition applies to all the sacred buildings of every land.

A group, gathered round a medium, was the nucleus of the first church; a special erection, at a later date, being given over to house the medium who was the intermediary between the gods and man. The first Lord's house was probably a cave, and then a tent, into which, or around which, gathered the tribe to hear the voice of the Lord as spoken through the tribe's medium, who, in trance, gave utterances from an intelligence believed to be apart from the medium's own mentality. By seeing apparitions, and from trance utterances, primitive man came to realise that there were men and women of a different order in his midst but beyond his ordinary power of sight. To them he attributed the phenomena of nature, as he could not imagine a force different from that exercised by an individual. He could imagine some one more powerful than himself, and to such supernormal beings he attributed the different phenomena of nature. These individuals, to him, were none other than gods, one being the rain god, another the thunder god, or the wind god, and so on throughout the entire range of observed natural phenomena.

Consequently these designations came to be associated with other-world men, believed to speak through the tribe's mediums, who received names such as Rain Cloud, Running Water, Big Wind, Lightning and other appropriate titles. To primitive man the men and women whom he called gods and goddesses were very real and near neighbours, with whom he was in close contact, and to whom he spoke aloud and made known his desires. Such was the origin of prayer, and in this manner religion came into being, to become the most potent influence in the lives of all future generations. Psychic phenomena, or what to the ancients was the manifestation of a god, can be duplicated by cunning and ingenuity. By mimicry and deception simple childlike people can be made to believe anything. So it was not long before unscrupulous men pretended to enter the trance state, and speak as if controlled by a god. By deception they duplicated the other supernormal manifestations which occurred in the presence of the medium, and were able to satisfy the people at all times, whereas the medium could only function supernormally when the gods willed it. Thus the medium lost his place to the magician, who, to support his frauds, attributed the genuine phenomena to devils.

The magician sat within his sacred magic circle, thus protecting himself from prying eyes, and, by fraud and cunning, made the people his devoted worshippers. So he became the chief, to develop later on into the priest-magician. Here we are at the opening of the Magic Age which was, and still is, world-wide. Here we are at the origin of the priesthood, as the priest has always had his mysteries and his magic tricks with which to mystify and control his simple flock.

The priest has always been the pseudo-medium, though accepted by all as genuine up to the Scientific Age, when increasing numbers began to discover his false claims. He has always claimed to be the medium between one or more gods and man, and, as the gods were believed to direct all the phenomena of nature, the importance of his office can be understood. The priesthood formed a class by themselves, and, apart from Greek and Roman times, the scanty knowledge of the past centred in their theological colleges. Consequently they were the only professional men, and to them was allotted the administration of the law.

The church was their office, or place of business, as here came the people to be mystified and make their offerings to the priests, who passed their etheric counterparts on to the gods by means of sacrifice. In the church the gods were fed to the accompaniment of the people's prayers for benefits in return for their offerings. Here the simple childlike people asked the gods for what they wanted, and uncritically believed all they heard. They were just like simple children, who make their requests to their father on earth, little realising that those they called the gods were none other than fallible men and women who had lived on earth and died, to continue their lives in another world interpenetrating this one.

It is strange to think of the world-wide effect the so-called dead have had on the affairs of this earth, but, if the dead had not survived death and returned to earth, there never would have been a church or a priest; in fact history would be so completely different from what it is that it is impossible to imagine what things would have been like.

So, outside of the family life and every-day toil, the Church to everyone was everything. To our ancestors it embraced the mental life of the community, as, until the Scientific Age, it was the university, the school and the centre of knowledge. Now each church is a monument to the age-old way of explaining natural phenomena, a monument to the Theological Age, the age of ignorance, when it was believed that the gods controlled the universe. So theology, the knowledge of the gods, claimed to encompass all there was to know, beyond which there was nothing.

The philosophers of Greece and Rome rose above this state of ignorance, because they sought for natural causes for the effects observed. They advocated a more rational outlook on life, their influence being in favour of a natural and not a theological education. This outlook met with so much success that the intelligent Greeks and Romans cast theology aside, and put philosophy in its place, religion to many being Neo-Platonism, whose adherents reached a higher standard of ethical conduct than ever before attained in human history.

This was the intellectual position when the Christian Church became the State Church of Rome, and it immediately set to work to abolish philosophy as the work of the devil. Then Rome fell to the Christian barbarians, and this tragic event gave to the Christian priests unlimited civil power. Had these two events not happened a high standard of ethical conduct might have become established, and the Scientific Age would have dawned a thousand years before it did. Unfortunately destiny decreed that the pall of ignorance would still darken man's stony road on earth, as, in place of knowledge which was leading to better health and greater comforts, arose the Christian Church, to abolish all philosophy, scientific enquiry, education and the rational healing of disease. Every book, moreover, which was found was burned as something pertaining to the devil.

This is probably the greatest tragedy of all times, and can be directly traced to the majority decision at the Council of Nicaea, the greatest event in history. Nicaea closed the schoolhouse of Aristotle, the lecture room of Socrates and Plato, the Greek and Roman hospitals, besides the consulting rooms of Dr. Galen and all other physicians everywhere, all of which, over the preceding centuries, had brought knowledge and the relief of suffering to mankind. Nicaea put out the light of reason, and consigned to oblivion the great and noble thoughts of the Greek and Roman philosophers and healers. Nicaea persecuted, imprisoned or banished into exile the philosophers, scientists and doctors who came after it for the next thirteen hundred years, its immediate effect being to scatter their pupils until learning and the art of healing vanished from the lands in which they had been born and nurtured.[1]

The supporters of universal law and order were thus liquidated. The gods once more reigned supreme, to perform miracles and answer prayer, to favour some and damn others for all eternity. Charms, images and sacred relics took the place of surgery and medical prescriptions; the Bible took the place of philosophy, belief that of conduct, and in the Confessional the people relieved their consciences. To

---

[1] Christianity, from its inception to within our own times, considered disease to be the result of sin, and curable only by repentance, the following being quoted against any attempt to cure illness by medical means:

"And Asa (King of Judah) was diseased in his feet, until his disease was exceeding great: yet in his disease he sought not to the Lord but to the physicians, and Asa . . . died." (2 *Chronicles* xvi, 12.) Jesus likewise is reported as attributing disease to sin, and telling a lame man whom he cured to sin no more or worse would come to him. (*John* v, 14.)

crown all, the priests claimed that by means of their access to the powers in heaven they could pardon sins, cure diseases and change the course of nature for all who were willing to pay the sums they demanded. Rome now became the centre of a very limited universe, which circled round this earth, and there the Pope, in the name of God, managed affairs for the good of all Christian people, every other person being an outcast and a child of the devil.

Thus did Christendom enter the Dark Ages, and black night descended upon the once illustrious Roman Empire. Rome became a holy city and a slum, an array of filthy dwellings, separated by moss-covered evil-smelling streets, on which mostly priests and holy men did walk. Into this foul hovel flowed much of the movable wealth of Christendom, brought by Christians from all parts of Europe in exchange for papal forgiveness of their sins. Prayer, instead of manure, was expected to produce better crops, and offerings, to bring rain, took the place of irrigation.

The papal possessions of land and wealth became so great that the Pope required an army for their protection. Each church throughout Europe, Asia and North Africa, as it ceased to be a Pagan temple, became a sub-office of this great ecclesiastical business organisation, and each priest an agent of the vast machine which sucked the people's money into the coffers at Rome. Every Pope, for the next sixteen hundred years, exploited the partnership he claimed to have with God, to the great enrichment of the Church, himself and all the major and minor clergy.

Such, then, is the age into which this chapter introduces us, an age when the belief continued that the other world is a supernatural world, the abode of gods, saints, angels and devils—the truth, that it is quite a natural place, with natural human beings as its inhabitants, being smothered over with theological speculation and superstition. Consequently, when we remember the black ignorance of the people, and their very restricted outlook on life, we shall better appreciate the foolish things they said and did. If this is kept in mind the Christian era will be better understood, and the limitations of our ancestors more appreciated. For more than a thousand years Christendom thought only the theological way, and then we reach the time when, very slowly but surely, some, with more developed minds, pushed it aside and laid the foundation for the Scientific Age in which we now live.

Now, in our day, amongst civilised people, only the few think the theological way. The clergy, and their churches, remain, but their old-time functions have gone, as doctors, lawyers, scientists and schoolmasters have taken their place, intent on removing the curse of ignorance which the purveyors of superstition did their utmost to maintain. Prayers and charms to many have lost their age-old meaning, while creeds and ceremonials have also ceased to appeal to intelligent people, to whom religion is no longer an organised affair but a personal matter between their God and themselves.

No longer do we rely on theology to explain the ordering of the universe and our destiny. We have ceased to divide humanity into Christians and heretics, into the damned and the saved. No longer do we live under the fear of divine wrath, and it is just because of this vast change in our mental outlook that it is so difficult for us to get back to the mentality of our forefathers. We must, however, do so if we are to understand past history, when the gods, and the priests, were for ever in the limelight. Up to the Scientific Age, history cannot be written without reference to their ideas and activities, but now we know that the universe, which embraces both the physical and etheric worlds, is based on natural law, and that the same cause always produces the same effect.

So let us go back in thought to that queer child-like 5th-century world which had been the Roman Empire, now dominated by Christian theology, and let us try to pick up the thoughts and ideas of that time, so as better to understand the reason for the sordid story about to be unfolded. Five events had brought about this new era in history: (1) the majority decision at the Council of Nicaea; (2) Christianity in consequence becoming the State religion of Rome; (3) the building of Constantinople, and the government being moved there, thus leaving Rome free to be dominated by the Church; (4) the collapse of the western Empire when Rome was captured by the Visigoths; and finally (5) the Pontifex Maximus, now called the Pope, stepping into the vacant imperial throne, thus giving the Christian Church undisputed power over the Empire's 120,000,000 inhabitants, besides the prestige attached to the Roman Empire. To Pagan Rome the Christian Church is indebted for the power and position it has held since the collapse of this widespread empire, a priest-monarch taking the place of the Emperor, with all the glorious traditions this entailed, and all the evil and wickedness associated with despotic rule.

The first four of these great historical episodes have already been recorded, and now we come to the time when the Pope took over the authority of the Emperor, and the Christian Church became all-powerful throughout the Empire.

(1) The Rise to Power of the Christian Church.

"Whatsoever things are true, whatsoever things are honest, whatsoever things are just, whatsoever things are pure, whatsoever things are lovely, whatsoever things are of good report, if there be any virtue" (*Philippians* iv, 8) they will be commended in the pages of this book. If the reverse, they will be condemned, quite irrespective of the veneration accorded to an individual, or of the age and tradition behind the institution which has been guilty of departing from the right way. Whatsoever things are true will be told honestly and fearlessly, with no attempt to pass over evil and absurdities because of hoary tradition or their venerable antiquity. We have suffered too much in the past from this historical dishonesty, but here the naked truth will be told and the lesson emphasised that we must draw from it.

The evil associated with supernatural religion will be recorded and condemned, because that which is founded on error and fraud produces wickedness. Natural religion, based on evidence and facts, on things as they are, and not on theological speculation, will receive no criticism, because true religion is natural and gives comfort and consolation to the weary and heavy-laden. Supernatural religion relies on tradition, on priestly dogma and on ceremonials which appeal to the emotions, but entirely lack truth and substance, whereas natural religion, based on psychic phenomena, relies on facts and knowledge to satisfy us as to our destiny hereafter. This is something much more substantial and to be desired than anything imagined by the theologians.

Most people, in some way or another, reach out towards the infinite, and strive to pierce the veil which separates the unseen from the seen. The attempt to bind the unseen to the seen, which the word Religion means, constitutes religion. The religious instinct is expressed by some through prayer, worship, and, strange as it may seem to many, most of all by attending séances, the oldest and most venerable of all the ways man has used to get into touch with the unseen world around us. From what mediumship revealed he first discovered the gods, and then he commenced to pray to them, to end by worshipping them. Religion has nothing whatever to do with ethics, which relates to our conduct one towards another on earth, and this difference between religion and conduct must be remembered when we read the pages which follow.

Religion, as such, is a personal matter for each individual, but we shall find much to condemn during the Christian era, because of the policy of religious leaders who attempted by force to make everyone think as the Church authorities in the 4th century decreed was the truth. The evil results which followed will be emphasised and perhaps appreciated as never before, because only now are some people sufficiently developed mentally to face the truth, and put aside the prejudice which came as the result of early training.

If the Church leaders in the 4th century, and those who followed them, had taken the moralisings of Seneca, Pythagoras and other philosophers, on which to build up a comprehensive code of ethics, to teach to both young and old, only praise would have been forthcoming for their efforts. If they had made practical use of the learning the Academy at Alexandria had accumulated from Greece, Egypt and Babylon, and had put knowledge before faith, medicine and surgery before prayers, and facts before creeds, then much of this book need never have been written. Instead of this the Church, through its clergy, not only entirely neglected ethics and learning, but explained everything in nature by the will of God, using the domination it secured over the people to keep them ignorant and consequently set in their evil ways. The standard it established for a good Christian was not righteousness, but belief in a false mystical theological creed.

The Church, however, was not founded to make the people good, but to protect and propagate a scheme for their salvation from their wickedness, which is quite another matter. This soothed the people's conscience, it nursed them to sleep, but it never stirred them to strive to live more righteous lives. It provided the whipping-boy, whose image, stretched out upon a cross, was, and still is, in most churches, prominently displayed. On him they relied for salvation, a belief which certainly made life easier but not more righteous, as why strive to be good when you believe that all your wrong-doing will be forgiven because "the blood of Jesus Christ his Son cleanseth us from all sin"? (1 *John* i, 7).

Thus the very basis of Christianity is vicious and immoral, but it never claimed to be established to improve conduct and raise the standard of thought and action. It never strove, as did the Greek philosophers, to produce the ideal man. The Church, which claims to be the interpreter of the faith, was founded to proclaim an easy way of salvation and to preserve the dogmas, doctrines, rites and ceremonies surrounding this belief. Its aim was to sooth the fear of death by an idea, and keep its members childlike in their faith. It produced thousands of fairy tales about the miraculous deeds of the saints, on the same lines as did the Greeks about the gods, but it never wished the people to be other than children, because it wanted to mother them, not to educate them. So it kept everyone childlike and simple, and never enlightened them, the consequence being that the curse of ignorance has afflicted Christendom throughout the entire Christian era, the great majority of its inhabitants being unable to read or write until within our own times.

Christianity, as we have discovered, was just a continuation of the Pagan mystery religions under another name. By the shedding of the blood of the god Dionysus the faithful believed that salvation was secured. At their eucharist services his body was mystically broken in the form of bread, which with his blood, in the form of wine, were handed round for the worshippers to eat and drink. That belief likewise soothed the fears of these devout believers, but it did not make them better men and women ethically, and it is just this lack of ethical development which has so retarded humanity up to our own time.

The Christian Church, however, did something no Pagan Church did, or had the power to do, and thus it made its teaching all the more dangerous to the well-being of society. Basing its authority on the curse God placed on Adam for eating from the tree of knowledge, it put back the clock of progress by closing all schools, persecuting the thinkers and philosophers, and supporting that which was evil while condemning that which was good. Instead of being, as we now are, at constant war, one nation with another, we, if the Church had done what was right and not what was wrong, would have reached a much higher ethical standard. This might have brought peace on earth to all mankind, because, if all the Christian nations had been determined to maintain peace, the non-Christians would have been forced to do likewise.

For fifteen hundred years, from the 5th century when it obtained domination, the Christian Church fought against progress, education and social improvement, it encouraged war, strife, persecution and intolerance, doing little to teach the people ethics, or the right way of life. It extinguished the lamp of reason, and put in its place the darkness of blind unreasoning superstition, its only form of education being theological. This taught men to despise progress, as the more they deprived themselves of comfort and enjoyment the greater would be their reward hereafter, a policy which brought to the Church an abundant harvest, and made it rich and powerful. That, for centuries, was the standard of Christian education, which dragged Christendom down to the depths of degradation. By this outlook the Church turned the people of Christendom into unthinking slaves, ready and willing to do the priests' bidding, and think only as they told them.

Only within the past hundred years has religious freedom of thought prevailed in the Western world, but many in Christendom still remain slaves to the Church. Only now have some been freed from the political bondage of leaders who adopted its methods. Centuries of tyranny have made it impossible for the human mind to develop as it should have done. Centuries of ignorance and fear have prevented many from learning the science of right living. Centuries of Christian rule have produced the mentality of the present day, as we are all products of the past, and are suffering from the ignorance in which our ancestors were kept throughout the Christian era.

So, when Constantine made his bargain with the priests, that, in exchange for a uniform Christian belief, he would raise their Church to the rank of a state organisation, the foundation was laid for the mental enslavement of a large part of the human race. Then the Christian priesthood, figuratively speaking, marched through the open door into the Imperial Palace, and, from that time onwards, the baneful rule of the priest spread itself over the then civilised world. That explains why the world today is in its present plight, as the most virile section of the human race has not yet recovered from the loss of education, both ethical and factual, which followed the dark age of Church rule. We, who today have just escaped a similar fate by the overthrow of totalitarian rule in Germany, will better realise the tragedy which befell the world when the Christian Church became dictator of civilisation, and extinguished the light of freedom. This will be made clear as we proceed.

So we have now reached the outcome of the greatest event in history, the decision reached at the Council of Nicaea, which established the Christian Church as the State church of Rome. At this fateful point in human history let us briefly retrace the main events which have brought all this about. In the previous chapter a section was devoted to the origin and growth of the Christian Church, and here we recall some important facts there mentioned because they are generally quite unknown. To emphasise them again is necessary, as Church history quite ignores them, Church tradition being based on error and fraud, and consequently the story the clergy give of the origin of their faith is quite untrue.

The psychic gifts displayed by Jesus, who was just as human as we are, his arrest by the priests, his violent death, his reappearance after death, and Paul's belief that Jesus was the Christ who was controlling him, gave birth to what became known at a later date as the Christian Church, but this great event came about in quite a different way from what we have hitherto been taught. In its infancy it was cradled in the Temple at Jerusalem (*Acts* ii, 46), where it was nursed by Peter, but, when this edifice was destroyed, that which was but a branch of the Hebrew religion separated to grow and develop on its own.

This might easily have been its end, but by this time Paul had lifted the young Jesuian sect over to Greece, where it took root, its Hebrew ancestry increasing its prestige. There it ceased being solely a Jewish cult, to become nurtured in the Greek Mystery religions, while that which had remained in Palestine branched out to form different denominations. Some of these remained separate and distinct for centuries to come, until all their adherents were finally exterminated by the Christian Church. Jesuism thus broke up into different groups, but the only one that expanded greatly was the one to come under Greek influence, as it absorbed the religious beliefs already held in the Roman Empire. In the lands influenced by Greece, Jesus was transformed into the Christ, and the new religion became known as Christianity, to find its chief centre eventually in Rome, where for a century it was a bitter rival to the Mithraic Church.

In these early centuries there was no fixed belief, no Christianity as we now know it, and the Jesuians, who believed in the early end of the world and the return to earth of their master, consoled themselves by prayer and séances during what they considered would be but a brief interval of separation. Amongst the Jesuians there was a common belief in the value to be attached to those psychic gifts to which Paul refers in his letter to the Corinthians. They believed that the mediums, who officiated at their services, were acting as the connecting link between earth and heaven. Thus the inspiration of the Apostolic Church came through natural law, through psychic phenomena, which was the cause that brought every religion into being, an undisputed fact however much it has been forgotten and smothered over by theology as time went on.

By the end of the 2nd century the organisation of the various Apostolic churches, dotted here and there throughout the Roman Empire, was for all practical purposes identical, as they adopted as their pattern that of the Roman and Greek civic senates, but for the first two centuries there were no priests. Ministers, who were laymen, conducted the services, reading from the Hebrew scriptures and leading the prayers and hymns, it being the medium in trance who delivered the address under what was believed to be the inspiration of the medium's spirit control, known as the divine or holy spirit.

Priests and mediums have always been deadly enemies, and, when Pagan and Jewish priests were converted to the new religion, they gradually made their influence felt. Moreover, the ministers resented the medium being the leading personality during the service, and, as this antagonism developed, the converts from Paganism gradually introduced their old beliefs, rites and ritual. These took hold, as they corresponded to what the people had been accustomed to in the Pagan temples, and, as churches grew in numbers, and mediums were scarce, what became Christianity grew and developed, so much so that by the 4th century to have a medium officiating in church was the exception and not the rule.

A natural religion had by now been changed into a supernatural religion, just as Jesus had been transformed into Paul's heavenly glorified Christ, and around this imaginary god were draped the Pagan beliefs relating to their saviour-gods. Here the story would have ended, and what was now called Christianity would have been but another of the supernatural religions which then abounded, with no influence on future world affairs. However, that was not to be, as other causes were at work which had their unfortunate effects during the centuries to come. In the 4th century Christianity received the powerful support of the wide-spread Roman Empire, when Constantine favoured this young rival of the older Mithraic form of belief, a rival which had not only changed the name of the god worshipped, but had also absorbed the beliefs surrounding Dionysus, Mithra and the other saviour-gods. This policy of combining religion and politics made future history, and the Christian Church became the State church of Rome, to continue the protection of the Pagan Eucharist and the beliefs, rites and ceremonies revered by the Romans and Greeks.

The next event favourable to the Christian Church was the collapse of the imperial power in Rome, when the Church established a dictatorship over the lives of the millions who lived in the Western hemisphere. It can rightly claim to be the successor to the Roman Empire, and the way it linked itself to the different states of Europe will be told as we proceed. France, in 507, was the first to bow to its authority, and, until last century, proudly bore the title of eldest son of the Church. This long period, during which the Church was in control of France, was one of reaction, suppression and persecution, and the same results followed in every other country on which it fastened its grip. The social conditions of the people were terrible, there was no education, and ethical instruction was entirely lacking, but this will become vividly obvious as our story unfolds.

Like the Nazis, the Church in the 4th century started off its inglorious career by being organised by a triumvirate made up of Augustine, Jerome and Ambrose, who launched the Christian totalitarian form of rule on Christendom. The malignant part played by them, in using every priestly invention to strangle all freedom of thought, will some day be appreciated, when they will come to be looked upon as unscrupulous tyrants of the worst type, and not as the saints they have always been presented to us.

They were paralleled in our own time by the Nazi triumvirate in Germany, Hitler, Goebbels and Himmler, who likewise banished all freedom of expression, and managed to maintain a stranglehold over the German people, the only difference being that the Christian grip lasted 150 times longer than did the one in Germany. Augustine, the intolerant ruthless aggressor, corresponds to Hitler; Goebbels, the liar and falsifier of the truth, to Jerome; and Ambrose, the Inquisitor, to the cruel and calculating Himmler, each one of these three Christian saints fitting perfectly the role played by their counterparts in our own time.

Though the Christian triumvirate spent much of its time speculating on the Godhead, it had no idea of human liberty, and looked upon humanity as slaves whose duty it was to do the bidding of the priests. On the foundation of the dogma, doctrines and tyrannical laws laid down by Augustine, Jerome and Ambrose, Christian rule was established, to be overthrown only partially in some of the more enlightened countries within our own time.

The words which the priests put into the mouth of Jesus that "He that believeth, and is baptised, shall be saved; but he that believeth not shall be damned" (*Mark* xvi, 16) brought about even better results than the interpolators imagined, and, at the opening of the 5th century, we are now witnessing, in the dogmas and doctrines these three men added to the religion, the culmination of all that had gone before. They claimed that what they decreed must be believed as the true Christian faith, and that only those who did so, as members of the Holy Catholic Church, could secure salvation. With this powerful weapon they swept the people into the Christian fold and exterminated those who thought otherwise.

Augustine (354–430) (who must not be confused with the priest of the same name who became the first Archbishop of Canterbury in 596) was the greatest of all those who were responsible for founding the Christian Church. He was active in exterminating and banishing heretics, justifying his deeds by the words attributed to Jesus: "Compel them to come in, that my house may be filled." (*Luke* xiv, 23.) This, and other similar texts in the Bible, explain the reason why Christians persecuted all unbelievers from this time onwards up to last century, believing, as they fervently did, that by so doing they were pleasing the god imagined by their cruel and ignorant minds.

The saying attributed to Jesus, "But those mine enemies, which would not that I reign over them, bring hither and slay them before me" (*Luke* xix, 27) gave the Christians the urge to carry forward their bloody work of exterminating unbelievers. Nothing could be clearer or more definite, and if Jesus said these words, which his followers attribute to him, he was the cause of more deaths, suffering and misery than any other man who ever lived. How irrational Christians are, because they believe that Jesus on another occasion taught them to love their enemies, and they call him "Gentle Jesus".

How much wiser it is to accept the opinion of the scholars who have studied the question deeply, and are able to prove to any unprejudiced person that we have no reliable record of what Jesus said or did. What is reported of him was attributed to him by those who came after him, but this was done in such an irresponsible way that he was made to contradict himself over and over again on the most vital issues. Consequently it is a fair assumption that the above wicked command was inserted by some zealous copyist, acting on behalf of the Church authorities in the 4th century, who wished to have the authority of Jesus for the persecution and massacres then being carried out by the priests. As we read on we shall discover how it was that these words, and other similar remarks attributed to Jesus, were made full use of by Christians during the next fourteen hundred years to exterminate all who thought differently from the orthodox opinion of the time.

Augustine, in his zeal for a world-wide uniform religious belief, laid down the rule that religious error was a crime against the State, and must be punished as if it were treason. This became the established policy of the Church. Further, he decreed that the unity of the Church must be preserved by physical force, and that all unbelievers in the Nicene Creed must be crushed out by the sword. He was responsible for the abolition of the Agape, or Supper of Remembrance, celebrated by the early Jesuians from apostolic times, which concluded with what we to-day would call a séance, when it was believed that Jesus, through the divine or holy spirit, the medium's control, passed on to them his messages and blessing. In its place was put the Pagan Eucharist, as we now know it, the gospels and epistles having been altered to conform to the changed outlook.

We are now quite accustomed, in our own times, to hear remarks over the radio disparaging Paganism and exalting Christianity, but these are made by people who are either quite ignorant of the truth or so prejudiced that they prefer falsehood to truth. Last century Lecky protested against this ignorance, or dishonesty, in his *History of European Morals.* The Pagan philosophers had far higher ideals than had Augustine and the other Church fathers who produced the Christian religion. Most of the philosophers taught that death, like birth, is a natural event, and that by virtue man could become acceptable to God, whereas the Christians believed that death was a curse placed on mankind in consequence of the sin of Adam. Many of the philosophers believed that death was a change for the better, whereas the Christians insisted that the vast majority of the human race would suffer eternal torment in hell.

Few people realise how completely Christendom has been misled by the clergy from the time we are now considering to the present day. Just as the Nazis poisoned the German mind against Democracy, so did the Christian priests pervert the minds of all Christians towards Philosophy. Already we have read of the high ethical standard reached by the Greek and Roman philosophers, but their theosophical ideas also attained to heights never yet surpassed by man. To some of them this earth was no narrow vale betwixt two bleak eternities, but the place for mental development to fit us for a larger and wider experience after death. Their intense belief in an after life, and the need to prepare ourselves wisely for it, produced thoughts never before expressed more clearly and sublimely. To represent the Pagans as barren of hope, as damned image-worshipping heathen, who lived for the present without a thought of the hereafter, is just another of the many falsehoods for which Christian propaganda has been responsible during its long inglorious career.

Pagan literature overflows with the belief that we are all the sons and daughters of God, from whom we came and to whom we return, our duty on earth being to fit ourselves to enter his presence at death. This idea and their belief in divine providence, divine love and care for everyone on earth—calamities not being sent as a punishment—supplied a constant and forcible motive for virtuous living, as everyone was urged to do nothing to dishonour his creator. No nobler teaching ever came from the mind of man, and only lack of space prevents quotation after quotation being given to support this assertion. Psychic philosophy of today is but a continuation of the teachings of the Pagan Spiritualist philosophers, who regarded death as a door leading to greater and freer mental refreshment, in a world of finer substance surrounding this earth 'where life would continue, as it does here, but freed from the limitations caused, by the physical body.

Because they were wise enough not to make entrance into heaven dependent on belief in a creed, because to them man must save himself and reap what he sows, the Pagan philosophers were one and all solemnly condemned to hell for all eternity at different councils of Christian priests, and the Church denied to Christendom their noble thoughts so long as it had the power to do so. To the enlightened Pagan the future life was a vivid reality, the earth body the restraining influence on the soul's fuller development, and death the escape to a purer and less restricted life in heaven where parted friends would be reunited.

Then came the conflict with Christian beliefs that only through the acceptance of Christ as saviour could heaven be reached, to be complicated by the idea of a bodily resurrection of the faithful on earth, an idea fiercely resented by the Pagans, who could not imagine a purified life in association with the carnal body. In the whirlwind of controversy and persecution following the rise of the Christians to power, Pagan philosophy and natural religion faded into oblivion, and a nebulous heaven became reserved only for those who accepted the doctrine of the Christian Church. The intolerance this caused reduced Christendom to a level so miserable and degraded that its like has no other historical parallel.

Augustine taught in his *Epistles* that "He that is not quickened in Christ must remain in that condemnation of which the Apostle speaks. To which condemnation infants are born liable to all the Church believes." Then he goes on to say how unbaptised infants, and all who die without partaking of the Sacrament, spend eternity in hell's eternal fire. From this doctrine came the saying, which the clergy of Christendom have used in one form or another, "The streets of hell are paved with the bones of unbaptised infants." Thus, by fear, they obtained a grip over the people whom they retained in their clutches from birth until death. On the other hand Plutarch, whom Christians term a heathen, writes in his *Ad Uxorem:* "No funeral sacrifices are offered for children who die at an early age. The law forbids us . . . because it is irreligious to lament for those pure souls who have passed into a better life, and a happier dwelling place.[1]

The Church has always falsely claimed that it was the basis round which the home is built, and yet Augustine, its greatest authority, basing his opinions on the words attributed to Jesus, that everyone and everything must be forsaken for his sake, wrote:—

> Fly to the desert, and though your wife puts her arms round your neck tear her hands away, as she is a temptation of the devil. Though your father and mother throw their bodies athwart your threshold step over them, and though your children pursue, and with weeping eyes beseech you to return, listen not. It is the temptation of the evil one. Fly to the desert and save your soul.

Augustine incorporated into the doctrine of the Church the worst of Paul's theology. Paul wrote that we are "by nature the children of wrath". Augustine

---

[1] Plutarch, on the death of his infant daughter, wrote to his wife as follows: "The death and resurrection of Dionysus teaches us that the soul is immortal, so why trouble unduly about our daughter, as her soul is with Our Lord, and, when our turn comes, we shall be with her again."

improved upon this by describing the human race as "one mass of perdition from Adam". He then elaborated Paul's doctrines of predestination, salvation by faith, justification by grace, and the remnant of the elect, thus abolishing all the comfort the reappearance of Jesus after death had given to believers. What misery these doctrines have caused to multitudes in the Christian community, and what arrogance they have produced through many thinking that they were predestined to be saved by grace, and counted amongst the elect!

Augustine was born in Numidia, and became Bishop of Hippo. No single name has ever exercised such power over the Christian Church, and no one mind has ever made such an impression upon Christian thought. His successful work in exterminating the Christian sects, known as the Donatists and Pelagians, so earned for him the gratitude of the Church that he was made a saint after his death, this being a good example of the standard of righteousness set up by the organisation which, in the centuries to come, was to be responsible for the morals of Christendom.

The Donatists were a powerful body of Christians who wished to exclude from Church teaching certain doctrines which had become orthodox, but which were not held by the early Jesuians. At the Battle of Bagnia, after thirteen years of bloodshed and persecution, they were finally defeated and largely exterminated, thus to suffer the fate of the Arians and many others who, in the 4th century, looked upon themselves as followers of Jesus. It will be remembered that when the Christian Church determined in 325 what exactly was meant by Christianity, many were excluded from the fellowship of the Church, to be told to change their beliefs and become orthodox, or be branded as heretics and take the consequences.

Augustine, who was one of the most reactionary figures in history, led the Church authorities in stamping out education, schools everywhere being closed and the teachers exiled or murdered. This was one of the greatest crimes ever perpetrated on the human race, as it brought Christendom down to the depths of degradation. Thus began the policy pursued by the Christian Church from that day till last century, to produce the slave mentality amongst the people, which, as time went on, reduced Europe to a state of mental darkness.

Augustine was its first outstanding tyrant, determined to keep every Christian ignorant and make him think as the Church decreed, his activities in this direction being concentrated not only on the Donatists, but also on the Pelagians, who incurred his wrath, because they believed (1) that man is not born in sin as the result of the disobedience of Adam, each one being free by his own effort to raise himself to greater heights of righteousness; (2) that infants are not eternally damned if they die unbaptised; and (3) that all good men and women who died before the death of Jesus reached heaven.

These heretical beliefs upset the basis of fear on which the Church was growing rich, and, by the blood purge carried out by Augustine, the Church liquidated all those Christians and Pagans who could not subscribe to the Nicene Creed and the orthodox outlook. Periodically, from now onwards, similar purges were organised to exterminate all who doubted its various dogmas, and the people were intimidated into servile obedience and increased liberality towards the support of the priests. By such tyrannical methods, which deprived Christendom of all freedom of thought, the Church became a powerful dictatorship, its treasury was always full to overflowing, the people became servile slaves, and the old Roman Empire was won over for Christ.

Next in importance in the Christian hierarchy is Jerome (341–420), who was a man in a good social position and possessed of considerable wealth. When he became a Christian he betook himself to the Syrian desert, where he lived a hermit life, as did a number of monks, each one in a solitary cell pondering over the Scriptures. He became an active, ruthless partisan of orthodox Christianity, and set his tongue and pen to work with extreme bitterness. From his secluded abode he poured forth a torrent of bigoted eloquence, and thundered with indiscriminate wrath against all who remained outside the orthodox fold. He vented against them a malignant calumnious rancour which continued until his old age, and which only death brought to an end, when he was made a saint in heaven for his painstaking work in translating and altering the gospels and epistles to make them correspond to what Christianity had become in consequence of the decisions reached at the Council of Nicaea.

This intolerant bigot, with his narrow monkish outlook, exerted his powerful influence to bring to an end the use of psychic gifts in the churches and elsewhere, thus denying to the people the comfort they had hitherto received from their belief in the gods, who were their guardian angels and to whom they prayed when in trouble. Now began the long era of medium extermination, which brought to so many innocent harmless people such dreadful misery and suffering. Since apostolic days mediums had taken the leading part in church services, but, as the power of the priests increased, their employment became less frequent, to come finally to an end in Jerome's time, the reason he gave for this discarding of the psychic gifts, so praised by the Apostle Paul, being

> We tell them (the mediums) that we do not so much reject prophecy (mediumship), as refuse to receive prophets (mediums) whose utterances fail to accord with the Scriptures old and new.

Jerome was a zealous believer in the Christian way of salvation, through the acceptance of Christ as the sacrificed saviour-god, all unbelievers perishing in hell, and when he talked with the so-called dead, who told him, just as they tell us today, that the etheric world is open to all quite irrespective of belief, he considered that he had been conversing with devils. Here indeed was a problem for the Church authorities to solve, and, in order to secure the continued devotion of the people to the Church, they came to the decision we would expect from men who were both fanatical and quite unscrupulous. Instead of deciding, as they should have done, to make the Church the protector of mediumship, they did just the opposite, the reason being that they were now so far along the road of error that they could not turn back without upsetting the entire organisation.

Before the time of the Council of Nicaea, Christian

beliefs had been in a state of flux, when Jesuism was gradually changing into Christianity. Then there was no central authority, and everyone believed as he pleased, but, when the priests began to organise a united Church with a belief common to all, the gospels and epistles were altered and brought up to the standard of belief which had been fixed at Nicaea. So we are not astonished to read in what remains of the writings of Celsus, the learned Platonic philosopher of the 3rd century, that he accused the Church authorities of forgery and fabrication in these words:—

> You utter fables, and you do not even possess the art of making them seem likely. . . . You have altered three, four times and oftener the texts of your own Gospels in order to deny objections made to you.

Truth and honesty have never been the guide of Christian priests, the result being that both ignorance and expediency produced an array of theological beliefs which were quite contrary to what is true. Consequently the medium was a continual menace to this great bastion of superstition, because of the fact that Christian doctrines were refuted by the men and women of the etheric world, who used this natural instrument when in trance, or by the Direct Voice, to speak to the people on earth. So Jerome advised the Pope to forbid all mediumship in the future, and a decree was issued abolishing the use of psychic gifts in the churches and elsewhere, mediums being degraded from their former high office of "Oracles of God" to that of "Servants of the Devil", by which insulting name they have been called by the clergy from that day to this.

Then, also, the authority of the Old Testament was invoked, convenient texts being discovered about the extermination of wizards, witches and sorcerers, and so began the long-drawn-out war between the Christian Church and the mediums, who, by successive edicts of different popes, were described as outcasts to be tortured, burned or drowned whenever discovered. After the Reformation, Protestant countries passed Witchcraft Acts to the same effect, and these are still in force, Britain today being a shining example of this reactionary form of legislation. Here, in a land which is proud of its freedom, mediums are fined and imprisoned because they are mediums, and not because of any fraud, their crime being that they were born with psychic gifts. This legislation had its origin in the 4th century, when the Church authorities clamped down nature's means of revealing the other world, so as to keep the people believing in their false and superstitious doctrines.

As has already been stated, Christianity is founded on fraud and forgery, and to this rotten foundation Jerome added his quota of dishonesty. On his return from Syria to Rome in 382 he became Secretary to Pope Damasus, an immoral and unscrupulous pontif, who rose to the height of his ambition over the bodies of hundreds of victims he had slain. He was made a saint after his death because of his activities in exterminating heretics. These unorthodox people were a constant thorn in the side of the orthodox Church, because so many different gospels and epistles were in circulation that every heretic could find a gospel or epistle to support his opinions. For three centuries such a variety of beliefs had prevailed that no two gospels or epistles were alike, each one having had deletions, interpolations and alterations made, as the scribe thought fitting when making his so-called copy from some previous doubtful copy, which was a dubious copy of earlier untrustworthy copies.

The orthodox Christian faith had now become so diametrically different from the original Jesuian beliefs, that Damasus decided that the time had come to revise the sacred literature to bring it into line with the now paganised Christian religion. So he commissioned Jerome to bring those gospels and epistles, which were in general use, into line with the now orthodox beliefs, and this work Jerome at once set about. First of all he commenced to edit and revise those writings which later came to be included in the New Testament, altering them to emphasise the new Christian beliefs and accentuate the fact that Jesus, the Jew, was none other than the Christ, the world saviour, now acting as mediator for sinful mankind in heaven.

So Jerome tells us that he carried through a systematic revision of the gospels and epistles, altering and adapting them as he thought right, to bring them into line with the new orthodox beliefs, thus continuing the dishonest practice against which Celsus so boldly protested. From his editing of the numerous different versions at his disposal we obtained the books now included in the New Testament, which represent those that Jerome brought up to the orthodox standard, and, as all the early manuscripts had perished centuries earlier, no one could question his decisions.

In those days no one was critical, literary honesty being quite unknown, and when Jerome had finished fixing Christian beliefs to his own satisfaction in the writings considered to record their history, he set to work to revise the Old Testament, a task to which he devoted his great abilities with the help of three Jewish scholars. The various different versions, the contradictions and the anomalies in the different manuscripts which he used as his material, so shook his faith in what he had hitherto looked upon as "the Word of God", that he informed the Pope, when his work was completed, that, though he had done his best, his translation must not be considered as other than a makeshift to overcome an impossible task.

Theologians do not regard truth and honesty in the same light as do ordinary men. Unlike scientists, who welcome facts, and are eager for new ideas which come from further experiment and greater experience, no matter what prevailing opinions may be upset, theologians prefer tradition to what is true. So the Church hierarchy of those days smothered up the fact that there was no solid basis for their religion, and Jerome and Augustine now set about to determine which of the many sacred writings (13 Gospels, 9 Acts and Teachings of the Apostles, and 31 Epistles, etc.), then revered, were to be considered orthodox, and those to be discarded as unorthodox, a matter which had been greatly simplified by Jerome's editorial efforts. Consequently we are not surprised to find that those he had adjusted to what the Church now proclaimed was the true faith were passed by the Council of Carthage in 397, to become known as the Latin Vulgate Version, the Pope, Innocent I, confirming its decision eight years later.

Then followed in 494 a decree by Pope Gelasius I,

that only those approved writings, which were termed canonical, were in future to be read in the churches, and that all who disobeyed this edict were to be tortured and put to death as heretics. By these fraudulent and brutal methods we got *The Holy Bible,* a medley of old documents whose authorship is unknown, which came to be looked upon as written by God through the hands of his inspired scribes, but it was not until after the 17th century that the priests ceased to tamper with its contents. Its evil effect on civilisation will become apparent as we proceed, because within its two covers there is to be found as much that is wicked as there is that which is good, both the good and bad being regarded as coming from the same divine source. Consequently the fanatical zealots, which most of the leaders of Christianity always were, had ample authority for their many evil deeds.

Jerome's idea of the morals of the Christian clergy was so low that he expressed the opinion that their lives were worse than those lived by the dregs of the population, and that no woman should remain alone in a room with a priest. His own influence over some of the women of Rome, whom he wished to take out to the east as nuns, so alarmed their relations that he found it expedient to leave the capital, accompanied by two of these women, and return to the east, where they founded three convents and a monastery at Bethlehem. In this monastery Jerome did most of his literary work, and finished his great task of producing the Christian Bible.

The third and last outstanding man, who figured prominently in the founding of the Christian Church, is Ambrose (340–397), who was born in Gaul, his father, a Roman, being then a prefect in charge of a district. He was trained as a lawyer, and became Prefect of North Italy, with his residence in Milan. His wise use of power won for him increased popularity, and, when the Arians and Catholics were creating uproar because they could not agree upon a bishop for Milan, the Emperor appointed him to the office. Then he became a Christian and espoused the Catholic faith, to develop into an intolerant despot.

During this time of religious conflict, when nearly every Christian was either an Arian or a Catholic, and despised and hated one another, Ambrose had to wait for the passing of two Arian emperors until the Catholic Theodosius I assumed the purple, when his great power in the Church commenced. Then it was that the Theodosian edicts were issued, to become later the Theodosian Code, which contained Article IX providing imprisonment, torture, death or banishment for the crime of heresy, and the establishment of a body of priests who were called Inquisitors of the Faith.

Heresy was therein described as treason against God and the State, and all the persecution and misery which came to the world from Christianity can be traced back to Ambrose, whose evil work against liberty of thought makes him one of the most sinister figures of history, a tyrant whom every good man and woman should loathe and detest. · His influence in securing the legislation contained in Article IX makes him the Himmler of the Christian Church, but he did not long survive the Emperor he had so greatly influenced. The Church regarded him as a noble devout Christian, and because of his great achievement in securing for it the power to persecute all unbelievers he was elevated to the rank of a saint in heaven after his death.

Ambrose was the founder of the Holy Inquisition and the Church Gestapo, as, from now onwards, up to the 19th century, the clergy, both Roman Catholic and Protestant, occupied the position of informer against all who were unorthodox in their beliefs. The modern dictators just continued what the Church commenced and practised for centuries, until rising intelligence only a few generations back forced it to abandon its terrorist methods. This being so, it can only be because of ignorance that so much attention is paid to the opinions of the leaders of the Church in our own times, because the clergy owe their present positions to the debased practices adopted by their predecessors, and they must maintain the fraud as long as possible in their own interests.

Such then were the three men who established the Christian Church on the foundation from which it quickly grew to greatness and power. Their record of evil was far greater than that of the German Gestapo chief Heydrich, whom all good people look upon as a monster of savagery. Yet Christians have such a low moral sense that they honour and sanctify these three outstanding Christians, and their biographers, as recently as last century, condoned their wicked deeds as justifiable in the interests of the orthodox faith and the unity of the Church. To their biographers the so-called spirituality of their heroes made amends for all their deceit, intolerance and cruelty.

Nevertheless they were responsible for the murders and banishments, the suffering, misery, persecution and torture of millions of innocent victims for a vastly longer period than ever was the Nazi gang of criminals, made up of men who were the products of Christian civilisation, and practised in politics what the Church had done in religion.

For centuries the aim of the Church authorities was to secure complete unity of belief, all liberty of thought being considered as quite out of the question. From the 4th century onwards the burning question was the definition of the Holy Trinity, a problem which Constantine thought he had definitely settled at Nicaea. On this question there still remained the two definite opinions there expressed when the leaders met under his direction in 325, and the malignity this controversy engendered is beyond belief. Zosimus, the Greek historian of the 5th century, who wrote the history of this period, declared that "the hatred of the Christians against one another surpassed the fury of wild beasts".

Marcellinus, another historian of the time, writes that "I have never seen wild beasts that were so cruel to each other as these Christians". Massacres occurred in which thousands were killed and maimed, and there was uproar and dissension in every city of the Empire. For centuries to come the attempt by the Church to make everyone into an orthodox Christian resulted in bloody wars and savage persecutions, while the princes of the Church were at times as much divided in their beliefs as the people at large. Robertson, in his *Short History of Christianity*, sums up the position in the 4th century in these words:—

At each episcopal election or expulsion, the most exalted sees of Christendom (Constantinople, Alexandria, Antioch) furnished scenes that would have disgraced a revolution. Julian (the Emperor) has told how whole troops of those who were called heretics were massacred, notably at Cyzicus and at Aamosata; while in Paphlagonia, Bithynia, Galatia, and many other provinces, towns and villages were utterly destroyed. In one massacre at Constantinople, the second in connection with the forcible reinstalment of the semi-Arian Bishop Macedonius, there perished more than 3000 people. The orthodox populace, divided in furious factions, fighting like savages in their very churches, were as brutal as their masters. Gregory of Nazianzun, whose own ferocities of utterance illustrate the character of the period, declared truly that he had never seen a synod do aught but worsen a quarrel.

After reading the various chronicles of this and succeeding centuries of the Christian era, we cannot escape from the opinion that the people had degenerated to be little better than animals. Much has come down to us in writing about the bestial cruelties they inflicted one on another, the different writers recording the cutting out of eyes, the cutting off of ears, the slitting of noses and tongues and much else too horrible to mention, as if these atrocities were the most ordinary and everyday affairs. Torture the Pagans never thought of was now invented and put into regular use. As for morality, there seems to have been none, both men and women speaking of, and displaying, their passions in the most blatant fashion, the nobles and priests leading the people in every form of carnal vice. This appalling state of affairs is not peculiar to one particular place, or one particular period of Christian history, but continued everywhere throughout Christendom up to the 18th century, when education amongst the upper classes began to dissipate the coarseness and brutality which came from ignorance.

To claim, as does the Christian Church, that Christianity raised the people from their Pagan wickedness is one of the many travesties it has made of history, most moralists being of the opinion that during the greater part of the Christian era morality was at a lower ebb than at any other time in history Reference in the pages which follow cannot continually be made to the way the people lived, but let it be clearly kept in mind, as we pass from century to century, that life in Christendom from now onwards was bestial to a degree, that ignorance was profound, and that many of the priests, abbots and monks took the lead in perpetrating cruelties and practising the most debased immoralities. Their deeds indeed shock and disgust the present-day historian who has to peruse these ancient writings, to form a correct conception of the way the people lived. The most convenient way for anyone to satisfy himself that the foregoing is no exaggeration is to read through Joseph McCabe's *The Testament of Christian Civilisation*, which records century by century the actual statements made by responsible writers of the time, and makes clear to what depths ignorance can degrade humanity.

To recapitulate, now that we are at the close of this section, let us remember that the Church eliminated by torture, persecution and banishment all who did not accept its opinions, and this continued somewhere or other throughout the time called Christian civilisation. Its history is a fitting sequel to the methods Augustine, Ambrose and Jerome adopted to secure unity of belief. The means it used to obtain this unity could not have been improved upon by the most barbarous savages, and, as it was by this institution that Christendom was to be guided in its moral life up to our own times, we need not wonder at the present ethical backwardness of those nations who have forced themselves forward as the leaders of the human race.

What will particularly strike us in the chapters which follow is the entire absence of justice, tolerance, mercy and kindness in the dealings of Christians one with another, in their treatment of the unorthodox, and in their attitude towards those they looked upon as heathen. The low moral standard set by the Church was faithfully followed by its members, from whom we of the present day are descended, their virtues and their vices combining to produce Christian civilisation and our present standard of ethical conduct.

(2) THE BEGINNING OF CHRISTIAN CIVILISATION.

Christian civilisation began in the year 381 when Theodosius (called the Great) issued his edicts for the purpose of making everyone a Christian, as defined by the Nicene Creed. Constantine, it will be remembered, bribed the Christian priests, in 325, to produce and agree to what came to be known as the Nicene Creed. This creed was the result of a bargain made between the priests and Constantine, to the effect that if they would agree amongst themselves as to what the Christian religion really was, he would make Christianity the religion of his empire.

Except for his persecution of the minority, known as the Arians, who were those Christians who could not accept the Nicene Creed, things went on very much as usual. The Christians were still in the minority, and Pagan beliefs continued without much interference. The emperors who reigned between Constantine and Theodosius were half Pagan and half Christian, and seemed quite indifferent as to what the people believed. The only exception, it will be remembered, was Julian, who tried to re-establish Paganism, but his reign was too short to make his effort successful.

Matters were in this undetermined condition when Theodosius became emperor in 379. With his reign began Christian civilisation, based on his famous edicts, which, in 438, became known as the Theodosian Code, and affected European law and order during the centuries this civilisation has prevailed. This terrible code brought misery to all parts of the world up to the middle of the 19th century, and, as we proceed, we shall read how it was applied everywhere in Europe and North and South America.

From now onwards the homes of the higher clergy became the centres of atrocities which no words can describe. Each had its dungeon and torture chamber, and, while the clergy lived on the tenth of the produce of the land, those who could not accept the Christian scheme of salvation lay languishing in their cells, to be brought out and tortured at intervals. Then they returned to their underground hovels, into which little light ever penetrated, to exist there until the time came when exposure, starvation, or burning at

the stake, mercifully brought their miserable existence
to an end.

In the *Encyclopædia Britannica*, under "Torture",
further particulars will be found, but the following
extract gives an outline of the new legislation against
all unbelievers in the Christian faith, as decided upon
at Nicaea:—

> As far as it could the Church adopted the Roman law, with
> the important and characteristic difference (dating from the
> severe edicts of Theodosius the Great in 381) that heresy took
> the place of treason, it being regarded as a kind of treason against
> God ("crimen laessae majestatis divinae"). The doctrine of
> confiscation for treason was so convenient and profitable that
> it was rapidly adopted by the Church.
>
> As most instances, in which torture was inflicted by ecclesi-
> astical tribunals, would be accusations of heresy, or Judaism—
> a specially revolting form of heresy to mediaeval Christians—
> this theory practically equalised all persons for the purpose of
> torture, in accordance with the doctrine that in treason all were
> equal. The Church generally secured the almost entire im-
> munity of its clergy, at any rate of the higher ranks, from
> torture by civil tribunals.
>
> Scourging was inflicted only on slaves; free men were
> exempt except in a few cases such as that of adultery, the penalty
> for which was scourging and cutting off the nose. On the other
> hand, where the interests of the Church were concerned, the
> tendancy was for greater severity; thus, by the Theodosian Code,
> a heretic was to be flogged with lead before banishment, and
> Justinian made liable to torture and exile anyone insulting a
> bishop or priest in a Church.

Crucifixion was excepted in veneration of the
memory of the one who was crucified for mankind.
When people can be so debased as to believe that God
gave his son, as a victim of torture, there is little to
cause surprise that the same people believed that to

torture unbelievers was pleasing in the sight of God. When Christians were so stupid and depraved to believe that their god had commanded the destruction of all who did not worship him (*Exodus* xxii, 20), the barbarity of the laws on which Christian civilisation was founded can be understood.

Moreover we can appreciate the dreadful plight of the millions of innocent Pagan victims, who were robbed of their possessions, exiled, imprisoned and massacred by the Christians over a period of hundreds of years. We, in our time, have experienced Europe in this tragic condition because of German brutality, but think of this state of affairs lasting for centuries, and we shall better understand the suffering of the Pagans under Christian rule, which was even more intolerant and savage than was German domination that lasted for only a few years.

Little wonder also that Paganism, under Theodosius, was exterminated in Rome, and Christianity took its place, the Church acquiring much of the people's wealth, as every unbeliever's property was confiscated. Thus did the Christian Church, which represented him who we are told had no place when on earth on which to place his head, lay the foundation of its great wealth. This it did so effectively that, from the time of its rise to power onwards to the present day, it has continued to be the wealthiest corporate body of all history.

All good people everywhere have been horrified at the Nazi persecutions in Europe in our own times, but the Nazis only continued the policy adopted by the Christians up to the middle of the 19th century; in fact 95 per cent. of the people of Germany profess the Christian faith. Up to last century, throughout Christendom, there was a recognised trade engaged in the manufacture of instruments of torture. In Britain those employed in this debased industry, which manufactured thumb-screws, iron coffins in which the victim could not move a muscle without suffering pain, and other devilish devices, petitioned Parliament last century not to abolish torture as it was "absolutely necessary to the proper regulation of heathen and infidels and highly useful to the propagation of the gospel of Christ". This happened in the lifetime of people whose children are living amongst us today, and what the Nazis have done over eleven years was practised with the authority of the Christian Church throughout Christendom from the 4th century up to last century.

So, when cardinals, archbishops, bishops, churchmen and the clergy of all ranks tell the people by means of the B.B.C., in sermons or newspaper articles, of the beneficence of Christianity, how it alone brought kindness, succour and pity to humanity, and that from it came hospitals, social welfare and all our institutions of charity and mercy, do not believe them. Like the Nazis, the Christian Church has always maintained a propaganda organisation for the purpose of maintaining these delusions, its clergy have performed the same services as the gestapo, and, in the theological colleges, which distorted their minds, truth, honesty and tolerance have been treated with the same contempt as they were in Nazi Germany.

Here, however, we are considering facts, and these are grim and sordid, as it was the fate of what became Christendom to experience the martyrdom of man in all its frightful hideousness. After Nicaea the Church increased its influence in the realm of politics, and, besides making itself responsible for the destruction of the Arians and other heretics, all books favouring this or any other heresy were destroyed, and all who published or read them banished.

When, however, Rome fell, and political power was taken over by the Pope, the Church became a political religious organisation, the way for this having already been prepared by Ambrose, Bishop of Milan, who is the first instance we have of a Christian priest taking up the role of a politician. Thenceforward politics, as much as religion, was the work of the Church, and, under his guidance, the Emperor Theodosius united the Christian churches throughout the Empire, thus materialising the dream of Cyprian, the Father of the Episcopacy, of one Church, one Faith and one Priesthood.

Augustine, however, carried matters much further. Deeply impressed and horrified by the influx of barbarism, and the break-down of imperial authority in Rome, he set to work to write the greatest of all his works, *The City of God*, in which he set out his vast conception of the Christian Church's universal ecclesiastical supremacy, and its domination over all the kingdoms of the earth. Innocent I (402–417) had the same idea, and it was taken over by Leo the Great, who became Pope in 440. Only the Church remained in those days to take the place of the Roman emperors in western Europe, to become, by sheer ruthlessness, the dominant power, until, under Charlemagne, the old empire was partially reformed under the name of the Holy Roman Empire.

Historians have found it difficult to determine exactly the number of victims who have suffered and died as the result of Christian persecution and slaughter during the reign of the Christian Church. An estimate was made by a distinguished German historian, and he arrived at the figure of 9,000,000, but he did not include the 16,000,000 who perished during the Thirty Years' War, when the Protestants and Roman Catholics fought for supremacy and devastated a large part of Europe. If we add the victims of this purely religious war to the 9,000,000 who were killed and massacred in various ways, we arrive at the truly appalling figure of 25,000,000 victims. The tragedy, however, is heightened when it is realised that all this loss of life and suffering was caused because of differences of opinion on Christian doctrine and dogma, the outcome of theological speculation, for which there is not a particle of evidence.

The number of so-called wizards and witches the Church destroyed probably reached over 250,000. These, we now know, were harmless people, many of whom had psychic gifts in a more or less developed state, most of them being quite ignorant as to why they were different from the rest of humanity. In this dreadful massacre of quite innocent people the Church gestapo, composed until the Reformation of Catholic, and thereafter of both the Roman Catholic and Protestant clergy, was very active up to the end of the 18th century.

So much for the direct action of the Christian Church in Europe, but we must not forget the 12,000,000 victims of Christian civilisation in South America. These perished from the brutality of the

Christian invaders, who regarded the natives as damned heathen and human outcasts, because they did not accept the Nicene Creed and the Christian Trinity. The various injunctions in the Old Testament about making the heathen bondmen, taking their inheritance, and other cruel commands, were believed to be the will of God, who desired to see that "the heathen are perished out of his land". (*Psalm* x, 16.)

For different reasons both Protestant and Roman Catholic Christians have found cause to liquidate other Christians, if in the minority, who held different opinions about the interpretation of Christian dogma. One difference which caused the slaughter, persecution, imprisonment and banishment of countless thousands was the exact relationship of the Son to the Father, or, in other words, the exact definition of the Holy Trinity. If present-day Christians were not so ignorant and stupid they would be ashamed to repeat the Nicene Creed, an assembly of words which has been the cause of such incalculable misery, suffering and horror. The mountain of agony and human suffering these words have brought on humanity would by now, if Christians knew more and were ethically minded, have consigned them to the limbo of oblivion, and the so-called Holy Trinity into the dark ages of the past, it being something fit only for minds unbalanced by religion to ponder over.

The first outstanding victim of the Theodosian edicts was Precillian, Bishop of Avila, a Spanish theologian who, with several of his followers, in the year 385, on the decision of Pope Damasus and Ambrose, was tortured and then burned alive at Tréves on a charge of heresy. He was accused of the

crime of communicating with the dead and holding
certain Gnostic doctrines, a form of Christianity, very
prevalent in the first three Christian centuries, which
rejected the Old Testament as its religious guide. The
last victim who was put to death at the instigation of
Protestant priests was Robert Aikenhead, aged nineteen, who was found guilty on a charge of blasphemy
(disbelieving in the Trinity) and hanged in Edinburgh
in 1696, but in Roman Catholic countries the priests
have had their victims up to our own times. They
tortured them, and then murdered them, up to last
century, and imprisoned them up to the present century, especially in Spain, their tyranny driving some
of the people into the arms of the Communists, whose
increasing numbers brought about the Spanish civil
war of 1936.

The mighty weapon of torture and death, which
Theodosius put into the hands of the Christian
Church, made it the supreme dictator of Europe and
the lands bordering the Mediterranean. Quickly it
set to work and framed its laws on the savage Theodosian Code, thus making them the most cruel and
barbarous any civilised people had so far known. The
Code moreover provided for the appointment of
groups of priests who were known as "Inquisitors
of the Faith", and thus was laid the foundation of the
Holy Inquisition.

These Inquisitors were the forerunners of the
German Waffen S.S. and Gestapo, as the office of
Inquisitors was maintained throughout the Christian
era up to last century. There was no period when it
can be affirmed that charity, forgiveness, or brotherly
love, existed between Christian sects. Differences of

opinion invariably led to charges of heresy, and heresy was invariably stamped out with ferocious cruelty. No pause, moderation, restraint or mercy was ever shown, and the contrast between the toleration of Paganism and the ferocious intolerance of Christianity cannot be passed by unnoticed.

Anything hidebound, which lays down rigid principles or beliefs, which chains the mind, or prevents progressive development, and keeps back the evolution of the human intellect, must be resisted. History is largely made up of action and re-action in this direction, and in all countries which have made any mark in history we find a record of the fight between tyranny and freedom. Ancient Greece is an example of this constant fight for freedom, the Christian era being likewise no exception.

The Christian Church took over the role played by the Roman emperors, some of whom were tyrants, while others were enlightened rulers. When, however, the popes secured the authority hitherto in the hands of the emperors, all enlightened rule vanished, as the Church has always had only one aim, the uniformity of belief, whereas civil rulers were mainly interested in maintaining order and were not generally religious fanatics. Now, under Church rule, we find fixed observances and stereotyped beliefs being imposed on all, and the penalties for unbelief applied to everyone who was unfortunate enough to come within its jurisdiction.

The Theodosian Code, which put all unbelievers of the Nicene Creed under sentence of death, made it impossible for human beings to profess other than the Church decreed. This code, which chained the mind for fifteen hundred years, had its counterpart in Germany when the National Socialist Party, adopting the same methods as the Christian Church, stamped out all freedom of thought and expression. We know the effect this policy has had on Germany, and we can well imagine the reaction this tyranny had on the Pagan world when the Christian Church came into power. All rational intelligent thinking was effaced, and remained obliterated up to within our own times.

This then represents what Christianity gave to the world, this only and nothing else that was new. On the other hand Neo-Platonic philosophy, under the leadership of the thoughtful Plotinus, a man endowed with remarkable psychic gifts, had been influencing intelligent people more and more in these early Christian centuries. The thoughtful minority were giving up the beliefs in their Pagan superstitions, and naturally looked upon Christianity as just another religion, out of which they had grown. Philosophy and Christianity could not, therefore, live side by side. So we are not surprised to discover that immediately the Theodosian Code came into operation, Christians set about, in a thorough manner, the extermination of all rational thought.

One of the most distinguished fathers · of the Church, the tyrannical Cyril (376–444), became Archbishop of Alexandria at a time when many were being attracted to a more philosophical outlook on life. He was a great theologian, and left many commentaries on the subject of Church doctrine, besides a treatise on the Trinity and the Incarnation. He presented to the City of Ephesus a statue of the Virgin Mary, which replaced the one to the goddess Artemis.

He was one of the most bloodthirsty ruffians we have to deal with in early Church history, as, shortly after his appointment to the See of Alexandria, he displayed his zeal against the Jews, Pagans and heretics. Immediately after he became endowed with the Holy Spirit, on his election to office, he closed all non-Catholic churches in his diocese. He assailed the Jewish synagogues with an armed force, drove the Jews in thousands from the city, and exposed their houses and property to pillage. Thirty thousand Jews are said to have perished as the result of his persecution, while another of his crimes was his liquidation of those with a philosophic outlook.

Archbishop Cyril's most notable victim was Hypatia (350–415), described by Socrates (385–450), the Church historian, as one of the most outstanding women of her time. (This historian must not be confused with his great namesake who lived in Athens nine hundred years earlier.) Hypatia was a very remarkable woman, as she was not only a philosopher but also a brilliant mathematician, being responsible for a commentary on the work of Diophantus, the inventor of Greek algebra. She was the daughter of Theon, the mathematician, astronomer and philosopher, and spent her early life studying in Athens.

She became a distinguished lecturer on philosophy in Alexandria, and came to be regarded as the recognised head of the Neo-Platonic school in that city. Her lectures attracted so many of the leading people of the city that the street, in which they were held, was always crowded with chariots when a lecture was proceeding. We are told that the "fascination of her great eloquence, the charm of her rare modesty and beauty, combined with her remarkable intellectual gifts, attracted to her classroom a large number of disciples, over some of whom her influence was very great".

This gifted woman continued to conduct her lectures during the time the Christians in Alexandria were ravaging, torturing and slaughtering the Jews, Pagans and heretics, and it does not, therefore, surprise us to read that she met a tragic end. Urged on by Cyril, the congregation from his church invaded her classroom and dragged her out, along the streets, into their church. There the Christians stripped her naked, cut her to pieces with oyster shells, and finally burned her body piece by piece. For this crime Cyril was responsible, though it was carried out under the leadership of Peter, a lay-reader in his church.

With her death died also philosophy in Alexandria, and a city which once flourished as the intellectual centre of the world became, under Christian control, a mere provincial town and of little importance. The fate which befell the intellectual life of Alexandria also overtook Athens, where the Christians likewise extinguished the light of reason, and put in its place the dark night of superstition. In both these cities theology replaced philosophy, and religious speculation took the place of scientific enquiry.

If the Arabs, outside of Christian authority, had not continued the pursuit of knowledge, carrying on elsewhere the good work done at the Academy of Alexandria, all learning might have vanished from the earth. Everything that the Babylonians, the Egyptians, and lastly the Greeks, had discovered might have been lost, never to have been recovered, because all Greek books were henceforth burned and banned in the west, where the Greek language was forbidden to be learned, so that philosophy could not be studied. Greek consequently remained a forgotten speech in the west until the 15th century, when it was relearned, as it was then that the Greeks fled westwards after Constantinople was captured by the Turks in 1453, an event which brought about that great period in history known as the Renaissance. The Ancient Greeks and the Arabs civilised Christendom, not Christianity, as is so loudly claimed, and this will become clear as we proceed.

The Arabs, during an age of Moslem unorthodoxy, fortunately preserved the knowledge stored up in Alexandria, and, when Constantinople fell to the Turks, Greek scholars carried to Venice the learning of the east, whence it spread all over Europe, to reach eventually the ends of the earth. Much good work had been done at the Academy of Alexandria prior to the rise to power of the Christian Church. There the books of preceding centuries were arranged and preserved, there languages were first studied and grammars and lexicons compiled. There anatomists examined the human body, medicine and healing were studied, geography became a science, and Euclid produced his famous mathematical and logical treatises. At Alexandria the earth was first measured, the heavens were mapped out, astronomy became a science, and the foundation was laid on which Copernicus, centuries later, built his conclusions of the movements of the planets. There chemistry and physics were studied, and practical inventions were made by Archimedes, but all this was now a memory. In place of scientific enquiry Alexandria became the centre where men wrestled with the puzzle of the Holy Trinity, its solution having become more important than the wresting of further secrets from nature.

Moreover the edicts against all unbelievers in Christianity, which were promulgated in the year 381, had naturally the effect of terrorising millions of the Empire's population. Unbelievers were banished, others were persecuted, tortured and burned to death, and many philosophers, scientists and schoolmasters had to find refuge in non-Christian lands. Gibbon, the historian, writes about these 5th and 6th centuries when the unfortunate Pagans were being mercilessly liquidated:—

From the extremities of Italy and Asia both young and aged were dragged in chains to the tribunals of Rome and Antioch. Senators, matrons, and philosophers expired in ignominious and cruel tortures. The soldiers who were appointed to guard the prisons declared, with a murmur of pity and indignation, that their numbers were insufficient to oppose the flight or resistance of the multitude of captives. The wealthiest families were ruined by fines and confiscations; the innocent citizens trembled for their safety.

Though, before the time of the Theodosian Code, there were many sects and differences of opinion as to what Christianity really was, none of these opinions was legally termed heresy at the time. They became heresy from the date the Theodosian edicts were issued, when all unbelievers in the Nicene Creed were branded as heretics. No savage beasts could equal the cruelty of the Christians towards everyone who would not subscribe to this form of belief, says Ammianus, the Roman historian who lived at this time, and even Pope Gregory the Great had to admit that Christianity had turned hell loose over an empire where there had previously reigned peace, tolerance, justice and concord.

Pelagius was the first outstanding heretic, and Pelagianism the first heresy. From his extant *Commentaries on the Epistle of St. Paul,* we discover that the Christian priests were encouraging the people to rely on a profession of the creed and the magical efficiency of the sacraments, while they entirely neglected to emphasise the need of cultivating a higher ethical standard of living. This state of things Pelagius denounced. He tried to break men's minds from the Augustinian doctrine of total depravity, as this belief made it impossible for anyone to maintain a high moral outlook. He substituted for Augustine's doctrine the maxim, "If I ought I can."

Pelagius thus stood up boldly against the greatest of all the Church fathers, Augustine, whose writings and preaching about man's total depravity exceeded, to a far greater extent, even those of Paul. This brought upon him the wrath of Augustine and the Church, the result being that he was taken before the Bishop of Jerusalem and charged with holding the heretical doctrine that man, if he only desires it, can be without sin.

The Synod, which was summoned to try him, found him not guilty, but Augustine pursued the matter further and would not let it rest. Another Synod was called which finally condemned Pelagius, and enacted that not only he but his co-worker Coelestius, and all who accepted their opinions, should suffer confiscation of their possessions and unrevocable banishment. In 431 this decision received the consent of the entire Church.

Pelagius is described in the *Encyclopædia Britannica* as "a man of blameless character, devoted to the reformation of society, full of enthusiasm, and that confidence in the natural impulses of humanity, which often accompanies philanthropic enthusiasm". Just the type of man history tells us the Church has never encouraged. Instead of this outlook on life receiving sympathy, all freedom of thought and expression were stamped out by Christian civilisation, all learning, education and social progress were banned as sinful, and everything to do with mediumship was heresy and subject to banishment or death.

In pre-Christian days knowledge was not looked upon as sinful. It was only when Christian civilisation came into being that knowledge was considered sinful and books were banned. In pre-Christian days books were much sought after. The early poets and orators publicly recited their effusions to induce their hearers to possess written copies of their works. Frequently these were taken down *viva voce*, and transcripts sold to those wealthy enough to purchase them.

As we have learned, the Sumerians, the pioneers of civilisation, encouraged the reading of books and had great libraries. In Athens and Rome it was the correct thing to have a library as part of the household furniture, and bookshops were to be found in the great cities of the Empire. At Alexandria there was a famous library founded by Ptolemy I in the 3rd century B.C., and it became the most important library in the ancient world. Under the enlightened rule of the Ptolemys, scholars and men of science were attracted to the Egyptian capital and made much use of the literature there available.

The first Ptolemy began this collection of books, and so laid the foundation for this great library, his successors sending to every part of Greece and Asia to secure the most valuable works. No exertion or expense was spared in enriching the collection. Books were translated by Alexandrian scholars into many languages for the benefit of the different nationalities which came to Alexandria to consult them. There were two libraries in this city, the Bruchium and the Serapeum, and both contained a large number of volumes. According to Callimachus and Eratosthenes, who were the librarians of this great collection of books, there were 42,800 volumes, or rolls, in the Serapeum, and 490,000 in the Bruchium. These figures agree approximately with those given by Seneca and others of the time.

In 389 an edict of Theodosius ordered the destruction of the Serapeum, and its books were pillaged and destroyed by the Christians. This act of barbarism was carried out under the direction of the Christian bishop Theophilus. Gibbon, in his *Decline and Fall of the Roman Empire*, tells the whole disgraceful story. All the books in Alexandria, available to the public, were thus destroyed by this act of vandalism, as by that time the two libraries had been amalgamated as one in the Serapeum.

With the destruction of all books, and legislation

against all knowledge apart from what is contained in the Holy Scriptures, there was naturally no need for education, the consequence being that all schools were closed. In Greece, prior to this time, where, according to the Apostle Paul, lived a heathen people, children in Athens were being educated up to the age of eighteen years, and there were elementary and higher-grade schools in every considerable town in the Roman Empire, but now, after the edicts of Theodosius, philosophy and knowledge were abandoned, and schools everywhere throughout the Empire were closed. Christendom thus entered its dark night of superstition, which was to last for fifteen hundred years. Had it not been for Christianity, philosophy, in time, would probably have increased its influence, and, if the Christians had not thought that all knowledge was contained in the Scriptures, education and enlightenment would doubtless have continued to expand. If this had been so what a different story the historian would have to tell.

Socrates, Plato, Aristotle and Pythagoras, to mention only four of the great Greek thinkers, laid the foundation of a philosophy of life which illumined mankind, and they were followed by a galaxy of men of intellectual splendour whose sayings and writings will glorify humanity for ever. Moreover, the Greeks were the first to establish schools for learning, as distinct from theological seminaries, but learning and Christianity could not live together, and this great opportunity for a nobler way of life was cast aside. Consequently Simplicius, in the 6th century, the last schoolmaster of Plato's 900-year-old Académy, was the last philosopher and thinker who dared to brave its deadening influence. Just as its grip tightened the bounds of scholarship narrowed, so much so that in 529, under Justinian, the Academy and all the remaining libraries and schools were closed, and all learning finally abolished. Thus the Dark Ages began, and intellectual night settled down over Europe.

All the remaining philosophers, Simplicius included, were expelled from Europe, because they would not accept Christianity, and many died in hunger and poverty. Everyone who put knowledge before superstition was murdered or exiled, until the thinkers and scholars were exterminated, Europe and the Middle East being occupied by Christian barbarians, ignorant and superstitious, who believed that all knowledge was sinful. Surely this was one of humanity's greatest tragedies, and one which baffles the imagination to envisage. Then, and for fifteen centuries, were enacted all the horrors which took place in Nazi Germany in our own times, but how ignorant most people are of these momentous events. The reason is obvious. The Christian Church was the victor and became the dominant power in the Western world. Consequently history was told as it directed, and Christian historians pass by the agony and torment Christendom went through. On the other hand Nazi Germany was defeated, and everything came to light, but, if Germany had been victorious, all the Nazi crimes would have been smoothed over and passed by, the victims carrying their sufferings to unknown graves.

Many Christian kings and popes were just as diabolically wicked as Hitler, but they were on the winning side and retained the power, whereas

Hitler played and lost. The famous Christian potentates were successful, and became great characters in history, not because of their goodness but because of their success. If Hitler had succeeded in his evil designs and become the autocrat of Europe, historians would have raised him to the rank of Hitler the Great. This is the great tragedy of life, because success, no matter how evil the motive behind it, brings greatness, and failure the reverse. Force over weakness, not good over evil, brings its reward, and so long as ethical values are so lightly regarded human affairs are doomed to failure.

Pomp and circumstance, when Christianity ruled, were purchased at the price of liberty and happiness. For every church built there was a dungeon. The clang of the fetters filled the air along with the music of the choir. The hand that lit the taper on the altar lit the faggot at the stake. For every cross there was a sword, for every blessing a curse, and the cries of the damned mingled with the hallelujahs of the saved.

If the numerous schools of philosophy, in existence before Christianity reigned supreme, had remained open to shed their light over Europe and the world, what might we not have been today? Everything certainly points to the probability that we would have been at least a thousand years in advance of what we now are, as the Dark Ages lasted for much longer than this period, during which time the minds of the people in Christendom were like a stagnant pool.

Innocent I was Bishop of Rome between the fateful years of 402 and 417, the most momentous pontifical period in the history of the Church, as within that time Rome fell to the Christian Visigoths, when he stepped into the place of the Emperor. He was the first to lay claim to the status of sovereign over the entire Western Church. Though the Eastern Church rejected this bold assertion it would still be correct to look upon him as the first Pope. From this time onwards the Bishop of Rome took the title of Pontifex Maximus, and succeeded to this Pagan office. He became the Chief Priest and the bishops were the high priests, all of whom claimed to be controlled by the Holy Spirit.

Each Pope further claimed to be the "Oracle of God", and so replaced the mediums supplied by nature, who were the oracles of the other-world men and women who controlled them in trance, they alone being the revealers of the etheric world and its inhabitants. Besides replacing the mediums, the Pope took the titles of "Father of Princes", "The Ruler of the World", and "The Vicar of Christ", the Empire being divided into twelve provinces, over each of which reigned an archbishop, then termed a Patriarch, each of whom also claimed to be controlled by the Holy Spirit.

So the priesthood, which the apostles considered was abolished by the coming of Jesus, came to life again in a body of ambitious, scheming men whose predecessors during the first two Christian centuries were ministers, and nothing more. These holy gangsters captured the Church organisation, just as the Nazis and Fascists captured the government of Germany and Italy. Once this was done the bishops assumed dictatorial powers, which they claimed to have received from Christ in heaven through the Holy Spirit, who was their control, and they his medium. This mediumship, they falsely claimed, was passed on by them from bishop to bishop when they were under divine control. This took place when they laid their hands on the head of every new bishop on his election to the position of a medium of the Holy Spirit. This is what has happened in the past, happens today, and will continue to happen, so the Roman and Anglican priests claim, until the return of Christ to earth, when he will then relieve his priestly mediums of the responsibility of revealing his will to mankind. Surely this is one of the greatest and most successful deceptions in all history, the most gigantic of all the holy swindles of the past, and it was, and still is, only made possible by the complete ignorance of their dupes.

When Rome fell to the Visigoths the Christian Church had been established for eighty-five years. No emperor in those days ruled in Rome, the seat of government being now in Constantinople, and when civil power collapsed the ecclesiastical organisation was all that remained. Consequently, when this momentous event occurred, the Pope, Innocent I, became the ruling power, receiving the veneration of not only the Christians within the Empire, but also of the Visigoths who were also Christians. Two causes brought about this extraordinary state of affairs, namely the capture of Rome by the Visigoths and the transference of the seat of government to Constantinople. Both these events enabled the Bishop of Rome to take the title and role of Pontifex Maximus, a revered position which had hitherto been held by the emperors.

By continuing this imperial office, with the support

of the invaders, he obtained the power and authority which no priest could otherwise have exercised. The Bishop of Rome, now to be called colloquially The Pope, thus took the place vacated by the Emperor, and Rome, though it ceased being an imperial city, became, like Babylon, the centre of a powerful political ecclesiastical organisation with a god-priest at its head. Thus Rome became a holy city, the Pope taking over the imperial palaces and receiving from the people the same unquestioning obedience as did a pharaoh or any other Eastern god-emperor.

At no time did the Pope's ecclesiastical supremacy reach a greater height than under Gregory the Great, who wore the papal crown from 590 until he died in 604. From now onwards the Popes had their own private army which they sent against those who questioned their authority. Its function was similar to the Waffen S.S. which Hitler employed to keep down conquered Europe, and which he intended to expand after he had won the war to keep all Europe under his domination.

Gregory was more powerful than was ever a Roman emperor, maintaining an establishment equal to that of an Eastern potentate, and he lived so sumptuously that he was the owner of a thousand slaves. This magnificence followed the Pagan tradition of a god-emperor, and it was continued by Christianity which, in its early days, had refused to acknowledge the Emperor as a divine potentate! How surprised Jesus, Peter, James and John would have been could they have foreseen how the ordinary everyday psychic events which they experienced would have been the cause, four hundred years later, of this great new ecclesiastical empire, ruled over by a so-called god-inspired priest, holding the ancient Pagan title of Pontifex Maximus, and claiming divine status and authority in the name of him who had so vehemently denounced the priesthood and all its evil ways.

Surely this is quite the most extraordinary transformation in human history,[1] and one for which there is no previous or later parallel. The whirligig of time has certainly worked some strange and remarkable transformations over the ages, but none more surprising and remarkable than this. Now a divine priest wielded unquestioned authority at the seat of the once mighty Roman Empire, and claimed to represent a humble Jew, now elevated to be one of a trinity of gods and regarded as the Judge, Saviour and Mediator of all mankind, the creator and ruler of the universe.

The simple disciples of this Jew have now become gods in heaven, endowed with supernatural power, and his mother has been transformed into a holy virgin and heavenly goddess, all of whom receive the same adoration and worship as was accorded to the great Pagan deities they have dethroned. The statues of these cast-off gods remain, the names of the old gods having been chiselled off and replaced by those of the new divinities, whose images are none other than those of the dethroned gods, in the churches throughout the Empire. Only the names have changed, all else being the same as before when Paganism reigned supreme.

It was an old belief that if the image of a snake

---

[1] The history of this transmutation, from its early stages to its completion, is given fully and clearly in *The Psychic Stream.*

were held before a person who had received a snake-bite, the poison would be transferred to the image by an act of faith. Then later the belief arose that a sacrificed lamb took over the sins of believers. Consequently, up to the year 680, the Christians venerated the Mithraic image of a lamb hanging from a pole, but, from this time onwards, it was decreed that this symbol of sacrifice be replaced by the effigy of the suffering and dying god of Paganism, the only change the Christians made being that they represented him hanging from a cross, a fitting emblem of the injustice and cruelty of the beliefs adopted by the adherents of the new religion. This figurehead of their faith the Christian priests eventually carried round the world, calling the crucified figure the image of Almighty God, by which fraud they gained much power and great wealth.

The cross as a religious emblem goes back to the days of savagery. Primitive man discovered that by rubbing two sticks together he could produce fire by friction. This new wonder he worshipped as a god, and so we find fire an object of worship from early times. It became the symbol of life, and the two crossed sticks which produced it came to be looked upon as sacred. Thus the cross became a venerated emblem to be worshipped by millions from early times for thousands of years, and it is found carved on the stone slabs over the graves of some of the most ancient races. In ancient Egypt, Assyria, Persia, India, Mexico and Scandinavia the cross occupied a prominent place in religious worship, the Mithraists using the sign of the cross to mark the foreheads of the newly initiated communicants, and to identify their consecrated Eucharistic bread. There is, however, little doubt that the Christian symbol was adopted from the Egyptian *crux ansata* which, to the Egyptians, was the emblem signifying salvation and eternal life.

Ancient stories tell of how the human victim, about to be sacrificed on the altar, was first bound to a cross, anointed with oil so as to burn better, and thus became the Christ, the anointed one. So the Christian emblem has behind it a long tradition, and Christians, from childhood upwards, have been taught that the victim hanging on it is the image of their god who suffered in their place. As already mentioned, Dr. Temple, the Archbishop of Canterbury, laid special emphasis, in his Easter 1943 broadcast, on the fact that Jesus, who was crucified, was God. No reply was permitted, no one was allowed to tell the people how the gruesome idea originated, no one was allowed to say that this belief is a relic of barbarism, derived from the time when the people sacrificed human beings and animals to feed the gods, and in return received their forgiveness. No one could denounce the Archbishop's savage conception of the deity, and say that it was an insult and blasphemy, because even today this is the Christian conception of God, the official national god of Great Britain and all Christendom. So everyone had to accept all that the Archbishop had to say without an opportunity to reply, as no freedom of religious expression is permitted by the British Broadcasting Corporation.

Christian teaching has prostituted the more elevated ideas of God propounded by the Greek philosophers and the Hebrew prophets, who told their people that to God righteousness was more acceptable than burnt offerings and sacrificed victims. Christianity, however, entirely changed this more exalted conception of the power that controls the universe, and, from the 4th century onwards, for centuries to come, all books discovered by the priests, which expounded a more noble religious conception, were burned, Pope Gregory being responsible for this decree and also for the destruction of Greek and Roman art.

The only book preserved was *The Holy Bible*, which came into being in the 6th century when the Hebrew scriptures, the gospels and epistles, were brought within one cover. Then, in 527, it was decreed when Jesus was born, after various monks equipped with astrological learning had been called in to decide the question. Ultimately it was decided that the 25th December, the birthday of the god Mithra, be accepted as that of the birthday of Jesus, who, as Christ the god, had deposed his former rival. However, we now know that Jesus was not born in the year one of the Christian era, as Herod, reported as alive at his birth, died four years earlier. So the Christian calendar, the only new idea which Christianity gave to the world, is false like all its other claims.

We have to go back much earlier than the beginning of the Christian era to discover the celebration of the first Christmas festival, as its origin is to be found in sun-worship, Christmas Day being observed by the ancients as the day on which the sun was re-born, when the days begin to lengthen, and its heat to strengthen. So to Mithra, and other saviour-gods, was allotted this day for their birth, when what we call Christmas trees performed their part on this Pagan holy day, and the people rejoiced and gave thanks for their saviour's birth. This decision to adopt Mithra's birthday, and the earlier appropriation by the Christian priesthood of the uniform of the Pagan priests, now completed the borrowing process from Paganism which had been in progress over the previous four hundred years.

The Christian Church, now completely Pagan under a new name, and backed by imperial authority from Constantinople, grew and flourished from this time onwards, just as culture declined, all Italy being now in a state of poverty, besides mental and moral decay. When the emperors went out to conquer, the defeated nations were butchered into acceptance of the new religion, until the time came when Christianity had complete control over a large part of Europe. All intellectual life vanished, and, in its place, the people venerated churches, altars and relics, and thought only about their salvation when not concerned with their ordinary occupations of husbandry and fighting.

After the fall of the Roman Empire, Europe was submerged in a sea of barbarism, and due acknowledgment must be given to the work of the early monks who kept themselves apart from the turbulence of the times. What civilisation there was at that time, and it was very slight, was to be found in the monasteries of Europe, but what a contrast to former times! It is difficult to imagine the ignorance of those days, or the depth to which man's mind had fallen from the heights reached at the zenith of the greatness of Rome and Greece. Barbarism was rife everywhere, and, mentally, Christendom was in the darkness of a night of dense superstition. Monastic life, in all parts of the world, had this advantage in those days, that the monasteries were holy ground, and those inside them were safe from devastation. The Christian Church took its idea of monastic life from Buddhism, and, in the early days, the copying and illuminating of the Scriptures took up much of the monks' time.

A study of the history of Christian civilisation, between the time it came into being in 381 until the Renaissance in the 15th century, reveals an arid desert of thought and intelligence. Little literature of any value was produced. There was no education, and all knowledge was considered sinful. Anyone who had an opinion different from that prescribed by the Church was looked upon as a heretic. Consequently we read that Jovinian, a Christian monk of the 4th century, was condemned and flogged by the Church Council because he stated that the Virgin Mary ceased to be a virgin after the birth of Jesus. After the flogging he was excommunicated and banished to a desert island. Discussions only took place with regard to the Trinity and other Church doctrines; in fact Europe mentally was quite uninterested in anything beyond theological problems.

Christian civilisation brought to Christendom nothing but misery and ignorance. The dogma that error of belief was heresy, doomed the unorthodox to persecution on earth and threats of eternal torment hereafter, all freedom of thought and the belief in the brotherhood and dignity of man being completely destroyed. Better to enter heaven halt and maimed but a true Christian (*Matthew* v, 29) was quoted in justification of this reign of terror, just as the people believed that whosoever "believeth not shall be damned". (*Mark* xvi, 16.) How could literature and free expression live in such an atmosphere? All public lecturing was also abolished, reading was condemned, science was heresy, including the Pagan belief that the earth was round. Medicine and healing had gone far under Pagan auspices, and in the Pagan world hospitals and sanatoria were everywhere to be found, but these were closed along with all the psychic healing institutions. Hospitals were re-established only after the Crusades, the idea being taken from the Moslems.

If German National Socialism had conquered Europe and laid its deadly grip on everything it touched, history would just have been repeated. In the days we are considering there was no freedom-loving Britain and America to stand up to the Church of Christ and stay its deadly advance, the consequence being that it not only behaved as did the Nazis, but it also falsified history and propagated lies which are still believed. Consequently, to give only one example, it is still generally thought that Europe was Christianised by saintly men who, by their piety and missionary zeal, brought over the heathen to the belief in the Gospel.

Such stories are told in Church literature, and a few are true, because, even amongst Christians in those days, there were some who were better than their fellows. The great majority in Europe, however, were converted to Christianity by force, as the priests then had the same zealous desire for power and wealth as had the. Nazis. The same insidious propaganda went on then as it did during the reign of National Socialism in Germany. Everywhere there were to be found quislings, and traitors, who undermined the power of the king, or chief, if he stood out for his own religion, and was against bowing the knee to the Church authorities.

Just as happened during Hitler's tyrannical rule, when nations, which would have stood out against the Nazi octopus, succumbed by treachery and defeat, so it happened in the time we are considering. Moreover Saint Boniface, the Englishman who converted part of Germany to Christianity, told the German tribes that they should come into the Christian fold because "the Christians have the bulk and the best of the world, possessing all the rich lands which yield wine and oil, while the Pagans are now confined to the coldest and most barren regions". Kings and priests became natural allies in this proselytising of Europe, and the advance of the Church was bloody or bloodless, just in accordance with the amount of resistance offered. As Robertson says in his *History of Christianity*, when writing of the time when all Europe had become Christianised:—

The summary of seven hundred years of Christian expansion in northern Europe is that the work was mainly done by the sword, in the interests of kings and tyrants, who supported it, as against the resistance of their subjects, who saw in the Church an instrument for their subjection. Christianity, in short, was as truly a religion of the sword as Islam.

The heathen, broadly speaking, were never persuaded, never convinced, never won by the appeal of the new doctrine; they were either transferred by their kings to the Church like so many cattle, or beaten down into submission after generations of resistance and massacre. The misery and the butchery wrought from first to last are unimaginable. If the Spanish conquest of Mexico and Peru, with their Church-blessed policy of suppressing heathenism, be added to the record, the total of evil becomes appalling; for the Spanish priest Las Casas estimated the total destruction of native life (in South America) at twelve millions.

All this slaughter took place by way of expansion, and is exclusive of the further record of the slaughters wrought by the Church within its established field.

Gibbon writes in the same strain. From the end of the 4th century onwards to the conclusion of the 17th century, Christian civilisation is a record of persecution, tyranny, cruelty, intrigue and everything that is evil, the history of the 18th and 19th centuries containing an account of the heroic struggle against all these wicked things we were up against in the last war. Finally, after the middle of last century, the fighters for liberty and freedom won the great struggle waged by their ancestors of the previous two centuries, when the people of most of Europe and America gained freedom to express themselves as they thought right. If this had not happened a book such as this could not have been published or sold today, as both the author and publisher would have been imprisoned, to end their days by torture or some other cruel death.

One of the most common delusions in the minds of Christians is that their religion brought to mankind all that was good, true and noble, and that before this divine revelation came to humanity the people were living in the darkness of heathenism, bowing down to gods of wood and stone. Christians believe that Christianity raised the world from savagery to a state of civilisation, and that before its time there was no such thing as loving-kindness, charity, works of healing and mercy, the virtues being unknown outside the Old Testament and the Jewish race. What has so far been said, and what will be told in the pages to come, should help to correct the misrepresentations assiduously circulated by those whose interests lie in misleading the people.

The foregoing gives a background of much of the history that is to follow. Ever winding in and out of our story we shall observe the repeated attempts made by the Church to achieve world domination, based on the scheme of Augustine in his book *The City of God*, which was the *Mein Kampf* of Christianity, to end in complete failure after thirteen centuries of effort. Both works envisaged a scheme of absolute world rule and both attempts relied on aggressive and ruthless methods. The Christian priests, to achieve their purpose, relied on torture, imprisonment, banishment, the Inquisitors of the Faith, intrigue and on Christian rulers, backed by their armies of cruel and plundering soldiers, while the Nazis relied on the gestapo, intrigue, concentration camps, ruthless brutality, quislings, tanks and bombers. The similarity of the two attempts by two organisations, made up of tyrants seeking power and wealth, at the expense of the liberty and happiness of their victims, is obvious and there is nothing to choose between them.

With this in our minds we can now go forward and understand better the story which is to follow. So we shall now take up the tale of mankind's ignorance and folly which, in the last chapter, had brought us to that great event in history, the collapse of the Roman Empire.

(3) EUROPE BEFORE AND AFTER THE FALL OF THE ROMAN EMPIRE.

To understand the immediate cause which brought about the fall of the Roman Empire we must go back some years to Central Asia, whence a wild Mongolian people started on their rough-haired horses to make their way into south-eastern Europe. Over the wide rolling steppes they came, slaying, pillaging and leaving behind them only a desert. Before them fled the Goths, who found their way into Britain, Gaul, Spain, Africa and Italy, the first bastion of the Empire to be pierced being Transylvania which, in after years, became part of the country now known as Rumania.

These merciless invaders were the Huns, and the Visigoths, who then inhabited Transylvania, appealed to Rome for shelter and protection. Eighty thousand Visigoths were generously given permission in 376 to cross the Danube, hitherto considered the one safe and formidable barrier against them, and settle in Thrace within the Empire. The arrangement was not a success, in fact it turned out to be a calamity, as it was the first breach in the Empire's line of defence. The Visigoths did not mix well with their new neighbours, who distrusted them and resented their presence, the land not being sufficient to support such an addition to the population. Poverty produced discontent, which developed into violence, to end in the newcomers, at Adrianople in 378, attacking those who had befriended them. Here these ruthless but valiant horsemen defeated the Roman foot soldiers, and established for the next thousand years the value of cavalry in battle.

Valens, the Emperor, was slain in this battle, and Theodosius, about whom we have already read, came forward to deal with a dangerous situation. Skilfully he changed the Visigoths from enemies into allies of the Empire, and satisfied them with a grant of imperial territory which provided them with their needs. If only the Gothic character had been different, and the successors of Theodosius had been wise and resolute, the safety of the Empire might have been secured by the Goths becoming incorporated within its structure. Unfortunately his death in 395 altered everything, as then the Empire fell into the hands of his two weak sons. Arcadius became emperor of the east and Honorius of the west, and with them the mighty Empire crumpled into decay.

The Visigoths, like their German descendants of the present day, were little better than savages, and could understand nothing but force. No partnership with them was possible, and they immediately took advantage of the weakness apparent in Constantinople and Rome to renew their aggression. Alaric I, a Christian in religion and a fiend in action, was elected King of the Visigoths. Nothing was too degraded for him to undertake, blackmail and dishonesty being his policy in peace, while in war it was massacre and plunder. He held Athens up to ransom, pillaged Corinth and Sparta, ravaged Greece, besieged Rome three times, finally to rob it and hand it over to his Christian barbarians to do with as they pleased. Fifteen hundred years later the present-day German Alarics followed faithfully in the footsteps of their ignoble ancestor. Time has not civilised them, and they are as much barbarians and outlaws today as they were then.

The sacking of Rome was only an incident in the great events which followed the breakdown of imperial authority. Everywhere the Roman legions were on the defensive, and the frontier garrisons were depleted to ward off attacks from all sides. Gaul was overrun by the Germanic Vandals, another tribe which had been converted to Christianity, and, after three years of mercilessly massacring and plundering the Pagan Kelts, they crossed the Pyrenees into Spain.

Meantime the Roman garrison in Britain had been evacuated, the country being left to the mercy of the Picts, Scots and the Saxons from overseas. Then followed the invasion of Gaul by other Germanic tribes, the Franks, the Alemanni, the Burgundians, and finally the Visigoths, the Gothic kingdom, at its height, extending from the Atlantic coast of Spain over the southern half of Gaul and what is now Austria, Italy and Sicily. The Burgundians had established a kingdom on either side of the Rhone, the Franks dominated all northern France to beyond the Rhine, the Vandals controlled Sardinia, Corsica and what is now Algiers and Tunis, the once mighty Roman Empire having shrunk by A.D. 500 to what we today call the Balkans, Turkey, Syria, Palestine and Egypt.

Very little is known of the early history of these Germanic tribes. They originally came from Central Asia, and, after emigrating west, settled in what is now Norway, Sweden and Denmark. Here they multiplied rapidly, a feature of the Germanic race, and overflowed into what is now Germany until they reached the Rhine, the Danube and the Black Sea, where they were held by the Roman legions. When they come into history the Goths are settled along the Danube, and the Franks and Saxons on the east bank of the Rhine, which separated them from the Kelts in Gaul who had come from the same part of Central Asia at an earlier date.

Before the civilising influence of Rome penetrated into the heart of Europe all these people, both in manners and custom, resembled the Red Indians of North America. They lived in round wigwams, a hole in the top permitting smoke from a ground fire to escape. Their peace-time occupations were hunting and stealing, their pleasures being heavy drinking and gambling, the women doing all the drudgery, bringing in the firewood, attending to their cultivated plots and the feeding of the cattle and pigs. The first trace of civilisation came to these people from the Phoenicians, later from the Greeks, and lastly from the Romans, the latter building their military roads in Gaul by the side of which they placed their colonies. Schools were opened in Gaul, and Roman manners, customs and mode of dress introduced amongst the Kelts.

In a few generations the savage Kelts had become respectable Roman citizens, and on the banks of the Seine and Rhone arose great cities watered by aqueducts, their streets being bordered by gardens, libraries, temples and schools. Beyond the Rhine the German tribes remained barbarians, often crossing the river to raid the fair land we now call France. Then the frontier was guarded by a chain of camps, and the poorly armed Germans, with only spears and wooden weapons, were driven back by the steel-clad and well-disciplined Roman legions. When the frontier defences broke down, and Rome fell, all this changed, and Gaul, with its culture and wealth, became a fruitful field for the plundering Germans, who played havoc with the civilisation built up by the Romans.

All these different Germanic tribes were classified by the Greeks and Romans as barbarians, though the Greeks, Romans, Kelts and Germans came originally from the same Aryan breeding-ground in Central Asia. Those who became Greeks and Romans came first, the former to be civilised by the Babylonians and Egyptians, and centuries later to pass their culture on to the Romans. The efforts of Ulfila (310–380), a Cappadocian missionary, first brought to the Visigoths, who were a branch of the Gothic people, a knowledge of Christ, his missionary zeal finally converting the Ostrogoths and the Vandals. He translated the Bible into their language, and Jehovah became their Lord of Hosts, all their atrocities from now onwards being justified by his instructions to the Hebrews. To the Pope at Rome they looked for religious guidance, to them Rome was a holy city, and, when the Visigoths sacked it, the authority of His Holiness was never questioned, the churches being left undamaged. Thus, these savages, fortified by the Christian faith, destroyed Roman civilisation, and prepared the way for Christian civilisation to spread over all Europe.

Though Rome, from now onwards, was the centre of ecclesiastical authority, Constantinople continued as the seat of secular government. Here lived the Emperor, and from this city, with its ideal situation, he ruled what remained of the old Roman Empire. A glance at the map will indicate the wisdom of Constantine in choosing such a strong bastion for his seat of government, as north, south, east and west could easily be reached by sea. Until the airplane came into use, travel by ship was by far the simplest means of long-distance passage.

The collapse of the Roman Empire was like the bursting of a dam. Slowly at first the barbaric stream poured through, to become a torrent carrying all before it, and when the flood had subsided the face of Europe was entirely changed. During the 5th century, after this great upheaval had taken place, the Franks, Germans, Visigoths, Ostrogoths, Lombards, Slavs, Burgundians, Huns, Alans, Jutes and Suevi had settled themselves amongst the Kelts and other Aryan races in this fashion.

The Angles, Saxons and Jutes were in eastern Britain, having pushed the Britons to the west and over into Brittany, but they never advanced far enough north to affect the Picts in Scotland. The Scots, who were later to invade Scotland, were left undisturbed in Ireland. In Portugal were the Suevi, in Spain the Goths, and in what is now France, Belgium and the Rhineland were the Franks. The Burgundians occupied the valley of the Rhone, the Goths were in Italy, Sicily and the eastern coast of the Adriatic, the Lombards in what is now eastern Germany, to settle finally in Lombardy. The Saxons were in Holland as well as eastwards to the Elbe, the Jutes in Denmark, and the Slavs farther east in what is now called Russia, some of whom pushed westwards into what we now call Yugoslavia. Bohemia and

Moravia were populated by the people now called Czechs, the Huns were in central Europe, and what remained of the Vandals were in North Africa.

Out of this conglomeration of various races has developed the different nations of Europe, whose frontiers have swayed backwards and forwards, as one or the other obtained ascendancy. There has been no settled development anywhere, as Europe since then has been perpetually in a state of flux, with armies marching backwards and forwards, destroying, plundering and causing misery and suffering.

Attila, the Hun, was the first to appear for the purpose of conquering and consolidating this mass of mixed humanity. He established his seat of government east of the Danube, and, at the height of his power, ruled for nineteen years (435–454) from the Rhine to Central Asia. His capital consisted of a great camp of wooden huts and tents protected by stockades, and only one building, a Roman bath, was made of stone. In 451 he declared war on the old Western Empire and invaded Gaul, sacking most of the towns as far south as Orleans. At Troyes he was defeated by a combined force of Romans, Franks and Visigoths, the battlefield being strewn with over 150,000 men killed on both sides. This was one of the decisive battles in history, as it saved Europe from the Huns who, it will be remembered, were a Mongolian race.

This defeat, however, did not end his aggression, as he then turned south and overran northern Italy, burning and pillaging wherever he went. Attila died in 453, leaving his tribe such a name for everything that was evil that the Kaiser, William of Germany, in 1900 adopted it as a symbol of ferocity, to encourage his troops to ravage and plunder the Chinese during the time they were in China helping to quell the Boxer rising. "Give no quarter," said this very orthodox Christian ruler who was inspired in his savagery by his daily reading of *The Holy Bible.* "Take no prisoners. Kill them when they fall into your hands, even as a thousand years ago the Huns, under their King Attila, made such a name for themselves as still resounds in terror, in legend and fable. So make the name of German resound through Chinese history a thousand years from now."

This command his brutal subjects faithfully obeyed, not only then but also in the wars the Germans brought on Europe and the world in after years. By their own ruler these warlike people have thus been branded with the vile name of Hun, which it will take generations of decent behaviour to live down. From the 5th century onwards we hear nothing more of the Huns in history, as they merged into the surrounding populations, and, if the Germans had not taken the name, they would have been remembered only as one of the smears across the path of progress, and nothing more.

Rome now lay helpless before the barbarians, and deprived of her principal source of food because the Vandals were now in North Africa, which had been her granary. Serious as this loss was to her, further humiliation was still to come, as Genseric, the first of the Vandal kings of North Africa, entered the Tiber in 455 with a fleet of ships, and landed an army which plundered the city more thoroughly than ever before.

These Vandals were no better than savages,

destroying everything and constructing nothing, one hundred years of their rule in civilised and prosperous North Africa being a record of havoc and destruction. The consequences were far-reaching, as, to meet the menace of this pirate state so close to Italy, the Roman legions were withdrawn from Britain and Gaul, after which followed chaos, disorder, and the Saxon invasion of Britain.

Ravenna in Italy still housed someone who called himself Emperor of the Western Empire, but the power rested with the leaders of the barbarian invaders. Their chief, Orestes, made his son emperor, but both were soon killed. Then a chieftain named Odoacer, who could have made himself emperor, preferred to send the imperial crown, purple robe and other insignia of office to the Emperor at Constantinople with the intimation that Italy had no further use for an imperial ruler. This happened in 476, and marks the end of the Roman Empire in the west, its place being taken by the Christian Church, whose empire expanded just as the numerous barbarian tribes submitted to its authority. These, from now onwards, coalesced amongst themselves to form ultimately the nations which now constitute the continent of Europe.

There was now no emperor in Rome, and in 489 Theodoric I established himself at Ravenna as the first of a line of Gothic kings. Here for thirty-seven years he worked to unite Gothic strength with Roman culture. His rule extended from the Alps in the north to Sicily in the south, and eastwards to what is now Yugoslavia, though he acknowledged himself as nominally subject to Constantinople. All that was now left to the Emperor at Constantinople was what is today called Greece, Bulgaria, Turkey, Syria, Palestine, Egypt and Cyrenaica, in fact nothing more than the stump of the old empire of Alexander. That was all that remained of the old Roman Empire, as nowhere else did the Emperor wield any authority, the division between the western and eastern empires being accentuated by the fact that in those lands ruled from Constantinople the people spoke Greek, while where Ravenna ruled they spoke Latin.

Elsewhere language was separating the people into new nations. In Gaul the Franks were mixing their own tongue with Latin to produce French, and in Spain and Portugal the old Latin was changing into what became Spanish and Portuguese. Even in Italy the Latin language gradually changed until it became Italian, though it remains the nearest approach to the old Roman form of speech. All these languages, however, maintained the Latin roots, and, in consequence, they differ widely from German, which was quite uninfluenced by either Latin or Greek, whose culture never reached so far north.

The roots of the German language are to be found in the other Nordic languages, which were likewise unaffected by either Greece or Rome, and the same is true of the old Slavonic languages, which even spread down to the Balkans. The Magyar invasion of Europe, in 900, introduced the Turko-Finnish language now spoken in Hungary and Finland, but Rumania kept its Roman name and form of speech. English grew out of a mixture of old French and old German, which accounts for the similarity of so many of its words to Latin and present-day French and German.

Language, as well as distance, separate people and

keep the nations from understanding one another. A time must surely come when everyone will be taught at school, not only their own language but one common to all, such as Esperanto, a language devoid of all unnecessary grammar. When we are intelligent enough to get thus far, then, as the result of the increased speed of travel and the consequent reduction of distance, the inhabitants of this earth will get to know one another better, and realise that it was only ignorance which made the different nations misunderstand each other.

Moreover, when the people of Europe get to know one another better, they will the more readily agree to a common form of federal government, and police force, to keep order and peace in this hitherto distracted part of the world's surface. Then we may see the sun of peace arise to shine over the United States of Europe, each one separate in the administration of its own affairs, but united in the common purpose of maintaining peace and order over the entire continent.

This great ideal, which has been the aim of many, has been for ever frustrated by evil-minded ambitious men, who, seeking power, besides increased wealth and glory, set about to force the people into one unified subject confederation, a thing which could never be permanent. We shall be reading of these various attempts which were never successful, as it is now quite obvious that different nationalities will not be forced, though they may some day be persuaded, to come together. Scotland and England came together by reason and not by force, after repeated attempts with force had failed. Britain could never reason the Irish into a common partnership, so force was used, with disastrous results.   These are only two examples, one how to accomplish unity, the other how not to do so, and Europe provides many others throughout the Christian era.

Augustine planned the unification of the entire known world, whose inhabitants were to submit to the domination of the Pope at Rome, but he made the mistake of advocating that if persuasion failed, force must then be applied.   In his book, already mentioned, *The City of God*, he envisaged the world as a kind of theological Kingdom of Heaven, "a spiritual society of the predestined faithful", which was to be brought about by political means.   The Church was to rule the world, and all nations were to be its subjects. The Pope was to be the divine ruler and the Nicene Creed was to be the common belief of all, His Holiness being given complete power over his subjects, from whom he was to receive abject and complete obedience.

From now onwards until the Reformation we shall find this scheme everywhere in practice, or attempted, throughout those lands which remained faithful to the Christian religion.   Just as the barbarians, living out in the blue, were conquered by the legions doing the bidding of both Pope and Emperor they either accepted Christianity or were massacred, until gradually all Europe became Christian and recognised the Pope as the over-lord of their kings and chiefs.   With each fresh conquest the power of the Pope grew, until he became to everyone the Chief Priest, Judge and Divine Monarch of all the lands which comprised the Roman Empire, besides those barbarian countries Rome failed to conquer, but which were subdued by

Christian soldiers under the leadership of Christian rulers.

While the Church was tightening its grip on everyone from prince to peasant, a very old idea entered the mind of a young man of good social position. His name was Benedict, and he was born in Italy in 480. Like Buddha he renounced the world, but unlike him he practised torment on his body for the salvation of his soul. Moreover he renounced all learning, preferring, as Pope Gregory said in praise of him, to be "knowingly ignorant and unlearned". Benedict retired to a cave in a gorge of the River Anio, some fifty miles from Rome, and here he lived for three years clothed in a hair shirt. In those days, to do such a thing made the people consider Benedict a holy man, the consequence being that as his fame spread he gathered around him more and more disciples.

From this humble origin we can trace the monastic mode of life being applied to the Western world, a common enough affair in the East but quite new to the West. In India the Buddhists had adopted it a thousand years earlier, and the Theraputae of Egypt had copied it, the Essenes of Palestine being their offshoot. From this source Benedict drew his inspiration, to such effect that before many years had passed he was no longer torturing his body but controlling twelve monasteries. Here flocked the young men who put contemplation before fighting, and they were the forerunners of those who, many centuries later, were to revive the learning now denounced by the Church.

This new effort was a very different affair from the free and liberal-minded form of education which had been carried on in Greece for eight hundred years and in Rome for four hundred years, but at least it was the best that could be done under the changed circumstances. Mixed up as it was with the superstitions of the time we find a real attempt at something constructive, and for the betterment of humanity. Benedict now denounced self-torture and put hard work in its place, but more than this was needed to raise the inmates above the common herd, and fit them to take their place as the forerunners of our present-day doctors and schoolmasters.

Fortunately Cassiodorus (490–585) saw what was needed, and can rightly be claimed as the first man in Christendom to appreciate the value of knowledge. He was a Syrian of good family, and had served the Gothic kings in an official capacity, but, after their overthrow, he took refuge from the Lombards in a monastery which he founded on his own estate. Here he set about the re-lighting of the lamp of learning by collecting, with the help of his followers, all the ancient literature he could find which the Church had not destroyed. Greatly concerned as he was at the entire absence everywhere of education, he produced a series of school books on the arts, and he himself wrote a history of the Gothic kings. He, moreover, employed his fellow monks in copying old manuscripts, making sun-dials, water clocks, and other contrivances, all of which seem commonplace enough to us nowadays, but in those days of mental darkness they were novelties indeed.

Such then is the story of monastic life coming to Europe. Until they became corrupt the monks did what little healing and teaching they could, but it was very slight, as few people anywhere thought of anything but husbandry, war and superstition. Nevertheless the monasteries were the only instruments in the Dark Ages to maintain even a semblance of social order, and, as the centuries passed, they increased in numbers and influence.

They were the only centres of light in a dark Western world, as they raised the standard of cultivation and preserved a simple kind of elementary education amongst the few who gathered within their walls. They encouraged the useful arts, collected and copied theological books, and for eight centuries were the only libraries in Europe. Out of them evolved the theological universities of the Middle Ages, but, until this development occurred, many of the priests were so ignorant that they could not even read the Scriptures or their service liturgy.

It was not until the 15th century that the Greek and Latin classics obtained a free circulation. This came about prior to the capture of Constantinople by the Turks, when much literature, for the sake of safety, found its way to Venice, and, for the first time in a thousand years saw the light of day. This fortunate event coincided with the invention of printing following the discovery of the way to make paper, all three happenings being the cause which in the course of time defeated the Church's settled policy to keep the people ignorant.

Until this happened, and for a thousand years, it ruled the people by fear, the fear of punishment here and hereafter, and it ruthlessly used its most potent weapon, that of excommunication, to have its decisions obeyed. To be excommunicated meant that one was not safe, as to kill one who was so cursed was not considered to be murder, the victim moreover being consigned to everlasting torment in hell, and this fear kept kings, nobles and peasants in subjection.

Whatever is based on force or fraud must fail in the end, and the first to awaken the Church from its fantastic dream of world domination was a desert merchant who was born in 570, in far-off Arabia, and given the name of Mahomet. Before, however, we come to this great event in history other things have been happening elsewhere, which we must consider in their correct chronological order.

(4) The Middle East after the Collapse of the Roman Empire.

It will be remembered that Chapter VII closed with the Empire divided between the two sons of Theodosius. Arcadius reigned in Constantinople and Honorius ruled from Ravenna, a town in Italy placed about sixty miles south of Venice, near the Adriatic coast, and situated amongst dreary marshes and fever-haunted swamps. Such an unenviable situation was chosen because Rome was then considered to be too difficult to defend from the north and from the sea, and this foresight was justified when, ten years later (410), it fell to the Visigoths.

The warrior responsible for the fall of the once powerful Roman Empire was the barbarian leader Alaric I, the most outstanding figure in all Gothic history. As told in the previous section, he had great ambitions, and was an aggressive plunderer besides being a very devout Christian. Prior to his capture of Rome he was foiled in an attempt to take Constantinople, but, after devastating Greece, he turned his attention to Italy. Honorius, the Emperor, jealous of his able general Stilicho, had him murdered, a deed which so angered the army that it went over to Alaric, who marched on Rome against little opposition. Thus Rome fell, and we must now concentrate our attention on Constantinople to learn the history of what remained of the once invincible empire.

Arcadius, the Emperor of the east, was succeeded by men of no outstanding merit, though mention should be made of the Emperor Leo I (457–474), called "the butcher" by the Arians. He was the first potentate to be crowned and blessed by a Christian priest, an event which did not improve his morals, as he slaughtered the heretics without mercy, murdered his sons, and also the man responsible for his reaching the throne. The court history of these days was painfully saturated with intrigue and vice of all kinds, morality and culture being almost unknown, and education a thing of the past.

With this evil background in mind, we shall now focus our attention on one of the most famous Christian emperors to sit on the throne of the much reduced Roman Empire. Justinian I (527–565), a native of Illyria (now Albania) of obscure origin, became emperor in 527, and reigned for thirty-eight years, during which time Christianity completed its work of exterminating Philosophy, and the Western world entered what we call the Dark Ages. He was ambitious and capable, his wife Theodora, a nymphomaniac, formerly a stage dancer and prostitute, round whom was woven numerous scandals, being equally so.

He and she reigned jointly, and they set about restoring the ancient glory of the Empire by turning out the Vandals from North Africa and the Goths from Sicily and Italy. They were both devout Christians, the perpetrators of many murders, the inflicters of much torture, excessively cruel and vicious, and sincere believers in the Nicene Creed, the bulwark of the faith. Eventually they built so many fine churches and buildings that the State became impoverished. The Church of Saint Sophia, built by Constantine, had been twice destroyed by fire during heresy riots, and the piety of Justinian prompted him to erect the present noble edifice which is now a mosque.

On the other hand Justinian closed the schools at Athens, which had flourished for a thousand years and had given so many sages and heroes to mankind. This once famous city was now overshadowed by a cloud of mental darkness, and barbarism was replacing its former glory. By imperial edict of 529 all schools and libraries throughout the Empire were closed, and towns once famous were forgotten, or rotted in decay, while fifty once splendid cities became no better than villages. Constantinople was suffering from dreadful corruption, and there, each day, terrible atrocities were committed, while Alexandria, a city so renowned under the Ptolemies for the beams of intellectual light it had cast on all the civilised world, was mentally dead, its once progressive outlook having been smothered by the deadly hand of Christian ignorance.

Learning, culture and social progress had now ceased to interest Christian rulers, who were much more concerned with the question of whether the divine and human natures of Jesus co-existed. The Council of Chalcedon (451) had decided that they did, and this meant that all who thought differently were heretics and marked down for slaughter. Besides these heretics there still survived the Spiritualists in Phrygia (now central Turkey), the descendants of the Apostolic Church, while in Constantinople and elsewhere there were many Arians and numerous Pagans who still retained their old beliefs. All these were doomed to suffer extermination, besides the Jews and other sects, including the Samaritans of Palestine, who were looked upon with hatred because of their unorthodox beliefs. All this great multitude the Church decided either to convert or exterminate, some being given three months in which to accept the blood-stained Nicene Creed and the Pauline doctrines elaborated by Jerome and Augustine, while others were put to the sword without delay.

During this time the Emperor Justinian was assiduous in holding vigils and fasts, besides spending much time in prayer, and the clergy were rivalling the Court with their wealth and magnificence secured from the gold, silver and treasure they had stolen from the Pagans. Elsewhere the imperial troops, under the guidance of priests, and aided by the Inquisitors of the Faith, were passing from one district to another torturing, massacring and banishing all those the priestly inquisitors decided were unorthodox. One hundred thousand Samaritans were either slain or sold as slaves to Persia or India and their land laid waste, while 70,000 Pagans in Asia Minor were either converted or exterminated, the same process going on elsewhere. The consequent hatred of the people of the Middle East towards the Christians became so bitter that when Mahomet commenced his crusade the Egyptians, Syrians, Samaritans and people of other nationalities became his followers, and cast off the religion under which they had been treated so cruelly.

The violence of the Christians was so savage that they scourged Procopius, the historian, for writing that "man, ignorant of his own nature, should not presume to scrutinise the nature of his God". Moreover a council of priests assembled to order the exhumation of the bones, and declare the damnation of the soul of the learned and humane Origen (whose body had been in the grave for the past three hundred years) because his Christianity did not now conform to the orthodox faith. The souls of Plato, Pythagoras, and all philosophers in general, both dead and alive, were likewise consigned to hell for all eternity, as a warning to those who dared to study philosophy instead of theology. Christendom was then a vast lunatic asylum, reason was dethroned, and insanity had full play to practise its abominations on humanity.

Thus was carried on the process of extermination of all heretics, one which had started in the reign of Constantine, was continued throughout the time of Saint Augustine to the period we are now considering, and was to last until the 19th century, a term of fifteen hundred years. By these barbarous methods the old Roman Empire was eventually brought to the knowledge of Christ, to be followed by all Europe and America, the same intolerance, cruelty and savagery being always noticeable from those early days right up to within our own times.

In this way Christian civilisation was established

and maintained, to preserve which our clergy, churchmen and politicians tell us we fought the last war with Germany. Such is the prevailing ignorance that the people believe this tale, because they have been taught the exact opposite to what is true. During its long span of tyrannical rule, the Church has suppressed all history which exposed its evil record, and, instead of recording the truth, it has manufactured numerous fables about early Christian martyrs, most of which are now known to be false, or grossly exaggerated and embellished.

Truly the Christian Church has outdistanced the Nazis every time in crime and fraud, and, while they had only some eleven years of gangsterdom, the Church of Christ flourished on violence down the ages, perpetrating its bloody crimes in the name of the Holy Trinity. In its zeal to establish the belief in the idea that Jesus was the Christ, and one of three gods, all equal in power and majesty, it caused the death and suffering of untold millions throughout the Christian era, but, by the way Christians speak and write, one would think that it has always been as gentle as a lamb, and as stainless as a dove in carrying to mankind a divine message of peace and goodwill.

Besides acting for the priests as the hammer to flatten out heresy on the anvil of the Church, Justinian had vast political ambitions, and for a time it seemed as if he would win back a large part of the old empire. His troops were under the command of Belisarius, one of the world's most famous soldiers, who, with comparatively few men but by rapid movements, conquered wherever he went. Supplied by the wealth which was pouring into Constantinople from the confiscated property of the heretics in his Asiatic provinces, his armies, with great speed, vanquished the Vandals in North Africa so thoroughly that from this time forward these human locusts pass out of history. Then followed a struggle for twenty-eight years to recover Italy from the Gothic invaders. First Sicily in 535, then southern Italy, and lastly Rome and Ravenna, fell to the Emperor's brilliantly led armies, and Belisarius returned to Constantinople in triumph, the Gothic fortunes being by now considered hopeless.

Justinian, by these victories, raised the imperial throne to the level it once occupied in Rome, but his building operations, and an expensive war with Persia, largely depleted his treasury. His financial difficulties, combined with famine, pestilence, crushing taxation, general misery and discontent in Italy, gave the Gothic power a chance of revival, and this was taken advantage of by Totila, who has come down to us as "a soldier of real power and a Christian of sincere piety", but who in reality was a cruel savage whose record is one of merciless devastation.

After severe fighting Totila was defeated and died of wounds, and some years later, in 553, the Goths left Italy, never to return. Following the deaths of Justinian, Theodora and Belisarius, the briefly revived empire collapsed, and all that remained of their conquests was Ravenna, Rome, southern Italy and North Africa, the rest of Italy being occupied by the Lombards, who found it a plague-ridden and famished land.

Besides his extensive building of churches, Justinian's other constructive effort was the conclusion of the work of codifying the laws of Rome, a splendid work which had been begun centuries earlier, to be carried on by leading Roman lawyers, and now at last it had reached its end. Gradually Roman law appealed to the other Western nations, who adopted it as the basis of their legislation, but unfortunately it included the section in the Theodosian Code which defined heretics as traitors against God and the State, and this gave the Church a powerful weapon in its war against all unbelievers.

We remember how this legislation became part of Roman law under the Christian emperor Theodosius, who was under the influence of Ambrose, Bishop of Milan, the Himmler of the Christian Church, a story already told, and now we notice the effect of this fierce enactment. Every country, as it became Christian, adopted the Theodosian law against heretics, and made it imperative for every Pagan, Jew or Christian heretic to conform to the creeds and doctrines of the Christian Church or suffer banishment, if he were fortunate enough to escape torture, imprisonment and death as a traitor to God and his country. Justinian tightened up still further this law against heretics, who were treated as outcasts, and the belief in the Nicene Creed became the law of his empire, an enactment which was copied by every other land as it became Christian, and so made possible the Holy Inquisition.

Here we are presented with an impressive picture of both ignorance and knowledge, of wisdom and folly, of good and evil, and it is one which faces us in every age and phase of history. Gradually, by using his reason, man had built up a code of laws and ethics which had by now reached an impressive stage. First came the jungle law that might was right, then came taboos and traditions that some things were right to do and others wrong. When writing was discovered these were tabulated to become the laws of Hammurabi, which, in turn, laid the basis for the Greek laws of Solon, and then the Romans took the idea of government one step further. Their knowledge and wisdom established law and order, justice and liberty, but everything changed for the worse with the coming of Christianity.

Disbelief in the Holy Trinity and the Nicene Creed became a civil offence; a mystical theological puzzle was made the test of a good Christian and a loyal subject, a reactionary development so different from the tolerance of the Pagan Romans in the days of the Empire, who only demanded the vague recognition of the divinity of the Emperor, after which everyone could believe what he pleased. So Justinian, by his legal code, did not confer a blessing on mankind, and wasted his substance on war and the building of churches. How much better it would have been if he had built for his people good sanitary houses, schools, hospitals, and halls for their amusement, thus to increase knowledge, wisdom, home comforts, health and happiness, but such ideas only developed when the curse of Christian ignorance was lightened in our own times, to the blessing of everyone.

Both his wars and church-building were for his own glorification, but his vast building programme did not end with him, as a mania developed throughout Christendom to build magnificent edifices for worship, an effort which consumed wealth and labour that should have been devoted to more useful purposes. These priceless cathedrals were surrounded by stinking hovels, housing illiterate, filthy, miserable, plague-ridden creatures, crawling with vermin, too poor to keep fit, too miserable to be happy, too ignorant to know better than obey the priests, who took all they could get in exchange for absolving them from the consequences hereafter of their wickedness. Europe was then, and for many centuries to come, one immense slum, and the people physically, mentally and morally were at a correspondingly low level.

How the curse of ignorance for ever follows the race, as the people themselves were to blame for being down-trodden, poor and miserable, the State and the Church taking conditions as they found them, and acting accordingly. We have a good example in our own times of how the people have their own welfare in their hands when we consider, for instance, the difference between the present-day Scottish and the Irish Roman Catholics. The former will not allow themselves to be priest-ridden to the extent that prevails elsewhere, and consequently they live better and fuller lives than their Irish co-religionists who do. The Scots, whether Protestant or Roman Catholic, are more independent, self-reliant and intelligent, and this reacts on their attitude to authority.

Here and now is the time to be healthy, comfortable and happy, and, if we are, the more we will develop, and so better fit ourselves for the next order of existence, which we enter just as naturally as we entered this one, without the need of priests, creeds or any other kind of passport.

The next outstanding character to attract attention is Heraclius (610–642) who, in the year 610, became

Emperor of the Eastern Empire. He proved himself to be one of the most successful soldiers of the imperial line, defeating the Persians, who, by entering Syria and Palestine, threatened Constantinople. In a brilliant campaign he drove them out and penetrated as far east as Nineveh, where peace terms were arranged. In later years, when past his best and suffering from dropsy, with his empire exhausted by the long Persian war, he lost what he had won to the Moslems, but this story will be told later on. His victory over the Persians was doubly welcome to the Christians, because he recovered that ancient relic, the Cross of Jesus, so often lost in the past, to be always conveniently discovered when the Christians possessed Jerusalem.

Heraclius returned the relic with much pomp and ceremony to Jerusalem, while what is called the true Cross was reposing in Rome, having been brought there from Palestine by Helena the mother of Constantine. The faithful, who were always receiving parts of the relic, did not worry over such a trifling matter as two such crosses being in existence, as they accepted the only possible explanation: that the wood possessed such a marvellous secret power of reproduction that it was for ever giving off new wood as the old was withdrawn. On such stories, and on other equally absurd legends and beliefs, the priests fed the people, but how could Europe, with this mentality, be other than poor and miserable? Superstition was crowned, and knowledge dethroned everywhere, while priests and relics took the place of doctors and medicine, legends always being accepted in place of **facts.**

It will be remembered how the Romans always found the Persians a thorn in their side, and how all their efforts to conquer them completely failed. The Persian Empire retained its vitality under the Arsacid dynasty of Parthian kings (250 B.C.–A.D. 228), to be followed by the Sassanid dynasty, and, as Rome grew weaker, it grew stronger. Like Constantine, who made use of Christianity to consolidate his empire, so Arsaces adopted the old Persian religion of Zoroaster for the same reason, making it the state religion, which had no serious rival until the coming of Christianity, when converts were bitterly persecuted because they would not recognise the divinity of the King. Eastern and western Christians grew more and more diverse in their beliefs, so much so that in 483 the Christians of Asia split off from the Church of Rome, to establish the Nestorian Church. Only then did they obtain freedom of worship in Persia, as the Persian monarch now considered that the divine Pope had ceased to receive the loyalty which he, as divine monarch, should receive from his Christian subjects.

Under Chosroes I (531–579) the Persian Empire was extended southwards to Arabia, and, northwards into western Turkestan, his aggressive methods bringing him into conflict with Justinian. Chosroes, for those days, can be considered an enlightened ruler, as he welcomed those oppressed in Christian countries. Because of this the schoolmasters, who were banished from Greece when Justinian closed the schools of Athens, found refuge at his Court. After his war with Justinian he, moreover, made it a condition of the Armistice that they be allowed to return to their native land and not be persecuted or punished for their philosophical beliefs. His successor Hormizd (579–590) was equally enlightened, religious toleration, impartial justice, and care of his troops being a feature of his reign, which throughout was one succession of wars and conflicts.

Chosroes II (590–628), who succeeded, was the Persian monarch who took the Cross from Jerusalem, and was later defeated by Heraclius. During his wars with the Eastern Empire he nearly captured Constantinople on three occasions, and succeeded in capturing Antioch, Damascus and Jerusalem. Only after a struggle of eighteen years was he conquered, during which time he had penetrated as far south as Egypt. He was, however, defeated at Nineveh in 627, but both sides were so exhausted that the Persians, who relinquished their conquests, were able to retire within their old boundaries, which then extended as far south as the Euphrates. Here in Mesopotamia, in spite of wars, misrule and corrupt government, the country supported a large population. Commerce and agriculture flourished, architecture was of a high order, and the dykes, which brought the life-giving waters to the land, were in good repair. This state of affairs continued until the 13th century, when the Mongol nomads destroyed this old irrigation system and the ancient civilisation, a tragic event in the story of the folly and ignorance of man which will be told when the time comes.

The prosperity in the east was in strange contrast to that prevailing in the west. The lands surrounding the eastern Mediterranean were prosperous, and the coast was studded with large wealthy cosmopolitan cities. Syria contained large and prosperous towns, such as Antioch, Apamea, Homs and Palmyra, which were the clearing centres of the trade between the east and the west. Baalbek, where is situated the famous temple of Jupiter, was then at the height of its glory. Good roads and great aqueducts were to be found running through these parts, and today anyone who visits Syria, Galilee and Mesopotamia is impressed by the ruins of this old Greek civilisation, rich in culture and beauty. In Mesopotamia, and farther north in Persia, flourished the great cities of Ctesiphon (near Baghdad), Seleucia, Hatra, Nisibin, Harran and hundreds more which are now forgotten. Greek was spoken in many of these, but their cultured citizens, who were fortunate to be outside the bounds of Christian civilisation, little realised the fate which was to befall their way of life in the years to come, or how Mesopotamia, with its enormous cereal wealth, was to become desert.

The East, of course, had a much older tradition than the West, as it had been civilised for thousands of years when the West was in a state of barbarism. Out of this Western primitive society Greece first of all emerged, then Carthage, and lastly Rome, but they were all newcomers compared with India, China, Egypt and the valleys of the Euphrates and Tigris. When Rome collapsed the younger civilisations perished, but the old remained, little affected by what had taken place in the West, and, if this be true of the Middle East, it was equally true of India and China, an interesting fact to remember being that Turkestan and Afghanistan had then a much higher civilisation than had England and France.

Farther east in Central Asia progress can be

recorded in literature and the arts, while Europe was living through the Dark Ages. True, nomadic invasions occurred, but towns and villages on the trade routes were prosperous, and from paintings discovered of this period the people dressed and lived much as did Europeans a thousand years later. They, however, have left only a small mark on history, as it was the Aryans of the West whose deeds and thoughts have been more amply recorded, as their geographical position in Europe enabled them eventually to dominate the greater part of the world. Most of our story now concerns this forceful race, but we must here break into their history to tell of the remarkable rise to power of quite another people, the descendants of those who first established civilisation.

CHAPTER IX.

MOSLEM CIVILISATION.
(A.D. 570–1939.)

Introduction. (1) *Mahomet Sets the Arab World Ablaze* (2) *The Rise and Fall of the Arabian Empire..* (3) *The Turks Become a Great Power.* (4) *India during Moslem Rule.* (5) *Moslem Spain Becomes a Beacon in Europe's Night.*

RELIGION and politics are the two subjects to which men and women devote most thought, apart from their own everyday occupations and home affairs. Religion has often been made use of by politicians, and politics by the religious minded, in order to advance their own interests, and this mixture of religion and politics was never more in evidence than in those early centuries of the Christian era.

The old Pagan religions, in all the lands surrounding the Mediterranean, were now passing into oblivion, all their main essentials being continued in Christianity, the Pantheon (the Temple of all the gods) in Rome being now used to house the images of the Christian gods and goddesses who had replaced their once Pagan rivals, the official dedication being performed by Pope Boniface IV (608–615) with much pomp and ceremony. In northern Europe the old beliefs still survived, as Charlemagne had not yet arrived on the scene to massacre their adherents into accepting the Christian faith. Apart from the Christians, the Jews retained their old confidence in Jehovah, and the belief that they were his chosen people, while in Mesopotamia, because of Persian influence, Zoroaster received the veneration of the people who had transferred their allegiance from Bel and the other gods of Babylon.

The belief in gods of various names waxes and wanes, as do the theological opinions surrounding them. The gods of one age become the bywords of the next. This fact emphasises the folly of ever taking seriously the theological dogmas of any religion, and yet millions of zealous believers have suffered and died rather than change their opinions on some theological question about which they, and the tyrants over them, differed.

How much more sensible it is to accept only those facts which come within the framework of natural religion. Nature's revelation, by means of psychic phenomena, requires no man-made theological beliefs which are produced for the purpose of dressing up and making mysterious a natural event, namely death and what follows hereafter. In this vital question many are interested, but their knowledge is limited because only the few have experienced the lifting of the veil which hangs between the two worlds. Once this is witnessed, in the presence of some highly developed medium, the driving force which produced every religion becomes clear as crystal, and we appreciate the powerful effect the men and women, who once lived on earth, have had on world events in consequence of what developed from their activities, namely religion.[1]

[1] In 1927 some Europeans living in Indo-China, mostly Government officials and their wives, met for the purpose of having séances in the presence of a medium. From this nucleus a new religion commenced which has now many churches, a priesthood and numerous adherents. This interesting modern religious development is fully recorded in *The Psychic Stream*.

Unfortunately, as we have discovered, religion departed from facts and evidence, and became, as the result of theological speculation, a matter of creeds and dogmas. Nevertheless the fact remains that however much natural religion has been distorted into supernatural religion,. natural religion still represents what the word means, a binding again, through mediumship, of the people of earth to the people of the etheric world. This, in early times, before priests and theologians came on the scene, was the only form of religion known to mankind.

In the previous chapter we read of how a new religion changed the history of Europe, and now we are about to learn how another brought about a tremendous convulsion in the Middle East, to reach as far east as India, but first of all let us picture the then religious setting so as better to appreciate what took place. So far we have, in earlier chapters, read of the religious opinions prevailing in India, China, Babylonia, Egypt, Palestine, Greece and Rome, but there is one important country which also played a powerful part in world religious history, namely Persia, whose people venerated Zoroaster. He ranks with Buddha as one of the world's greatest religious teachers, and is reputed to have laid the foundation of the widely renowned wisdom of the Magi, who were the custodians of all that pertains to mediumship and psychic knowledge, which in their days was known as the Wisdom of the East.

Zoroaster is supposed to have lived about three thousand years ago; some ancient authorities place him much earlier, but we know nothing about his life on earth. All we know about him is what was told by the priests in after years, of how the holy spirit, the "Vohu Mano", meaning the divine spirit, descended upon him in his thirtieth year, after which he went into the wilderness to be tempted by the spirit of evil, who offered him all the nations of the world if he would only renounce the worship of Ormuzd. Today we would say that this account of the descent of the holy spirit relates to the time when he developed into a medium, as then, in trance, he would be controlled by an other-world man, then called the Holy Spirit, to be used by him to speak to the people on earth. What this etheric man said through his medium Zoroaster we do not know, just as we are quite ignorant of what was said through Jesus in trance when he was controlled by the Holy Spirit. These words have not come down to us.

What Zoroaster is reported to have taught is contained in the *Zend Avesta*, and this briefly is that the god Ormuzd, the god of goodness, light and purity, was at constant war with the god of evil, Ahriman. To read these teachings, hopes and warnings is just like reading the Christian gospels, which latter just repeat what was said and believed a thousand years earlier.

Round these ideas developed a priesthood, temples, altars, sacred fire, sacrifice and the usual theological forms and ceremonies which go with priestcraft. The Parsees of India are the last remaining Zoro-astrians, their method of leaving the dead body in their Towers of Silence, to be eaten by vultures, being a well-known characteristic of their faith. The Zoro-astrians were originally monotheists like the Jews, and the worship of Ormuzd was the state religion of

Persia, whose chief priest came next to the divine king, the earthly representative of the god.

As Christianity was an off-shoot of Judaism, so likewise did Zoroastrianism send out a branch in the form of Mithraism, with Mithra as its Saviour-god and Ormuzd as the Father-god. It became a trinitarian religion, and its beliefs were in many ways like those adopted by Christianity. Mithraism spread rapidly in the centuries just before the Christian era, and in the 1st Christian century found its way to Rome, where it became very popular. It was a serious rival to Christianity, and was the state religion of Rome at the time when Constantine made his bargain with the Christian priests to put their religion in its place if they would settle on a creed.

The religious picture of these times would not, however, be complete without reference to Mani, the founder of Manichæism, who was the son of a family of good standing. Born in Media in A.D. 216, and educated at Ctesiphon, he lived his early life in a psychic atmosphere which had such an influence upon him that he felt compelled to proclaim that he had received a revelation from heaven. He accepted the ideas of the great religious teachers of the past, whose opinions he believed had been corrupted by the priests, and it now remained with him to set forward the gospel, as proclaimed by these ancient prophets, in the true light.

His theological views need not be considered here, but it is interesting to record that he went through Persia, Turkestan and into India, preaching his gospel, which spread everywhere with great rapidity, right into the heart of Christendom, to become the cause of many heresy hunts in the centuries to come. On the return of Mani to Ctesiphon he was arrested by the Zoroastrian priests and crucified, his followers being persecuted everywhere, but this did not prevent the spread of the new religion.

In the 6th century four religions, Christianity, Judaism, Zoroastrianism and Manichæism, were playing their part in the history of the Western hemisphere, but another new idea was gathering force which was soon to engulf a large part of the race, and take from the already established religions, as far east as India, a large number of their adherents. This new mental revolution, which had such far-reaching consequences, now becomes the theme of our story.

(1) Mahomet Sets the Arab World Ablaze.

The new religious storm began by a cloud of small dimensions, in the form of a child born in Mecca in the year 570, who was given the name of Mahomet. As a boy he tended sheep, becoming later a commercial traveller, and then the agent of a rich widow whom he married at the age of twenty-five. They lived in Mecca, had several children, and there was nothing eventful in their lives until he reached the age of forty.

Latent in this seemingly ordinary being simmered something deep down which then reached the surface, as he became convinced that God had given him a message to deliver to mankind. From what he wrote about himself he was evidently a medium, as he went into trance when he was controlled by a mind other than his own. He was clairaudient, but in those days of ignorance he mistook the other-world man who spoke to him for an angel, a messenger from God, who had delivered to him a message for him alone. Moreover, he was evidently clairvoyant, because he saw those who had passed through death to the etheric world. One especially he called by the name of Gabriel.

All this may well be true, as this claim to hear supernormal voices is made by some today, and it is also claimed for all who were the pivot round which every new religion first revolved, to enlarge in circumference as the years passed and miraculous and marvellous tales accumulated. Jesus, we are told, believed in one God only, his father in heaven, but that did not prevent him being eventually deified. In Mahomet's case the surroundings were different, his followers being ardent monotheists, a belief with a tradition going back for thousands of years to Abraham, whereas what became Christianity was nurtured and reared amongst the polytheistic beliefs of Greece and Egypt.

Mahomet, as the result of his psychic experiences, felt the call to purify the religion of his time, and abolish the superstition so prevalent in his midst. He proclaimed (1) the return to the simple faith of Abraham in one God, one which he declared had been polluted by Paganism, Judaism and Christianity, and (2) that he had been appointed by God to deliver this message, the acceptance of which would save the believer on the fateful Judgment Day, which followed the Resurrection Day, when the physical body and the etheric body would be reunited. In these early days he was just a successor of the Hebrew prophets, whose message was the same, each prophet interpreting his revelation as he thought right. Mediums are only transmitters, but, when they also become the interpreters, as did those who make up religious history, their message, whatever it was, becomes no more than their own personal opinions.

When Mahomet was proclaiming his faith to a hostile city, when his friends were few and his opponents many. his life was irreproachable. In looks he was tall and handsome, with flowing beard, his manner was frank and courteous. In character he was a good and kind husband and father, who lived simply, was temperate in his habits, kind and considerate to all, the poor receiving his charity. Then it was he wrote in the Koran: "Use no violence in religion." When, however, his power increased his virtue declined, and his zeal to put in place of the old beliefs that which he considered to be a true and purer faith, changed him into a tyrant who considered every unbeliever an enemy of God who must either be converted or perish. Then it was that he expunged from the Koran the instructions to use no violence in religion, and also other verses advocating toleration and indulgence.

At the outset, this story is a tale of two cities, Mecca and Medina,[1] situated in Arabia not far distant from the Red Sea, and at equal distance from Suez and Aden. Mecca contained the sanctuary of the Kaaba, meaning House of God, a small square temple, the corner stone of which was a meteorite. This stone was considered by the inhabitants to be sacred,

[1] Medina means the town of the prophet.

and the centre of the worship of Allah Taala, the Most High God. Here also had grown up a form of idolatry, the images and pictures of the Virgin Mary, Christ and other deities decorating its walls. The temple was under the control of a tribe of Bedouins, who made great profit from the multitudes who came to kiss the sacred stone and worship before the images. The people of Medina, farther north, greatly envied Mecca, because of the lucrative trade it enjoyed from this regular flow of pilgrims, and, in consequence, there were continuous raids and skirmishes between the two towns.

Mahomet, we are told, slowly came to realise the evil of this traffic in sacred things, and one day announced to a few friends that he had been called to proclaim the only true God. Moreover, he assured them that an angel had given him a message to this effect, and that only through righteousness could God be approached. This was the basis of his teaching, but, like all fanatics, he further declared that everyone who did not accept his message was destined for hell. On the other hand all who accepted it would reach heaven. He acknowledged Abraham, Moses and Jesus as his forerunners, whose teachings had been corrupted by the priests. Mahomet, however, had received the final divine message for mankind, and he had been appointed by God to complete the revelation which his forerunners had announced.

Gradually those who accepted his beliefs grew in number, much to the annoyance of the majority of the inhabitants of Mecca, who realised that, if these new ideas took root, their profitable pilgrim trade would be seriously affected. Naturally they did everything they could to silence the self-styled prophet, but, as the opposition grew, he became bolder and preached his new doctrines with such effect that his followers steadily increased. As Mecca was a centre of pilgrimage no blood could be shed inside its walls, so his opponents could only be disagreeable, to end in boycotting him and confiscating the belongings of all who became his followers.

Matters became so uncomfortable that Mahomet recanted amidst great rejoicings, but this weakening was only of short duration, as the fear of God returned, and he cursed himself for having, as he said, given way to the promptings of the devil. So he put on again the mantle of a prophet, and resumed his missionary efforts, this time there being no turning back. Even his threats of a future in hell could not, however, induce the majority of his townsmen to forsake the profitable present. On their part, as persuasion had failed, the elders of the town now decided that there was nothing left to be done but to dispose of the seditious prophet in the most effective way possible.

A plot was consequently hatched to murder him in his bed. Mahomet, however, was forewarned and escaped, only to be followed by those who sought his destruction. With his faithful friend Abu Bekr he found refuge in a cave, and eventually arrived at Medina where he knew a welcome awaited him, as two years earlier its people had invited him to come and rule them as the prophet of Allah, the Jews in their midst having convinced them that he was none other than the Messiah.

Mahomet arrived in Medina in 622. His probation was over, and he had been tempted only to become stronger. He had had his wandering in the wilderness, known to the faithful as the Hegira (the flight), and now his power began. He believed, be it remembered, that he had been appointed by the creator of the universe to convert and rule the people on earth, which shows that he was a man with the power of imagination highly developed, and, besides this, he possessed a clear, rapid and decisive judgment and had unbounded confidence in himself. We know this Hitler type only too well in our own times, and one wonders if the human race will ever become sufficiently intelligent to ignore or confine these megalomaniacs, and not be led by them to commit the excesses they plan.

In this case the Arabs were the people who believed that they were the chosen race, destined to conquer the world and bring about a new order, and here again their Führer wrote a book to explain his mission. We all know that *Mein Kampf* was written for the same purpose, but, in its case, the Germans were the chosen people who had been appointed by God to rule the world under Hitler. We read in the previous chapter that *The City of God* was written with the same end in view, the difference being that it was the Christian Church which was to dominate the world under the Pope at Rome. Mahomet's literary effort became known as *The Koran* (meaning, in Arabic, recitation, as he claimed that it was a repetition of what he had heard from God), and few other books have had such an influence in moulding the opinion of great multitudes living in many lands.

These three books have been responsible for the

shedding of rivers of blood, and for the torture, imprisonment and banishment of millions of innocent victims. They have been the cause of bitter, bloody and destructive wars, and have brought misery and desolation to Europe, Asia and the Americas, but the stupid multitude goes on bemoaning the evils and misery of their times, never learning the lessons the past has to teach. As the people of this earth are quite ignorant of history, knowing little of the misery and destruction caused by the megalomaniacs of the past, the Alexanders, the Napoleons, the Charlemagnes, the Suleymans and the Mahomets, is it surprising that the Italians were beguiled by their Mussolini and the Germans by their Hitler?

Some day another nation may go down the same wrong road, but the world will only be saved from another catastrophe such as we have just experienced if knowledge and wisdom everywhere take the place of ignorance and folly, if the people think for themselves, and do not allow unscrupulous fanatics to think for them.

Mahomet began his reign in Medina to bring righteousness and the knowledge of the only true God to mankind, by a series of raids upon the caravans of Mecca, and this led to the Meccans convoying their merchandise. An army of 700 men on one occasion was so employed, and they encountered 300 of the faithful out on one of their plundering expeditions. A battle followed in which Mahomet was successful, and he returned in triumph to Medina where he was inspired by God, so he said, to order the assassination of all the people of Medina who had not accepted his message.

Battles between Medina and Mecca continued with varying success, and the Koran contains what the faithful term sublime passages written by the prophet during the periods of his distress, when every battle was not a victory. Then it was that he called upon Allah in his trouble, then it was that the faithful were not faithful enough, then did he write many words of encouragement, and then did he become more than ever convinced that all unbelievers must either be converted or exterminated. Here is one passage taken from the Koran:—

We will cast terror into the hearts of those who disbelieve, because they set up with Allah that for which he has sent down no authority, and their abode is the fire, and evil is the abode of the unjust.

We need not follow the course of the inconclusive battles waged between Mecca and Medina, or the massacres Mahomet carried out, one being the slaughtering of 900 Jews and the enslavement of their women and children. Finally, a treaty was signed between them in which the Meccans agreed to recognise the prophet if Mecca be made the centre of the new faith. So Mahomet won over Mecca, and what the Meccans lost through pilgrims ceasing to kiss the holy stone they made up by the faithful coming to see the place where the prophet of the only true God was born. Another item in the treaty was that the faithful were to turn towards Mecca when praying and not towards Jerusalem, the idea doubtless being that this would for ever make Mecca the Holy City and keep the people from ever forgetting it. The same idea was behind the Nazis adopting the greeting "Heil Hitler", so that the Germans would never forget to recognise him as their leader.

In 629 Mahomet entered Mecca as the victorious prophet who had subdued his enemies, and, from now onwards, we read of his treachery, massacres and wars until all Arabia acknowledged him as its master. Then he died (632) at the age of sixty-two, leaving to his followers his unscrupulous aggressive methods, which they faithfully carried into effect until they had established an empire, the extent of which will be given a few pages farther on. Mahomet used religion to lay the foundation of an empire. Righteousness, which he said he was bringing to the world, is noticeable by its absence. His sanctimonious humbug blinded many to his true character, just as Hitler deluded the great majority in Germany with his programme of social welfare. Nothing in the public or private life of Mahomet points to him being other than an unbalanced zealot, who used both men and women for his own purposes.

His interest in women was Eastern to a degree. He had quite a number of wives and concubines, who caused much trouble and confusion in his household, and, although Allah tried to help him in straightening out his domestic worries, excuses for some disgraceful episodes still remain to be found. Like all Easterners of those days, women to him were just chattels, to be picked up and dropped according to his moods, and to us the account of Mahomet's marriage to a Jewess on the evening of a battle, just after her husband had been made a prisoner and executed, reads very like the story of David, Uriah and Bathsheba.

We read of Moses, the founder of the Hebrew

faith, being a murderer, and yet the laws the Hebrews believed he delivered from Mount Sinai included one against murder, and so also with Mahomet. His latter life was that of an unscrupulous aggressor, but either he, or someone else, incorporated some sound and enlightened teaching in the Koran which has inspired millions of good Mahomedans to live better lives, just as many Christians have been helped by the good passages in the Bible, while ignoring those that are evil. He advocated restraint and self-control, which he did not practice, but however inconsistent he was there is no question about his influence. He abolished drunkenness, gambling and infanticide, but not slavery, as all but Moslems could be enslaved. He made no laws against polygamy, but easy divorce was abolished, thus preventing men from casting away unwanted wives.

Besides being a great law-giver he was an outstanding rule , as, by convincing the people that he was God's medium, and that the Koran was the only divine message received by mankind, he united Arabia for the first time in history. His burning zeal and fierce intolerance infected his followers, who, ardently believing that they were waging war for God, used every possible device to bring Jews, Arabs and Christians to the knowledge of Allah, the only true God. What began as religion developed into a political system by the power of the sword, Mahomet proving himself to be an able soldier and politician, who, by appealing to the emotions, and by the use of force, forged loosely knit communities into a nation of fanatics intent on spreading their creed over all the earth.

The idea of a personal God in the image of man
has caused slaughter and suffering so extensive that
no words can make the mountain of misery comprehensible. An anthropomorphic God is no more
than a mental picture formed by each individual, who
imagines a god like unto himself. If the individual
is cruel and unjust his god is likewise cruel and unjust. When he believes in only one divine being there
is no latitude for more than his own conception, but,
when there is belief in many gods, greater room
exists for a diversity of ideas. A multitude of gods
cannot all think alike, any more than a crowd of
people, and consequently in polytheistic religions there
is more toleration, gods being added to, and withdrawn from, the pantheon from time to time without
upsetting the prevailing beliefs.

To the Moslem Arab, however, there was only one
God, and one opinion about the way he must be
worshipped. In his mind this being was none other
than an invisible Arab, endowed with almighty
supernatural powers, who had taken the Semite race
under his special protection and looked with favour
only on those who worshipped him.

Here we are not concerned with individual
religious beliefs. There have been, and are today,
both good and evil men and women professing all
the different world faiths. The narrow-minded
orthodox, the proselytising zealots and the bigots,
are those who bring trouble to the many who are
quite content to go along without interfering in, or
troubling about, what their neighbours think concerning the mysteries of this or that religion. Likewise we are not concerned with individual political

opinions, as here again the great majority are quite satisfied to allow everyone to hold any political creed he thinks right. What we are concerned with is the effect on history of the fanatics, the zealots and the bigots, both in religion and politics, as these are the people who have changed the course of events for good or ill. At no time in history is this more evident than during the period we are now considering.

Mahomet, the one-time shepherd boy, completely changed the mental outlook of millions by a religion which ultimately spread over much of North Africa and Asia. Schools were part of each mosque, where the children were taught to read the Koran, Arabic thus becoming the language of the Middle East. His followers, and their army, carried this book into distant lands, and snatched from Christianity some of its most treasured possessions, finally to capture Constantinople, the bastion of Christianity in eastern Europe.

The words which he first spoke to jeering crowds in the city of Mecca are still, after the lapse of more than thirteen centuries, pondered over by his followers in that holy city. They are reverently studied by over 200,000,000 of his faithful devotees throughout more than half of Africa and all Central Asia, all Arabia, Turkey, Iran, Iraq and northern India. This indeed is a great achievement for one man, whatever we may think of his character and mental balance.

Most people have heard of Mahomet, but few, except Moslems, know about Abu Bekr, his ever-staunch friend who always supported him throughout his tempestuous career. Abu Bekr was the guiding mind behind the movement, the thinker and sustainer of it all, and so it was natural, when the prophet's career ended, that he became the Kalifa, which means the successor, or, as we term it, the Caliph. His great capacity, his organising ability and fanaticism, welded the Arabs into one united race, intent on two things only—to conquer the world for Allah, and secure all the loot and booty possible from those they looked upon as unbelievers. He ruthlessly stamped down insurrections, schisms and all disunity, and, when this was accomplished, he organised an army to carry out his purpose.

Just as there was in Germany, in our own time, a fanatical desire to rule the world by first of all conquering all Europe, and then the British Empire, so there was then in Arabia the same grandiose idea of conquest, based on the belief that every other political and religious system was wrong, and that only the Arabs had the truth and the right way of life to guide them. When it is remembered that the Christian zealots had then the same fanatical opinions about their system of life and belief, we can well understand what all this was to mean to the future peace and happiness of the millions who wished only to live quietly and peacefully all the days of their time on earth.

(2) THE RISE AND FALL OF THE ARABIAN EMPIRE.

With Medina as his headquarters, and all Arabia behind him, Abu Bekr laid his plans, and carried them out with brilliant success with the help of zealous, resolute and sagacious collaborators. He was fortunate to have Khalid as commander of his troops, because this outstanding soldier was victorious in every battle. The Arabs moved their armies simultaneously in 635 to the Syrian and Persian borders, and to both countries they sent the same ultimatum giving them three courses of action: (1) to pay tribute to the Caliph, (2) confess the true God and adopt the Moslem faith, or (3) accept death by the sword of Allah. All resistance was ruthlessly crushed and all who accepted the true faith were spared.

Large armies were encountered and defeated, the people accepting the new faith after a victory without much resistance. Christian Arabs became Moslems, as did many Jews. Mesopotamia, Syria, Egypt, and finally Persia, were conquered, and their people changed over to worship Allah as the only true God. Inspired by the belief in Allah, the conquering armies continued effectively their missionary effort, and the people either accepted the new faith or were massacred. Truly this was a religious and social revolution which, for its swiftness and thoroughness, has few parallels. By 656, or twenty-four years from the death of Mahomet, Egypt, and the north African coast as far as Tripoli, were under Arab rule, as were also Armenia, Syria, Palestine, Persia, Mesopotamia and Arabia. By 750 the Arab Empire extended, in the east, to the frontier of India, in the north to Turkestan, and westward right along North Africa, including Spain.

The Christian armies were encouraged by great parades of priests and chanting monks carrying holy relics, crosses, sacred banners and pictures. Prayers and fastings were also tried to stem the Infidel's onward rush, but all in vain. Christendom thus lost most of its sacred places: the Holy Land, including Jerusalem and the Holy Sepulchre, the place of pilgrimage where rested the Cross; Damascus, so closely associated with Paul, the founder of Christianity; Antioch, where the first Christian church was established; Alexandria and Egypt, which were responsible for the doctrine of the Trinity, and Nicaea and Carthage, the meeting-place of so many important Church councils. Out of what had seemed a cloudless sky this black cloud had rolled up to defeat the Emperor Heraclius, whose armies were the bulwark of the Faith. Little wonder that this rapid change in the situation brought amazement and consternation to the popes at Rome. It was indeed a set-back to their dreams of world domination.

In 634 Abu Bekr died, and his place as caliph was taken by Omar, the prophet's brother-in-law, during whose reign (634–644) the principal Moslem conquests were effected. His penetration into Egypt cut off Abyssinia from the rest of Christendom, and for 800 years its very existence was forgotten. It still remained Christian, so much so that greatly to the surprise of the Church at Rome a deputation arrived there in the 15th century to enquire about certain points of doctrine. Elsewhere, though the Moslems imposed their own culture and civilisation on their conquered lands, there was no set-back, rather the reverse, as what they found in some countries could scarcely have been made worse. In places they encountered people apathetic because of the unjust and reactionary Christian or Persian rule, whose subjects were oppressed, disheartened, overtaxed and ignorant. Though the Moslems had conquered by force they at least freed the people from tyranny and injustice, and put in their place a more enlightened system of government.

Othman became the third caliph after the death of Omar. During his reign the Arab simplicity of living gave place to greater luxury. As with the Christians, world domination, for the purpose of material gain, took the place of the earlier impulse of winning the world for God. From now onwards plunder and riches, pomp and circumstance, gorgeous finery and worldly aspirations, determined those in charge of guiding the destinies of the Moslem Empire.

Like the Pope in Rome, who became Pontifex Maximus, with all its divine traditions, those who succeeded the Prophet of Allah became oriental monarchs surrounded by the display associated with an Eastern Court. Internal quarrels arose; in fact intrigues, murders and everything that is sordid became the order of the times, largely due to the domestic mess Mahomet left for future generations to clear up.

The trouble arose in determining who had the right to be caliph. There were several claimants to the throne as time went on, but the first was Ali, the husband of the Prophet's daughter Fatima. He resented Othman being chosen caliph as he was not one of the family, and he considered that the caliphate should remain a family affair. Ayesha, the Prophet's favourite wife, on the other hand, thought otherwise, and round these two, Ali and Ayesha, grew two parties for and against Othman, to end in him being mobbed, chased to his house and murdered when an old man of eighty. The Moslem Empire, triumphant abroad, was now suffering from civil war at its centre, and this division in its ranks remains to this day, because the Shiites, the orthodox Moslems of Persia, look on Ali as the rightful caliph while the rest, known as the Sunnites, accept Othman as such.

In the next phase of this quarrel, Hasan, the son of Ali, was poisoned, and Husein, his brother, was also murdered, and they are looked upon by the Shiites as their two outstanding martyrs. The rivals being thus liquidated, the Omayyad family, the one to which Othman belonged, was able to retain the caliphate for nearly one hundred years, but thereafter it went to the man who was clever enough, and sufficiently unscrupulous, to seize the power. Under the rule of Abdal Malik (685–705) and Walid I (705–714) the Omayyad dynasty rose to its greatest height, with the western boundary of the Empire on the Atlantic coast of Spain, and the eastern on the Indus river, the boundary of India.

Suleyman, who became caliph in 715, attacked Constantinople two years later from the sea, but failed, a victory for the Christians which was even more important to Europe than Charles Martel's success at Tours (732), because Constantinople was so close to the centre of Moslem power, whereas Christianity in France was by then too well established to be easily overthrown. So far all the other Moslem attempts to capture the city by land had been equally unsuccessful, the Taurus mountains always forming an insuperable barrier. If Leo, the Emperor, had failed on this occasion to retain this bastion of Christianity in the East, the Moslem faith would probably have swept like a whirlwind over Europe from the plains of Hungary and the Balkans to the Ural mountains, as there, in those days, religious beliefs were fluid, and Christianity, where it was accepted, was somewhat lightly held.

This Christian victory, moreover, checked Moslem expansion, and, from then onwards, the enthusiasm for the cause of Allah gradually dwindled. Millions of people of different races, creeds and languages had by now been incorporated within the Moslem Empire, and acknowledged Allah as the only true God. The Koran had now become his revelation to them, and was looked upon as their handbook for life on earth and guide to the life beyond, just as the Bible had become to Christians the only revelation of God to mankind. These two books were considered by the followers of both faiths as God-inspired, and the only literature deserving any attention, all else being unsuitable for study. Literary effort thus received no encouragement in the Christian world for more than a thousand years, but, during the height of Moslem rule, which was an age of unorthodoxy, this was not so, as we shall discover. With this exception these books became more like icons to the faithful, as every word was considered as having been written by God. Consequently they played a great part in moulding the Christian and Moslem outlook on life.

Damascus was now the capital of the Empire, Mecca being geographically unsuitable, and here reigned Walid II, but the time of the Omayyad caliphs was getting short. In 749 the last of the dynasty was slain in Egypt, and the family of Abbasids, which was responsible for the crime, set itself up as the true line because it acknowledged Ali, and not Othman, as the rightful successor to the caliphate.

The Abbasids adopted a black flag as their emblem, as a sign of mourning for the two martyrs, Hasan and Husein, in contrast to the white banner of the Omayyads. The crescent, now the Moslem emblem, was originally a Christian emblem. It was first used by the Christians of Constantinople as signifying an expanding Christianity, and it was only after that city came under Turkish rule in 1453 that it became the symbol of the Moslem faith.

Abul Abbas was the first of the new line of caliphs, and he commenced his reign by inviting every male belonging to the house of Omayyad to a banquet, only to massacre them. Then, we are told that he placed their bodies in his dining-hall, covered them over with a carpet, and, on this improvised table, he and his principal supporters had a great feast. Everything belonging to the Omayyads was either confiscated or destroyed, their tombs were entered and their remains burnt and scattered. In such fashion were the two martyrs avenged, the means adopted being similar to those pursued by Mahomet himself, to whom righteousness meant aggression, domination and brutal ruthlessness for the purpose of securing his own fanatical ends.

This slaughter by Abul Abbas was of course carried out in order to secure his own position, as he cared nothing for the rights or wrongs of the long-standing dispute. Clearing off the Omayyad family was not, however, sufficient, as he was still confronted with the descendants of Ali, who were likewise a source of danger. All who could claim descent from Mahomet were therefore exterminated, and only then did this criminal feel secure.

During his reign the Moslem Empire lost command of the sea, and, in consequence, its control over Spain and North Africa, where independent Moslem states came into being. In the time of his successor, Mansur, the capital was moved from Damascus to Baghdad, which town became immortal as the scene of some of the stories in *The Arabian Nights*. These were supposed to have been told to the Caliph Haroun-al-Raschid (786–809) by one of his wives, who thus preserved her life, as she retained his interest for a thousand and one nights. For this there is no historical evidence, and similar tales, told in like circumstances, can be traced far back in both Persia and India, the story of Esther in the Bible being set in a similar environment in Persia.

Under the reign of Haroun-al-Raschid, Moslem civilisation reached its height. We are now in the age of unorthodoxy, when the teaching and warnings contained in the Koran went unheeded. Court life was polished and luxurious, the Caliph and his courtiers being surrounded by every luxury money could buy. Baghdad was then a great mercantile city carrying on a large trade with the East, and this was supplemented by the loot and plunder secured by the Moslem armies ever raiding their neighbours' lands.

These state-organised robbers went as far north as Asia Minor and Turkestan, and eastwards to India, thus producing an unending supply of slaves and riches of all kinds. This source of abundance, combined with its legitimate commerce, made Baghdad the richest city of its time. Wealth was plentiful, and literature, philosophy, poetry and the arts were encouraged. Schools and colleges abounded where philosophers, students, scientists, doctors and poets gathered from all parts of the then civilised world.

Large public buildings dominated the city, with its many luxurious and comfortable dwelling-houses. Hospitals and their doctors were under government control, and what is true of the capital embraces all the provincial cities of the Empire. There were many hospitals and a large asylum for the insane, sixty medical stores, 900 doctors and 6000 medical students, while the poor received free treatment.

Every department of administration had its own well-ordered office under the control of ministers and officials, such as the Ministry of Posts, of Finance, Privy Seal, Crown Lands, Justice and the Army, where each day a large concourse of clerks, scribes and accountants assembled to conduct the affairs of state. The army was loyal and efficient, all strategic points being well protected, and the ministers of state and officials were honestly devoted to their duties. No distinction of race or creed was made—Jews, Christians and Moslems all finding equal opportunity to do their part in the administration of the vast empire.

There was complete freedom and liberty of expression, and consequently philosophic thought and free discussion about all the problems of the time were in evidence. Here the scientific attempts of the Greeks to understand natural law received fresh encouragement. Here also science, which had died in its childhood in Greece, was reborn, to light once again the torch of knowledge which, eight hundred years later, was to illuminate the Dark Ages of Christendom and finally bring to humanity the knowledge we now possess. The Moslems produced eminent historians, opticians, astronomers, biographers, poets, writers of fiction, and mathematicians, the science of Algebra and Trigonometry being their invention.

Al-Mamun (813–833), the son of Haroun-al-Raschid, succeeded his brother as caliph. He secured a period of tranquillity, during which he patronised and fostered the cultivation of literature and science throughout his empire. He founded colleges, which attracted the most eminent men of his day, and, under his rule, Baghdad became the seat of academical instruction and the centre of intelligence. He had all the classical literature of Greece, Persia and Chaldea translated into Arabic, and he, himself,· devoted much of his time to the study of mathematics and astronomy, founding an observatory at Baghdad and one near to Damascus.

He appointed the most learned men to be the principals of the colleges, quite irrespective of their race and creed, and besides this he repudiated openly the claims made in the Koran, and advocated philosophy in its place. His closing years were disturbed by revolts throughout his empire, and a conflict arose with the Eastern Empire, it is said, because the Emperor Theophilus objected to a Greek Christian being appointed as professor to the college at Baghdad. The death of Al-Mumun ended an important epoch in the history of science and literature, and to him, and his father, Europe owed much when, centuries later, light began to shine through barbaric darkness.

This was an age of great men. In the 9th century

lived Khwarizim, then claimed to be the greatest mathematician of all times, a genius who contributed greatly to the advance in the science of trigonometry. He was followed by Avicenna (980–1073), who was physician to the Persian court, his outstanding contribution being a treatise on medicine, which remained the standard medical work for centuries. Avicenna was one of the most learned and brilliant men of his age, and, by his writings on philosophy, mathematics, astronomy, physics and music became famous throughout the entire Moslem world. Rhazes (860–932) was famous for his works on medicine, and was the first to diagnose small-pox and measles. He was a pioneer in work on bacteria, a science to be finally mastered many centuries later by the experiments of Pasteur and Lister. Al-Hazen, in the 10th century, laid the foundation for our present-day knowledge of Optics and Vision, the refraction of light and the height of the atmosphere.

Omar Khayyám, who lived in the 11th century, is best known as a poet and for his *Rubáiyát*. He was one of the greatest mathematicians of these days, besides being an outstanding astronomer and geologist, his belief that large tracts of land were once covered by sea being now everywhere accepted. Edrisi, in the same century, was the most eminent astronomer and geographer of his age, and spent fifteen years compiling a book on geography which was more comprehensive than any so far produced.

By men like these, and many others, the knowledge of the past was regained and widened. Their medical and scientific achievements certainly raised the Arabian world of 100,000,000 people well above the

mark civilisation reached in the time of the Greeks
and Romans, and the knowledge they accumulated
gave birth to the Renaissance in Europe centuries
later. This knowledge came to Europe by three
routes—the East, Sicily and Spain. The Crusaders
made contact with it (1) in the East; (2) Frederick II,
the German Emperor, the most advanced European
of his time, was greatly influenced by it in Sicily, his
domain, where Moslem culture and learning flourished;
and finally, (3) through the Arab occupation of Spain,
where its effect on Europe was most pronounced.

Instruction in how to read and write was the basis
of the Moslem educational system, and the children
were supplied with grammars and lexicons. The
University of Baghdad was founded and endowed in
1065, and colleges devoted to knowledge and science,
as distinct from theology, were established throughout
the Empire. These attracted students from all parts,
and in all the large towns free education was given to
the children of the poor, the Arabic language thus
replacing Greek, Persian and other forms of speech.

Only under Moslem rule was learning encouraged
in Spain, and the light the Moslems lit in Europe
flickered until it burned into flame at the Renaissance
six hundred years later. Only then did Christendom
begin to acquire knowledge, and Moslem civilisation
contributed much to bring about the establishment of
the universities of Europe when light began to shine
through the Dark Ages. In the Moslem universities
a sharp distinction was made between religious superstition and scientific facts, and this prepared the way
for the Renaissance when scientific research led the
way to knowledge, and theology was left to be pursued

only by the priests. Very few realise the debt the world owes to the Moslem Empire for rekindling the light of knowledge, and adopting the scientific method of approaching the laws of nature.

To the Christians, the Arabs were damned infidels and consequently this religious barrier prevented their contribution to science being appreciated in Christian lands, so much so that even seven hundred years after this era of Arab enlightenment Christendom was opposed to every form of scientific enquiry. The Moslems encouraged the scientific approach to an understanding of nature, the Moslem doctors laying the foundation of our present-day knowledge of medicine and hygiene, and many there were who helped to alleviate human suffering. Anaesthetics were used for surgical operations, a science which then had developed to a remarkable degree.

What a contrast with the position as it then was in Christendom, and as it remained for centuries. Seven hundred years after the time we are now considering, the first man in Christendom who studied the structure of the human body was sent by the Pope to do penance in the Holy Land, and died in poverty, a story which will be told in Chapter XI. When Christians were forbidden by the Church to practise any kind of healing, and were employing sacred relics and priests to pray the devils out of the afflicted, the Moslems had their well-equipped hospitals and highly trained doctors relieving sickness and suffering.

Their scientists included chemists who discovered many new substances. Their craftsmen produced works of art in the metals, surpassing anything then known. In the manufacture of paper, glass work, pottery, dyes, fertilisers and numerous commodities they were far in advance of their times. They introduced to Europe many new trees and plants, they farmed their land scientifically, and excelled in producing new varieties of fruit trees, plants and flowers. Scientific treatises were written on the right and the wrong way to farm the land, and they knew how to make tinctures, essences and syrups.

All this was going on, from Spain to the frontier of India, while the Christian Church was keeping the people poor, miserable and ignorant. Likewise the increase of knowledge did not appeal to the orthodox Moslem mind, as progressive thought never does to orthodoxy of any kind, but the people as a whole had become quite unorthodox and had put the Moslem Church aside. Consequently, while Christendom remained mentally dead under the blight of orthodoxy, the Moslem world progressed, and produced an age of splendour which had not been equalled since the days when Greece was at the height of her glory.

While there was no freedom of thought in Christendom, bound in mental chains because of the Theodosian Code, free discussion in those days was always possible under Moslem rule, and to this liberty of thought their high culture and standard of life was due. The numerous cities within this empire were clean and sanitary, supporting a vigorous, intelligent and educated population, so much so that in the 10th century there must have been something like 100,000,000 people benefiting from enlightened Moslem rule in this its unorthodox era.

Nevertheless this remarkable people were unable to govern themselves, and left their fate in the hands of one man, the Caliph, with the result that when Haroun-al-Raschid died in 809 the Empire became convulsed in civil war. Then followed intrigue, murders and the disorder which always comes about when the sole directing mind is withdrawn, this state of affairs continuing for five years until Al-Mamun restored order out of chaos. Democracy, with all its faults, has solved this problem, and, if the Moslems had adopted this form of government, their civilisation might not have perished.

The Roman people could not govern themselves, and their empire passed away, and we, in our day, know the fate which has come over dictator-governed Germany and Italy. In a democratic state there is no place for the political or religious fanatic who seizes power and rules only as he thinks right, murdering or imprisoning all who oppose him. Where the people can choose their rulers, more balanced thinking prevails and mistakes are less likely, though it follows that decisions are made more slowly and this exposes them to sudden and swift attack. Democracy seldom plans aggression, and is often slow to realise its coming, a recognised fact which makes dictatorships dangerous to all freedom-loving people.

As in the case of the Roman Empire, barbarians stood outside the Moslem frontiers awaiting the right moment to strike down its civilisation. At the beginning of the 11th century, two hundred years after the death of Haroun-al-Raschid, the Turks, of Hun descent, poured out of Turkestan and captured Baghdad and its dominions. Coming as they did from the north, they were able also to occupy Asia Minor, hitherto inaccessible from the south because of the

Taurus mountains. These Turks were orthodox Moslems, primitive and fanatical, and they revived the old hatred between the Christians and the Moslems which had died down amongst the latter during their age of unorthodox splendour. Now, however, the old bitterness blazed into a long series of disastrous. religious wars, known as the Crusades, about which the story will be told in the next chapter.

(3) The Turks Become a Great Power.

We need not blame the barbarians for their crime of destroying the Moslem civilisation of the Baghdad Empire, as they suffered from the curse of ignorance and knew no better. Moreover, they had been cruelly treated by the Baghdad Moslems in their raids for plunder and slaves, and many old scores were due to be paid off. Civilisation then, as now, did not put international righteousness before wrong-doing, and, where the treatment of foreigners was concerned, the unorthodox civilised Moslems were not a whit better than the uncivilised orthodox Turkish Moslems.

Early in the 13th century the small tribe which was to found the Ottoman Empire settled in Armenia, under its leader Suleyman, its hereditary chief. For the aid he gave to the Seljuk Turks against the Mongols he was given a tract of land on the Byzantine frontier, where settled his tribe, to become known as Osman Turks, corrupted to Ottoman, after the name of their chief, Osman, the grandson of Suleyman. Osman, for his conquests, was raised to the rank of prince by the Seljuk sultan, and, when the Seljuks were conquered by the Mongols in 1300, the Osmans took the lead in consolidating the ten Turkish tribes settled in Asia Minor into one nation, to which they gave their name.

At the beginning of the 14th century Osman (1301–1326) was acknowledged as the Sultan of the Turks, and to him the Ottoman Empire owed its origin, as, before he died, he had extended his domains as far west as the Bosphorus, and was in possession of many towns hitherto occupied by the Greeks. His son Orkhan (1326–1359) continued this policy of expansion, by crossing over the Dardanelles and capturing Gallipoli and many neighbouring towns and villages. Besides being a conqueror, he was also passionately devout, many mosques and public buildings being built during his reign, and a standing army of paid soldiers was organised which was the first regular army in Europe.

His successor Murad I (1359–1389) next formed a bodyguard of Christian captives, who, from an early age, were taught the Moslem creed. They lived in camps under strict military discipline, and were taught to glorify war and hate everyone holding opinions contrary to the Moslem faith, especially the Christians. Thus, like the Hitler Youth, they became fanatical warriors, carrying all before them. As all Christian families living under Turkish rule had to contribute one boy or more, this bodyguard swelled into an army to be known as the Janissaries, meaning "new troops". Like most proselytes they were more fanatical than the genuine Moslems, and success after success followed their conflicts, so much so that in time they dominated the Empire, many sultans being appointed, deposed or murdered by them. Not until 1826 was their power broken, but, to us, they stand out as an historical example of what can be done by false education.

So far the young have too often been educated to hate, fight and steal, but surely the time has now come to educate the youth of all the earth in the principles of righteousness, and not of evil, and, if this is done, it will be found that the desire to do what is right will become just as strong as has hitherto been the desire to do evil.

Under Murad I the Ottoman Empire greatly enlarged its bounds, which now embraced Asia Minor, Bulgaria and Serbia, while Turkish penetration into Greece, Albania, Hungary and Rumania continued slowly but surely, to end in the great victory at Kossovo (1389), when the invaders defeated a combined force of Balkan Christians. Here Murad was slain, to be succeeded by Bayezid I (1389–1403), who set about making preparations for the conquest of Constantinople, which, like a Christian island, stood out alone in this great sea of Moslem rule, bounded in the east by the Euphrates, and the west by the Danube.

However, before his arrangements were complete, a check came to Ottoman expansion from the fierce Mongol warriors whose empire by now comprised Persia, Mesopotamia, Afghanistan, Armenia, Turkestan and part of northern India. Under their savage leader Timurlane, whose pastime was religion, and whose profession was destruction, a vast horde of Mongol horsemen swept westwards and utterly defeated the Turks in 1402 on the plains of Angora. Bayezid was made a prisoner, and, as he proceeded under guard eastwards, he saw his victorious foes streaming west, devastating everything they could destroy up to within a short distance of Constantinople.

Now surely was the right time for all Christian Europe to unite to drive the Turks out of the Balkans, but the opportunity was not taken, The Turks were given time to recover from their great disaster, as Timurlane did not follow up his victory, but withdrew from Asia Minor. Then arose Mahomet I (1413–1421), who fought his way to the throne, and set about restoring Ottoman rule, a task which was fully accomplished by his son Murad II (1421–1451), who had then to turn westwards and face the most formidable opposition from Europe so far encountered from that direction. The interval of peace, when the Turkish power was shattered, had been used by the Christians to build up a formidable force, including a body of Crusaders led by a cardinal, and when it attacked under the leadership of John Hunyady, the illegitimate son of Sigismund, the King of Hungary, the Turks were utterly routed and driven out of Serbia and Bulgaria.

Again the opportunity to expel the Turks from Europe was lost, and 477 years had to pass before another such occasion occurred. Instead of the Christians following up their victory by capturing Adrianople, the last Turkish European stronghold, peace was made and the Turks again obtained the necessary time to recover. Then the Christians saw their mistake, and, as in these days treaties between those professing different religious beliefs were not considered binding, they recommenced the war, and thus broke their promise not to advance farther east. The

Turks reassembled, in great force, and, with the broken treaty fixed on the point of a lance, bore down on their enemies, to defeat them utterly at Varna in 1444. Thus was Hungary for a time eliminated as an effective defence of Christian Europe.

Now we come to the time when another of these human pests arose, a world conqueror, intent on subduing everyone to his will. Just as the Christian Church set out to conquer the world for Christ, as Lenin did likewise for Bolshevism, as Hitler did for National Socialism, as Napoleon did in the name of Liberty, Equality and Fraternity, so Mahomet II (1451–1481) was determined to convert all the earth to the Moslem faith within the framework of a great Turkish Empire. His first move was to realise the dream of former sultans, the capture of Constantinople, a stronghold which to him was the ideal capital for his new empire.

He had all the conditions necessary for empire-building, a docile and obedient people trained to hardship and war, but quite lacking in the gift of independent thought. Before them was dangled the carrot of plundered wealth, but, donkey-like, they did not see the string which was tightly held in their leader's hand. He, and his fellow gangsters, as always happened in the past, and was to happen so often in the future, obtained the wealth and power his simple-minded subjects fought for, worked for, suffered and died for. Empire-building meant nothing to these serfs but hardship, and yet the glamour of conquest lured them on, the carrot always held before them by their leaders, who made sure that the substance of conquest always fell to them only. We search the pages of history in vain to find if the people, beyond a favoured few, ever benefited from the victories of their conquering heroes.

The position then was much the same as it was in 1939, when a divided Europe was faced with a strong fanatical Germany, and it will happen again so long as powerful nations are composed of people who lack the gift of independent thought. The Turks bowed to authority so abjectly that their sultans had only to command to secure obedience, and when the òccasion for conquest arose every Turk was ready and willing to make any sacrifice to meet the will of his lord and master.

What a tragedy it is that the human being is not endowed with intelligent, rational, critical and independent thought! So long as this sheep-like attitude continues the storm of conquest will arise periodically and sweep the earth, to the profit of the few, if they are victorious, and the suffering of the many, whatever happens. The only way to stop this is the development in everyone of a highly ethical, independent, critical mind, and this can only come about by education on right lines. Owing to ignorance the majority of the people lack the character necessary to think for themselves as individuals, preferring to follow tamely after the strong-minded outspoken minority. This weakness can only be cured by mental development, which alone will bring the peace and happiness nearly all desire, and end the career of world conquerors, who will find no soil in which to plant the tree of conquest.

At the time we are now considering the soil for conquest was favourable to Turkey, as the Christians in Constantinople were divided on questions of doctrine when the call came to save the city from the Infidel. Had there been concord within this ancient bastion of the Christian faith it could have successfully withstood the Moslem onslaught, but, because there was not, it fell. Constantine XI (1448–1453), the Emperor, and the last of the Caesars, was a statesman and a hero in the hour of peril. To secure unity amongst his Christian subjects he tried in vain to persuade the Catholic Church authorities in Rome to send him help, on the understanding that he and his people would in future believe that the Holy Ghost proceeded from the Father and the Son and not from the Father only. On this one word "Filioque" (and from the Son), which the Catholics had added to the Creed in 1054, hung the fate of the first and greatest Christian city. The Emperor, to save his city, was now prepared to accept a belief which he had been brought up to consider to be untrue, and against which the Greeks had protested vehemently since its quite unjustified insertion into the Creed of the Christian Church.

While Mahomet's artillery was battering at the city's walls, the Greeks turned in fury against the Emperor for making such an outrageous offer, as to them such a belief was nothing less than blasphemy. Moreover, he had permitted a Catholic celebration of the Eucharist to be held within St. Sophia, at which the hateful word "Filioque" had been heard by the congregation for the first time. Such shocking heresy made the beleaguered citizens forget their peril, and many hoped for a Turkish victory rather than experience such unbelief within their walls. The correct interpretation of Christianity meant more to the orthodox Greeks than the salvation of their city, and so the theological conflict continued between the Greeks, on the one hand, and the Catholic Spaniards, Germans and Italians who helped to make up the garrison. Meantime, as this dispute continued, the Turks, profiting by it, worked their way into the city, subduing one defence after another, intent only on its capture, and the subjection to their will of the Christians within who could not agree upon the definition of their faith.

The same cause which brought about disaster to the Crusades, this conflict over the Creed between the Greek Church and the Catholic Church, probably lost to Christendom the first Christian city and the bulwark against the Infidel, just as a dispute over the celebration of the Eucharist permitted the Turks to settle in Europe. If Hungary, Poland and Bohemia, the most threatened countries, had only united they could have cleared the Balkans of the Turks and re-established the Christian faith, but they would not join forces because a united opinion on a point of doctrine could not be reached.

Instead of agreeing to differ, Hungary quarrelled with Bohemia because the Czechs, who had become Protestants, had evolved their own ideas as to the celebration of the Eucharist. But for this difference of opinion they would have fought side by side against the common enemy, as they had everything else to secure the unity which would probably have meant victory. Two remarkable men were at this time on the thrones of Bohemia and Hungary—George of Podiebrad (1458–1471), a Czech noble, being King of

Bohemia, while Matthias Corvinus (1458–1490) reigned over Hungary. George had won for himself national esteem for his defence of the Hussite faith, and no man up to the time of Masaryk had such authority or respect from his people. Matthias likewise was much esteemed in Hungary, he having been the right-hand man of his father Hunyady when the Turks had been driven from Belgrade.

If these two men had only worked together, the history of Europe from this time onwards would have been entirely different. Though united by marriage, they quarrelled over religion, to end, as we shall just be reading, in Hungary and Bohemia going to war. No help came from Bohemia when Hungary went down before the Turks, because George of Bohemia believed that the laity were entitled to partake in the ancient mystical ceremony of eating the god's body and drinking his blood. Up to now all Christendom had stood up in church and gaped in wonder at this magical ceremony derived from cannibalism, the priest alone participating in the sacred feast.

On the other hand Matthias of Hungary believed that the laity should be only spectators and not partakers, but no one really had any authority on which to base an opinion, the account which has come down to us of the Last Supper containing no instructions, because it was copied from the Pagan eucharist. This borrowing process commenced in the 2nd century, and, as those Greeks who became Christians understood the traditional ritual, no set form was put down in writing, thus leaving future generations to celebrate the sacred feast as they thought right.

The Pope fanned the flames of hatred between

the two countries, by excommunicating George of Bohemia and giving his crown to Matthias of Hungary. A terrible war followed in 1468, but Bohemia remained undefeated, though, when George died, the Czechs were forced to accept as their king Vladislav Jagellon, a Polish Roman Catholic prince, who became King of Hungary and Bohemia in 1471, a union which was to be the cause of violent revolts in both countries. Under such adverse conditions Hungary had to resist the onslaught of the Turks, who were united, fierce, and determined to convert all Europe to their faith.

The greater part of Hungary eventually fell to the Turks, as will be told a few pages farther on, the remainder being taken over by Austria, who also seized Bohemia, to hold it in subjection until 1918, when the Czechs obtained their freedom and called their country Czechoslovakia. Only after the French Revolution, when the desire for freedom again became pronounced, did the Balkan nations, which were groaning under Turkish misrule, strive to regain their liberty. Until then the Ottoman Empire faced the Holy Roman Empire, centred in Vienna, and to the latter fell the defence of Christian Europe, a circumstance which gave the Hapsburgs additional prestige, and the discredited Holy Roman Empire a new lease of life. The ramshackle Austrian Empire nevertheless weakened in cohesion as the centuries passed and the Turkish peril lessened, to end in final collapse when, along with her German ally, defeat came to the Central European alliance at the end of the First World War.

In the Spring of 1453 Constantinople, the seat of the Eastern Empire and the Greek Orthodox faith, fell to the blows of the Infidel, as, by means of various cunning devices, Mahomet II overcame the city's formidable defences. By this great victory he mesmerised his people with the idea of an all-powerful Moslem Empire, which he and his successors eventually brought into being, but meantime he had an important duty to perform. In gratitude for Allah's help, Mahomet bowed himself in reverence in the cathedral of St. Sophia, where, for the last time the previous evening, the Emperor, who fell in the fray, partook of the Sacrament, a celebration never again to be performed within its walls, as its treasures were plundered and it became a mosque.

Then Mahomet, "the conqueror", as he is called, proceeded to subdue Italy, Serbia, Bosnia, Greece, the Crimea and the islands of the Greek archipelago. At Belgrade, however, he was severely defeated by Hunyady, an event which did not prevent him from sending an army across the Adriatic to Italy, prepared to march on Rome, but its progress ceased with his death in. 1481. From this time onwards Turkish penetration westwards did not get farther than Vienna, the Turks turning their attention to the lands of the Middle East, which they successfully exploited.

Bayezid II (1481-1512), Mahomet's son, was faced on accession to the throne by a revolt organised by his brother, who eventually fled from the country, to be murdered by the notorious scoundrel Pope Alexander VI, who received from the Sultan 300,000 ducats in payment for his crime. In this reign the Turks built a powerful fleet which defeated the Venetian navy, and finally dominated the Mediterranean, but Bayezid was not sufficiently aggressive to please the Janissaries, who forced him to abdicate in favour of his son, Selim, whose warlike qualities they much preferred.

As an empire-builder Selim (1512–1520) was one of the greatest of all the Ottoman monarchs, courageous, tireless, and a scholar with great political sagacity. He made Constantinople, which was called Stambul, his capital and the centre of the Moslem faith, Baghdad, the former seat of authority, sinking to the position of a provincial town. He became the Caliph, the successor of Mahomet the Prophet, and to him was given the keys of the Kaaba at Mecca, the symbol of his supremacy over the Moslem world.

He was both cruel and merciless, and, fortunately for Europe, he set his face eastwards and marched on Persia because the Shah was the pillar of the Shiite Moslems, whereas Selim was the bulwark of the Sunnite Moslems. Forty-five thousand Shiites were massacred by Selim, a crime which caused a battle between the forces of the Shah and the Sultan, in which the Persians were routed, and a slice of their territory was lost to the victors. Selim next proceeded south to Syria, Palestine and Egypt, which countries, after determined resistance, were conquered in 1517. If he had not died three years later he would have attacked Rhodes next, for which campaign he was making preparations.

Then followed Suleyman I (1520–1566), known as "the Magnificent", the son of Selim, who was soon at war with Hungary, in which campaign he succeeded in capturing Belgrade, the key to Central Europe. Then his fleet captured Rhodes from the Knights of St. John. Again he invaded Hungary, annihilated the Magyar army at Mohacs (1526), slew their king, and occupied Budapest, a battle which altered the entire structure of Central Europe, as Hungary now lay a helpless wreck to be partitioned by Austria and Turkey. Besides that, this famous battle altered the entire religious history of Europe, because it prevented the Holy Roman Emperor Charles V from having the forces available to crush the Reformation in Germany. Consequently this great religious movement was able to get its roots well down before the Emperor later attempted its destruction. So the Protestants have the Turks to thank for the religious liberty they now enjoy, a freedom which in its early stages trembled in the balance.

Three years later Suleyman advanced on Vienna, to meet such determined resistance that after a four-days' battle his mighty host was compelled to retire from the walls of the principal city of Christendom. Only once again did the torrent of Turkish might sweep round the walls of the city, but it was now at full tide and never again did it get farther into Europe. Suleyman next turned to Persia, capturing Armenia, and then Iraq, with its famous old capital Baghdad. By the time he had finished his grim work of conquest he had occupied all Algeria, Libya, Egypt, Palestine, Syria, Mesopotamia, Armenia, Asia Minor, Greece, Rumania, Bulgaria, Serbia, Albania, Dalmatia and Hungary, which represents the height of Ottoman greatness and the summit of its power.

Then the Turks were the terror of everyone around them, the achievements of their navy being as remarkable as those of their army. But this flowing tide of conquest was not to last for ever. Malta was their first check after the one they received at Vienna, as, from this natural fortress held by the Knights of St. John, they were driven off with great loss and slaughter in 1565. The following year Suleyman died at the age of seventy-six. His son Selim II (1565–1574) attacked Russia, but failed miserably, and, after a treacherous attack on Cyprus, the Christian fleet utterly routed and destroyed the Turkish navy at the important battle of Lepanto (1571), a victory which changed the course of history, because the Turks never recovered from the disaster.

From now onwards the Empire began to decay, corruption and inefficiency prevailing in official quarters. Murad III (1574–1595) was followed by Mahomet III (1595–1603), who, when heir to the throne, was the last to enjoy his liberty, the reason being that all the sons of the sultans who followed were kept in confinement within a walled prison, to prevent them becoming rivals to the throne on the death of the reigning sultan, a system which was very prejudicial to the character of future rulers.

Not until the reign of Murad IV (1623–1640) did life again come into the decaying bones of the Empire. His vigour and courage stayed for a time the decomposition, but he had to murder many disloyal and corrupt members of his retinue before he secured implicit obedience. He thus cleared the government of the intrigue and corruption which was bringing the Empire to ruin. Then he successfully attacked Persia to recover Baghdad, when he slaughtered most of its inhabitants. He died in 1640, to be succeeded by his brother Ibrahim (1640–1648), under whom all the evils Murad had curbed broke out afresh. This new potentate plundered his people and wasted the country's wealth in every imaginable extravagance, until at length he was deposed, his young son Mahomet IV (1648-1687) becoming sultan. He was fortunate in his grand vizier, who set such an example of integrity to his successors that they did much to counteract the pernicious influence of degenerate sultans. For a time this new influence acted as a prop to the declining empire, but its great weakness lay in the fact that the Turk had no aptitude for industry, and took little interest in trade. As he was indolent, and often stupid, both Christians and Jews consequently thrived under his rule as shopkeepers, artisans and merchants, they alone supplying what culture there was to be found within the Empire. Now that the zeal to bring all the world to the knowledge of Allah had burned itself out, Mahomet IV permitted both Christians and Jews to worship as they thought best, many a Protestant electing to live under the tolerant Turkish rule rather than suffer from the persecutions of Roman Catholic Austria.

On the other hand Roman Catholic Austria and Poland hated the Turks with a bitter hatred, and, while the Roman Catholic and the Protestant factions were at grips in western Europe on the question of doctrine and supremacy, John Sobieski, King of Poland, joined in the fight to "conquer and curb the monster", as he exclaimed, "and hurl him back into the deserts to exterminate him". This powerful man, genial, cultured and a devout Roman Catholic, forced the Turks to surrender to Poland Podolia and two-thirds of Ukrainia which they had just conquered, but, while Christendom was debating as to whether or not to follow up this victory and drive the Turks out of

Europe, the Sultan took the opportunity to launch an attack against Vienna (1683) with 500,000 men. The fall of the city seemed imminent, but the timely arrival of Sobieski, with his army, drove off the invaders and inflicted upon them one of the most decisive defeats in their history.

Encouraged by the weakening of Turkish military might, the Venetians, urged on by the Pope, commenced a campaign to conquer Greece. With the help of German mercenaries they drove the Turks out of Dalmatia and Morea (southern Greece), and when they reached Athens they so bombarded the city that the famous shrine, the Parthenon, received irreparable damage. The damage remained, but not the Venetians, as, after nineteen years, they were driven out of Athens by the Turks, with the help of the Orthodox Greeks, who preferred the liberty of worship they enjoyed under the Turks to having Roman Catholic Venetians as their overlords. Besides this the Venetians established a trade monopoly which was not to the liking of the Ægean traders.

After the Turkish defeat at the gates of Vienna, misfortune followed misfortune, as city after city, and district after district, fell away from the Ottoman Empire. Austria was now in occupation of Hungary, and Italy had regained Morea. Then the Sultan was deposed and his brother Suleyman II (1687–1691) succeeded him, to be faced with the difficult problem of quelling a serious rising of the Janissaries, who plundered Constantinople and created a reign of terror. Meantime the Austrians were carrying all before them, but, with the appointment of Mustafa as grand vizier, a wise, able and patriotic man, and one who was trusted by all, the position changed, when thousands flocked to join the army which succeeded in driving the Austrians out of Serbia and occupying Belgrade.

With the death of Mustafa, who was killed when fighting the Austrians, the hapless empire, besides continuing to suffer defeat after defeat, was visited by pestilence and domestic insurrection. Then it was that Prince Eugène (the friend and ally of the Duke of Marlborough in the Spanish Succession war) at the head of an Austrian force in 1697 at Senta, near the Hungarian-Yugoslavian frontier, utterly routed the Turks and thus ended their long sustained attempt to conquer Europe. For the next hundred years territories were gained and lost, and good and bad sultans followed one another.

A repetition of the places won, only to be lost, would be wearisome, and so we pass on to the year 1774, when the Russians, after losing ports and territories around the Black Sea, regained them after decisively defeating the Turks. Then it was that the Russians obtained acknowledgment from Turkey that they were the protectors of the Christians within the Ottoman Empire, which protectorate we shall later discover was to become intimately connected with the outbreak of the First World War.

Elsewhere we shall be reading about Turkey's contact with her neighbours, and how it was that, one by one, the separate nations she had conquered were either seized by other countries or rebelled, and, after much suffering, broke the chains which bound them to her. Here, in the collapse of the Ottoman

Empire, we have another of the many instances recorded in history of force producing force, as tyranny
always creates reaction.   Millions, for centuries,
suffered from the Turkish gangsters, who, to enrich
themselves, kept down multitudes by means of the
Janissaries, the well-paid body of ruffians trained to
kill and terrorise all who stood in their path.   Eventually they got out of hand, which was fortunate as this
gave the oppressed victims an opportunity to cast off
the Turkish yoke.   Likewise the Turkish people
themselves, who had been kept poor and ignorant,
having gained nothing from the imperialism of their
rulers, overthrew the old order and the Moslem faith,
when both had brought to them defeat after defeat.

After seeing the remainder of the Empire dis-
membered, following its defeat in the First World
War, the old gang was overthrown, and then Mustapha
Kemal, who saved for Turkey the Dardanelles, rallied
his countrymen to form a new and independent
Turkish state, freed from the barbarities of the
Koran.   In this he was helped by the Greek attack on
Smyrna (1919), disgraced as it was by the brutal
barbarities of the Greeks.   Mustapha, a fierce, tough,
disagreeable, dominant man, was the creator of modern
Turkey.   If his debaucheries were sordid, his head
in any crisis was clear, his judgment independent and
his military gifts brilliant.

These qualities he used to make a new Turkey for
the Turks on up-to-date lines, based on modern law
and the abolition of polygamy.   He hated the old
gang, their religion, and the evil sultan Abdul Hamid,
while behind him was ranged the influential Committee
of Union and Progress, secretly formed for the pur-

pose of terminating the old order and the creation of a modern and efficient Ottoman state. It was composed of the most enlightened Turks, who had been influenced by education, and, through defeat, had come to realise the folly of pursuing imperialistic conquests. All that was virile in the Turkish race rallied round Mustapha at Angora, where he defied the Sultan and pursued his policy to build up a new Turkey, free from the old traditions, internal tyranny and foreign interference. First of all he defeated the Greek invasion, and sent her troops in disorderly rout to the coast, whence they returned home with the knowledge that their presence had caused the massacre of thousands of men and women of their own race settled in Asia Minor. More than 1,000,000 Christians fled from Turkey, and out of the smoking ruins of Smyrna, where they had congregated before their flight, a new era arose for both Greece and Turkey. Their old monarchs disappeared, their differences were wisely settled, and Turkey, after centuries of autocratic caliphate and sultanate rule, became a democratic state, happy, contented and prosperous, to show its sympathy for freedom, and its hatred of tyranny, when again the world was plunged into war in 1939 by another criminal gang, intent on pursuing the same evil policy which had brought to the Turks only ruin and misery.

When will humanity cast off for ever the curse of ignorance, and cease to allow itself, first in one country and then in another, to be dragged to destruction by wicked men intent on their own glorification and enrichment? Only when mental development, by means of education, reaches a point

which enables the people to have and keep a wise
control of their own affairs. Then will be laid a basis
for peace and prosperity; but this constitutes only the
first step, as education must continue to direct these
free people along the path of righteousness, which
alone leads to happiness, as any deviation from it
brings conflict, misery and eventual destruction.

(4) India During Moslem Rule.

In Chapter IV we read the story of India's
early civilisation up to the time of King Asoka
(264–227 B.C.). Little is really known of India's early
history, and the Greeks and Romans began to take
notice of this vast continent only after Alexander
entered it in 327 B.C. Few records remain in the
country, as the climate quickly destroys all literature,
but from this time onwards we begin to know more
from outside sources.

About 126 B.C. the Greeks, who had settled in the
Punjab, were driven out by the Tartars, who were
followed by Scythians. These latter played an important part in the history of northern India, following
an empire established by Kanishka, who became the
royal founder of Northern Buddhism, which extended
to Tibet and Hindustan. The Scythians poured into
India in such masses that they supplanted the previous
population, but, by A.D. 100, Vikramaditya, a native
prince, had succeeded in driving out the invaders.
He is the central royal personage of the Hindu population, and from his reign dates the highest efforts of
Indian intellect and the greatest era of Sanskrit
literature.

During the next seven centuries three powerful monarchies, the Sahs, Guptas and Valabhis, succeeded each other in northern and western India, the last being overthrown by the Arabs in the 8th century A.D. From the 2nd century, until the Moslem conquest, the earlier races secured an ever-increasing importance, retaining some of the fairest tracts of northern India, but few facts are available. When, however, the Moslems supply an historical footing after A.D. 1000 things become clearer, but it is impossible to do more than just mention some outstanding features until the time came when the country was occupied by the British.

The first serious Moslem invasion of India occurred in 977 under Sabuktagin, whose son Mahomed was the first of the great Moslem conquerors—names which still ring throughout Asia. During his reign he extended the limits of his kingdom from Persia to the Ganges, and, for the next two hundred years, we read of further Moslem conquests, until the entire northern plain from the Indus to the Brahmaputra lay under their rule. Kutab proclaimed himself Sultan of Delhi in 1206, founding a dynasty which lasted until 1288. Then came Allah-ud-din, who extended his conquests into the still unsubdued southern part of the continent. Next followed the Tughlak dynasty, which lasted for seventy years, to be succeeded by the fourth outstanding Moslem conqueror of India, the fiendish scoundrel Timurlane (1398), about whom we have already read, and about whom more will be told in the next chapter.

In 1525 Baber, the fifth in descent from Timurlane, and also the fifth Moslem conquerer, invaded India and founded the Mogul Empire,[1] which lasted, at least in name, until 1858, when Queen Victoria became first the ruler, and then Empress of India in 1877. She took the Mogul title of Kaisar-i-Hind (Caesar of India), which, at the time this history is being written, is still held by her descendant George VI, the only remaining monarch to hold the ancient title of Caesar, now that the German Kaiser and the Russian Tzar are no more.

The most outstanding and enlightened of all the Mogul monarchs was Akbar I (1556–1605), who reigned simultaneously with Elizabeth of England. He became the undisputed ruler of a larger portion of India than had ever before acknowledged the rule of one man. Not only was he a successful conqueror, but his name is still cherished because of his ability as a civil administrator. He introduced a new state religion, became its prophet, and every morning in public worshipped the sun as the symbol of the divine soul which animates the universe, while at the same time he himself was worshipped as a god by the ignorant multitude. His attitude towards all religious beliefs was liberal, as he believed in religious toleration, because all should try to tune in with the Infinite in the way which best suited their mental development.

His son Jahangir (1605–1627) followed, and it was to his court that the English sent their first representative when they occupied Surat. During the reign of his son Jahan (1627–1658) the Mogul Empire attained its greatest magnificence, when Delhi was

---

[1] Mogul is the Arabic and Persian for Mongol, and came to be applied to the Moslem invaders of India.

founded, and the magnificent Taj Mahal at Agra was erected as a mausoleum to his favourite wife. Twenty thousand workmen, it is said, laboured on this work for many years.

Then followed his son Aurangzeb (1658–1707), and it was in his long reign that the Mogul power reached its culminating point, and commenced to decay. He extended his dominions to the extreme south of India, but even during his lifetime the Mahrattas, the Sikhs and the Nawabs (= Maharajas) of the Deccan, of Oudh and of Bengal, raised themselves to practical independence. On the death of Aurangzeb in 1707 the decline of the Mogul Empire set in with extraordinary rapidity, when, in 1739, Nadir, Shah of Persia, the sixth and last of the great Moslem conquerors of India, swept like a whirlwind over Hindustan and carried off plunder worth about £20,000,000 sterling. From now onwards the Great Mogul became a mere name, though the hereditary succession has continued unbroken down to our day. Out of the dismembered empire the power passed into the hands of Moslem courtiers and Mahratta generals, who carved for themselves separate kingdoms until at last British authority placed itself supreme over all.

Before this time India is largely a closed book, only its most prominent experiences being known, but, from the 18th century onwards, recorded history reveals the doings of its seething multitudes, a tale which will be told in the later chapters of Volume II.

(5) Moslem Spain Becomes a Beacon in Europe's Night.

During the reign of Omar, the land of Egypt, a province of the Eastern Empire, was conquered by the Arabs. These Arabs of the 7th century were virile and greedy for blood and loot. So they looked round for more lands to conquer, and decided to go farther west along the north coast of Africa. After conquering the Byzantine army they finally reached Morocco, with some ten miles of sea between them and Spain. Under their leader Tarik they crossed over to Spain in 711 and defeated Roderic, the last king of the Visigoths.

After occupying the greater part of Spain the Arabs entered France, and were defeated at Tours in 732 by Charles Martel. If, instead of venturing farther north beyond the Pyrenees, into France, they had consolidated their position everywhere in Spain, they might have been there to this day. Instead of so doing they left a part of northern Spain in the keeping of the Christian Visigoths, who eventually drove them out eight centuries later with the help of the Pope. By one of those curious freaks of fate, some of their descendants in 1936 were brought back to Spain by Franco, to help to save the Church which had brought about their expulsion in 1492.

The period of the Arabian occupation of southern Spain is one of fascinating interest and importance, as they were the first to bring civilisation, culture and learning to Christendom, to develop, centuries later, into what is called the Renaissance. Forty years after their first landing, a new Arab leader came to Spain. He was Abd-al-Rahman, a member of the house of Omayyad, who had been warned not to accept Abul Abbas's invitation to the banquet at which all his relations were killed, and their bodies used as a table for the feast. He escaped to Egypt and, after many adventures over five years, reached Morocco, whence he despatched a message to the Arabs in Spain. A vessel was sent for him, and he crossed over to be acclaimed as Emir. He it was who founded the Moslem civilisation in Spain, though he only secured a firm throne by dispatching his enemies in the usual brutal way of those days.

Once his authority was recognised he devoted himself to the prosperity of Spain, giving all Christians, Moslems and Jews complete religious liberty, building and repairing roads, and establishing a postal service. He made Cordova his capital, and began the erection of its great mosque, but, what was even more important, he encouraged learning, the circulation of literature, and established institutions for the work of charity and mercy. His statesmanship and perseverance gained for him the admiration of the entire Moslem world, and he left a prosperous cultured Spain to his son Hischem.

Hischem (788–796) first put down the rebellion of his elder brothers, who had been passed over because their father considered them unsuitable as rulers, and then he marched against the Visigoths, now called Spaniards, in the north, and across the Pyrenees into France. This was a plundering expedition, and he gave a fifth part of the booty towards the completion of the mosque at Cordova which his father had commenced to build. He then continued his father's work of ennobling Cordova by building stately palaces, public baths, and laying out gardens interspersed with palms, lawns and fountains. Orchards, vines and crops were planted, bridges were built, sanitation was improved, and the natives were persuaded to discard their heavy Gothic tunics in favour of the more colourful Arab robes. By the end of his reign Cordova was the cleanest and most spacious city in Europe, and the Western centre of Arab learning and culture.

His son Al-Hakem I (796–822) succeeded him as Emir. His evil life and impiety aroused the orthodox Moslems to rebellion, and this encouraged the Christian nobles, many of whom the invaders had displaced, to threaten his throne. They were invited by the Emir to a banquet, only to be murdered. The Moslem rebels were treated with equal ferocity, thousands were massacred, and many thousands exiled, but it is probable, if we judge from the stories of the Emir's orgies, that he was mad, though he lived to misrule the land for twenty-six years.

The constructive work interrupted by Al-Hakem was continued by Abd-al-Rahman II (822–852). His court at Cordova was marked by its brilliance and learning, outshining in wealth and magnificence any other in Europe. This reign of thirty years was progressive, trade flourished, and Cordova's population rose to 100,000. On either side of the banks of the Guadalquivir, on which it is situated, stood fine mansions surrounded by beautiful gardens, while the city itself was served with a good water supply and provided with many public baths, its streets being clean and its gardens well kept.

Abd-al-Rahman II was greatly helped by his enlightened chief minister Ziryab, whose wise counsel and progressive ideas did much to help forward Moslem civilisation in Spain. This outstanding man brought from ·the East delicacies, perfumes and also new flowers and shrubs to adorn further the public and private gardens. Cordova, and the other cities, he decided must have better houses, improved drainage, more baths, and the people must have better and more courteous manners. Every city must have a pure water supply and new roads connecting each, all of which was carried out. New and better hospitals were built, improved drugs were used, and new and more advanced medical schools were started.

Besides his social achievements Ziryab was a notable poet, musician and scholar, and he so encouraged learning that Cordova became the seat of science. The teaching of philosophy, history, medicine and geography received his special care, and Aristotle was translated from the Greek into Arabic. So enthusiastic was he in favour of education that he infected the people with his thirst for knowledge. Work was found for all able-bodied men, and those in need were taken care of in the various charitable institutions throughout the land.

Ziryab now passes out of history, and the closing years of the Emir are marred by intrigues of the orthodox, who resented this backsliding from the teaching of the Prophet. So his son and heir, Mahomet, was educated in the doctrines of the Koran, and when his father died progress ceased. For eleven years Moslem civilisation in Spain decayed, unbelievers were persecuted and dismissed from public offices, public funds were devoted to advance theology, and the country slipped into disorder. This state of affairs continued during the next two reigns, and Arabian Spain returned to poverty after her all too brief period of prosperity.

Her recovery came with Abd-al-Rahman III (912–961), who followed as the next emir. He found Spain in chaos and he raised it to order and prosperity. He came to the throne when the different towns and cities in the land were fighting one another, and the governors of provinces were in conflict. Brigands infested the roads and life was nowhere safe. The Christians pillaged and destroyed the property of the Arabs, who retaliated. Agriculture and trade were ruined, and the country was bankrupt. Such was Spain in consequence of two reigns of bad emirs, and yet, from the depths, Abd-al-Rahman III raised his country, during his long reign of just under fifty years, to a condition of prosperity never before reached. During this period lived Abulcasis, the greatest surgeon of his time, and the first to produce an illustrated work on surgery which set a standard for several centuries, while Isaac, a Jew, wrote the most learned treatise so far produced on fevers.

Eighteen years were required to pacify the country, the Christian nobles in the north, who were at constant war with each other, being the chief source of trouble. Finally Theuda, Queen of Navarre, subdued them, and entered into an alliance with the Emir, who now took the title of Caliph. With peace established prosperity commenced, the fields were ploughed and agriculture flourished. The roads again became safe, trade revived, and the national income increased to such a degree that large and magnificent palaces and public buildings arose in the cities throughout the land. Taxation was everywhere uniform, based on the value of agricultural produce, which was so encouraged that every acre of land was cultivated. Irrigation received special consideration, until the land became "one glorious garden" filled with corn, vegetables, fruit and flowers, some of the warm moist valleys in the south bearing three or four crops a year.

An industrious and contented people took all the wealth the land could give, and what was not required at home was exported abroad in exchange for those goods which Spain did not produce. A large assortment of fruits and vegetables went to the East in exchange for its delicacies and spices. Numerous prosperous villages studded the banks of the Guadalquivir, inhabited by peasants living in clean and tidy white-washed cottages. These villages were connected by well-paved roads which centred in an easily accessible town, whence went their surplus produce. Serfs and slaves were rare, as money, consisting of minted coins, was available to pay for the necessary labour, whereas, in the rest of Europe, 90 per cent. of the people were serfs and there were thousands of slaves.

Mines were opened up and developed, silver, gold, iron and quicksilver being won from the earth, while marble and alabaster were hewn from the quarries, to produce the material for the palaces, mansions, public buildings and baths. Ships sailed from Spain to India, China, Asia, North Africa and Constantinople, returning with amber, furs, tea, coffee, spices and ivory. Many villages cultivated the silkworm to produce the silk required for clothes, and elsewhere, for the same purpose, cotton and wool were grown. Embroidered silks, gold and silver brocades and velvet, added to the elegance of the clothes of the people. Craftsmen became famous for their work in leather, pottery, porcelain, glass, gold, silver and brass. Handsome carpets and beautiful tapestries were also produced in great number, and weaving was extensively carried on.

Cordova, situated in the midst of a fertile plain through which flowed the winding Guadalquivir, became the most beautiful and prosperous city in the world, and all Moslem Spain rose to a level of civilisation and culture not attained elsewhere in Europe until well on in the 18th century. Seville, Granada, and other large cities, had likewise all the elements of culture—fountains, public baths, public libraries, schools, and all that we now associate with modern civilisation, including mile after mile of well-paved streets lit with lamps, and an abundant supply of pure water and good sanitation.   .

Southern Spain, under Moslem rule, now supported a population of 30,000,000, spread throughout the land and inhabiting 80 large and 300 smaller towns, Cordova's citizens numbering 1,000,000, and every child in the land was taught to read and write. Rome, on the other hand, with its palaces, theatres, mansions, temples and public baths rotting in decay and covered with grass, a city which in the days of its glory had maintained a population equal to that of Cordova, had now only 40,000 ignorant, impoverished inhabitants, a large proportion being priests who lived like parasites on the earnings of the people.

Few in Christendom could even read or write, schools there being non-existent, while soap and baths were unknown. Towns were squalid, with streets of mud, undrained, unlit, unsafe, without public water or regard to hygiene and sanitation. Paris and London were no better than any of the other towns in Europe, and even the Christian towns of northern Spain were in the same squalid condition, the Spaniards evidently disdaining to copy anything from the Moslems, preferring ignorance and filth to knowledge and comfort. An example of the way Christians lived is found in an account of a monk who was sent with a letter from the Archbishop of Cologne to the Caliph. On arrival at Cordova he was so filthy and smelly that objection was taken to his being brought into the palace, but he stoutly refused to wash or change his clothes for the clean ones the officials set before him.

Elsewhere in Europe, for the first fifteen centuries of the Christian era, conditions were semi-barbaric, the people being without any idea of cleanliness. Baths and soap were unknown, even the nobles living in conditions of indescribable filth. No one in Europe, outside of Moslem Spain, wore underclothing which could be washed, or used handkerchiefs, or had any of the refinements to which even the poor of our day are accustomed. Everyone slept in their every-day clothes, which were alive with vermin. Culture was unknown, manners were crude and coarse to a degree, and yet, in this age, within one hundred years, the Arabs had raised themselves, and also the Spaniards they had conquered, to a height of refinement unknown since Roman times.

Cordova had, according to the records of the time,

more than 250,000 houses, so its population of a
million could not have been overcrowded. For
twenty-four miles the suburbs extended along the
river, each house within its own palm-shaded garden.
Public gardens, with every known shrub and flower,
promenades, public baths, fountains, cascades and
lily-ponds were interspersed over this wide area.
Music was provided, and famous musicians came to
the capital from the East. Flowers and shrubs were
in such abundance that a hill near the palace was
known as the Mountain of Flowers, and the banks of
the river as the Vale of Paradise.

Sewers ran under the streets, some so large that a
cart and bullocks could pass through them, and these
were constantly flushed with water. The stone streets
were well policed, and imposing and stately bridges
crossed the river, the largest still being capable of
supporting modern traffic. The citizens of Cordova
were justly proud of the fact that their city contained
two of the largest and most majestic buildings on
earth: the Caliph's palace and the Great Mosque.
The latter remains to this day, to testify to the building
capacity of the Spanish Moslems, but the palace, which
was said to have cost a fabulous figure, was destroyed,
and little now remains.

Ten thousand men and 28,000 horses, mules and
bullocks worked for forty years to construct this
marvellous palace. The walls were built of marble,
and its interior was decorated with exquisite frescoes
and magnificent sculptures. In this beautiful building
there were columns of rose and green marble and
alabaster, besides priceless works in rock-crystal
onyx and ebony, studded with pearls, rubies and

wondrous mosaics. Great domes in the ceilings added to the lighting effect, and the doors were made of rare wood inlaid with jewels, ivory, gold and ebony.

This was the edifice Abd-al-Rahman III built to house himself, his numerous wives and concubines, and his thousands of retainers, the money to pay for which came from taxation, as the rulers everywhere in those days received the nation's revenue and spent it as they pleased. Besides all this massive and glittering display he had seven other palaces. The Great Mosque, now a Christian church, is 600 feet long and 400 feet wide, its roof being supported by numerous columns of marble, jasper and porphyry, interlaced with arches. It is entered by nineteen large doors and is adorned with exquisite mosaics.

All the splendour of Arabian Spain did not centre in the capital, as the other cities were equally prosperous and attractively set out. Six other towns had populations of from a quarter to half a million. Seville, the second city of importance, had a population of over 500,000, and for thirty miles along the Guadalquivir, whose banks were rich with fruit trees, there were prosperous villages interspersed with the houses of the nobility and middle class, each within its own garden. Here in Seville, ships loaded and unloaded their cargoes brought from foreign lands. Like the capital, this city had imposing shops and spacious markets, but only the minaret of its great mosque still remains to declare its size and beauty.

Almeria, the most beautiful of all the Mediterranean coastal towns, was the chief port, with a population of 500,000, and there some of the thousand ships belonging to the Caliph entered and departed. Malaga, Valencia, Toledo and Granada, each with its special charm, were large and prosperous towns, but enough has been said to show how Spain, under Moslem rule, reached a level of prosperity and culture unlike any other land in the continent of Europe, which was then slumbering in a deep sleep of ignorance during the time so aptly called the Dark Ages.

Material prosperity did not mean that these unorthodox Moslems neglected mental culture. Cordova, for nearly two hundred and fifty years, was the greatest city of Europe both materially and mentally, during which time there was a period of regression just prior to the reign of Abd-al-Rahman III. Other Moslem cities in Spain continued this great achievement for a further four hundred years. All races and religions were free to live together, and, just so long as this toleration lasted, material and mental progress continued.

Learning was encouraged and books were collected, the library at Cordova containing some 500,000. New and rare books always found their way to the capital, original copies being often bought at high prices. The spacious library was the great attraction for scholars from all parts of the world, and it also housed a large number of men trained in copying, illuminating and binding. Here paper of fine quality, and not parchment, was used, and this was bound into handsome leather-covered volumes. Women took a large share in the intellectual life of the community; some were learned in the arts, crafts and science of the time, and one of the chief librarians was a woman, while another, herself an authoress, travelled abroad in search of new books. In Moslem Spain, educated women often earned their own living, and some made literature their career.

Cordova had at one time seventy public libraries, and twenty-seven schools for the poor, when in Christian Europe only ône per cent. of the population could read or write. Books contrary to the Moslem faith circulated alongside those which were orthodox, there being no ban on the expression of opinion, and the Greek classics were as eagerly read as the Koran. Enlightened Moslems did not take their holy book seriously, and they grew vines, and drank wine, which was quite contrary to its teaching.

Medicine and surgery made great progress, the maintenance of health and the relief of suffering receiving special attention in hospitals staffed by doctors trained in medical schools. Special attention was given to hygiene and sanitation, and the poor received free treatment for their ailments, besides being supported by alms in their poverty. Cleanliness was part of the life of the people. Public baths were plentiful in all the cities and towns, Cordova having 900, and soap was in general use.

Education was not state-endowed, but the majority were taught at home to read and write, and teachers, for all who wished to become educated, abounded, their fees being small. Most mosques had a school attached where children were taught to read the Koran, after which there were numerous books of all kinds available. The children of the middle and upper classes attended college lectures, which were also available for the poor, who received grants from endowments. Learning was encouraged by the authorities, and the keenness for knowledge amongst the young of all classes is an outstanding feature of this time. A list of authors of those days has survived, containing 10,000 names, and the numerous books in circulation ranged from those devoted to theology, surgery, geography, geology, agriculture, biology, botany, medicine, biography and zoology to those concerned with poetry, lyrics and stories.

In their knowledge of geography the Arabs reached a point never so far attained, and maps on paper, silk, and in the form of globes, were plentiful. Zoological and botanical gardens were maintained, and agriculture received special consideration from students, who made it a scientific study. Astronomy reached an advanced level, and with this science went the knowledge of the higher mathematics. Arab physicists were the pioneers in the science of optics, and their chemists made many important discoveries which also resulted in the production of new medicines. Surgeons and doctors, both Jews and Arabs, in Arabian Spain specialised in fevers, obstetrics, eye diseases, hernia, cataract, tumours and many other afflictions.

In the atmosphere of toleration and freedom of thought, which characterised this age, the Jew had scope for his talents, and added greatly to the mental wealth of these times. Prior to the coming of the Moslems to Spain the Jews were persecuted by the Christian Visigoths, but, under the Moslems, they were given complete freedom to practise their religion. Many rose to high positions, and contributed their share to the culture of these times. The Christians, likewise, were free to worship as they pleased, and

Cordova had a cathedral, with a bishopric attached, eleven monasteries and six churches.

This was the land which in the years to come was to be conquered by the Christians, who immediately introduced the Inquisition to stamp out all liberty of religious and political thought, a state of affairs which lasted until the 19th century.

The great love the Moslems had for beauty is very noticeable. Their taste lay in things which were refined and dainty, and this is especially noticeable in their silken colourful robes and velvet slippers. While Christians, outside of Moslem Spain, were content with rushes, which their dogs and other animals polluted, the floors of Moslem houses were covered with beautiful carpets, and their rooms were adorned with graceful ornaments. Everything, from their architecture to the simplest things they used, was embellished to please the eye. In their entertainments the same characteristic is noticeable, as they found no pleasure in watching animals suffer and die for their amusement—juggling, music, dancing, chess and backgammon being more to their taste.

Such, then, is the setting in which life went on in Moslem Spain during the age we are now considering. Though its history is filled with war, yet its civilisation and culture managed to endure and recover from all set-backs, until the last phase came when the Christians secured the Moslem's last foothold, Granada. Then the Arabs were driven from Spain, and Christian priests, by means of the Inquisition, dragged the country down to the low mental level in which they kept the rest of Europe.

Al-Hakem II (961–976) succeeded Abd-al-Rahman

III, and to him more than to any other of the Caliphs the encouragement of knowledge is due. He was a liberal ruler in all he did, and to him is due the great advance in the social and cultural services of his time. He was followed by his son Hischem II (976–1013), a brainless dandy who had a larger wardrobe of luxurious clothes than anyone before his time or since. He was buried naked when he died as a punishment for his extravagance. This coxcomb was quite overshadowed by Ibn-abi-Amir, known as Al-Mansur, meaning the Victorious, the greatest soldier and statesman of the 10th century. Under him Moslem Spain reached even greater heights of prosperity than ever before, and he brought it to a state of splendour never contemplated by any of the earlier Caliphs.

He, the son of a farmer, worked his way through school to employment in the palace, where his advancement was rapid. As Minister of Finance, at the age of twenty-seven, he acquired both power and wealth, and then, after occupying other important positions, became commander of the army and Vizier to the Caliph. He built for himself a strongly fortified palace close to Cordova, to which he removed the government offices. Here he conducted the affairs of state and welcomed ambassadors and foreign envoys. The army also received his attention, to reach over 500,000 men, mostly composed of Christian adventurers and Berbers. These latter were called Moors, their place of origin being Morocco, and they had the reputation of being hardy warriors, but they were quite distinct in race from the Arabs of Arabia.

Scholars from all parts of the world were welcomed

by this remarkable man, who attended their lectures and encouraged all branches of science. Roads were widened, new bridges were built, and graft in the public services abolished. He, however, could not rest with only these activities when his great army awaited his bidding. So he pushed the Christians in the north close up to the Pyrenees, and captured or destroyed their towns and villages. Everything was plundered, and what remained was destroyed. Then he moved against Catalonia, and, after capturing Barcelona, he crossed to North Africa to subdue a revolt. Soon he returned to stamp out intrigue at home, and, in order to unite the Arabs and the Berbers, who were in conflict, he started for Galicia in the north-west corner of Spain with promises of more loot for his organised army of thieves. Churches and convents were destroyed, the nuns removed to the harems, and wholesale slaughter and pillage followed everywhere. Everything movable was put on the backs of the Christian captives and brought to Cordova.

Feeling that his end was near, he decided to loot Castile, so as to receive even more abundant mercy from Allah, as all good Moslems felt that to die in a holy war against the Christians was the sure and certain way to obtain everlasting bliss in paradise. He, however, died in 1002 before he reached Castile, and so passed away this outstanding man, whose spectacular career of constructive effort was impaired by his aggression and destruction in war.

During the rule of Al-Mansur the caliphate reached the height of its power and the extent of its domination. From now onwards disintegration followed, and the various cities became independent states, but, in spite of the disorder of the times, science advanced and the cities continued to be prosperous and civilised. Al-Modhaffer succeeded his father Al-Mansur as Grand Vizier, and, for seven years, ruled the greater part of Spain. Under him prosperity continued, and literature and learning were encouraged. He unfortunately died and was succeeded by his brother, Abd-al-Rahman, a frivolous and drunken youth, who forced the Caliph, Hischem II, to surrender to him his office. So he reigned for a short time as Abd-al-Rahman IV, but a revolt brought about his death.

Now followed a scramble for the caliphate, when law and order ceased. Then the rumbling rage of the Orthodox Moslems, who had hated all the glamour and splendour, considering it as quite contrary to the Koran, broke out in all its fury. The magnificent palace of the Caliph was stripped of all its decorations, and then set on fire. The mania for destruction then passed on to the mansions along the river, many of which were likewise destroyed. Civil war followed, the Berber and Christian mercenaries offering themselves to whichever side paid them best, and for a time it seemed as if Moslem civilisation in Spain was doomed.

Help was asked from the Christians in the north, and this was given in exchange for the surrender of all the forts Al-Mansur had built to keep them from coming south. With civil war at· home, and the Christians coming in from the north, the land was in a sad plight, once prosperous towns and villages being now ruined and desolate. Out of this confusion and desolation grew the city states ruled by powerful governors. A caliph reigned for only twenty years more at Cordova, the last being Hischem III, when, in 1031, the nobles proclaimed the end of the caliphate, and their intention to rule the land themselves.

For two hundred and fifty years Emirs, and then Caliphs, had ruled, first of all the southern part and then most of Spain, during which time, except for fifty years, their subjects had enjoyed a high degree of civilisation while the rest of Europe was living in the depths of degradation. Ethically the Arabian Spaniards were not much better than their contemporaries, but, at least, they were the first during the Christian era to make life easier and happier, to erect hospitals and cure the sick, to have homes for the poor and needy, to encourage the study of medicine and surgery, and to promote the sciences and literature. For these great achievements they can be truly thanked, as they brought light into a dark and ignorant Spain, only in the end to have it smothered under a load of Christian superstition. The torch which the Arabs lit in Spain was, however, never quite extinguished, and, after lying dormant for the next six centuries, it again began to glow, to produce eventually the light we have today.

From now onwards, for the next two hundred years, the history of Moslem Spain centres around its great cities, where the sciences and arts continued to flourish amongst these prosperous communities. Under a President and a Council the city states thrived and developed, while the zealous orthodox Moors, the principal cause of the downfall of the caliphate, were suppressed. Cordova once more became prosperous and famous for its School of Medicine. Granada was a flourishing prosperous city for the next four hundred years, and on the hill above the town successive emirs built the famous palace, the Alhambra. Toledo, one of the great centres of culture, had a population of 250,000 people, many active traders, and an upper class living in mansions along its river banks. Here lived the astronomer Al-Zarkal, one of the many learned men of the time.

Almeria, about the same size as Toledo, was an active port and trading centre. Valencia, of like size, was the home of many famous scholars, but, at the end of the 11th century, it was captured by the Spaniards. Seville, another large and wealthy city, likewise prospered, and here also science flourished. These, and other cities, were centres of learning, and each, in friendly rivalry, tried to pass the other in scientific achievement. The 10th, 11th and 12th centuries can be regarded as the time when Arab culture and knowledge reached its highest level, an era when both Arabian and Jewish historians, astronomers, and writers on medicine and science were most numerous.

The other side of the picture is less pleasing, as we read of the most appalling cruelties and massacres during the frequent wars to which this land was subjected. Lying as it did between the Christians in the north and the Berber Moors in Africa, it was just another Palestine or Belgium, the battlefield of countless adventurers and plunderers. Here rich spoil was always to be found, and the Spanish Arabs turned for help sometimes to one side and then to the other. In 1086, hard pressed by the Christians and their

King Alfonso, they sought help from Yusef, the Moorish leader whose city of Morocco was the centre of these fierce fanatical Berber Moslems, a man who hated the more cultured Arabian Spaniards as much as did the Christians. He came to their aid and defeated the Christians, only to settle down and take possession of the land he came to help. Then it was that Christians, Arabs and Jews were ravaged and persecuted, and all culture and learning were discouraged.

Civil war in Morocco depleted Spain of the best Berber troops, and Alfonso, taking advantage of this, again invaded the south in 1134, only to be defeated. The Spanish Arabs then revolted against the Berbers, who, on this occasion, asked the northern Christians for help. Cordova was captured with the help of Castilian Knights, and the long-awaited opportunity for the north to take possession of the south of Spain had come at last. The Christians, however, quarrelled amongst themselves over the division of the loot and returned home, leaving the south to fall again under the domination of the Moors.

For one hundred and forty years this grinding of southern Spain between the Christian north and the Moslem Africans went on, and yet, whenever there was peace, both civilisation and culture returned, to spread to North Africa, the city of Morocco planning its public services on those of Cordova. Seville now reached the height of its prosperity when its magnificent mosque was built, its majestic minaret still remaining to remind us of the city's past glory, though the mosque itself has vanished, as it was destroyed by the Christians.

At this time lived Averroës (1126–1198) in Seville, the most outstanding Moslem philosopher, physician and scholar of his day, who, for twenty years, was governor of the city. He separated religious superstition from scientific facts, and developed the teaching of Aristotle. Thus he laid the foundation for the break between the scientist who relied on facts to increase his knowledge, and the priest who was satisfied with tradition, holy relics and superstition for his guidance. Then also flourished Avenzoar, the teacher of Averroës, the greatest physician of his age, and if the people of Christian Europe had co-operated with these great Moslem thinkers, instead of devoting their thoughts only to theology and religious dogma, we today would certainly be many centuries ahead of our present-day knowledge. Not until the 16th century did Christian Europe begin to give consideration to the higher culture adopted by the Moslems.

In 1196 the Spanish and Portuguese Christians, encouraged by disturbances in Morocco, again set out to ravage the south, but the Sultan of Morocco gathered his forces together and forced them back with great slaughter. He captured Lisbon, and returned with thousands of captives and enormous booty. This bloody conflict between the Moors and the Christians did not end here, as, when another revolt developed in Morocco, the Christians again attacked, and the Sultan, with another great army, crossed over from Africa. The Pope appealed for a Crusade against the Infidel, and 60,000 knights from Germany, France and England rallied to his appeal. This time (1212) the Christians were victorious in the decisive Battle of Las Navas de Toloso, and Moslem power in Spain was shattered; five centuries and hundreds of battles having been necessary to secure this triumph, which was followed by an age of reaction the passing years have done little to mitigate. How Spain became Christian, and how the Spanish Moslems fared for the next two hundred and fifty years, will be told in Chapter XI, but here the melancholy fact has to be recorded that the sole ray of intellectual light in Europe was extinguished by this battle, and was not to be relit for another four hundred years.

Before closing this story of great achievements, interspersed with bloody wars, massacres, plundering and so much that was evil, let us remember the enduring benefits which Moslem civilisation left to slumber in Spain, until Europe was ready to rouse the giant of knowledge. The Arabs advanced civilisation and culture one stage further, when the torch of knowledge, which they re-lit and kept burning for seven hundred years, was taken up centuries later by the rest of Europe, at the time known as the Renaissance, about which we shall be reading later on.

Like humanity in our own time, they were plagued with war, while cruelty and suffering were their portion as the result of their own and other people's ignorance. Yet, in spite of this ever-present blot, there runs through their history, like a golden thread, the desire for knowledge which raised their civilisation and culture to a high level, such as was quite unknown elsewhere in Europe at that time.

The Spanish Arabs, with their love of the beautiful, of luxury and learning, became, as time went on, the victims of their geographical position. They were in constant danger from the Christians in the north, who hated and envied them, and the savage Berbers in Africa, who looked on their fellow religionists as backsliders, because they had strayed from the orthodox path as laid down by the Koran. Knowledge did not appeal to the Christians or the Moors, as to them all who could read and write, all who loved literature and culture, were despised as effete. So let us remember what we owe to the Spanish Arabs, because much of what we enjoy today can be traced to these intelligent people who lived for nearly eight hundred years in southern Spain.

CHAPTER X.

CHRISTIAN CIVILISATION.
(352–1270.)

Introduction. (1) *Europe Takes Shape as Separate King-doms.* (2) *Christendom's Holy War on the Moslems.* (3) *Germany and Italy in the Middle Ages.* (4) *France During the Crusades.* (5) *England Becomes a United Nation.*

HISTORY has certainly been badly distorted in our own times, and the British Broadcasting Corporation has been the medium to convey to the people everywhere an entirely erroneous idea of the past. The speakers consistently speak as if from the year one of the Christian era, light, for the first time, illumined humanity, that Paganism was then overthrown, and that only in our day has Paganism been re-born in Germany. The impression sought to be conveyed is obvious, namely that during the Christian era, which dates from the year Jesus was supposed to be born, what came to be known as Christendom became civilised. Something like what we, outside of Germany, are today, and that the birth of Jesus brought to an end an age when the heathen lived in utter darkness, as do the savages and cannibals of the South Sea Islands, their gods being idols of stone.

The influence of the Christian Church on history is largely the cause of this ignorance. Naturally the Church wished to glorify the age for which it was largely responsible, at the expense of all that went before, with the result that nearly everyone has an entirely wrong idea of the past. Its propaganda has been as distorted as anything the Nazis or Fascists ever produced, and, while the latter flourished during only the past ten to twenty years, the Christian Church, with its vast wealth and its huge clerical army, intent on its glorification, regardless of the truth, has been at work since the 4th century to the present day.

This great religious organisation secured from different monarchs immense power over the lives of the people, who looked to it for guidance in their religious and social life. As its boundaries grew, when more and more of Europe was Christianised, these powers were extended until they eventually covered most of Europe, besides all north and south America, South Africa and Australasia. It was a State within the states of Europe, with its own law courts, and all matters concerning birth, marriage, death and burial came under its jurisdiction. Priests, monks, theological students, crusaders, widows and orphans had their grievances and difficulties settled in these courts. Everything to do with the disposal of property left by deceased people, heresy, sorcery, witchcraft and blasphemy came under Church law. There were numerous Church prisons where the priests placed those they considered had contravened Church law, and where they pined, often for life, without the right of appeal.

The Pope was the supreme law-giver of Christendom, and from his Court at Rome there was likewise no appeal. He could issue excommunications and dispensations to anyone as he pleased, which meant that he could set aside the law of any country. He could allow a man to have two wives, or marry a cousin, or do whatever he thought was right. Church law borrowed much from Roman civil law, but it was also based upon expediency, which, in the hands of the religious fanatics who mostly made up the papal dynasty, brought about endless cases of injustice, cruelty and misery.

The Church levied various taxes and imposed the tithe tax on all land, which meant that one tenth of all the produce of the soil came into the hands of the priests. It owned then, as it still does, vast possessions in the form of land, houses, and wealth of all kinds, but this was exempt from all taxation, as were the priests, who were only subject to Church law, and not to the laws of the country in which they lived.

In this chapter we are now entering the age when the influence of the Church on Western world affairs becomes dominant. Having under its power a great multitude of illiterate and superstitious people from kings, princes and nobles downwards, its threat of excommunication was always a most effective weapon. Next came the immense power it obtained by means of the Confessional. The Church indeed held the keys of life and death, which very keys are represented on its crest, and only through implicit obedience to its commands could anyone hope to save his soul hereafter. This being so it is perhaps appropriate that this chapter should open with some consideration of the popes at Rome, who wielded authority above and beyond any earthly monarch.

Just as the Nazi and Fascist organisations seized power by a number of ambitious and unscrupulous men getting together after a time of crisis, so the Christian Church rapaciously snatched political power at the beginning of the 5th century after the fall of Rome. The methods employed were the same in both cases: intrigue, fraud, torture, imprisonment and banishment of all who opposed the will of the dictator. In the case of the Church the dictator was the Pope, and he based his authority on a reported saying of Jesus:—

> Thou art Peter, and upon this rock I will build my Church, and the gates of hell shall not prevail against it. I will give unto thee the keys of the Kingdom of Heaven, and whatsoever thou shalt bind on earth shall be bound in heaven, and whatsoever thou shalt loose on earth shall be loosed in heaven. (*Matthew* xvi, 18.)

This remark was never made by Jesus, because it was attributed to him by means of an interpolation in the Gospel at a much later date, when the Church required divine authority for its claims. Anyone who thinks will realise at once that such a remark could not have been understood by Peter or the other disciples. Petra is the Greek for rock, whereas Jesus spoke Aramaic, which language contains no word for Church, and the idea of a Christian Church only evolved slowly during the first three centuries. On this fraud, and the story that Peter founded a church at Rome, for which there is not a shred of evidence, the popes have based their authority as the representatives of Peter, to whom had been given by Jesus the keys of heaven and hell.

Another equally blatant fraud perpetrated by the Church is known to historians as "the Donation of

Constantine", which enabled it to claim temporal power from the 8th century onwards. In 752 Boniface, the English missionary, anointed and crowned Pepin II at Soissons as King of the Franks, thus bringing to an end the effete Merovingian dynasty, and inaugurating the Carlovingian monarchy. In exchange for according him this divine recognition of his kingship, Pepin, at the request of Pope Stephen (a cruel and wicked pontiff, who cut out the eyes of his enemies), conquered the Lombards and handed over to the Holy See all their territory in the centre of Italy. This large tract of land, comprising 16,000 square miles, became known as the Papal States, which from now onwards divided Italy in two. This intrusion prevented Italy from becoming a nation until the 19th century, these states, moreover, being a cesspool of degradation, and the centre of the gross ecclesiastical wickedness which cursed Europe from the 8th century for eleven hundred years.

Whenever Pepin withdrew his troops the Lombards again occupied their stolen land. Then followed passionate requests from Rome for Pepin to return and again drive out the owners, but he would do nothing more. So the Pope took an ingenious course, and wrote a letter to Pepin, dated from heaven and signed by Saint Peter, demanding that this territory be again conquered and given over to the Church. Pepin, an ignorant barbarian, believed that the letter had come to him direct from heaven, and did as he was told to do, the consequence being that a third of Italy, comprising twenty-three towns, became the property of the Christian Church.

The Pope had no title to this stolen property. So

he set about to forge one. He conveniently discovered, sometime between the years 752 and 777, that
Constantine had conveyed all Italy over to Pope
Sylvester (314-335), the then Bishop of Rome, when
the capital of the Empire was removed to Constantinople in 330. In the 8th century, which was a time
of savage ignorance, anything the Pope said was
accepted, and it was not until the 15th century that
the fraud was made public, when Lorenzo Valla, the
pioneer of historical criticism, exposed the forgery so
thoroughly that no reply was ever attempted. No
contemporary document referred to the donation, no
original deed had ever been seen by anyone, in fact
the entire affair from beginning to end was a pious
forgery, and one which takes its place alongside the
clerical forgeries in the Gospels and Epistles, now
part of the Bible. Instead of burning this bold critic
of the nefarious doings of the Holy See, Pope Nicholas
V made Valla his private secretary, and thus disarmed
further controversy, which, under the circumstances,
was probably the simplest way out of an impossible
position.

Here there is not the space to expand on the
numerous frauds and intrigues which ultimately
raised the Pope to the position of supreme dictator
of Christendom. The origin and history of the
Papacy is a sordid story from beginning to end, and
would require volumes to encompass. From the
time the first Pope obtained control, there commenced the work of representing the past history
of the Church in the light in which it has now
come down to us. Then followed the falsifying of
past history, to represent the Greeks, Romans,

Egyptians and Babylonians as heathen savages lacking both civilisation and culture. Saints and martyrs sprang into being, legends took the place of history, and false stories were told of Christian martyrs, some of whom were depicted as being torn to death by beasts in the Colosseum. Few saints or martyrs emerge into reality, according to those historians who have made the investigation, as practically all the stories told about them are now known to be fictitious.

The divine origin of the Church was likewise invented, and history was distorted with this end in view. Forgeries became so numerous that Pope Gelasius, in 494, timidly, and somewhat haltingly, rebuked their authors. Pope Benedict XIV, in the 18th century, was so ashamed at the extent to which fraud and forgery had contributed to produce Church history, that he ordered it to be rewritten, but the cardinals so obstructed the work that it had to be abandoned.

The British Broadcasting Corporation is dominated by Church influence, as those who control its broadcasts, and those who are allowed to speak, have been taught history at school based on the bogus stories of the Christian Church. In consequence, listeners obtain an entirely false idea of the world before and during the Christian era. Unless we can get a true perspective of the past we cannot be correctly informed, and this affects our judgment. History has always been too much influenced by the interests of both Church and State. In Germany and Italy, for the past generation, the youth have been taught false history by the scoundrels who seized power after the First World War. Thus they secured the help of the young by telling them the old stories, so often told in the past, of plunder and glory to be obtained by war, but they never informed their dupes that if, and when, such success came the leaders only would reap the harvest. Those who fight for war lords pay the cost, suffer the destruction or meet death, wounds, pain, suffering and misery, but seldom do they see the plunder or obtain the glory.

If only history were truthfully told, and intelligently understood, the pious frauds of priests, and the glittering promises of zealous politicians or would-be conquerors, would cease to be believed. Then the people would turn their attention to securing their own happiness, and material comforts, by honest methods and leave aside for evermore the path trodden by the thugs and the highwaymen. Only by following the way of righteousness can happiness be obtained, but this will be discovered solely by knowledge and wisdom, and, if the people lack both, how easy it is to slip into the road that leads to destruction.

The first thirty bishops of Rome were men of no merit or distinction, quite ignorant, and with a very small following. Then came the beginning of the Golden Age of the Church, when Constantine recognised it as the State Church of the Roman Empire, and the Bishop of Rome later became the Pope. Then the popes and cardinals began to live in palaces and don the gorgeous dress of state officials. Then came competition for the holy office. The followers of Pope Liberius (352–366), and those of his rival Felix II, fought bloody battles in which many people were killed. After Liberius, the conflict was renewed between Damasus (366–384), a Catholic, and Ursinus, an Arian, both of whom were elected Pope. In one church alone, after a terrible siege, 160 Christians killed each other in support of one or the other, and the deadly conflict spread all over Rome and lasted for weeks, with the result that in October in the year 366 the Church secured more martyrs than ever fell in the days of Pagan persecution.

Christianity had, so far, not made better the lives of the people, and Jerome, some years later, wrote of the priests, nuns and the laity as sordid, greedy and unchaste. Hymns, chanting, altars, images, incense, holy water, candles and silk vestments, copied or stolen from the Pagans, and the duplication of the Pagan form of worship at the Church of St. Peter, the Church of St. Paul, and elsewhere, constituted the religious life of the people of Rome. When the Christian Visigoths broke down the imperial rule they peacefully adapted their religious life to what was then prevailing, and so the Church progressed in wealth and power, drawing within its fold, by force or persuasion, the barbarian tribes and those who still remained Pagans.

The papal power in Rome was further consolidated by Pope Leo I (440–461), though the Bishop of Constantinople claimed equal status in the east. To this claim the false reply was made that Constantine, when he left Rome for Constantinople, had declared that the Bishop of Rome was to be both the secular and spiritual ruler of Christendom west of Greece. After the death of Leo two popes, one a Catholic and the other an Arian, were again elected, and again the same bloody feud ensued, this time for three years. Pope Gregory (590–604), of all the popes of this age, did raise the prestige of the Holy See. He was one of the most able and energetic of all the popes, and was responsible for missionaries being sent to England.

He it was who established the liturgical music of the Church. He ruled in Rome as an independent monarch, made treaties, and had his own standing army, but some of the things he said and did are quite revolting. He put down all attempt at education, closed the Roman schools, and believed the most absurd stories about devils and miracles. It was he who started the Church on its policy of keeping the people ignorant, and he was therefore one of the causes which brought about the Dark Ages. He persuaded a large number of nobles to leave their estates to the Church, in view of the imminence of the second coming of Christ, and this very superstitious but shrewd priest thus became the richest man and largest slave-owner in Europe.

When we come to the 7th century we find six popes in its first quarter, some of whom were probably murdered. From then onwards, during the Dark Ages, there is little that is good to say of the Papacy. The records which have come down paint a dismal picture of the morals of the popes and the clergy, as they just constitute one story after another of licentious living, of contested elections, with bribery, corruption, bloody riots, intrigues and quarrels between the popes and the bishops. Twenty popes thus darken the pages of history until we reach the close of the 7th century. In the 8th century the popes begin to win temporal power, and this will be realised as we proceed, because from that time onwards they become intertwined with the rest of our story.

Temporal power, which led to the lust for wealth and increased territory, reduced the Holy See to the depth of degradation. From the 9th century, when Pope Nicholas I declared that each pope was God on earth, to the time when the French, disgusted with the conduct of successive popes, removed Clement V to Avignon in 1305, there is little good to be told and much that is bad. Forgeries abounded, and cruelty, vice and brutality stained the lives of successive pontiffs, while immorality and licence were open and unashamed from the popes downwards to the humblest amongst the clergy. Those who opposed the wishes of the Pope were too often subjected to violent and cruel deaths, the cutting out of eyes and tongues being a common practice.

Murders were common in the Lateran Palace, and much blood reddened the streets of Rome, especially during episcopal elections. Anathemas were scattered far and wide. Forty-two of the eighty-five popes who ruled from 600 to 1050 had each a reign of less than two years, quite a number suffering violent deaths because of their outrages. Thousands of victims languished in the papal dungeons, without trial or reason, and there many ended their days. Ecclesiastical offices were sold to the highest bidder, no matter who he was. Vice and crime in Rome during these centuries were so common that the chroniclers of the time took for granted much that took place, and only became interested when a character like Pope John XII (956–963) committed every evil deed in the calendar of crime.

The crime-stained pages of the Papacy have unfortunately caused to be passed over the popes who were sincere, saintly and eager for the reform of the wickedness so prevalent everywhere throughout the Church. Their attempts at purification and reform were largely ineffective, as the whole ecclesiastical system was rotten from top to bottom. Morality rested on theology and not on ethics, the consequence being that "the will of God" was interpreted to suit individual tastes, which meant that there was little justice or toleration because these virtues were quite neglected.

There was no ethical standard in the Church, which was a money-making affair that could only prosper by keeping the people ignorant. Consequently, from the popes downwards, the clergy and people were vicious, bigoted and intolerant, even the so-called good popes believing that all heretics deserved torture and death.

This being so, we need not be surprised that Lecky described Europe of the Middle Ages as "a society which was absolutely anarchical", and Gibbon remarked that "it would be difficult to find anywhere more vice and less virtue". Such, then, is a brief résumé of the terrible history of the Papacy during the first thousand years of the Christian era, but another system was at work which exercised a great influence in these degenerate times. It is called Feudalism, and is incorrectly known as the Feudal System, but it was a system in name only, as there was little systematic thought in its development and operation.

With the break-up of the Roman power confusion prevailed everywhere, there being neither states nor rulers as we understand by these words. Europe was in chaos without law or administration, and numerous princes, dukes, chiefs, bishops and adventurers ruled the area they were able to control from their castle or stronghold, to be continually fighting one against the other. Christians and Jews had fierce feuds in Spain, which were quelled only when the Moslems in 711 invaded and took over control of the country. In Britain the Anglo-Saxon invaders fought amongst themselves, and in Italy and France lawlessness and disturbance were everywhere.

Out of this boiling turmoil a new order gradually evolved from sheer necessity, as no one felt safe and crimes were left unpunished. It was a time for leadership, but, owing to the breakdown of communications, it could only be of a local nature. So the weak joined up with the strong, the man of no substance joining with others like him, to become the vassals of the man who had a following. They agreed to do his bidding in exchange for his protection, and this process went on up the social scale, each weaker individual, or group of weaker men, joining up with someone stronger than themselves. The Lord, or whoever he was, thus obtained the service, for his protection and aggression, of a large force of vassals, grouped under a number of minor protectors, who all looked to him to protect them. It was a kind of mutual service organisation, and out of this developed the social life of Europe, with its different grades of society.

The strong man invariably took the lead, and became the king, with the nobles of different degrees under him. Amongst these he divided the land of his kingdom, which he considered he held on behalf of God. It was like a pyramid, with God at the top, who granted the King the · life-rent of the land, and he in turn leased it out to his nobles in exchange for service and payment in kind. As it was believed that the Pope represented God on earth, we can understand how powerful the popes became, as they considered themselves, and were looked upon, as the final court of appeal by kings, nobles and the people. So long as the vassals fulfilled their obligations they, and their heirs, held their property, or fief, as if they were the owners. Thus Europe was converted into numerous fiefs, rising in graded ranks from the knight's fee or benefice at the bottom to the King, and God, represented by the Pope, was over all.

(1) Europe Takes Shape as Separate Kingdoms.

It will be remembered that in Chapter VIII we arrived at the year 642, when Heraclius died an old man. That was the last point we reached in European history, and we now take up the story in France, to learn how it will all work in with the Eastern Empire over which he ruled. Various kingdoms had now been set up in Europe, the kingdom of the Franks holding a dominating position in the centre of the Continent.

The founder of this kingdom was Clovis (481–511), who, when a youth of fifteen, succeeded his father as King of the Franks, the tribe then occupying the country now called Belgium. He was a vigorous and fierce warrior, and did not rest until he had extended his dominions nearly to the Pyrenees in the south, and in the east to about half-way between the rivers

Rhine and Elbe. He was the first to create some kind of national order out of the wreckage everywhere in Europe, but, for other reasons, his reign and achievements were of paramount importance to the future of Europe.

Besides being the architect of France, and changing the capital from Soissons to Paris (named after the Parisii, a Keltic tribe which settled on the banks of the Seine in the 3rd century B.C.), he established Catholic Christianity in Gaul, now to be called France. Hitherto, since the fall of the Roman Empire, it was doubtful whether Catholic or Arian Christianity would prevail, as the different Germanic tribes were not unanimous on the vital question as to whether the theological Christ had come into existence at the same time, or after his father Jehovah; in other words, whether Jehovah or Christ were equal, or Jehovah the older and more important god of the two.

To these ignorant savages this was a burning question which could be settled only by war. From the time of the Council of Nicaea, which established Catholic Christianity as the state religion of Rome, numerous conflicts, massacres and deportations had occurred, according to the way those in power viewed this theological dogma. The Catholic popes never lost a chance to promote the Catholic opinion in its conflict with the Arian belief that Jehovah had existed prior to Christ, who therefore was not equal with his father. The manner in which the former triumphed should be known by everyone, as then was settled the way the people of Europe, and those lands still to be discovered, were to think as regards their salvation.

Realising that Clovis was a formidable warrior, who would be useful to the Catholic cause, the Pope arranged that he be introduced to a Catholic maiden, the niece of the King of Burgundy, a bishop being instructed to do everything possible to bring about a marriage between these two young barbarians. When Clovis fell for the girl's charms the wedding was celebrated, and then began the task, under the bishop's direction, of changing her husband into a Catholic Christian. Finally her influence induced him to make a vow that if he succeeded in driving out the Allemans, who had invaded his lands, he would adopt the Catholic instead of the Arian form of Christianity.

Clovis successfully drove out the invaders, and then he, along with thousands of his wild warriors, accepted Catholic baptism without thought or question. Now followed the climax which was to have tremendous effects all down the centuries. Here indeed we are at one of the turning-points in history. Catholicism and Arianism were now so definitely ranged against each other, that only by the ordeal of battle would one or the other predominate. Clovis now became the champion of Catholic Christianity, and against him were ranged the Visigoths, who held Spain and much of Gaul. Their King was Alaric II, who was an enlightened and tolerant man, and quite content to allow everyone to define the Trinity as he thought best.

Clovis, now a fanatical Catholic, and full of zeal to spread the Catholic faith, had no such refined feelings, declaring that "with God's aid" he would attack these heretics and rid Gaul of every Arian. So it came about that on these two men depended whether the Christian faith, as defined at the Council of Nicaea, would prevail, or whether the minority opinion, which was there outvoted, would at this late date win the way to acceptance. On them was to rest the solution of the puzzle which for the past two centuries had occupied the mind of all Christendom, the correct definition of the Trinity. A bloody battlefield was to settle for Christians, for all time, the intimate details concerning the creator and sustainer of the immeasurable universe!

On the field of Vouillé, near Poitiers, the Franks, led by Clovis, attacked the Visigoths under Alaric II in the year 507, and in this momentous battle Clovis decisively defeated, and personally killed, his enemy. Thus was definitely settled for Christendom this tremendous question of the nature of God, the belief from now onwards prevailing that Jehovah and Christ had always co-existed, and were of equal standing, power and majesty. Catholic Christianity was now supreme, every Christian from that day to this being brought up in the Catholic faith, which teaches the necessity of everyone accepting its definition of the Trinity if heaven is to be reached and hell avoided.[1] After the Reformation the Protestants continued to believe in the Catholic faith, in its definition of the Trinity, and the damnation of all unbelievers.

So Clovis, an ignorant savage, takes a very high place in the Christian Church. To have settled this question of the godhead to the satisfaction of all Christians from his time to this is no small achieve-

---

[1] This is the substance of the Athanasian Creed, which was produced about the 8th or 9th century by someone unknown, for the purpose of correctly defining the Trinity from the Catholic point of view, thus amplifying and stabilizing the statements contained in the earlier Nicene Creed.

ment, especially as the Church has always proclaimed
that the acceptance of the Catholic interpretation
alone leads to salvation.   If this be so, the chance of a
single battle decided the destiny of the millions then
unborn, and consequently makes the Battle of Vouillé
one of the most important, if not the most important,
in history.   The fate of all non-Catholic Christians,
who died prior to this vital conflict, can best be left
to the imagination.

Clovis, this ardent Christian soldier, for ever
marching on to war, continued his missionary crusade
until his death, and, as he advanced towards the Rhine
and Elbe in the east, and to the Pyrenees in the south,
his plundering army massacred all who would not
accept the Catholic faith, priests accompanying the
marauders and urging them on in their bloody work.
Clovis never showed pity or mercy to anyone, and,
not without reason, French historians, when writing
the first page of their country's history, brand him as a
plunderer, an unscrupulous liar, a murderer and one
of the most debased and wicked amongst men.

From his time French history begins, and so also
do two factors which were to have a powerful influence
on European history.   The first, as we have read, was
the consolidation of Catholic Christianity, and the
second the establishment, by Clovis, of feudalism and
serfdom, with which the Church allied herself by
becoming the feudal lord of much of Europe, to the
deterioration of what little morality she still possessed.
A matter which was, however, of more importance
to the Catholic priests was the fact that these two circumstances greatly increased their power and influence,
the Pope becoming the dominant force in Europe, as

the barbarian kings, realising that Catholic Christianity was now on the winning side, came over to the acceptance of the creed of Nicaea, and gave the Catholic Church their support. From this time onwards Christianity and the Christian Church stand for Catholic Christianity, and not Arian Christianity, which fades into the background.

Not only did Clovis first establish the long alliance between the French monarchy and the Church at Rome, which did not end until the down-trodden people of France drove out of Páris the last despotic Bourbon king in 1830, but he established Church rule from the Mediterranean to the English Channel, and from the Atlantic to the Rhine. Bishops now became the influential dignitaries at Court, their business being to see that the Pope's will and pleasure was carried out by the sovereigns who now held their kingdoms from him on behalf of God. Most important of all the clerical duties was the supervision of the collection of a tenth of the produce of the land. This was used to meet the needs of the clergy, and the balance was transferred to the Papal Treasury in Rome, legislation to this effect being the first business of the Church whenever a king was converted to Christianity.

Churches were then built by serf labour, and on them were carved images of hideous faces to drive away the devils, the Church being as much an affair of this earth as the means of eternal salvation. Here the devils were prayed out of the sick, and prayers were offered for freedom from plague, for rain or fine weather, the three Christian gods being looked upon as responsible for the welfare and maintenance of the people. The Pagan temples, which the Christian churches replaced, had been built for the same purpose, the change from Paganism to Christianity only meaning a change in the names of the gods worshipped, and not in the deeds they were expected to perform.

Clovis was the first warrior chief to place himself in alliance with the militant Christian Church, and, from now onwards, the Pope used the sovereigns of Europe to carry out the policy of Augustine—that all must accept the Christian faith or perish by the sword. Thus did the faith spread until, by persuasion or force, it was eventually accepted by a third of the world's inhabitants.

The four sons of Clovis succeeded to the lands their father had conquered, but, as each one was determined to secure supreme control, a bitter feud developed between them. Gradually the Franks of the west, those who occupied what had been Gaul, and spoke a form of Latin, split off from the Franks of the Rhineland, who continued to speak what is now called low German, the language once common to both. This difference in language was the cause of the rise of two separate nations, composed of people who otherwise would probably have remained as one, if those who became the French had not had their language changed as the result of the conquest of Gaul by the Romans. Julius Caesar, who conquered Gaul, and imposed on it Roman culture, was therefore primarily responsible for two separate nations arising out of what was originally a kindred people. If they had been one they might have kept the peace of Europe, instead of being hereditary enemies and constantly at war with each other.

What is now France then became Neustria, and the

region from the Rhineland eastwards towards the Elbe became Austrasia. Just north of the Alps were the Bavarians, farther west in the Rhone valley were the Burgundians, while the Lombards were south of the Alps in North Italy. For one hundred and fifty years the Franks were divided into Neustria and Austrasia, and the language of each became ever more different, to emerge finally as French and German. Those who became Dutch and Flemish retained the low-German tongue, while those who became Germans were influenced by the Swabians and Bavarians, who spoke high German. The Saxons, north-east of what is now Holland, retained their low-German language, bringing it over to England, to be mixed later with the French spoken by the Normans, and thus produce the basis of the English language.

The Merovingian dynasty, founded by Clovis, became quite effete, its kings became priest-kings to become known as "do-nothing kings", and when this dynasty ended much the greater part of France was in the possession of the Church. In 687 Pepin I conquered Neustria, and once more united the Franks. He held the position in Austrasia of Mayor of the Palace, an hereditary office which exercised even greater power than did the king. Pepin I was succeeded in his office (721) by his son Charles Martel, who, it will be remembered, prevented the Moslems occupying France. At Tours in 732 he utterly defeated them and drove them back to Spain, after which they never again crossed the Pyrenees. He left his office of Mayor of the Palace between his two sons, but, as one of them entered a monastery, Pepin II, the other son, succeeded to this exalted position.

Pepin II (752–768) was an ambitious man, and objected to have to do all the work, and take all the responsibility, because the king was too stupid to exercise any authority. So he told the Pope that he wanted to become king, and to this the Holy Father agreed. In consequence all the Frankish nobles gathered at Soissons in 751 to approve of Pepin II as their king, after which he was anointed and crowned. Thus Austrasia and Neustria became a kingdom under one king, and, if only all their inhabitants had spoken the same language, they might have remained so to this day. If they had, then Europe would probably have had a more peaceful history, and England would not have had the power to make her influence felt in European politics; in fact, it is unlikely that there would ever have been a British Empire.

The work of consolidation was continued by his son Charlemagne (768–814), or Charles the Great. He was an active man, and could keep going at the same time various love affairs along with his constant military and political activities. He was deeply religious, fond of pomp and ceremony, and had numerous wives and mistresses. Full of self-confidence, and with many varied interests, he was an outstanding character, though quite ignorant, and he never could master the art of writing. He was always anxious to learn more, and what little knowledge there was in those days centred round his court.

This was entirely of a theological nature, and priests, in consequence, were his teachers. They were his guides and instructors when first he visited Rome, where he saw all the wonders the Church had assembled to impress the faithful. There this semi-savage, the greatest of all Christian missionaries, was shown the heads of Peter and Paul, the blood and tears of Jesus, his cradle and purple robe, his cross, his portrait painted by St. Luke, the table on which was laid the last supper, the milk of the Virgin Mary, and much else of a like nature. Much impressed by all he had seen, Charles returned home to Aix-la-Chapelle, now known as Aachen, to start a theological school, which attracted all the so-called learned men of the time.

Charles would sit for hours and listen to passages being read from the Bible, thus becoming such a theologian that he decided to add his contribution to the endless discussion relating to the definition of the Trinity. In 381 the Council of Constantinople substantially altered the Nicene Creed, one addition being that the Holy Ghost proceeded from the Father, and, in 589, the Council of Toledo made a further addition to the effect that the Holy Ghost proceeded from the Father and from the Son. Between 787 and 796 three Church councils debated this burning question, and Charlemagne now wished this new idea of the Holy Ghost proceeding from the Father and the Son to become part of the accepted creed of the Church, but his desire was opposed by the Pope, Leo III, though adopted at a later date in 1054.

The decision to adopt the addition made by the Council of Toledo had great historical effects, as it split Europe into two religious camps, and divided the Christian Church in two, the Western Church retaining the old name Catholic (= universal), and the Eastern Church becoming known as the Orthodox Eastern

Church, commonly called the Greek Church. Besides thus splitting the Church, this controversy revealed ever more clearly the lack of foundation on which Christian beliefs rest, as, up to the present day, these two great Christian communities, which comprise all Christendom, are at variance over the question of the godhead and the wording of the Christian Creed, the foundation on which the faith rests.

From the time of the Council of Nicaea to that of Charlemagne, the uncertainty as to the definition of the Trinity had caused endless confusion. This intricate puzzle had confounded Christendom from the time of that fateful gathering, when the Unitarian Arians, the name then given to the Jesuians, lost their amendment to the effect that the Father was the supreme God. Except for short periods when they were in power, persecution, death and banishment had been the fate of the Arians from that day onwards, and now Charlemagne set the cauldron boiling once more, to bring disruption, hatred, wars and persecution to Europe up to the 19th century, as we shall discover in the pages which follow.

Charles's Bible study so impressed him with the savagery of Jehovah that he set about to copy this god's injunctions, as was then believed had been delivered to Moses, Charles making it an offence punishable by death for anyone to refuse to become a Christian and be baptised. He encouraged architecture and church music, started the building of quite a number of cathedrals, which he lavishly endowed with vast areas of land, and gave large grants of land to found abbeys and monasteries. He conscientiously went through his kingdom dispensing a crude form of justice, and corresponded with Haroun-al-Raschid, the Moslem emperor, who sent him gifts and the keys of the Holy Sepulchre, thus recognising him as the protector of Christianity. Pope Leo III (795–816), a wicked and dissolute man, also had this idea, and developed a plan to make Charles the Emperor of Christendom, but before recording this event something must be said to explain why the Pope made this decision.

The policy consistently maintained by Charles was to conquer all the non-Christian European people, and give them the choice of accepting Christianity or perishing by the sword. In this he had the cordial approval of the Pope at Rome, who had before him Augustine's *City of God*, and dreamed of a world united under one faith and ruled by one emperor who accepted the Pope as his divine master. Charles had this book read to him, and he also formed the same idea. Both men saw that the first step necessary to carry out their ambitious scheme was to reconstruct the Roman Empire by converting everyone to Christianity, and this Charles set himself to do.

His first aggressive moves were against the Saxons, Bavarians and Slavs, and wherever his army went it carried the Christian faith. All who accepted it were spared, and those who preferred their old form of religious belief were slaughtered. By these barbarous methods Christian civilisation spread over Europe, countless thousands perished, and the Saxons, who suffered terribly, showed for long their bitter hatred of the Christians.

Then Charles quarrelled with his father-in-law, the King of Lombardy, and subdued Lombardy and

North Italy, carrying his conquests into Dalmatia. After fifty-three campaigns over all western Europe, he was now in command of France, except Brittany, down to the Pyrenees, besides Dalmatia and all Germany up to the Baltic and east to the Danube. He made his son Pepin III King of Italy and had him crowned at Rome. Pope Leo III then sent to Charles the keys of St. Peter's tomb and a banner, to represent his recognition of this ardent Christian monarch as sovereign of all Italy.

Some time later the Pope became so unpopular in Italy that he had to escape to Germany, where he put himself under the protection of Charles, who restored him to his throne in Rome. Now was the time to act, decided the Holy Father, and, on Christmas Day in the year 800, as Charles rose from prayer in St. Peter's in Rome, the Pope set a crown upon the monarch's head, hailing him, at the same time, as Caesar and Augustus amid great popular applause. This act of recognition of Christianity's greatest missionary rather forestalled Charles's intentions, as it was then believed by some that he proposed to gain the Eastern Empire by marrying the Empress Irene, then reigning in Constantinople. This dreadful creature, now a Christian saint because of her devotion to the faith, gouged out the eyes of her son when he came of age to prevent him taking her place, after which crime we are told that her reign continued for another five years in prosperity and splendour.

Charles was annoyed at the Pope's action in St. Peter's, as he was now under an obligation to His Holiness. Moreover, Constantinople refused to recognise their new emperor because the Greek Church disputed the authority of the Pope to confer this dignity, and this might have been the end of the scheme had not the Bulgarians in 811 defeated the army of the Eastern Empire, and overrun much of the Balkan peninsula. This event decided the East to accept Charles as Caesar and Augustus, and so it came about that part of the old Roman Empire, in the following year, returned to life under the name of the Holy Roman Empire, to be continued over the centuries by Austria and Germany until 1806. These were the two countries, it is interesting to remember, whose inhabitants, known to the Greeks and Romans as barbarians, brought the old Roman Empire crashing to the ground.

The Holy Roman Empire of Charles the Great did not, however, include Britain, Spain, North Africa, Egypt, Palestine, Syria, Mesopotamia and Persia, all but Britain being by now under Moslem rule. So it was Roman only in name, and by no means Holy, but it included Central Europe, which was now open to Christian domination. Missionaries from Rome and Britain were quick to seize the opportunity of consolidating the conversions to the new religion which Charles had secured by the edge of the sword, persuasion always being combined with force. A few more centuries passed, and all Europe, outside of Moslem rule, had given heed to the Church's command "Join us or be damned", a challenge which was later changed to "Remain with us or be damned", when all had been gathered in and some wanted to have the freedom to exercise their own thoughts free of ecclesiastical interference.

Charles died in 814, and left his empire to his only

legitimate son Louis, called the Pious, a weak creature who was the slave of the Pope and the perpetrator of cruel deeds. On his death in 840 civil war broke out between his three sons. Charles the Bald had received Neustria, another, called Lewis, had been left all the lands bordering the Rhine, while Lothair had been given Austrasia, Burgundy and Italy. After the important Battle of Fontenay, when Lothair was defeated, the three brothers met at Verdun in 843 and agreed to divide amicably their father's inheritance. This compact is called the Partition of Verdun, which placed a new kingdom between what is now called Germany and France, comprising all those lands which ever since have been the cause of so many bloody battles involving Spain, France, the Netherlands, England, Austria and Germany. This bone of contention, which lay between a number of snarling dogs, comprised what is now called Holland, Belgium, the Rhineland, eastern France and northern Italy, on which territory more battles have been fought than in any other place on earth.

In this way the great empire built up by Charlemagne dissolved, and not until 962 was there a succession of Holy Roman Emperors, though now and again the title was revived. The Kelts and Franks of Neustria thus again became separated from their race in Austrasia. Language and tradition in this case rose superior to race, and France, as we now know it, took shape. What is now Germany likewise began to appear, somewhat as it is today, but both countries were split up into principalities and dukedoms. Until 987 the Carlovingians, representing the dynasty founded by Charles, retained nominal power throughout France, but in this year Hugh Capet founded a new dynasty.

Likewise in Germany Henry the Fowler, a Saxon, and not a Frank, was elected King of Germany in 918 and founded a new dynasty. His fame rests on the victory he secured at the Battle of Unstrut in 933, which checked the Magyar penetration into Central Europe. He was succeeded by Otto (936–973), called the Great, who pushed the German frontier beyond the Elbe and carved out a new empire, comprising all that is now Germany, Holland and Italy. He was the creator of the First Reich (realm), and was crowned Holy Roman Emperor by Pope John XII in Rome in 962. Thus did Italy come under the domination of the Germans who plundered her, and have tyrannised over her people from that day to the present time, this fair land for the next two centuries being moreover the battle-ground for the quarrel which raged between the Emperors and the Popes on the question as to which ruler was to be supreme in Italy, the Emperor or the Pope.

This period of papal history is known as "the Rule of the Whores", when for forty years harlots guided the popes, and Rome was a brothel. The most wanton women, especially two sisters named Marozia and Theodora, spread their evil influence from the Pope downwards to the clergy and people. Their mother was equally wicked, and during their shameful time of influence three popes, John X, Leo VI, and John XI pass before us, to be followed twenty years later by John XII, the pontiff who crowned Otto, as told in the foregoing paragraph.

Pope John XII (956–963) was one of the greatest

scoundrels in history. There was no crime that he did not commit. The palaces of Nero or Caligula, two of the worst Roman emperors, never witnessed more wanton scenes than took place at the Lateran Palace, the Pope's residence in Rome. Amongst his many misdeeds were murder, perjury, adultery, incest with his two sisters, rape and sacrilege. He turned his palace into a brothel, cut out the eyes, or castrated, those who criticised him, and raped girls and women who came to pray at St. Peter's. He gambled, cursed, and drank to the devil.

These were the crimes proved against him when Otto deposed him. His Holiness fled to Tivoli, where he excommunicated all his enemies, and, by bribery and corruption, secured his re-election to the Holy Office. His enemies then suffered from his savagery, when noses were cut off and tongues were cut out, but this lasted for only three months, as he then died, murdered, it is thought, by a jealous husband. We read of three further popes during the reign of Otto, whose records are filled with crime, murder and intrigue, and what took place at the Lateran was going on amongst the priests everywhere. The moral life of most of the clergy was foul and degraded, and the only reason John XII stands out as a monster is because he outdid in crime and degradation all his contemporaries.

It must not be imagined that the way adopted by Charlemagne to bring converts into the Christian fold was the only one employed. Kinder and more humane methods were used by others who were zealous for the spread of the Gospel. Many Bavarians and Frisians were baptised by the efforts of Saint Boniface (680–755), who came from England, and, during the 7th and 8th centuries, similar work went on elsewhere. There were Christians in England during the Roman occupation, their first martyr being Alban, who is remembered by the town of St. Albans being called after him. Saint Patrick converted the Irish, and from Ireland came Columba to preach the Gospel to the Kelts in Scotland. Pope Gregory sent missionaries from Rome to England at the end of the 6th century, and, by the end of the next century, a part of England was Christianised, though Mercia, today known as the Midlands, held out to the last.

This is the best side of the story of the spread of the Gospel, but unfortunately it is not the whole story. It is not what people believe about the gods that matters but how they live, and history proves that those holding quite different theological beliefs can be both good and bad according to their characters. Although Europe was what is called Pagan before the advent of Christianity, that does not mean that the people were barbarians because they were Pagans. The Romans and Greeks were Pagans and not barbarians. When the barbarians became Christians they still remained barbarians, and Rome, it will be remembered, was conquered by the Christian Visigoths, who were barbarians.

Christianity did not humanise or civilise Europe, because Europe remained savage and uncivilised for centuries after the people became Christians. The part Christianity played in the eventual civilising process was of a secondary nature, in that it linked up Christian Europe with Rome and Constantinople, where lingered all that remained of Greek and Roman civilisation. The semi-savage tribal kings, after becoming Christians, visited these cities and gaped in wonder and amazement, to return home impressed by the splendour of the clergy, the magnificence of the churches, and the grandeur of the public buildings. That constituted the first step, the second being the spread of classical literature. Pagan Rome, and later Pagan Greece, civilised Europe when their literature eventually found its way into Christendom, their great philosophers, moralists and lawyers being the source from which sprang all the culture we now enjoy.

The Paganism of Europe did not differ much from the Paganism of Greece and Rome, its gods being known under Nordic or other names. All Pagan Europe, including Greece and Rome, believed much the same about the gods, yet Greece was cultured and civilised for centuries, long before Christianity was born. Europe could have remained Pagan, and been civilised, if the people had had the mentality and the education of the Greeks. Because they had a lower mentality they were barbarians, and the only reason Paganism is so much denounced in our day is for the purpose of elevating Christianity, which, nevertheless, is only Paganism under another name.

The Pagans had their Father god, Mother god, gods, goddesses and devils, temples, priests and sacrifices, and so have the Christians, the only difference being that the latter call their numerous gods and goddesses saints and angels, the Eucharist, representing one big sacrifice, taking the place of the daily offerings of animals by the Pagans. In place of the uncivilised outlook of the barbarians, Christianity substituted the savagery of the Hebrews. Consequently the ethical teaching of the great moral philosophers of the past was smothered by the theological doctrines of the Church, all of which were borrowed from the Pagan beliefs surrounding Mithra, Osiris, Dionysus, Bel and other deities.

The Christian belief in hell for all unbelievers stimulated missionary enterprise, but the idea was also taken up by kings and princes for the purpose of controlling and keeping their people under subjection. Thus Church and State worked hand in hand, and Europe became Christian as much by force as by persuasion. For centuries there was much bitterness and intense feeling of hatred, the desire amongst the Pagans being for revenge because of the cruel treatment they received from the Christians.

All Europe, which is now Great Britain, France, Denmark, Germany, Norway, Sweden, Bohemia, Hungary and Dalmatia, was an arena of bloody conflict between the Pagans and the Christians in the 8th and 9th centuries. Entire tribes were converted by the sword, and the Christians, in their zeal to extend their faith, treated the Pagans in just the same way as did the fanatical Moslems those who believed differently from them. Intolerance and ignorance always work together hand in hand, because they are twin brothers.

Egbert, who became the first king of all England in 828, pursued the same methods as did his patron Charlemagne in Europe, but a reaction followed. The Pagans in northern Europe retaliated for the cruelty meted out to their co-religionists in Britain and Europe, by making raids by sea along the coasts of Britain and northern France. From the deep fiords of

Scandinavia the Vikings came south in their long-shaped galleys, and took their revenge on all monasteries and nunneries, slaughtering priests and monks on every occasion. These seafaring people spread down the coasts of northern Europe and Britain, and in 911 an expedition under Rolf the Ganger settled in the north of France, giving the name to the land which from now onwards became known as Normandy.

The Vikings and Danes not only settled in Europe and Britain, but Eric the Red founded settlements in Greenland, and his son Leif Ericsson, about the year 1000, reached America and was probably the first European to discover the new world. They also settled in Iceland, and then later found their way down to the Mediterranean. By 866 the Danes had conquered a large part of England, and it was against this invasion that Alfred, the English king, so valiantly fought. By now Angles, Saxons, Jutes and Danes, all much the same in race, had settled in Britain, to be later conquered by the Normans in 1066, after which they all amalgamated with the Britons to make the British race as it is today.

The Normans had shed their northern uncouthness during their hundred and fifty years' stay in Normandy, and with them there came to England a more civilised way of life. William, Duke of Normandy, their leader, established a new dynasty in England, and rewarded his followers with large grants of land. He retained his connection with northern France, and thus the two countries were joined, only to be finally separated in the reign of Mary Tudor, when the English lost Calais in 1558.

These virile northmen were not satisfied with their

conquests of northern France and England, so some went much farther afield. Their knowledge of the sea, and how to build ships, enabled them to reach the Mediterranean in search of a great and wealthy city which their legends had for long told them was to be found there. The glory that once belonged to Rome, and now surrounded Constantinople, had reached far north, and been pictured to these hardy Norsemen as something rich and alluring. So, by way of the sea, and the wide deep sluggish Russian rivers, they reached the Caspian and Black seas and the Mediterranean, raiding Persia, threatening Constantinople, and capturing the town of Kiev, which in our day is the important wheat and sugar centre of Ukrainia. In fact it was two northmen, Rurik and Oleg, who, in the 9th century, laid the foundation of Europe's largest nation, Russia.

The plunderings of the Normans greatly worried the Emperor at Constantinople, and also Pope Leo IX in Rome, as they were roaming over southern Europe as bands of robbers, pillaging wherever they went. Some went on a pilgrimage to the Holy Land, but they were just as ready to fight as to pray. Thence they moved on to southern Italy and Sicily, to fight the Saracens, who had settled there in considerable numbers. These fertile lands also attracted the Normans who had settled in Normandy. They flowed south in increasing numbers, and this went on until a man came on the scene who ranks next to William the Conqueror in Norman history.

Robert the Guiscard (1015–1085), this Norman hero, earned for himself the sobriquet of *guiscard*, which means cunning or sagacious. He was not only an adventurer but also a great warrior, and, in company with his brother Roger, succeeded in defeating the armies of the Greeks, Lombards and the Pope at the Battle of Civitella (1053), the Holy Father Leo IX being captured. Six years later His Holiness gave Robert the duchies of Apulia and Calabria, and promised him Sicily if he would drive out the Saracens from the island. After a long-drawn-out struggle, extending over thirty years, Robert and Roger conquered both the Saracens and Greeks in Sicily and southern Italy.

Sicily flourished under Norman rule, when science, architecture and literature were encouraged. Here the Normans made their deepest impression, and its most settled period began under the rule of the Rogers I and II, who united the island, which became a Norman kingdom. When Robert considered that Norman rule was firmly established in these parts he set about to subdue the Eastern Empire (1081), crossing over the Adriatic to capture Durazzo. Thence he marched on Constantinople, driving the troops of the defeated emperor before him, but before he reached the capital he was summoned back by Pope Gregory VII to rescue him from his German enemies— Henry IV, the Holy Roman emperor, being now outside the walls of Rome. Robert returned, defeated Henry, and then himself sacked Rome, after which he resumed his attack on the Eastern Empire, defeating the combined Greek and Venetian fleets, but he died before he reached the capital.

The Normans, however, were not the only danger to the security of these parts, as new enemies, the Turks, appeared from the east. The Moslem Empire by now had dissolved into separate nations. Egypt was independent under its own caliph, Persia was now a kingdom by itself, and Spain and North Africa had their own independent rulers. This strong bulwark against the eastern barbarians of Central Asia had therefore disappeared, and Europe was again open to attack.

We read in the last chapter about the Turks sweeping down on Baghdad, and destroying Moslem civilisation in Mesopotamia. These nomadic people, prior to this time, had extended their penetration into Europe by settling in what is now Bulgaria. They were then Pagans, and thus they lived between Christian and Moslem influence. Their king Boris (852–884), after considering the adoption of the Moslem faith, decided to become a Christian because this was his wife's religion. So he adopted the Christian faith, and, without asking their consent, he declared that his people were also to adopt the same belief. This high-handed way of dealing with such a personal matter as religion was the usual practice in those times, when the people followed their rulers in religion as they did in war. They knew nothing about the merits of either Christianity or Mahomedanism and, like children, did as they were told.

Another Turkish tribe, the Magyars, invaded Hungary, retaining their Turko-Finnish language, and Stephen, their king, adopted Christianity for himself and his people about the year 1000. Coming behind the Bulgarians and Hungarians into Europe there followed another Turkish tribe, the Khazars, and, following them, another, the Petschenegs. With the Khazars came many Jews, who were to be the founders of the large Jewish settlements in Poland and Russia. When we remember the large number of Norsemen who settled in Russia and mingled with the Slavs, and how the country was also populated by these eastern migrants, we realise the mixed nature of the present Russian nation, especially in the south.

By now a bird's-eye view will have been obtained of the mosaic formed by the different tribes which, since 1000 B.C., had invaded the European peninsula from Central Asia, that breeding-ground of the Western world whose climate produced such a virile stock. More were still to come, but, from now onwards, the Europe as it is today gradually took shape. Its rich plains and valleys were the bait which ever attracted these migrants westwards. The first-comers settled down in Greece and Italy, and later they reached the most westerly point of Spain. Always there followed others, strong and tough, though poor and hungry, who plundered as they journeyed to the west. They fought all who opposed them, to settle down finally and intermingle with the earlier settlers. No nation in Europe is composed of one stock only, every one is mongrel, and the claim made by the Germans that they come of pure Nordic stock is untrue. Only the Semites have not to any extent intermixed, and Europeans who are not Jews are predominantly of Aryan extraction.

(2) CHRISTENDOM'S HOLY WAR ON THE MOSLEMS.

We have now reached the time in European history when, in the 11th century, the Moslem Empire was shattered by the onslaught of the Turks from the

east, who came west along the southern shores of the
Caspian Sea. They first struck at Baghdad, and
destroyed the centre of this high civilisation. Under
the lead of the Seljuk tribe, who were orthodox
Moslems, the Turks overran Armenia, Syria and
Asia Minor up to the gates of Constantinople. Led
by their chief Alp Arslan, they decisively defeated the
Eastern Empire at Manzikert in 1071 and captured
Nicaea, where the Christian form of belief was first
produced under the· dictation of Constantine. Now
the Moslem faith again arose in its most fanatical
form, and, when this clashed with Christianity,
sorrow and misery came to many in Europe and the
Middle East. This clash is known as The Crusades,
about which we are now to read.

This gruesome story, to be correctly understood,
requires some preliminary explanation, and the
first part centres round the belief in a trinity
of gods, an age-old belief which first originated,
probably in India or Sumeria, in connection with the
mystical beliefs which came to surround the first
saviour-god. To trace its progress and development,
from one saviour-god religion to another, until it was
finally incorporated into Christianity at Nicaea, is too
long and intricate a problem to attempt here, but this
much can be said: the idea of the Trinity came from
man himself.[1]

Man is a triune being, made up of physical body,
etheric body, and mind which is the directing, thinking and reasoning part of his make-up. This discovery was made in the early days of religious con-

---

[1] The origin and evolution of the belief in the Trinity is fully explained
in *The Psychic Stream*.

templation, and came about as the result of mediumship. In trance the medium's duplicate etheric body separates from the physical body and functions by itself, while the physical body is quite inert, and, besides this, clairvoyants can see the etheric body parting from the physical body at death.

By seeing apparitions of the dead, and from other psychic manifestations, our primitive ancestors, who may have been more psychic than we are now, came to believe in the gods who were either their companions and friends or their enemies. This belief developed into Ancestor Worship, a form of devotion which prevailed everywhere from early times, and still continues in many places, as the gods are none other than those who lived on earth and now live in a world of finer substance interpenetrating this earth. Ancestor Worship was the first and earliest religion, and, from it, mystical and priestly minds evolved many weird theological beliefs, including the belief in a personal God made in the likeness of man himself. Alongside of this theological development evolved the belief in this anthropomorphic being separating himself, and emanating his spirit from his body, as happens when the spirit of the medium leaves his body in trance.

This emanating spirit became known as the Divine Spirit, or Holy Spirit, whose mission was to convey the will of God to mankind, by taking control of a medium while in trance and using his or her mouth to speak. To the Greeks this spirit was known as Mercury, the messenger of Zeus. The saviour-god, who came to earth to suffer for mankind (the origin of which belief is too complicated to consider here but will be found clearly explained in *The Psychic Stream*), was the mind of God, or, as the Greeks called it, the Logos, meaning reason. Thus we arrive at the composition of the Trinity, made up of the Father God (the body), the Son (his mind) and the Holy Ghost (the emanating spirit), three parts of one God, a trinity and unity like man himself.

This very old mystical speculation, the origin of which was forgotten when the priests replaced the mediums in the early Apostolic Church, has caused rivers of blood to flow. It has filled the prisons, banished men and women from their native lands, and produced every evil device for torture and cruelty. It has been the reason for numerous Church councils being called for the purpose of bringing about an understanding of a puzzle which cannot be understood without a knowledge of its origin.

The first split in the Christian Church came about when Arius, in the 4th century, took a different view of the meaning of the Trinity from that adopted by the Bishop of Rome. This caused such a cleavage in the Church that Constantine called all the priests together at Nicaea to settle the question. From this council followed the Nicene Creed, but the division remained, and, from that date onwards, there were two forms of belief about the Holy Trinity—the orthodox, as contained in the Creed, and the Arian. This was the cause of endless disputes, and the reason for two popes at times being elected to fill the same office.

To strengthen the trinitarian position the Athanasian Creed was produced about the 8th century, and given the name of this outstanding champion of the Trinity who lived in the 4th century. This fraud was for the purpose of increasing the Creed's prestige, but he was certainly not its author. This creed caused untold misery for many centuries, and the fact that many Christians repeat it on their special feast days proves how ignorant or morally backward they are, as it is drenched in the blood of millions of innocent victims. The Apostles' Creed likewise made its appearance about the same time, but, like the Athanasian Creed, its origin is unknown. All that is known about its origin is that the Apostles knew nothing of it, and that it was given their name to increase its authority.

Catholic Christianity, as centred in the Pope at Rome, believed then, as it still does, that the Divine spirit, theologically termed the Holy Spirit, emanated from the Father God and the Son, whereas the Greek and eastern Christians believed, as they still do, that the Holy Spirit emanated from the Father God only, the latter belief inclining towards Arianism. Charlemagne, we remember, decided to make the Catholic belief applicable throughout Christendom, but to this the Pope of his day objected. This suggested imposition, in what was considered to be a fundamental belief in the Christian religion, so angered the eastern Christians that they refused to acknowledge the Pope's authority to create Charlemagne the Holy Roman Emperor, and only did so later for political reasons.

From this time onwards Christendom retained a kind of nominal unity, but when, in 1054, the Pope decided to add the word *Filioque*, meaning "and from the Son", to the Creed, the eastern and western Christians divided, and from that date the eastern Christians have not been in fellowship with those of the west. The Pope excommunicated the eastern Christians, who formed what is now called the Greek Orthodox Church, the fabric of which had been in being since the 5th century, when the Christians of eastern Syria, Persia, Central Asia, Egypt, Abyssinia and India had refused fellowship with the Catholic Church because of disagreement over the definition of the Trinity. The Abyssinians and Egyptians were called Coptic Christians and the others Nestorian Christians.

So it came about in the 11th century that the Greek, Russian and Balkan Christians refused to have any further fellowship with the Western Church, and they called their chief priest by the name of Patriarch. Consequently, half of those who professed the Christian religion in Europe were not on speaking terms with the other half. Europe was split in two by the word *Filioque* and by this vain attempt to define the Infinite. This great event had important reactions on European history up to our own time, as we shall discover as we proceed.

When the Turks in 1071 defeated the Eastern Empire, the Emperor Michael VII appealed in vain to Pope Gregory VII for help, and again the same appeal went out to his successor, Pope Urban II, by Alexius Comnenus, the Emperor who followed. Now was the opportunity, thought the authorities at Rome, to reunite the Church once more under the leadership of the Pope, and bring about the never-forgotten dream of Augustine of a world ruled by the Christian Church with its centre in Rome. Popes, cardinals and priests were for ever pondering over this mighty problem, and now, once again, it seemed as if an opportunity had presented itself to bring all their dreams to fruition.

Likewise those who traded between Genoa, Venice and the East were anxious to reopen the trade routes closed by the Turks, and they gladly gave their support to a war which would weaken Turkish influence in the Near East. This was a minor influence, as was also the poverty of Europe, which produced numerous adventurers always ready for a war which would enable them to loot as they pleased.

The influence of Gregory VII (1073–1085) on world affairs was profound. He was a coarse, ignorant and passionate peasant, but nevertheless an exceptionally able man and an outstanding statesman. He is better known as Hildebrand, and there was scarcely a country in Europe which he did not claim as vassal to the Holy See. His internal activities were equally drastic, as he instituted celibacy amongst the clergy, which had the effect of greatly increasing their immorality, mistresses now taking the place of legal wives. Many priests, from then onwards, including the popes and cardinals, produced illegitimate children, who were always called their nephews and nieces.

Doubtless the reason for this unnatural legislation was for the purpose of transforming the priesthood into a body of holy men, who had cut themselves off from the joys of life, as in these days the lives of the priests were so debased that no woman was safe in their presence. So Gregory set about to improve the prestige of the Church, and sweep away the corruption which had so tarnished the Church at large, including the Papacy, over the previous seven hundred years.

No more foolish way could have been adopted to purify the Church, but in the Age of Faith there was much folly and little reasoned thought. The married clergy consequently had their home life destroyed, and were separated· from their wives and children. Many rebelled against this harsh treatment, and received much public sympathy, as so far there was no Church law against priests marrying. Many bloody scenes followed, Hildebrand using his great authority and wealth to organise armed bands of hooligans, who went from place to place looting what they could, and dragging the wives and children away from their husbands and fathers. Abominable cruelties were perpetrated on fathers, mothers and children, and a terrible price in human happiness was paid by this mistaken way of going about the purification of the Church.

What the married priests felt we must imagine, but a written outburst by one of these wretched wives has been preserved, in which we read of her agony, despair and bitter hatred towards all responsible for this cruel separation of husband and wife. She predicted that the priests, now deprived of their legal wives, would live with mistresses, and the number of illegitimate children would increase. Just as this miserable and angry woman expected, morality declined and celibacy turned many convents into brothels, the nuns becoming the mistresses of the priests, while sodomy continued as heretofore in most of the monasteries.

Moreover, Gregory's vain attempt to reform the Church led to a dispute with the Holy Roman Emperor on the question of appointing bishops, and, because of this, the first appeal from Constantinople for help against the Turks did not receive a decisive response. Then Gregory died in 1085 in exile, where he had been driven because of his cruelties and many unscrupulous deeds. His successor, Urban II, a prelate zealous to make the Greek Church subject to Rome, now foresaw the realisation of his desires, and took this opportunity to further his policy. The appeal from the Eastern Emperor, he calculated, would now make possible the welding of Christendom into one Church directed by the Pope at Rome, as with the Emperor as his ally his task would be simplified. Consequently a holy war was declared on the Moslems, two Church councils being held, and propaganda against the Moslems commenced. All Hitler's methods were effectively employed, and, before long, Western Christendom was united for one purpose only—to destroy the Infidel.

Hitler used the port of Danzig and the Polish Corridor as his excuse to bring about war in 1939, and all his hateful propaganda was employed to stir the feelings of the Germans to the uttermost. He made use of unscrupulous people to tell how cruelly the Germans in Poland were being treated, and Pope Urban made use of a fanatic, called Peter the Hermit, to tell how the Turks were desecrating the Holy Sepulchre in Jerusalem. This man, who by self-imposed austerities had deformed his body, wandered through Europe with his story, which was probably exaggerated and embellished, to the effect that he had just returned from a pilgrimage to the Holy City and had seen pilgrims there persecuted and ill-treated. He rode on an ass, barefooted, wearing a coarse garment, while in his hand he bore a large cross, and everywhere he told his tale to large crowds throughout France and Germany.

Then there was no radio to rouse the mob, but, though the method was slower, it was not less effective, and Peter, now the popular hero, did for Urban what Goebbels did for Hitler. He made Europe insane on one idea: to free the Holy Sepulchre from the hated Infidel, and drive the Turks out of the Holy Land. Europe was united, for the first and the last time, on the prosecution of one of the greatest religious wars in history, the priests quoting to their flocks the passage from their sacred book, which had always stimulated unreasoned fury in the past and was to do so often again in the future, when there were heretics to slaughter:—

Do not I hate them, O Lord, that hate thee? I hate them with perfect hatred; I count them as mine enemies. (*Psalm* cxxxix, 21.)

This conflict was not against the things that are evil, not against cruelty, poverty, crime, injustice, intolerance and all unrighteousness, but against a nation of unbelievers in the Holy Trinity which was in possession of a piece of ground wherein Helena, the mother of Constantine, said the body of a member of that Trinity was buried. Her information was valueless as it had been obtained by means of bribery and corruption. No one has the faintest idea where the body of Jesus was buried, the whole extraordinary story of his burial and resurrection being the repetition of an ancient myth, belonging to earlier saviour-god religions, which was added to the gospel story in the

2nd century to replace an earlier story of his reappearance as an apparition.[1]

The foregoing explains the reason why the princes of the Western Church organised this holy war, and they prepared all western Europe for a bloody conflict. The people became as inflammable as parched grass, and all that was needed was a spark to set them alight. Pilgrimages to the Holy Land had at that time greatly increased, because the thousand years mentioned in *The Revelation* had just expired, it being believed that the time had come when the Christ would return to Jerusalem to gather in his faithful people. All Christendom was on the tip-toe of expectation that at long last their ever-present dream was about to materialise.

> And then shall appear the sign of the Son of Man in heaven, . . . and they shall see the Son of Man coming in the clouds of heaven with power and great glory. And he shall send his angels with a great sound of a trumpet, and they shall gather together his elect from the four winds, from one end of heaven to the other. (*Matthew* xxiv, 30.)

The origin of this extraordinary idea can be found in the beliefs surrounding ancient sun-worship, when the priests held a service of welcome to the sun at dawn every morning. For thousands of years the ancients pursued their astronomical studies, during which they elaborated their various systems of solar worship. The heavens to them were a stage divided into various scenes of astronomical time. The heavenly bodies were the actors, and their movements

---

[1] The original story, and the mystical interpretation of the one which took its place, will be found in *The Psychic Stream.*

were their performance during each act in a great heavenly drama, which lasted for all eternity, the audience being the people of earth, which was the auditorium. Theology, with all its rites and mysteries, is intertwined with astronomy as it appeared to those of long ago, and ecclesiasticism is the play, composed of myths and legends, wound round real or imaginary lives to whom were attributed all that was believed about the sun.

As the sun god returned each day, so the belief arose that the various saviour-gods, whose deeds on earth were made to resemble the wonderful stories surrounding the sun, would likewise return, and to each saviour-god a longer or shorter period was attributed. The Christian belief in the return of the Christ undoubtedly came from India, where it was believed that Krishna, from which name the Greeks got the word Christos, was the reincarnation of Vishnu, the second person of the Brahman Trinity.

In Alexandria, Brahmans and Buddhists mingled with the early Christian theologians, who became convinced that what was believed about Krishna would also happen to Christ, round whom had been draped the same legends as surrounded his Indian prototype. Consequently, as Krishna was believed to have returned to earth as the deliverer of his people, so would the Christ, to establish his kingdom of peace and justice. This idea originated in India at a time when the Hindu faith was in danger, just as it came to be attached to Jesus, who was given the heavenly name of Christ. These Alexandrian theologians were mostly all converted Jews, whose ancestors had longed for a deliverer against foreign oppression. In the person of

Jesus, now accepted by them as the Messiah, they recognised the deliverer of their homeland from Roman domination, just as did the Brahmans, in their legends about Krishna, who was believed to have destroyed the tyrant King Kamsa and ruled justly in his place.

In the 2nd Christian century the belief in the return of the theological Christ was so widespread, that it found its way into the Gospels and Epistles when copies were being made by scribes who had become enthusiasts of the idea. Thus they put into the mouth of Jesus the words just quoted from the Gospel attributed to Matthew, to represent a situation he would certainly have been one of the last to appreciate or understand Nevertheless the idea worked well in the interests of the Church, and that was what mattered to those who, in the 2nd century, were laying the foundations of this great institution.

Doubtless, in their ignorance, they believed it, and, by their zeal, made others do likewise, until by the 5th century all Christendom accepted the second coming of the Lord as something that was bound to happen. From that time onwards up to last century this fantastic idea ruled the minds of almost every man and woman in Christendom, it affected all they did and thought, it separated families, created monasteries and convents, and filled the churches, all being prepared for the fateful event to happen on any day and at any hour.

When people were really and truly ardent Christians, not like the lukewarm Christians of the present day, and when everyone wholeheartedly and zealously believed in the Christian religion, this belief in the second coming of the Christ profoundly influenced history. Progress ceased, as to trouble to improve one's lot on earth was stupid when any day everything would change for the better, "in a moment, in the twinkling of an eye, at the last trump". (1 *Corinthians* xv, 52.)

Today it is difficult for us to realise the effect this idea had on everyone, many selling all their possessions, and spending their time in poverty and filth, in prayer and hymn-singing. Only those of us who have witnessed the irrational and emotional scenes enacted during the religious revivals at the close of last century can form a faint impression of what it meant in the 11th century, when everyone believed that the time had come at last to join their Lord at Jerusalem. There his arrival was daily expected, and it became everyone's sacred duty to clear the Holy Land of the Infidel before this long-expected event took place.

The Christians of these crusading days certainly showed none of those noble qualities which present-day believers consider has always accompanied the acceptance of the Christian faith. They were intolerant and ignorant, savage and cruel, dishonest and treacherous, pious and filthy, and when first they turned their faces eastwards in 1096 their minds were filled with hatred towards the infidel Turk. The first unorganised Crusade, known as the People's Crusade, was made up of a huge leaderless rabble of 200,000 men and women, who set out for Jerusalem by way of the Danube valley and Constantinople. Entire families, and their belongings, were piled into carts, and at every town where they stopped they enquired if they were at Jerusalem, and some wanted to know if the Lord had yet arrived.

When this fanatical horde reached Hungary, which had just accepted Christianity, they committed such excesses that they were massacred by the inhabitants, while another multitude, passing through the Rhineland, slaughtered all the Jews they came across, to experience the same fate when they likewise reached Hungary. Peter the Hermit, and another equally degraded creature, known as Walter the Penniless, successfully reached Constantinople with only 7000 survivors behind them, but there they committed such atrocities that the Emperor shipped everyone across the Bosphorus to Asia Minor, where they were either slaughtered or made slaves by the Turks.

The first organised Crusade reached Constantinople in 1097, and this was composed of soldiers, adventurers, fanatics, priests, monks and escaped serfs from England, France, Flanders, Italy and Sicily, their leaders being mostly Normans. On crossing the Bosphorus they were prevented by the Emperor from looting Nicaea. Passing on they reached Antioch, which they besieged and finally captured after encompassing it for nearly a year. A relieving army, which came from Mosul, was then defeated, and this enabled Godfrey of Bouillon to take a small force to Jerusalem, which was captured in 1099 after a month's siege, during which time the Christians marched round the city, led by Peter the Hermit and the priests, to the accompaniment of much hymn-singing.

The time in history we are now considering is called the Age of Chivalry, but in truth this is just another pious fraud which has been propagated down the centuries to enhance the Christian faith. The deeds of the Christian knights, as told in these pages, will reveal the truth in all its hideousness. When Jerusalem surrendered, the massacre of the citizens commenced, and their blood ran down the streets until the Christians splashed each other with it as they rode hither and thither. Few were spared, some 10,000 being killed around the Temple court, and when the Christians had finished their wholesale butchery they prepared themselves by prayer and hymn-singing for the purpose of their mission.

When night came, after treading the wine-press of slaughtered humanity, from which had poured so much innocent blood, the Christians devoutly approached the Holy Sepulchre, and, putting their blood-stained hands together, they all knelt down in prayer to express their gratitude to their Lord for having so mercifully spared them to reach his tomb. Christian priests were kept busy all night, and, when day came, the Catholic and Eastern Orthodox Christians fell out amongst themselves on the question of which Church, the Western or the Eastern, was to take charge of the Holy Sepulchre. Until now, in their eagerness to reach the holy place, they had forgotten all about their differences as to whether the Holy Ghost proceeded from the Father or from both the Father and the Son. It was a case of priestly thieves falling out, and this gave the Emperor Alexius of Constantinople his opportunity to come again into what he considered was his own territory.

Alexius played the part of the jackal, just as did Mussolini after the fall of France in the Second World

War. In spite of his agreement to help in defeating the Turks, he followed the fanatics, and then devoured their leavings, as both the Turks and the Christians were so occupied fighting each other that the Emperor was able to win back the islands of Rhodes and Chios, the land and cities of Asia Minor, and strengthen the frontiers of Syria and Cilicia. In 1101 the Pope despatched reinforcements from Venice and Genoa, and, for a time, established his authority in Jerusalem, while the treachery of Alexius still further widened the breach between the East and the West; in fact an army was raised to attack him, but, owing to famine and the approach of winter, it withered away.

The earlier enthusiasm of the Christians in Jerusalem to exterminate the Infidels gradually waned, and for the next forty-six years there is not much to tell, the return of the Christ being awaited in prayer and hymn-singing. In 1144 the Turks captured Edessa (now called Urfa), close to the Syrian northern frontier, and Bernard, now a saint, declared that the time had again come for a second Crusade. The Eastern Emperor, Conrad III, secured the help of Louis VII of France, and, in 1147, a new expeditionary force was organised and despatched to the East. This ended in failure, which Bernard put down to the sins of the Christians and as a punishment from God.

One large force of Germans decided that more plunder was to be found nearer home, and, instead of going east, they attacked and conquered the Wends, a Pagan tribe east of the Elbe. Another Flemish and English force went west and attacked Pagan Portugal, capturing Lisbon, and so Christianised that country. Both these expeditions received the blessing of the

Pope, as they were considered as of equal value to the Church as a crusade against the infidel Turk, because the more lands conquered and Christianised the greater was the revenue which flowed into the Church Treasury.

The Christians in Jerusalem were still quarrelling bitterly as to whether the Eastern or Western Church would be in control at Jerusalem, but this was brought to a temporary halt by the arrival of Saladin (1174–1193) on the scene, the man who had conquered Egypt and become the Sultan. He was an able soldier of great courage, generous, magnanimous, merciful, honourable, humane and blessed with great self-control. He had welded together the various Moslem states, and now he commenced a holy war against the Christians. The Moslems, under his leadership, now became as fanatical in their project as the Christians had been in theirs, so much so that in 1187, after a battle near the Lake of Tiberias, the Christians were defeated. What was claimed to be the cross of Jesus had been brought from Jerusalem and carried into battle, but this availed nothing, and when Saladin secured the surrender of Jerusalem he treated the citizens humanely, quite unlike the way the Christians had done when they captured the city.

Only the sea coasts of Palestine now remained to the Christians, all the lives sacrificed, the bodies maimed, and the treasure lost, having brought nothing of any value in return. So the cry went up for another Crusade, and this was organised in 1189 by Frederick I, the German Emperor, better known as Barbarossa, in company with Richard Cœur de Lion of England and Philip II of France. They were all much occupied by home affairs, but the Pope insisted, and so they left their troubles and quarrels at home to fight a new Holy War, now known as the Third Crusade.

This likewise ended in failure. Frederick was drowned, and Richard and Philip quarrelled on the way out. Though they captured Acre on their way to the Holy Land they could not regain Jerusalem. Philip returned to France, and Richard finally returned to England, after being retained as a prisoner in Austria for more than a year, leaving behind him in the East a memory of great courage and military ability, but also one of great cruelty, because he killed over 4000 prisoners, in contrast to Saladin who set free all those he captured in Jerusalem.

The Christians were now beginning to wonder where all this loss of life and treasure was leading them. Men left Europe never to return; mostly the kings, princes and nobles came back, and some of these only after heavy ransoms had been paid for their release. The fire of hatred against the Moslems now burned with intense heat solely amongst the popes, cardinals and priests, and, when Innocent III became Pope, he organised in 1202 a new Holy War, now known as the Fourth Crusade. The three principal characters who figured in this effort were Theobald, Count of Champagne, Baldwin, Count of Flanders, and Simon de Montfort, who, some years later, butchered the Albigenses and Waldenses, a monstrous crime to be related a few pages further on. He was the father of the man who helped to lay the foundation of the first English Parliament, about which we shall be reading at the close of this chapter.

Venice, and the other Adriatic ports, had performed their part in the previous Crusades, and had profited greatly thereby. They had secured trading rights in the East, Venice particularly benefiting by obtaining valuable commercial facilities at Constantinople. Within a few centuries Venice had grown from being nothing more than a few scattered bleak islands of refuge from the savage Huns, into a throbbing workshop whose ships sailed to every port carrying her wares. Her once fugitive inhabitants had now become rich merchants, with banking establishments in all the principal towns of Europe, and, under the sign of the three golden balls, today the perquisite of pawnbrokers, they financed the Crusades.

Venetian ships carried the Crusaders, their equipment and their food to the Holy Land, bringing home the plunder and those who were fortunate enough to return. Besides being amply rewarded for their services they demanded trading concessions in every town captured from the Turks, as the Lord might not come so soon as some expected, and, in any case, it was wise to continue having as lucrative an interest as possible in the affairs of this world until he did. They were fortunate to be able to continue these trading rights after the Moslems had driven the Christians out of their land, and recovered their possessions. So Venice alone, in all Europe, benefited from the Crusades, as elsewhere they only brought misery and ruin.

The merchants of Venice therefore played an important part in this holy war, as they had the goods, the ships, the seamen and the money, all useful assets which enabled them to dictate their own terms to the zealots whose one object in life was to reach the Holy Land, drive out the Turks, and then await the coming of their Lord. Now the Venetians decided that the time had come to crush a rival, and they used their new-found power to the full. For long they had resented the rivalry of the Christian city of Zara on the Dalmatian coast, and they bargained with the Crusaders that they would only furnish the necessary ships if they first captured Zara, and handed it over to the control of Venice. Zara was captured in 1202, many of its inhabitants perished, and then the prospect of quite a new adventure opened up. Alexius, the son of the late emperor, asked the help of the Crusaders against his uncle, who occupied the throne in Constantinople, and, in exchange, he promised trading concessions and the union of the Church of the East with that of the West.

So the Crusaders of the Fourth Crusade, who had set out to defeat the Moslems, moved off instead to depose the usurping uncle. In this they succeeded, but the nephew, who became Alexius IV, was slain by an enraged mob which rose against him. This gave the Crusaders an excuse to attack the capital, which, in 1204, fell because the defence was weak and corrupt. Thus this great city was captured for the first time during its nine centuries of existence, and never did a gang of adventurers secure such rich booty. Priceless treasures and works of art were destroyed, and all that was movable—the gold, silver and precious tapestries—were divided amongst the plunderers, who slaughtered the inhabitants without mercy. "No one was spared," says a contemporary historian. "In the alleys, streets and churches you heard nothing but the mourning of women and the groans of men. You saw nothing but rape, the taking of captives, and the severing of families."

The Crusaders set up a new government, and the Greek Church was replaced by the victorious Catholic Church, with the Pope at Rome as its head instead of the Patriarch at Constantinople. Baldwin, with the Pope's approval, became emperor, and the Venetian merchants took over a large part of the city. The new state, which His Holiness declared had been delivered over to him for the greater glory of God, existed from 1204 until 1262, but it never received popular support, and finally collapsed. Then a new empire was set up with the support of the Greek Church, but the Eastern Empire never regained its strength, and to the abominations of the Fourth Crusade can be attributed its downfall two centuries later when the Turks captured Constantinople.

The holy war against the Turks had been welcomed at its outset in Constantinople after the city's defeat at the Battle of Manzikert (1071), as the position had then become desperate. Nomadic hordes threatened it from the north, and the Turks were pressing in from the east, but never had its inhabitants believed that it would fall to the Christians from the west. To the Eastern Empire the war was for the purpose of driving back the Turks from the lands of the Empire they had invaded, but to the popes at Rome the unification of Christendom was as much their aim as the capture of the Holy Sepulchre. They wanted to heal the difference in belief on the question of the Trinity, one which had created a deep gulf between the Christians of the West and those of the East, the Catholic Church holding the Greek Church in horror and contempt, while the Greeks retained their age-old scorn of everything Roman.

Constantinople considered itself the heir to ancient Hellas and the Roman Empire. To the Greeks, Rome had lost her claim to Christian leadership by the scandals surrounding so many of the popes, and by the Papacy being supported by the French and Germans, whom the Greeks still considered to be barbarians. This attitude greatly angered the Holy See at Rome, which looked upon the Patriarch at Constantinople as an upstart, and the Greeks as damned heretics. The Greeks, in turn, rightly claimed that Christianity was born and nurtured in Greece, and that the brilliant conquests of her famous Macedonian emperors, Basil I, Phocas, Zimisces, and Basil II, over the past hundred and fifty years, had carried Greek Christianity into southern Italy, Bulgaria and Asia Minor. Besides all this Russia had now accepted the faith from her, and organised her Church on Greek lines.

The bloody sack of Constantinople by the soldiers comprising the Fourth Crusade was the Pope's reply to all these Greek claims to leadership of the Christian Church. For the next fifty-eight years, up to 1262, the Pope ruled in Constantinople, and the Greek Church priesthood was abolished, all of which led to such bitterness and hatred that the sore was never healed and the union of the Christian Church made impossible. The failure of the Crusaders in their mission to retrieve the Holy Land can therefore be put down to this division in the Christian ranks, as, if the Crusaders had been united, organised and well led, Asia Minor and Palestine could have been recovered for Christendom.

The Fourth Crusade, it will be seen, never reached the Holy Land, and, from now onwards, the Crusaders were used by the popes against all and sundry. The next crusade was against the Albigenses in the south of France, for which in violence and cruelty there is no parallel. The Christian Church has perpetrated countless crimes, but one of its worst is the extermination of the Albigenses, a sect which had beliefs different from those held by the Catholic Church. It was one of a number of such sects which developed in the Middle Ages, and its fate is typical of the others. This sect took its name from Albi, a town of southern France, and held unorthodox opinions on the definition of the Trinity, infant baptism, and other generally accepted doctrines.

In spite of all the persecutions to which its adherents were subjected, after the Christian Church became supreme in Europe, its form of belief had survived since Apostolic times, and, as the centuries passed, they had increased in numbers and influence. Consequently we find that at a council held in 1165 the Church decided to stamp them out entirely, and from this date the history of the Albigenses is written in blood, to reach its climax when Pope Innocent III ascended the papal throne in 1198, the fateful year in which he began his infamous campaign for their extermination. Inquisitors (the Gestapo of the Christian era) were appointed wherever the sect was known to exist, and the bloody massacre which followed revealed how true was the saying attributed to Jesus, that he had not brought peace on earth but a sword.

As town after town was taken in southern France the inhabitants were put to the sword without distinction of age or sex, and the numerous priests who led the army distinguished themselves by a bloodthirsty ferocity. At the taking of Beziers in 1209 the Abbot Arnold, on being asked how the heretics were to be distinguished from the faithful, made the outrageous reply, "Slay all; God will know his own." The war was carried on under the command of Simon de Montfort, the elder, with undiminished cruelty for a number of years, all the leaders of the sect being imprisoned, tortured and then executed. The establishment of an Inquisition at Languedoc in 1229 accelerated the extermination process, and in a few years the sect was all but extinct, hundreds of thousands having perished. Further particulars of this massacre will be given later on in this chapter, when we come to the history of France during this period.

Excommunications and curses were being hurled right and left from the Holy See at Rome, and Christendom was plunging everywhere deeper and deeper into the mire of crime, but all that has been told so far is overshadowed by what now happened. In 1212 occurred one of the worst crimes ever perpetrated by the fanatics at Rome, and this is known as the Children's Crusade. It was organised by the Church, the reason being that the failure to retake the Holy Land from the Turks was considered to be due to the Crusaders being too worldly for such a holy project, and that only innocent children could secure the prize.

The children of France and Germany were organised into an army, and 50,000 boys and girls were brought to Marseilles, and the ports of Italy, for shipment to the East, they being promised miraculous experiences, even that the sea would dry up to enable them to walk all the way on dry land. Many died before they reached the coast, but those who survived found the sea still there, and ships waiting to embark them. Thus began the Fifth Crusade, its aim being the conquest of Egypt because the Sultan of Egypt was then in control of Palestine. Few of the children ever returned from this insane expedition, thousands died of disease, many were captured and made slaves, and some were drowned, the adults who accompanied them straggling back with nothing to show for their folly except that some claimed to have with them a few pieces of the Cross. All that the devout tyrant, Pope Innocent III, could do, when he heard how his expedition had failed, was to exclaim that the enthusiasm of the children had put everyone else to shame.

If the Fifth Crusade was the height of folly and cruelty, the sixth reached the limits of absurdity. The Emperor Frederick II made a bargain with Pope Innocent III, to secure his election as Holy Roman Emperor of Germany in return for his organisation of a fresh Crusade. Some years later Frederick started off, only to return in a few days complaining that he did not feel well enough for such an undertaking. For thus breaking his promise to the Church the then ruling Pope excommunicated him, but this did not prevent him eventually sailing in 1228, to arrive in Palestine, not as an enemy of the Sultan but as a friend, and thus win more privileges for Christian pilgrims visiting Jerusalem than had been won by the sword.

Besides this he secured from the Sultan the nominal Kingdom of Jerusalem, but, as no priest would crown an excommunicated sinner, he took the crown in his own hands and crowned himself in a church devoid of priests. For this act the Pope declared a Crusade against him, and the Emperor returned home to find the papal army ravaging his possessions in Naples. This he defeated, and then made peace with the Pope, who withdrew his ban of excommunication.

Frederick's success with the Sultan, when all else had failed, was a triumph of wisdom. Neither monarch cared in the least for orthodox religion, and both considered that the Pope should confine himself to his own legitimate business and keep out of politics. Frederick was a good linguist and spoke six languages fluently, including Arabic, and when the two rulers met they were more interested in discussing how to repel the threatened Mongolian hordes which were gathering strength farther east, than the question of the Holy Sepulchre; in fact it is doubtful if Frederick ever took the trouble to visit it.

The Christians, however, lost Jerusalem again in 1244, because they started intriguing against the Sultan, and this was the cause of the Seventh Crusade under Louis IX (Saint Louis) of France, who was taken prisoner in Egypt, to be finally ransomed. The eighth and last Crusade was undertaken at a later date by the same monarch, but he died of fever in Tunis, and not until 1918 did the Holy Land return to Christian keeping, when British and French troops captured it from the Turks during the First World War.

Thus ended this long-drawn-out series of campaigns, waged by one portion of the human race against another because each defined God differently, one thinking that only one God lived in heaven, and had never come to live on earth, while the other believed that a third part of the deity had, for three days, occupied a tomb situated in Jerusalem, and was now about to return to earth. Christendom accepted the Pagan and Jewish idea of sacrifice as a means of salvation, and also adopted the Eastern mysticism which imagined a god of three persons. To the Moslems this was no better than polytheism, which they considered was the greatest of all religious sins. So once again we find that a disagreement on a definition of the Infinite, which no finite mind can ever define, brought about these centuries of crusading warfare, involving countless thousands killed and wounded, immense loss of wealth, and enormous suffering and misery.

The Church certainly gained by this insane enterprise against the Turks, because landowners, and those possessed of wealth, handed over their riches and lands to its keeping while they set off to the east. The Church became their trustee in their absence, and, as many did not return, it became the perpetual owner of their possessions. Consequently the more Crusades there were the Church benefited to an ever greater degree. Every parish during this mad age was a recruiting ground, and every priest a recruiting sergeant, who promised a safe entry into heaven for all who became Crusaders. All such were freed from their debts, the serfs were released from the land, and the prison doors were opened to all prisoners who agreed to wear the crusading cross and carry the sword.

Relying on the words attributed to Jesus:—

> And everyone that hath forsaken houses, or brethren, or sisters, or father or mother, or wife or children, or lands for my name's sake, shall receive an hundredfold, and shall inherit everlasting life. (*Matthew* xix, 29.)

wives left their husbands, who wisely stayed at home, and found another man to take them on the sacred enterprise. Husbands left their wives and families to fend for themselves as best they could, everyone starting off in the belief that by undertaking this holy mission they would be doubly sure of salvation. All semblance of law and order was thus abolished by the bribe of heaven to those who would commit themselves to this insane adventure. Society consequently crumbled to pieces, and centuries passed before the evil results of the Crusades wore away.

The effects were however not entirely evil, as indirectly some good came from this long-drawn-out struggle for the Holy Sepulchre. It opened up an interchange of thought between the East and the West which slowly, during the intervening centuries, ended in the Renaissance, produced by Moslem learning and culture finding their way to Europe. Thus the Christians, who had never heard of hospitals or medical treatment, copied from the Moslems their method of treating the sick in these institutions. Christians then looked on the sick and suffering as people afflicted by devils, but, from now onwards, Moslem medical knowledge influenced Europe, which slowly abandoned its ignorance and commenced the study of healing by means of remedies for ailments, thus depriving the priest of one of his occupations: the praying of the devils out of the afflicted.

Out of much that was evil followed that which was good many centuries later, and the Christian Church, which, by this long-drawn-out conflict, had brought immense loss and misery on mankind, was in the end the greatest sufferer. The knowledge which came from the East was the cause which ultimately broke its power and gave to Christendom religious liberty. Another result was the decline in the influence of the nobles, who had mortgaged much of their land to pay for the expeditions they had organised. The town now became more important than the castle, the burghers becoming the loyal subjects of the King, to end in securing representation in the national assemblies, where they determined their own taxation.

Thus did a middle class come into being, to be a powerful influence on the mental development of the people as a whole. They lived chiefly by trade and commerce, which required a practical education in law, the arts, and all there was to know. Theological education, relating everything in nature to the caprice of God, and so far the only form of instruction in Christendom, thus received its first set-back, from which it has never recovered. It was pushed ever more into the background as each century passed, and is today reserved only for a class of men entirely out of touch with practical everyday affairs.

Wars have been waged for many reasons, mostly for plunder and power, but this one, for the multitude, was purely emotional, in support of an idea that was only a figment of the imagination. Could the curse of ignorance be more clearly demonstrated than in this Holy War, in support of a theological speculation which brought no immediate good, and only suffering and destitution to humanity?

Christian civilisation was an age of abomination and wickedness for which no decent-minded person today would lift a finger to have revived, and the repeated assertions during the Second World War that this struggle was a conflict waged to preserve Christian civilisation reveals the ignorance of the people, who accepted as true what they were told by the clergy and zealous churchmen.

War at all times brings out the worst in humanity, but its very wickedness produces the nobler qualities of bravery and courage which gleam through the surrounding darkness. This is all that can be said for war, and that is not much, as these virtues can shine equally well in ordinary daily life. The mountaineer, the explorer, the coal-miner, always in danger, the sailor, battling against the storm, and many others show the same high degree of disregard for danger without inflicting destruction, injury and death on others.

Only within recent years has war produced those kind, unselfish healers, from whom flow words of comfort and cheer, and whose deft hands try to cure the damage that hate and ignorance have caused. Prior to last century little or nothing was done for the wounded. Then there were few hospitals, doctors or nurses, and the wounded suffered and often died alone. There was no pity, no succour, no exemption from death either offered or granted. It was slay or be slain, and, if a combatant survived, he carried his wounds and disabilities with him to the grave.

All the savagery and hatred which man at his worst can generate came to the surface in this terrible crusading war. Enthusiasm became hatred, and the lust for blood on both sides seemed unquenchable. In grim reality the people carried into effect the words of the famous hymn "Onward, Christian soldiers, marching as to war, with the cross of Jesus going on before". In Rome the Pope and his cardinals coolly and deliberately planned the whole diabolical enterprise, and the ignorant mob, who did their bidding, endured the suffering and misery. The Turks suffered likewise, and, as the victims to this unprovoked aggression, their misery was no less bitter. Intolerance was everywhere rampant, and the curse of ignorance ground poor humanity down to the very lowest depths.

The B.B.C., in a series of talks during 1942 on "The Church and Society", gave the British public an entirely false, misleading and distorted account of the record of the Christian Church throughout the Christian era. Moreover, Viscount Halifax, in a broadcast (20–9–1942) which was given great prominence in the B.B.C. News Service, and in the newspapers the following day, announced that the real issue for the United Nations in fighting the Second World War "was whether Christianity, and all it means, is to sur vive or not". Millions of good, kind and righteous people, who were not Christians, were just as anxious as the Christians, outside of Germany and Italy, to have German tyranny destroyed, and many of them fought in the war to that end. We certainly did not fight

the last war to preserve Christianity, but to save ourselves from German domination.

Halifax further told his audience that Christianity
had been responsible for all the hospitals, and deeds
of mercy and kindness, which we now enjoy, and
"that every one of the things we value is rooted in
Christian thought". Education was encouraged by
the Pagans and banned in Christendom. Surgery
was practised in ancient Egypt, whereas the first
Christian surgeon was banished from Europe in the
16th century. Hospitals and curative centres in considerable numbers existed in Greece and the Roman
Empire long before the Christian era, in which lands
the virtues were expounded by their great philosophers,
and their numerous followers, from the time of
Pythagoras onwards. Galen, the first outstanding
doctor, was a Pagan, and there were many others who
healed the sick long before the Christian era. In
both Greece and Rome there were widespread organisations for charity and mercy, the ancient Greeks
especially being renowned for their kindness and
sympathy towards those in distress.

Christians speak and write as if charity were
something which was the outcome of the Christian
religion, and, as most Christians know little about
history, or the origin of their religion, this is the prevailing belief in the Western hemisphere. "Christian
charity", which is nothing more than humanitarianism,
first made its appearance in Christendom in the 18th
century of the Christian era (eighteen hundred years
after the birth of Jesus, which is a long time between
the alleged cause and the effect), and it was in no way a
novelty, because the charity claimed by Christians took

place in Pagan Greece and the Roman Empire long before Christianity was born.

The Oxford Dictionary's definition of Charity is "Christian love of fellow men", but this is quite wrong, as the word comes from the Latin *carita* meaning high regard, and if Christians would only take the trouble to read the writings of Aristotle, and other Greek and Latin writers on Charity, they would realise how ignorant they are of the charitable ideas and deeds of the Pagans towards the poor and needy. Love of our fellow men is in no way confined to Christians and Christendom, as it is just the practice of kindness, and kind deeds are confined to no one religion, race or place.

This dishonest Christian propaganda has now been going on since the 4th century, and Christians should be ashamed of the lies and fabrications which seem inseparable from their faith. The clergy are notorious for the false claims they make for their religion, but, when a leading statesman, such as Lord Halifax, associates himself with priestly lies, and the B.B.C. gives his mis-statements world-wide publicity, the time has certainly come for the people to study history for themselves. They most assuredly cannot rely on either politicians or the clergy to tell them the truth, and the foregoing is only one example of many, to which the B.B.C. permits no reply from those who put truth before falsehood.

(3) Germany and Italy in the Middle Ages.

It will be remembered that we had reached the time of Otto I, the creator of the First Reich who died in 973, when we broke into the regular sequence of events to tell about the Crusades. Otto I was followed by Otto II (973–983), and he was succeeded by Otto III (983–1002). All that need be mentioned about these uneventful periods was the foundation of the new state of Poland through Papal influence, and that the Magyars, now known as Hungarians, accepted the Christian faith.

European history now revolves round the struggle for power between the Emperors of the Empire created by Otto I and the Popes at Rome. Then, as on many later occasions, Germany's policy was the domination of Italy. This state of affairs was no more successful than it was in our own times, because both countries disliked each other and had widely different traditions, social conditions and language. Italy had behind her the culture and history of the Roman Empire, which Germany completely lacked, and feudalism flourished in Germany, but not in southern Italy.

Since the fall of Rome, and the collapse of the Roman Empire, Italy's history had indeed been full of tragedy. We remember Justinian's successful efforts to regain her from the Goths, which came to nothing after his death when his empire collapsed. This long bitter struggle was a terrible calamity for Italy, as great atrocities were committed, millions died from war, starvation, pestilence or massacre, the entire male population of Milan, some 300,000, being slaughtered in 539. Rome became a wilderness, the last circus had been held, the last Senate elected, the water supply cut off, and trade was extinct. In this desert lived the Christian priests, quite incapable of restoring the prestige of the once great city.

Justinian's destruction of the Gothic power was a great disaster for Italy, as under the Goths the country was prospering. He uprooted them, putting nothing in their place, and the Lombards, who replaced the Goths, had not outgrown their barbarian heredity. From this time onwards Italy became the bone of contention of the Germans, French and Spaniards. For centuries she was partly dominated by one or other of these alien races, and, up to last century, was split in two by the Papal States, a grossly mismanaged community, governed by priests, devoid of all decency and humane principles.

From the year 753, when the lands belonging to the Lombards were wrested from them by the Frankish king Pepin II and given to the Pope, to become known as the Papal States, they were a running sore for eleven centuries to the Italian people, who have every reason to curse the day this happened. Germany, until the time of Otto I, had co-operated with the Papacy since the time of Charlemagne, but, when her kings became emperors of the combined German and Italian empire, the popes resented German interference in their government. The popes were not only the divine rulers of the Christian Church, but also the temporal rulers of Italy, and the German attempt to usurp their rule was bitterly resented.

Then nationalism, as we understand it today, was unknown. Mediaeval institutions were international in a way we hardly realise, and Latin their common language. The Crusades show how united Europe was on one common purpose. Her leader and superior was the Pope, with his representative priest in every parish, and the people followed him blindly until the Renaissance, when some began to realise for the first time that their spiritual leader only led them down a blind alley and left them there.

The attempt made by the popes to unify Europe dismally failed, just as nationalism has failed to bring unity and a common purpose to the human race. How unfortunate it is that the people of our own time cannot find something true, honest and of good repute to rally round, and become one in thought and deed, instead of glorifying narrow nationalism which inevitably leads to war. Some day this something may be found, but, if it is to bind the people together and keep them united, it must conform to natural law, and not be based on ignorant theological speculations or imperialistic dreams.

If Religion had always been in the hands of men of high character, honest in their purpose, and indifferent to wealth, power and position, what a force for good it could have been, as it touches the very vitals of humanity. If it had never been stereotyped into rigid creeds, and had developed as knowledge increased, what a power for the advancement of humanity it might have been. If nature's revelation of the life hereafter had never been distorted by priests into saviours, creeds, dogmas and doctrines, how the knowledge that we live hereafter as we live here, and that we reap as we sow, would have stimulated ethics and morality. Instead of this simple fact, the people of every religion have been promised heaven if only they believe the dogmas produced by priestly minds, and hell if they reject them. The priests, from early times everywhere, have traded on man's ignorance about his destiny, for their own ends, and they could only retain their power by keeping ignorant the masses who trusted them.

Nature's revelation, through prophets, or, as we call them today, mediums, conflicted with this false theological teaching, and the clergy consequently branded all mediums as servants of the devil, and had them destroyed. The destruction of mediums by priestly organisations runs into hundreds of thousands. The priests have always looked upon the prophets as their rivals, and taught their ignorant followers to ignore the only revelation which has ever come, or can come, from heaven. This only can come from those who have preceded us, and the only instrument they have for their communications is the one provided by nature, the prophet, the individual who is so made that he or she can be used by the men and women of the other world to reveal themselves to us on earth.

This is nature's one and only unifying channel, which, when the curse of ignorance passes, should bind mankind together, as we all have the same destiny hereafter, and are thus linked together by this uniform vital bond. This common heritage of mankind, which should have bound humanity together, has, because of ignorance, separated them, and, in the form of supernatural religion, produced hatred and intolerance. Under wise guidance man's common destiny could be used for unifying the entire human race, and developing the idea of the dignity and brotherhood of man.

If only the Christian Church had not destroyed,

from the 4th century onwards, nature's method of revealing the hereafter to us, what a power for good this knowledge would have been to mankind. That, and its obliteration of education, its two greatest crimes, will never be forgotten. Instead of acting as the protector of nature's revelation, by shielding and developing these invaluable sensitive beings endowed with psychic gifts, and wisely guiding the people into a right understanding of mediumship, it destroyed the mediums supplied by nature and put itself in their place, securing domination by every evil device it could conceive.

In place of nature's means of revealing our destiny the Church put forward a rigid false creed, which conflicts with all the other false creeds believed in by other sections of the race. As each creed considers that belief in the doctrines of any other religion leads to hell, isolation and intolerance, which produces conflict, were inevitable. Instead of religion, properly understood, unifying the race, it has had exactly the opposite effect. This being so, the people of Europe, at the time we are now considering, turned to local unification by glorifying nationalism. By teaching the young embellished stories, and traditions of the land of their birth, they produced a national spirit which made each group of people, who spoke the same language and had the same traditions, a nation, beyond whose frontiers lived the ever hated foreigner.

Where boundary questions were concerned each nation considered itself right and the others wrong. Each nation was quite ignorant of the others, and feared the community stronger than itself. Disputes continually developed over territory, and Europe became a mass of humanity honeycombed by fluid national boundaries which swayed hither and thither, her sons suffering and dying to secure the aspirations of their respective nations, as determined by each national ruler. Nationality, like religion, has separated the people and led to misery and unhappiness, and the national-minded politician has been as great a curse to humanity as has the zealous priest.

Now we are coming to the time when it was becoming evident that religion would not unify the people of Europe, and the dream of a great ecclesiastical empire was fading. The Church is still supreme and nationalism is in its infancy. The Italian people are, however, resenting the German domination of their land, because they have different traditions and a different language. The Crusades consequently represented the last united effort of a people with different traditions and languages to work together. From now onwards the Pope, instead of directing the policy of the rulers of Europe, is often at variance with them, nationalism has taken root, and religion slowly loses any unifying power it had over the people of Europe.

Otto III was succeeded by Henry II (1002–1024) as Holy Roman Emperor, his special trouble being with the Saxons because he was not of their race. The events in the reign of the two emperors who followed, Conrad II and Henry III, call for no special mention, but, with the accession of Henry IV (1056–1106), we come to the beginning of the struggle between the secular rulers of Europe and the popes. Henry claimed to be the secular head of Europe, which bold assertion Pope Gregory VII disputed, although he himself interfered in the internal affairs of nearly every country in Europe.

Each claimed the same powers of government, as in those days there was little difference between the authority of Church and State. The Emperor claimed the power to invest the newly appointed bishops, and to this the Pope objected, as he claimed the right to invest them with ring and staff as they attained their office at his direction, and were subject to his commands. The Pope, therefore, declared that all bishops must give obedience to him and not to the Emperor, and that any ruler who appointed a bishop would be excommunicated.

When it is remembered that in those days the bishops were the political administrators of their districts, we can better understand what this decision meant to all present and future rulers of Europe. Henry replied to Gregory, calling on him to resign as an immoral and false monk, and relinquish the Chair of Saint Peter to one who would teach sound doctrine and not interfere with politics. In those days such state documents did not end with a polite flourish, so Henry concluded "Be damned throughout all the ages", and to this the Pope replied with an anathema and excommunication. Such were the methods adopted in the Age of Faith, and, just because it was such an age, the Pope won because all Italy rallied round him, and even Germany was not united in its support of the Emperor. Henry, fearing the strength of opinion behind the Pope, who claimed to have the keys of heaven and hell in his pocket, surrendered and sued for pardon, which was only granted, so the story goes, after he had stood for three consecutive days bare-footed in the snow at the door of the castle of Canossa, in the Apennines, where the Pope was staying on his way to Germany.

This humiliation of the Emperor marks the zenith of Papal despotism, and Henry bided his time to take his revenge. When the quarrel was resumed the Pope again excommunicated him, to which Henry replied by appointing another bishop as Pope. Henry would have captured his enemy, who had retreated within the walls of the castle of Saint Angelo in Rome, had not the Norman, Robert Guiscard, returned from Durazzo with his army of Norman adventurers. This Norman soldier of fortune feared Henry's punishment for his plunderings, and, by aiding the Pope, he curbed the Emperor's power in Italy. Henry was consequently forced to leave Rome, and the Normans immediately proceeded to sack the city more thoroughly than ever Alaric the Goth, or Genseric the Vandal, had done.

The death of the despotic Gregory VII, who died a discredited exile to become a saint in heaven, did not end the struggle, as it was not a personal dispute but one between Emperor and Pope, and it continued for two centuries. Henry IV died in 1106, and his successor Henry V (1106–1125) went to Rome to be crowned, on the understanding that a compromise had been reached, but the Pope, Paschal II, broke his word, and, after the coronation, there were riots and bloodshed, during which Henry fled from Rome. A temporary truce, called "The Concordat of Worms", brought the struggle in 1122 to a close, when it was agreed that the Pope could elect his bishops, but only in the presence of a representative of the Emperor, who had the decision in the case of a dispute. All bishops, moreover, had to do homage to the Emperor for their lands, and be appointed by him as rulers over them. Thus they became what the Church likes to call spiritual bishops, on the authority of the Pope, and temporal bishops on that of the Emperor.

Peace between the two thrones was, however, impossible, as both Pope and Emperor claimed universal sovereignty over the people. By cunning political diplomacy, the Pope always managed to secure the support of an ally of great military strength and so maintain his claim, but here we must leave this ever recurring issue until we return to it again in the 14th century, when such help failed to materialise.

With the election of Conrad III, in 1138, commenced the Hohenstaufen dynasty. He was followed by his nephew, Frederick I (1152–1190), known in later years as Barbarossa, or Red Beard, one of the most outstanding and strongest of all the mediaeval emperors. During his reign Cologne, Mainz, Augsburg and other cities, with their own municipal government, became important centres of trade and the arts, similar to Milan, Florence and Venice. In France and England the cities were also freeing themselves from feudal restrictions by securing charters of privileges, and the kings sometimes adopted a friendly attitude towards their aspirations, but the nobles, who had no say in their administration, were their enemies. With this development came the practice of Roman law, produced in the age of the godemperors before feudalism was known, and this gave the king final authority in everything, much to the resentment of the great nobles who ruled over large areas. We shall soon be reading how the English barons settled the matter to their own satisfaction.

The reign of Frederick Barbarossa was by no means peaceful. On five occasions he entered Italy in force, to quell the resentment of the Italian cities against a German ruler. Milan and Rome were the storm centres, the resistance of the former representing the dislike of the cities towards his rule, and that of the latter because Pope Alexander III, a man whose election was secured by bribery and bloody massacre, supported the cities against the Emperor. In self-protection nearly all the cities of northern Italy formed themselves (1167) into "The Lombard League", which eventually defeated the Emperor at Legnano, the dénouement being that he, like his predecessor, knelt before the Pope and asked forgiveness. The cities thus secured their independence, their own armies, and their own jurisdiction, but in Germany Barbarossa was more successful, as he broke the power of his great rival Henry the Lion, the head of the powerful Guelf family and owner of the duchies of Bavaria and Saxony.

German influence extended both to the east and south. Eastwards it now reached far beyond the Elbe, its old boundary, to form the state of Brandenburg, and southwards it spread down the Danube, where a new duchy came into being. This southern outpost of German civilisation against the Magyars came to be known as Austria, which country was to play such a large part in future history (under the rule of the Hapsburgs, who succeeded the Hohenstaufens) and eventually dominate Germany and then Europe. Though Barbarossa's influence declined in

Italy, Germany increased in territory and influence, and the foundations were then laid for the Germany as we know it in our own time. Towards the end of his reign, the Emperor accompanied the third Crusade to the east and was drowned in Asia Minor in 1190.

This period of history produced not only one of the great popes, Gregory VII, a man who threatened war, and set armies moving on the slightest provocation, but also one of the notable figures in Church life. He is now known as Saint Bernard (1091-1153), and during his life he dominated Church politics, being one of the most powerful influences in European affairs. He was reponsible for the Second Crusade, and was an active enemy of all the heretics of the time. The monastic movement was then in full swing, spreading on a great wave of enthusiasm throughout Europe, and he raised the Cistercian order to the height it attained. These religious orders, such as the Cluniac, the Cistercian, the Carthusian, the Franciscan and the Dominican, always came to the help of the popes in their time of trouble, and supported the Holy See in its long struggle with the emperors and kings of Europe. Some were also active agents in the suppression of heresy, acting for the Pope as did the gestapo for Hitler.

These religious orders appealed to the masses in a way the Church did not do, their teaching being more simple and easily understood than was the Latin service in church. It was to recover those who had become indifferent, and to root out heresies, that these religious orders were founded, their members being influenced by the words attributed to Jesus :—

If any man come to me, and hate not his father and mother, and wife and children, and brethren, and sisters, yea, and his own life also, he cannot be my disciple. (*Luke* xiv, 26.)

These pitiless words, which were probably inserted in the Gospel by Jerome, or some other monkish zealot, broke up families and caused countless desertions of both men and women from each other and their children. The monastic orders flourished on the breaking-up of families, their recruits believing that by cutting themselves adrift from all earthly ties they were obeying the will of their Saviour and fulfilling the injunctions of God. This text, which is an obvious priestly interpolation in the interests of the Church, as it is not to be found in the oldest manuscripts, has exerted an evil influence throughout Christendom, as did also the belief in the imminent second coming of Christ, which dissipated all urge to work and improve one's lot in life. Little do we realise today the profound effect these two false ideas had on the outlook of Christendom, and the deadening consequences which followed from their taking a grip of the minds of the people, who normally would have given thought to the improvement of their social conditions, which in those days were sordid and deplorable.

Saint Francis and Saint Dominic, each of whom gave his name to the order he founded, were men of quite different character, Francis being kind and lovable. He wandered about preaching and doing deeds of kindness, the idea of forming a new monastic order only coming to him slowly. His outlook on life was so different from the one adopted by the Church that the Pope only sanctioned his scheme with reluctance, eventually giving his consent in 1209. Others soon took charge of the new order, and, because of their materialistic outlook, Francis withdrew and refused to have anything further to do with it.

Saint Dominic was cast in quite a different mould. He wished to crush all who differed from Church authority, and he was one of the leaders in the massacre of the Albigenses to which reference has already been made. He founded his order in 1213, to preach orthodox Christianity and use force where persuasion failed, the Dominicans becoming known as "the Bloodhounds of the Church". These two orders differed from those founded for meditation and contemplation, because the friars belonging to them went out and mixed with the people, obtaining their sustenance by begging. The Franciscans became known as the Grey Friars, and the Dominicans as the Black Friars, every town in western Europe soon becoming familiar with their distinctive dress.

Other Christian organisations came into being in those days. These were the military religious orders, which were the outcome of the Crusades, they being formed for the protection of pilgrims to the Holy Land. They paraded the gallantry of their members, who went out on their expeditions with the cross in one hand and the sword in the other, the best known of these being the Knights Templars and the Knights Hospitallers, but there were others, such as the Teutonic Knights, about whose activities something must be said.

German progress eastwards had continued beyond the Elbe, and now had reached to the Oder, where, still farther east, were non-German races, some of whom were still Pagans. The principal Pagan tribe was the Prussians, situated on the shore of the Baltic, with Danzig as their chief town and port. Here were, therefore, large territories for the Christians to plunder under the guise of missionary zeal, and, when the Teutonic Knights were turned out of the Holy Land by the Moslems, the Church directed them in 1228 to Prussia, where they were told that they could retain any lands they conquered.

In Christian eyes the Pagans had no rights, being looked upon as outcasts, and, with this divine authority, the Teutonic Knights proceeded, under Hermann of Salza, to do the Church's bidding, and bring more tithes into the Papal Treasury. Wherever they went they exercised the utmost brutality, massacring the inhabitants, and dispossessing them of their lands and dwellings, thus winning Prussia for Christ in a series of long-drawn-out campaigns.

In this manner was laid the foundation stone on which a united Germany was built six hundred years later, a task which the Hohenstaufen dynasty tried to do but failed to accomplish. The conquest of Prussia, moreover, marked the completion of the conversion of Europe, outside of Spain and Turkey, to Christianity. In the Middle East Mahomet had conquered, but the Gospel of Christ had certainly triumphed in Europe, and the priests could point with satisfaction to at least a partial fulfilment of one of their predecessors' most blatant interpolations: "Go ye therefore, and teach all nations, baptising them in the name of the Father, and of the Son, and of the Holy Ghost" (*Matthew* xxviii,. 19.)

The Christians had stolen most of Europe from the Pagans, and imposed on them their religious beliefs, because they had the support of more powerful rulers, who had more and better armed soldiers. Had it been otherwise, Europe would probably have been at least nominally Pagan to this day. As the Europeans discovered America, Australasia and other lands, where they imposed their culture and religion, Christianity spread round the world. The story of their missionary efforts in these parts will be told further on, though here it should be noted that the claim is false, that its expansion proves its divine origin, both force and good fortune being the cause.

Henry VI (1190–1197), who succeeded his father Frederick I, married Constance of Naples, the heiress of Sicily. Thus this great Norman stronghold became part of the Hohenstaufen Empire, much to the alarm of the Pope, who greatly resented Naples and Sicily entering the ranks of his German enemies. After seven years of conflict in Germany and Italy Henry died, but not before he had succeeded in overcoming all his enemies. His greatest contribution to Europe was the son he left behind him, the intellectual wonder of his age, as we shall soon discover. This son, who became Frederick II, was then only a child, and Pope Innocent III made Otto IV emperor, to depose him later because he claimed Sicily as part of his empire.

During the youth of the young prince, Innocent III (1198–1216), profiting from a temporary eclipse of the Holy Roman Empire, brought the Papacy to the summit of its power. He was undoubtedly the most powerful of all the popes, a man of great strength of character, considerable ability, treacherous, cunning and deeply religious. During his eighteen years' reign he claimed to be able to do "nearly all that God can do", and, although this was rather an exaggeration, he nevertheless accomplished more than any other pope before or since, his most outstanding achievements being:

The organisation of the Fourth Crusade.

The capture of Constantinople, its sack, and the massacre of its inhabitants.

The overthrow of the Greek Orthodox Church in Constantinople, and the imposition of the Catholic Church in its place.

His influence brought about a united Christian Spain, and led to the eventual ejection of most of the Moslems.

The securing from the kings of England, Portugal and Aragon the surrender of their respective countries as fiefs of the Holy See.

The placing of England, France and Venice under papal interdict.

The excommunication of King John of England, whom, at a later date, he encouraged to set aside the Magna Charta.

The excommunication of the barons who supported the terms set out in the Magna Charta.

The clearing of the Germans from Italy and Sicily.

The fomenting of a terrible civil war in Germany.

The making and unmaking of emperors on terms most favourable to the Church.

The intensification of the activities of the Inquisition, which lasted until the 19th century, and finally,

The crushing of the Albigensian heresy in southern France, thus obliterating the civilisation of an intelligent and virile people, hundreds of thousands of whom were brutally slaughtered.

During an age when Christendom was in a state of profound moral corruption, when its laity, clergy, monks and nuns were living degraded and bestial lives, Innocent, moreover, instituted a campaign throughout Christendom against all heretics. He mercilessly put to death everyone having opinions different from those proclaimed by the Church, making use of the Dominican friars as "Inquisitors of the Faith", as set down by the Theodosian code. From now onwards these Inquisitors play a large part in the intellectual life of Europe, their activities reminding us of the early centuries of Church rule. After the various early heresies had been suppressed the Church gestapo had not been in great use, because for nearly eight hundred years all intelligent thought had been stifled. It had been truly an Age of Faith. None had wondered, and, as knowledge comes from wondering, ignorance had reigned supreme during this time of intellectual coma.

Now, however, men's minds were stirring slightly, and Innocent determined that this must not be allowed. So it came about that in his reign the Inquisition was re-established, and the Church, by this instrument, did many of its foulest deeds over the next six hundred years. By fire, torture and imprisonment during the coming centuries it attempted to chain the mind of man to its own false beliefs, and, from now onwards, in every market place in Europe the cardinals, bishops and priests watched their victims expire by torture and at the stake, repeating to them that:—

If thy right eye offend thee pluck it out and cast it from thee . . . and if thy right hand offend thee cut it off and cast it from thee: for it is profitable for thee that one of thy members should perish and not that thy whole body should be cast into hell. (*Matthew* v, 29.)

During the age of Christian civilisation, when faith took the place of reason, during the period when "the Christian way of life", about which we hear so much in our own time, was being lived, Christians, when unable to make the unorthodox think exactly as they did, resorted to every method of torture which the human mind could devise. They crushed the feet of heretics in iron boots, roasted them on slow fires, plucked out their nails, gouged out their eyes, cut out their tongues, cut off their ears, and placed them on the rack, thus drawing every bone out of joint. There was a new torture for every new doubt, and no one except the victims seemed to think it wrong, even when Montaigne (1533–1592) raised his voice against it in France. What could one humane man do amongst these millions of savages?

People were dismayed by the reports of German cruelty during the Nazi regime, and many thought that the race was consequently degenerating. German brutality lasted for only about twelve years, and was no more than a continuation of what happened during the time of Christian civilisation. For fifteen hundred years no one could speak or write differently from what orthodox Christians believed, without risking torture or imprisonment, and at least 100,000,000 innocent men, women and children suffered in one way or another as the result of Christian bigotry.

They perished by the sword, by torture, at the stake, in prisons, or by famine; they died wandering homeless on the moors or in caves, Britain and Europe being everywhere pitted with their graves. Countless families were broken up, wives became widows, children became orphans, multitudes were exiled to die in poverty or slavery, and numerous wars were engineered by the Church, which caused untold millions to mourn. Gradually, over the centuries, more and more risked their lives for the sake of liberty to think as they thought right, the first outstanding heretic being Frederick II of Germany. Ultimately their fight for freedom was victorious, so much so that today no ecclesiastic anywhere, except in Spain, Eire, the Balkans and some South American states, would dare to lift a finger against anyone exposing the frauds and errors of the Christian faith.

The thoughtful and gifted Frederick II (1197–1250) became Holy Roman emperor in 1215. He was a cultivated and intelligent ruler, and from Sicily, which he made his home, he dispensed justice over southern Italy and Sicily which he inherited from his mother. He controlled the excessive liberties of the clergy and nobles, and built up a system of government without equal anywhere, his democratic Parliament anticipating what was later to come in England.

He was the first prominent man of the Middle Ages to doubt the truth of Christianity, and, if he had not been a king and emperor, would doubtless have shared the fate of all heretics. Other heretics so far had only interpreted Christianity differently from the Church, but he was the first to proclaim openly that its claims were based on fraud and ignorance, Jesus having been a human being like other men, and not a god. His anti-Christian opinions were doubtless due to the fact that he had received a remarkably good education for those times, so much so that his knowledge earned for him the title of "Stupor mundi", the amazement of the world, and time has in no way diminished this description. He it was who made friends with the Sultan of Egypt, instead of fighting him, when he went out on the sixth Crusade, and, as he spoke and read Arabic as well as five other languages, he was able to look on Christianity from the aspect of a scholar. Consequently he came to the conclusion that all supernatural religions were priest-made systems of belief, and that Christianity was a form of ancient belief, dressed up under a new name, which the priests were propagating for their own ends.

Frederick's anti-Christian opinions developed later in life, but, when he was a young man, Innocent III supported his election as emperor, because he agreed to the papal demand that, when elected, he would relinquish his possessions in southern Italy and Sicily, ruthlessly stamp out heresy in Germany, and free the clergy there from coming under the law and from all taxation. Frederick did none of these things, and neither Innocent nor his successor Honorius III (1216–1227) could ever get him to do so. Gregory IX (1227–1241), the next Pope, · excommunicated him because he turned back the sixth Crusade, making his health the excuse, but nothing the popes of his time could do altered the fact that he was the greatest intellectual force of the Middle Ages, a brilliant light in a black night, which shone brightly for thirty-five years to disappear in darkness.

The Emperor eventually went east, to exchange opinions with the Sultan of Egypt on the Mongol invasion from Asia which threatened both Egypt and Europe, taking also the opportunity to express his views on the Pope, and his religion, to the Sultan, who had similar ideas about the Moslem form of belief. Frederick, of all the Crusaders, was interested in the Greek classics and Arabian science and literature. These he studied and fostered at a time when all Christendom gave thought only to the destruction of the Turks, and the recovery of the Holy Sepulchre.

On his return home he wrote to Innocent IV (1243–1254), who had succeeded Gregory IX, a candid letter denouncing the lives and claims of the priests. As the controversy increased he became bolder, he accusing the Pope and his priests of living in vice, in luxury, and by fraud on the earnings of their ignorant dupes. Frederick contrasted their lives with the way Jesus and his disciples had lived, and threatened for the good of the Church to confiscate its vast possessions. As this wordy contest increased in intensity, the Emperor threatened to establish a new Church based on poverty and simplicity, this being what he took to be the purport of the message delivered by Jesus, to be told in reply that the Council of Lyons (1245) had solemnly deposed him and elected a new emperor. The controversy was still proceeding when the Emperor died.

Frederick gathered round him Jews, Moslems and Christians holding unorthodox opinions, and thus some of the knowledge and wisdom of the East reached

Europe (excepting Moslem Spain) for the first time since the collapse of the Roman Empire. His Court was the refuge of the persecuted, as there all opinions were freely expressed. Arising from this liberal assembly, which was more Eastern than European, as the Emperor lived in oriental splendour and maintained a harem, Arabian culture and knowledge were planted in Italy just as they had been in Spain some centuries before.

Consequently the Arabic numerals, which we use today, and Algebra were introduced into Europe, as were the writings of Aristotle, which, from this time onwards, were to act as the foundation of learning for the new universities, now to come into being all over western Europe. Aristotle had been unknown up to now, as, to keep western Europe ignorant of Greek philosophy, the Greek language had been forbidden, but, though this ban remained, a translation of Aristotle's works was now made from Arabic into Latin, together with a Moslem commentary thereon.

Being desirous of introducing Arabian science into Europe, Frederick founded in 1224 the University of Naples, for those, as he said in the charter, "who have hunger for knowledge". He also financed the school of medicine at Salerno, which, with a struggle, had survived from the time of Greek occupation, and thus he made it one of the great institutions of the time. Arabian science was also responsible for the foundation of the medical school at Montpelier. To the Arabs Europe is indebted for her universities, though it was not long before the Church degraded them into theological colleges, where the students were forbidden to study medicine, science or law.

Frederick also started a Zoological Society for the collection of wild animals, wrote poetry, also a book on hawking which showed his knowledge of bird life, and he revived the old Carthaginian system of issuing bank notes made of leather. His advanced thinking was doubtless due to his knowledge of Arabic, and the contact he had with Moslem civilisation.

This man, unique for his time, was reviled by three successive popes, but his novel opinions sank into the minds of others and laid the foundation of the Renaissance of the 15th century, all the universities of Italy being founded by secular bodies mainly for secular purposes. Frederick was the first ruler to be a thorn in the side of the Christian Church, which, from now onwards, was to receive other and greater pricks until it split in half at the time called the Reformation. Then others saw the sham of excommunications and interdicts, and took heart, while students began to think less of devils causing illness, and more of practical cures instead of prayers.

Frederick disturbed Europe in her long sleep, which had been caused by her being drugged by orthodox religion, and for this he ranks as the first thinker in Christian Europe, the first to loosen the chain the Church had bound round the mind of Christendom. What he did for Europe his contemporary Roger Bacon likewise did for England. From now onwards it will be found that where medical or educational schools, hospitals and universities are founded, the Church had no part in their establishment, just as happened in the Moslem world, where science flourished during its age of unorthodoxy.

Frederick II loved the sunny south, and lived

much of his life in Sicily. Here he found an existing Arabian culture, as Sicily, from the 9th century, had been under Saracen rule until 1060, when it was conquered by the Normans. There, as in Spain, the Moslems had produced a civilisation above anything experienced in Christendom. Frederick, however, neglected Germany, with the result that its clergy, princes and nobles obtained such power that some became his dangerous enemies. Under the leadership of his son they rose in insurrection against him, and were defeated, but not before they had gained sufficient power to make it impossible to restore the prestige of the Crown. This event had its repercussions down the centuries, as not until the 19th century did Germany secure a central government, a fact which accounts for the Germans of today being so backward in self-government. Politically Germany is hundreds of years behind Great Britain, where a central authority has been in control of affairs for more than a thousand years, and the people have not been corrupted by evil rulers as have the Germans.

Frederick's experience as a Crusader was more that of a statesman than of a soldier. His friendship with the Sultan displeased the Pope, who also took the opportunity of his absence to weaken his attempt to rule over all Italy, because the Pope considered that this land was his own preserve. Frederick consequently found on his return that the army of the Pope had ravaged southern Italy and Sicily, but it was not until his death that the Pope regained his sovereignty over the Papal States, a position the Holy See was able to retain until the 19th century, and thus keep Italy a divided country.

If the rich cities of Lombardy had sided with Frederick against the Pope, this dream of a united Italy might then have been accomplished, but they preferred an autocratic Pope, whose claims and deeds were meekly accepted in those days, in preference to the hated Germans, who were then as much feared by the Italians as in our own times. Frederick's determination to crush the northern cities into subjection caused bitter conflicts, which, to begin with, went in his favour, but, after his deposition as emperor, when the Pope ranged his armies against him, he was defeated at Parma (1247), then besieged by his army, and when he died three years later the struggle was still undecided.

Frederick was a man of strong will, with the power of organisation, but, after his death, the efficient government he had developed in Naples and Sicily gradually fell into decay. His son Conrad IV came to Italy after attempting, without success, to establish his control in Germany. His early death enabled Pope Urban IV (1261–1264) to offer the crown of southern Italy to Charles of Anjou, the brother of the King of France, on the understanding that if he failed in his payments to the papal treasury his kingdom would be laid under an interdict. Naples and Sicily thus fell to a cruel tyrant, but the Pope had succeeded in ejecting the hated German rule from Italy, and from now onwards the house of Hohenstaufen, which had played so great a part during the Middle Ages, quickly faded out, its last representative, Conradin, Frederick's grandson, being murdered in 1268.

The Papacy had triumphed by using every possible

device to secure its temporal authority. Religion had been cunningly used for worldly power, but retribution was to come within the next fifty years, when the Holy See received the most severe humiliation in its long inglorious career.

(4) France During the Crusades.

With the fall of the house of Hohenstaufen, France stepped into the place occupied by Germany as the leading power in Europe, to carry on the quarrel with the Papacy and deliver to it a blow from which it never recovered. Before, however, this story is told we must go back some three hundred years, and see how this western half of Charlemagne's empire has fared since his time.

It will be remembered that Louis the Pious (son of Charlemagne) divided his empire between his three sons. They fought one another for supreme power, but, in 843, the Treaty of Verdun was drawn up, dividing the empire into three, (1) France, (2) Rhineland, Switzerland and North Italy, and (3) Bavaria and Saxony, as we now call these lands. Though, from this time onwards for a century and a half, the history of France is one of continuous disturbance, this date is generally taken as the time when France, more or less as we now know it, was born. Here feudalism developed, and for long this remained the only form of government.

In 885 the Normans, who had occupied the Channel coast, besieged Paris, but Odo, Count of Paris, drove off the invaders and so saved the city and the throne of a weak king, for which service he himself was made king. He, however, received only a vague acknowledgment of his sovereignty from the great nobles, of whom the chief ruled over Burgundy, Aquitaine, Toulouse, Flanders, Normandy and Champagne. Each of these possessed authority equal to that of the king, and this state of affairs continued for many years until the time of Hugh Capet, a hundred years later, when the authority of the throne came to be everywhere recognised.

Capet, who had ruled Paris and the surrounding country, was appointed king in 987, and, as he was a devout Christian, a close alliance developed between France and the Papacy. This continued, and when the conflict between the German Emperor and the Church began a hundred years later the King of France supported the Pope, to receive in return his help to establish the throne on a secure basis against the feudal nobles. Thus the monarchy became supreme, and the nobles became the subjects of the king, a position the emperors in Germany had tried to achieve, but could not. From possessing only feudal territories around Paris the Crown gradually, over the next three hundred years, took over the feudal control of all the other domains controlled by the nobles until this form of government ceased, though even then they continued to retain their wealth and their lands.

During this time, when Germany remained divided into dukedoms, when Italy was under German rule, and Spain was in Moslem hands, England, Scotland and France had acquired unity as kingdoms, a development which made for settled government. Germany remained weak because of her disputes with the Church, and, in after years, she was torn to bits by another religious war engineered by the Church, all of which kept her from acquiring a commanding position in Europe during the period when new lands were being discovered. Thus she was deprived of the opportunities which others had, and this poverty in oversea possessions explains one of the reasons for the bitterness amongst some of the Nazi hierarchy towards the Catholic Church.

The first to be termed Sovereign of the French was Philip I (1060–1108), and several causes can be put forward as the reason. In 1066 William of Normandy conquered England, and was so pleased with the nice big peach which he had stolen, that his French plum, Normandy (likewise stolen, but at an earlier dáte) received less of his attention. In 1095 the first Crusade took from France many of the most dangerous rivals of the Crown, few of whom ever returned, and Philip took advantage of these two events to reduce the feudal power of those who gave him scant respect. He thus increased the prestige of the royal court, the central government became better organised, all authority now concentrating round the King, who had as his advisers the loyal nobles, the chief priests and the leading lawyers. As happened elsewhere, the new cities which were developing looked to the King for protection against those claiming feudal authority, and this further strengthened the power and prestige of the throne.

At this time both religion and morals in France were at the lowest depths of degradation. The people, being quite illiterate, had no means of mental refreshment, and spent what leisure they had in playing games or quarrelling. With little to occupy them in their spare time, sexual affairs took a prominent place in their lives. Modesty, as we understand it today, did not then exist, and consequently the most disgusting sights were to be seen. Religious services until the Reformation were burlesqued by what is called the Feast of Fools, held for the purpose of joyously celebrating the Nativity. Then it was that the priests, wearing monstrous masks during divine service, both sang and danced indecently, played dice on the altar steps, and behaved in other unmentionable ways so obscenely that the entire congregation was carried away and followed their example.

If the people had only been able to read and write, and if there had been paper and the knowledge of printing, they would have found their enjoyment in more dignified ways. However, they were ignorant and knew no better, and when Peter Abélard (1079–1142) tried to raise them to a higher level of thought he was shamefully treated. This man, the eldest son of a noble Breton house, fixed more decisively than anyone before him the scholastic manner of teaching philosophy, his object being to expound a rational religious doctrine. Through him the way was prepared in the Middle Ages for the ascendancy of the philosophic authority of Aristotle. This became firmly established fifty years after his death, which was brought about by the mutilation and persecution he received, because he lived to try and shed some intellectual light on a Europe then in the throes of theological ignorance and moral depravity.

The evolution of the power of the Crown, which began in the reign of Philip I, continued throughout the reign of Louis VI (1108–1137) until the time of his son Louis VII (1137–1180), who had an unfortunate reign. He bowed unconditionally to the Pope, who acted as if he, and not Louis VII, were the King of France. Then Louis went east with the second Crusade, only to suffer defeat and loss; and, by divorcing his wife Eleanor, he lost Aquitaine, of which she was the heiress. No greater blunder of the Middle Ages exceeded this one, as this disagreeable lady then married Henry II of England, who already possessed Normandy and Anjou, and thus brought to the English crown another large slice of France. However, Philip II (1180–1223), who followed, changed everything, as in a series of successful wars he added largely to his dominions.

He took Normandy, Anjou, Maine and Touraine, from King John of England, but the Battle of Bouvines in 1214 really decided the question of English participation in French affairs. At this decisive engagement, Otto IV of Germany, with whom John was in alliance, was decisively defeated, and this destroyed the English plans for the recovery of her lost possessions. Two centuries later the question of England's sovereignty over any part of France was put to the test of war, the Hundred Years' War definitely settling the ownership of the lands brought to the English crown by William of Normandy and Eleanor of Aquitaine. John's prestige fell so low in England that he was forced to grant the Magna Charta, an event which is of such importance that it will be referred to in greater detail when we come to consider English history.

On all sides Philip was victorious and, by his alliance with the Church, the monarchy at his death had reached a height never before attained. Paris rose to be the greatest and richest town in France, while many other towns received charters. Trade everywhere increased, the army was efficiently organised, and the middle class replaced the nobles in the country's administration. During this reign feudalism and English influence had been seriously weakened, and the prestige of the Crown greatly enhanced. The dynasty was now firmly established, and the Kingdom of France had come definitely into being.

It will be remembered that in the introduction to the chapter on Moslem civilisation reference was made to Mani, who founded the Manichaean faith, and was crucified in A.D. 277 by the Zoroastrian priests of Persia. Like Mahomet, he tried to clarify what he considered were the teachings of the great religious leaders of the past, Moses, Zoroaster, Buddha and Jesus, and his beliefs spread to the east and west with great rapidity. These took root in southern France, and, during the reign of Philip II, its adherents were known as Albigenses and Waldenses. Both sects considered themselves genuine devout Christians, and are reported as living lives of purity and virtue, but they criticised the orthodoxy of Rome, its interpretation of the Bible, the luxury and licence of the priests, and advocated the return to early Jesuism.

Why, we may ask, did southern France rise above the rest of Europe then sunk in the depths of mental darkness? To get our answer we must go back to Chapter IX on Moslem Spain, where we read about its splendid civilisation, its science and high culture. Rays of intellectual light from Spain had by now commenced to enlighten southern France, its nearest neighbour, to spread later to northern Italy and then to far-off England, where Roger Bacon lit the lamp of learning. Barcelona was the gateway through which Arabian culture reached southern France, then the most civilised place in all Christian Europe, and where-ever there is intelligence there is heresy. Heresy and culture did not appeal to the authorities at Rome, who were isolationists and did not want Europe to be influenced by outside thought. To maintain their authority the people must be kept ignorant, and consequently Innocent III, the Pope, engaged every possible wandering scoundrel to carry the sword and destruction amongst these peace-loving and harmless people.

The accounts of the cruelties and abominations of this Crusade for the furtherance of orthodox Christianity are amongst the worst in history. Every conceivable brutality was practised, and what was a fair and pleasant land, with prosperous towns, was laid waste, a flourishing culture being thus wiped out. Raymond, Count of Toulouse, led the reformers, and Saint Dominic and Simon de Montfort were the agents of the Church. Not only were the towns and villages devastated, but their inhabitants were exterminated by being massacred wholesale, quite regardless of their beliefs, and before every holocaust the orthodox Christians prepared themselves for the bloody slaughter by prayers and hymn-singing.

The city of Beziers was reduced to a heap of ruins, and 60,000 inhabitants were murdered, as were all the 5000 inhabitants of Miromand. Christian knights and footmen of all nations, numbering 300,000, and an army of priests massacred the inhabitants of "hundreds of towns and villages" over a period of two years, and when they had finished their bloody work hundreds of thousands of victims had perished by their swords. The Christian Church has many crimes to regret, but this was one of its worst, in which Philip II took no part, as it was organised and directed from Rome, though it brought about an increase in his dominions. Simon de Montfort died in 1218, after taking possession of the lands of the defeated Count of Toulouse, but this event in no way relaxed the persecution and oppression, the result being that the remaining inhabitants rose in revolt, and the lands were transferred to the protection of the Crown.

We remember reading about the Church destroying Greek and Roman education and culture in the 4th, 5th and 6th centuries, and how this brought about the period known as the Dark Ages. Once again culture and education had found its way into Europe, and once again the Church destroyed this attempt to raise the standard of living and enlighten the surrounding mental darkness. So the curse of ignorance remained, and from now onwards we shall observe the ever growing struggle between the powers of darkness and those who fought for increased mental light.

After a short reign Louis VIII was succeeded by Louis IX (1226–1270), to become known as Saint Louis, because he devoted a large part of each day to attending church services. He dressed and lived simply, washed the feet of beggars, and introduced the Inquisition into France because he hated heretics. His saintliness, however, did not prevent him being a strong ruler, as all who opposed him quickly discovered, and at the Battle of Saintes (1242) he finally overthrew the last vestiges of feudalism. On two occasions he joined the Crusaders, being completely defeated on the first expedition, and on the second he, and a large part of his army, died of plague.

On his return home from the first Crusade he found that his people, maddened by poverty and injustice, had risen in fury against the luxurious-living priests, whom they blamed for all their misery. Then, just as we have today in Liverpool, where two magnificent cathedrals have arisen from the squalour of slumdom, money was spent on great churches and cathedrals while the people living around them were ignorant, squalid and diseased. Schools did not exist, as on theology only the people relied to secure their happiness here and hereafter, the misery which its mistaken ideas caused being sufficient proof of their folly.

We can well imagine why some people in those days cried out, "O Lord, how long can these abominations of thy priests continue without punishment?" So far the clergy had carried everything before them for nine hundred years, having wielded everywhere unquestioned authority, and the Papacy had now reached the highest pinnacle of power. By this authority kings and emperors had been humiliated and excommunicated, and those of lesser degree tortured, imprisoned, murdered and massacred. The Papacy had conquered in its fight against the German emperors, and been fawned upon by the royal house of France, but, if its power was great, its prestige was in the depths.

Germany was now divided and incapable of united

effort, and the Italian cities, hitherto in fear of the emperors, felt that the time had come to loosen their alliance with the Holy See. In spite of mass massacres the feeling was growing that the Church was plundering everybody for its own ends, and piling up an immense fortune in lands and wealth of all kinds. The churches of Rome in those days were so littered with money and jewels after each pilgrimage, that men were regularly employed collecting the scattered wealth into barrows with shovels, whilst others were busy selling fraudulent relics at high prices, the satisfaction the faithful received being the general absolution granted to everyone who visited the holy city.

Boniface VIII, a man stained with every vice and crime, was the Pope from 1294 for the next ten years, and he continued to pursue the aggrandisement of the Church, declaring that "God has established us above all kings and emperors that we may in his name pull up and destroy, bring to nothing and disperse, or build or plant." Furthermore, he declared that God had set the Pope over all nations and kingdoms of the earth, to whom alone they owed obedience, and that no one on earth could be his judge. He claimed that he possessed two swords, the spiritual and the temporal, and he appeared before the people, first in the robes of a king and then in those of the Pope. His evil character can best be appreciated when we remember the way he treated his predecessor in office, Celestine V, who could not find it possible as Pope to secure "the desire for humility, for a purer life, for a stainless conscience, and for the tranquillity of his former life". So, after five months, Celestine resigned the holy office which had been forced upon him, only to be imprisoned by Boniface VIII in a foul dungeon, where he languished for ten months and then died as the result of the impure air.

Even the devout royal house of France thought that the time had now come to curb this cruel fanatical priest, and, as it had now no one to fear, Philip IV (1285–1314), a grandson of Saint Louis, in the year 1301, attacked the Pope with a fierceness never before adopted by a reigning monarch, the Chief Minister of France, Pierre Flotte, quoting Roman law to prove that the Sovereign, and not the Pope, had supreme power. The King, moreover, set about taxing the priests, who had hitherto been exempt, and this brought a reply from the Pope to the effect that they were to pay no taxes. The King replied by refusing to allow any money to pass out of France into the Papal Treasury, thus bringing to an end the vast revenues it was receiving from his subjects. Philip next arrested the Bishop of Pamiers, whom he accused of plotting against the throne, to which action the Pope retorted that no ecclesiastic could be tried by laymen, and that the Bishop must come to Rome to be tried by an ecclesiastical court.

The contest grew hotter as time went on, and culminated in a plot by the King's agents to capture the Pope, and bring him to France to be tried as a criminal. The Holy Father was in his castle near Rome when an armed force, under the King's agent Nogaret, forced its way into his presence. All the cardinals fled, and the invaders found the Pope sitting on the papal chair, robed in the mantle of Saint Peter, with the crown of Constantine upon his head, the cross in one hand, and the keys of heaven and hell in the other.

Dante, writing of the scene, says "Christ had been again crucified among robbers, and the vinegar and gall had been again pressed to his lips". That was evidently the feeling amongst the people, because a popular rising released the captured Pope, who died shortly afterwards. He was followed by Benedict XI, who likewise would not bow to the King of France, but this stalwart occupied the papal throne for only a year, when Clement V (1305–1314) succeeded him, with the backing of the King, on the condition that he would leave Rome and set up his papal court at Avignon in France. For seventy years the popes, under the domination of the kings of France, lost their independence, and Church history refers to this period of humiliation as "the Babylonish captivity".

Avignon, a large and prosperous town, and also the surrounding country, was passed over to the Holy See by Joanna, Queen of Naples, for the meagre sum of 30,000 florins, on condition that the Pope would absolve her for murdering a former husband. This he did, and then began a period of degradation such as few towns have ever experienced. The famous scholar Petrarch describes the horrors in detail, the following being some extracts:—

At the moment I live in the Babylon of the West (Avignon) amidst the most hideous scenes the sun shines upon.

Vice has reached its zenith. . . . The city is now the cesspool of all crimes and infamies, the hell of the living . . . swept along in a flood of the most obscene pleasures and a veritable storm of debauch.

The streets of this abominable city are not less hideous and painful than the people. The men and the place are obscene, ugly, horrible.

This modern Babylon, burning, boiling, obscene, terrible. All you ever read about perfidy, cunning, callousness, pride, obscenity and unbridled licence, all the instances of impiety and evil conduct that the world offers, or ever offered, you will see piled up here.

Truth passes for folly, abstinence for rusticity, chastity is a reproach, the more crimes one commits the more glory one acquires.

These old men (the Pope, cardinals and bishops) wallow in vice, as if all their glory was in the pleasures of the table and the orgies of impurity that follow in their bedrooms.

At the time when the priests were turning Avignon into a cesspool of iniquity, Philip IV directed his attention to the Knights Templars, whose order was founded during the first Crusade to protect pilgrims. This organisation had become immensely rich, numbering 15,000 members, and, like the monasteries, it was now very corrupt. Charges of murder, usury, profanity and many other crimes were brought against them, many being arrested and tried in Paris. Fifty-four were burned at the stake, and the Pope was forced to abolish the order entirely, the Crown taking over its great wealth. In those days it was an all-round game of beggar-my-neighbour, and both land and wealth could only be retained if the possessor was strong enough to keep them.

Philip IV adopted the methods of Henry VIII of England against organised religion, but he acted more than two hundred years earlier. In order to bring the people over to his side in his conflict with the Church, he set up the "States General", consisting of representatives of the clergy, the nobles and the people, each of whom met separately and expressed their approval or disapproval of the King's actions. This was a fairly representative body, and corresponded to a similar one then acting in England, but it was not destined, like the English counterpart, to become a really representative assembly.

Here in France, at last, was the germ of something constructive, a gleam of intelligence in a long night of ignorance, during which time the people had no rights and privileges, all liberty of thought and action being always suppressed by the divine King or the divine Pope. What follies and cruelties man has inflicted on man in the attempt to curb his evolution towards complete individuality. What misery has been caused to mankind by the lust some have for power and domination, how intolerance has often made life unbearable, how ignorance has deprived the people of the happiness which, by wisdom and knowledge, would have been theirs had they only known how to attain it. Ignorance of how to obtain happiness explains the many black pages in the story of the race.

(5) England Becomes a United Nation.

Set in the Atlantic Ocean, with twenty miles of water between her and the continent of Europe, Britain enjoys a unique and in some ways enviable position. She is near enough to Europe to be closely affected by what goes on there, and yet sufficiently isolated to be able to order her own doings as she pleases. Being an island, blessed by numerous excellent anchorages and harbours, her destiny has depended, and always will depend, on the sea, a heritage which means that her connections are world-wide and not only with her immediate neighbours. To understand the history of this favoured island, her geographical situation must always be remembered, as, though she has experienced all the main phases of European political and religious history, her frontiers have always remained the same, and her people have always been enclosed and protected by the sea.

This does not mean that she has not had unwelcome visitors from time to time. In her early days (100 B.C. –A.D. 50), when England was enjoying the most brilliant phase of prehistoric Keltic civilisation, her shores were the landing-ground of different tribes, anxious to settle on her fertile soil. One of these, the Belgae, introduced the plough in 75 B.C. These new-comers were not met by painted savages, as historians have told us in our school history books, because the ancient Britons were sufficiently cultured to absorb the invaders, which fusion finally produced the British people, who have the blood of many different tribes and nations in their veins.

The first powerful invader of her shores was Julius Caesar in 55 B.C., who received a hot reception from the Kelts, then the island's inhabitants. Both in race and language they were akin to the Gauls, from whom they must have come at an earlier date, but Caesar did not stay for long, and no further invasions occurred until A.D. 43, when the legions of the Emperor Claudius landed and made a much more permanent occupation. In spite of great bravery, and a stiff but sporadic resistance, the Romans

succeeded in conquering the British, who were dis-
united and had no military organisation, but the invaders were never able to reach far beyond the
estuaries of the rivers Clyde and Forth, between
which they erected a rampart to protect the south from
the Picts, a Keltic tribe which took to the mountains.
South of this line the country was governed in
much the same way as were the other Roman provinces. Roman law and culture were established,
and the remains of their towns and houses point to a
civilised life similar to what existed elsewhere throughout the Empire. After the brave and fierce attempts
by Boadicea and Caractacus to prevent the Roman
occupation, peace reigned and the inter-tribal conflicts of the Britons came to an end. Good roads
were built, connecting up all the principal towns,
which grew in size and importance. Traders, soldiers
and officials, with their families, came from Rome and
settled down in villas and camps, intermarrying and
mixing on friendly terms with the native Britons, some
of whom they educated sufficiently to enable them to
make the journey to Rome and learn something of the
world.

This state of affairs continued for nearly four
centuries, until the fall of Rome in 410, when the Visigoths captured the heart of the Empire. Then the
Romans left the island, without leaving much impression on the natives, who retained their Keltic
speech, as it was not until later that the Latin roots,
now to be found in the English language, came into it
through the French language, which was brought over
by the Normans. Fortunately, as English developed,
the gender of all inanimate things was taken as neuter,

and so English-speaking people have not this quite unnecessary complication in their language as is to be found in so many others.

Even in Roman times the northern Germanic tribes raided the British coast, and, when the Romans left the island, its inhabitants were at their mercy, as the British received no military training or experience during the Roman occupation. This weakness, and the island's fertility, attracted swarms of raiders during the 5th and 6th centuries from north Germany and Denmark, these bold adventurers making the hazardous journey in small craft, bringing with them their women and children. Intermarrying with the natives, these strangers produced the stock which became the English people, but, from now onwards for the next four hundred years, their history is broken by periods of uncertainty. When a connected record returns we find Roman civilisation obliterated, the Anglo-Saxon race supreme in the lowlands, and the Britons forced back into the mountain regions where they were better able to defend themselves. The Jutes had settled in Kent, the Saxons in Sussex and Essex, to which they gave their name, and the Angles in the centre and north up to the River Forth, to give their name eventually to the land of their adoption.

The Battle of Deorham in 577 enabled the invaders to occupy the Severn valley, and thus drive a wedge between the Britons in Wales, Cornwall and Devon, while the Battle of Chester, in 607, divided the Britons in Wales from their fellow tribesmen in north England. Then followed the establishment of the kingdoms of Northumbria, Mercia, Wessex, East Anglia, Essex, Kent and Sussex. The kingdom of

Mercia occupied what is now termed the Midlands, and for long its King Penda fought for his Pagan religion, while elsewhere Christianity made progress. In 655 Christian Northumbria eventually defeated Mercia and forced upon it the new faith.

The coming of the Anglo-Saxons destroyed all the culture and refinement left behind by the Romans. The only use they had for towns was to sack and destroy them, because villages of log huts, presided over by a chief, were much more to their liking. So the Roman villas fell into decay, leaving only their foundations to be discovered by later generations. Instead of encouraging intercommunication, as did the Romans, the newcomers preferred isolation, so much so that villages became the exclusive dwelling-places of those born there, no strangers being admitted. Continual enmity existed between these isolated habitations, and village fought against village composed of timbered houses which replaced the wattle and mud dwellings of the Britons. In these smoky crude dwellings, without chimney or ventilation, and crawling with vermin, the villagers ate to excess, drank to excess and were for ever quarrelling, when curses, blows and often worse became the order of the day.

The dispensing of a crude form of legislation took place first of all at the local moot, where equal justice was administered to everyone, as in these days every man was regarded as free and having equal rights. The moot was also responsible for taxation and providing military service. Then followed the dividing of England into bishoprics, which were sub-divided into parishes enclosing the village church. Monasteries sprang up everywhere, but it was the local church and the parish priest which left an enduring mark on English life.

In the 9th century began in England what was also happening in Europe, the degrading of the free men into villeins or bondmen. Pagan England was a land of free men, with equal rights and justice for all, but feudalism and Christianity joined hands to degrade the status of the individual to the level of a slave. The Church took a leading part in the development of feudalism. Gradually the village community ceased to be the homes of free men, and either the Church or a powerful nobleman became the owner of the soil, the houses, and the lives of the volk, or folk, which was the Saxon word then used for what we to-day call the people. The free township ceased to exist, and the feudal manor or monastery took its place. The kings, to save their souls, gave large grants of lands to the Church, while the wealthy, for the same reason, built monasteries and convents to which they frequently retired with their servants, and their belongings, to secure safety from the prevailing disorder.

Next came about, for administrative purposes, the dividing of the country into shires ruled over by ealdormen (to become known later as earls), under whom were the thegns (later to be called barons, a word which originally meant free men), who were the owners of one or more manors. They, together with the leading priests, were regarded as the nobility, but the earls became so strong that England, like Europe, was fast drifting into a land of independent rulers who ignored the Crown, when a halt was called by the Norman invasion. In those lawless days, feudalism was the outcome of rapine and injustice, and the poor defenceless free man, to secure a livelihood and safety, allied himself to a nobleman or a monastery. Thus he became a mere chattel, by sacrificing his liberty and his possessions in order to live.

What the Church got it kept, as the nobles died, some without heirs, but, though the bishops and abbots were likewise mortal, the Church was not, and its lands, its wealth, its taxation, its jurisdiction and its serfs went on from generation to generation, nothing ever being relinquished. Steadily it grew ever more wealthy, its lands often increasing by means of forged title deeds and the fear it developed amongst the landowners, hell fire being their portion if they did not leave one or more of their manorial possessions to God's Church on earth. Thus manor after manor, in increasing numbers, passed into its possession over the centuries, until in Tudor times it owned a large part of England, and possessed both the bodies and souls of her people.

At the time when the Church was beginning to fasten its grip upon England, lived the Venerable Bede (673–735), a monk of Jarrow-on-Tyne, who, with 600 other monks in his monastery, shed some light on the history of England for the first time since the Romans left the island. His work *The Ecclesiastical History of the English*, and his other writings, became widely known throughout Europe, his method of fixing the date by the number of years which had elapsed since the time it was believed Jesus was born being adopted by others, to become the common practice.

Little did this venerable monk realise that by this novel and simple action he performed what was probably the greatest benefit his faith has ever received from a single individual. His invention had a powerful influence on all Christendom, because, by thus dividing up time into pre-Christian and Christian, the natural conclusion was drawn that there were two ages in world history, the first of mental and religious darkness, and the second when a divine revelation shone its beneficent rays over a savage heathen world. To Christians there were these two periods in time, the one of wickedness and the other of righteousness, and this fixed idea had a marvellous propaganda effect throughout the Theological Age of ignorance, and it still has in our own times.

England was now becoming a Christian country, as missionaries who had come from Rome in 596 with the monk Augustine had converted some, while the sword had converted others. He was welcomed in England by Ethelbert, King of Kent, because his wife was a Christian, and then followed the conversion of Edwin, King of Northumbria, the subjects of both monarchs meekly accepting the religion of their rulers. Even in these early days true Christianity was in doubt, as missionaries were preaching different doctrines, and, for a time, it seemed as if two Christian sects would spring up. Oswy, King of Northumbria, then played the part Constantine did at Nicaea, as he called all the priests together at Whitby in 664, and, at the Synod of Whitby, after hearing both sides, decided that the Christianity, as believed by the Pope at Rome, and not the Arian interpretation, was to be the Christianity for England.

He was strong enough to force his decision, and, from that date, the Church of England came into being, to become a great political and religious power in the land, and the link between Rome and the monarchy. Thus, for the second time, England was bound to Rome, this time ecclesiastically, from which city she received her law and form of Church government.

After many conflicts Wessex dominated all the other kingdoms of England, by gaining the decisive Battle of Ellandun in Wiltshire against the Mercians in 825. This made Egbert of Wessex (800–836), who was a man of great ability and political wisdom, overlord of all England, an event which can be considered as the beginning of England as a kingdom and a nation. England was now ruled by a king who was advised by his witan or council. She was now well abreast with the rest of Europe, the same religion uniting her people, who, like many others on the Continent, were shortly to suffer from the attacks of the northmen.

Egbert, the first English king, was followed by Ethelwulf (836–858), and he was the father of England's greatest king, Alfred (871–901), rightly called the Great. Alfred became king at the age of twenty-three, after his three brothers had experienced short and troubled reigns, but he likewise was to suffer from the burden of care and anxiety. He was soon called upon to defend his country against the Danes, the first large invasion, under Hingwar, carrying everything before it from the Thames to the Clyde. In defence Alfred built "burhs," or strong camps, which later became towns, and thus postponed the barbarians control of England until they had become accustomed to a more civilised form of life.

Then in the seventh year of his reign (878) he defeated the Danes at Edington, when Guthrum, their leader, agreed to retire to the north-east of England and, with much bitterness; accept the despised and hated Christian faith for himself and his people. The Danes now held the greater part of England, namely southern Northumbria, Mercia and East Anglia, known as the Danelaw, and soon they were strong enough to attack again, but over a hundred years had to pass before they dominated the entire country.

Alfred was the wisest, the best and greatest king that ever ruled in England. He was a constructor, not a destroyer, a defender and not a plunderer, as were so many who carried the title of Great. He organised the country's naval and military resources, and built the first English navy, which consisted of better ships than had the Danes. He possessed much of the culture of his time, and supported what learning there then was. He tried to educate the priests, who were illiterate, he built and restored churches, and encouraged the translation of Latin literature into English, the *English Chronicle*, which he founded, being our best authority for the history of these times.

He died in 901, and for the next hundred years the good work he had done was carried on by his successors. His son Edward (901–925), who reconquered the Danelaw, eventually reigned over a united England, and each succeeding king, Athelstan, Edmund, Edred and Edwy, consolidated still further the country's unity, which was completed in the reign of Edgar (959–975). Scotland then likewise emerged, because northern Northumbria, beyond the Tweed up to Edinburgh, was ceded to her to become known as the Scottish Lowlands. In these days lived Dunstan, Abbot of Glastonbury, and later Archbishop of Canterbury. This exceptionably able man greatly influenced Edgar's policy, and now begins in England the close alliance of Church and State, a union which is such a feature of Christian civilisation.

In those days the rulers made a country great if they were strong and good men, just as the reverse happened if they were not. In our own times, in democratic lands, the people get the leaders the majority desire, but, in those bygone days, they had no say in political affairs, a fact which explains why history centres round emperors and kings, while the people receive little notice. The rulers did the things that became historical, and the people, like children, accepted their decisions.

History is more the story of nations, and not so much of the people as individuals. Throughout the ages many individuals, more intelligent than the majority, thought their own thoughts and lived their own lives, apart from political and religious control, and, as knowledge takes the place of ignorance, this type of individual thinking will increase for the good of everyone. Our time on earth is intended to teach us to become individuals, and not just units of a nation.

Nature is working out a great and profound scheme, in which each one of us plays a part, and gradually, with many set-backs, we are rising from the herd level to that of self-thinking individuals. We are slowly passing out of the flock and herd stage, when most people thought alike and were directed by a master mind. The race must some day pass from the age of childhood into youth, with each one an individual, capable and able to think for himself. When this time comes war will cease, as war is not the result of individual thinking but of individuals in the mass allowing warmongers to control the affairs of their nation, while believing all they are told without thinking for themselves.

The more each one thinks for himself the more one is independent; the more one is not mass-minded the better it is for the character, as after all it is only character, individuality and personality which count both here and hereafter. The politicians and priests are seldom the representatives of the best in the nation, as the zealots, the intriguers, the seekers after titles, the place-hunters, the political and social climbers, often come prominently before the ignorant public, which gapes in wonder at their so-called leaders. Little do the masses realise that many of the really great men do not advertise themselves, being quite content to accumulate wisdom. and knowledge, help others to do likewise, and thus raise the standard of living and culture to a higher level. That, and that only, is of value, because it pertains to the mind, which never dies, and we carry over to the next order of existence that which we learn here on earth—that and nothing more.

The foolish, untrustworthy, feckless Ethelred (978–1016), known as Redeless, meaning unwise in council, succeeded his father Edgar after the death of his brother Edward, to be confronted with a second Danish invasion better organised, and much stronger,

than the first. Those who landed were massacred
by the English, and this so angered their king Sweyn
that he himself, with a large host, landed on the English
coast. This time numbers overpowered the English
resistance and Ethelred had to find refuge in Normandy. Sweyn, a brutal and ruthless man, became
king, and the war continued between him and Edmund
Ironside, Ethelred's son and successor. When
Sweyn died the conflict was waged between Edmund
and Canute, who was the son of Sweyn, and only after
the death of Edmund did Canute become the undisputed king of all England.

He was as good a king as his father was bad. He
did not rule England as a military conqueror, but
retained only a bodyguard of Danish troops. He so
merged himself into the ways of the people that he
became in effect an Englishman. By his conquest of
Norway he became ruler of Iceland, Orkney and the
Hebrides, all of which, including Denmark and
England, became one kingdom. This consequently
linked England up with the then flourishing Scandi-
navian trade route, which, in those days, passed
through the Baltic and Russia to as far south as Constantinople, an event which brought the country into
close trade and cultural relations with northern Europe,
and this lasted for the next seven centuries. From
this time onwards London was a great commercial
centre; to become, and ever afterwards retain its
place as the principal port of the country, Danish
merchants being amongst its leading citizens. After
the death of Canute in 1035 civil war began in England
and his kingdom dissolved, but not before Christianity,
which he introduced into Scandinavia, had taken

root there, to supersede eventually the worship of Odin.

After this short time of Danish domination the Wessex dynasty returned to rule, and Edward the Confessor (1042–1066), son of Ethelred, became the next king. He was more a monk than a king, and, when he died childless, Harold, the son of Godwin, Earl of Wessex, an able, kind and lovable man, succeeded him. His was a tragic reign, as it lasted for only nine months, during which time he had to face two separate invasions from Europe. The Danish Royal House thought that a Dane should have been chosen, and this brought about an invasion under Tostig, the disloyal brother of Harold, and Hardrada, the King of Norway, who were defeated and slain by Harold at Stamford Bridge near York. Three days after Harold had gained this decisive victory, some 5000 Normans, accompanied by French soldiers and priests, landed at Pevensey in Sussex, and within a fortnight he and his army, by forced marches, reached Hastings, where he was killed and his army defeated.

All this happened in 1066, and the effect of the decisive Battle of Hastings was to bring to an end the six hundred years of Saxon rule in England, and create a new dynasty, in fact a new era in England, because William, Duke of Normandy, who led the invaders, became King of England (1066–1087) and divided the land amongst his faithful followers. He was the bastard son of Robert, Duke of Normandy, by a tanner's daughter, a union which produced this strong, ruthless, fearless man. His venture was a tremendous gamble which, fortunately for him, was successful, but if that fatal arrow, which deprived the

English of Harold's brilliant leadership, had only gone a few inches to the right or left, how different the outcome might have been. That one arrow seemingly changed England, and entirely altered future European history.

To begin with the battle went well for the English, who in numbers˙ equally matched their opponents, and they repelled all the Norman attempts to break through, so much so that over-confidence spurred them on against orders. They attacked, only to be cut to pieces and lose their leader. Had Harold lived, or if his two brothers had not also been killed, the disaster could have been retrieved, because the English had three considerable armies in reserve, and the Normans had lost heavily, but lacking leaders the day was lost, and the reserves were useless without them. That fatal day changed human destiny in the west, it ruined the Saxon ruling class and put foreign adventurers in its place, men who brought with them European feudalism in all its soullessness, and wove it into English life. The victory was so swift and unexpected that the transformation was complete before anyone realised it, and proud Saxon England lay helpless before the invader, quite unable to do more than accept unconditional surrender.

During their short occupation of northern France, the Normans had picked up some of the Roman culture which still remained, they now spoke the French language, and, when they came to England, they brought this culture and their language with them, French becoming the official language of the country. Thus the two tongues, the Saxon and the French, intermingled to produce after three centuries the beautiful literary language of Chaucer. ·That is what England gained, but she lost her isolation, because from now onwards she became part of war-distracted Europe. Today we may well question whether increased culture was sufficient compensation for the numerous wars in France which the Norman victory brought upon England, especially as from now onwards England became tightly bound to the Pope in Rome.

William's conquest of England was also the conquest of Pope Alexander II, as the plunder was shared between these two thieves who had plotted her subjection. William, like all Christian rulers of those days, was very devout, and, like the Hebrew warriors of old, believed that he was carrying out the will of Jehovah in undertaking the conquest of England, a country which had not shown sufficient submissiveness to the Pope at Rome. The Pope was responsible for William's idea that he was serving the Lord, and His Holiness not only issued a Bull declaring him to be the rightful heir to the English throne, but also sent him a ring and a banner as symbolic of the blessing of heaven.

By now the Church had been completely successful in securing the entire subservience of both Germany and France, much of their fairest lands being in her possession. In England the position was different, as the Anglo-Saxon Church had shown no inclination to submit humbly to all the commands of the Holy See. The land of England was rich, and the Holy Father was determined that she likewise must yield up more of her wealth to the Papal Treasury. What he could not accomplish by persuasion he did by force, he and William becoming allies for the purpose of conquering and pillaging England. The Pope financed and blessed the enterprise, on the understanding that he shared the plunder, and the banners of the Vicar of Christ mingled with those of the Normans as the invaders bore down on the English on the bloody field of Hastings.[1]

Over the previous thousand years Britain had been conquered by four successive waves of invaders, the Romans, the Angles and Saxons, the Danes and now the Normans. Though others since then have made the attempt, none have succeeded. Since 1066 England has worked out her own salvation, and this freedom from foreign invasion accounts for British institutions having such a long tradition behind them. It also shows that war is not necessary for progress and national development, as some claim it to be. The British, since then, have fought many wars, civil and foreign, but never since that date have they had to fight for their freedom against a foreign enemy on their own soil. Britain nevertheless has made as great, if not greater, progress without foreign interference than have those nations of Europe which, century after century, have had to fight for their liberty and see devastation in their midst.

The British have not deteriorated in character because they do not now fight duels, one with another, on every possible occasion. Neither have they declined because their towns no longer fight each other to cripple or destroy competitors. Civilised people do not now fight one another over some

---

[1] In Pagan times images of the gods were carried on poles into battle, but this custom later gave place to flags on which emblems were painted.

political issue, such as the man who is to be their King or Prime Minister, and Great Britain is no longer in bitter conflict on the question of whether Catholicism, Episcopalianism or Presbyterianism is the right form of Christianity to believe. Her national life is now peaceful, without loss, in fact with great gain, to the character and happiness of her people.

The same peaceful relations must now be established between nations, so that some day our descendants will look back with astonishment at the folly of fighting over matters which are always subject to a settlement fair to all. As mental development made national peace possible, so will further mental development make international peace possible. It is all a question of time, provided ethical education, combined with knowledge wisely applied, progresses in the years to come. It is all a matter of mental development. That and nothing else.

To the illiterate mentality of 1066 all such reasoning would have fallen on deaf ears. It would not have been understood, because the Norman barons and their followers had the debased minds of thieves. They were out for loot, and they had got it in France and England by superior force and cunning. They were like the Germans of our time, quite devoid of any international morality. Might was right, and land and wealth went to the one who could seize it and keep it.

To prevent those with thieving minds taking things within the nation we have evolved the criminal code, backed up by a police force, as force must always be met by force, but it took countries now civilised many centuries before the mentality of the people rose sufficiently to make this possible. This mentality has now to rise still further and produce an international police force, so that nations, with the German marauding instinct, shall be kept in check and prevented from arming for the purpose of despoiling Europe, or any other part of the world, every generation.

Whatever economic methods our descendants adopt for wealth production, protection must be given to everyone. Even if private ownership is some day abolished, law and order, backed by force, will be necessary to prevent the strongest taking and keeping land and wealth for the benefit of themselves alone. Land, and the wealth it produces, is limited, whereas the population and the desires of the people are unlimited. All theoretical schemes of land division, or the common use of wealth, break down because of that vital fact, and only when, by mechanical means, wealth can be produced with the minimum of labour will it be possible to think out a communistic form of society. Meantime, the incentive to work and produce wealth is the gain therefrom, and, unless the producer is protected, production is impossible.

Along with further developments in protective measures, intensive international ethical propaganda must be carried on, until future generations have absorbed the fact that happiness can only come from doing to others as we wish to have done to ourselves, and that only misery comes to those who do otherwise. The Normans were too undeveloped to realise that this is always true, but, at this distance, we can look back and see that what is true today was equally so then. As so often happens, the Norman thieves fell out amongst themselves, and William, now King of England, had his hands full to keep them from disowning him and fighting one another.

The lands these Normans robbed were taken from Saxon or Danish robbers, who, in turn, had taken them from earlier robbers in previous years. In barbarian society title deeds do not exist, the strong arm wielding a stout sword being the only title to possession, but, when civilisation came, legal owner- ship followed and the thief was punished. Who would go back to the barbarian method of obtaining and holding property and wealth? Is our present method of exchange not the best? A fair exchange is no robbery, and, on this basis, civilised society developed, to be broken into continually by one nation adopting the barbarian method towards another. Consequently there has never yet been an international civilised society, a state of affairs that must come about as the human mind develops. The same human mind, which produced a national society, or national civilisation, is quite capable some day of producing an international society, and an inter- national civilisation.

The Normans, it will be noticed, were by no means a happy family after their victory at the Battle of Hastings, even though they had all England, and her million and a half inhabitants, at their feet. Who was to get this and who was to get that? The numerous disputes which followed must have given William much anxiety, as he had to deal with the English nobles on the one hand, who were being plundered, and with the plunderers on the other. The English people, strangely enough, proved more amenable than the Normans, and, except for local risings, they settled down quietly under their new rulers, so much so that a writer of the time could say that "a man could travel throughout the realm with his bosom full of gold".

This ancient record may have referred to one particular district, but it could not have applied to all England, where, until the 18th century, travellers were always in danger from robbers. Not only lawlessness prevailed but manners continued to be rough and coarse, and this form of behaviour continued until a century after the Renaissance. Consequently we can picture the English from now onwards as being like their forbears and people elsewhere, brutish in their sports, their ways and table manners.

The rich dressed well, their enjoyments lying between bear-baiting, cock-fighting, football and tournaments on the one hand, and sitting round a well-spread board, lacking forks and knives, quarrelling to get the most from the common pot. Drinking to excess, spitting everywhere, slobbering over their faces and clothes, they would now appear to us more like animals than men and women. Cuffs and blows were common in the home, while outside aggressive neighbours lay in wait to seize the manors and lands of all who could not defend them, heiresses being kidnapped and made the wives of the strongest, who thus became heir to their lands.

In these days the English had no tradition behind them, and little national feeling. The Normans brought new institutions into being, and old ones were altered and modified. The women of the Saxon nobility were given to those who wanted them. Land was taken from the conquered and divided amongst the conquerers, but the masses were little affected by these changes, and life went on much as before. The new-comers, who were comparatively small in number, some 12,000, were gradually absorbed into the English nation, accepting its customs and speech, which in time became English, the language of a mongrel Aryan people made up of Kelts, Latins, Angles, Saxons, Danes and Norsemen.

William was quick to realise that a country could not be efficiently run by a gang of robbers, having only the thieves' moral code to guide them. So, like other master crooks who had got all they wanted, he settled down to try and live an honest decent life, and make his gang do likewise. This was not easy, as many felt that the loot had not been evenly distributed, and this caused much heart-burning and strife. To secure his authority he retained for the Crown by far the largest area of land, and thus obtained the feudal services of so great a number of men that his power was unquestioned. The lands he gave to the individual barons were not all together, but in different parts of the country, and this made it difficult for them to centralise their power.

William, moreover, cut into the traditions of feudalism, which prescribed that the vassal of each noble swore allegiance to his lord, and not to the king. At the Moot of Salisbury, in 1086, he demanded fealty from all landowners, tenants or subtenants, on the understanding that if they broke their oath confiscation of their lands would follow. By means of the Doomsday Book, William recorded every acre of land, house and animal for the purposes of taxation, thus obtaining a basis for a sound financial structure, because in those days, land, houses and animals were the principal forms of wealth.

William's strength also lay in his co-operation with the Church, which had been his ally in his conquest and plundering of England, and, when the time came to divide the spoils, the Pope made certain that he received ample compensation and reward for his financial and moral help. Consequently he secured for the Church such vast tracts of land that a man well versed in the management of real estate had to be appointed to supervise these great new possessions. The holy land agent, who was made responsible for this tremendous business undertaking, was the able Prior of the Abbey of Bec in Normandy, Lanfranc by name, who was appointed the thirty-fourth Archbishop of Canterbury so as to increase his power and authority.

The chief duty of this wise Italian prelate, one of the most astute churchmen of his time, was to make secure for the Church her new acquisitions, and to organise the payment of tithes from every landowner, great or small, everywhere. This system brought in annually to the coffers of the Church enormous wealth from the labour of the poor downtrodden toilers, who never obtained any rights or privileges, and were always kept in bondage and ignorance so as to maintain better the security of their overlords.

In return for their servitude on earth they were promised happiness hereafter if they obeyed the priests, who also claimed the power to send them to hell if they were not subservient. Consequently the winning of souls for Christ was always of prime importance, as obedience and revenue were impossible without first of all having the faithful within the Church. We cannot fail to see, that the motive behind the zeal of the clergy for the conversion of the people to their way of thinking was too often the lust for power and wealth, a fact which was candidly admitted by Pope Urban IV to Thomas Aquinas in the 13th century, to receive an appropriate rebuke.

The Norman conquest of England was a diabolical plot hatched by two gangsters, William and Pope Alexander II, who shared the plunder between them in one form or another, and to this day the landowners of England, whether they are churchmen or not, have to pay heavy tithes to the Church of England for the benefit of its priests.[1] The priests, moreover, were placed above the law in that they were given separate ecclesiastical courts, in which they administered their own form of legislation and in which only they could be tried. The clergy paid no taxation on their land, and deemed themselves above the

[1] In 1936, because of the rising public indignation against this method of supporting the priesthood, an Act was passed in the House of Commons abolishing the tithe payment. In place of tithes, fixed annuities became chargeable on land until October, 1996. These annuities are for the purpose of paying for the 3% Government Stock which has been handed over to the Church of England authorities in exchange for their waiving the right to the tithe rent. The Church has thus capitalised its right to this tenth of the produce of the land, and has now become the owner of £51,650,000 Government Stock, which makes the Church of England one of the richest close corporations in the world. This money, which it has received from the people, is the direct result of its priests preaching hell in the days gone by, and so frightening them into placing a lien on their land. To release the people from this lien the Church has now made this exceptionally good bargain of cash down, and the landowners, to get out of the net in which their ancestors were caught, have now to pay, until the year 1996, for the Government Stock handed over to the Church. Thus is continued till then the increase on the price of all foodstuffs, as the producers recoup themselves for what they have to pay to the Church by charging more for their produce.

dictates of the Crown, but William refused to become the vassal of the Pope, or to do him homage.

Out of the English Witan, the assembly of barons and bishops to whom the King looked for advice, which he generally accepted, William formed the Great Council, including all the Crown's chief tenants and ecclesiastics. This was the beginning of the English Parliament, and explains why it is that, to this day, we have unelected bishops and nobles legislating for a democratic people in the House of Lords. Some pages further on we shall find how representative government made an unsuccessful beginning, and how the first House of Commons came into being, to commence a controversy which runs through much of British history, as many centuries were to pass before true democratic government was generally accepted.

William realised to the full the dangers of feudalism, and, by strong and ruthless measures, he deprived the nobles and great landlords of the power secured by the nobility in Europe. There they had almost sovereign powers, and could engage in war against each other and against the King as it pleased them. Besides this they had supreme judicial power, a state of affairs which William was determined would not happen in England, but his policy was not appreciated by the nobles, who, when his strong hand was removed, made repeated attempts to secure for themselves the feudal rights to which they believed they were entitled.

In the year William died (1087) there was much misery throughout the land—famine, distress and lawlessness being general. Churches, including St. Paul's in London, were burned down and many towns set on fire. His extensive church-building had not improved the well-being of the people, but they indeed despaired when his unworthy son reigned over them as his successor. Rebellion followed and William II (1087–1100), to be followed by Henry I (1100–1135), and finally Stephen (1135–1154), were continually fighting to maintain the power William I had secured for the Throne. This task was by no means easy, as, during the life of Robert, King of Normandy, and son of the Conqueror, who thought he should be King of England, William and Henry had to fight him as well as their own nobles. If the Throne had not obtained the support of the people, feudalism in England would have become as powerful as it was in Europe.

When, to everyone's delight, William II died, his brother Henry, a hard efficient man, set off for Winchester to seize the treasury and the crown. He successfully met Robert's invasion of England, defeated him, and kept him in prison until he died. His reign brought greater peace and justice to England, so much so that some of the worst abuses of the previous reign were removed and he became known as the Lion of Justice.

As Henry I had no son to succeed him, the nobles gave the crown to Stephen, who was the grandson of William. Stephen was a brave, chivalrous, popular king, but too mild to rule the lawless barons. He had a troubled reign because Henry, the son of Matilda (daughter of Henry I, who had married Geoffrey Plantagenet, Count of Anjou), claimed the throne. Owing to this struggle, Stephen had to give the priests and nobles all they demanded in exchange for their help, the consequence being that the nobles established themselves securely in their castles and behaved as they thought feudal lords should · do. Crime and desolation consequently spread throughout the land, and only on the death of Stephen's son was peace made between Henry and Stephen, on the understanding that he, Henry, would be his successor. Consequently, as Henry II (1154–1189), he became king on the death of Stephen. He had no rival, and brought with him the family name of his royal house, Plantagenet. As Count of Anjou, Duke of Aquitaine and Duke of Normandy he was, moreover, ruler of the western half of France, possessing a greater area than the lands belonging to the King of France. Hadrian IV, the only English Pope, gave him Ireland in 1155, which he invaded, to proclaim himself Lord of Ireland, and then King William "the Lion" of Scotland, who was defeated at Alnwick, was forced to do him homage. Henry II, who inherited all these great possessions, was one of the most outstanding monarchs of the period known as the Middle Ages (600–1500). He was strong, just and ruthless, and built up such an autocratic form of government that it produced its reaction in the following century, to end in the Magna Charta, after which followed the formation of a national Parliament.

He revoked many grants of land, destroyed the newly built baronial strongholds, and established the foundations of the country's administrative and judicial systems, thus raising England to a position which France did not attain until the 19th century. The Church, pursuing its settled policy, worked against all his reforms, and the Pope was his greatest enemy. In spite of clerical opposition he gave the common men in England a sense of dignity, so much so that his taxes were honestly paid, an achievement which was something the French kings could never secure, the consequence being sound finance in England and always the opposite in France.

Henry's greatest accomplishment was the development of Common Law, supported by the evidence of witnesses who later became known as Jurors, and the institution of itinerant justices, two reforms which grew into the present-day system of Local Assizes. The Law now became a learned profession, and the lawyer, who stood for justice and order, became the rival of the priest. The new judges whom the King appointed were made responsible to the Crown, and the national army which he organised was likewise under his authority. By these means the King deprived the barons of their former power, and thus again gained a march on France, where the King's authority was always being challenged by the great nobles. These strong measures so restricted the power of the feudal lords that they drew ever more closely towards the common people, to produce finally the first attempt at democratic government.

In this reign was written the first page of the tragic story of Ireland's relations with England. Her troubles, however, began much earlier, her greatest misfortune being that the Romans stopped short at Anglesea, and thus deprived her of their culture, good roads and a civilised way of life. Her only touch with Rome came through Christianity, which reached Ireland from Britain in the 4th century, at a time when the Irish were in possession of many places in the south and west of England. Pelagius, and his disciple Coelestius (who raised the wrath of the eminent Church father, now called Saint Augustine, because of their heresy, as told in Chapter VIII), were Irishmen, and then came Patrick in the 5th century, about whom nothing reliable is known, though he is now believed to be a saint in heaven.

Patrick is the reputed founder of the Christian Church in Ireland, which was then, and has remained, orthodox Catholic to this day, but the culture Ireland received from Rome was soon extinguished by a series of invasions, first from Norway, and then from Denmark. These swept the people back to primitive barbarism, where they remained until Henry II made them realise the existence of England, by sending over two of his leading generals to secure the island, which had been given to him by the Pope for the annual payment of a penny a house. The Irish, divided by tribal jealousies, and quite unprotected by armour, fought with great bravery, but were quickly subdued by a picked force of mailed knights. Their settlements were garrisoned by the English, who took their land and settled down as Irish landlords, marrying Irish women, and taking on the characteristics of their new environment.

So the Anglo-Norman Butlers, FitzGeralds, and others, gave to Ireland a new aristocracy who owned the land, ruled the people, but were never regarded as · either Irish or English; the natives, shorn of their ancient pride, always remaining wedded to their early laws, customs, language and literature. Ireland's misfortunes were not, however, at an end, as in 1315 Edward Bruce, the brother of Robert Bruce, tried to snatch the country from the English to make it a province of Scotland. He, and his fellow barbarians, ravaged the land from north to south, and any prosperity English rule had brought withered away. England now became involved in the Hundred Years' War, and, being thus busy in France, she allowed the country to relapse into a wilderness, almost forgetting its existence until the 16th century, when the religious differences, caused by the Reformation, made English politicians resent the fact that Ireland did not come within the orbit of the Anglican Church.

The Church and State, during Norman times, worked for a time together for their own mutual advantage, but the day came, as it did in Europe, when a definite decision had to be made as to whether the King or the Pope was to appoint the bishops. The trouble first arose with the simple but stubborn Anselm, on his appointment by William II as Archbishop of Canterbury in succession to Lanfranc, because Anselm thought that this holy office should be the gift of the Pope and not of the King. William II was adamant, and, after a conference of the leading priests and nobles at Rockingham Castle, Anselm was exiled to Normandy.

Henry I, however, at a later date accepted a similar compromise to the one adopted at the Concordat of Worms, whereby the sovereign renounced his right of appointment on the understanding that the Archbishop did homage to him for all the Church lands. Thus did this clerical attempt to gain equality with the sovereign fail, though it was renewed in after years. The King, however, retained his status, and though the Church increased in wealth and power it was never regarded as other than subject to the Throne.

In the reign of Henry II a new quarrel with the Church developed. Thomas Becket, a very peculiar man, but possessed of a certain charm, was then the Archbishop, and he objected to priests, found guilty by the Church Court, being handed over to the civil authorities to receive their punishment. Henry would not transfer the law and justice of the land to the Church, and he was also determined to put an end to clerical excommunications which had not his authority. Becket stirred up endless trouble, and then escaped to France, to be later reconciled, though he never wavered in his assertion that the Church and not the King should rule England.

So arrogant was he that on his return he excommunicated the Archbishop of York, and the bishops of London and Salisbury, because he considered that they had exceeded their powers during his absence, a deed which made Henry exclaim, "Is there no one who will free me from this turbulent priest?" Four knights immediately set off for Canterbury, without the King's knowledge, and murdered Becket in the Cathedral, a crime which produced a great sensation, and Henry, the ruler of England and half of France, was forced by misguided public opinion to do penance at the victim's tomb at Canterbury. The priests henceforth were leniently tried by their own courts, the Pope's authority was re-established, and Becket was revered in England as a saint and martyr up to the time of the Reformation. His tomb became a place of miracles and the most popular of all the pilgrimages, it being laden with jewels and gold placed there by the simple, ignorant people, who failed to realise that he, and not the King, had been their real enemy.

On Henry's death his son Richard I (1189-1199), who was given the title of Cœur de Lion for his bravery, succeeded, and inherited all his father's vast dominions. His coronation was celebrated by his subjects massacring all the Jews they could find, and this continued for over a year. All the romance which has gathered round this stalwart cannot conceal the fact that he was a bad king, most of his reign being spent either crusading in the East, as a captive in Austria or fighting for Normandy against the King of France. Had his father not welded England together under his strong rule, and left the administration in the hands of trained officials, nothing could have prevented a collapse. Richard conquered Cyprus and sold it to the Knights Templars, but his repeated attempts to capture Jerusalem failed. His visits to England were mostly for the purpose of raising money for his war in Normandy, a conflict which was not concluded when he died.

In those days of ignorance, when the people were just children devoid of any kind of education, a strong ruler was essential to the maintenance of peace. Like children, the people were always quarrelling and fighting amongst themselves, and, if we keep in mind that history is the story of the nursery age of the race, much that happened will be understood in its true light. We try to train children out of their passionate and foolish ways, but, except by the Greeks and Romans, the education of the people was never seriously considered until our own times, with the result that history is just a record of childish folly and cruelty, caused by greed, intolerance, hatred and sadism. Most kings were ruthless because they knew of no other way to keep order, few had any ethical qualities, and liberty, as we now understand it, was not then known. We have made some progress since these times, though the average human mind is still childish, and largely devoid of the power of independent thought and action outside its everyday routine.

Consequently, Norman autocracy then served the country better than any milder form of government, as it established law and order, combined with a sense of national unity, but seldom did the Crown in England receive the support of the people as it did in France. In England both the Lords and Commons joined together, and often fought together, for greater liberty, and this was no exception during the reign of John, who succeeded his brother Richard.

John (1199–1216) was probably one of the most despised of all the kings of England, being possessed of all the vices of his ancestors and none of their virtues. Victory and successes had so far crowned the efforts of the Norman war lords, and these had carried them over obstacles which would have brought down others lacking their tradition. The people were prepared to accept and follow the rule of tyrants, if only they succeeded in all their various enterprises. The average mind did not reason out the right and wrong of their war lord's actions, if he could win every battle, and this is evident all down history. Napoleon and Hitler are two examples close to our own times. Both were obvious master criminals, and yet their successes blinded their supporters until defeat opened their eyes.

The Romanoff, Hapsburg and Hohenzollern dynasties fell during the First World War because of defeat. Their long-established prestige was shattered in a few weeks, as the people prefer a strong, autocratic, successful ruler to a weak one who cannot maintain order, or protect his country's frontiers, however high and noble his character may be. Neither John, nor his enemy the Pope, were worthy men, but the latter was successful and the former was not so, because the combination against John was too strong. Pope Innocent III was determined on his destruction, and, in company with Philip II of France and Frederick II of Germany, he decisively defeated the forces of Otto IV, the Holy Roman Emperor, and John at Bouvines in 1214. This was one of the most important conflicts in European history, as it helped to consolidate the national state of France, foil John's plan to recover his lost French dominions, and gave to Frederick the imperial crown.

As John had previously lost Normandy to Philip in 1204, and Anjou, Maine and Touraine in 1206, many of his nobles, disgusted at the loss of their possessions in these parts, decided that they preferred a strong and ruthless ruler like Henry II, who, at least, could keep his domains intact, even though they had to bow to his authority. Besides these losses and humiliations, the old quarrel broke out again between the King and Innocent III on the question of the appointment of the Archbishop. Again the Church asserted its claim to be above all kings, and never before was it nearer its goal.

Let us pause for a moment and think of the meaning of all this, as it is a subject which has never so far received rational thought. If, however, we do get down to facts, we find that there is a connecting chain, made up of links of cause and effect, right back from this world-domineering pope to a ghost being seen in Palestine some twelve hundred years earlier. From seeing a ghost to the claim of world-wide authority, there is an unbroken connection, step by step, without a break, a cause having produced an effect, and that effect in turn a cause, until finally a man reached the position of Pontifex Maximus and, as the Pope, became the greatest power on earth. Other religions have come into being from the same cause, but certainly none obtained the power and majesty secured by Christianity, which happened to develop and spread amongst a strong and virile people.

So we have now reached the time in history when His Holiness, claiming to represent a priestly victim who was seen on earth after his death, wielded an authority over Europe such as was never previously exercised. He decided that Stephen Langton was to be the new Archbishop of Canterbury, and John not only refused to agree but seized all the Church land of Canterbury. Innocent then excommunicated the King and everyone in England from communion with the Church, and this, in the opinion of every Englishman, not only meant everlasting torment but being boycotted by all Christendom. This holy curse did not complete the revenge of the Holy Father, because Innocent followed it up by encouraging rebellion in England, and instructing the King of France to invade the island.

John, with everyone in England his enemy, surrendered completely. He did homage to the Pope, they became friends, and he agreed to have Langton as Archbishop of Canterbury. His humiliation, however, did not end there, and he further agreed that in future England would be a vassal state to the Holy See, besides which he promised large indemnities to the Church in England, including an annual subsidy to the Pope. Defeated in battle, hated by everyone for his cruel misdeeds, and his country now a vassal state; never before had England fallen so low, and never previously was a king so despised. With the Church his overlord, and the barons ceasing to fear him, conferences commenced between Langton, who was a man of great ability, and the nobles, to end in the King being brought to Runnymede in 1215, and made to grant the Great Charter safeguarding the rights of the nobles, the priests and the free men.

The principal points in this historic document can be summed up briefly as follows:—

(1) Before the King could levy more taxes beyond the ordinary feudal dues he must call together the Great Council.

(2) The existing privileges of the Church in England were guaranteed.

(3) No free man shall be arrested or imprisoned except by the lawful judgment of his peers, or by the law of the land. To none will justice be denied.

(4) The liberties of London, and the other towns or harbours of England, were confirmed.

(5) A Commission of twenty-five barons was appointed to enforce the sixty-three clauses of the Charter.

Too much has been claimed for the Magna Charta. It made few lasting innovations, and asserted no new liberties. It contained, however, guarantees for the greater security of all free men, but nothing was said of the vast majority who were bondmen, whose bondage was further tightened. The Church secured her ancient liberties, and the barons obtained greater privileges, both of which were reactionary developments. The limitation of the power of the King to tax without the consent of the Great Council was in the interests of the barons, though ultimately it was for the good of all.

Magna Charta, however, never became the law of the land, but, instead, a somewhat similar Charter took its place in 1225. This, however, omitted the obligation of the King to call together the Great Council before new taxes were imposed, and the new Charter remained the basis of the law throughout the Middle Ages. Magna Charta did not guarantee trial by jury, nor give the people any political power; in fact it was a feudal document designed for the benefit of the Church and the barons, and is not the liberty-giving document it is so often represented to be.

In spite of the guarantee that the privileges of the Church in England would be preserved, Pope Innocent III was not satisfied, and he vehemently denounced the new Charter as "a diabolical document" and an impudent infringement of the King's right over the people. He evidently expected even more privileges for his Church, and, by absolving John from keeping his oath, he encouraged him to break his promises, which is just what the King did. The barons consequently declared war against him, and offered the crown to Louis of France. This he accepted, but fortunately John died in 1216, and this happy event prevented England from becoming an appendage of

France, as Louis had by then arrived in London with ships of war, and French troops were already in England supporting the barons.

Magna Charta, to its framers, must have been looked back upon as simply a scrap of paper which had only fanned the flames of civil war, and introduced a foreign king as claimant to the throne of England. Its failure, however, brought about the necessary reaction, which laid the foundation of something better and more enduring. We can compare this set-back to the one suffered by the League of Nations in our own time, a failure which may lead to something better. It, however, required a Hitler and a war to expose where its weakness lay, just as it required a John and a civil war to make the more intelligent of his time realise that law and order were to be preferred to lawlessness and injustice. Evolution sometimes follows a great catastrophe, and one of our problems is to find the way to progress without being first whipped into the way of knowledge and wisdom.

Henry III (1216–1272), who followed John, his father, at nine years of age, turned out to be a better man. He could hardly have been worse, but he was a weak-minded, devout, futile creature. In his reign the revised Magna Charta was issued and accepted without protest, even though it gave the King the sole power to levy new taxes. He commenced the re-building of Westminster Abbey, most of the early church having been destroyed. Then he angered the barons by his introduction of foreigners to the Court, because they came between him and them. Another grievance the barons had against him was his support of the Pope's schemes to expel from Italy and Sicily the house of Hohenstaufen. Moreover, he subscribed heavily to the Papal Treasury, and in doing so he greatly overtaxed the people to obtain the money. What was bitterly resented in England was joyfully received in Rome, and His Holiness enthusiastically exclaimed, "Verily England is an unexhausted well, where much abounds and much may be extorted."

So the disgusted barons found a new and great leader in their resumed war against the Crown, and one moreover who had sufficient imagination to devise a scheme which enabled some of the people to take part in their country's government. Though the plan was only a skeleton, lacking in fleshy substance, yet it was one which never for long remained shut up in the cupboard, as it was always coming out in after years to impress on the people the necessity of it being more decently clothed.

The man, in whose mind first simmered the Greek method of democratic government, was Simon de Montfort (1200–1265), Earl of Leicester, whose father, a French nobleman, had dealt so ruthlessly with the Albigenses in the south of France. He was the first man to summon representatives of the boroughs to a Parliament, based approximately on the foundation of the present British parliamentary system. He was hostile to the King, which may be the reason for what followed, but he was a man of progressive ideas, and these included both political and Church reform. The Pope supported the King in his attitude against the introduction of these reforms, and absolved him from his oath to observe "The Provisions of Oxford", which provided for a Parliament of twelve delegates and a Council of fifteen to control the King's actions.

This scheme had not proved a success, as the barons quarrelled amongst themselves, and civil war followed. The King was defeated at Lewes, and, though he was not dethroned, Simon de Montfort ruled England. In the following year, 1265, Simon produced his completed scheme of parliamentary government, by summoning a new form of Parliament, consisting of a representative of every county and borough to consult with the nobles and the chief ecclesiastics. Many of the nobles refused to agree to this drastic innovation, and Edward, the King's son, joined them in the civil war which followed. At Evesham, the same year, Simon was defeated and killed, and the nobles who had supported this outstanding reformer, who, in some degree, can be called the Father of the British Parliament, pleaded for mercy from their now liberated king. Henry was again given full authority to exercise his royal power without hindrance, and this the country accepted without opposition. England was not yet ready for representative government.

Christian civilisation in Europe, in the 13th century, was no further forward than was civilisation in the days of Hammurabi of Babylon three thousand years earlier, whose code of laws was certainly in no way inferior to those in use in Christian countries up to last century. The example shown by the Church, which claimed to represent Christ on earth, was so terrible that all the misrepresentations and mis-statements of a subsidised priesthood cannot for ever keep the people from knowing the truth. This awful record, moreover, continued to within our own time amongst all branches of the Christian organisation.

Christian ethics, about which we hear so much, have certainly left a foul smell on the pages of history, and Lecky, the historian, is fully justified in describing the Christian era as one of the most contemptible periods in history.

The kings and nobles of England, like the priests, were for ever working in their own interests, and the voiceless ignorant masses had to do as their superiors told them. Within our own generation the British people have come into their own after a hard and long struggle, with little help from either priests, nobles or gentry. Developing mind has made this advance possible, as this dynamic force brought about the beginning of education in Christendom, a power for righteousness which is still in its infancy. Most people are still grossly ignorant of the vital truths of life, and, if this be so today, we can better understand the history we have so far been reading, and the story yet to be told. So let us proceed with this, our world-wide survey of humanity's achievements and follies, by giving some thought to a terrible menace which had threatened to engulf both Christian and Moslem civilisations during the previous fifty years.

CHINESE CIVILISATION.
(311–1405.)

The Mongols Spread Themselves Over China, Asia and Europe.

THE conquest of the Moslem Empire by the Turks destroyed a barrier which protected Europe and the Middle East from a great and growing nomadic horde gathering strength in Central Asia, and here we must break into our review of Christian civilisation to tell of its world-wide conquests. So far our history has been mostly confined to Europe since we last dealt with China in Chapter IV. A thousand years have passed since then, during which time stirring events have been happening in the Far East, but to understand better the danger now overhanging Europe and the Middle East we must again take up the story of China, to see what has taken place there since we left her at the time when the Emperor Theodosius had sent envoys from Constantinople to the Chinese capital.

At the beginning of the 4th Christian century the Huns, at a time when Chinese power was at its lowest depth, renewed their incursions into China, and this gave an adventurer Lew Yuen the opportunity amidst the confusion to proclaim himself emperor in A.D. 311. China in those days was in a state of chaos, as the hand of every man was against his neighbour. Nothing was permanent, as new states came and went in bewildering confusion. The Eastern Tsin dynasty collapsed, and then, for more than two hundred years, all semblance of united authority vanished. Finally, in 590, the Suy dynasty brought order out of chaos, new and improved laws were decreed, and literature and culture spread, the imperial library containing 54,000 volumes.

Then followed years of external wars, and great internal extravagances, which laid such a heavy burden on the country that the Emperor on his return from a successful expedition against Korea found his people in revolt. The Emperor was assassinated, the leader of the rebellion, General Le Yuen, proclaiming himself emperor of the Tang dynasty and taking the name of Tai-Tsung (617–649). He reconquered much of China which had been lost to invaders during the centuries of internal chaos. Besides this he extended the frontier as far west as Persia and the Caspian Sea. So great now (643) was the position of China that ambassadors were sent to its capital from Nepaul, Persia and elsewhere, besides a Nestorian priest who so won the Emperor's favour that he built for him a church, and permitted him, and those he converted, to preach this particular brand of Christianity.

Architecturally China is the same today as it was two thousand years ago. In the 4th century A.D. it produced its greatest painter in Ku-Kai-Chih, and some of the beautiful work of this master artist, and other great craftsmen, have come down to the present time. In contrast to the Renaissance art of Europe, which confined itself to portrait-painting, the Chinese produced landscape pictures in water-colour, their pottery and bronze work being unmatched elsewhere, and very skilfully produced. Fine buildings and decorations were to be seen, and block printing was in use, while the people refreshed themselves with tea, which, by the 6th century A.D., was drunk everywhere throughout the land.

Quite the most interesting item of news of these parts in that age was the distances people covered when going from one country to another. In 628 there arrived at Canton, Arab messengers bearing a message from Mohamet to the Emperor calling upon him to acknowledge Allah as the only true God. A similar message was sent to Heraclius at Constantinople, and to the Emperor of Persia. These Arab envoys travelled by sea from Arabia to China by a trading vessel, which points to East and West being linked together by trade.

A year later Yuan Chwang, a devout Buddhist, made the greatest journey so far recorded. He was away from China for sixteen years, having, during this time, crossed the Gobi desert and entered India through the Khyber Pass. After journeying through India, from Nepaul to Ceylon, for fourteen years, he returned home by way of Afghanistan. He recorded his travels and adventures in a book, now a Chinese classic, wherein is described much that is marvellous and unbelievable. India, like China, was then much as it is now, and he tells of considerable centres for education. The picture he draws of Buddhism depicts it as having become a religion of impossible marvels, so unlike what we imagine was the intention of its founder. On his return home he received a great reception, and ended his days in a monastery translating the Buddhist literature into Chinese.

In this land of bewildering changes we now find, on the death of Tai-Tsung, that a woman gained supreme power, a fact all the more strange as women were considered in the light of slaves. Woo How, the wife of the new emperor, pushed aside her husband, and then, after his death, became his successor, and took possession of the throne. She governed well and wisely for fifty-five years, and, at her death, her daughter-in-law, whose husband had been deprived of the throne by his mother, played a similar role, as she poisoned him and ruled through her son whom she set on the throne.

The history of the next few hundred years is too monotonous to give in detail, as it is a repetition of civil war at home and conflicts with the Tibetans and Arabs on the frontiers. For the most part it is a record of bad and feeble government, intrigues, oppressions and rebellions, only to be relieved by the iconoclastic policy of Woo-tsung (841–847), who abolished all the temples and closed all the Buddhist monasteries and nunneries, sending their inmates back to their homes. All foreign priests and missionaries were expelled, but his death brought this persecution to an end, and Buddhism again revived during the reign of his successor, who was greatly elated to discover what he thought was a bone of the Buddha. This he brought to his capital in great state.

Religious intolerance has been the exception and not the rule in China, because her religion is based on Ancestor Worship, the most uniform and tolerant of all supernatural religions, and, if we except Spiritualism, the one that comes nearest to natural religion. The Chinese constitute the largest exclusive human group on earth, but they have shown the least tendency to aggression outside their own boundaries. They are revengeful and constant in their hatred of those who make themselves their enemies, but they prefer to follow the guidance of their great moral teachers, Confucius and Lao-tsze, to requite evil by justice and kindness. Invaders have conquered China, but she has absorbed them, and, in company with India and Egypt, likewise peace-loving people, her civilisation remains while that of aggressive nations has vanished into history. China still continues her own way of life, in spite of internal disruptions, and her millions have pursued their own way of evolution without resorting to aggressive war.

While internal anarchy has been the prevailing feature of Chinese history, the fact still remains that its multitude of decent hard-working peasants have for ever plodded on at their rice patches, and supported their families just·beyond the border line of starvation. They have been a peace-loving simple people, whose lives were the same year by year, century after century, the glamour, if one can call it such, resting with the bands of brigands who plundered the land under leaders, who were honoured by being called generals when they led their warriors against some unruly prince, or attacked some foreign foe. Such, then, was China, deep down in the slough of ignorance, until we come to the beginning of the 13th century of the Christian era.

During this period the Mongols, who came from the same stock as the Huns, began to acquire power in eastern Asia, and make their dual nature conspicuous. Like the rest of mankind, they had two aspects in life— amity and enmity—being friendly, mild and kind at home, and fiercely antagonistic and vindictive to strangers. Formerly vassals of the Kin dynasty, the Mongols ultimately grew so powerful, under their ruthless leader Jengis, that the position was reversed. Then followed the Mongol invasion of China in 1212, when the Kins were completely defeated. Entering China from the north-west, the invaders advanced southwards, destroying everything as they went, until the provinces of Honan, Chih-li and Shan-tung, including their ninety cities, were devastated. It was their boast that a horseman could ride over their sites and never stumble. Year after year the war dragged on, Peking being occupied, and one city after another fell to the invader.

The only rule in the life of Jengis, their notorious leader or Khan, meaning chief, was to take what he had the power to take and keep all he could, which gangster code has been faithfully followed by the numerous conquerors who made use of their ignorant followers for their own ends. The barbarian Mongols never professed to be other than thieves of the lowest order, and their opportunities had never fitted them for anything different, a fact which makes the comparison between them and the modern barbarians all the more striking and disgraceful. The Germans and the Japanese in our day have repeated in the 20th century what a wild ignorant savage race, without learning and culture, perpetrated in the 13th century, The depredations of the Mongols ring through the ages, and, if the deeds of these barbarians are so well remembered, what will history have to say of the devastations and massacres of the Germans and Japanese in our own times?

Desperate was the Chinese resistance to the invaders, and for years cities were besieged and destroyed. men, women and children being wiped out. Jooning Foo held out until every animal had been killed for food, and every person unable to fight was put to death to save useless mouths. When the invaders finally stormed the walls, the Emperor burned himself to death in his palace, an act which brought to an end this imperial line until the Manchu family came four hundred years latei to claim the throne as the rightful heir to the brave defender of Joo-ning Foo. Such is the story as told by Chinese historians, and now let us look at the position as it affected the Western world. We remember reading earlier in this chapter about Frederick II, the Holy Roman Emperor, who led the Sixth Crusade against the Saracens. This enlightened monarch had ho animosity towards the Infidel, and evidently cared little about freeing the Holy Sepulchre from his keeping. In reality Frederick went east to consult with the Sultan of Egypt about the danger overhanging Europe, and the Middle East, from the growing horde of Mongols now at the gate of Europe.

When Frederick met the Sultan as a friend in 1228 this danger had become very acute, so much so that these two monarchs, instead of fighting each other to decide whether the Christians or the Moslems were to occupy the Holy Sepulchre, talked over the means to be adopted to prevent the nomads encroaching farther west. Already they were threatening Kiev and Constantinople. So there is little wonder that this subject, more than the question of the ownership of the Holy Sepulchre, occupied all their thoughts.

History, up to now, records one nomadic invasion after another against those people who had decided that living in houses, in one place, was to be preferred to the more adventurous and less comfortable life of wandering from place to place in search of food. Such people feared these wild migrants, and they, in turn, hated and despised the sheltered form of life, and the people who lived it. All our ancestors were once nomads, and those of us who like hiking and camping out, who prefer the countryside, the hills and the glens, to living in towns, have inherited their love of country life. Those who prefer to live in the country, rather than in towns, have a touch of the nomads outlook on life, and can understand their preference to living close to nature, which the town-dweller, with his streets and squares and never a green field, cannot do.

As we have just been reading, a host of nomadic barbarians, the Mongols, forced themselves from obscurity in Mongolia into the light of history at the beginning of the 13th century. Their place of origin was somewhere in Asia, north-east of China, near where the Turks and Huns had increased and multiplied. They lived under a chief whose son Jengis, to whom we have just been introduced, was a great military genius, and, under his direction, they became a formidable horde. He realised that in both the East and West there were opportunities for loot and plunder, and he prepared his people to make the most of their opportunities.

A glance at the map of the world, as known in the year 1200, reveals great tracts of land under unified rule in the East, and much smaller tracts in the West. Starting from Portugal, we find Spain half Christian and half Moslem. France is half English and half French. Germany rules from the North Sea to Sicily. Next to her in the north is Prussia on the Baltic, Poland immediately south, then Hungary and, farthest south, the Greek Eastern Empire. England, Scotland, Ireland, Norway and Sweden were then much as they are now, except that Sweden ruled Finland. Russia occupied the same place as it does now, though she was divided up under different influences. North of the Caspian Sea were the Tartars, and east of the Urals in Siberia were the nomads under Jengis the Khan.

Farther east were the Chinese, divided up into the Hsia Empire, the Kin Empire and the Sung Empire. Working back to the west, keeping south of Siberia, we come to Tibet and India, which were divided into kingdoms. From the Himalayas to Persia, including northern India, was the Kharismian Empire under the rule of a Turkish emperor. The Seljuk Turks ruled Turkey, while Syria, Palestine and Egypt had been divided between the sons of Saladin. The Caliphs ruled Mesopotamia, and southwards lay Arabia, sparsely populated by the nomadic Arabs.

The foregoing is a bird's-eye view of the then known world, the world Jengis Khan was about to rock, as much as it has been shaken in our own times, by his host of highly trained warriors who were as much at home on a horse as we are on our feet. They lived in tents, and their lives were occupied tending their animals and hunting, drifting northwards as the snows melted and southwards in winter. His first success was to secure an alliance with the Tartars, which thus extended his influence to the Black Sea. Then, as we have just read, he attacked the Chinese Kin Empire and captured Peking, which increased his influence to the Pacific Ocean, but there were still great tracts of country lying to the south and west rich in possible plunder.

The Kharismian Empire, under Turkish rule, which embraced northern India, Afghanistan and Persia, was a new but progressive state, and to its emperor at his capital, Samarkand, Jengis sent envoys in 1217. These were murdered, which was the way they had in those days of showing that the Emperor looked upon Jengis as an outlaw and a bandit, with whom he would have no diplomatic relations. The bandit's reply was swift and terrible, as immediately a vast collection of horsemen, probably armed with cannon and guns (as the Chinese whom they had over-run knew by then the use of gunpowder), swept through the Kharismian Empire, taking town after town, until they reached the capital, which surrendered.

Thence they swept westwards, past the Caspian Sea and also south into India. Near Kiev they encountered a force of Russians, whom they defeated, taking the Grand Duke of Kiev a prisoner. The Mongols were now on the shores of the Black Sea, and panic swept through the inhabitants of Constantinople. Meantime in the East still more of China was conquered, but, at the height of his success, Jengis the Khan died in 1227, and followed his 6,000,000 victims to the other world. In 1228 Frederick II and the Egyptian Sultan met to talk over what all this meant to them, as, though this ferocious Mongol leader was now out of the way, his vast empire was still vigorous and expanding.

At the death of this brilliant soldier and master plunderer, the Khan of Khans, or King of Kings, the Mongol Empire in the west reached to the Black Sea, and eastwards it stretched through Afghanistan, Lahore in India, skirting the northern slopes of the Himalayas, on to Peking. Into the able hands of Yeliu Chutsai the administration of this vast territory now devolved. He was a great statesman and administrator, in fact one of the outstanding men in history. He ruled with moderation, allowing complete freedom in religion, and saved many cities and priceless works of art from destruction. Unfortunately he was unable to use his influence wherever his armies went, but he made no attempt to amass wealth, and died a poor man.

At Karakorum in Mongolia, the capital of the Mongol Empire, a great barbaric town, the chiefs elected Ogdai, the son of Jengis, who was just as cruel and ruthless as his father, to be their military leader. He was fired by his father's last wish that he would complete the conquest of the world, and under him the Mongol hosts poured into Russia in 1235. Kiev was captured and destroyed in 1240, and nearly all Russia became tributary to him. Poland was overrun and ravaged, and an army of Poles and Germans was defeated at Liegnitz in Lower Silesia in the following year. The Mongols showed great strategic skill, and out-manœuvred the Europeans, more by their brains than their numbers. Their military machine moved with clock-like precision, a feat quite beyond the power of any European army of those days. Their spy and intelligence system was excellent, and it knew all about the intentions of its opponents, who, on their side, were quite ignorant of those of their enemies. There was no military leader in Europe to match Ogdai, who probably could have overrun the entire continent had he wished.

He, however, decided otherwise, and moved southwards into Hungary, his men massacring or mingling with the inhabitants as they passed on from place to place. What would have happened to Europe had Ogdai lived we can only imagine. Fortunately he died in 1241 at the age of fifty-six, having reigned for thirteen years, and, as there was trouble about his successor,. the great undefeated army began to move back towards the East, leaving, as Mongol islands, dotted in an Aryan Sea, the Finns, the Lapps, the Magyars, the Bulgars and the Turks to remind us of this great flood of humanity which swept westwards from the mountains and plains of Mongolia.

Ogdai was followed by Kwei-Yew, who became the Great Khan, then by Mangu (1251-1259), the eldest son of Too-le, the warrior brother of Ogdai, who made his brother Kublai the Governor of China, and slowly the entire Sung Empire was conquered, thus bringing all China under Mongol rule. Tibet was then invaded, and this was followed by the conquest of Persia, Syria and Mesopotamia. Mangu in turn was succeeded by Kublai (1259-1294), who ascended the throne to become the sovereign of all China. Never in its history was the nation more illustrious than it was during this reign, and at no time was its power more widely felt than under his rule, as his dominions extended "from the frozen sea almost to the Straits of Malacca", or, as we would say today, from the Arctic Ocean to Singapore and from the Pacific to the Caspian. He was the ruler of most of Asia, comprising a third of the land surface of the earth, and only India, Arabia and the most westerly parts of Asia did not acknowledge his sovereignty or pay him tribute.

Kublai made Peking his capital, where he devoted his attention to Chinese affairs. His brother Hulagu ruled over Persia, Syria, Asia Minor and Mesopotamia, which became an independent empire. He was prevented from entering Africa through being defeated in Palestine by the Sultan of Egypt in 1260, and this led to the Mongols losing their influence in the Middle East. Likewise the Mongols in Russia and Siberia became separated from their eastern relations, and formed new states, the consequence being that when Kublai died in 1294 no new Great Khan was appointed, and the once great empire dissolved, leaving Mongolia and China under Mongol rule directed from Peking. In Russia the Mongols took as their capital Kipchak, where they ruled over that country. Persia likewise became a distinct Mongol empire, embracing the Seljuk Turks, while Siberia formed a separate state, and so did Turkestan.

This remarkable Mongol penetration now ceased, so far as Europe and the Middle East were concerned, but it was not yet exhausted, as they next invaded northern India, where they set up a monarchy, which lasted for about a century, when it was driven out by the Afghans. The Mongol dynasty in China was finally overthrown when the Ming dynasty took its place in 1368, to last for nearly three hundred years. This was replaced by the Manchus, who ruled China until 1912, when the Emperor abdicated in favour of a republic.

The Mongols might have come and gone, or been absorbed into the existing populations without much permanent harm. Houses can be destroyed and rebuilt, but these human locusts devastated one great engineering scheme which was never replaced, much to the permanent economic loss of the world. The Mongols destroyed the wonderful irrigation system in Mesopotamia, first built by the Sumerians some five thousand years earlier, and one which had made the land such a fertile paradise that these early people, in their legends, placed there the Garden of Eden. Here, in the cradle of civilisation, the Mongols deliberately destroyed this wonderful engineering feat which had added so much agricultural wealth to the world. For five thousand years there had been continuous bountiful harvests in these fertile regions, which had supported a great population and many large cities, such as Eridu, Babylon, Nineveh, Ur, Ctesiphon, Nippur and Baghdad. What we all owe to the early civilisation of this fertile region few realise, and its loss was another of the many tragedies mankind has had to endure because of ignorance.

Now it was all obliterated by a rabble of stupid barbarians, who despised all forms of civilised life, and looked on those who lived in houses, and by agriculture, as detestable and depraved. Never since then has Mesopotamia yielded its great rich harvests, and, from being a well-populated land, it became a wilderness in which wandered a few scattered nomadic tribes. Mud swamps took the place of fertile fields, mosquitoes that of wheat, and the waters of two great rivers flowed on to the sea without in any way benefiting mankind. Fortunately the victory of the Sultan of Egypt in Palestine, in 1260, prevented the Nile valley from sharing the same fate, but the great prosperity which has come to Egypt in modern times, by scientific irrigation, will come again to Mesopotamia, as the Iraq government is now building dams, digging ditches, and installing pumps to restore this "sea of verdure", as Herodotus called it, to its former glory.

Those Mongols, who did not mix with the people they conquered, reverted to the same tribal form of life in which they were when Jengis turned them into an organised army of plunderers, and, from now onwards, they lived in small independent groups each under a Khan. Their descendants wander through central and western Asia and the Middle East to this day, and their dislike of a settled life has in no way decreased.

This plague on the lives of decent people seemed at last to be dead, but a dying flame spluttered up in 1369 when Timurlane, a descendant of Jengis Khan, spread his savage rule over northern India, Afghanistan, Turkestan, Persia, Mesopotamia, Armenia and a slice of Asia Minor. He ravaged everything of value wherever he went, and, in place of the houses which he destroyed, he erected pyramids of skulls. He took the title of Great Khan, and wherever he ruled there were destruction, devastation, desolation, fiendish cruelties and wholesale massacres. This monster of iniquity tried to restore the old Mongol Empire, but failed, and, when he died in 1405, all that remained to mark his rule was a tale of anguish, and a name which reeks with every abomination known to mankind.

With the passing of this danger to civilisation we shall now return to Europe and take up our tale much nearer home.

CHAPTER XI.

CHRISTIAN CIVILISATION.
(862–1642.)

Introduction. (1) *England and France at War for Over a Hundred Years.* (2) *The Kings of Europe Command and the Servile People Obey.* (3) *Spain Under Christian Rule.* (4) *Exploration and Colonisation Beyond the Sea.* (5) *The Torch of Knowledge Begins to Glow in Europe.* (6) *The Basis is Laid for Parliament and Education in England.* (7) *Europe Prior to the Reformation.*

BEFORE every deed comes a thought. History thus embraces the billions of thoughts of the millions of individuals who have lived during the past six thousand years, during which time history has been recorded. We came into this world without being asked whether we wished to or not, and we get slowly but irresistibly caught up and carried forward in the stream of thought of the time in which we are born. What is natural to us would be strange to our ancestors. Each generation lives and thinks differently from the previous one, and, as history records their deeds, we realise ever more clearly that they were, and we are, the creatures of circumstance. What we think and do depends upon our environment and heredity; the minute cell at conception containing the potential of what we each become.

History also teaches us that when people are ignorant they generally do what is wrong, the word we give to an action which upsets the harmony and aspirations of life. Thus they are unrighteous, because they do that which is not right. When they are enlightened and wise they more often do what is right, and are consequently righteous. Wrong-doing comes from unbalanced and undeveloped minds, and, in its final analysis, can be reduced to selfishness, to the consideration of only our own wishes and the ignoring of those with whom we come in contact.

Selfishness, which causes all the different phases of wrong-doing, comes from unenlightened minds, as a truly enlightened person, one whose mind is evenly balanced and well developed, is not selfish. Selfishness comes from minds which are coarse and unsensitive, as the finer or enlightened mind could not find peace and harmony if others suffered from actions produced by its thoughts. The enlightened mind is so tele-pathically in touch with the minds of other people that it is upset if it produces disharmony in other minds. As the mind develops it becomes ever more sensitive to the thoughts of others, and adjusts itself to prevent the disharmony which leads to quarrels and unhappiness.

If all minds were better balanced, more developed, more enlightened and more sensitive, selfishness would decrease and happiness would increase. It is because this is very slowly taking place amongst a large part of the human race that there is less cruelty now than formerly, and much more is done for the poor, the sick and the suffering than was done in former times when minds were coarser and less responsive to the thoughts of others. In the Middle Ages minds were coarse and unresponsive, selfishness predominated, and cruelty and intolerance brought misery where there would have been happiness if mental development had been greater. As it was, the minds of the people of the time we are now considering in this chapter dovetailed into the mental level of the times, and they accepted as natural what we now look back upon with horror and repulsion.

Much of what is, and has been, happening in our own times will receive the same condemnation by generations yet unborn. Each generation only develops slowly to a higher level of thought, if conditions are favourable for such improvement, and, if they are not, retrogression takes place. Material conditions affect the mind, and can be so unfavourable that it does not develop as it would if its environment were more favourable. It is like a tender plant which makes the most of the soil from which it grows, but, if deprived of rain and sunshine, withers away for want of nourishment.

History is the story of unfolding mind in the form of a spiral, as this unfolding is not continuous but subject sometimes to long reactions. It is one of those periods of long reaction that we are now considering, and it continued until the 17th century. The soil was poor, and little intellectual rain or sunshine fed the mind in those long dark centuries during which Christianity dominated men's thoughts. It was an age when faith was at its zenith, when the Church was the only school, and the priest the only teacher. In this arid desert of ignorance mental development was impossible, and the parched mind of Christendom was stunted by lack of sustenance.

What, then, was the ethical standard of instruction

in those days, and how exactly did the people look upon life? They had their own crude ideas of right and wrong, just as a savage has, but they had no incentive to strive for something better, as they were taught and believed that their wickedness had been forgiven by God, because "By the righteousness of one the free gift (of salvation) came upon all men . . . so by the obedience of one shall many be made righteous." (*Romans* v, 18.) This being so, they had no reason to worry over their shortcomings.

The foregoing represents the sum and substance of Christian ethics, membership of the Church securing salvation, the consequence being that there was no incentive to do right and nothing to fear by doing wrong. The partaking of the Eucharist cleansed the wicked of his sins, and only when the would-be partaker was an adulterer, murderer or thief was it withheld for a time. By means of the Confessional, minor failings were expiated through various forms of penance. These were mostly sexual lapses, or religious sins which were outside the ethical code, such as doubting the dogma preached by the priests, not going to church or keeping Sunday and the feast days holy, while others included the neglect of having a priest to baptise a child or perform the marriage or funeral service.

Christian morality had reached no higher a standard than that attained by the Hebrews two thousand years earlier, the reason being that its very foundations are based on error, namely the assumption that man is a fallen being, to be raised only through belief in a sacrificed saviour. Original sin was considered a chronic canker which only a supernatural god could remove, man himself being incapable of rising above his carnal nature, which is evil. This distorted and degraded estimate of human nature had a baneful effect on ethical conduct, as wrong-doing was taken for granted, and little effort was made to improve one's way of life, that being considered to be beyond human endeavour.

What a contrast to this exaggerated idea was the outlook of the Pagan philosophers of Greece and Rome, to whom the attainment of righteousness was the main object in life. To them the duty of everyone was to discard vice and attain virtue, as on each one individually rested the responsibility to improve character and reach a nobler way of life. The Pagans extolled the wisdom of righteousness, while the Christians revelled in the remorse which followed the sinner who had not accepted the Christian way of salvation. The former appealed to all that was good in human nature, to the intellect, to reason, to evolutionary development, while the latter pandered to the lowest qualities in man, urging him to rely on a saviour and carry on as best he could.

Consequently Christian civilisation was based on a wrong interpretation of human conduct, because there is more good than evil in most people, and, by encouraging the good, the evil can eventually be overcome. As this was not done, ethical conduct is noticeable by its absence; the fear of God, and the attempt to please him, dismally failing to produce good results because everyone imagines God according to his own imagination. Though it was considered wrong to murder, commit adultery and steal at home, it was thought to be right to kill, attack and plunder the people of neighbouring countries, and rape their women. No restraint was exercised anywhere on cruelty, and justice everywhere was corrupt and often ignored. Most people were intolerant and fierce towards all who disagreed with them, children, both boys and girls, servants and animals, being lashed on every occasion, and the upper classes looked upon the lower classes as serfs and outcasts.

Plato argued that women should be treated as equal to men, but both as husband and father the male, as has always happened, predominated throughout the Christian era, and deprived the female of many rights or privileges. Marriage was a necessary convenience, and not necessarily related to love, as the woman was forced to marry the man the father chose as suitable. Amongst the upper classes marriages were arranged during childhood, and neither son nor daughter was expected to have any say in the matter. Not until the 19th century did marriage become a matter of affection and personal choice. Little was done in those days for the sick and suffering, and no attempt was made to raise the social and mental condition of the people, who lived their debased and degraded lives for ever toiling, while lacking comforts and decent living conditions in their humble homes built of logs, rubble and clay, the bare earth being their only floor.

Theology, up to now, had satisfied the people in its explanation of the ordering of the universe. It had conceived a weird and unnatural destiny for everyone after death, and was freely used to help rulers to keep the people servile, but there was now a stirring in a hitherto mentally indolent Europe. A few of the most intelligent were beginning to wonder if all its claims and assertions were true, and if something better could not be put in place of priest rule, which had kept the people submissive during the childhood of the race. Here and there a few were beginning to look upon priests as a nuisance and a hindrance to progress, as they lived on past tradition and hated any change or novelty, but such an idea to the vast majority was nothing less than revolution, which would end in social disaster. Theology, thundered the Church, contains all there is to know, and the expounding of this knowledge is reserved for the priests alone, the people's duty being to obey and not to reason.

So long as this night of mental darkness lasted no progress was possible. The king felt more comfortable with his subjects simple, and so he left them ignorant. The priests did not wish their opinions questioned, and consequently they did nothing to make the people more intelligent. There were no schools, no schoolmasters, no books, and the people went from the cradle to the grave with only a very meagre idea of the meaning of existence. There was no one to stimulate thought, as anyone who tried to do so was at once imprisoned, tortured and burned at the stake.

Such, then, was the mental level of the inhabitants of Europe at the beginning of the 14th century of the Christian era, and it will consequently be no surprise to find that wars, famine and pestilence ravaged Europe, whose people had no other remedy for their suffering beyond prayers, kissing holy relics, and penances. A streak of dawn was, however, visible on the dark horizon, and before this chapter ends a new day will have dawned for mankind. Truth and knowledge will have challenged theology, and a corner of the dark curtain of ignorance will have been lifted. So let us go forward to meet the dawn, noticing on our way the inevitable wars, poverty and misery produced by ignorance.

(1) England and France at War for Over a Hundred Years.

It will be remembered that in the reign of King John all the northern and central English possessions in France were lost. It would have been fortunate if France and England, from that time onwards, had remained apart, as, by race and situation, they are not natural partners. In those days, however, when the land was owned by the king, and passed on to his heir at death, all kinds of complications followed. A king would marry another king's daughter, who was his heiress, and in this way large slices of land were transferred to foreign ownership. As time went on this caused endless trouble, and so we find constant wars over successions and boundaries, in which the people, with no say in the matter, were the innocent victims. Countless lives have been lost because of this way of owning and transferring land.

We can easily imagine a more ideal state of existence than the one in which we find ourselves. Space is limitless and has no boundaries, and, if life could have been sustained in such an environment, it could then have produced new life without limit. Again, if life had remained in the sea and never come on to the land, in fact if there were only sea and no land, the constant trouble over boundaries would never have arisen. Birds and fish do not quarrel amongst themselves over boundaries and frontiers, as do human beings, who have a limited amount of land on which they are confined, and yet have limitless reproductive powers. When life reached the land in the Palæozoic age its productive capacity should have been reduced to conform to its more cramped environment. The productive organs, which were suitable for populating the vast oceans, were much too generous when used on land, the consequence being that the greater proportion of life produced on earth died for want of sufficient nourishment.

We must, however, take things as we find them, as here we are, and we may as well make the best of what we experience. Life consists of experiences, and our happiness depends on what each one makes of these mental sensations. Life lives on life in both air and sea, as well as on land, a condition which to many seems cruel and wrong, but, as nothing in nature is destroyed or wasted, this, and other such problems, may become clearer to us hereafter when we have a fuller vision. Here on earth we do not see the finished pattern but only a crude outline of the design. Here our mind both images and senses physical vibrations by means of physical organs, but, when functioning in the duplicate etheric body, apart from the physical, it will appreciate a new range of vibrations from which physical limitations and experiences are absent, and boundaries, as we now know them, will cease to be.

The part cannot comprehend the whole, and it is

useless to attempt to encompass the universe from only a physical aspect, but we may conclude from the fact that we live in a cosmos, where everything is changed but never destroyed, that what seems to us to be wrong and unjust may straighten itself out elsewhere. As life, guided by mind, persists and continues its experiences, death is no more than a change in its environment.

If this were not so the universe would be a purposeless robot, lacking everything to which we aspire. Fortunately our mental cravings have received satisfaction from the accumulating evidence that we are destined for another order of existence where mind, freed from physical limitations, can attain ever greater and wider experiences, and wander in new regions of thought and understanding. There we can order our existence more in accordance with our thoughts, and there, as we think, we shall be. Hence the importance of developing our minds aright, as all recent discoveries point to the fact that mind culture is the purpose of life.

When we read of the wickedness and martyrdom of mankind in the pages that follow, the thoughts recorded since this chapter opened may help us to adjust our outlook by enlarging the perspective. We must always think of the physical and etheric orders of life as co-related, and this will again become evident as we proceed.

The time we are now considering is the 14th century of the Christian era, when the kings of England and France were quarrelling over the ownership of France. All this trouble came about because the daughter of a French king married an English king, but, in order to understand how this caused what is called the Hundred Years' War, a few words of explanation are necessary. In the previous chapter we reached the time when Louis IX (Saint Louis) of France was followed by Philip III, after whom came Philip IV, who had three sons and one daughter, Isabella. Each of these three sons reigned in turn for only a few years and were known as Louis X, Philip V and Charles IV, the last dying in 1328, none leaving a son to succeed to the throne.

Now we go back to Isabella, the daughter of Philip IV. She married Edward II of England in 1308 and produced a son who became Edward III. He was therefore the grandson of Philip IV, King of France. When Charles IV, who was the last of the sons of Philip IV, died, Edward III claimed the throne of France, but the French were determined not to have an English king, and they found legal support in an old law of the Franks, known as the Salic law, which was once in use by a Frankish tribe known as the Salians. This law prescribed that "no portion of the inheritance shall come to a woman, but the whole inheritance of the land shall come to the male sex".

The French, however, had no need to consider the female line, because Philip IV (the king with the three sons who all died childless, and one daughter, Isabella, the mother of Edward III) had a brother whose son, after the death of Charles IV, the last of the three sons, became Philip VI (1328–1350). He in turn followed by John (1350–1364) and then by Charles V (1364–1380). Against these three kings, and their successors, the kings of England fought for the throne of France for over one hundred years (1337–1453), leaving France at the end a wilderness, and her people in abject poverty and misery. This is one of the blackest pages in English history, a story of savagery, greed, cruelty and plundering, to end finally in England being defeated and France exhausted.

Much the greater part of the English population in those days, and throughout the Middle Ages, lived in London and East Anglia. Here dwelt the most prosperous and advanced of the English people, who thrived on their trade with the Netherlands, Cologne, Scandinavia and the Baltic, but most of all with Flanders, her prosperous cities of Bruges and Ghent being the principal purchasers of English wool. There it was worked up into cloth, which found its way all over Europe, but now happened an affair which makes clear how folly, caused by ignorance, never ceases to interfere with the prosperity and happiness of mankind.

In 1336 Philip VI, envious of England's prosperity, due to her free trade policy, persuaded Louis of Flanders to arrest and imprison every Englishman resident or travelling in Flanders, to which outrage England replied by stopping the export of wool to Flanders and ceasing to purchase her cloth. A Flemish brewer, van Arteveldt, a wealthy and influential man, preferring economic prosperity and free trade with England to the ruinous economic policy pursued by France, prevailed on Edward III to establish his claim to the crown of France by force of arms. The brewer received the support of his countrymen, who allied themselves with this dangerous project which brought death, destruction and misery to everyone concerned, but especially to France, where the fighting and devastation occurred.

By concluding an alliance with Flanders, the English obtained allies and a valuable base for an attack on France. Moreover, in consequence of their genius for invention, the English were better equipped than the French, and often, in spite of having to fight an enemy superior in numbers, secured victory after victory. The war commenced when a voluntary, but paid, English force of adventurers, intent on loot and sexual satisfaction, crossed the Channel under the leadership of the Black Prince, the son of Edward III, everyone believing that it was his sacred duty to rule and plunder France. His generals and commanders consisted of nobles, bishops, abbots and the higher-ranking clergy, it being part of the Christian social order of those days for the leading priests to lead the troops in battle. The Black Prince was a great soldier, quick to take opportunities when they offered, and daring in adopting new and improved methods of warfare.

England secured command of the sea in a naval engagement fought in 1340, and, six years later, the English, speeded by the prayers and blessings of the clergy, landed in Normandy just as they did in 1944, the same towns and villages being occupied within a month in 1346 as happened in 1944. The French and English armies met at Crecy, just north of Abbeville, but in these days war was no blitzkrieg, it being a much more leisurely affair than it is today. By using the long bow, with its greater range and more deadly effect, the English outshot the French, whose armour could not stop its piercing power. The long bow brought feudal chivalry down with a crash, as, by killing his horse, it dismounted the knight.

Consequently, in spite of great bravery and dash, the French knights, and their horses, were mercilessly slain, and the English gained a great victory with small losses to themselves. Calais was then captured after famine forced the inhabitants to surrender, but this did not end their misery, as they were turned out of their homes, which were occupied by the English, so that the gateway to Europe would always in future be in English keeping.

The Black Prince, and his followers, ravaged the land, butchering many of the citizens of the towns he passed through, and, after him, followed a bubonic plague, known as the Black Death, a terrible affliction which completed the misery this devastating war had brought to France. Again, in 1356, the two armies met at Poitiers, and again, by superior weapons and tactics, the English were victorious, the French king John II being captured and taken to London. Wandering bands of English soldiers now roamed the land, plundering and destroying as they went, and everywhere the plague was reaping the country of its inhabitants. In Paris both representative government and national compulsory mobilisation were suggested, but the country was not sufficiently well organised to make either scheme practicable.

In 1360 a compromise peace was arranged which gave to England Aquitaine and Calais, on the understanding that Edward III renounced his claim to the French throne. It proved to be only a truce, because in 1364 John II died, to be succeeded by his son Charles V, who was fortunate to have as his general

Du Guesclin, a Breton knight, who had put into practice with great success the English methods of warfare. Du Guesclin proved himself to be a soldier of great skill, and he assembled an efficient army by promising that each man could keep the booty he secured. So this devastating war between two armies of avowed thieves was renewed under his direction, and gradually Aquitaine was recovered. In a naval battle off La Rochelle, France was victorious, and, when Edward III died in 1377, only Calais, Bordeaux, Bayonne, and the country in their immediate neighbourhood, remained to the English.

Deep as France had fallen in those evil days, even worse was to come from civil war. Charles V died in 1380, leaving as heir his son Charles VI, a child of eleven, who was insane. A scramble for power followed when Philip the Bold, who was Duke of Burgundy, and Louis, Duke of Orleans, with their followers, fought each other in savage contests to secure the Regency and the wealth and power this position carried. This civil war had now lasted for over thirty-three years when, in 1413, Henry V of England renewed the war by invading France with a fresh army, this time with Burgundy as an ally. He captured Harfleur at great cost, and, with an army further reduced by disease, he was met by the French at Agincourt in 1415 on his way back to Calais.

The English were in a dangerous position, and only the skill of leadership displayed by their king, and the courage and discipline of the men, saved them from disaster. The English archers once more proved themselves superior to the French, who, moreover, suffered from bad generalship, the consequence being that the English were again victorious, even more so than they were at Crecy and Poitiers. Still the civil war continued, to the accompaniment of quarrels between the various French leaders, which led to one murdering the other. So it is not surprising that under such circumstances the English made rapid progress, and soon all Normandy was in their possession.

In 1420 the Treaty of Troyes was signed, which made Henry V of England the Regent during the lifetime of the imbecile king, and King of France at his death, the heirs of Henry V to succeed him as kings of France for ever afterwards. Moreover, it provided for his marriage to Catherine, the mad king's daughter, a terrible misalliance as it turned out, because through this woman France struck a deadly blow at England, and one which was indeed just retribution for all she had suffered.

The following year Henry V entered Paris, only to die in 1422, leaving a son of nine months old to become Henry VI of England, but the tragedy lay in the fact that this boy inherited through his mother the insanity of his French grandfather. A long regency, and a weak-minded king, led to riots and civil war in England, during the time which is now known as the Wars of the Roses, but all this will be told when we come to the English history of this period.

When the mad King Charles VI died in the same year as his son-in-law Henry V, France was in the throes of defeat, as the English renewed their devastation of the land by one victory after another. Charles VII (1422–1461) succeeded his father, but found himself with only Orleans and the south of France, all of which the English and Burgundians were making plans to capture. His mother, moreover, to secure favour with the English, made his position more difficult by casting doubt on his legitimacy. Orleans was besieged, and it seemed only a matter of time before starvation would make the city surrender. The French monarchy appeared to be tottering before its final collapse, and France, as an independent kingdom, looked like disintegrating completely.

More than once we have had occasion to notice that the mind of man has directed human actions as much from events relating to heaven as to earth. History is as much made up of incidents springing from religion as from material causes. So far as history is concerned the two worlds, heaven and earth, are one, and to think otherwise would be to write off half the happenings in the story of mankind. True, the historians of the past have not emphasised this, and the majority of people today are woefully ignorant of this fact, so much so that they are unable to understand intelligently the causes which have brought about some of the great events in history.

A psychic experience brought into being the all-powerful Hindu religious system, which has had such a determining effect on the lives of the majority of the people of India. This experience was the seeing after death of a man in his etheric body, who, because he had previously died as a priestly victim, and was believed to have returned to his followers after death, became to them a god, the Christ, to be known as Krishna,[1] who had conquered death for all believers.

Likewise a psychic experience brought into being the Moslem religion, as we discovered when reading about Mahomet. This form of belief spread throughout the Middle East, reaching as far east as northern India. Another psychic experience produced the Christian faith when Jesus, a priestly victim, was believed by some to have been seen after death, and, like Krishna, was looked upon as the conqueror of the grave.

Three psychic experiences thus changed the lives and outlook of more than half the world's population, and to ignore the causes which brought these three religions into being, as historians do, presents history in a false light. Doubtless this is due to ignorance, but, when knowledge enlightens our vision, we find that these three causes were in reality one and the same. Nature's revelation does not change, however much it may be distorted, and the supernormal voices, the apparitions, and the trance utterances through mediums, have always come about by the exercise of natural law, to produce the same revelation no matter when or where it occurred on earth.

Priests and theologians have distorted this natural revelation, the consequence being that from the same root grew different branches. When this is remembered, how foolish it is to quarrel over religious questions! The Hindu hates the Moslem just as bitterly as the Moslem hates the Hindu, and until Britain intervened and put down religious strife in

---

[1] The Greek word Khristos, translated Christ, is thought by some to have been derived from the name Krishna, but this is doubted by other authorities.

India, persecution and massacres by one religion or the other were the order of the day. Likewise Christians and Moslems have hated and fought each other. Nevertheless the fact remains that if we go back to the beginning of all three religions, the origin of each one was the same. These psychic happenings changed the course of history, and other similar psychic occurrences have done likewise.

One of these changed the course of European history in the 15th century when Jeanne d'Arc (1412–1431), known in English as Joan of Arc, came forward in the crisis of her country's history and led the French army to victory, thus making possible the ultimate unity and independence of France. If Joan had not acted on her psychic experiences there is little doubt that England would have conquered and occupied all France, and what a tremendous effect this would have had in the years which followed!

The history of England, Scotland, and much of Europe, would have been completely different; the effect of the West on the Americas would have been different; in fact Joan, a girl of seventeen, illiterate and ignorant, changed the entire course of world history. True, women, by their influence on men, have been the cause of dramatic changes, but, in this case, a young peasant girl rises within a few months to supreme power, and brings about such a stupendous change in the affairs of two great nations that world-wide repercussions followed for centuries to come. Surely we have reached one of the most interesting events. of history, one which is as extraordinary as it is unique, and one which has never been repeated.

How was it possible for a young peasant girl to

bring about such immense results? Let us briefly review the events, all of which were carefully recorded at the time.[1] We are here dealing with facts, well-attested facts, and considering their ever-widening effects the initial cause is well worth investigating. At Domremy, in a secluded valley of the Vosges mountains, a girl was born in 1412, her father being a small farmer, and her mother a devout woman who came from the adjoining parish, both being upright people and much respected. They had three sons and two daughters, Jeanne,. or Joan as we call her in English, being the third child, who grew up into a strong, healthy, handsome, vivacious girl, endowed with great physical energy. In household work she was specially proficient, and during her short life the needlework she produced could not be excelled.

When Henry V of England concluded the Treaty of Troyes, to which reference has already been made, he little thought that on the banks of the Meuse lived a little girl of eight years, who, before many years had passed, would shatter all his plans for uniting France with England, and change the course of history. As this child grew up her hearing and seeing powers developed beyond the normal, so much so that she saw men, women and children about her who were not of this earth; she heard them speak to her and she replied; in other words she became clairvoyant and clairaudient, much of her time being spent in the

---

[1] Jules Quicherat, the Keeper of the Archives of France, discovered the actual manuscripts recording Joan's trial at Rouen, and other records relating to the different enquiries into her supernatural powers, which took place during her lifetime and after her death. He published these in five volumes between 1841 and 1849, and it is on them, and other documents of her time, that the facts given on this and the following pages are based.

local church or woods, where she was quiet and could experience their society.

To her the etheric world had become as real as this earth, it was no dream world, as by the time she was thirteen she was told by "Messire" (my Lord), the name she gave to the etheric man who was the leading spokesman, that she had a mission to perform, one which, with heaven's help, would rid France of the invaders, who were creating devastation and misery all around. Protesting that such an idea was impossible to realise, as all she had ever been taught was the Creed, she was told to follow the guidance she would be given, and this would convince the King, and his generals, that she was the agent working for minds higher in intelligence than this earth contained. Then the plan of campaign would be unfolded to her, and she, as their medium, would be responsible for its execution.

Joan was then only thirteen years of age, and for the next four years her etheric friends prepared her for the great task ahead, it being largely due to her strength of character that she achieved such remarkable results. If she had not followed obediently everything she was told, humiliating failure must have been her lot. She dedicated herself to their service, refused to marry when she reached the age of seventeen, learned to ride a horse, and was deaf to all the entreaties of her parents to give up her mad enterprise, her father going so far as to tell her that if she did not settle down as a respectable young woman, and marry her lover, he would drown her as a witch in the Meuse.

Now that Joan had reached the age of seventeen,

her four years of supernormal preparation having passed, she was told by her etheric guide to see Sir Robert de Baudricourt, then fighting for the French against the English. He lived in his castle near to Domremy, and there she was told to go and say that she was the agent appointed by heaven to drive the English out of France. Her family naturally thought she was mad, just as Jesus (*Mark* iii, 21) and Paul (*Acts* xxvi, 19–24) were thought to be mad when they made claims to be guided by minds other than their own. This, however, did not deter her, and, after a short interview, Sir Robert realised that he was speaking to no ordinary peasant girl. She unfolded to him his past, and showed remarkable knowledge of the then existing military situation, even telling him of important events which at the moment were happening a great distance away, all of which he discovered later to be true.

After much hesitation Sir Robert decided to await events, and, if Joan were right in what she said was taking place in far-off Orleans, he would arrange for her to see the King. As everything Joan had said turned out to be correct, and quite beyond her normal knowledge, Sir Robert arranged with the Duke of Lorraine to take this strange maiden to Chinon to see her timid, weak, pleasure-loving King, but, on arrival there, before a meeting was arranged, conference after conference took place, conferences of priests, conferences of military leaders, at each of which she appeared, to confound their hostility by her answers and supernormal knowledge.

Finally, after much delay, the military chiefs decided that Joan should see the King, who was to take a place amongst the crowd of court officials, dressed as a servant; another, arrayed in the royal robes, taking his place on the dais. On entering the royal presence Joan did not go forward to the substitute king but straight to the real king, whom she had never before seen, and to him she made her obeisance.

Then followed what must have been the strangest interview between a monarch and a subject, as in the private audience that followed Joan laid bare the King's past private life and thoughts. Charles VII had charming manners, and a kind and winning personality, but he lacked strength of character, he being a debater but not a man of action. Joan, on the other hand, chafed at delay and wanted immediate action against her country's enemies, being disappointed when told that a council would now be called to consider her proposals. A desperate position required unconventional decisions, and, just because the French position was so desperate, the council decided that Joan be given a chance to carry out her plan to save her country.

Four months after her arrival at Chinon she was made Commander-in-Chief of the French army at the age of seventeen, all the generals agreeing to be guided by her in their future military decisions. At an age when Napoleon, Julius Caesar and Alexander the Great were still in the schoolroom she was given this exalted and responsible position, installed at Court, treated with royal dignity, and given pages to wait upon her, her graceful womanly bearing, her charm, simplicity and sweetness of disposition winning for her the affection of the Queen and the ladies at the

Court. What a transformation for an ignorant, illiterate peasant girl, who knew nothing about war, its strategy and tactics, and just as little about life at the royal palace! Had she not been endowed with an unusual amount of good sense, her head would have been turned by all the attention she received.

Joan hated war, hated killing, and turned sick at the sight of blood, and yet, because of her psychic gifts, she was the instrument used by "Messire" and others to change the course of history. She, little more than a child, had been chosen to defeat and confound the best English generals, who, for the past eighty years, had experienced only victory and never defeat. Now the time for action had come, and, on the instructions of "Messire", she made known her plans to raise the siege of Orleans, its 20,000 inhabitants, after six months' investment, being on the point of surrender. Her plan for its relief was not carried out as she instructed, and, as this failed, her generals grudgingly allowed her full power over future operations, the consequence being that within ten days Orleans was relieved on the very day Joan said this would take place.

Then followed one fight after another for the forts outside the town; Joan, now twice wounded, with her own specially designed standard held always in her right hand, being ever in the thick of battle, but never as a slayer, only as a guide. Her generals told her that these forts would take months to capture; she said days, and foretold the day when each would fall. This they did, when the English retreated north closely followed by the French, who captured one town after another, to defeat finally the combined

English force commanded by the ablest generals of the day on the field of Patay, Sir John Talbot, who became the Earl of Shrewsbury, the terror of France, being taken prisoner. To account for this great victory Count Dunois, Joan's Chief of Staff, declared that only one under supernormal guidance could have planned and acted as she did on that fateful day.

This decisive battle, which Joan herself directed, and which she foretold would end just as it did, opened up the way to Rheims, and brought many wavering Frenchmen over to the side of the King. Her enthusiasm, and her generalship, had already won over the army, just as her victories had roused the King from his lethargy by convincing him that he was the legitimate king of France, heaven having heard his prayer that if he were the rightful heir to the throne his army would be victorious. Her enthusiasm for the cause of France, and her courage, made brave those who had been weak, and, with the daily arrival from all over France of new recruits, her army grew into a force numbering 12,000 men.

For eighty years England had experienced continuous victories, and France never-ending defeat, but now the tide began to turn, the French being encouraged by the belief that a heaven-sent being had been given to them who would recover the soil of France from the cruel invader. Joan, in her eagerness to follow up her victory, could not rest, because she felt that her work was only half done until the King was crowned at Rheims. When she accomplished this, in 1429, she had performed the master stroke of her short but brilliant public career, because the crowned monarch gradually brought all France together as one united nation. So let us now follow the French army, under its remarkable leader, on its march to Rheims.

From the time of Clovis the kings of France had been crowned at Rheims Cathedral, the Westminster Abbey of France, and on Rheims Joan now decided to march, though the 150 miles were through hostile territory, the towns being garrisoned by English soldiers. To this proposal there was strong objection, as to the timid Charles, and his advisers, the idea seemed utter madness. Joan, however, overcame all objections, and the advance began, Troyes being the first town reached. "You will have Troyes tomorrow," she told the King, and with all energy she made her preparations, but no fighting followed. When morning came, the city gates were opened and Charles entered in triumph, only to wish to go no farther, to which ever-recurring desire Joan's reply always was "Forward to Rheims".

When Chalons was reached the gates were opened and the keys of the town brought out to the King, who now feared that even if he got as far as Rheims it could never be captured. "March boldly. Your kingdom will soon be given back to you again," was Joan's reply, and when her army stood before its gates a siege was unnecessary, as it capitulated at once. Charles, in company with Joan, entered in triumph, to receive an enthusiastic reception, sixteen days only having elapsed since the fateful march had begun after the English defeat at Patay. The next day Charles VII was crowned King of France, the illiterate peasant maid standing by his side. Her triumph was complete, and the seemingly impossible had been accomplished. She had fought and won, and France was once again on the way to becoming a nation, all this wonder-working having been accomplished within the space of eleven weeks since Orleans had been relieved.

Joan had always said that only treachery could spoil her plans for complete victory, and now she was to experience this in full measure. Her plan to capture Paris was delayed by the King signing a truce with the English contrary to her advice, and this gave them time to switch an army of 8000 men, originally destined to fight the Bohemians, to the defence of Paris. Six weeks were thus wasted, Joan's opportunity for a bloodless capture of Paris being lost, and, when the truce ended, and the attack was made, the treacherous King did everything possible to thwart her plans. Severely wounded, she had the mortification of seeing a bridge, built for her army to enter the capital, destroyed by royal command, and then hear the order given to the army to retire.

The feeble Charles VII wanted peace, and to return to his hunting on the Loire. Now that he was the crowned head of France he seemed to have no further interest in the conflict, and the Maid of Orleans was relieved of her command. Her use to him was over; she received no reward nor recognition, but was allowed to remain at court. Her active military career, which had lasted for three months, May, June and July of 1429, was now finished, but never did she complain or reproach her sovereign. Instead she returned with the Court to the Loire, feeling like a sucked orange, now cast aside as she was no longer wanted. The pity is that she did not decide to go home, marry and live a natural life, but, after her crowded hour of adventurous living, to settle down to humdrum existence in Domremy was impossible.

Hoping that the King's attitude would change towards her, as she still had her plans for complete victory, she remained on at court, to be told one day by "Messire" that the time of her capture by the enemy was approaching. She could even then have avoided this fate by keeping out of danger, but, instead, she went to Compiègne, then infested by Burgundians, to visit the French troops, who were attacking towns held by the English. Joining in with a detachment, sent out to discover the strength of the enemy, she was surrounded and captured. She could have escaped, but refused to leave the others, and fought with them until she was pulled off her horse, and taken into the presence of the Duke of Burgundy, to be placed in a tower, her room being sixty feet above ground. From this she jumped to the ground, to be picked up unconscious but unhurt, and then, after four months' confinement, she was removed to Rouen.

Thus ends the active part Joan played in European history, but she still hoped that she would find a way to escape, or be given her liberty on her own terms. Because she could not get these terms she remained in prison after Sir Aimond de Macy had persuaded the English authorities in Rouen to liberate her, on condition that she would never again fight against the English. He, along with the Earl of Warwick, Governor of Rouen, the Earl of Stafford, Constable of France, Bishop Therouanne, Chancellor for England in France, and the Lord of Luxembourg visited Joan in prison to offer her this conditional liberty, but she flatly refused to consider it, and told them that if she ever regained her freedom she would fight on until the last Englishman had left the soil of France.

The English offer was magnanimous, especially when we consider the feelings her victories had aroused, and how deep England felt her humiliation. To us today it is impossible to imagine the relief felt by the people in England that this "agent of Satan", as she was called, could do them no further harm. This woman, in male attire, was a terrible creature to the English, and now that they had her in their possession the desire for revenge was strong. If only it could be proved that she was a witch, if only they could say that they had been defeated by the devil working through this sorceress, their humiliation would not be so great as to feel that they had been outfought and outwitted by a girl of seventeen. Moreover, if that were proved, it would discredit the coronation of Charles VII, and make it thought that the devil had been behind it all, using her for his evil purposes.

This being the prevailing feeling, we can now understand why the English authorities, after Joan had refused their offer, acceded to the demand made by the Church that she be handed over to the Holy Inquisition to be tried for witchcraft. The clergy of English-occupied France were mostly traitors to their country, and in league with the English. They it was who had encouraged the belief that Joan was a servant of the devil. They it was who said that she must pay the penalty at the stake, and they it was who were both her accusers and her judges, Pierre Cauchon, Bishop of Beauvais, claiming as his right and privilege the honour of presiding at her trial because she had been captured in his diocese.

So Joan, a devout Catholic, was handed over by the English to these cruel and ignorant men, on the understanding that if she were found innocent she was to be returned to the English civil authorities. Never did the English make a greater political blunder, as the cruel treatment she received from now onwards, and her terrible death, produced such a feeling of horror and pity throughout France, that eventually the French forgot their internal disputes, and united against the English, who were held responsible for the death of an outstanding saint and patriot. Joan, by her death, did more to create a new France than she accomplished by the sword.

When Joan was captured, the Lord of Luxemburg, who claimed her as his captive, quite expected Charles to ransom the girl who had done so much to make him the crowned King of France. But the King did nothing, and from now onwards adopted an attitude of complete indifference, not even securing her parents from want in their old age. The reason was doubtless because the Archbishop of Rheims, his closest adviser, and the clergy in the part of France over which Charles ruled, were just as convinced that Joan was a witch as were the clergy in occupied France. If Charles had not been in such a plight before Joan arrived at court, we may be sure that instead of being made chief of the army her fate would have been death at the stake.

So Joan remained at Rouen, an English prisoner, and Charles lost the only chance he had to repay her for all she had done for him. Surely we would have to seek the pages of history in vain to find such base ingratitude. For such a man there seems to be nothing bad enough, and Joan, all alone, had to face the ferocity of the Christian Church, now determined to utterly destroy her. Though her honesty and sincerity were proved beyond question, even her enemies admitting that she sought no self-glorification or fame, the independence of her country being her only desire, she was found guilty of the crime of pretending to communicate with the spirits of the dead. This offence still remains on the statute books of most Christian countries, Britain taking the lead in our own times in applying this peculiarly Christian piece of legislation. Honest respectable mediums of the 20th century, instead of now being burned or drowned, are heavily fined or put in prison, and they are, moreover, generally denied the right of a trial by jury. All attempts to alter this unjust law have proved abortive, as the evil influence of the Church is still decisive.

Since the 4th century, when the priests turned the mediums out of the Apostolic Church, the Christian Church has proclaimed unceasingly that to communicate with the denizens of the other world is impossible. Consequently the law of Christendom is based on the pronouncement of this ignorant institution, and every medium, honest and dishonest, is treated alike and pronounced guilty, because, by pretending to do what is called the impossible, fraud is taken for granted.

The balance has always been, and still is, heavily

weighted against nature's way of revealing the after life, and in favour of superstition, because it is quite legal to pretend to turn bread and wine into the body and blood of a god by mumbling over the Sacrament some sacred words. Likewise, a priest is within the law by pretending to wash away original sin by sprinkling a baby's face with water, by pretending to obtain forgiveness of wickedness at Confession, by pretending to secure the release of souls from purgatory if paid enough, and by pretending that by the death of a man some nineteen hundred years ago all believers will reach heaven.

All this, and much more, is quite legal, but when Jesus, Socrates and Joan of Arc, to name only three of the great psychic figures of the past, made use of their mediumistic gifts, they were confronted by the priests of their day and treated as criminals. So Joan, when she got into the clutches of the Church, had no hope of escape, everything being done to humiliate her and break her spirit. For nine months she was in prison, always heavily chained, and denied guards of her own sex—five soldiers, night and day, being always present. Little wonder that she refused to discard her male attire, even though her judges made it clear that this was one of the most damning proofs of her association with the devil and his angels.

The arraignment of Joan of Arc was the greatest ecclesiastical trial in history, and here Christian justice was revealed in all its sordid brutality. The accused, after being confined for the previous nine months, was brought from her dungeon to court to face some fifty priests, mainly bishops, abbots, priors and canons, who were learned in all the arts and cunning of the Inquisition. Heavily manacled, denied counsel, friends or witnesses, and deliberately reduced in health by want of food, she had to stand for hours while questions were shot at her for one purpose only: to confuse and trap her into saying something her accusers could fasten upon to determine guilt. From the first she was considered guilty, by men whose avowed purpose was her destruction, and the marvel is that in spite of every distraction, three questions sometimes being put to her at the same time, she never faltered nor slipped. She baffled them all, because she replied in the words given her by her etheric companions.

There is nothing recorded in history to compare with Joan's demeanour under this severe pressure and strain, an ordeal, lasting three months, which would normally have broken the strongest and most heroic, but she never lost her self-control, being ever courageous and courteous. Her replies to subtle and insidious questions dumbfounded their authors, so much so that her virtue, nobility, sanity and intelligence stand but clearly from the reports of the proceedings produced by her avowed enemies. This limb of Satan, as she was called, standing before men who claimed to be administering divine justice, with no case against her, proved herself to be innocent and her accusers guilty. Divine law, as administered by the Church, took no thought of confining evidence to the precise charge, its object being to force the accused to admit what her accusers wished her to admit, by building up a case against her as the trial proceeded.

Surely nothing in history resembles this long-drawn-out, calculated cruelty. Bodily torture can only last as long as there is physical endurance, but the cunningly calculated mental torture which was imposed upon this young girl lasted for three months, to end in an agonising death at the stake. The most debased savages never invented a more terrible death for anyone, and the despised heathen, who had been denied all the blessings which Christians claim their religion brought to mankind, never sank so low in moral depravity. Nevertheless the authority these Christian judges claimed for their evil deeds was the highest possible. According to their debased religion, God himself, when he walked this earth as man, showed no pity to backsliders when he declared:—

Whoso shall offend ... it were better for him that a millstone were hanged about his neck, and that he were drowned in the depth of the sea. (*Matthew* xviii, 6.)

Behind all this Christian savagery was the authority of the verses in the Sermon on the Mount, and elsewhere, advocating the destruction of unbelievers. These quotations, and numerous other theological questions, were hurled at Joan, who never ceased to vow her deep devotion to the Church and her religion, besides repeatedly answering questions concerning the voices she heard and the visions she saw.

Time and time again she was asked, What did they say to you? What language did they use? When did you first hear them speak? Did they speak to you today? Are they speaking to you now? When you see these other-world people, what do they look like? Have they clothes on or are they naked? Are their faces and bodies like ours? Have the men beards and the women long hair? Do these men's and women's voices resemble the voices of men and women on earth? Are the men and women you see the same as earth men and women? How do you know they come from heaven and not from hell? Are they helping you in answering all our questions? And so on, her descriptions of what she experienced closely resembling what mediums claim today.

Then came the question to which she could not give an answer that was understood. How can a voice be produced when its body is in the grave? This paradox has perplexed many people in the past who have experienced the phenomenon. The knowledge which has come to us within the past fifty years on the subject of vibrations, to which reference is made in Chapter III, was not then available to make clear that it is quite possible for us to have two bodies occupying the same space. The fact that our physical body is visible and tangible because its vibrations appeal to us, and our etheric body is not because its vibrations are beyond our physical senses, clears up an age-long mystery and makes understandable the seemingly impossible.

Though Joan did not know anything about vibrations, and could not have understood the subject in those days which were devoid of all scientific knowledge, she knew well enough that other-world people were around her, because, by her developed etheric sight and hearing, she could see them and hear them speak. Even when she was taken into the torture chamber and threatened with the rack, the contracting boot, and the thumb-screw, she refused to deny what was to her part of her everyday experience. Consequently sentence of death was pronounced upon her in the name of Jesus Christ. She was found guilty of sorcery and heresy, because she claimed to be a true Christian when she was not, and had given thanks to God for his guidance when she should have thanked Satan.

For her grievous sin she was to be burned at the stake until she died. This was a great event for the Christians of Rouen in the year 1431, platforms having been erected for the leading priests and soldiers to see better what was being enacted in the middle of the square. There Joan, wearing a paper mitre hat on which was inscribed in large letters "Heretic, Relapsed, Apostate, Idolator", was chained to a stake surrounded by faggots and priests, each priest holding aloft a cross, and each mumbling something in Latin. Ten thousand people watched this gruesome spectacle, and when it was over her charred and blackened body was flung into the Seine.

For England this was a black day, and one which sealed her doom. Joan became a martyr, even the ignorant multitude soon becoming convinced that an outstanding patriot, and not a witch, had been murdered, one whose short public life had been devoted to the cause of her country's freedom. Her death, at the tender age of nineteen, did more to unify France than all her other heroic deeds. She became a symbol of unity, as all France came to love her as much as the English hated her. She is the greatest woman France has ever produced, her courage, her devotion to what she considered was her duty, her strength of character, her tenacity of purpose and her originality being remarkable. She passed by tradition and precedent if better methods were discovered, her innovations in the use of artillery in war being as striking as those she introduced in her dress.

Her conduct seems always to have been irreproachable, her enemies never being able to discover a flaw in her behaviour. Despite the torrent of abuse she received, her character was never soiled. Instead of this making her hard and bitter, she remained kind and gentle to the last, never a reproach being uttered against her former friends who had abandoned her, and she prayed only for forgiveness and pity for her unjust judges. When chained to the stake she spoke words of tenderness and compassion, pardoning all who had injured her, and particularly her judges. Brave and courageous to the last, she rose above earth's sufferings as one destined for a life of greater and wider service, her last words being, "Tonight, by God's grace, I shall be in paradise."

As so often happened with men and women, different from the rest of humanity, who were murdered by their contemporaries, only to be worshipped by those who came after them, Joan was no exception. Moreover the Church, which committed this foul deed, was forced by public opinion to reopen the case and re-examine the evidence in 1455. Many of Joan's companions were then still alive ; Count Dunois (1402–1468), her former Chief of Staff, by now the foremost man in France, being emphatic in his evidence that Joan was supernormally guided throughout her life. Only by accepting the fact that she was clairaudient and clairvoyant could he explain her superhuman knowledge, her foresight, and her genius in achieving seemingly impossible victories on the field of battle. He it was who finished the work Joan began, as he captured Paris and cleared the English out of France, his success being due to the fact that he never forgot the lessons he had learned when serving under her command.

When the Commission, which sat in the Church of Notre Dame in Paris, had finished re-examining the evidence, Joan was unanimously declared innocent, though only within recent years has her greatness been really recognised. In 1894 she was declared Venerable by the Church which 463 years previously had declared her to be "a servant of the devil"; in 1908 she was Beatified, and in 1920 she was elevated to the rank of Saint. This meaningless nonsense, however, cannot atone for foul murder and all the misery and injustice she experienced.

Her short life was such a tragedy, all the suffering she endured being the result of ignorance, from which comes cruelty and injustice, but what Joan experienced was neither new nor strange, as what she suffered many millions of victims endured before and after her time. The English generals feared her for her military skill, the priests hated her because she was a medium, and some of the French commanders were jealous of her popularity and accomplishments, which were in such marked contrast to their own.

That Joan was a clairaudient and clairvoyant medium there is no doubt, as our knowledge of this form of psychic phenomena is now considerable, and all that is told about her confirms this conclusion. On this subject of clairaudient and clairvoyant medium-ship there is now a voluminous literature. That some have these gifts can be discovered by anyone who

takes the trouble to attend a Spiritualist service, when
one of the many outstanding mediums in our midst
today is conducting the proceedings.[1] Though these
mediums are liable to immediate arrest for exercising
their psychic gifts, ever increasing numbers of people
attend Spiritualist gatherings, which more nearly
correspond to the early Apostolic Church services
than any other. What Spiritualism stands for is not
new, as all ancient literature, including the Bible,
contains many similar instances of people endowed
with supernormal gifts, which the Greeks termed
charismata, the early literature of the Apostolic
Church giving much space to advice on their development for the furtherance of knowledge of the after
life.

The noble-minded Socrates made claims to supernormal guidance, by means of clairaudience and clairvoyance, which were no different from those made by
Joan, and the story of Deborah, the Hebrew clairaudient woman medium, who led the Israelites to
victory guided by a voice, is a parellel case to what we
have just read, except that she was not destroyed by
the priests. As in the case of Elijah, the other-world
men and women who spoke to Joan were not in the
earthquake, the wind or the fire, but manifested by

[1] On over one hundred occasions the author has personally heard different
clairaudient mediums, in different brightly lighted halls throughout the
British Isles, giving to different people present, many intimate messages
relating to their friends or relations who have died. The mediums, who
were not in trance, and whose honesty is unquestioned, declared that those
"dead" people, who gave their full names, were standing beside them telling
them what to say. In this way more than two thousand different personal
messages, many long and detailed, were given, in the author's presence, to
people on earth, whom these mediums had never seen nor heard of before,
all of which were acknowledged at the time to be correct and only known
to the recipients.

means of the "still small voice". Clairaudience and clairvoyance were generally accepted until the Christian Church, in the 4th century, turned out the mediums and put priests in their place. Then the priests, to protect themselves and their false theology against nature's method of revealing the other world, used some barbarous texts in Exodus and Deuteronomy against witchcraft, and denounced all psychic gifts as coming from the devil, which decision was responsible for some quarter of a million innocent people being murdered under their direction.

Joan's military strategy and tactics, her skilful planning, are today acknowledged by experts to be quite beyond the range of a young girl's intellect. Her own explanation, that she was guided by others, who were unseen to all except herself, therefore remains the only possible solution of the problem. Probably one or more other-world men, who had a wider range of knowledge than was possessed by the French commanders, besides a gift for the military art, made use of Joan to accomplish the independence of what had once been their country, which they still loved and desired to see free from a foreign invader.

We do not immediately forget our earth life when we pass into the etheric world, and some for many years take as much interest in this earth as they do in their new surroundings. The mind does not die, it is the seat of memory; earth memories persist, and only slowly do we forget earth experiences. Only within recent times, due to the decline in clerical power, is this vast subject now being intelligently studied, with results which are as remarkable as they are astonishing.[1] Here, however, is not the place to enlarge further on this subject, and so we return to the closing stages of this devastating war in which Joan figured so brilliantly and all too briefly.

Joan's military achievements loosened England's hold on France, but much remained to be done before the country was cleared of the invaders. The withdrawal of the Duke of Burgundy from his alliance with England was the next step towards freedom, and then followed bitter strife in England, which country was quickly moving into civil war owing to the mental weakness of her king Henry VI.

England was beginning to reap the misery she had sown in France, and this encouraged her victim to even greater effort. In 1436 Charles VII entered Paris, and, with the help of a few able men, re-organised the army and administration of the country. Its finances, which were in a deplorable condition, were reformed and placed on a firmer basis, the large sums which were going into the coffers of the Church being diverted to national purposes.

Bands of brigands, made up of disbanded soldiers and other criminals, roamed France and made life impossible outside the walled towns, but, with the increase in the power of the Crown and an efficient army, they were gradually rounded up. This power, which the throne now won, was never lost, as the King obtained the right to tax the people to maintain a standing army, which was always available to crush

---

[1] *On the Edge of the Etheric* gives an account of the author's experiences with one of the most outstanding mediums of the present day, and also a scientific explanation of how they all conform to natural law. *The Psychic Stream* also contains many references to clairvoyance and clairaudience in ancient literature.

democratic aspirations. The English crown never secured this privilege, and, while France became saddled with an absolute monarchy until the revolution of 1789, England worked her way slowly towards parliamentary government.

In 1439 Normandy rebelled against English rule, and, with the help of the French army, Rouen was captured. At Formigny (1450) the English were again defeated and lost all northern France, with the exception of Calais. Then slowly the English possessions in the west were lost, and finally Bordeaux was captured. At Castillon, the last battle of this long-drawn-out struggle, the English were finally defeated in 1453, their archers being shot to pieces by the superior French artillery, and, though her knights charged and charged again, it was all in vain, as they could not win the day.

Thus ended the Hundred Years' War, and also the close intimacy which had existed between the two countries for nearly four centuries. The effect this had on England was to encourage the development of her own resources, her long and prosperous career as a manufacturing country commencing from this period. The devastation on the Continent reduced production, and she was forced in consequence to supply her own requirements, the manufacture of cloth being her first industrial enterprise, to become, next to agriculture, her greatest industry until the 19th century. Moreover, it created the wealth which built up her shipping, erected the luxurious manor houses and relieved the poverty of the cottage, besides spreading her trade all over the world.

Ten years of depression followed the conclusion

of hostilities, after which trade revived to bring into greater prominence both the mercantile and artisan classes, who, from now onwards, took an ever more important part in the economy of the nation. Across the Channel Charles VII, with the help of his faithful and able generals and statesmen, was now firmly settled on the throne. They it was, not the King, who carried France successfully through the difficulties, dangers and distress which come after every great conflict, and very slowly did she recover from the devastation. Only Calais remained in English hands, and the invaders returned home to lick their wounds and prepare for the evil time which was now to be their portion.

Burgundy, during these black days, had been no friend of France, and when the war finished she became her determined enemy. More than once the French must have regretted the action of their King John II in making Burgundy an independent duchy. The first duke inherited Flanders through his wife, and also other lands in these parts, which territory was further increased in 1420 by the third duke's invasion and occupation of Holland, Friesland, Zeeland and Hainault. Alsace and Lorraine now stood between Burgundy in the south and her new possessions in the north, and the first opportunity was taken to incorporate these two rich provinces within the Burgundian domains. This was done when Charles the Bold (1467–1477), Duke of Burgundy, the last great leader of the feudal barons, obtained Alsace in security for money he advanced to its overlord Sigismund of Austria, and then he took over the protectorship of Lorraine during the minority of its duke.

For centuries the French monarchy had been in danger from the great nobles, but never before had one become so powerful, the consequence being that the Burgundians were regarded with fear and distrust throughout all France. A new and powerful state was arising on her eastern frontier, and Louis XI (1461–1483), the crafty but shrewd King of France, now set about to frustrate its consolidation. First of all he reduced the French nobles to submission, and then he was free to act. England was still the enemy, but, owing to civil war at home, she could now do no more than levy blackmail by means of landing troops in France, and then withdrawing them when a cash indemnity was paid. So Louis made his preparations without having to look back across the Channel. Then the Burgundians foolishly became involved in a war with the Swiss, who invaded Alsace, and this brought about a rising in Lorraine. Here the Duke of Burgundy came up against the Swiss, to be beaten and slain at Nancy in 1477, leaving a daughter but no son to succeed him.

Now we have come to one of the important crossroads of history, where the way of destiny points in two opposite directions. To take one or the other means so little at the time, but the decision ultimately means so much to mankind. Small causes lead to tremendous effects, and here we are at the time when the future of Europe hung in the balance, the scale being moved by a woman's emotions. Would Mary, the Duke's daughter, marry Charles, the young heir to the French throne, or Maximilian of Austria, the son and heir of the Emperor Frederick III?

No woman had ever such a fateful decision to

make, as the balance of power in Europe depended on her choice of the man she would marry. With her went a large slice of northern Europe, a territory rich in minerals and with many prosperous towns: Brussels, the capital, gay and fashionable; Antwerp, about to flourish from the discovery of America; and others such as Bruges, Ghent, Ypres and Tournai.

Mary rejected the proposal of Louis XI that she become betrothed to his young son, deciding instead to marry Maximilian of Austria, the consequence being that her great inheritance was joined to that of the house of Hapsburg in 1477. Like a snowball its territory increased in size, as her son Philip married Joanna, who became Queen of Spain, whose son Charles inherited Spain and all her vast possessions in America. Thus was evolved the great empire of Charles V, who, like his grandfather Maximilian, was to wear the imperial crown of the Holy Roman Empire.

European history for sixty years centred round this great Spanish-Hapsburg empire, consisting of Spain, her colonies, the Netherlands, Luxemburg, Switzerland, Tyrol, Austria, part of Hungary, Bohemia and Silesia, and it would have been even greater had Burgundy, Picardy and Artois not reverted to the French crown because Charles the Bold had no male heir. Fortune also favoured France, as Maine, Anjou and Provence fell to her on the death of their ruler without male issue. Consequently, when Louis XI died in 1483, France, which for a time was so greatly threatened by the rise of the power of Burgundy, was compact, powerful and securely guarded on nearly all fronts. He it was who created a united France, which from now onwards was ruled by an absolute monarchy that unfortunately gave little regard to the true welfare of the nation.

Charles VIII (1483–1498), who succeeded his father, proposed marriage to Anne, the Duchess of Brittany. She accepted him, and this rounded off the French boundaries with the exception of the feudal state of Bourbon. Charles was a man of doubtful sanity, and, realising this, Louis XI, on his death-bed, entrusted the government to his daughter Anne, Duchess of Bourbon. During the eight years of her regency France benefited by her able rule. Her prudence, and high intelligence, overcame all difficulties, to end in the Crown completely triumphing over the feudal barons.

She was in truth a very remarkable woman, wise, just, honest and successful in her difficult task. So long as Charles reigned, and she ruled, the government of France was good, her territories compact, while her commerce and wealth increased. France had by now recovered from the ravages of the war with England, and was destined to play her part as a nation in future European affairs.

(2) The Kings of Europe Command and the Servile People Obey.

One thing is very clear from our study of mankind, up to the age we have now reached, and that is that man is a plundering, thieving, predatory creature. He will take what he wants if he can. Material things attract him more than mental wealth. Material wealth is much more real to him than knowledge,

He has no feeling about taking from others the product of their labour, their land, their animals and their wealth. He will kill or wound anyone who resists him in his thieving expeditions, and shows no pity or mercy to anyone who crosses his path.

Further, men of like mind band themselves together for mutual protection and greater strength, in their marauding raids, and are willing to be led by a master crook, who takes a larger proportion of the plunder than the lesser crooks, because he has the intelligence to think out the expeditions and plan their success. So long as he is successful he is always sure of followers who will do his bidding, and accept what he gives them. These men are called robbers, and the gang is known as a robber band.

Higher than the robber in the social scale is the super master-thief, the chief gangster, who organises these robber bands into an army under his direction, for the purpose of plundering large communities of people instead of isolated groups. When he has trained his men in the art of killing all who resist them, he sets out to capture a large tract of land, rich and fertile, which has been cultivated and contains houses, animals and the needs of a settled community. He is met by another similar army, in being for a like purpose if the opportunity arise, but ready to defend what is already possessed. A battle ensues, many are killed and wounded, but one side is able to disperse the other and victory follows. When men defend their possessions they are called the victims, but when they try to take other people's property they are called aggressors, though the victims often become the aggressors, and the aggressors the victims, according to their strength and the capacity of their leaders.

When the master crook was successful in conquering a country he became king, and in Christendom the Church gave him the title of "Defender of the Faith", or "Very Christian Majesty" or "Eldest Son of the Church". When he succeeded in conquering several countries he became emperor. When he was an outstanding criminal and impressed the people with his spectacular successes, he was honoured in after years with the title of "The Great" after his name.

His generals were known as Dukes, the other leaders being called Marquises, Bishops, Earls, Counts, Barons and Knights, and the land and wealth stolen was parcelled out between them, and the entire gang of thieves, in proportion to their rank.[1] The dukes, earls, counts and barons were called nobles, the bishops spiritual princes, the knights were the gentry, and the rank and file became small landowners, generally known as freemen, those who were conquered becoming bondmen to those who had secured the spoils.

Most of the common people were consequently bondmen, but this historical fact seems to be little known today, as the vast majority in our own times are quite ignorant of the way their ancestors lived during the Christian era. An example of this ignorance was the assertion, prominently displayed in a leading English newspaper, in October 1946, by a well-known man who was writing about the outcasts in India.

---

[1] The rates of pay per day for the army which besieged Calais in 1346 was as follows: Dukes 10*s*., Earls and Bishops 6*s*. 8*d*., Barons 4*s*., Knights 2*s*., Esquires 1*s*., Archers from 3*d*. to 6*d*., Gunners 3*d*., and the rank and file 2*d*., all of which had a much greater purchasing power than it has now.

With much pride he remarked that there had never been any outcasts in Christendom, because such treatment was contrary to the Christian faith, and doubtless his readers accepted this as the truth.

He evidently had never heard of Christian slavery, of Jews in ghettos, of the negroes in America, of serfs, villains, heretics, infidels and "the damned heathen", all of whom were regarded as outcasts by Christians up to within recent times. However, to the ignorant and the foolish, the name Christian can only stand for everything they consider is good. Such is the effect of intensive Christian propaganda on the childish mind; it withers the intellect, which accepts but never thinks nor reasons when considering religious matters.

The people as a whole—that is to say the vast majority until our own times—had no voice or say in what went on. They did as they were told, and, if they did not, were killed or imprisoned. The land they lived in was ruled by someone they never appointed, and, at his death, it was left to a son or daughter's husband to rule or dispose of as he pleased. The eldest son generally followed his father, but, at times, his brothers claimed what they considered was their birthright, and each gathered together followers who were promised their share of the spoils, if successful, in the fight which followed. The daughters passed their inheritance on to their husbands and sons, and in consequence large areas were sometimes ruled by men who knew nothing of their people, not even their language.

Such, then, was the state of things wherever kings and emperors ruled, but the great majority, then as now, preferred a settled form of life to taking from others without producing. It was more comfortable, and they did not grudge the adventurers the excitement of war, when they could stay at home with their families and make a living by hard work without risking their lives. Circumstance produced civilisation, and civilisation produced morality. Fear produced conscience, and conscience produced the virtues. The greatest number consequently became peaceful, hardworking serfs, anxious only to make a livelihood and live their family life as best they could. They knew nothing about what is called politics, the grouping of people together under one single direction, or war, and the training or direction of armies, they being equally ignorant about the world in general, their travelling consisting of a pilgrimage to see the bones of some dead saint.

This, then, is how we find Europe at the beginning of the 14th century. Those whose ancestors had been master crooks are now kings, and the descendants of their leading men are dukes, earls, barons and knights, who now conduct the affairs of their various domains. These are passed on from father to son, or from daughter to husband or son; the freemen pay the tithes and taxes demanded, the kings and nobles live in as much luxury as they can, and the bonded masses plod on making a bare living, lacking everything connected with decency and comfort.

Europe, including England, at the opening of the 14th century was controlled by the descendants of those who were successful thieves of earlier times. Now that they had all the land, and its revenues, they carefully protected their possessions against other thieves, but gave little thought to the condition of the people who produced the wealth. The Church had likewise come off well by encouraging, and following after, the conquering armies, as, by working on the fear of the unknown, which is latent in everyone, it had secured a priority everywhere over the people's earnings in the form of tithes. The Church and State had now the same policy, to protect what they had won, and keep the people from thinking about anything beyond their everyday affairs.

Keeping this background always in mind, we shall now roam round Europe, and see how other lands are faring since we left them in the previous chapter. England and France, we have discovered, acquired national unity by slowly consolidating round the throne. In Germany exactly the opposite happened, as, after the collapse of the Hohenstaufens, the nobles obtained the power, and the country was divided into petty states under the direction of a number of noble families, such as the Wettins, Welfs, Wittelsbachs, Hapsburgs and Hohenzollerns. These noble houses and the Church elected the Holy Roman Emperor, always referred to by historians as the Emperor. Thus there was no continuous hereditary rule in Germany, and the nobles were able to keep their feudal power in their own hands. The nobles, and not the Emperor, were the hereditary rulers of the German states, it being their actions which make up German history, and not so much the doings of the Emperor.

In 1273 Rudolf of Hapsburg became the Emperor, and it was he who laid the foundation of the Austrian Empire. This effort took up all his attention, and so he abandoned his sovereignty over Italy, his place being taken by the Pope, who now took possession of Tuscany and Sicily. King Ottokar of Bohemia had occupied Austria and neighbouring lands, and refused to do homage to Rudolf. War followed, when Ottokar was killed in the Battle of Marchfeld in 1278, and his possessions in Germany were taken by Rudolf. Austria, from now onwards, remained a separate state, to be often an imposing and dominating influence on European affairs.

The next emperor was Louis of Bavaria, whose reign was embittered by civil war and a long-drawn-out quarrel with the Pope, who finally excommunicated him. His successor was Charles, King of Bohemia, who became emperor in 1347, as Charles IV, and published what is known as "the Golden Bull" for the purpose of regularising the political life of Germany, though no attempt was made to unify the people, the law or the government. It established the method of election, declaring that the choice of emperor was to be determined by seven electors. He made Bohemia the strongest state of Central Europe, its territories reaching to the Danube in the south and close to the Baltic in the north.

Under his rule trade flourished, the people prospered, and the desire for knowledge increased to such a degree that he established the University of Prague, which became one of the most important seats of the arts and learning in Europe, drawing students from all over Germany and Poland. Thus the way was prepared for the Renaissance, and here it was that John Huss, one of its professors, who was greatly influenced by the opinions of John Wycliffe, helped to lay the foundation for the Reformation.

Charles IV was succeeded by his son Wenzel (1378–1400), a drunkard, who undid some of his father's great achievements, but he shielded the Hussites from the attacks of the Church, and indirectly was responsible for the foundation of Leipzig University. Like all Bohemians, he disliked the Germans, and excluded them from having any authority at Prague University, an action which made them leave and found their own at Leipzig. There the age-old hatred of the Germans for the Czechs was poured out, and their unorthodox religious opinions ridiculed, to deepen the intense racial animosity which is always to be found when two uncongenial races intermingle within the same area.

Wenzel was followed by his brother Sigismund (1410–1437), who, on becoming King of Bohemia, adopted an attitude of such bitter enmity towards the Hussites that he was driven out of the country. He was instrumental in the death of Huss, as he broke his promise to the reformer that he would be safe if he went to Constance, where he was murdered. Hateful as the Bohemians were to the Austrians, yet, according to the ways of those times, they were incorporated within the Austrian Empire at Sigismund's death because his daughter Elizabeth married Albert II of Austria and brought Bohemia with her. The Austrian Empire thus grew large and powerful, as much by various fortunate marriages as by conquest, to embrace finally within its frontiers various different races holding diverse political and religious beliefs.

Consequently the Hapsburgs flourished, so much so that from the election of Albert II as emperor in 1438 onwards until the time of Napoleon, who destroyed the Empire, only one emperor was elected outside their house. Thus it enjoyed an almost unbroken succession of imperial rule for about four hundred years.

The Hapsburg Empire was not sufficiently strong to protect the coast towns and ports of northern Germany from enemies from overseas. Pirates made the seas unsafe, and seaborne trade was carried on with difficulty. Consequently, Lubeck, Hamburg, and seventy other towns in these parts, joined themselves together for mutual protection under the name of The Hanseatic League, which union greatly increased their prosperity, as it secured the monopoly in the sale of furs, timber, hemp, pitch and corn. Such a combination gave great offence to the merchants of Norway, Sweden and Denmark, who fought it fiercely until finally the league faded into insignificance in the 15th century, leaving as a legacy to Britain the word Sterling, by which name her currency is now known. This word is a corruption of Easterling, the name the English gave to the prosperous Hanseatic merchant, with his business fortress where now is Cannon Street Station, who, to them, represented wealth and everything synonymous with sound finance.

Farther to the north-east in Prussia developments were taking place. Mention has already been made of this country, and how the Pope sent the Teutonic Knights to rob the inhabitants of their land, win the people for Christ, and their tithes for the Church. In every country in Europe the cross accompanied the sword, and the difference between the sword and the cross is slight, because it all depends how one holds it. To the Church it was a very effective weapon, whichever way it was held, and great was the material gain therefrom to the coffers of the Papal Treasury.

Prussia was now a Christian country contributing its quota to the Church, and the Christian German knights had done their work so well that Germans now owned the land in place of the former Pagan Slavs. The Teutonic Knights ruled the country until they were overwhelmed by Poland in 1410 at the Battle of Tannenberg, when most of their possessions were incorporated into those of the victor. There was no strong united Germany in those days, in fact German influence east of the Oder was now seriously threatened, and this reminds us of the words of Pope Pius II to the German people some years later:—

"You might be masters of the world as heretofore, were it not for your division of sovereignty, to which wise men have long traced all your disasters."

Unity, we would say today, has been far more disastrous to Germany than her division into principalities, but Pius was also right, and Germany's unity came too late for her to have the place in the sun to which she believes she was destined. The German people were hundreds of years behind France and Britain in securing unified government, and, when at last it was obtained, they reverted to the methods of the Middle Ages in their different attempts to make up for lost time, all of which has now ended in her second great defeat within twenty-six years, to the accompaniment of misery, destitution and enormous loss of life and wealth to all Europe.

The Danes, Swedes and Norwegians were the last

to adopt the Christian faith. Under Canute they were united, and under him they became Christians because he accepted Christianity. This unity did not last beyond his life-time, as at his death in 1035 they broke up into three separate kingdoms, Denmark, Sweden and Norway. Under Waldemar III (1340–1375) Denmark became a strong power, a position which was maintained by his daughter Margaret, who, in a successful war with Sweden and Norway, reunited the three countries. Norway and Denmark remained united for some time, but Sweden broke away and became hostile to the other two sister states.

In the middle of the 15th century, north-western Europe consisted of the Kingdom of Denmark and Norway, including the Orkney, Shetland and Faeroe islands. The Kingdom of Sweden embraced Finland, south of which was Prussia. The position in Russia is more difficult to explain, but, if we draw a line due south from Archangel to Rostov, we shall be able to visualise it. West of this line were the Republic of Novgorod, the Duchy of Moscow, the Duchy of Lithuania, the Kingdom of Poland and the Kingdom of Hungary. East of the line was the Kipchak Empire, made up of the Mongol Tartars, who had settled there, as recorded in the previous chapter, and founded a separate kingdom of their own, to become known as the Golden Horde.

From the time when Rurik the Northman established himself as ruler of Novgorod in 862, some approach to settled order gradually developed over the vast area now called Russia, so named because in those days the Swedish influence was so strong that the word Ruotsi, the Finnish for Swede, became Russia, the name of the country the Swedes first civilised. These hardy northmen completely dominated the land from the Baltic to the Black Sea, Novgorod and Kiev being their trading centres, the rivers their means of communication, and the docile Slavs their slaves. Six times they failed to capture Constantinople, and once they tried to conquer Bulgaria, the Emperor in Constantinople being glad to give them trading concessions to keep them away.

The ferocious fratricide Vladimir (980–1015) holds an important place in Russian history, because it was he who Christianised the country. This barbarian, in one of his marauding expeditions, entered a town in the Crimea belonging to the Eastern Empire, whence he commanded the Emperor to hand him over his daughter in marriage or everyone would be massacred. This demand was granted on the understanding that he was baptised a Christian. Accordingly he went to Constantinople to marry the princess and become a member of the Church.

We remember how impressed Charlemagne was with all he saw in Rome, the relics of the cross, and hundreds of other fakes, besides the impressive services, the singing, and the mysticism surrounding the religious ceremonials. Vladimir, on his visit to Constantinople, was equally influenced by its handsome buildings, the beautiful statues and paintings, the lavish decorations, carvings, mosaics and colouring in the churches, the shrines and altars bathed in candlelight, and the weird chanting of the priests. Relics of everything sacred abounded, and this ignorant savage was so dumbfounded that he could not rest until priests had accompanied him back to

Kiev, to set up the entire ecclesiastical organisation there.

If Vladimir's conversion had made him a better man, the way it came about could be passed over, but it had no such effect, and he remained a monster of iniquity to the end. His record is terrible—murder, cruelty, vice, blackmail and everything wicked continued up to the last—but all was forgiven the prince who had made Kiev a city of churches, and had increased the influence, the power and the wealth of the Church by forcing the Russians to become Christians by the edge of the sword. So, in spite of the fact that he was nothing better than an ignorant, wicked, fiendish brute, whose harem consisted of 3500 concubines, the Church, at his death, made him a saint in heaven, and thus added the name of another scoundrel to the Christian pantheon of gods.

So much for Vladimir, but we must not overlook the fact that his conversion to Christianity was a very important historical event, just as outstanding as was Charlemagne's acceptance of the Christian faith. The fact that Christianity and Paganism were originally twin brothers meant that when the former replaced the latter, Pagan civilisation and culture marched forward under the Christian name. It was not Christian doctrines and beliefs that civilised Europe, but the Greeks and Italians who passed on the civilisation and culture they had inherited from their Pagan ancestors. The Church organisation at first acted as the carrier of their civilisation, but, when the trade routes were opened, commerce took its place, spreading through Europe the ancient civilisation of Greece and Rome.

Charlemagne introduced Roman civilisation into

western Europe, and Vladimir introduced Greek civilisation into Russia, with this difference: that in the west the Church and State were separate organisations, whereas in the east the Church and State were one. In the west a conflict between the two was not only possible but of constant occurrence, to lead to the Reformation and the liberty we now enjoy. In Russia, on the other hand, to reform the Church meant the overthrow of the Tzar, and, until that happened, as the result of the Revolution of 1917, the corrupt Russian Church flourished, and kept the people in servile ignorance and misery long after much of Europe had freed itself of Church rule.

Great as has been the evil influence of the Christian Church throughout Europe, Russia, as much as any other country, has been its victim to a greater degree than some others. There, as in Spain and the Balkans, its grip lasted longer than it did amongst more enlightened people, to frustrate all progress and reform, whereas after the Reformation those countries called Protestant slowly but surely broke down its deadening influence, to become finally free and independent.

The house of Ruric supplied the princes who ruled over the Russian city states, but, after the death of Jaroslav, the legislator, in 1054, endless family quarrels sapped its strength. Then happened, about two hundred years later, the crowning catastrophe for Russia, the Mongol Tartar invasion consisting of some 500,000 disciplined and trained warriors on horseback, against whom the Russians were powerless. These nomads, who ravaged and burned as they passed by, were nominally Moslems, and their chief, the Khan of the Golden Horde, ruled óver the Kipchak Empire. As we read in the last pages of the previous chapter, Kiev, Moscow, and other cities, were subdued, and forced to pay tribute to the Khan, while their rulers, who were either Russian dukes or Tartar governors, were made responsible for its collection.

For two hundred years the Tartars dominated Russia from their capital Sarai on the Volga, and, though the Russians retained their religion and customs, they were no better than bondmen to their Asiatic masters. Finally, the Grand Duke of Moscow so gained the confidence of the Khan that he obtained a more favoured position than the other tributaries, and, when the Grand Duke Ivan III (1462–1505), known as Ivan the Great, became the ruler of Moscow, he felt himself strong enough to throw off the Mongol yoke, refusing to pay further tribute.

Thus was established the Kingdom of Moscow, and, as the Turks were now in Constantinople, Ivan appropriated the coat of arms of the Eastern Empire, the double-headed eagle, claiming to be the successor of the Caesars because of his marriage with Zoe of the imperial house. Next he subjugated the Republic of Novgorod in the north, and thus laid the foundation for the Russian Empire, his grandson, Ivan the Terrible (1533–1584), a cruel and brutal tyrant, claiming not only the eastern imperial title but also to be the head of the Eastern Christian Church, taking the title of Tzar, the Russian for Caesar.

Now that Constantinople was in Moslem hands, Moscow became the centre of the Greek Church, the Tzar becoming its divine head and responsible only to God, the Metropolitan Bishop of Moscow becoming the Pope of the East. Only the priests and monks were exempt from taxation, and they only profited from the ignorance and superstition of the people. At a time when the most intelligent of the inhabitants of Europe were partially emerging from the slough into which theology had kept the Continent for over eleven hundred years, Russia was plunging ever deeper into the mire of ignorance, to become so begrimed with superstition that until the 18th century she was looked upon by all civilised countries as a land of barbarians with whom diplomatic relations were impossible. There, churches, monasteries and convents rapidly multiplied, and every despotic act had the support of the Church, which, in no instance, ever considered the common man. This soul-destroying rule of the priest, who acted along with the tyrannical nobles, shackled the people, who were only able to throw off this bondage within our time, to the consternation of the rest of Christendom.

While the Russians became the subjects of an absolute monarch, the Poles, who were also Slavs, and had a language similar to the Russians, became subject to independent nobles, their king never becoming an absolute monarch. This want of unity made Poland the prey of Russia, Germany and Austria until she finally disappeared altogether off the map in the 18th century. Poland adopted orthodox Catholic Christianity, and this widened the difference between the Poles and the Russians, but one thing she was spared: she never became subject to the Mongols. In Ukrainia the people were Christian nomads, known as Cossacks, who were continually raiding Poland, and constant warfare continued between them and the Polish nobles, whose serfs, moreover, took every opportunity to join the invaders and partake of their free and adventurous life.

Throughout the 13th century, in the fertile valleys of what we now call Switzerland, prosperous towns, such as Zurich and Berne, were developing, which gave allegiance to different overlords, but everywhere there prevailed a spirit of independence, helped by the strength of their mountain fortress. Cantons evolved round the towns, which joined together for mutual protection. This action angered the Hapsburgs, who laid claim to these districts, and, in 1315, Leopold attacked them at Schwyz, only to be defeated, a victory for the Swiss which gave the name to the country they were hammering out on the anvil of war.

For over one hundred years the Swiss fought stubbornly and successfully against the Hapsburgs to secure their independence. This conflict finally produced a close Swiss confederation in 1648 that broke off all its connections with Austria, and later established itself in 1798 as the Helvetic Republic. Switzerland was the first state in Europe to ignore the old aristocratic ruling class, and secure political and religious liberty for the people within her frontiers, thus becoming the pioneer of democratic government.

Further south in Italy, we find quite a different state of affairs, a position more like the political condition of Greece in the 4th century B.C. Italy was not a kingdom, and there was no national unity. It was a land of individual city states, having their own government with only two exceptions. The Kingdom of Naples stood by itself, with its monarch supported by all the old feudal institutions. We remember how, after the fall of the Hohenstaufens, Charles of Anjou, brother of Saint Louis of France, was made King of Naples and Sicily by Pope Urban IV, only to have his troops massacred by the enraged inhabitants of Sicily.

The royal house of Aragon then accepted the crown of Sicily, and this started a bitter feud which lasted for two hundred years between the kings of Naples and Sicily, to end eventually in the two kingdoms being joined (as the result of a marriage) under Alfonso, who reigned for twenty-three years until 1458. The crimes and intrigues of the two royal courts during these years of rivalry need not here be recounted, as they followed closely to the Christian way of life of those days, so much so that if the record had been other than sordid it would have been an event well worth mentioning.

The Holy See was still situated at Avignon in France, but the States of the Church remained, occupying the entire centre of Italy, bounded on the south by the Kingdom of Naples and the State of Florence in the north. Rome enjoyed an independent municipal government, but it was a city in strange contrast to the one which flourished during the days of the Roman Empire. It had neither peace nor unity, and this state of affairs ended in a revolution (1347) led by Rienzi, a bitter opponent of the aristocracy whose rule and evil lives at last made the people rebel. In 1354 this eloquent reformer was murdered, and his efforts to raise the city to its once proud position came to nothing. Twenty years later the Holy See was once again centred in Rome, when the Papacy returned from its exile in France.

Against the abuses and evil of his time Girolamo Savonarola (1452–1498) shines as a light in the surrounding darkness. Amidst the corruption of this age, when the Church ruled supreme, he alone stood for righteousness, and few names in Italian history give out a greater lustre. He boldly denounced the prevailing corruption in both Church and State, and thundered forth the prediction of heavenly wrath. His life was in constant danger, but his influence in Florence rapidly increased, so much so that the priests decided that he must be put to death. Amidst great popular indignation he was arrested, to be cruelly tortured day after day on the rack, and then, weakened in body and mind, he was burned at the stake along with a number of his faithful followers. Thus did the Church stamp out righteousness, because all the reformers in Italy now scattered and fled.

In the Italian cities there was a hum of active trade, but the rivalry between them was intense. Within each city, party fought against party, morality amongst all classes was at zero, and, politically, everything was fluid and unstable. The citizens were too much occupied in their own affairs to protect their boundaries, and in consequence each city hired mercenary troops for its protection, many of whom were foreigners. Florence is an interesting example of an Italian city state of those days, and we have to go back to the city states of Greece to find a parallel. Politically the people swayed between oligarchy and democracy, both of which ended in tyranny. Parties formed and broke up quickly, and, after an attempted revolution in 1382, the rich and powerful trade guilds became stronger, to succeed eventually in bringing some order out of chaos.

Two families, the Medici and Albizzi, were keen rivals for power, and, after Maso and Rinaldo Albizzi had been the uncrowned rulers of Florence from 1382 to 1434, Cosimo de Medici established himself in control, this great family ruling Florence for nearly two hundred years. He brought peace, security and prosperity to this beautiful city, where, from now onwards, the arts and literature took root and flourished. Here, as elsewhere in Italy in the 15th century, masterpieces in painting, sculpture and literature were being produced, because we are now at the beginning of that great new era, known as the Renaissance, about which more will be said before this chapter closes.

Milan, farther to the north and situated in the plain of Lombardy, was ruled by brutal force, first by the house of Visconti, and then by the Sforza dynasty, who have left behind them a terrible record of crime and cruelty. Venice, on the Adriatic, as the result of the Crusades, had greatly increased in wealth, and her ships sailed the seas far and wide. Gradually the rich families monopolised political power, they being keen on the prosperity of their city, and they displayed great ability in its management. Under their rule the city remained a prosperous republic with a stable government.

The Doge (meaning, the leader), to begin with, held the reins of power, but, by the creation of the Grand Council, consisting of the nobles, this was curtailed, and the people were excluded from any participation in the government of the city. Venice consequently developed into an oligarchy, which form of exclusive rule became more restricted by the establishment of the Council of Ten. This was given full executive power, thus making the Doge a mere figure-head.

Venice now developed into a state by defeating Genoa, Padua, Vicenza and Verona, thus leaving Milan as her chief rival. Her fortunes, however, were soon to change through the capture of Constantinople by the Turks in 1453, when she lost her influence and trade in the eastern Mediterranean. The discovery of America also diverted commerce to the ports farther west, which important event, and its effect on European trade, will be told a few pages farther on.

(3) Spain Under Christian Rule.

In Chapter IX we read the interesting story of Spain under Moslem rule, and how gradually the Spanish Moslems were crushed by the combined attacks of the Berbers from Morocco and the Christians from northern Spain. Weakened by the invasions from Africa, Moslem Spain eventually succumbed to the Christians, who had by now established two powerful states in the north, Aragon and Castile. Ferdinand I (1037–1067) commenced the consolidation of Castile by driving out the Moslems, and this was completed by his son Alfonso, who made Toledo his capital. Ramiro I (1035–1063) likewise cleared Aragon of the Moslems, and then Aragon and Castile united to attack Navarre, which they divided between them.

Up to now Christian Spain had been isolated from the rest of Europe, but the all-powerful Pope Gregory VII (1073–1085) was determined that this must cease, and plans were laid to bring her under the closer direction of the Church. From this time onwards Spain became the most faithful and servile of all her subjects, Aragon agreeing to pay tribute, and Castile finally doing likewise from fear of isolation from the Mother Church. The Holy See had, however, further and more ambitious plans, namely the gathering of all Spain within the Christian fold, which meant the expulsion of the entire Moslem and Jewish population. Successive popes did not cease their holy war against them, Innocent III being the most aggressive, until all Spain eventually came under Christian domination, and paid tribute to Rome.

From the 11th century onwards for the next two hundred years, Spain was a bloody battle-ground, as the Moslems did not relinquish their hold without a fierce struggle. Moreover, the Christians were at constant war between themselves, and this greatly delayed the final issue. For a time the Christian states united under Alfonso I (1104–1134), but this did not last for long, as civil war followed, and Aragon and Navarre separated from Castile and Galicia. When Alfonso died Navarre declared its independence, but we must pass over these interstate quarrels, and briefly consider the history of Christian Spain as a whole, until the country eventually found unity in the 15th century.

This story centres round the states of Castile and Aragon, which, during the 13th, 14th and 15th centuries, dominated Christian Spain, and ultimately, when they united in 1479, drove out the Infidel. To tell of their civil wars, quarrels, achievements and atrocities during this period would be wearisome. Its historical interest lies mainly in the long-drawn-out struggle between the Christians and the Moslems, who now came to be called Moors, as they in turn were dominated from Morocco because Moslem Spain had by now become part of the Moorish state, the Sultan of Morocco being its overlord. With its centre of power removed across the Straits to Africa, Moorish Spain lost its cohesion, and this gave the Christians their long-awaited opportunity, but it was not until the year 1212 that the issue was decided.

Then, at the important Battle of Las Navas de Tolosa, the fate of Spain was settled. There the Christian army, under the lead of Alfonso VIII, and drawn from Castile, Aragon, Leon, Navarre and Portugal, with large numbers of foreign adventurers gathered together by the Pope from Germany, France and England, gained a decisive victory. From now onwards the triumphs of the Christian armies were unbroken and complete, Cordova being captured in 1236. Then followed the conquest of Seville and other cities, which brought the frontier of Castile down to the southern coast, when Cadiz was occupied. Christian persecution drove out most of the Moors, who found refuge either in Granada, their last stronghold, or in Africa.

Meanwhile Aragon had taken an important part in the struggle, her accomplished sailors being responsible for driving out the Moslems in 1229 from their long-held stronghold, the Balearic Islands. Then she occupied Valencia and Murcia, the last of the Moorish territories in Spain except Granada. Now it was that the Iberian peninsula, with this single exception, was divided between three Christian states, Castile, Aragon and the Kingdom of Portugal, which latter country has been able to maintain its frontiers with Spain, with little change, throughout the centuries, from those times to the present day.

From the latter half of the 13th century the crusading energy of the Spaniards came to a sudden halt, and the Moors were allowed to retain Granada for another two centuries. Here they were strongly entrenched, as its natural defences made invasion difficult. Moreover, for the next two hundred years, Castile and Aragon found their own internal troubles sufficient to engage their energies, and this brought to an end, for the time being, the unity of the Christians for a common cause. Granada had likewise its own internal trouble, in one perpetual struggle for power between members of the same family. Even during its final fight for existence, when the only hope lay in unity, the city's cause was sacrificed to the jealous rivalry of three claimants to the throne.

Both Castile and Aragon now evolved a constitution under Church domination. The religious character of the war had enabled the priests to obtain even greater powers than they had secured throughout the rest of Europe, but the war also increased the strength of the nobles at the expense of the monarchy. These two classes met together, along with the elected deputies of the chief towns, to form the national assembly of each kingdom, the Cortes as it was called. Its functions were the approval of legislation and taxation when the monarch required this additional authority, but, as both the nobles and the clergy were exempt from taxation, this question interested the deputies only, who, on more than one occasion, debated on it alone.

Unlike the English Parliament, there was this wide gap between the aristocracy and the people. The priests and nobles were two classes apart from the rest of the community, and there was a complete absence of any class like the knights of the shire— the gentry as they came to be called in England— to form a link between the burgesses and the nobles. The nobles, with their judicial powers, and the priests, who administered ecclesiastical jurisdiction, were the real rulers under the King of all but the large cities, where the administration of justice and local affairs were in the hands of the elected corporations. In theory there existed in all cases the right of appeal to the Crown, but this was rarely exercised, and always resisted by the priests and nobles whenever the monarch attempted to assert his authority.

Such, then, was Spain during this period, and it remained divided until it became one by the marriage of Ferdinand of Aragon and Isabella of Castile, who ascended the united throne in 1479. Each province, however, retained its own institutions and laws, just as happened when James VI of Scotland became the King of England. Their first care was to reform the existing laws and system of government, the curbing of the power of the nobles being their chief aim. Trade was encouraged by breaking down the customs barrier between Castile and Aragon, while, at the same time, the currency was reformed, all of which added greatly to the prosperity of the country.

Both sovereigns were loyal subjects of the Church, and the political unity of the nation came from all having a common belief. No freedom of thought or speech was possible, and, much to the horror and indignation of many who had inherited the tolerance of the unorthodox Moslems, Pope Sixtus IV, a man notorious for his corruption, decreed the establishment of the Inquisition in 1478, under the presidency of Torquemada, the Himmler of those days. The activity of the Holy Inquisition, under the direction of this priestly Inquisitor-General, was primarily directed against the Jews, whose obstinate adherence to their faith, in spite of persistent persecution, greatly angered the Spanish priests. Finally, despairing of their conversion, they had them ultimately expelled from the country in 1492, thus depriving it of many industrious inhabitants.

From now onwards torture was applied to all having liberal political or religious opinions, and this continued until Napoleon's generals, when in Spain, put a temporary end to this ghastly institution founded by Saint Ambrose in the 4th century. The Spaniards thus exchanged the liberal and tolerant rule of the Moslems for the cruel intolerance of the Church, and, from now onwards, they have been its abject slaves, all having an enlightened outlook being tortured, murdered or banished.

Two other important events occurred in this reign: the discovery of America, which gave to Spain a great colonial empire, and, in the same year, the capture of Granada (1492), which followed after ten years of war. The Moors, who fought with the courage of despair, received very lenient terms from the Crown, being permitted to retain their religion, laws, customs and language. This, however, was more than the priests could countenance, and soon they obtained a law that all Moslems must either become Christians or perish, the result being the bloody massacre of all who retained their old beliefs.

So it came about that all Spain became a Christian country, and, on the highest point in Granada, arose a great silver cross to symbolise that Spain was at last freed from the hated Infidel. If the Moslems could not remain in person, they certainly left behind them some of their culture and learning, drawn originally from the great Moslem universities of Baghdad, Basra, Kufa and Cairo, and this spread to France and Italy, to develop into the Renaissance. Further, they left behind them their mills for manufacturing paper, which trade Italy developed until the discovery of printing made it a widespread industry. Finally, they left behind them soap, a substance the Christians needed more than anything else, as, so far, their godliness had gone far in advance of their cleanliness.

The history of Spain up to this time again emphasises the powerful influence which religion has had on both the great and small issues that determine the happiness or misery of mankind. Here we find in one country three different religious beliefs, and the adherents of each were firmly convinced that they alone had been favoured with the truth, all who thought differently being damned sinners. The Jews believed that God, on Mount Sinai, had revealed to them only his message for mankind, the Christians that to them alone this revelation had come in Palestine, and the Moslems that it had been given to them

solely in Arabia. Nevertheless, if we remember what
we read in earlier chapters, each revelation came about
by the same kind of psychic experience. Though the
origin was the same, the time, place and circumstance
were different, the consequence being that three
different religions evolved whose adherents believed
that they alone were the chosen people.

Only during the unorthodox Moslem age was
Spain free and tolerant. Then Jew, Moslem and
Christian were free to think and worship as they
pleased. When the orthodox Moors arrived, the
unorthodox Moslems, the Christians and the Jews
suffered, and this was followed by the Christian conquests, when both Jews and Moslems either perished
or were banished. Such is the curse of ignorance,
because the Kingdom of Heaven or the Limbo of
Hell is within us, they being the result of our
thoughts. It does not in the least matter what we
believe about the hereafter, but it matters very much
how we live and think on earth, because by thought
we create our own happiness both here and hereafter.
That, however, was beyond the mental range of those
days, as it still is to many in our own times.

(4) Exploration and Colonisation Beyond the Sea.

The discovery that a magnetised needle on a pivot
pointed to the magnetic north was certainly one of the
great, though not the greatest, discoveries of man.
Who first realised this fact we know not, but the
Chinese now claim to have known it for over four
thousand years. They made use of this knowledge

for travelling by land, but not until A.D. 300 did they use it at sea. How this knowledge came to Europe is unknown, but some say that the compass was known in the 12th century, and that the priests prevented its use because it was an invention of the devil.

Others think that Marco Polo, about whom we shall be reading, brought it from China. Though it is doubtful how Europeans came by the knowledge, it is probable that without it the world would not have been discovered and explored by sea. To the compass we owe our knowledge of the geography of the world, and all that this has meant to mankind over the past five hundred years. Instead of hugging the shore, and being guided by the stars, sailors felt safe, with the help of this little needle, in setting a course away from land, as they knew that they could keep on a straight course and reach their destination. Before, however, European sailors made use of this invention a great land explorer brought to Europe some very startling information.

In a naval engagement between the fleets of Venice and Genoa, in 1298, one of the 7000 prisoners captured by Genoa was a Venetian, named Marco Polo, who greatly enthralled his captors by his travel tales. These stories were all written down at the time, and they form a remarkable narrative which came to be known as *The Travels of Marco Polo*. It was then the greatest book of travel so far written, completely changing all past conceptions of the size of the earth, and it influenced Columbus to set out to find the world Polo said he had visited. Polo journeyed to China with his father and uncle, who were

Venetian merchants of repute living in Constantinople. They started off in 1271 to Palestine, and thence to Armenia, Mesopotamia and the Persian Gulf. There they did not take to the sea, as we would expect, but, instead, turned north through Persia, and then eastwards through Afghanistan, along the north of Tibet, until they reached the source of the Hwang-ho (Yellow) River, which they travelled down to find their way eventually to Peking.

There they were welcomed by the Great Khan, and Polo was given an official position, being sent on several missions to south-west China. He described wide rolling plains of fertile country, good hostelries on the way, vineyards, Buddhist monasteries and abbeys, thriving trade in silks and cloths, and a constant succession of cities and towns. Then he told of Burmah, to which land he went on another mission for the Great Khan, of its elephants and forests, of Japan and its wealth in gold, and lastly, most wonderful of all, of Christians in China, evidently referring to the Nestorian Christians, to whom reference has already been made. Then comes the story of their return home by sea, by way of south China, when they visited Sumatra and India, whence they returned home to Constantinople by land.

What a remarkable story for those days, when people thought that the world was flat and ended on the horizon or thereabouts! Nevertheless it was true in all essentials. These travellers took three and a half years to get to China, and there they stayed for about sixteen years, when they began to long for home. Their return voyage occupied two years, and when they arrived home, dressed in Tartar clothes, they were refused admission. It was some time before they could prove their identity, but, when they produced a great display of diamonds, rubies, sapphires, emeralds and other precious stones their tale came to be believed. This started people thinking that the world was not only something quite different from what it seemed to be, but that there were developed civilisations outside of Europe and the Middle East. Polo made adventurers ardent to see the wonders he described, and, two hundred years later, his experiences made Columbus believe that he could more quickly reach these rich lands by way of the Atlantic. Marco Polo made Christendom sit up and think!

Prince Henry of Portugal (1394–1460), surnamed the "Navigator", was the European pioneer of exploration by sea, and it is to his enlightened foresight and perseverance that the great maritime discoveries of the next hundred years are due. In those days the young Portuguese nobles were engaged in seeking new opponents from neighbouring lands to overthrow on the tilting-ground, and the priests, with their army of militant monks, sworn to exterminate all unbelievers everywhere, were intent on following up the slaughter of the Moslems in North Africa, where they had recently been driven from Portugal.

So the Prince did not find much encouragement from his contemporaries in his endeavour to seek out new lands across the sea, but his enthusiasm was still further roused when, on an expedition to North Africa, he heard of the prosperous and learned cities of Morocco, and of a rich land south of the Sahara inhabited only by negroes. To discover this new world beyond the desert, which hitherto had been taken to mark the southern extremity of this earth, now became his ambition.

As the son of John I, King of Portugal, by Philippa, daughter of John of Gaunt, and as Grand Master of the Order of Christ, he had the influence of the Court, and the great wealth of the Order to sustain him in any effort to convert the heathen to the knowledge of Christ. First of all, however, he had to find these souls to be saved, and this meant the discovery of the coast of Africa, which was his immediate purpose, and then, if fortune favoured him, he hoped to find the sea route to India, which was his goal. So he devoted himself to the study of astronomy and mathematics, perused the works of the Greek geographers, founded a school for naval instruction, erected an observatory, and set about making maps and nautical instruments.

In spite of the contempt in which he and his affairs were held by nearly everyone, the ships he sent out from Portugal gradually reached ever farther south, to return with captured natives, who were sold as slaves, 10,000 slaves a year being thus imported to Europe. By 1433 his captains had discovered nearly half the west coast of Africa, and, within the next twelve years, all the numerous islands, including the Azores, lying off that coast.

This was Henry's reply to his critics, because, to begin with, he received much abuse, especially from the priests, for spending sacred money on building ships and sending them to places not mentioned in the Bible. He was on a fool's errand, they declared, as no one could live on a globe, as Henry believed we did, because those underneath us would fall off. In any case, no one there could see the Lord's return in glory to Jerusalem, as he had promised. Consequently the inhabitants of these parts must be animals, and not men with souls to save.

Though his ships never reached India, which was his life's dream, and the Pope absolved him for trading with the heathen, besides granting permission to the King of Portugal to keep all the land discovered, his fame rests on the great results which followed from what he commenced. His genius and perseverance gave the primary inspiration to maritime exploration, and, from his time onwards, the mariners he trained and infected with his enthusiasm, sought for and reached still more distant goals, teaching others the art of seamanship until all the earth was finally discovered.

Portugal, because of him, was the European pioneer of overseas discovery, as her king John II (1481–1495) took up the quest after Henry had passed on: Pedro Covilham, on his instructions, going to Alexandria, whence he sailed down the east coast of Africa, touching at one large and prosperous town after another where Arab traders lived and ruled. Here he heard of what we now call the Cape of Good Hope.[1] Then he crossed over to southern India, and passed from one seaport to another.

Astonished and bewildered at all he saw, the riches and the magnificence of everything, he returned to Cairo, whence he wrote to his king to tell him of his

[1] This name was given to it by King John II of Portugal after it was discovered by Diaz in 1486, because of the hope John now had that his ships would reach India, he then having dreams of adding this vast continent to his possessions.

discoveries, and that India could be reached by sailing down the west coast of Africa, rounding the Cape and thence sailing north. Covilham next proceeded to Abyssinia, where he was detained as a prisoner, but, before he died, he heard that Portugal had risen to the rank of one of the great European powers, her ships and seamen having rounded the Cape, reached India, and the lands and islands washed by the Indian Ocean, where trading centres had been established. The Indian Ocean, in fact, became for a time a sea bordered by Portuguese settlements, but other great events were to take place before that happened.

Spain, it will be remembered, became united through the marriage of Ferdinand of Aragon to Isabella of Castile, when followed the final expulsion of the Moslem Moors in 1491. Spain was now a united Christian country, through the common devotion of the people to this form of belief. Moslem rule, and the Pyrenees, had hitherto separated her from the rest of Europe, but in the 15th century this isolation ceased when the House of Aragon accepted the throne of Sicily. Her interests were thus enlarged beyond the mountain frontier barrier, and this was further increased when Joanna, the daughter of Ferdinand and Isabella, and heiress of Spain, married Philip, the son of Mary of Burgundy and Maximilian of Austria, who were the owners of vast possessions. Finally Spain reached the height of her power the following century, when Charles, the son of Philip and Joanna, became King Charles I of Spain and Emperor Charles V of the Holy Roman Empire. Spain thus became the head of a great empire as, by then, America had been discovered.

The daring explorer who discovered the islands fringing the American continent was Christopher Columbus (1436–1506), one of the first men to shed light into the darkness of Europe. A native of Genoa, he began to wonder if Christian geography was really correct in declaring that the world was flat, and Rome the centre of the universe. No one in Europe then knew that America existed, but, after studying the writings of Ptolemy of Alexandria, who made his astronomical observations between A.D. 127 and 151, Columbus came to the conclusion that the world was a sphere, and that Asia could consequently be reached by crossing the Atlantic. Marco Polo had told of the immense size of the Asiatic continent, and Columbus, adopting the miscalculation of the world's circumference made by the Greek Astronomer Posidonius, plotted out India on his chart as situated somewhere in the Gulf of Mexico. He had been to Iceland, but no farther, and now he was determined to discover what was to be found over the wide horizon where set the sun.

So Columbus put his project before the Senate of Genoa, to have his request for help refused. Why should the Genoese, the Venetians, or anyone in Italy, help him to discover a western route to India that would so seriously compete with the Mediterranean, which carried the trade to the East on which these northern Italian ports thrived? Undaunted, Columbus set out for Portugal and placed his proposition before King John II, who listened to him, and then, without saying more, despatched a ship on his own. This underhand attempt on the King's part to get first into the great unknown failed, as the crew mutinied. Columbus saw no more of John, and went to Spain to put his project before King Ferdinand.

At that moment Spain was clearing the Moslems out of Granada, and the King was not interested. He, however, introduced him to the leading ecclesiastics, who assembled to consider his plan, but soon over- whelmed him with Biblical texts to prove that it was contrary to Scripture and consequently impossible. Columbus was now in despair, as he had already approached Henry VII of England, by messenger, but without success. What an opportunity England thus missed, and how history would have taken a different course if Henry had been more enterprising!

With the help of some merchants of Palos in southern Spain, three ships were at last provided, one the *Santa Maria,* a decked vessel of one hundred tons, and two others undecked of fifty tons each. With these, and 120 men, Columbus set out on his great adventure in 1492, hoping to reach India. He did not lack foresight, as besides fine clothes he also took with him a letter of introduction from Ferdinand to the Great Khan of Tartary. After touching at the Canary Islands, Columbus, now raised to the rank of Admiral, set his course to the west, and, for over two months, he sailed without sighting land.

So far he had discovered nothing new, as the Canary Islands, Madeira and the Azores had been discovered by the Portuguese in 1445, and Bartolomeu Diaz had sailed round the south of Africa in 1486. His fame rests on what he discovered through going on farther into the unknown blue, knowing nothing of his destination. The sea, for all he knew to the contrary, might have extended westwards for ever, or, even worse, he might come to the end of everything and topple over into an abyss.

Many doubts and fears prevailed on this momentous voyage, the most important and far-reaching in its effect of any voyage of discovery, and yet courageously they sailed on, comforted by seeing birds and some wood on which was human markings. This latter, however, caused some misgiving, as, if they were about to meet a new race of men, what would be their reception, even if they survived the perils of the sea?

A light was seen on the night of 11th October, 1492, after they had been out of sight of land for sixty-nine days, and, when they awoke the next morning, land was seen. The ship dropped anchor, and Columbus, gorgeously attired, landed, bearing in his hand the royal banner of Spain. He received no opposition from the natives of what is now San Salvador, one of a group of islands to become known as the Bahamas. Other islands were discovered, the most important being Cuba, and Hispaniola, now called Haiti or San Domingo. To the day of his death he believed that he had discovered India, which accounts for the entire archipelago of Central America, enclosing the Caribbean Sea and the Gulf of Mexico, being now known as the West Indies.

Early the following year Columbus returned to Europe, bringing with him gold, cotton, beasts, birds and two natives for baptism into the Christian Church. Soon he again set out, this time with seventeen ships and 1500 men, and the permission of the Pope to take over the lands for the Spanish king, who had promised the Holy Father that the Church would share in the spoils. As governor of all the islands he had discovered, he instituted slavery, with the support of the Christian priests he took out with him, and developed a large trade in buying and selling the natives. He was deeply devout, and all his actions were preceded by prayer, but his diabolical cruelty made the natives, who had shown him kindness and friendship, hate and fear him intensely.

He made four voyages in all, his other principal discoveries being Martinique, Trinidad, Jamaica, Honduras and the mouth of the Orinoco. He received many honours for his great discoveries, becoming a grandee of Spain and a very wealthy man, though, because of his misgovernment, he was suspended by an emissary from the King, who put him in chains and sent him home, but he was released on his arrival and the action repudiated by the King and Queen. Western Europe became wild with excitement at these great discoveries, and other adventurers set out to find the land of gold and precious stones— India, as they thought.

In 1497 Vasco da Gama (1460–1;24), a Portuguese, sailed from Lisbon down the west coast of Africa round the Cape of Good Hope, and up the east coast to Zanzibar, whence he struck across the Indian Ocean and reached Calicut in India. In 1499 Vicente Pinzon, a wealthy Spaniard, who had encouraged, financed and accompanied Columbus on his first voyage, discovered Brazil, but hard on his heels came Cabral, a Portuguese. Magellan (1470–1521), another Portuguese sailor, next determined that he would outdo all the others, and circumnavigate the world.

Following the discovery of the Pacific Ocean by Vasco Nuñez de Balboa in 1513, when he crossed over the Panama isthmus, Magellan started off from Lisbon in 1519 with several ships, setting his course for the coast of South America. This he sailed down, and then through the bleak and fearsome straits now called by his name, into the Pacific Ocean. Thence he continued for some distance up the west coast, and then struck out to the west across the Pacific until he reached the Ladrones Islands. For the first time a European had crossed and named the deepest and widest of oceans, twenty-three times the size of the United States, its greatest depth, 32,000 feet, being deeper than Mount Everest is high.

Magellan next discovered the Philippine Islands, where he, and several of his captains, were killed in a fight with the natives. Passing by Borneo and Java, the expedition entered the Indian Ocean with its course set for the Cape of Good Hope, round which it sailed, and then the ships went north, up the west coast of Africa to Seville in Spain. This was a more heroic enterprise than that of Columbus, as Magellan was much longer out of sight of land. His crews were ill with scurvy from lack of vegetables, and suffered so much from lack of water that they were starving and parched when they reached land. Of the five ships which left Lisbon, with 280 men, only one, the *Victoria*, returned, with 130 men on board.

The earth, for the first time, had been circumnavigated and proved to be round, a feat which had taken from August 1519 to July 1522 to accomplish, and one which was not again attempted until Sir Francis Drake repeated the performance in 1577. It was so far quite the greatest enterprise ever carried out by man. This was indeed an event of world-wide importance, as, for the first time, the people of earth knew the shape of their habitation. After knowing its shape they next learned its geography, and thus trade and commerce increased as a vast new and rich expanse of land was opened up for development. Trade by sea, hitherto confined to the Mediterranean, now expanded over the seven seas, and, as by the sea every coast is washed, so every continent was now open to inspection. To every land there was now a road waiting and ready for use.

All this came about by the courage and leadership of a few really great men—great, not because they plundered their neighbours better than others, but great because they conferred on mankind lasting benefits which have made life fuller, happier and more comfortable. They rank amongst the real bene-factors of the human race. They used their courage and skill not solely to plunder, kill and destroy, but to discover the world's wealth, so that others might develop it, transport it, and organise an exchange of produce between all the nations of earth. One immediate result of their discoveries was to alter the entire course of the world's trade. Hitherto, since civilisation began, the Mediterranean and the Middle East had been the route through which trade had passed between the east and the west. Now the Atlantic and Indian oceans carried this traffic, the effect being that Alexandria, and the great cities of Mesopotamia and Central Asia, fell into decay, and Lisbon took the place of Venice as the market for the dispersal of Indian produce.

Since those days world trade has increased many thousandfold, as has wealth, comfort and speed of transport, so much so that the labourer of today has more comfort and luxuries than had kings and queens in the Middle Ages. There is, however, another side to this picture, and one which should not be forgotten. Europe certainly benefited from all these discoveries, but they were obtained at a terrible cost to the inhabitants of these newly discovered territories.

In America, lived races which had a culture and civilisation of their own, some even having an advanced development. All these people were completely ruined, their civilisation and ancient literature destroyed, and their mode of life changed. They were plundered, enslaved, tortured and ill-treated. Las Casas (1474–1566), the Spanish historian of the time, and the first outstanding humanitarian to be produced by Christian civilisation, did his utmost to prevent the extermination of native life, but to little effect. He puts the number of deaths in South America, as the result of the European invasion, at 12,000,000, all of whom had as much a right to live as anyone else, while those natives who survived became subject to, and the bondmen of, their conquerors.

This was especially the case in Mexico and South America, though there the Spaniards and Portuguese intermarried with the natives, which was something that did not happen in North America, where the aborigines were mostly exterminated. All the benefits of the new world could have been obtained without this cruelty and destruction, but the methods of mankind are not in the interests of one another—taking by the strong from the weak being always in evidence at all stages of history.

English, French and Dutch sailors attempted without success to reach the east by sailing round North America and North Asia. These efforts followed the discovery of 1800 miles of sea coast of the mainland of North America by John and Sebastian Cabot, father and son, Venetians who lived in Bristol. They sailed in an English ship with an English crew, on the authority of the English King Henry VII, starting off from Bristol in 1496, four years after Columbus had discovered the West Indies. Thus they were the first of their time to discover the American continent, and Henry VII in this way retrieved to some degree his mistake in turning down the request Columbus made to him for financial help.

This discovery of America was not in reality something quite new, as other Europeans had been in these parts five centuries earlier. The Vikings from Iceland, under Leif Ericsson about A.D. 1000, had settled for a short time somewhere in the neighbourhood of what is now New York, calling the land Vinland. When Columbus visited Iceland he may have heard of this adventure, and perhaps he had a shrewd idea of his destination before he started, some years later, upon his famous voyage of discovery. Spain and Portugal had a few years' start of other European countries in both the east and the west, but, though they obtained South and Central America, England and France did well in North America, so much so that Antwerp and London became great and prosperous, the world's trade moving from the

Mediterranean to the Atlantic, an event which brought about the ruination of Venice and Genoa.

Germany never had a chance, even though her emperor Charles V was also King of Spain, as the Pope, acting on behalf of God, gave the monopoly of all America, except what is now Brazil, to the Spanish royal house of Castile. Charles's interests in the new world came to him through Spain, and Germany never got a look in. A century later Germany was in the grip of the Thirty Years' War, a conflict which left her a weak impoverished land, and all this time Spain, Portugal, England, France and Holland were snapping up every place they could get throughout the world. This land-grabbing was never forgotten by the German people, it was drilled into her children at school, to be the cause of much of their bitterness and resentment towards France, Britain and Holland, who had gained so much from their enterprise overseas.

In 1494 Pope Alexander VI tried to avoid disputes between Spain and Portugal over many of the new territories they both had discovered, by dividing the newly found world between them. This wicked man, one of the most degenerate of the popes, was looked upon as the authority appointed by God to parcel out the earth to the different nations, but his divine decisions pleased only Spain and Portugal. He was a Spaniard, which may be the reason why he gave all North America and much of South America to Spain, the rest being allotted to Portugal, while India was divided between them, every other country in Europe being ignored.

If we take a map of the world and draw a straight

line due southwards from the southernmost point of
Greenland we find that to the east of this line lies
the extensive territory now known as Brazil and to
the west of it all the rest of North and South America.
This dividing line is known as The Pope's Line, and
he gave all the land west of this line to Spain and all
east of it to Portugal. That is why Brazil once
belonged to Portugal, and its people speak Portuguese.
All the rest of South America once belonged to Spain,
and there the people speak Spanish. North America,
likewise given by the Pope to Spain, came mostly
under British and French influence, as the Spanish
and Portuguese had their hands full in South America
and could not be everywhere.

The 16th century witnessed a rush of explorers,
traders, adventurers and criminals across the Atlantic
Ocean, all out for the plunder they could obtain.
Basing its authority on the divine promise contained
in the Word of God:—

I shall give thee the heathen for thine inheritance, and the
uttermost parts of the earth for thy possession. Thou shalt
break them with a rod of iron, thou shalt dash them in pieces
like a potter's vessel. (*Psalm* ii, 8–9.)

the Christian Church, likewise. eager for greater
wealth and power, quickly organised bands of priests
to accompany this great army of adventurers. A
multitude of non-Christians numbering millions had
been discovered, whose contributions would sustain
a fresh great army of priests and contribute to the
Papal Treasury.

First of all they had to be converted to the new
faith, and the Christian method, so successful in

Europe, was put into practice from Mexico in the north to Patagonia in the south. Those who accepted the gospel message were spared, while those who preferred their old form of belief were massacred. Thus it was that the inhabitants of these parts were brought to the knowledge of Christ, to the great material enrichment of the Christian Church

The Spaniards were well fitted to conduct this holy war, as they had just successfully finished one in their own country. They had driven out the Moslems, after years of conflict, and had brought all Spain into the Christian fold. Now they thought that God had entrusted them with a further and greater mission. Full of blind bigotry, and greedy for plunder, they allowed their passions full play, and terrible is the story of their conquests in the new world. No anthropologists, geologists or biologists accompanied this rabble, because the Spaniards had driven out all the Moslem scientists from Spain, and consequently we have no scientific records of the kind of people they encountered in America. Few intelligent observations have come down to us of the natives, their habits and ideas, they being looked upon as "damned heathen" to be robbed, liquidated, enslaved and baptised.

The Spaniards and Portuguese were no exception, as all the other Christian invaders of new lands treated the natives in much the same way. In Tasmania, for instance, the British shot off all the Palæolithic people they found there, or left poisoned meat about for them to eat. In the Americas, nomadic tribes, resembling the later Palæolithic people of Europe, were discovered who were living much as did their primitive ancestors. They were given the name of Indians, as the invaders thought that they had landed in India, but, besides them, two other separate great civilisations were discovered, the Aztec of Mexico and the Inca of Peru.

How the Americas were originally populated is still a mystery, as there is so little to guide anthropologists in their quest. There is a considerable resemblance between the natives and the Mongols of North and East Asia, but, if they came originally from these parts, it was so very long ago that there is now no affinity between their languages. The original peopling of America may well date from the time when there was continuous land between it and Asia, but what took place in the far distant past, when primitive man wandered over an earth having land where there is now sea, no one can say.

It does not follow, however, that between these remote ages and the time of the discoveries made in the 16th century no fresh immigrants reached America, but, so far as history goes back, we know little of what happened earlier than the 12th Christian century, when the Aztecs migrated into Mexico, to commence the founding of their cities, which so astonished the Spanish invaders. Here the Spaniards found nations with organised armies, official administrators, courts of justice, high agricultural and mechanical arts, besides stone buildings whose architecture and sculpture were often of dimensions and elaborateness to astonish the builders and sculptors of Europe.

The Aztec kingdom embraced what is now the central part of Mexico, and it followed an earlier civilisation, the Maya, the remains of whose cities in

Yucatan date from A.D. 300, though an even earlier culture dating from the 3rd centuy B.C. has been recently discovered. The Aztecs were deeply religious, employing all the cruel rites, and accepting all the superstitions associated with priestcraft. They had their sacrificed saviour-god, who had died for their sins, a eucharist service of remembrance, and human sacrifice. Like Christianity their religion embraced a blood sacrifice for sin, the main difference being that it called its gods by different names, and practised human sacrifice. The holocaust, which took place on each of their great feast days, destroyed hundreds of human beings, and their butchering priests left the ceremony, after a day of slaughter, under the belief that they had given to the gods a good square meal by sending the etheric bodies of so many victims into the other world.

In 1519 Cortez (1485–1547) landed in this strange land, hitherto unknown to the Western world, his army of 700 Europeans, 200 Indians and 14 cannon disembarking on a wide sandy beach where now stands the city of Vera Cruz, rather less than 200 miles from the capital. The simple inhabitants welcomed him as their Christ who had come to gather in his faithful people prior to the Day of Judgment, their religion in all important respects resembling Christianity and the other Pagan saviour-god religions.[1] Montezuma, the King, was not so overjoyed to hear of their arrival, and foolishly sent to Cortez rich gifts of gold and silver with the request that they return whence they came. The effect of this generosity on a gang of plundering adventurers was only to strengthen

[1] The explanation of this similarity will be found in *The Psychic Stream*.

their determination to press inland and secure even greater quantities of these precious metals, despite the risks, which were great.

This certainly is one of the world's greatest adventure stories, and, although it is marred by massacres and abominable cruelties, the Spaniards displayed remarkable courage. Cortez prepared for his advance by destroying all his ships, with one solitary exception, as to him it was to succeed or die. He and his men had two aims only—to obtain gold and convert these heathen to Christianity, his prayer being that the cross would rise above every temple in the land. So, after a solemn service, when all had dedicated themselves to the cause of Christ, they moved forward into the interior.

As they ascended to the high tableland where stood Mexico City, they met the Tlaxcalans, the people of an independent republic, who attacked, and, after two days fighting, were defeated, because they could not withstand the cavalry and artillery, which mowed them down in thousands. Next the Spaniards arrived at Cholula, which Cortez described as "a more beautiful city than any in Spain", and here it was that the massacring of the people began, his purpose being to impart such fear to the inhabitants that no one would dare to molest him during his unwelcome visit. The defenceless people fell in thousands, and when the ghastly holocaust was over Cortez gathered together those who had survived, and, through an interpreter, told them of the wonders of the Christian religion, its saving power, its heaven and its hell. Then he erected an altar and a cross, and went on his way to the capital.

Mexico City had a population of about 300,000, its streets were wide, and the market square could accommodate a sixth of the population. Its royal palaces excelled in magnificence any in Europe, and the numerous richly furnished temples, dwelling-houses, and the aspect of the inhabitants declared their comfort and contentment. Here the Spaniards were received by Montezuma with magnificent hospitality, and given one of his palaces in which to live during what he thought was only a visit. Hardly had Cortez arrived before he started his missionary activities, he being as much a missionary as a brigand, and the King was quickly instructed in the leading doctrines of the Christian faith. Lacking in tact and courtesy, Cortez told the King that the Mexican gods were devils, but, as he could not convince His Majesty that this was so, he decided that he could only effect his mission by force combined with cunning.

The Spanish position was certainly dangerous, but, if they had acted honourably and peacefully, they would doubtless have been accepted as honoured guests and allowed to depart in safety. Cortez, however, was determined to convert the Mexicans to Christianity, and this achievement was as much to him as was the rich plunder all around him. So with calm decision he rode to the palace, with his own escort, kidnapped the King and took him back to his own residence. The plot was quite successful, as within a few days Montezuma and his nobles professed themselves vassals of the King of Spain.

For six months Cortez ruled Mexico, during which time he abolished her religion and human sacrifice, though he murdered everyone who would not worship Christ. Much gold did he accumulate, but how it was to be removed to Spain did not become a question, as the Governor of Cuba, jealous of his success, sent 1400 soldiers with twenty guns to take over the country and send Cortez back to Cuba. When Cortez heard of this he hastened to the coast to meet them, leaving one of his men, Alvarado, to conduct the government in his absence.

During this period the people of Mexico began to grow restive, but still they proceeded to hold their annual festival, only to be pounced upon by Alvarado, and his men, during its celebration, 600 being put to death. Immediately the people rose in revolt, and the desperate situation of the invaders, blockaded within their own quarters, would have become hopeless had Cortez not returned with the army sent from Cuba, he having won it over to his side. An attack at once commenced on the city, which was defended by the Mexicans with the greatest gallantry, though they had only stones and arrows to meet the shot and shell of the besiegers.

The hatred of the Mexicans towards the Spanish invaders was now so intense that thousands willingly sacrificed their lives if only they could kill one Spaniard, but all their courage and numbers could not prevail, and the city was captured, Montezuma being killed by a shower of arrows when he appealed to the people to accept their fate and cease resistance. This tragedy convinced Cortez that the game was up, and that the Mexicans were intent on their destruction. So he and his men slipped away when night came, only to be followed and caught at a great disadvantage because they had to cross water over which the bridges had been destroyed. Here they were met by the Mexicans in their canoes, and the retreat became a bloody rout, 450 Spaniards and half their horses perishing, besides all the cannon being lost.

Cortez was not a man to be turned from his goal by one defeat, and he resolved to regain what he had won. He united many of the small states on the borders of the Aztec kingdom into a league for the purpose of its overthrow, and, with reinforcements from Hispaniola, he was again before the capital in six months' time with 1000 Spaniards and 100,000 native allies, including horses, muskets and cannon. He ravaged the land, the cross in one hand and the sword in the other, sparing neither man, woman nor child, but the capital held out for three months, and neither famine nor disease would induce the Mexicans to surrender.

So Cortez determined to destroy the city, and day after day it was shattered house by house, the half-starved defenders perishing in its ruins. Diaz, the Spanish historian, who was present at this destruction and slaughter, could not find words to describe the indescribable horror, all that he could say being that what happened at the time Jerusalem was destroyed by the Romans could not have been worse than what took place when the great Mexican capital was razed to the ground. Thus was Mexico conquered, and its inhabitants brought to the knowledge of Christ. Thus it was that all America, from Mexico south-wards, was conquered and Christianised, the same barbarous methods as were applied in Europe centuries earlier, to change the religious beliefs of the Pagans, being adopted in this new-found land.

Cortez was now lord and master of all Mexico, and, as his brutal methods became known throughout Central America, ambassadors came from other tribes and nations of these parts offering him their submission. The rich state of Guatemala in the south, with its large and well-built cities, whose people were cultured and civilised, and where the arts were encouraged, alone showed little cordiality towards the conqueror. So she must next be destroyed, as Cortez and his followers were zealous to bring all the heathen sheep they could find within the Christian fold, and besides that there was much rich booty to be had for the taking.

An expedition of 280 men with four cannon now set out under the brutal Alvarado, and, by the time their ghastly work was completed, the cities, towns and villages of Guatemala had been devastated, thousands had been massacred, the King murdered, and his chiefs gathered together and burned in one huge holocaust. Those who remained were forced to become Christians and slaves, and when his ghastly work was accomplished the devout Alvarado sent a message to Cortez. This requested him to arrange in Mexico City for a solemn service of thanksgiving to Almighty God for all the mercies he had showered down on his faithful Christian soldiers, who, by their zeal, had still further spread the glad tidings of salvation amongst the heathen. To this request Cortez duly complied.

An equally devout criminal was Francisco Pizarro (1471–1541), a Spaniard, who found his work as a farmer too monotonous. When thus occupied in Panama he heard of the riches of a land farther south, whose shores were washed by the Pacific Ocean. Here, over the past five hundred years, the Incas, a civilised race, had built up a prosperous community. They had many fine cities and their land was rich in minerals. Pizarro heard tales of this wonderful region away in the southern blues of the Pacific, and decided that if there was gold to be found, and souls to be saved, he was the one to carry out this noble mission.

So, in 1524, he crept down the Pacific coast with eighty men and four horses in a small ship, and, after overcoming incredible dangers and difficulties, he arrived at his goal with only fourteen survivors. Gold was to be seen everywhere, the walls of the temples were lined with it, and the palaces were filled with ornaments made of the precious metal, but with only fourteen men he could but gaze at the sight with greedy eyes. He therefore returned to Panama, and thence home to Spain to tell the King of his marvellous discovery. On hearing this the King created him Governor of Peru, and elevated an unscrupulous adventurer De Luque to be Bishop of Peru, because the King, like his subjects, was intent on bringing the natives within the Christian fold.

So these two scoundrels set sail to secure the prize with 239 men and sixty-five horses, being fortunate to arrive eventually at their destination (1530) at the termination of a civil war, a fact which considerably lightened their task of getting a firm footing on Peruvian soil. We remember how the Pagans believed that a god always directed their various enterprises. Likewise every adventurer of these days believed that a saint guided his efforts, an idea which accounts for so many towns and places in South America bearing the names of saints, and Pizarro was no exception. His first act on landing was to build a fort and a church which he dedicated to San Miguel, who, he believed, was directing the expedition from heaven. As he proceeded inland the natives had the option to become Christians or die, a policy which he said "would serve the cause of religion and tend greatly to the spiritual welfare" of the people.

What unflinching courage was required in this wild adventure, as twelve days' journey inland, across the great Andes mountain barrier, was encamped the King of Peru with an army of 50,000 warriors, flushed by their victory in the civil war which had just ended. But Pizarro knew the stuff his men were made of, and that he had vastly superior weapons. Moreover, they were all fortified by the sacred words attributed to Jehovah, when he encouraged the Israelites to advance into the Promised Land:—

> The Lord thy God, he will go over before thee, and he will destroy these nations from before thee, and thou shalt possess them. . . . Be strong and of a good courage, fear not, nor be afraid of them, for the Lord thy God, he it is that doth go with thee, he will not fail thee, nor forsake thee. (*Deuteronomy* xxxi, 3.)

Prosperous well-built towns were passed through on their hazardous journey across the Andes, and everywhere the people were friendly and hospitable until they experienced the invader's brutality. After seven days of climbing they looked down upon the fertile valleys and plains beyond, while, in the distance, they saw the tents of the great army of the Inca Atahualpa, whom they had come to destroy. On the horizon arose from the plain the splendid city of Cassamarca bathed in the rays of the brilliant sun. After the celebration of the Eucharist the invaders joined together in prayer and praise, their chant being "Rise, O Lord, and judge thine own cause". Being thus strengthened, they now set to work to perpetrate one of the foulest crimes in history.

The Inca was prepared to meet the invaders as friends, and, expecting a friendly reception, he arrived in great state at the square of the city where they had encamped. After him came his nobles, retainers and citizens until an assembly of over 5000 filled the square. The first to meet him was Pizarro's chaplain, who began immediately to expound Christian doctrine to the astonished monarch, but, as the King would not accept his offer of a Bible, the priest shouted to Pizarro: "You see the attitude of this haughty heathen dog. At him—I absolve you all!"

This exclamation was followed by the firing of the Spanish guns, which had all been trained on the vast multitude. Then came the charge of the Spanish cavalry, supported by volleys from the invader's muskets. Soon the swords of the cavalry, the bullets from the muskets, and the balls from the cannon had done their deadly work, and the square was piled high with dead, so high that those within could not get out.

Gallantly did the defenceless multitude try to save their king, but he was quickly taken prisoner, and, after no more could be found to kill in the square, the cavalry swept through the streets, slaughtering all on their wild onward surge, until finally they were massacring those who had escaped beyond the city's walls. The Peruvian army fled in panic, and within an hour the city was captured, the once powerful king, the possessor of vast treasure, being a prisoner in the hands of the Spanish gang of ruffians.

He sought to regain his liberty by a costly ransom, offering to fill a room 17 feet broad and 22 feet long with gold 9 feet high, all of which the invaders could take back with them, including double the amount of silver. The offer was accepted, and for two months the natives brought from the temples great golden vessels, large plates of gold, and golden ornaments of every description which the people had given to save their king. At last the gold and silver had accumulated to provide the promised amount, but Pizarro broke his bargain and retained the Inca a prisoner, as a Christian's word to a damned heathen never counted for anything during the first eighteen Christian centuries.

The value of this treasure is estimated to have been worth over £4,000,000, allowing for the greater purchasing power of money in those days. This provided a handsome fortune for each of the robber band, now increased to 400 by recent arrivals from Spain, but they could not move it, and, as the Inca was still a prisoner, rumours circulated that the army had re-formed and was moving on the capital. So Pizarro staged a mock trial and had the King convicted of being a heretic, a usurper, and of attempting to incite an insurrection against the Spaniards. He was found guilty and sentenced to death by burning at the stake, this method of dying, he was told, being the fate of all who disbelieved in the Christian faith.

Under the stress of great emotion the King pleaded

for his release, but nothing would change the decision of his captors. Bound hand and foot in chains, the once proud monarch was led into the city square where stood the stake surrounded by faggots. Alongside him came a priest instructing him in the tenets of the Christian religion, and promising him that if he accepted Christ he would be hanged instead of burned. The miserable victim, to secure release from the agony of the flames, turned to Christ, to be at once baptised, after which he partook of the Eucharist. Then followed immediately his murder, he being strangled by a cord, his last words being that pity be shown to his young children. This final request was, however, drowned by the surrounding band of Spanish Christians chanting the Nicene Creed, and offering up praise to the glory of God.

Slowly this new form of religious belief spread throughout both North and South America, a new triad of gods forming the basis of the religious beliefs which came to be accepted by many millions of simple creatures who, like children, did what they were told or were punished for their disobedience. Gunpowder, which was unknown to this vast throng of humanity, was the means destiny employed to bring them to the knowledge of Christ, just as the sword in the preceding centuries, in the hands of the Christians, had brought the gospel message to the Pagan Europeans who could only handle a bow and arrow.

Next morning the Inca was given a Christian burial, and immediately thereafter Pizarro marched south and possessed himself of the capital, the city of Cusco, which he thoroughly plundered, removing eleven life-size statues of pure gold, "beautiful and well formed as if they had been alive". The Temple of the Sun was cleared of everything worth moving, the mummies of former Incas being stripped of their gold and cast aside, their thrones of gold on which they were seated, and a golden image of the sun, being removed to add to the booty. Then followed the destruction of every temple in the land, and the setting up of crosses along the highways, to end with a proclamation that the land now belonged to the Christian Church and the King of Spain, the fate of all who did not become Christians being torture and death. A Christian church now arose in the capital, and before long every town and village had its Christian place of worship.

Cusco, the capital, was a city of considerable size, its population being about 300,000; its streets were wide and regular, on each side of which were built stone houses. Its numerous palaces were of imposing construction, and more magnificent than anything to be found in Europe. This noble city was to the Peruvians what Athens had been to the Greeks, Rome to the Romans, and Jerusalem to the Jews, and now it was theirs no longer. Strangers from a strange land, who could kill with lead bullets, and whose armour protected them from arrows, had taken it from them, and not only it but also their king, their land, their liberty and their religion. Superior force and not righteousness determines history, and until mental development reverses this process the curse of ignorance will remain, and our goal of happiness will not be reached.

Every evil which it is possible for man to inflict on man was perpetrated by the Spaniards on the victims of their conquest, who were deprived of their possessions and liberty. Every possible indignity was heaped upon these unhappy people: their women were dishonoured, and the entire population reduced to slavery, so severe that many died from the unaccustomed toil, until at last they could endure their misery no longer. Then they dashed their unprotected bodies against the armour of their oppressors, preferring to die rather than live under such conditions.

The Spanish garrison of Cusco numbered 200 Spaniards and 1000 natives, a force which was considered sufficient to protect the city, whose palaces were now occupied by a small Spanish population living in luxury on the labour of their slaves. Silently the natives gathered in the neighbouring mountains, armed with lances and axes, prepared to die to the last man to recover the land they had lost. When the signal came in 1535 they rushed the city, set it on fire, and forced the Spaniards into the great square. Great was the slaughter and nearly did the Peruvians exterminate their hated foe. Unfortunately their javelins, stones and arrows became exhausted, and, after six days' struggle, they had to retire defeated.

Much misery was still in store for this unhappy country, as the criminal gang, whose numbers increased with new arrivals from Spain, fell out amongst themselves because they could not agree on the division of their great possessions. For twelve years Peru lacked all semblance of government, while fierce conflicts amongst the Spaniards ravished the land, and peace did not come before a large part of the population had perished. The chief criminal, now known as the Marquis Pizarro, was finally murdered after all the rest of the original invaders had met violent deaths.

The tide of Spanish conquest. flowed on, Chili, Argentina, and other lands, one by one, falling under her domination. Within forty years of the discovery of South America all the coastal regions of this vast southern continent, with the exception of Brazil, were in Spanish possession, and explorers were penetrating inland bent on converting the natives and securing their land and labour. Later on will be told how disgracefully Spain misused her new responsibilities. It is a story of enslavement, injustice, robbery, cruelty and treachery. Nowhere do we find kindness, mercy, justice, righteousness or charity, only one long miserable tale of forcible conversion to Christianity, on the one hand, and enslavement and plundering on the other. Very slowly was the rule of the armed brigand replaced by that of law and order, but centuries had to pass before liberty took the place of bondage.

Everywhere the invaders enslaved the natives, who received no justice and were treated with great cruelty. It never occurred to these newcomers into the Americas to pay the rightful owners for the land they took, and treat them humanely, honestly and justly. These invaders were all deeply religious, but they entirely lacked the sense of right and wrong, their hope of salvation hereafter depending on belief and not on deeds. The Church authorities were equally unscrupulous, the increase in its wealth and power being their principal aim, so much so that not many years passed before it owned half of all the newly discovered land in Mexico and South America.

Within one hundred years the Church had a firm grip over the minds of the simple natives, on whom was levied a tenth of all they produced—baptism having produced millions of additional Christians who were now sure of salvation no matter how they lived. Twelve hundred monasteries and nunneries flourished, the convents in Lima covering more ground than all the rest of the city. From Europe had flowed a regular stream of priests and monks, many sincerely bent on the conversion of these heathen millions over whom they exercised a profound influence. Consequently, the natives by the million turned to Christ, either through fear of their overlords, or from persuasion by the priests, and the wealth of the Church became so fabulous that the entire continent fell completely under the rule of the Church hierarchy, composed of cardinals, archbishops and bishops, each one in receipt of a princely income. Moreover, the magnificence of the churches and convents everywhere became so dazzling, that it was said no European could possibly imagine their grandeur.

It was many years before law and order were everywhere established, and meantime plantations sprang up, mines were worked, and gold and precious metals flowed across the sea to Europe from this new land which the Spaniards and Portuguese had transformed into one vast slave camp for their own material advantage. These great possessions made Spain and Portugal rich beyond all the other states of Europe, so much so that Spain became the leading power for over a century, but their population was not large enough to take care of the entire newly found continent, and great areas in the north fell to adventurers from other lands.

Ferdinand de Soto, who had been with Pizarro in Peru, returned to Spain greatly enriched by his adventure, but still thirsting for more. North of Mexico he believed there was much plunder awaiting the first adventurer, and, encouraged by this idea, he fitted out an expedition consisting of 600 men, all eager for the quest. They took with them priests, fetters, bloodhounds to prevent captives from escaping, and an array of weapons and instruments of torture. They made for the land now called Florida, and, after landing, proceeded inland to reach finally the Mississippi river, a mile in breadth, a sight never to be seen in Spain.

Many conflicts occurred with the natives, but nowhere could they find gold or any great city to loot, only Indian towns and villages composed of logs of wood. Crossing the river on rafts, they continued their eastward march, but their revolting cruelty to the natives, who at first were friendly, created such hostility that they found themselves in constant danger. After three years of hazard and privations, half of those who set out returned home, the rest, including de Soto, having died in adding yet another possession to the Spanish crown.

Far up in the icy north lay a vast stretch of country. Cabot was probably the first to discover Newfoundland, but he passed by these bleak and desolate coasts and those containing what came to be known as the Gulf of St. Lawrence. Though he reached as far south as Florida, he took no formal possession of any territory in the name of the King of England. Many years passed before England made her claim to these parts; in fact their very existence was forgotten until 1576, when Martin Frobisher, in an attempt to find a passage through to the Pacific Ocean, again brought them to mind. Sir Humphrey Gilbert, then (1583) formally occupied Newfoundland in the name of Elizabeth, but France laid claim to all the territory north of Mexico and based her title on the earlier landings made in 1524 by John Verazzani, a mariner in her service.

One hundred years later both France and England fought each other fiercely for the possession of North America, but that story will be told as we go on. Meantime, in 1534, a Frenchman Jacques Cartier discovered the River St. Lawrence, and planted a cross in the name of France on the rocky promontory where now stands Quebec. There, in 1759, a decisive battle settled the long-drawn-out conflict, and decided that the Anglo-Saxon race was to guide the destinies of the North American continent. Penetrating farther inland, Cartier reached Hochelaga, the native capital of an extensive territory, on which site later arose the city of Montreal.

Cartier returned to France bearing with him, as a present to the King, a chief and three minor chiefs, which was his way of returning the kind hospitality given him by the native Indians. France was however quite uninterested in his discoveries, Frenchmen then being much more interested in killing off the Protestants in their midst. Not until 1608 did France concern herself with these northern regions, and, but for the zeal of Samuel de Champlain (1567–1635), she

might never have done so. He was the founder of
Canada, and for thirty years toiled incessantly to foster
settlements for the purpose of converting the natives
and establishing a fur trade. His efforts only succeeded
in destroying the natives by raising inter-tribal conflicts, and, when he died, the fort which he built,
and called Quebec, was in English hands, being
captured in 1629.

France brought only misery to Canada, the muskets
and liquor, exchanged for furs, in the end utterly
destroying the Huron Indians. Champlain's missionary efforts likewise failed, as he took with him
both Roman Catholic and Protestants, who quarrelled
and fought violently amongst themselves, but he
never wavered in his desire to see the natives embrace
the Roman Catholic faith, especially as the English
were equally zealous to make them Protestants.
Happy would he have been to know that a few years
after his death an attempt was made to meet his
wishes, by the Jesuits sending eight priests to lay the
foundation of a movement to convert the numerous
tribes of natives living in villages made up of log huts
in the western prairies.

Though increasing numbers of Jesuits laboured
in deep earnestness, and endured much privation and
suffering, they could not convince the Indians that
Christianity was superior to their crude form of
Spiritualism. Moreover, the natives could not forget
the unfortunate expeditions of Champlain, who had
supplied the Hurons with muskets to use against the
Iroquois, now, in turn, armed with this deadly weapon.
This the latter now used against the French, many
missionaries perishing, and then the remainder

returned to France. Their labour had been in vain, and their policy to change the Indians into good Catholics, industrious farmers and loyal subjects of France had failed.

If it had been successful France would probably have populated Canada more profusely than she did, and become solidly established on the North American continent. Roman Catholicism would then have obtained a firm grip, and cast its blight over a people who were finding refuge in these new-found lands from the tyranny in Europe. The fierce Iroquois thus in reality secured the political and religious liberty of Canada, preserved North America for Protestant and Nonconformist exiles, and indirectly were the means of securing Canada for Britain. If the Jesuits had succeeded in building up a powerful Canada under French rule, the entire history of North America would have been different. French influence would have spread south and west until Canada, and all North America, had come under her domination. Instead of this the Iroquois, by their anti-Jesuit attitude, prepared the way for the conquest of Canada by the British, and enabled the British-American colonists to take root and thrive until they became a powerful nation.

The colonisation of the continent north of Florida came about from very different reasons than those which took the Spanish into the lands lying to the south of this their most northerly penetration. Britain was ruled by tyrannical kings who claimed divine authority for all they did, and only two men so far had protested against this claim, John Knox and George Buchanan in Scotland, but they were like two voices crying in the wilderness. The people bore this despotism in silence, until the idea came to some that they could obtain the religious and political freedom they desired by emigrating to the land across the Atlantic.

Sir Walter Raleigh had for years devoted his wealth and labour to attract colonists to that region, to which the name Virginia had been given, but only a few "dissolute persons", as they were then called, had taken him seriously. Had it not been for the ability and resolution of John Smith, whose strength of character and power for organisation overcame all difficulties and dangers, this, Britain's first serious attempt at colonisation, would have ended in failure. Instead of so doing, this young plant took root and ultimately flourished, being nourished by both political and religious rebels who were banished from, or voluntarily left, the land of their birth.

While this young community was struggling to survive, persecution by the Anglican Church drove some Nonconformists over to Holland, though repeatedly their embarkation was stopped by soldiers, who scattered, captured and imprisoned them for daring to leave the country. Finally some hundreds found refuge amongst the Dutch, including John Robinson (1575–1625), one of the founders of the Nonconformist Church in England, who settled in Leyden and there ministered to his exiled flock. Later Brewster, one of his elders, led some of these across the Atlantic in 1620 in the *Mayflower*, to find a permanent home in the land they called New England, Robinson's health preventing him from accompanying them. This trickle of men and women seeking religious liberty grew into a flood, and, in spite of great privations and danger from neighbouring Indian tribes, the colony grew and prospered.

Religious intolerance likewise caused the foundation of Pennsylvania in 1682 by William Penn (1644–1718), a much persecuted Quaker, who received this great tract of land from Charles II in exchange for money Penn's father had lent to the King. Penn opened this territory to all the persecuted Quakers and Nonconformists, but he did more than that, as he attracted to it the oppressed of all the nations of Europe, his honest kindly dealing with the natives ensuring the safety of the colonists who, in earlier times, got back from the natives just what they gave. To them the natives were "damned heathen", who could be robbed, tortured and deceived, and they retaliated in like manner, but Penn, by his kindness and justice, made the Indians his friends and good neighbours.

These strangers, who found a sanctuary in a strange land, had left their homes in Britain and elsewhere because others there who thought like them had been hanged, imprisoned and tortured, their ears being cut off, noses slit, or they had spent many weary hours in the pillory. Those who had escaped from this persecution gave up all that was dear to them to obtain political and religious freedom, but, whenever they became organised communities, they commenced the very same persecution towards everyone who differed from the opinions of the majority, the Bible being their sole guide in both religious and political wisdom.

So it came about that the very same persecution from which they had fled was re-established across the Atlantic,[1] all heretics and witches being treated in the same cruel way. A new arrival, Roger Williams, defied this tyranny and was banished from New England. He received a grant of land from the Indians, and there founded the State of Rhode Island as "a shelter for persons distressed for conscience". Alone of all the states of Christendom, Rhode Island has no taint of persecution on her statute book, and into this really free state fled all the heretics who were persecuted, or driven out, of the lands to which they had come in the hope of finding liberty and justice.

How the great continent lying west of the Atlantic seaboard was explored and colonised will be told later on. So far we have reached the period when the European people had spread themselves over the seas, and brought under their domination a large part of the surface of the earth, their last and greatest acquisition being this vast territory hitherto quite unknown except to those who dwelt upon it. Much more was still to follow, as Jacob Lemaire, a Dutchman, in 1615, sailed round Cape Horn and reached New Guinea and the Moluccas. Then, in 1642, the famous navigator Abel Tasman discovered New Zealand, Tasmania, the Fiji Islands, New Britain and Batavia, and a year later he explored part of the coast of Australia. Wherever Europeans went they brought with them their laws, culture and religion. Consequently the number of Christians greatly increased, and the influence of what took place at that momentous Council of Nicaea, thirteen centuries earlier, spread to such an extent

[1] In Virginia there was no coinage, tobacco being the medium of exchange. Absence from church cost the delinquent tobacco weighing 50 lbs., refusing to have his child baptised 2000 lbs., and for entertaining a Quaker 5000 lbs.

that the beliefs there formulated came to be accepted by almost a third of the human race.

Moreover, the discovery of the compass, which enabled the sea to be crossed in safety, changed the whole aspect of world affairs. Both good and evil, to begin with, came from the new discoveries which followed from its use. Much material wealth came to Europe from both East and West, where lands and mines were now put to more productive use, and increased mental wealth also followed because the mind develops according to its environment. Enlarge the scope of the mind and its power increases. This was now being done, and it is interesting to consider the effects which followed.

(5) THE TORCH OF KNOWLEDGE BEGINS TO GLOW IN EUROPE.

We have now reached the beginning of the greatest mental revolution in the history of the human race. This volume has been almost entirely devoted to what we might well term the Theological Age, and it ends with the beginning of its decline, the next volume recording the growth of its decay, to end with its passing from the minds of all intelligent and educated people. As the theological age decayed, the scientific age increased in strength and power, and we now hope that this new era will be accompanied in its further achievements by the Ethical Age, when righteousness will secure a place never before attained in the social order.

In the foregoing pages we have witnessed the curtain of ignorance being slightly lifted, first by the

Babylonians and the Egyptians, whose efforts were continued by the Greeks and Romans, but the enlightenment which followed was soon extinguished by the coming into power of the Christian Church. Fortunately the Arabs continued what the Greeks and the Hellenised Jews had accomplished in Alexandria and elsewhere, though this was in turn submerged by the Moslem Church when the orthodox regained the power they lost for a time. Now once again light broke through to a world shrouded in darkness, and soon we shall be reading of how some books containing Arabian and Greek knowledge found their way into Europe, through the barrage of Christian hostility, to bring eventually the dawn to a world sunk deep in the slough of theological ignorance.

So far a theological reason had been given for every phenomenon of nature. God and Satan, at the head of a multitude of saints and devils, were considered by Christians as responsible for everything that happened. This age-old explanation of the cause behind the phenomena we experience had held its ground since the time of primitive man, only a few of the more intelligent realising that it did not fit into reason and facts. Unfortunately these more enlightened people had no instruments to help them to demonstrate that their logic and reasoning were sound, and consequently they could not prove the truth of their opinions.

Theology therefore remained firmly entrenched, and to it there was no law and order in the universe, all that happened being due to the whims of the gods. Saint Patrick is today appealed to by a Roman Catholic Irishman as readily as was Apollo by the

Greeks, and the Holy Virgin Mary, by some Christians, is still expected to perform the miracles attributed to the Greek goddess, the Holy Demeter, the mother goddess, the names of both goddesses signifying productivity. The theological structure was the same throughout, the hierarchy of the gods being always alike, only the names being different. This will be clear from the following:—

Religion.	Father-god.	Virgin Mother-goddess.	Saviour god and son of the Father-god.	Heavenly messenger.	Entourage.
Greek	Zeus	Demeter	Dionysus	Hermes	The gods and goddesses
Roman	Jupiter	Ceres	Bacchus	Mercury	The gods and goddesses
Christian	Jehovah	Mary	Christ	Holy Spirit	The saints and angels

The Aryans, who invaded India and Greece about 1500 B.C., brought with them their gods. So Brahmanism is closely related to Greek theology, which was taken over by the Romans, and then later by the Christians, but, if we go still farther back to the origin of these religious beliefs, we find that theology is just a caricature of Spiritualism. Theology is Spiritualism twisted out of shape, in consequence of man's ignorance of nature's psychic laws. Theology grew out of the psychic phenomena produced in the presence of the medium, which phenomena have only to be experienced to be appreciated as something beyond the physical order. That, in the early days, gave rise to Ancestor Worship, but, when the priest replaced the medium, for the reasons already explained in an earlier chapter, the medium was persecuted and the phenomena discredited.

Consequently theology, which claimed to be the knowledge of the gods, grew into a twisted, gnarled tree, lacking nourishment, as it ignored the source from which psychic knowledge comes. Being thus a distortion of the facts which gave it birth, theology has never sought for truth. Ignorance is the soil in which it flourishes, and, relying as it does on speculative mystical contemplation, it turned something quite natural into the supernatural for which there is no evidence. Supernormal psychic phenomena were thus passed by in favour of the supernatural, while nature's revelation of the hereafter, and man's psychic bodily structure, as revealed by psychic science, were misinterpreted under the names of Theology and Mysticism. Mystery was worshipped instead of facts being studied, and ignorance flourished while reasoned thought languished. Truly the theologians have always been utterly mistaken in their conception of the etheric order, and they have only their own folly and selfishness to blame for their stupid blunders. On error and fraud they have thrived from primitive times to the present day, truth never being their goal.

It was always in the interests of the priests to keep the people believing in the supernatural gods. If their flocks had come to know that the other order of life is natural, that it is made up of men and women who once lived here on earth, and got there quite naturally without a special passport, there would have been no need of a priesthood to act as inter-mediaries between the gods and mankind.

Only by the people being kept in ignorance could

priestly rule continue, as the truth would have freed everyone from the fear of the gods, from the fear of death, and from the fear of the unknown which comes from ignorance. The search for truth is not, however, a priestly occupation, and, as we shall learn in the next volume, the clergy, even in our own times, will descend to any depths to prevent psychic knowledge spreading amongst the people, most of the leading Protestant clergy in Britain being implicated in this wilful smothering up of facts which all should know.

As the policy of the priesthood, from early times to the present day, has been to belittle reasoned thought and ignore facts, education and knowledge were always hateful to the clergy of every religion, ignorance and servile obedience to their dogmas being much more in keeping with their twisted outlook on life. All our present-day troubles spring from the fact that the priesthood, which made itself responsible for the mental life of the people down the ages, grossly abused its position in order to secure for itself power, privilege and wealth.

On the priesthood alone is the blame for the fact that the curse of ignorance still hangs over mankind. On the stupidity of the human race they thrived, on the stifling of all rational enquiry into the vital facts of life and death they secured belief in their evil superstitions, and, by representing every novelty as a work of the devil, and contrary to the will of God, they prevented mental development and social progress. Under ecclesiastical rule there never has been any advance, as one or more gods were always represented as thinking in the way which best suited the clergy. Consequently the people were kept from wondering and enquiring, through fear that if they did so something dreadful would happen to them.

Psychic knowledge would have put the gods in their right place, as the men and women they are, and nothing more. This being so, they would not have been considered responsible for all the forces of nature, and the fate of each individual after death; they would not have been feared, and the pursuit of knowledge and social progress would not have been hindered. Psychic phenomena, as modern science makes clear, fit in with the natural law governing the universe, and, although they relate to an unseen order of life, we now realise that our senses perceive only a fraction of what exists. Investigation and experiment on the part of the theologians would have demonstrated how everything on earth, and in the heavens, is natural, but, as this was never attempted, whatever happened was regarded as a mystery and related to supernatural beings called gods.

The intellectuals of Greece and Rome had so developed mentally that they despised theology, they had ceased to fear the gods, and some openly declared that they were men and women just as we are. They had come to recognise law and order in the universe, and philosophy was consequently taking the place of superstition. This was the mental outlook of the times amongst the thinkers when Constantine became emperor. There was then no real national religion, as religious freedom in the Empire permitted the gods of all nations to be worshipped, and from Alexandria philosophy was sending out its beams of greater intellectual light, disintegrating the old national religious beliefs.

Constantine, on becoming emperor, sought for some binding force to cement a loosely woven empire into one solid block, and he decided that this could best be done by returning to theology under a new name. He was a politician and not a philosopher, and he realised that to the masses supernatural religion appealed in a way philosophy never could do until education had made much greater headway. His policy was to bring unity throughout his wide domains, one Emperor and one Faith, and so place his empire on the same solid basis of religious unity as had sustained the empires of the past.

The Christian Church consequently became the State Church of the Empire, and, by the extraordinary set of circumstances already recorded, which no one could possibly have foreseen, it secured dictatorial powers within the short space of one hundred years. Then the theologians became the rulers of what had once been the Roman Empire, the consequence being that the scientists, the philosophers and the schoolmasters were liquidated. Mediumship, through which psychic phenomena were revealing the true nature of the gods, was likewise abolished and smothered under a mass of superstition.

Theology was now triumphant, militantly triumphant, triumphant as never before, as always in the past there had been a king, a pharaoh, or an emperor, to preserve to a degree some rational outlook on life. Now unfortunately the people were drawn into an entirely new social order, one that was regulated by Church law, by which justice was conditioned by belief in theological doctrines and dogmas, and all who refused to accept these were branded as traitors to

God and the State, and made to suffer accordingly. Ignorance was robed and crowned.

Such, then, had been the position from the 4th century to the time we have reached, but, from now onwards, we shall learn of the conflict between science and theology being renewed. Hitherto in Christendom theology had always triumphed over every heresy, but this time it was to be a fight to the finish, to end, after much suffering and misery, with theology defeated, ignorance dethroned, and knowledge firmly set upon the throne of reason.

We have now reached one of the most interesting periods in world history, when, for centuries to come, the great intellectual battle was waged between the thinkers and the theologians. Hard and unscrupulously the theologians fought to maintain their fanciful speculations, which lacked the support of facts and evidence. Instead of argument they used torture, imprisonment, banishment and death, and to retain their power and wealth they plunged Europe into a sea of frightfulness so deep that we have not yet recovered from the effect.

Constantine's dream of an empire united by one religion had not materialised before it collapsed, and an imposed religious belief did not bring unity and harmony to Europe. Up to the time we are now considering, Europe, for some two thousand five hundred years, had been a seething cauldron of unrest, and it can best be compared to a grandstand at a football match which had no reserved seats. A crowd of nomads from the East was ceaselessly pressing in to secure the most favoured places, which, after much jostling, were obtained by some and not by others.

Then another rabble followed which turned out those who had obtained the best seats, and these it occupied. Fighting followed, to be intensified by a third, a fourth, and a fifth mob coming in one after the other, until finally all the seats were occupied. All this time the spectators took different sides about the game that was being played, and free fights ensued, so that pandemonium prevailed from the time the game began until it ended.

Europe not only suffered from these recurring nomadic invasions but also from its inhabitants for ever quarrelling amongst themselves. Under these conditions mental development was impossible, but, as the invasions became less frequent, and the kings obtained control of the human masses, as nations took shape, and law and order was established, some men began to think of things other than fighting, stealing and superstitition. A small but new class developed who began to wonder, to doubt and to reason. These men were individual thinkers, whose minds were sufficiently developed to think and reason on a line of their own, quite unlike the masses, who were no better than sheep, as all thought the same way, just as the Pope or the King decreed.

In those days the number of thinkers was very very small, but between then and our own times it has grown, though the real thinkers are still greatly in the minority. This was ever so, as always the few have led the many, who, too often, have followed grudgingly behind. On these rare leaders the future happiness of the race depends, as only by taking reason as our guide can humanity climb out of the pit of ignorance in which it has for ever wallowed. Not until the great majority of the inhabitants of this earth have intelligent, well-balanced, individualistic minds can we expect settled peace and real happiness. The mass mind, admired by the drill sergeant, means that when nations hate one another war generally follows, because all think as a unit and fight united.

Meantime the comparatively few, those who are endowed with well-balanced minds, those who are intelligent, well informed, wise and prudent, must live their lives alone, while deploring the crimes and follies which come from ignorance. They are not counted amongst the great of this earth, whose inhabitants worship wealth, titles, pomp and ceremony. They are mostly unknown, although they belong to all classes of the community, but the masses of inferior intellect do not understand such advanced thinking, because the thinkers think as individuals and not in company with the mass mind of the common herd. Those who are thus blessed with individuality, knowledge and wisdom live in the heights, but have the satisfaction of knowing that by their thoughts and deeds they are helping in the great work of drawing all men and women upwards unto them.

Socrates was one of these individual thinkers, and the people of his day failed to appreciate his wisdom. They put him on trial like any ordinary criminal, and, in his defence, he said:—

During my life I have not been ambitious for wealth or position. I have not sought to adorn my body, but I have endeavoured to adorn my mind with the jewels of patience, justice, knowledge and liberty.

These words aptly describe the life of this notable individualist, and, because he was unique, because he was really great, because he put what is real and enduring before the transitory affairs of this earth, he was made to drink the hemlock. Thus he was removed from this order of existence into one for which he was better fitted, his presence on earth being objectionable to his intolerant contemporaries, who could not understand his thoughts and language. He was one of the first intellectual martyrs, one of the first to realise that the mind as well as the body requires nourishment, and that only by this being honestly supplied could harmony, progress and happiness come to mankind.

Europe, up to the time we are now considering, had enjoyed no progress, little happiness, and less harmony, because the minds of the people were undeveloped, but, as mind is a developing substance, very real indeed though it does not pertain to the physical order, a few individuals, in spite of the ban on rational thinking, developed mentally more rapidly than did others. They had receptive minds which were ready, when opportunity offered, to absorb further knowledge when it came their way, and it is about these new opportunities for mental development that something must here be said.

Now we have arrived at the beginning of the greatest era in man's long and chequered history. Now it was that the most momentous changes began to take place in his outlook on this earth and the universe, more important than have ever occurred since our ancestors left their primitive jungle existence. Knowledge, which for centuries had been quietly and patiently waiting outside the ramparts of ignorance, at last obtained an entrance, and swept before it the forces of superstition. The piercing of the enemy lines was slight to begin with, but, as the years passed and scientific instruments improved and increased, the breach widened, and, as it did so, theology declined and science progressed. Natural law displaced the gods in the ordering of the universe, and knowledge took the place of ignorance.

Quite the most daring and original thinker of those early days was Roger Bacon (1214–1294), whose speculations and experiments disclosed his advanced and comprehensive mind. He was an Englishman, and one of the first men in Christian Europe to have a scientific outlook, panting after knowledge, the search for which was largely denied him because he was a Franciscan friar. His opinions constantly led him into trouble, but still he experimented, thought and studied. He was put under surveillance and confined for many years, but all the time he was thinking and writing, attacking the ignorance of his time, and making suggestions for increased knowledge by means of experiments. "Cease to be ruled by dogmas and authorities; look at the world," he wrote, and this was the tenor of his message to mankind. He forecast the steamship, the motor-car and the airplane. Little wonder that he was considered dangerous in those dark days, and kept in confinement out of harm's way.

During the intellectual night of the Dark Ages, there also emerged another figure who did more than anyone since the time of Augustine to fashion the theological outlook of the Christian Church. Thomas

Aquinas (1225–1274), of noble birth, and now elevated to the rank of a saint in heaven, devoted his tireless energies to bring all departments of knowledge
under the domain of theology, his various books to
this end being crowned by the comprehensive work
entitled *Summa Theologica*, which, as its title suggests,
endeavoured to summarise everything worth knowing within two covers. The influence of this book
was decidedly bad, because therein he fanned the
flames of ignorance against heretics, who must be
exterminated, and also those harmless women called
witches, who, in reality, were endowed to a greater
or less degree with psychic gifts. From now onwards
no woman was safe, Joan of Arc being burned at the
stake on the strength of the arguments contained in
this ignorant theological treatise, which was based on
quotations from the Bible. The Church took *Summa
Theologica* as its guide, and intensified its campaign
against witchcraft, when women, and not men, were
the special object of its fear and hatred.

Moreover, theology poisoned mythology by black-
ing out, with threatening clouds of ignorance, all the
beauty and romance the Pagans had associated with
the gods in heaven. These imaginative creations
were divine beings who came to earth as friends to
fraternise with mankind. These immortals were
transformed by Christian theology into devils, who
came to earth only to injure Christians and divert
their thoughts from the true faith.

Christianity therefore obliterated all the joy and
romance from religion, and removed the comfort the
people had obtained from their beliefs relating to the
gods. Fear took the place of confidence and serenity,

when the gods were chased away from Mount Olympus, and, in their place, the sky was filled with demons ever on the look out to find some woman through whom they could injure the faithful on earth. Such was the teaching imparted to the clergy at every theological school in Christendom up to the 19th century, the evil influence of theology, moreover, stultifying the mental development of our ancestors, and making them cruel and vicious.

Aquinas taught his doctrines at the theological schools of Cologne, Paris and Rome, to occupy finally the professor's chair at Naples. Round the Christian Church he wound all he considered was worth knowing, because, as the expounder of Christian theology, it represented the sum and crown of science. He ranks with the first of a class known as the Schoolmen, a name which comprises those men who occupied their time interpreting the writings of Aristotle into theological language. Science to them had to be made to fit into theology, and so they misconstrued the pages of this great Greek scientist with their own interpretation of his opinions. Something the same happened last century when the attempt was made to show that the first chapter of *Genesis* was in agreement with modern scientific discoveries.

The Schoolmen were really very ignorant of everything we now know to be true, as, in their time, a theological explanation was given for everything. Though they groped for the truth, they had little to guide them. Still, by breaking slightly the theological crust of ignorance, they were the pioneers of the Renaissance, and, by translating an Arabic version of Aristotle into Latin, they set men thinking. Hitherto Christian Europe knew not even the name of this great Greek scientist, as he had been committed to oblivion by the Church in the 5th century. He, and all the other Greek and Latin philosophers, had then been consigned to hell as damned heathen. Now, however, this hitherto banned scientist was read by a few Christians for the first time, to such effect that two centuries later his writings were accepted by some as he meant them to be, and not as interpreted by the Schoolmen.

For about fifty years (1350-1400) an oasis of religious freedom existed in England, to be followed by the persecution directed against the Lollards. During this period of liberty lived a logical and rational scholar, John Duns Scotus, who, from his lecture room in Oxford, challenged the claim made by Aquinas to have merged faith and reason. Orthodox religion, Scotus asserted, was quite unintelligible, theology being barren of rational and logical thought. Observation and experiment only could lead to truth, and, on this scientific basis, he first led a band of thinkers in Oxford, and then in Paris, in their endeavour to discover more about the physical universe, the study of optics, and all that was embraced by natural law, being their one concern.

Contemporary with him lived William of Ockham, he being thus designated by the name of the village in which he was born in Surrey. He was one of the most prominent intellectual leaders of his age, his religious beliefs centring round the imitation of the life of Jesus, and not on the doctrine surrounding the theological Christ. He, and others like minded, were excluded from the fellowship of the Church, and regarded as heretics. At the height of his fame he lectured at the University of Paris, and probably died in 1349 at Munich, but the light he lit was soon afterwards extinguished by bitter persecution, and not relit until greater toleration gave a place to science in the 17th century.

Men such as these were the pioneers of our present-day professors and schoolmasters, and, as the centuries passed, teachers very slowly replaced the priests, hitherto the self-appointed mediums through whom the gods made their revelations to mankind. The thinkers, the researchers and the discoverers only gradually came to be recognised as the real benefactors of humanity. Natural law was found to be rigid, but, when understood and obeyed, good health, comfort and happiness followed. From the time knowledge first broke through the long established fortifications of ignorance, the representatives of the gods have receded ever farther in public estimation, the reputation of the scientists increasing in like proportion. The Scientist is the real saviour of mankind, and this will be realised when the human race learns, through ethical development, to use his discoveries only for its comfort and happiness and not for its destruction.

The discovery of how to make paper must rank, as the foundation on which the new era of knowledge was built. Parchment was too limited for wide circulation, and something more suitable was necessary. We have already learned how the Moslems brought to Spain the knowledge they had obtained from China of the way to manufacture paper, and how the Italians discovered the art from them. Something more than this knowledge was still necessary before books could be produced in more than limited numbers, and this was also first thought of in China, namely printing by movable type, an invention which can be traced back to A.D. 868. Whether Europe got the idea from China or not is uncertain, but we do know that Coster of Haarlem in Holland was the first to print on paper by this method in 1446. He it was who produced a machine that was destined to batter to pieces the old order of society and build up the one we know today.

Doubtless the production of paper stimulated the idea of printing, a method which to us seems so simple and obvious, but that is because paper and printing are now part of our lives. Before they were known the scribes laboriously and inaccurately copied one papyrus document after another, the vast majority of the people being quite uninterested in their circulation because papyrus was so limited and few could read or write. Coster was followed by Gutenberg of Mainz in 1455, and then others in Italy (1465), Paris (1470), Stockholm (1483) and Madrid (1499) took up the novel trade. Caxton set up his printing press at Westminster in 1477, when the first book was printed in England.

William Caxton (1422–1491) was indeed an outstanding man, a pioneer of the new learning, besides being a successful business man who had spent thirty years of his life in the Netherlands as the agent of The London Mercers Company. There he learned the art of printing, which he introduced into England, while at the same time he translated book after book from French and Latin into English, until, during the remaining fourteen years of his life, he produced, without even a dictionary to help him, nearly a hundred small books in his mother tongue. Others did likewise in Europe, and soon the passing of knowledge from mind to mind ceased to be a trickle and became a stream, to grow in size year by year until in our own times it has become a flood. Knowledge is now available to all who take the trouble to read.

The Bible was one of the first books to be printed, and, as in those days there were few authors, it was for long the only book to be read in Protestant countries. Consequently it took a place in literature far beyond its merits. As it had no competitor, claims were made for it which were quite baseless, but, as no one knew better, they were accepted and still prevail in our own times. Its real literary merit lies in it having standardised words and phraseology, so much so that words in most European languages have changed little in their meaning over the past four hundred years.

Scholars now began to write books, and the knowledge of how to read increased just as books multiplied in number. Thus was European literature born in the 15th century, and very slowly ignorance gave place to the knowledge of many things now accepted by nearly everyone. Italy was the land where first shone the sun of knowledge in Europe, and the reason for this is not difficult to discover. Its geographical position was closest to the home of ancient learning, just as was ancient Greece to the wisdom and knowledge of the Babylonians and the Egyptians. As Greece gave knowledge to Pagan Europe, so Italy did likewise to Christian Europe.

As ancient Greece was the source of the learning and culture of Rome, whence schools spread out over the Empire, so Italy performed the same function to Europe lying in the depth of intellectual darkness.

Impressed by the learning and culture of ancient Greece, and depressed by the prevailing ignorance of his time, Dante (1265-1321), born in Florence, and eager for further knowledge, called for the return of Greek literature, though two centuries passed before his call was answered. He was the prophet of the classics, but his was a voice crying in the wilderness. During this age, when some intellects were for the first time gazing past the ramparts of orthodox theology, and wondering as to the nature of the forbidden land which lay beyond, this mystical genius wrote his great epic poem, *Divine Comedy*, which told of an imaginary journey he took, under the guidance of Virgil, through the realms of Hell and Purgatory, to meet at last his beloved Beatrice, who led him through Paradise into the heart of the celestial mysteries.

Dante was interested in the political problems of his day, read voluminously, and wrote lyrics, but his fame rests on the *Divine Comedy*. His mastery of words and phrases fixed the Italian language, and raised it above a patois. Influenced as he was by the writing of Virgil, he produced this poem, filled with tenderness and humanity, qualities which were quite alien to his times. Of all medieval poets he stands closest to Virgil, and introduced to Christendom the humanism of this great Pagan. On this achievement rests Dante's fame as a herald of the Renaissance. Though he contributed nothing to the knowledge of the times he saw the dawn ahead, and stretched out his arms towards it.

In those days it was always dangerous to read the works of Virgil, and Petrarch (1304–1374), one of the founders of Italian literature, was persecuted as a wizard by a cardinal for so doing. This great literary pioneer exercised a great influence over the Schoolmen of his time. He advocated knowledge of the Greek language, which was banned by the Church to prevent the ancient Greek philosophers being read, but the time had now arrived when this prohibition could no longer be enforced, as the Greeks were now seeking refuge in Italy, bringing with them their language and the classics. When a deputation came from Constantinople, asking for assistance against the advancing Turks, one of the members remained behind in Florence, and commenced to teach the long-forgotten speech. Then others followed, until the time came when the knowledge of Greek became the mark of an Italian gentleman. This fashion spread from Italy to France, Germany and England, so much so that a knowledge of the literature of Greece and Rome became part of the education of the upper classes.

The conquest of Constantinople by the Turks in 1453 greatly increased the number of Greek classics in circulation, as many Greeks fled from the doomed city to Italy, carrying with them their possessions. Hundreds of precious manuscripts thus came into the hands of the noble-minded Aldus Manutius (1449–1514), the historian, moralist, educational pioneer, and the founder of the Aldine Press of Venice. These he had translated, and then published, in the form of cheap and beautifully bound printed books. He, and other printers elsewhere, thus aided the birth of the new knowledge which came to life slowly as the result of a combination of influences, such as discoveries by land and sea, the use of paper, and most of all the invention of printing.

Arabian scientific literature had by now found its way from Spain to Italy, and, with the revival of the study of Greek, the writings of the foremost Greek thinkers gave a further impetus to the desire for increased knowledge. Scholars consequently turned over, with wonder and relish, the newly printed pages of Aristotle, hitherto known to few outside the Moslem world, which alone had kept alight the torch of knowledge during the age of darkness.

Seven hundred years after the time of the advanced civilisation of Baghdad and Moslem Spain, Europe was being reborn into a new world, away from superstition, priests, feudalism and all the evils of the Dark Ages. Those who were eager for increased knowledge, found in the works of Greek and Latin authors all there then was on which to feed their hungry minds. Consequently, in the 16th century, books became the daily companions of those who were able to read, and a room was set aside in the houses of the well-to-do Italians, round the walls of which were placed these new treasures, which brought a fresh outlook into the lives of their owners, who, from now onwards, lived in a new atmosphere of thought and dressed with greater elegance.

Though life outside was by no means safe, police being unknown, Italian manners at home became more refined, this being particularly noticeable at meals, as the rich sat round a table covered with a white linen cloth, each one being provided with forks, spoons and a table napkin. So Roman culture was revived, and on the table were placed beautiful vases and cups of porcelain, while crystal ornaments decorated the different rooms, which contained handsome carved chairs placed on delicate carpets and rugs.

The welcome arrival of the Greeks in Italy had been preceded by the time when the popes were resident in Avignon (1309–1377), which was an age when the Church was at the height of luxury and in the depths of corruption, the popes, cardinals and bishops being in receipt of incomes of £100,000 a year, which in those days was worth five times what it is today. Then followed the Great Schism when one Pope ruled in Rome and another at Avignon (1378–1449), and when for a time three different popes claimed to be the Vicar of Christ. The corruption, disunity and wickedness in the Church weakened its authority, and gave opportunity for the people to think with greater freedom, so much so that when the Greek scholars arrived in Venice, Milan, Mantua, Padua, Verona, Florence, and other Italian cities, they were gladly welcomed.

Under the lead of Florence these cities consequently developed a new intellectual life of their own, and, as they were rich and powerful, they could defy the Pope when he expressed his displeasure. In consequence the first schoolmaster arose in the person of Vittorino da Feltre (1396–1446), the pioneer of secular education. He was the pioneer of our present-day system of education, his school at Mantua becoming famous throughout all Italy. Though he was cursed by the priests from the Pope downwards, who hated education with a bitter hatred, he carried on training his pupils of both sexes in mind and body, developing their characters to make them wiser and better men and women.

Turkish misrule, which drove out the Greek intellectuals, combined as it was with the weakened authority of the Church, thus gave western Europe the opportunity to acquire knowledge, so long banned by the theologians. After eleven hundred years of Christian rule, Italy once again took the place intellectually which she had occupied when the Roman Empire was at its height. Consequently, during the two hundred years from 1340 to 1540 the cities of northern Italy produced an output of literature, scholarship and art such as had not been seen since the golden age of Rome and Greece. Men, starved of intellectual nourishment, feasted with delight on the mental food she now supplied, and naturally looked on with increased horror and disgust at the claims, the voluptuous, luxurious living, and the evil lives of the priests.

In those days northern Italy was wealthy and prosperous, as her cities were the first to be reached in the trade route from the East, and a glance at a map makes clear how well situated they were to distribute all over Europe the wares which flowed into them. Along with the commodities which her cities distributed throughout Europe went the knowledge that came from the East, so much so that the new learning gradually made its way everywhere, and by the time Venice and Genoa had lost their importance by the divergence of trade, in consequence of the opening up of the new· world, Europe had been impregnated with a fresh outlook which slowly gave birth to the Renaissance.

Unfortunately Italy was not privileged to reap the glory of the harvest from the seed she had sown, as, with her declining prosperity, due to the discovery of America, the Church again fastened on her the grip of its evil tentacles. Prosperity brings learning and comfort. Ignorance is the companion of poverty. So, when poverty returned to Italy, the grip of the Church tightened, all the more so because northern Italy fell under the domination of Spain in 1538, following her success in the conflict between Francis I of France and Charles V of Spain over the ownership of the Duchy of Milan. Then night again fell all over Italy, the Jesuits, the Holy Inquisition, and the Index, which prohibited all but theological literature, replacing the scholars, the thinkers and the Greek classics. Then ceased the broad and fruitful stream of Italian thought and art, its place being again taken by the muddy sluggish theological mysticism which had kept Europe in ignorance since the 4th century.

The achievements of the great Italian humanists must never be forgotten, as they led the way to the discovery of natural law from which developed the sciences. They brought again to light the beauty and greatness of the Pagan world, when Plato and Aristotle received the place which was due to their outstanding intellects. To the Italian pioneers we owe all that brings us intellectual satisfaction and our present comforts, the houses the Italian architects built being designed for comfort and not for defence as heretofore. Though her great painters and architects of the 15th and 16th centuries passed away and were not replaced, though her prose and dramatic writers died and none were found to take their places, other lands took up the good work she commenced, and centuries later brought it to a fruitful conclusion.

France now became the refuge of prose, England sheltered the creators of poetry and drama, while music found a home in Germany, and art in the Netherlands. So we have a galaxy of great men to thank for all we have today, Italians, Germans, French, Dutch and English. The intellectual light they shone on darkened Europe brought about that period known as the Renaissance, or new birth, the name we give to the time when these great artistic and literary achievements flourished. Then lived outstanding poets, painters and sculptors, when those things which are beautiful came to be revered in a way unknown since the golden age of Greece.

This poetic and artistic movement in Italy commenced before even printing was invented, in fact the Renaissance was a gradual development towards a higher type of life and thought. Dante, Petrarch and Boccaccio wrote before the Renaissance reached its zenith, while Giotto (1266–1337) and Angelico da Fiesole (1387–1455) were the first to give impetus to art. Then followed Michael Angelo (1474–1564), who was as great a sculptor as he was a painter, and, contemporary with him, lived Raphael (1483–1520), both of whom chose religious subjects because the Church was then their principal patron.

Italy was rich in master painters, the most famous

exponents of Venetian or Florentine art being Filippo Lippi (1412–1469), Mantegna (1431–1506), Signorelli (1442–1524), Botticelli (1447–1510), Ghirlandajo (1449–1494), Perugino (1446–1524), Titian (1477–1576), Tintoretto (1518–1594) and Palladio (1518–1580). In Germany were born Durer (1471–1528), Holbein (1497–1543) and Rubens (1577–1640), while Holland produced Hubert van Eyck (1366–1426), Jan van Eyck (1380–1441), Anthony van Dyck (1599–1641) and Rembrandt (1607–1669), and Spain Velazquez (1599–1660) and Murillo (1617–1682), but space does not permit more than just a mention of their names.

It is however noteworthy, as illustrating the limited knowledge of the times, that all artists and dramatists up to the end of the 18th century portrayed their characters in the dress of their own period, the actor representing Alexander the Great, for instance, appearing on the French stage, in the time of Voltaire, dressed in the costume of Louis XIV. Likewise religious plays took the setting of the time in which they were performed, the actor representing God, who came down from heaven by a ladder, wearing a beard, a tiara, a white cope and gloves, while Mary Magdalene was represented as a very fashionable lady of the times and Jewish priests were dressed like bishops.

In England Geoffrey Chaucer (1340–1400), a Londoner and cultured courtier, produced poetry in narrative verse, but, owing to wars and conflicts, it was not until two centuries had passed that there was here a rapid development of classical learning. Then Edmund Spenser (1552–1599) wrote the *Faerie Queene,* and literary effort was crowned by Shakespeare (1564–1616), the greatest dramatist of the Christian era and master literary mind of the age. In Europe Cervantes (1547–1616) wrote in Spain, Rabelais (1490–1553) and Montaigne (1533–1592) in France, and Erasmus (1466–1536) in Holland, each of whom were representative of the literary movement of the time, when authors gave free rein to their imagination and depicted life in all its aspects.

Christianity had always taught that all knowledge, culture and morals were contained within the Scriptures, and that before its advent the world was living in a state of heathen darkness. The revival of classical learning, and the return to the Greek method of imparting instruction from the stage, profoundly affected many fresh and simple enquiring minds, now brought for the first time to the knowledge of the truth, the great discovery being made that highly civilised nations existed long prior to the Christian era. Moreover they found, to their great surprise that the great Pagan thinkers, who had been represented to them as debased heathen, whose abode was now in hell, had advocated a code of ethics, and a way of life and thought, far higher than anything taught by the Christian Church.

In the works of Pythagoras, Plato, and the other philosophers, they found set down a much higher standard of ethical conduct than had ever been envisaged by Christianity, and one, moreover, which had not been debased by the inclusion of an innocent victim whose sacrifice had relieved all believers of the need to live righteous lives. Herein they found a new and noble philosophy, a wider and grander range of ideas, a beauty and vision far beyond anything they had ever known. Out of this mental garden grew the sciences, the philosophy and sociology which is now part of our daily lives. Truth consequently came to be sought for in place of the blind acceptance of the theological speculations of an ignorant priesthood, and Christian civilisation thus received its first setback. Nevertheless, its representatives fought hard and long before it was finally overthrown.

From this time onwards Europe took the leading place amongst all the other continents, and the prospect of the Mongols overlording the world. began to recede. From the 16th century Europe became a vital and powerful force in world affairs, and, instead of the East dominating the West, as at one time seemed possible, the reverse happened as Europe spread her influence over the entire globe. Progress quickened, but to advance only in material things does not comprise all that the word "progress" means to the humanists, those rational thinkers who put the welfare of mankind before all else. Knowledge of material things does not contain all there is to know, as matter is the crudest form of known substance. The study of etheric and mental substance is just as important, and, as man on earth comprises all three, a knowledge of them all is necessary to secure the comfort, happiness and harmony of human society.

Europe, from now onwards, certainly progressed materially, its people now used gunpowder and cannon to kill each other instead of swords and arrows, and they learned more of their place in the universe and the properties of matter. Something became known of the human frame, of the remedies necessary for better health, and, as the centuries passed, better houses, roads and public buildings were built, though travel and communication remained as they had been since the horse became the means of locomotion. The standard of living rose, the people dressed better, and altogether man was getting to grips with nature by making its forces work for him to his greater ease and comfort.

Along with this the means of human slaughter went on increasing, until today we have highly perfected mass-murder machines capable of blowing to pieces towns and villages in a single night. So material knowledge is not everything. There is something just as important for the human race to learn, and only when this knowledge comes will the curse of ignorance be removed. The nations must now learn how to live peacefully and happily as a world family. Our ancestors, in the 16th century, knew not how this could be attained, in fact they never gave the subject any thought. The difference between then and now is that we are at least thinking about it; in fact the future historian may write about the Renaissance of the 20th century, when the people were reborn into the realisation that happiness can only come when honour, truth, justice, kindness, and all that righteousness stands for, take first place in everyone's outlook on life.

Printing and paper also made more widely known the thoughts and activities of those men, with enquiring minds, who delved into the mysteries of nature, and tried to find the reason for the phenomena we daily experience. We have noticed how the works of Aristotle, who made the first attempt to systematise knowledge, were eagerly read by enquiring minds. From his time onwards to the 16th Christian century little further, outside the scientific work done by the Moslems, had been attempted, but now we are at the period when his influence again made itself felt, and others took up the work of scientific research. They were, however, handicapped in a way Aristotle and the Moslem scientists never were, because Church influence against them was strong and the Inquisition very active. Every enquirer knew that if he propounded something new and strange, then prison or banishment or torture and the stake might be his punishment. The Church was determined that knowledge should not increase, and it used every cruel and brutal method for its suppression.

All the same, some rare people went on thinking and experimenting, the alchemists being the forerunners of the chemists, as the astrologers were of the astronomers, and the herbalists of doctors. Their researches laid the foundation of the knowledge which produced the scientific mind so longed for by Roger Bacon.

The first great scientist of the Renaissance was Leonardo da Vinci (1452–1519), one of the really great men of the human race, who was the illegitimate son of a Florentine lawyer and a peasant woman. He was probably the most complete man of any age, a brilliant all-round man of science and the arts, as he surpassed all his contemporaries as an artist, sculptor, naturalist, chemist, anatomist, engineer, geologist, botanist, architect and musician. His knowledge was so in advance of his time that he anticipated in hundreds of ways the great masters of discovery who were to follow him. He was a genial companion, a generous, honourable and loyal friend, kind and considerate, never aggressive, and quite philosophical in his religion. His most celebrated picture depicts his idea of what is called "The Last Supper".

Niklas Koppernigk (1473–1543), better known as Nicolaus Copernicus, the great Polish astronomer, discovered that the earth and the planets revolved round the sun, but, knowing what his fate would be if he made public his knowledge, he withheld it until he was an elderly man. The first printed copy of his book, *On the Revolution of the Heavenly Bodies*, explaining his discoveries, reached him a few weeks before he died, but he was too ill to read it. Taking advantage of the great astronomer's enfeeblement, a Lutheran theologian, who had undertaken to read the proofs, inserted a preface to the effect that this new unsettling hypothesis need not be true or even likely, but this treacherous betrayal of confidence could not keep back the truth.

Both Luther and the Pope denounced Copernicus as an agent of the devil, and the Christian Church placed his book on the *Index Expurgatorius*, where it remained until 1835. Now indeed the first round had commenced between the theologians, basing their opinions on the Bible, and the scientists, and, although the priests did their utmost for seventy years to prevent his book reaching the people, torturing, imprisoning and burning at the stake many who accepted the new heresy, the Copernican theory was universally accepted within one hundred and fifty years.

While honouring Copernicus we must not forget that Pythagoras, Aristotle and Ptolemy of Alexandria, by their speculations, stimulated the famous Polish astronomer to fashion his ideas. Neither should we overlook the fact that the astronomers who followed him hastened their final triumph. Now we know that this illustrious man was right, and that our earth is but a satellite of a mediocre star, which we call the sun, itself a member of a galaxy of some hundred thousand million stars, this galaxy being again one of a system of galaxies numbering 50,000,000 so far as our present knowledge goes. How puny does this immensity make us feel as physical beings, but how great does it prove us to be mentally, to have been able to discover and envisage what these vast depths of space contain. We can think of the universe, and this is something the universe cannot do of us. Truly the human mind is boundless in its explorations, to it boundaries do not exist, and, as it develops, it is able to grasp and encompass ever more of its seemingly limitless environment.

The work commenced by Corpernicus was carried on enthusiastically by Joachim Rheticus (1514–1576), and then by Tycho Brahe (1546–1601), the illustrious Danish astronomer, who, under royal patronage, built an observatory and chemical laboratory. He was a nobleman, and in those days the aristocracy looked upon knowledge as beneath their dignity, only politics, theology and war being their occupation. All the more honour to him that he devoted his life to science, to become one of the outstanding pioneers of modern astronomy and the master of the famous Kepler, though unfortunately his early religious training made him twist facts to conform to old ideas. Thus he confused rather than clarified existing difficulties, which his celebrated pupil finally elucidated.

The famous German astronomer, John Kepler (1571–1630), might well be claimed to be the Father of Modern Science. This was born when he discovered his first law, that the planets do not move in circles, but maintain in the heavens a regular oval path, known as an ellipse. Then he propounded his second law, that they describe equal spaces in equal times, which was followed by his third law, that the squares of their periodic times are proportioned by the cubes of their distances. By these three laws he gave to mankind the key to unlock the mysteries of the heavens, and finally established the fact that the universe is governed by law, his effort being rewarded by him being excommunicated from the Protestant Church.

While this brilliant man was thinking out these deep problems, his contemporaries were torturing heretics and burning witches, his studies being often interrupted for this reason. His mother, for instance, who was a medium, was arrested at the age of seventy-four, after being under supervision for five years, when she was imprisoned and then taken to the torture chamber on the charge of witchcraft. For thirteen months thereafter she was kept in prison, awaiting the carrying out of the death sentence, which was only averted by the exertions of her son. To read of the long-drawn-out misery this woman endured is quite revolting, and the records which have been preserved make clear that the Protestant Church was in no way behind the Church from which it dissented in its cruelty and methods of torture. For centuries in Germany a veritable epidemic of fear of witches existed, and more perished there than in any other country in Europe.

The greatest of all the natural philosophers was undoubtedly Sir Isaac Newton (1642–1727), the first mathematical physicist, and a master of exposition, who, a century later, made comprehensible the three Kepler laws by his discovery of the law of gravitation. He, the most outstanding scientific figure of all time, and endowed with the greatest mind of his age, when a poor student at Cambridge, discovered the properties of light which led him to perfect the telescope. Thus began his study of astronomy, which made him wonder why the heavenly bodies kept their ordered course, and did not fly off into space. One day, seeing an apple fall from a tree, he came to the conclusion that the earth was a magnet which drew to it things smaller than itself. On this theory he worked out the law of gravitation, by which he explained how mass and distance affected the pull of gravity, one of the most stupendous achievements of the human mind.

Nevertheless theology in his day reigned supreme, and, unlike the Greek scientists, he did not dare to advocate a natural universe of law and order which operated apart from divine intervention. Descartes, his immediate predecessor in France, had his great work *Principia Philosophiae* held up for eleven years because he could not make his science fit in with the first chapter of Genesis. Newton, however, compromised with theology, and in a peculiarly subtle manner he rewrote the creation story in a way which least offended the Church, and so escaped the fate of earlier scientists. Consequently his fame spread, and from 1703 onwards he was president of the Royal Society until he died, though he also found time to be Master of the Mint and reform his country's currency.

Here indeed we have arrived at the beginning of a new age, the age of natural law, and have left behind for ever the theory that the gods are responsible for all the phenomena of nature. History can be divided into the Supernatural Age and the Natural Age, the theological and the logical, the former so far having burdened man's time on earth. Now we are at the beginning of quite a new conception of everything. Man, instead of considering himself the puppet of the gods and devils, to be pulled this way and that at their will and pleasure, now discovered that nature works according to fixed laws which when understood could be used to do his bidding. The gods were now banished from a place in the ordering of the universe, their functions had always been mistaken, and, besides this, the etheric realm, to which we all pass at death, had been imagined as quite different from what it really is.

This quite new and revolutionary outlook on life and the universe, came first of all to only a small number of men, and, for the next two hundred years, the clergy were able to keep it from the people by opposing their education and keeping them illiterate. Now only in the most backward priest-ridden countries can this be done, and the belief in miracles, which, during the Theological Age, was such a help in maintaining the priesthood, is now proving its undoing. When miracles cease to be believed, the end has come to all organised orthodox supernatural religion.

In ignorance man thought the sun moved round the earth, that the earth was flat, that matter was solid and space was empty, all easily understandable mistakes, as nearly everything in nature is different from what it seems to be. Likewise, in ignorance, it was believed that one or more supernatural beings could give or withhold rain, produce thunder and lightning, and control all those phenomena of nature which make life easy or difficult, comfortable or unpleasant. On them it was believed we depended for our food and clothing, and all the blessings and misfortunes which come to mankind.

We have only to read of the unpleasant experiences suffered by Spinoza (1632–1677), the Jewish philosopher, who lived in Holland, to obtain a glimpse of the mentality of our ancestors only some three hundred years ago. This brilliant thinker, who wrote on law and ethics, had placed upon him the most dreadful and comprehensive curse the theologians of his day could produce, and he moreover suffered much persecution because he regarded the Bible as naturally produced, and not dictated by God to certain scribes in Palestine. He was the forerunner of those scholars who, during the past hundred years, have separated facts from fiction in this ancient tome. By his arguments, he laid the foundation of rational thought which has freed the mind from those theological chains that, until now, had kept the people in mental darkness and the misery which comes from ignorance.

When it was discovered that the word translated

as God meant "the gods" in the original Aramaic, the *Book of Genesis* found its true place alongside the mythology of the Pagans. Then followed the scholarly work done by Ernest Renan (1823–1892), the great French thinker, his investigation into the composition of the New Testament bringing to light the fact that over a period of three centuries a Jew had been transformed into another Pagan Christ. It is difficult for us today to appreciate the mental revolution which followed when it was discovered that beliefs, hoary in age, supported by tradition thousands of years old, and all the wealth which had accumulated around them, were founded on myths and not on facts. Hitherto every church, pagoda, temple, mosque and shrine had been the meeting-place where man had made the best terms possible with the gods, through their agents the priests. Millions upon millions of prayers had been offered, vast wealth had been subscribed, countless ceremonies had been performed, millions of men, women and animals had been sacrificed as food to placate these potentates of the skies, and now it was discovered by some that all this effort, all this waste of wealth and time, had been unnecessary.

Truly we are here at the dividing line between ignorance and knowledge, between theology and science, between the priest and the schoolmaster, between the priest-magician and the medium, between miracles and facts, and between error and truth. No longer need man cringe and fear, as he has only to work in combination with knowledge, to think and to reason to obtain his needs. The more he mingles his reason with his work, and the less he relies on the gods for help, does his progress increase, his reward being the comforts and bounties nature has in store for all who understand her laws.   Man is his own saviour, and, as he lives here, so will he live hereafter, our life after death, in an etheric body, a duplicate of our present body, being a natural continuation, in a natural world, of the one lived on earth.

It was not until last century that physical and psychic science unfolded the secrets so long hidden in mystery.   Now we know man's physical and psychic construction, and his destiny.   Now we know enough of natural law to comprehend how marvellous is the universe in which mind is for ever struggling for expression.   Now we realise the omnipotence of Mind, the architect of the universe, the cosmic designer and sustainer, but three centuries had to pass from the time of the Renaissance before theology was replaced by science, and man found his true place in the universe.

Much of history from the 16th to the 19th century is concerned with the bitter fight which was waged between the theologians and the thinkers, between those who relied on the gods and those who held that man must save himself and rise superior to his surroundings by thought and action.   This volume has recorded the depravity caused by the curse of ignorance, though lightened here and there by the attempts made for its removal.   The next volume relates to the new era which the scientists, who are mentioned in this section, opened up for mankind, and records the bitter fight which followed for its realisation.   From now onwards we shall emerge from darkness, through the dawn, to welcome finally the day, illuminated by the sun of knowledge ever gathering strength and brightness.

One of the most distinguished men of science of the 16th century was William Gilbert (1540–1603), who made numerous experiments, chiefly in magnetism, and these helped Sir Francis Bacon (1561–1626) to form his ideas. Bacon is called the "Father of Experimental Philosophy", and more will be told of his life and work in Chapter XIII. The Greeks and Romans argued over and discussed the causes which created natural phenomena, but now we have come to the time when men began to experiment. Consequently they obtained positive information on questions which hitherto had been mysterious, to bring about a great advance in science during the next three hundred years. By applying this method to the human body, William Harvey (1578–1657), an Englishman, furthered the science of anatomy, and advanced the work of Servetus, who discovered the pulmonary circulation of the blood. Harvey's doctrine was completed by Leeuwenhoek (1632–1723), a Dutchman of remarkable scientific ability, who discovered the capillary circulation of the blood from the arteries into the veins.

Besides this, Leeuwenhoek arranged lenses so as to produce the first microscope,[1] and Lippershey, also a Dutchman, invented the telescope in 1608, which Galileo (1564–1642) perfected until he obtained a thirty-twofold magnifying power. Galileo published the result of his discoveries in a book entitled *The System of the World*, wherein he proved the

[1] The recently invented Electron microscope makes visible an object no larger in size than one millionth of an inch.

insignificance of the earth and the immensity of the universe. He made use of the leaning tower at Pisa to demonstrate his theories on the effect of the earth on substances of different size and weight. Because he asserted that the earth was not the fixed immovable centre of the universe, and that the sun was larger than the earth, he was condemned to imprisonment by seven cardinals, and made to recite seven penitential psalms once a week for three years.

He was fortunate not to be treated like Giordano Bruno (1548–1600), "The Morning Star of the Renaissance", one of the most genial of men, who was burned at the stake in Rome. He was tried and convicted because of his philosophical opinions, which embraced the discoveries of Copernicus, but was offered his liberty if he would accept the Scriptures as God-inspired. This he refused to do, and, after seven years of imprisonment, he was taken to the place of execution, draped in a robe adorned with paintings of hideous devils. He was chained to the stake, around his body being piled faggots, which the priests lit to the glory of God, and the mob, which had come to enjoy the entertainment, performed their function by repeating the creed produced by an assembly of ignorant quarrelling priests at Nicaea.

Thus perished one of the noblest and grandest men who ever trod this earth. He was the first martyr to science, and met his death without thought of reward or punishment hereafter, his great achievement being that he helped to lay the foundation of our modern science of astronomy.

When a young man, Bruno discarded all belief in

Christianity, for which decision he was excommunicated and treated as an outcast in Italy, the land of his birth. So he wandered throughout the cities of Europe absorbing the new learning and expounding his philosophy. Like the great Greek philosophers, he was always seeking for unity in the universe, for the one and only principle which binds the cosmos together. He postulated an ever active agent, infinite and eternal, expressing itself in unlimited forms of activity. He bitterly attacked the Christian faith and the Catholic and Protestant priests, who fed the people on lies and entirely neglected to raise them to a higher ethical level—truth, justice, knowledge and wisdom being to him the aim of those who seek for righteousness.

Wherever he went he was persecuted by the priests, to find refuge finally in England, where he became the friend of Sir Philip Sidney. He was much disgusted with the coarseness and brutality of English manners, and at the gross superstition everywhere throughout the land, but here at least he was permitted to live in peace, to produce the best of his philosophical works. He was one of the great pioneers of learning, one of those who had the imagination to see how the discoveries of Copernicus would alter the entire conception of the universe, but, though he was offered the Chair of Philosophy in Paris, he refused this tempting offer because it was conditional on him becoming a Christian.

After reading the foregoing tragic story, the following remarks made by the Reverend M. C. D'Arcy over the radio (when engaged in giving one of its numerous Christianity propaganda talks, a copy of which appeared in *The Listener*, 22-10-1942) make a travesty of history and treat truth with derision:—

> There is no end to the things we owe to Christianity, hospitals and our type of schools and university, a passion for learning, and laws which emancipated us and gave us our freedom and rights as free men . . . new kinds of spiritual beauty as displayed by a Venerable Bede, a Benedict, or Bruno, or Francis of Assisi; a new idea in truth, of human nature, with the accompanying virtues of brotherliness, respect for woman, and innocence and humility.

Those who have read this book so far, and read on to the end, will be able to judge for themselves how far this zealous propagandist has strayed from the truth, by attributing to Christianity the fact that we now have hospitals, schools, universities, a passion for learning, laws which gave us our freedom, and the virtues of brotherliness, respect for women, innocence and humility. In many ways the B.B.C. has been a great force for good; its honesty in providing Britain and the world with truthful news and propaganda during the Second World War brought it the gratitude and respect of all freedom-loving men and women everywhere throughout the world, and the hatred of all the tyrants. Its secular work is honest, clean and straightforward, but when it enters the realm of religion the position is quite different. Here it is under the authority of the Christian Church, whose B.B.C. Religious Advisory Committee is composed of orthodox Christians to whom their religion comes first and truth second.

So long as the clergy and churchmen have the power to control religious broadcasts, the people will never be told the truth, and no discussion will ever be allowed. Religious services will remain orthodox, none but the orthodox will be permitted to broadcast on religious subjects,[1] and the people will be told blatant lies to which no reply will be permitted. Not until the B.B.C. rids itself of Church domination, and the influence of the priest, will its religious broadcasts be fair to all, and free of theological bias, which is the enemy of truth. Not until then will it perform its function of expressing freely the honest opinions of all sections of the community. In a democratic country there can be no regimented religious thinking, and, as all are free to think and express their thoughts as they consider right, the radio should not be exclusively reserved for one shade of opinion, whose only claim is that its traditions go back to antiquity. Truth comes before all else, no one brand of religion or philosophy should have a monopoly, and the clergy should not have the liberty to tell the public their pious lies for the greater glory of their religion without fear of reply.

Vesalius (1514–1564), a native of Brussels, nearly suffered the same fate as Bruno. He was the pioneer of a comprehensive and systematic study of human anatomy, and only his position as imperial physician to the court of Charles V saved him from torture and the stake, because he dared to cut into a dead human body which it was believed was destined to rise again on the Resurrection Day. He was arrested by the Church gestapo, though he had received the consent

[1] Since this book was set up in print the B.B.C. has announced a new series of talks embracing the beliefs of men holding both orthodox and unorthodox religious opinions. It is to be hoped that this constitutes the beginning of a more latitudinarian policy for the future.

of the relatives of the deceased to make his investigations, and only the King's personal intervention
saved his life. He was, however, deprived of his
position, and forced by the Pope to undertake a
pilgrimage of penance to Jerusalem, to be wrecked on
an island and die there in poverty. Thus died this
great explorer into the composition of the human body,
a victim of the ignorance of his time, but he lit the
lamp which guided future anatomists on the way of
knowledge. What a contrast to the way surgeons
and doctors were treated in Pagan Greece and
Rome!

Persecution, as we have already discovered, has
always been associated with the Christian religion.
Up to the 10th century its victims were Pagans, Jews
and Arian Christians. Then, after an interval, when
the Church was occupied in organising one crusade
after another to overthrow the infidel Turk, the all-
powerful Innocent III (1198–1216) recommenced the
massacre of heretics by exterminating the Albigenses,
when hundreds of thousands of innocent people
perished, as was told in the last chapter. From this
time onwards one pope after another stands out as the
saviour of orthodoxy, by the power of the sword and
the torture inflicted by the Inquisition. Clement V
(1305–1314), a craven, cunning and worthless
pontiff (who was forced by France to remove the
Holy See from Rome to Avignon), carried on the
ghastly work of exterminating the unorthodox. All
heretics, mediums and those anxious to reform the
Church were burned at the stake throughout Europe,

at the time when the Holy See revelled in gaiety, licence and luxury surpassing any royal court elsewhere, Clement himself accumulating over £1,000,000 sterling.

The corrupt, cruel, passionate, hard-drinking Pope Paul IV (1555-1559) tightened up the existing torture organisation in all Christian countries, declaring that no distinction was to be made in the victim charged, no reports were to be made public, no witnesses were to be called, and that the names of all informers were to be kept secret. In other words there was to be no justice, only the verdict of the presiding priest, to whom everyone was a heretic who did not think as he did. Nazi Germany never reached to lower depths of iniquity than did the Christian Church throughout the 16th and 17th centuries, and only because of the ignorance of the people of its past evil record does it have a place in present-day society. Such, however, is still its influence that this book, which tells the story of the past honestly and fearlessly, will be kept out of our schools and universities by the authorities, and consequently only in later life will those with enquiring minds discover the truth.

During the Renaissance the Church gestapo was very busy. The Inquisitors of the Faith were everywhere hunting down heretics, thinkers and scholars, and few countries of Europe were safe for other than orthodox Christians. Since the Council of Toulouse in 1229 the Holy Inquisition (founded in the 4th century) had been everywhere firmly established, and few thinkers escaped from its deadly tentacles, as every parish priest was its active agent.

In Spain it was working hard, and every conceivable form of torture was being employed to force people to think as the priests desired. Having driven out the Moslems and the Jews, Spanish industrial and artistic talent had become negligible, and now every latitudinarian who remained was tortured, imprisoned or burned. In Portugal, and elsewhere, women and children were being burned for eating meat on a holy day. In Italy the flames rose ever and anon from the stakes set up in the market square of every town. In Germany and France all liberal thought was being stamped out with ferocious cruelty, while in England the flames from the stakes erected in London, Oxford, Canterbury, and other centres, were being fed by a regular supply of fresh victims, but it was reserved for the Netherlands to undergo such a systematic reign of terror and persecution as has hardly its equal in history.

Hundreds of volumes would be required to record the names of the victims of the Christian Church up to as late as the 19th century, as the numbers who were persecuted and murdered run into such astronomical figures that it is difficult for the mind to grasp them. Voltaire, in the 18th century, branded this evil institution "The Triumphant Beast", a sobriquet which epitomised its ghastly record for fourteen hundred years. When thinking of all the fiendish cruelty throughout the Christian era, and long before that time, one comforting thought comes to mind. Nature so arranges things that after the curve of pain has quickly risen to a certain definite height, it becomes level, and then gradually sinks to zero, as the victim becomes unconscious and feels no more.

Many, however, were never allowed to become unconscious, and the torture was repeated from time to time, with the never-ending mental agony from which the victim suffered by being told to recant and repent. But it must be remembered that this treatment was not inflicted for the purpose of only causing suffering, as there was a motive behind it all. Torquemada, the priest in charge of the Inquisition in Spain for many years of the 15th century, and the gangs of murderers and torturers in every Christian country, sincerely believed that it was better that unbelievers in the Christian creed and doctrines should be made believers by pain and suffering here on earth, and so be saved from everlasting torment in hell for all eternity. Their authority for this was the god they believed had saved them and founded their religion. (*Matthew* v, 29–30.)

This is the way Christians interpreted the brotherhood of man, so longed for by the noble Pagan idealists, who were fortunate to have lived before the time the Western world was blighted by Christian doctrines. During the time Christian civilisation prevailed nearly everyone believed that anyone holding heretical opinions was certain to suffer eternal pain in hell, this evil conception of God blinding them to all humane and rational thought. When such an idea was drilled into the minds of all Christian children when they were plastic and receptive, we can better understand the reason for the intolerance which darkened Christendom.

To these warped minds it was quite impossible to tolerate heretical opinions, which were to be the cause of the heretic's own personal everlasting damnation, and also the means of leading others off the only way which leads to salvation. Such is the bitter fruit that is produced by supernatural religion, which transforms the other world into two fantastic places, one for believers and one for unbelievers, and the men and women who inhabit it into saints and devils.

Man makes his god or gods in his own image. Cruel men have cruel gods, and Jehovah, taken over from a savage eastern tribe, is a merciless, pitiless deity, but he suited the Christian mentality, which believed that he had given each man, woman and child, one, and only one, chance of salvation. If this were rejected there was no way of escape from eternal perdition. When this is kept in mind, the motive which influenced these fiends, who so believed, can be better understood. Ignorance produced the Inquisition, and ignorance directed the unenlightened priests and their accomplices to adopt these cruel and inhuman methods.

All this evil came from a misinterpretation of nature's laws. A fundamental theological belief places right and wrong on God, who wills and desires this or that. This error is implied in every sermon in our own day, and runs through the prayers and hymns sung during worship. It is a mistake to be found in every religion, as each one declares that our beliefs and conduct must be directed to please God or the gods. This theological doctrine is fundamentally wrong, and has been the cause of so much of the misery and suffering which has afflicted humanity. Here the curse of ignorance has lain heavily on the human race.

To direct our conduct to please God means that we take the ancient theological idea of an anthropomorphic God as our guide, and not our duty to our fellow men. God to everyone is a mental creation, the evil-minded man imagining God like unto himself. What he does pleases the god of his own creation, whereas the ethical code is based on observation and experience, which means that there is a solid basis for conduct, namely to increase harmony, comfort and happiness throughout the human family. When this fact is well and truly learned, the God idea (the mental image the devout make of God) will conform to this higher aspect of thought, and right and wrong will be judged by the ethical and not the theological standard. Let us hope, however, that the time will some day come when the God idea will pass away, so far as conduct is concerned, and that our thoughts and deeds will be based solely on the welfare of mankind. When this advance is made everyone will realise how far astray theology led the people, its evil results being so apparent to everyone who makes reason and experience his guide.

The Church, led by ignorant and often wicked men, brought misery and confusion to Christendom, because its leaders believed that they were acting in accordance with the dictates of the god produced by the theologians of old, who imagined a god like unto themselves. Wicked as many of them were, they were devout, and honestly thought that heresy was something the god of their imagination loathed and hated, to stamp out which received his blessing and approval. Ignorance reduced heresy to a minimum, but, with increased intelligence, heresy flourished, and now we have reached the time when the Church authorities had to face the fact that only by increased persecution could their age-old authority be maintained.

After a thousand years of undisputed rule, after this millennium of mental darkness, during which time its power and dictates were unquestioned by its servile subjects, we can well imagine the attitude of the Church hierarchy towards everyone who now questioned its authority. Since the time the Christian Church had taken the place of the Roman emperor in 410, all criticism of its pronouncements had been curbed by brutal violence, until a uniform mode of thought had eventually been produced. Heretics in the past had interpreted Christianity differently from the Church authorities, but now these revolutionaries were striking at the very foundation of Christian doctrine. Well can we imagine the serious outlook which was then taken by the Holy See, and how grave the question seemed to men who had always been accustomed to unquestioned obedience.

To them the "will of God", as proclaimed by his Church on earth, was being undermined, and their duty called them to remove this danger by every possible means without delay. Schism and heresy were bad enough, but to cast doubt on the truth of the Holy Scriptures, which were considered a full and final divine revelation, was the greatest of all the sins. How could all these new discoveries be true when no mention had been made of them in God's Holy Word? Consequently they must be false, and, this being so, their authors were the agents of the devil working contrary to the divine plan.

With this opinion held by almost everyone, from the highest to the lowest, we can easily imagine the position of the man with a scientific outlook. A false step, an unguarded utterance, and he was immediately brought before his local Inquisition. The wonder is that some were brave enough to think, to wonder and to experiment. Developing mind, however, proved itself superior to unthinking brutal force, and truth slowly fought its way through the ramparts of theology. This conflict lasted over the next four hundred years, until the 19th century, and the persecution which accompanied it makes pale in comparison all the misery which theological ignorance had already brought on Christendom.

The leaders of Christianity, from now onwards, pass before us one by one, their chief characteristic being bigotry and intolerance, vices which caused them to perpetrate deeds so foul and shocking that even the Germans of our own time have not been able to equal them. Up to the Reformation this terrible cruelty found its source in the popes at Rome, but, as the reformers were equally bigoted, both Roman Catholic and Protestant Europe suffered from religious persecution so severe that it surpasses anything ever recorded in history.

All the popes have believed in torture as a means to combat heresy, as every priest holding high office has to swear on ordination that he will persecute all heretics, and Pius IX (1846–1878), as late as last century, in 1864, publicly declared his belief in torture. The belief in torture has always been amongst the declared beliefs of every Holy Father, each one having considered it as the means appointed by God to secure the salvation of unbelievers, and during the time we are considering this policy was considered by most people as right and proper.

What, however, disgusted a much greater number

was the sale of offices, the corruption, wickedness and luxurious living of the clergy, and from the 16th century onwards their licentious living, and lust for wealth and power, did more to lower the prestige of the Vicar of Christ in public estimation than anything else. As Europe advanced mentally the Papacy declined in respect and influence. Mental development, by lightening the curse of ignorance, decreased the power of those who thrived on cruelty and ignorance, and, as the Papacy waned, civilisation and culture increased.

How could it be otherwise? An institution, a system, which believed only in theological teaching and not in education, that progress was contrary to the will of God, and that the desire for improved social conditions was inspired by the devil, could not flourish in an age of greater enlightenment and freedom. Because "Semper Idem" has always remained its policy, the Church has never advanced beyond the age of ignorance it clamped on Christendom. In the barbaric age, which followed the fall of the Roman Empire, it expanded and flourished, as its dogmas and doctrines were primitive, but, if the Church stood still, men and women did not, the consequence being that it has now fortunately lost its once great power and influence.

What an influence for good it might have been if truth and righteousness had always been its aim, and progress and reform its watchword instead of Semper Idem, though it must be realised that this assumption was impossible for an institution built up on fraud and maintained by fear. Good cannot be produced by evil, but if an organisation, founded on righteousness, had been possible, one always devoted to the mental development of mankind, what a blessing it would have been for everyone! If only such an international institution had been in being for the purpose of furthering education and culture everywhere, what a different world we would be living in today! Now that supernatural religion has so failed to regenerate humanity, we must try other methods, and these will be discussed as we proceed.

Meantime, in the 15th century, the hierarchy of the Church saw danger ahead. They feared the loss of power, wealth and position if their teaching came to be disbelieved, and they imagined that God was equally concerned as to the future prospects of his one and only Church on earth. They heard the cracking and rumbling in their holy edifice, and were determined that nothing would be left undone to keep it from collapsing. Their minds were like those of all tyrants who put self before all else, and looked upon humanity as slaves who had been born for no other purpose than to do their bidding.

(6) THE BASIS IS LAID FOR PARLIAMENT AND EDUCATION IN ENGLAND.

When we left England in Chapter X we had followed her story up to the time when Simon de Montfort, the younger, was killed at the Battle of Evesham in 1265. He had attempted to give the country its first Parliament, but the barons would not support him, and this battle followed. It seemed as if all his work had been in vain, but this was not so, as Edward I (1272–1307), who succeeded his father

Henry III, carried de Montfort's ideas to a satisfactory conclusion. Edward I can rightly be considered as the most outstanding English king since the time of Alfred. He was a strong, capable, and, for the times, a wise ruler, and, by putting parliamentary government on a stable foundation, his reign of thirty-five years was a period of such fundamental importance that it has left its mark on English history.

Edward voluntarily developed the parliamentary system into a partnership between the Crown and the people, and, in 1295, he summoned a Parliament based on de Montfort's principles of representation. It was composed of the nobles, bishops, abbots and two representatives from every shire, city and borough, the latter standing to hear the decision of their peers, only one of them, called the Speaker, being allowed to speak for them. These voiceless men then gathered together alone, to form in time the House of Commons (from the old French word Comun—Community) where they decided what their speaker was to say on their behalf.

This form of representation continued with few modifications until 1832, and throughout these years Parliament controlled the raising of revenue, thus effectively curbing the power of the Sovereign. This control of taxation was the cause of its power, and, though France had her States-General, she never secured this weapon which gave the English Parliament its authority and the right to claim for itself to be the Mother of Parliaments.

Besides establishing parliamentary government in England, Edward curtailed the power of the ecclesiastical courts, reforming both the law and judicial procedure. Moreover, he appointed men from amongst the local gentry, who in the reign of Edward III became known as Justices of the Peace, an innovation which worked wonderfully well in the centuries to come. In those days this was an experiment forced on the King by the lawlessness which everywhere prevailed. Shocking crimes were perpetrated throughout the land, and new laws, judges and magistrates did no more than keep crime in check, the country being so badly served by roads that it was impossible to bring more than a proportion of the criminals to justice. Then, as always, war encourages crime and criminals, which increase in numbers after every conflict, and the wars of our own time have been no exception.

Edward made it illegal for the Church to receive grants of land without the permission of the King, because this was becoming dangerous to the country's finances. The policy of the Church had always been to accumulate wealth by frightening property owners with hell, but to promise them a safe entry into heaven if they left some or all of their property to the Church. All Church lands were free from taxation, they being termed "Spiritual Land", and consequently the remaining land outside its jurisdiction was bearing a greater burden of taxation year by year, as more and more land was passed over to the Church.

Edward's other land legislation was of more doubtful value, as he permitted landowners to entail their property, which meant that it could be handed down intact from eldest son to eldest son. Large tracts of land thus remained under single ownership, and were not available for purchase, the consequence being that the people generally were denied the privilege of becoming landowners. However, this concentration of land in the hands of the rich rather helped than otherwise the reclamation of waste spaces, so much so that more and more land came into cultivation to support a population of some 4,000,000, a figure not again to be reached for another two centuries because of the devastation caused by the Black Death.

The rich merchants of London now took as prominent a place in the country as the great nobles. They commanded the city's militia, and owned most of the ships which traded round the coast, besides acting as bankers to the King. So, when Edward expelled the Jews (1290), hitherto the royal moneylenders, England financially was unaffected, and it was not until the time of Cromwell that they were allowed to return. Hitherto it had been considered sinful for Christians to lend money (*Deuteronomy* xxiii, 19), but the Jews had interpreted this law more liberally and considered that it was meant to apply to everyone but themselves. Consequently they had been the money-lenders of Christendom, but the English now came to regard this moneylending monopoly as both unfair and unbusinesslike, and they likewise entered the profession and so freed themselves from dependence on the foreigner within their gates. This was something the rest of Europe did not do, and it is one reason why the Jews have not been so hated in Britain as they have been elsewhere.

War, as usual, played a large part in Edward's reign. He fought Philip IV of France over territory he inherited there, and finally, with nothing gained or lost, he married Philip's sister. His policy at home was to secure unity throughout the entire island,

and make Westminster the seat of law and justice. The Welsh, under Prince Llewelyn, bravely defended their mountainous country for six years, and, after being conquered, were appeased by Edward creating his eldest son Prince of Wales. Next he turned his attention to Scotland and arranged that the Prince of Wales was to marry Margaret, "the Maid of Norway", the grand-daughter of King Alexander III.[1] She was the heiress to the Scottish throne, and this union with England was all that was necessary to create the United Kingdom of Great Britain. Unfortunately she died in 1290 before the marriage could take place, and Scotland and England remained separate kingdoms, John Baliol (1292–1296) becoming King of Scotland and vassal to Edward.

No more untimely death, or greater tragedy, ever

[1] The Scottish Royal House commences with Kenneth Macalpine (844–860). He was followed by Donald I (861–863), Constantine I (863–877), Grig (878–889), Donald II (889–900), Constantine II (900–940) and Malcolm I (943–954). Then followed between 954 and 971 three kings, Indulf, Duff and Colin, after which came Kenneth II (971–995), son of Malcolm I. Three insignificant kings quickly passed, when Malcolm II (1005–1034) became the accepted ruler. Then followed Duncan (1034–1040), who was killed by Macbeth, the son of Findlay, Chief of Moray, and grandson-in-law of Kenneth II. This relationship gained Macbeth the throne, and he proved himself an able ruler during his reign of seventeen years (1040–1057).

Malcolm III (1058–1093), better known as Malcolm Canmore (meaning Great Head), the son of Duncan, succeeded, and from his time onwards we have a clearer idea of Scottish history. So far it has been a story of conflicts which produced a united Keltic kingdom comprising the greater part of what is now Scotland. From now onwards the invasions from Europe produced an Anglo-Norman feudal monarchy, Scotland, unlike England, not passing through a period of Saxon rule. Malcolm's wife Margaret raised the Church to the level it has since occupied in Scotland. Then, after a four years' conflict for the crown, followed Edgar (1097–1107), Alexander I (1107–1124), David I (1124–1153), Malcolm IV (1153–1165), William I (1165–1214), Alexander II (1214–1249) and Alexander III (1249–1286), who married Margaret, daughter of Henry III, and whose daughter Margaret married Eric II of Norway, their daughter being Margaret, known as the Maid of Norway.

occurred in this island's story, as from now onwards a strong national feeling developed in Scotland which led to war, border raids, and hatred between two groups of people who should have had no antagonisms. Her isolation from England brought centuries of grinding poverty to Scotland, which would have been avoided if the two countries had been united. The death of this young girl indeed changed the entire history of Britain, a small event, but one with tremendous consequences.

Draw a line from Glasgow to Aberdeen. North of it lived the Kelts, who spoke Gaelic and belonged to the same race as the Welsh, Irish and Cornish people, they being akin to the Gauls who inhabited France in Roman times. Like the Welsh and Cornish, they were the remains of the inhabitants of Britain before the Nordic invasions, which reached as far north as the Scottish highlands. South of the above line, known as "the Highland Line", the people are mostly Anglo-Normans, speaking the same language, believing the same religion, and of the same race as the English, but for nearly eight centuries Britain was divided into two kingdoms, which fought each other, intrigued against each other, and, instead of working as one, schemed against each other. The early death of Margaret was one of the greatest disasters which ever befell any country, as, if she had lived, Britain would then have been united under one king, and Scotland's history would have been England's history.

The Scots resented the fact that their king was vassal to Edward, and war followed. Baliol resigned, and Edward declared the annexation of Scotland to the English crown. Sir William Wallace (1270-1305), the Scottish leader, replied by defeating the English at Stirling Bridge in 1297. Next year Wallace was defeated by the English long-bowmen at Falkirk, to be taken prisoner later and executed in London under circumstances of exceptional cruelty. Robert Bruce (1306–1329) now became the Scottish leader, to be crowned King at Scone in 1306.

Most people look upon Bruce as an outstanding Scotsman, but this is far from being the case. Wallace certainly was a Scotsman, a cadet of the landed gentry, but Bruce sprang from a family in which for more than two centuries the finest Norman blood had flowed, he moreover having inherited estates in both England and Scotland which his Norman ancestors had taken from the Saxons. His Scottish estates made him one of the most powerful nobles in Scotland, but for long he was a loyal subject of the English king. Like many other barons with estates in both Scotland and England, he was lukewarm in his support of Wallace, being more often than not on the side of Edward. Then came the change. He began to distrust Edward, to become finally his enemy and the stalwart supporter of Scottish independence. One man's decision determined British history for the next four hundred years!

After his coronation as King of Scotland he lived for the next eight years between defeat and victory, at times a fugitive, but always determined that the English must be driven from Scotland. Finally victory at Bannockburn in 1314 crowned his effort with success, and Edward II, the son of Edward I who had died an old man on his way to Scotland in 1307, was forced to withdraw his army south of the border.

Thus began and ended the Scottish war of independence, which, by welding Scotland into a nation, gave great satisfaction at the time to the Scotch, but, if they had been wise, they would have joined up with England and made a united nation. Instead of so doing, the two countries drew apart, and wasted their substance in fighting and pillaging each other. In those days, however, London was a long way off, and Perth seemed to the Scotch to be the right place for the capital, as there the king could best direct affairs. Roads hardly existed, and communication between England and Scotland was slow and precarious, all of which makes their decision understandable though regrettable. Rapid communication makes for unity and understanding, and may some day unite the human race under a comprehensive plan for its social and economic welfare.

Edward II (1307–1327) never recovered his prestige after his defeat at Bannockburn, and the rest of his uneventful and weak reign was spent in the midst of civil war. In 1327 French troops landed in England to receive the support of the people, when Edward fled, but he was captured and deposed, to be later murdered. One interesting event during this reign was the enactment that the "commonality of the realm", together with the prelates, earls and barons, had their say in Parliament, and this secured a place for the people in the management of the nation's affairs, to develop, as the years passed, into democratic government conducted by the House of Commons.

The Crown in those days actively associated itself with the trade of the country, and in this reign the importation of cloth from abroad was prohibited. Foreigners, skilled in its manufacture and possessing trade secrets, were invited over to London and East Anglia, where they received government protection and help. Special privileges were likewise given to English clothiers, to such effect that the production of broadcloth in England trebled, and its export was increased ninefold. Sheep in large numbers were to be seen wandering over the country's hedgeless pastures, and these gave to English cloth manufacturers such good wool that they first secured the European market and, as the centuries passed, the cloth market of the world.

It is interesting in our day to look back and see how government control and planning in those days made England rich and prosperous, because, between then and now, the State has at times supported and encouraged trade and industry and at other times entirely neglected it. In our own day and generation Socialist policy is in line with that pursued in the 14th century, in striking contrast to the policy adopted in the 18th and 19th centuries, when the country's trade and industry received no government help or encouragement, such a policy being then considered as quite outside the functions of government.

Such then was England when Edward III (1327–1377), the first English king to be able to read and write, ascended the throne in succession to his murdered father. He reigned for fifty years, and we have already learned something about him, as he was responsible for the Hundred Years' War through his claim to the French throne, because his mother Isabella was the daughter of Philip IV of France.

Much of Edward's time was spent in this conflict, and his victories in France gave a glamour to the English throne. His character was debased, and it does not reflect highly on the chivalry of the age to think that he was considered one of its outstanding exponents. He was a good soldier and a great leader, which qualifications, with the help of his marvellous archers, well equipped with the long-bow, contributed as much as anything to his victories at Crecy and Poitiers against the French armoured knights, who displayed incredible bravery but little skill and feeble tactics. These two battles destroyed for ever the legend of invincibility attached to knights in armour, and from now onwards they gradually disappear from the battlefield.

Before the war with France commenced, Edward was at war with the Scotch, who wished David, the son of Robert Bruce, to be their king. Edward wanted Edward Baliol, who had agreed to be his vassal. At Halidon Hill in 1333 the English long-bow prevailed and the Scotch were defeated, Berwick was captured, and Baliol acknowledged Edward to be his overlord. The war, however, continued, and David invaded England (1346) but was defeated at Neville's Cross and taken captive. So the two countries remained at war for ten years, but the Scotch would never admit defeat, and when Edward ultimately realised that his effort to conquer them was hopeless he liberated David, after eleven years' captivity, in exchange for a large ransom.

Scotland thus remained independent, while in England the hatred of France reached such intensity that the French language ceased to be spoken at court, in the Law Courts, and in Parliament. Instead Geoffrey Chaucer (1340–1400), by his beautiful narrative poetry, established English as the national language, his *Canterbury Tales* being rich in humour, wit and charm. Chaucer caustically attacked the gross abuses then rampant in the Church, and expressed what the more intelligent were thinking, that the Church had excessive privileges and was utterly corrupt because of its colossal wealth. Dislike of the Pope developed alongside the detestation of the French, as the people believed that he was the power behind their refusal to acknowledge Edward III as their king. Parliament therefore withdrew the papal power to nominate priests to their parishes, making it a punishable offence to petition the Holy See as a final court of appeal for cases in dispute, and cancelled all further payment of tribute.

Here we notice the rising power of the people, whose anti-papal feeling enabled them to avoid the mistake made by the French of having three separate legislative chambers, one of which was composed entirely of ecclesiastics. Instead of this arrangement, the English included the bishops and the nobles together, and formed two chambers, the House of Lords and the House of Commons. So Parliament became established in this reign as we know it today, and, as the King was immersed in war, its power increased, the people obtaining greater control in the management of their own affairs.

Mental development was likewise responsible for another important event which occurred in this period. Secular education was then unknown, theological instruction being considered the only way to knowledge, but, in the centuries to come, as the former increased in importance, and the latter declined, some theological colleges became great seats of learning, to produce many men who became famous in their day and generation. Now we are at the time when one great man saw the need of giving both the priesthood and the laity an opportunity to increase their then scanty knowledge and improve their crude culture. By so doing he laid the foundation for those great secular institutions devoted to the instruction of the upper classes of Britain which, to this day, are unique and to be found only in this country.

This illustrious pioneer of education was William of Wykeham (1324–1404), who built, founded and generously endowed New College at Oxford in 1379 and Winchester College in 1387, the latter to become a model for future schools, Eton College being founded on similar lines in 1440 by Henry VI. Wykeham started life in humble circumstances, and, as in those days the road to advancement was only through the Church, he became a priest, his first appointment being Surveyor of Works at Windsor. There he looked after the royal establishments so well, and was so liked by the King, that he was made Bishop of Winchester with a salary of over £60,000 a year.

Soon he became a powerful and wealthy man, and one of the few really great men of the Middle Ages, his talent for finance and business being remarkable. If he had lived today he would probably have been the head of one of our great industrial combines, employing thousands of workers and controlling millions of capital. He rose to the highest position in the land when he became Chancellor, but his fame really rests on the fact that he was the first man in England, since Alfred the Great, to encourage education, which turned the cleric into the clerk and then into the student. His enterprise prepared the soil from which grew the plant of knowledge, as he was the pioneer of the schools and colleges which, centuries later, became devoted to the quest for truth, in place of the seminaries of the Theological Age confined to pondering over religious subjects.

(7) EUROPE PRIOR TO THE REFORMATION.

Now we again take up our review of affairs in Europe where we left them at the end of Section 2. Here we are approaching the first and most momentous repercussion of the Renaissance, when rising intelligence split the Catholic Church in two. To understand how it was possible for such an event to happen to this ancient institution, with its traditions running back to Roman imperialism and Greek Paganism, we must realise the depth of depravity to which its clergy had sunk during their thousand years of undisputed power.

Their refusal to consider any reform of the Church, in an age which was awakening from its long period of slumber, and not the discoveries of science, brought about the Reformation. Knowledge in time would have reduced its membership, but not split it in two, and, if the long-overdue reforms had been effected, it would probably have remained whole to this day, because, to begin with, there was little disagreement anywhere on the question of beliefs and doctrine. The Reformation brought about the second great cleavage in the Christian Church, as we have already read about the Eastern Church separating from the Western Church, to become known as the Orthodox or Greek Church, the Western portion retaining the name Catholic.

All this will become clear as we proceed, but, first of all, let us discover what indeed the Renaissance effected and what it passed by. An historian looks upon life from a much broader and wider aspect than do most people. Everyday affairs are all-important to everyone, as they constitute our experiences, pleasures, happiness, disappointments, and all that makes up life, but only when we look back can we see the completed picture which is being painted day by day. Only by an examination of the already finished canvas can we form a right judgment of the events which are daily making up our lives. So, if we train ourselves to consider current events in this broader aspect, we are more likely to form a balanced opinion on what we experience day by day.

Thus we broaden our outlook, and also better appreciate the mistakes and achievements of our ancestors, who, like ourselves, lived day by day interested only in what to them were the pressing problems of the time. The 16th century was a time when these problems seemed all-important, as the mental development, which came about because of the discovery of paper and printing, was creating a great cleavage of opinions between those who thought for themselves and those who accepted the dictates of their superiors. To us today, looking back, everything seems far different from what it was to those who lived through the transition stage from darkness to light.

To one living in the light of day it is difficult to understand the feelings of the individual, born and bred in a dark cavern, who first experiences the earth bathed in radiant light. Such must have been the feelings of those who, in the 16th century, made their acquaintance with the writings of Aristotle for the first time. They found themselves living in a new world, a world of reasoned sequence and not one ruled by the caprices of the gods.

Copernicus and Galileo had uncovered the heavens, and the minuteness of the earth, including its creatures, was now contrasted with the vastness of the universe. The earth was found to be but a speck in immensity, and not the centre of the universe. Man, at last, was beginning to know something about himself and his surroundings, but this new mental outlook had no effect on his carnal nature, and it did not make him stop and reason as to the wisdom of continuing his past insane way of living.

The vast majority remained in ignorance of it all, intent only on their own everyday affairs, and bent on making the most they could within the orbit of their own circumscribed existence. So, when kings quarrelled, the people followed their rulers, and men were always found willing to sacrifice their lives on some field of glory and honour, plundering, killing and maiming their neighbours so that, if fortune favoured them, they might add something to their possessions.

The Renaissance only brought further material facts to light, as new knowledge is just the uncovering of what has always been. To the ignorant the universe is no more than a cavern into which little light penetrates, but, as the mind develops, we proceed towards the light of day, ever seeing and comprehending more of our surroundings. Not here on earth will we ever encompass the wide expanse which stretches to view when we reach the light, but slowly, as we move forward, we realise that the universe is far different from what it seemed when we were within our gloomy cave.

Everything (such as space, time, matter, etc.) is relative and determined by our place in the universe, our appreciation of our surroundings being decided by the velocity at which the earth is travelling through space. On earth we can only interpret the universe from our own point of view, namely the earth standpoint, but to someone in some star or planet it would be different because of the different velocity of his travel. A delicate experiment with a beam of light confirmed this, and laid the foundation for Professor Einstein to develop his revolutionary metaphysical theory of the universe, which gives a new conception of natural law, and lays low the old orthodox scientific materialism so long accepted without question. A more complete understanding of the unification of nature is now being attempted, as reality must always be the same everywhere throughout the universe, and science is coming to realise that this is only possible by regarding the universe as a mental conception.

Plato, whose opinions were for long overshadowed by those of Aristotle, has come into his own again.

Here on earth we can only appreciate physical reality, but other realities are before us which we shall experience after death. Then our consciousness will regard its environment from a new angle, the physical outlook being a purely relative one, and our earth experiences consequently likewise so. After death our new environment will become real to us and the earth unreal. Now the earth is real to us, but much occurs in our environment to which we are blind and deaf. What we do not see, feel or hear we consider unreal, but that is because of our physical limitations, and only when we are freed from them will the unseen become the real and what is now seen the shadow.[1]

Those things which we learn as something new have existed previously, they being only new to us. The knowledge we acquire is something we have uncovered that was already there. What we have still to learn is now in being, but not yet revealed to enquiring mind. The universe, and all we now know, existed when we were still in our dark cavern of ignorance, and from this fact emerges a vital truth. Infinite mind and substance have been from all eternity and will be to all eternity. The mind of man, which constitutes the individual, can only appreciate its true environment by development and unfoldment, and, as this proceeds, we reach ever closer harmony

[1] This new but important subject of universal vibrationary activity has placed this earth, and the entire universe, in an aspect different from that previously accepted, and has made comprehensible life and substance interpenetrating and surrounding this world which to us are rarely sensed. The subject is explained and made clear in the author's work *The Unfolding Universe.*

with the infinite and eternal Mind which manifests all that is and ever will be.

So the Renaissance only revealed to mankind more of the ever present and ever existing universe. It was a physical revelation only, as no progress was made in the knowledge of man himself, a subject which to Socrates, we will remember, was the all-important subject. Only within the past hundred years have some discovered scientifically that the real man is the etheric being, who for a time is clad in a physical covering which he sheds at death. Another Renaissance is now needed to develop this new knowledge to its logical conclusion, because, as we are here, so shall we be after death.

Who then best fits himself for the experiences he will have in the etheric world, when each one, to an ever greater extent, will become as he thinks, and our mind will control our conditions in a way which is impossible while we are contained within physical vibrations? Will it be the man with the Hitler mentality or the one mentally constituted as was Socrates, who considered this earth to be a preparation for a better and fuller life after death?

This is a subject worthy of a new Renaissance, as we must decide now who is better qualified to handle the new knowledge the human mind is now opening to receive. Are our discoveries to be applied for the good of mankind or the reverse? Is the Hitler mentality, which has prevailed in the past, to continue and the Socratic outlook to be for ever ignored? The time has indeed come to give heed to the great Greek sage, and those who have thought like him, and so usher in a mental Renaissance when our children will be taught the great ethical truths propounded by the thinkers of the past and present. Only then will we become qualified instruments to handle the powerful forces of nature for the good of the human race, and, at the same time, prepare ourselves for the experiences which will come to us when we cast off the physical garment, and find ourselves in the etheric world which at first will be to us as we made it here on earth. As we sow here, so do we reap there.

We are not yet ethically fitted for the knowledge scientific research has put at our disposal, and, until we are, much of its usefulness will continue to be turned to evil purposes. We have so far only passed through the first stage of man's development from an animal into a human being, and we today stand at the door of a new era which will either lead us to greater happiness or greater misery. Now we must choose whether our ethical knowledge will progress side by side with our material knowledge, or, on the other hand, whether we intend to remain as only advanced beasts with our greater knowledge devoted to perfecting means of destruction to life and property.

This history of mankind has traced the progress of the race step by step from the time of primitive man, and our story is now approaching a new age, one which is quite different from any that has preceded it. In this new era man conquers the forces of nature, and makes them do his bidding, but unfortunately he uses them for destructive as well as for constructive purposes. War is just as prevalent today as it was thousands of years ago, and the ethical standard of the race still applies only to the nation to which we belong. When we compare the international ethical conduct of many in the world today with that of our ancestors in the 16th century, we find little to cause satisfaction. What has happened in our lifetime is only too familiar to the present generation, as is also the misery which comes from ignoring the moral law.

Education over the past fifty years has certainly improved our individual conduct, our manners and our way of life, which important fact gives us hope for the future, as it shows how a further advance is possible by increased mental development. In the 16th century, and on to the 19th century, the manners and customs of the people were coarse and degraded, only to improve with the coming of education at the end of last century. Moreover, during the time to which this chapter relates, all Christendom, except the prosperous, was living in filth and squalor, only the well-to-do being decently clad. The houses of the poor were just hovels, and the people generally were treated by their superiors as no better than cattle, being spoken to as we would not now speak to a dog. Oaths accompanied most remarks, the husband cursed his wife, the wife the children, there being nowhere much self-control. Tempers were easily roused, brawls and fights were common, and the sanctity of life received little respect. Truly the social conditions of Europe during the Christian era would have horrified the philosophically minded Pagan Greeks of two thousand years earlier.

As with the people, so likewise with the rulers, whose complete lack of morality and ethical conduct can best be realised by reading the writings of

Machiavelli (1469–1527), and learning of the reception they received from the kings, princes and chancellors of Europe. Monarchy is such a pose that we know not what sovereigns really think, only what they do, but here was a man who revealed the thoughts, ideals and purposes of statecraft. After serving in the diplomatic service of Florence, this man of good position passed from embassy to embassy, absorbing the diplomatic methods of his day and formulating what he considered was the ideal method of statesmanship. When the Medici family secured the power he was tortured on the rack and expelled from Florence, but he settled down nearby, and, in his enforced leisure, wrote a number of books which claim to reveal the thoughts of the rulers of his day.

He found his hero in Cardinal Caesar Borgia, the son of Pope Alexander VI, whom he idealised in his book *The Prince.* Backed up by the wealth of the Papal Treasury, Caesar secured a large area in Italy. He had murdered several relations, and quite a number of other enemies, to become, with the help of his holy father, the Duke of Valentino. He lived magnificently, had considerable political ability, and was a hardened scoundrel. In him Machiavelli found his ideal ruler, and on his methods he developed his political morality, which he said must be followed by all rulers who wish to be successful.

The complete abandonment of the ethical code by the State formed the basis of Machiavelli's teaching, as whatever succeeded was right. To this forerunner of the Nazi and Fascist creed no promise is ever binding, and lies are always useful. How familiar this is to our own generation, and also the chaos which follows the breaking of the ethical code. Power, riches, glory and privilege, to this moral outcast, were far superior to righteousness, as only by its abandonment could these great prizes be won at the height of Christian civilisation. To him freedom of thought was impossible, as repression, force, intrigue and dishonesty were his gods, and he mirrored the prevailing ideas of the rulers of his time so well that his writings received their unstinted praise.

For eleven hundred years Europe had looked to the Holy See for moral guidance, and the state of moral corruption which everywhere prevailed reflects its evil influence. Machiavelli was just a product of his time. "We Italians," he declared, "are irreligious and corrupt above all others, because the Church and her representatives set us the worst example." All around him were evil men, ignorance abounded, and Europe, for a thousand years, had reaped the harvest the Church had sown when it swept away the Roman educational system, and banished the schoolmasters in the 4th, 5th and 6th centuries. Christianity, by replacing the great Pagan moralists with theological dogma, now had a pope in Alexander VI (1492–1503) who was the inevitable result of this policy. Before he bribed the Sacred College to make him pope, he was known as Rodrigo Borgia, a wealthy Spaniard, and during the eleven years he held the holy office his mistresses and children occupied the Vatican.

Alexander was one of the wickedest men of his time, treacherous and cunning, and, if he were paid enough, he would put anyone not wanted out of the way by murder or imprisonment. His intercourse with married women was notorious, but it was in crime that he had few rivals. He sold the leading ecclesiastical offices for large sums, and permitted his children to turn the Vatican into a brothel of vice and crime in which he played a prominent part. The Diary, kept by a trustworthy inmate of the Vatican during these years of unbridled lust, contains a record of so much evil and obscenity that the pages of this book will not be soiled by recounting what took place. He himself participated in these scenes of obscene revelry up to an advanced age, but nothing was too bad for him to do, two cardinals being poisoned by him so that he might secure their great wealth, and he committed other murders for which he was paid large sums. Of this period of wickedness Savonarola, who lived at the time and denounced it all, wrote:—

The scandal begins in Rome and runs through the whole clergy. They are worse than Turks and Moors. In Rome you will find that they have one and all obtained their benefices by simony. They buy preferments, and bestow them on their children or brothers, who take possession of them by violence and all sorts of sinful means. Their greed is insatiable, they do all things for gold. They only ring their bells for coin and candles, only attend Vespers and Choir and Office when something is to be got by it. They sell their benefices, sell the sacraments, traffic in masses. . . .. If a priest, or a canon, leads an ordinary life he is mocked and called a hypocrite. It has come to pass that all are warned against Rome, and people say, "If you want to ruin your son make him a priest."

Ethically, Europe at this time was more backward than in the period considered in the chapter relating to the oldest civilisations. Christians had been morally starved by the Church, which put belief in its creed before righteousness. The moralisings of the great Pagan philosophers of the past had been kept from the people, who sought their happiness from material things, and neglected a fundamental law that happiness only comes from righteousness, whence proceeds mental freedom, mental harmony and contentment. The Machiavellis, all down the ages up to our own times, and the sages of the past, have always been in two opposite camps, and, as the people too often have followed evil instead of good, misery has been the portion of mankind. Only ethical development will remove the blight of moral ignorance, and only education along non-political and non-theological lines will raise the race to the mental level necessary for all to live together in harmony.

So the 16th century continued like its predecessors to be a period of wars, misery and destruction. Italy, when the century opened, was the victim of a strong, united and greedy France, which ravished its weaker neighbour as she herself had been devastated, off and on, for a hundred years by England. Just as Hitler felt himself strong enough to fight the rest of Europe, because he had developed the tank and airplane beyond that done by his neighbours, so the young and licentious hunchback Charles VIII (1483–1498), who succeeded Louis XI of France, was the aggressor because he had developed the use of artillery beyond anything so far known in Europe.

Conscious of his strength, he invaded Italy in 1494, with 30,000 mercenaries, intent on looting and ravaging, and, as they met with little resistance, Florence, Pisa, Rome and Naples were quickly captured and plundered. He might have occupied the entire peninsula indefinitely, had not Ferdinand of

Spain and Maximilian of Germany decided that too strong a France was a danger to their interests, the consequence being that for over sixty years a long-drawn-out war was fought to decide whether Germany, France or Spain was to dominate Italy.

The ever-recurring problem of the balance of power, which, from now onwards, was to bleed Europe white, had been altered by the increased strength of France, and so these two monarchs united against Charles VIII, forcing him to withdraw the following year (1495) from Naples, to meet their combined armies at Fornovo. Here Charles defeated the allies, but he did not return to Italy, and died three years later.

He was succeeded by Louis XII (1498–1515), who returned to the conquest of Italy in 1499, this time in alliance with Spain, as they had decided to divide between them the kingdom of Naples. The King of Naples was made a prisoner, and then France and Spain fell out over the division of the stolen lands. France was defeated and her armies driven north, but the two robbers made it up and joined with the city of Florence and Pope Julius II to rob Venice of its possessions. Julius, a debased and loathsome creature, was always ready to use his standing army in a fight if there were land and booty to be secured.

The Christian Church was then the owner of about one third of Europe, apart from those Balkan lands overrun by the Turks, the largest contributors to the Holy See being Germany, France, Spain, Italy and Britain. The Greek Church had secured for itself an equally favourable position in Russia and elsewhere, but here we are considering the Catholic Church, which, besides owning, free of all taxation, vast possessions of what it terms "Spiritual land" and "Spiritual wealth", had an annual income of a tenth of the produce of all the land. On this the priests lived, tax free, producing nothing, and keeping Europe in poverty and misery up to last century.

None of this great wealth had been honestly acquired, as every acre of land and penny of money was stolen from the people by two subtle methods: (1) as the result of the Church co-operating with the great Christian conquerors of Europe and sharing in their spoils, and (2) by means of the greatest swindle of all times, the preaching of everlasting hell and the promise of heaven to all who handed over some or all of their possessions to the Church. The keys of heaven and hell, which the Church falsely claims to have received from Jesus, through Peter, certainly unlocked for its benefit a greater quantity of wealth than has ever been at the disposal of any other organisation. Never was there a blatant fraud so profitable to the defrauder, and never has the people's ignorance been used by evil men for a more devilish purpose in the history of the human race.

Still, with it all, the Holy See was not satisfied and wanted more. Not content with its own vast possessions, comprising a third of Italy and much of Europe, it had for long coveted the lands and property of Venice. Now came the opportunity to join up with these other three robbers, and plunder this prosperous neighbouring state. Venice was defeated and her possessions divided between the conquerors, but this unholy alliance, known as The League of Cambrai, led to bitter quarrels, so much so that Pope

Julius formed a Holy League consisting of England, Germany, Spain and Venice for the purpose of expelling France from Italy. By 1513 only Milan remained to France, and then Louis died in the same year.

It is remarkable how Italy and Sicily, once strong and united, became the prey, century after century, of France, Germany or Spain. The people who lived in the land called Italy had no cohesion nor unity, there was really no Italy and there were no Italians in those days, as the land was divided into small kingdoms, or city states, which hated and were constantly at war with one another, and this was never more evident than during the 16th century.

Francis I (1515-1547) succeeded Louis XII and immediately recommenced the war in Italy. Venice became his ally, and Germany, Spain and the Holy See joined against them. At Marignano (1515), near Milan, Francis defeated his enemies, and then entered into an agreement with the evil-living Pope Leo X, who had been meeting his heavy expenditure by the sale of indulgences and lucrative positions in the Church. His Holiness required more money, as his many luxuries and dissipations were very expensive.

Consequently he sold to Francis the right to appoint the leading Church dignitaries in France, the King paying the Holy See annually in cash, an arrangement which continued until the end of the 18th century. Francis then put himself forward as the successor to the Holy Roman Emperor Maximilian who had died in 1519, but Charles I of Spain (1516-1556), who had inherited the vast possessions of Maximilian, his grandfather, and his grandmother Mary of

Burgundy, was chosen instead, to become Charles V Holy Roman Emperor, thus joining Spain and the Empire under one sovereign.

Never before had one man ruled over such a vast empire. It included Germany, Austria, Silesia, Styria, Bohemia, Switzerland, the Netherlands, Milan, the southern half of Italy, Sicily, Sardinia, Spain and North and South America, excluding Brazil. Truly the balance of power was heavily weighted against equilibrium, and the only comfort for the rest of Europe lay in the fact that it was a ramshackle empire at the best and loosely held together.

The real danger lay in the East, as the powerful Ottoman Empire had conquered Hungary in 1526, and now comprised Asia Minor, Greece, Hungary and the Balkans. A few years later, under the leadership of Suleyman the Magnificent, it was pressing on towards Austria and threatening Vienna. This threat caused Charles great anxiety, and, though he did his best to stem the advance, he was greatly handicapped by having France, which was an ally of the Turks, as his enemy. France, "the eldest son of the Church", allied with the Infidel Turk seems an anachronism, but to France in those days any alliance was encouraged which helped to weaken the feared and hated Hapsburg Empire.

France now invaded Italy in 1525, only to meet a German army under the Duke of Bourbon, the last of the French independent nobles. At Pavia, France was utterly defeated, and her king, Francis I, made a prisoner. He was taken to Spain, where he signed away much French territory, only to repudiate the treaty later, and this led to a fresh war, but nothing could now prevent Lombardy, Naples and Sicily from coming under the Spanish yoke. This great misfortune prevented Italy from taking any further part in the Renaissance she had mothered and tended since its birth, as from now onwards the Holy Inquisition stamped out all free and independent thought.[1]

War makes the wheels of history run quickly, and other vitally important events were to follow from this long-drawn-out conflict which was to shape the course of things to come. A mutinous German army in Italy entirely altered the mental outlook in England from this time onwards. A small insignificant event produced this profound change, which came about because the German soldiers were in arrear with their pay. They mutined, sacked Rome, and made Pope Clement VII their prisoner. After six months' captivity this unfortunate but foolish pontiff, who was always in trouble, was released upon very onerous conditions, and for some years followed a policy of subserviency to the Emperor Charles V. One momentous consequence of the Pope's dependence on Charles was the breach between the Vatican and England, as Henry VIII had meantime petitioned His Holiness for an annulment of his marriage with Catherine of Aragon.

Clement VII did not dare to give it because she was the aunt of Charles V, and in consequence Henry broke with the Pope and so made possible the Reformation in England, which country for long had

---

[1] A perusal of the extant *Index Librorum* of prohibited books, which was published by the Holy See in 1557, contains all the then known books on history, geography, philosophy, science and medicine, but no mention is made of the numerous obscene and debased books which were then in circulation.

resented papal interference in English affairs. The capture of the Pope, and the break between England and Rome, are two closely related events which changed the course of English history, to react eventually over much of Europe and the rest of the world. If England had not stood firm in the difficult years ahead, the Reformation might easily have been crushed in Europe, and, if this had happened, we might still be wandering in theological darkness.

The growing opposition in Germany to the Pope had an important influence on the war between Francis and Charles, as the heretics in Germany sided with Francis against their own emperor, who found himself in constant difficulties because of their intrigues and opposition. These internal troubles in Germany prevented Charles from pursuing the war against France to a successful conclusion. That, however, can be passed by, as what was really important was the far-reaching results which came from Charles's preoccupation in war. This enabled the heretics to gain a firm footing in Germany, which they might never have succeeded in doing had Charles been free to stamp them out.

Charles and Francis made peace at Cambrai in 1529, but this lasted for only seven years, as they again fell out over the vacant Duchy of Milan, which both claimed. By now both sides were getting tired of this senseless never-ending war, and, in 1538, the Truce of Nice suspended hostilities for ten years. This lasted for only four years, as fighting began again when Charles gave the Duchy of Milan to his son Philip. Though France was successful, yet, when peace returned in 1544, she had gained nothing from her victories, and then, three years later, Francis died. His son Henry II (1547–1559) pursued the struggle with the help of the German heretics, who hated Charles because he was a Burgundian and not a German, to defeat him finally at Metz.

By now Charles was broken in health, and he decided to abdicate in favour of his son Philip. The Germans, however, had no wish to be further tied to Spain, and they elected as emperor his brother Ferdinand, who now succeeded to the imperial title and the Hapsburgs' great Austrian possessions. Philip became King of Spain as Philip II (1556–1598), and inherited its vast territories in America and the Netherlands. He continued the war against France while his deeply religious father Charles, surrounded by every luxury, watched his career with great interest from inside the walls of a monastery, cursing all heretics to the last, and urging the intensification of the Holy Inquisition.

After a series of important victories, Philip, instead of reaching Paris as conqueror, was finally vanquished, which defeat was the means of breaking England's last remaining link with the Continent. His marriage to Mary Tudor had made England his ally in this war against France, and his defeat in 1558 meant to England the loss of Calais, her last remaining possession in Europe.

The peace which followed secured Italy for Spain, but France obtained the valuable bishoprics of Metz, Toul and Verdun, and this gave her a foothold in Lorraine, which she firmly occupied two centuries later. But the peace was only a truce, and for the next hundred and fifty years war continued between

France and Spain. By the time it ended these two great powers had been at war, off and on, for two hundred years, with nothing to show for all the treasure and lives wasted. Other lands in Europe likewise continued to settle their differences by means of the sword, which quarrels, for many years to come, were brought about by religious intolerance, to which we shall soon devote our attention, as it dominates European history for the next two hundred years.

The foregoing pages give the political background of the Reformation, but, like the Renaissance, no precise date can be fixed for its commencement. Dissatisfaction of social and religious conditions had been going on for some time, following a thousand years of servile obedience to authority. During this epoch the uneducated masses, lacking in communications and information beyond their immediate surroundings, accepted conditions just as they found them. In this period of mental inertia, faith and obedience took the place of knowledge and aspiration, but now we have come to the time when the glimmer of a new outlook, a hazy vision of something better, was seen by some whose minds had unfolded sufficiently to enable them to think somewhat differently. Nature, in one of her ruthless moods, caused this change when she forced those she spared to either think or die. Once again she perpetrated a wholesale holocaust which brought death as does a reaper to the standing corn.

The germ of the Black Death, which swept the earth and nearly destroyed the human race, came from the Crimea in a ship to Genoa. Other pestilences of lesser virulence had decimated mankind, but none can be compared with this one which swept from Central Asia westwards over Europe in the 14th century, reaching England in 1348. Upwards of a third of the population of England perished, and throughout Europe the death roll reached 25,000,000, an enormous figure when we consider that the total population in those days did not exceed 100,000,000. The plague spread eastwards as well as westwards, 13,000,000 perishing in China, and it caused such a social upheaval there that the river embankments were neglected, great floods and famine adding to the destruction and misery.

This disease is endemic amongst rodents around the districts north of the Caspian Sea, and mankind now faced either destruction or knowledge. All the faith and prayers, the relics and holy water, could not stay its deadly course. Where filthy and undrained conditions existed its ravages were worst. So the people in the towns and villages suffered severely, as there they had no sanitation. Animals and human beings lived together, the dung-heap was at the door, the streets were narrow, and the stench revolting. Everything, everywhere, was disorganised by this plague, and the scarcity of workers made cultivation impossible. Cattle, pigs and sheep strayed about the countryside, picking up what they could. Foodstuffs, and all kinds of necessities, became unprocurable, and famine followed the plague.

Scarcity of labour made those workers who remained more independent, as they were much in demand and better able to make terms with the landlords. Revolts for better conditions and higher remuneration became common, the people developing a consciousness of the injustice and inequality which prevailed. The towns became a refuge for the serfs who escaped from their masters, and there they found new employment to become free men. Serfdom, which was often little better than slavery, only came to an end slowly in Europe, as it lasted up to the present century, but here we are at the time when some of the peasants began to wonder whether they could not improve their lot in life. Thus gradually, as the result of mental development, and with the help of economic changes, the position of the toilers improved, but this did not come about as the result of religious or political influence, as both Church and State countenanced serfdom to within our own times, Russia being the last to end this system of bondage.

In 1360 the first labour agitator appeared in England, John Ball, preaching Communism, and expressing opinions about the nobles and gentry which Robert Burns put into poetry four hundred years later. Ball explained to the people that without their labour there would be no crops, and that their toil was needed to produce the harvest just as much as land and implements. Five hundred years, however, had to pass before the workers were intelligent enough to think of combining to obtain their rights, and until then their cry was unheeded, all agitators being either imprisoned or executed.

Wat Tyler next led the labour movement in England, but he was assassinated in 1381. A similar movement occurred in France in 1358, and a century later Germany was in the midst of the devastating Peasant Wars. There, religion and social reform combined under a sect called the Anabaptists, who tried to realise the Communism of the early Christians. They proclaimed their objection to infant baptism and their desire to sweep away the existing religious and social order. In their name John of Leyden captured Munster, made himself dictator (1532–1535) and evolved plans to conquer the world. Polygamy was instituted, and for twelve months the city was a scene of unbridled profligacy. After a determined resistance against a besieging force, under the Bishop of Munster, the city finally surrendered, when the bishop tortured the leaders by every conceivable devilish device, executed them, and then hung their mutilated bodies from a church steeple.

᾽ The Church has always demanded implicit obedience and acceptance by the labouring classes of their social conditions, while its priests and the nobles lived in comfort on their toil. The great plague stirred the minds of the masses as never before, because it altered the balance of supply of, and demand for, labour. Now the labourers began to realise the hollowness of the pious platitudes about social inequality being part of the divine order, and, though all attempts by the workers to improve their conditions were met with terrible cruelty and ruthlessness, their minds never returned to the former condition of childlike obedience. Finally they flared up to produce the French Revolution, and from that time onwards a new era opened up for the toiling masses.

Throughout all these centuries of poverty and unrest, millions of people, many with kindly dispositions, were going about their ordinary occupations, honestly producing their daily needs while kings and popes plundered and slaughtered. These peace-loving people were interested only in their work, their homes, their families and their destiny. About the latter they cared much, but knew little, and they eased their doubts by accepting the assurances of the priests that obedience to the Church would secure their salvation.

As mental development slowly proceeded, some were not satisfied with this assurance and began to think for themselves on the deeper problems of life, only to be treated as outcasts by the Church. Torture, death or imprisonment was their punishment, but still others followed who did likewise. All that was now required was some outstanding men to lead these unorthodox thinkers forward into a new religious outlook, and, as the need arose, the leaders duly appeared.

In England the gifted Malvern poet William Langland, in the latter half of the 14th century, wrote a book entitled *Piers the Plowman,* which criticised the Church, its priests and their evil deeds. We will remember reading that the Church in England possessed one third of all the land, on which no taxes were paid, the consequence being that the rest was heavily burdened by not only having to bear its undue proportion of taxation, but also because it had to pay the first tenth of its produce to support the priesthood. For three centuries the Church had flourished in England, following its profitable partnership with William I, when between them they took possession of Saxon England in 1066, and now a few courageous men began to ask what the country was receiving in exchange for all this wealth vested in a corrupt and exclusive institution.

Even more important than those scattered and un-influential criticisms was the Lollard Movement, led by John Wycliffe (1320–1384), a strong-minded out-spoken Yorkshireman, who not only attacked the scandals of the Church but also its claims and doc-trines. He condemned the abominations of the clergy and friars for the misuse they made of the Confession, Pilgrimages, Relic Worship, and the selling of Indulgences for the forgiveness of sin and wickedness, advocating a form of Church government and worship which differed little from that later adopted by the Presbyterians. Wycliffe was an out-standing theologian, being Master of Balliol at Oxford, and he took the line (1) that the Scriptures were the only basis of religious knowledge, (2) that they should be available to the people, (3) that the doctrine of transubstantiation is false, and (4) that the Pope was not the head of the Church.

He translated the Bible into English, and organised preachers to go throughout the country expounding his opinions. Strangely enough, this morning star of the Reformation was allowed to die in peace at Lutter-worth, where he was the parish priest, but later Henry IV, urged on by the priests, passed a statute in 1401 authorising the burning of all heretics, and some of his followers thus became martyrs. On the command of Pope Martin V, Wycliffe's bones were dug up in 1428, and burned so that they would cease to foul holy ground.

No less an influence for reform was John Huss (1369–1415) in Bohemia, where he started a new religious movement after reading the writings of Wycliffe. Here we notice the effect of the University of Prague, in which he held a good position, as better education was making the students think away from orthodox lines, and develop a widespread opposition to Church authority. Consequently his teaching fell upon fertile soil, especially amorgst those students whom he knew personally. He expressed the opinion that the vices of the priests were the curse of the Church, that all had the right to think as their conscience guided them, that transubstantiation is false, and that only the Bible is true.

He was denounced and excommunicated, but given a safe passport to Constance, so that his views could be heard there by a Church council set up by the Emperor Sigismund, for the purpose of bringing unity within the Church. The "safe passport" proved to be but a trap to get him to Constance, as, on arrival, he was put in prison and shockingly treated. Promises to heretics, he was told, were not binding. In 1415 he was burned to death outside the city walls, and the Council next set to work to crush the reform party in Paris University and banish its leader, after which it broke up without seriously considering the ever-growing demand for reform in Church administration and doctrines.

The martyrdom of Huss roused the Czechs to bitter anger against the Church, and it also marked the beginning of five Crusades launched by the Pope against this small but valiant nation. Fighting as a poor and independent small republic, Bohemia not only withstood these attacks but also repulsed one imperial army after another, and then so devastated Germany that His Holiness was forced to cry a halt.

Why was all this bloodshed and devastation

caused? Because the Czechs wished to read the Scriptures, and have the bread and the wine of the Eucharist handed round the congregation and not partaken of only by the officiating priest. When dealing with these old theological problems, the thinking person of today can only feel thankful that education has lifted the curtain of ignorance sufficiently in most lands to enable us now to read freely, to think as we please, and take these ancient mystical ceremonies seriously or not according to our mental development.

What became known as The Four Articles of Prague, published in 1420, also demanded the removal of the temporal power of the Pope, that the clergy be subject to the secular court for the punishment of crime and misdemeanour, and that they return to the simplicity of the Apostles. The reading of the Scriptures, when printing became general, brought all these questions to a head, but, if the reformers had known how much the early Church leaders had tampered with the original Gospels and Epistles, how much they had added to, and deleted from, them, their demands would have been even more far-reaching.

Then the reformers were unaware that Jerome in the 4th century had altered the Gospels and Epistles, to make them correspond with the Paganised Jesuism accepted by the Church authorities in his day, the consequence being that the Reformation made no change in the fundamental Christian beliefs. Unfortunately the fraud and error of the early Christian centuries were unknown in the 15th and 16th centuries. This being so, the Protestants did not go back to the simple beliefs held by the Jesuians of the Apostolic Church before all the Paganism, and its accompanying priestcraft, were introduced into the original Jesuism, to transform it into Christianity. If they had only known enough to model the reformed Church on the simple unitarianism of Apostolic times, what a different story historians would now have to tell! But it was not so, and the mistaken conception of everything connected with our life after death remained, to continue the suffering and misery which always comes from ignorance.

Behind the common programme as set out in the Four Articles of Prague, there were violent and extreme differences of opinion amongst the reformers, such questions as prayers to the Virgin and the saints, laymen and women preaching from the pulpit, and whether there should be a priesthood, finding no unanimous answer. To Pope Martin V all these questions were heretical, and to stamp them out he burned at the stake Jerome of Prague, a colleague of Huss, at the same time issuing a Bull proclaiming a Crusade of destruction by death on all who departed from orthodox tradition.

The intense feeling that the Church was depriving the people of their right to partake in the Eucharist was the pivot round which the reform movement swung, and when John Ziska (1360–1424), a Bohemian nobleman, marched to the municipal offices at Prague in 1419, and butchered the orthodox Catholic burgo-master and his colleagues, the first blow was struck in the twelve years' Hussite War against the Church. Round him gathered an army of religious and racial puritanical fanatics, who denounced every pleasure

and nicety in life. Ziska was a born general, and by
some is considered to be the greatest tactician of the
Middle Ages. Though he quite lost his sight in the
early stages of the war, he was amongst the first to
make full use of artillery, and was victorious in every
battle he fought. With his fanatical disciplined army,
which went into every conflict bearing before it the
sacred chalice and singing their weird battle psalm,
he struck terror into the ranks of his enemies.

In 1424 Ziska died, and this set all Bohemia in
confusion, to be calmed only when a man just as remarkable as the blind general arose to carry on the
conflict. Prokop, a priest, who took no part in the
fighting, organised the Czechs for victory by one
combined offensive effort, and, at the Battle of Tauss
in 1431, inflicted on the Papal army such a defeat that
the Holy See was forced to concede the right of the
new reformed Bohemian Church to take its place
within the Catholic fold. All Europe was made
aware of the victory which had been won, as the propaganda of the reformers was brilliantly carried out,
pamphlets setting forth their case being distributed
far and wide.

The defeat of the omnipotent Christian Church
came as a great shock to Christendom, the more so as
the victors in the full flush of victory destroyed everything held sacred, monasteries, churches and holy relics
being consigned to the flames. Horror-struck at the
sacrilege, Christendom gave no welcome to this new
vandalism, and Bohemia, desolate and impoverished,
was left alone to sink into a bitter civil war which
ended with the moderates victorious in 1434. The
fiery fanaticism, which had made the name of Czech

odious and terrible, passed into history, to add yet another page to the foul and evil deeds done in the name of Christ.

Such, then, was the prologue to the great drama known as the Reformation, a momentous event to which the first chapter in Volume II will give the consideration its importance deserves. Then all Christendom was at war over questions which to the intelligent person of today are purely theological, and lacking in any basis of truth or reason.

The Hussite War was, however, also inspired by something real and enduring, a factor of long standing which we in our time have been unfortunate enough to experience, namely the bitter hatred which exists between the Germanic and Slavonic races. Though primarily it was a religious war, racial antagonism increased its frightfulness, the Germans being intent on destroying the Slavonic Czechs, who, in turn, relished the massacre of the race the Pope had set upon them. For two centuries Bohemia retained its reformed religion, to lose it in 1620 at the Battle of White Mountain. This defeat brought her under Austrian domination and the Roman Catholic yoke, when her people, who did not become orthodox Catholics, were tortured and slaughtered, over 100,000 finding safety in exile, many settling in Britain and Ulster.

Besides being defeated on the field of battle, we now realise how the Papacy never recovered from the shock suffered to its prestige when Philip IV of France forced Clement V in 1305 to leave Rome, and come more directly under his direction at Avignon. From the time of the return of the Holy See to Rome in

1377, the popes claimed as much as ever, but never could they wield the power of Gregory VII or Innocent III.

On the home-coming of the Holy See to Rome "The Great Schism" broke out in 1378, when rival popes were elected amidst great tumult, the reason being the feeling in Italy that an Italian only should be Pope. The Italian, Urban VI, a cruel debased criminal and murderer, was elected. He remained in Rome while Clement VII, a native of Geneva, was later elected by the cardinals to satisfy the French and those who opposed the Italian because of his arrogant wickedness and disreputable methods. These two popes now hurled against each other anathemas and the foulest accusations, Wycliffe describing them as "two dogs snarling over a bone".

Rival popes continued to reign for thirty-eight years, one in Rome and the other in Avignon, each having an army which plundered and massacred without restraint. To heal this sore, which inevitably meant intrigues and European support being divided, great councils of the Church were called. This caused a further weakening in papal authority outside of Italy, as, when the popes now claimed to be the Regent, whenever the throne of the Holy Roman Empire was vacant, the imperial candidates stoutly objected, claiming that their election, and that of their successors, was in the hands of the German princes appointed as Electors, and that Rome had no say in the matter.

What is called the Conciliar Movement had now been in progress for some years, its object being to reform the Church by means of councils whose duty would be the supervision and control of the clergy, and the healing of the Great Schism by electing a pope all would accept. Pisa, Constance and Pavia had been the places where councils had met, to disperse without having accomplished anything of lasting benefit. In 1431 a new Council was summoned to Basel, and, though it continued in existence for eighteen years, its deliberations were thwarted on every occasion by successive pontiffs, until at last (1448) the Emperor Frederick III and Pope Nicholas V fixed everything up at the Concordat of Vienna to their own satisfaction. The arrangement made there was to the effect that the Emperor recognised Nicholas as the only pope, and Rome as the only Holy See, a state of affairs which was to continue as of old without reform, change or control. For this recognition the Emperor received from the Pope certain concessions with regard to episcopal elections, besides a hundred of the most valuable benefices, and a tenth of the monastic revenues within the imperial domains.

This was indeed a triumph for the Papacy; the Great Schism had ended, and no reform had been achieved, Nicholas V (1447–1455) being now recognised as the only reigning pope. Rome was once again the centre of Christendom, and Avignon, having played its ignoble part in the papal drama, now disappears from religious history. The Papacy did not easily adapt itself to the new conditions, as much of the old tradition and loyalty had gone, so much so that a strong feeling of hostility and disgust was expressed by some in Italy who had no wish to see Rome again befouled by priestly rule. So they rose up against Nicholas V, but failed to drive him into exile as they had done to Eugenius IV, his immediate predecessor.

Then followed a reign of terror in the Papal States, all disorder meeting with the harshest treatment, the mercenaries of the Pope slaying, hanging and torturing all who demanded more freedom and greater justice. When this ghastly massacre ended the Papacy again felt secure on its old throne in Rome, the resolution passed at the Council of Florence in 1439 giving it confidence that Rome would never again be questioned as the only place possible for the Holy See, its words being:—

We define the Holy Apostolic See and the Roman pontiff to have primacy over the whole earth, and the Roman pontiff to be himself the successor of the blessed Peter, chief of the Apostles, and the true Vicar of Christ, and to exist as head of the whole Church and father and teacher of all Christians, and that to him, in the blessed Peter, our Lord Jesus Christ has committed full power of feeding, governing and directing the universal Church.

This being so, there were to be no more councils called for the reform of the Church. As the true Vicar of Christ the Pope was above all criticism, and Pius II (1458–1464) consequently issued a Bull which described the formation of councils "as an execrable abuse", all who called such gatherings together being automatically excommunicated. Some, however, still thought and criticised the popes and priests for their wicked lives and erroneous teaching, some rulers even welcoming the holding of councils, if only for the purpose of curtailing the power of the Pope, and stopping the never-ending flow of money to Rome. Only in Italy had the Holy Father the same unquestioned power as of old, and there the Holy See devoted itself to widening its territorial boundaries, amassing wealth, and securing for itself a dominant place amongst the other states in Italy.

The Christian Church since the time it obtained power in the 4th century had always been prepared to further any wickedness provided its interests were thereby advanced. If it were paid enough it would undertake any evil deed, its lucrative ecclesiastical offices being bought at high prices by disreputable characters to whom righteous living was of secondary importance, their aim being power, position and wealth. Those who paid the most received the highest appointments, and, when vacancies occurred in foreign courts, those who paid the best received the support of the Church, this being all that was necessary to obtain preferment or position. Dispensations were sold at high prices; in fact the propagation of supernatural religion was, and still is, a profitable business to the entire priesthood.

From the time of Jerome in the 4th century, luxury, immorality, vice and iniquity of every description sums up the lives of many of the priests, an official report of the 15th century declaring that "Scarcely one priest in every thousand will be found chaste." The monasteries, like the priesthood, were completely corrupt, and the friars were for ever torn by disputes. The divorce between religion and ethics in those days was final and complete, and this continued until the time we now call the Reformation, a momentous event which somewhat altered the religious beliefs of half of Europe, but had little or no effect on the ethical conduct of the people.

Religion continued, as heretofore, to be the only remedy for all the troubles of mankind, theological beliefs and not conduct being the standard. The evil effect of this teaching is now becoming realised in our own time amongst intelligent people, although the devout still retain the belief that the acceptance of the creeds, dogmas and doctrines of the Church are necessary for salvation. Only when this false teaching is finally removed, and in its place is put a high standard of conduct, will a firm foundation be laid for the better world we all hope will be the heritage of those who come after us.

So far religion and conduct have been interlocked, belief securing salvation irrespective of the life lived. Now the well informed know that just as we sow here we reap hereafter. Now they know that selfishness is the cause of most of the world's troubles, and that only by improving our ethical conduct can we have peace, prosperity and happiness. Now they know that our life after death will be spent in a natural world like this one, in company with men and women who once lived on earth. Now they know that all the tragedies which accompanied supernatural religion came from error due to ignorance, its gods, saints, angels and devils being the product of theological imagination. Now the well informed know that whenever we go off the road of truth disaster follows, and that only through righteousness, knowledge and wisdom can this world become a fit place in which to live.

These truisms were, however, not appreciated at the time we have now reached in our history of mankind, the consequence being that disaster still pursued ignorant stupid humanity right on to our own time. This volume has been entirely concerned with the Theological Age, and only when we come to the end of Volume II will we emerge somewhat from its deadening influence, though its evil effects are still with us. So let us proceed, and always keep in mind the story so far recorded, as it forms the background of much we have still to read. In the next chapter we are at the beginning of a new age, when developing mind gradually frees itself from the shackles of theology to produce the environment in which we live today.

END OF VOLUME I.

CONTENTS

SECOND VOLUME

CHAPTER XII.
CHRISTIAN CIVILISATION (1377-1610).

Introduction—The Catholic Church splits in two—England suffers from a long and savage Civil War—Britain during the Reformation—The Effect of the Apostolic Church on the Reformation—Britain and Ireland after the Reformation.

CHAPTER XIII.
CHRISTIAN CIVILISATION (1513-1796).

Introduction—Germany is devastated for Thirty Years—France becomes the Dominant Power in Europe—Parliament gradually replaces Absolute Monarchy in Britain—Spain Falls from her high position—Russia becomes a Great Nation.

CHAPTER XIV.
CHRISTIAN CIVILISATION (1611-1802).

Introduction—Prussia becomes a Great Power—Injustice in France prepares the way for Revolution—The Old Order in France is Overthrown—Britain is Ruled by her First Prime Minister—The British Empire grows in size and power—Britain experiences her greatest humiliation—The first comprehensive Social Welfare Scheme.

CHAPTER XV.
CHRISTIAN CIVILISATION (1780-1858).

Introduction—Science and Invention increase Wealth, Trade and Industry—Pioneers of Modern Literature, Music and Art—The Rise and Fall of Napoleon Bonaparte—Tyranny and Injustice cause Revolution in Europe—Independent Republics arise in America—The United States grows rich on Slave Labour—Sordid Social Conditions in Britain cause Unrest—Social Reform in Britain while her Empire expands.

CHAPTER XVI.
CHRISTIAN CIVILISATION (1791-1901).

Introduction—A Revolution in Thought ushers in a New Era for Mankind—France under the Rule of Napoleon III—Italy

At a time when newspapers and periodicals were greatly reduced in size, because of the shortage of newsprint after the Second World War, and few were publishing reviews, "The Curse of Ignorance" received considerable prominence. The following are extracts from some of the many reviews it received.

"Mr. Arthur Findlay spared no trouble to make his history accurate. Into his narrative, ranging from primitive times to the end of the Second World War, he has packed a life-time of learning. To this wealth of knowledge he gave the title *The Curse of Ignorance*, because this was a history with a purpose, a monumental work, a monument, in fact, to mankind's folly—and mankind's hope."—*Daily Mail*.

"Arthur Findlay's *The Curse of Ignorance* is monumental in that it ranks him as a first-class historian, to be compared with Gibbon and other great writers. In one respect it puts him ahead of them—his lucidity. He not only gives a more enlightened interpretation of the past, but deals excellently with modern events and trends. If you will get these two volumes and spend delightful hours absorbing them, you will have promoted yourself to the level of a well-informed person, and will consider them worth many times their price."—*Educational Guide*.

"Mr. Arthur Findlay, who ranks among the leading historians of our day, has now given us *The Curse of Ignorance*, a lucid history of mankind from primitive times to the end of the Second World War—a truly monumental task. Throughout this competent and very readable work he strives, in vividly written pages, to show how ignorance and selfishness have led to wars, resulting in untold misery. All will agree with him as to the need for increased knowledge and an advance in our ethical standards."—*Staffordshire Advertiser*.

"Mr. Findlay is a brilliantly clever man and a most able advocate. . . . There is a tremendous amount of good, solid and dexterous historical analysis in his stupendous world history."—*Essex Chronicle*.

"Mr. Arthur Findlay (for many years a magistrate of Ayrshire and Essex, and a partner in one of the leading firms of Chartered Accountants and Stockbrokers in Glasgow; Chairman of several companies; a member of the Order of the British Empire and who farms 400 acres of his estate in Essex) writes history with a skilful pen, and tells his story in a way that both fascinates and captivates the reader. *The Curse of Ignorance* is destined to make its mark in historical literature and will undoubtedly become a classic."—*Psychic News*.

"*The Curse of Ignorance* is a very remarkable book. Mr. Arthur Findlay gave seven years' devoted labour, six hours a day, every day of the week, to writing this compendious history of mankind."—*Liverpool Daily Post*.

"Mr. Arthur Findlay has given us a compendious and most lucid work. Any writer who can creditably complete such a task has achieved no mean feat, and this Mr. Findlay has certainly performed. We cannot withhold a feeling of gratitude from a writer who has the monumental energy to give us 2,328 vivid pages marked by almost Gibbonian role but less verbosity. Here we have history of quality."— *Wolverhampton Express and Star*.

"The author is well known all over the world for his books on psychic phenomena, and this his latest work—a fascinating record of human activity throughout the ages— deals with the history of the human race from the psychic aspect. This book is a work of erudition and a mine of historical information and fact, written in a clear and lucid style. It is of absorbing interest. I recommend it to all thinking men and women, as much can be learned from a perusal of its pages. Its two volumes will be an asset to the home library."—*Essex County Telegraph*.

"This massive work is history presented from a new and wider aspect, and this more modern approach clarifies the many difficulties with which historians have been faced in the past. It is certainly a stimulating and thought-provoking analysis of the development of mankind, written from the psychic angle of thought."—*Northampton Chronicle.*

"Mr. Findlay, in telling mankind's story—religious, political and social—from primitive times to the present day, has addressed himself to this important problem with great knowledge, discernment, wisdom and a conviction born of unquestionable sincerity."—*Cambridge Daily News.*

"The condensation, even in two such large books, of this vast subject is in itself a commendable feat, but even more interesting than the author's summarizing of historical events is the angle from which he approaches them."—*Leicester Mail.*

"The deep wide sweep of his human survey gives the book, which is profound and sincere, a strong general appeal, and enables the author to bring out, time and time again, his main theme that ignorance is the root of most evil and unhappiness, particularly so in the case of war."
—*Carlisle Journal.*

"This is a history, a labour of love, written with a purpose. These two volumes may well find a place on the busy man's bookshelves, for they afford an opportunity for the easy study of the history of the world in the light of current events. They avoid religious prejudice which has so often represented the Christian era in a too favourable light."—*Stock Exchange Gazette.*

"These two stupendous volumes bridge the whole history of mankind on this earth. The contribution of the Hebrew, Greek, Roman and Christian civilizations is most carefully assessed. To say that *The Curse of Ignorance* will stimulate thought and provoke discussion is a gross under-statement."—*Head Teachers' Review.*

"Here are two volumes, a veritable cyclopaedia of world history, a perfect library of themselves. Mr. Findlay has written a challenging and widely informative book for which we cannot but be grateful."—*Paisley Express.*

"Arthur Findlay marshalls facts clearly and vigorously in his two-volume world history."—*Northern Echo*.

"In this history of mankind the past follies of the race are recorded with painstaking research."—*Newcastle Journal*.

"Mr. Findlay has accomplished his task with outstanding success, and his work will live in the annals of history as one of the greatest contributions to our literature."—*The Two Worlds*.

"*The Curse of Ignorance* appeals to the mind that is seeking, not for theological inexactitudes, but for a reasoned scientific formula of life . . . it is a book far more formidable and imposing than his previous works, both in size and content."—*Hertfordshire Mercury*.

"*The Curse of Ignorance* has been a labour of years and a labour of love, a vast monument of industry. None can deny that if we were to follow its positive principles the sword might be sheathed in England's green and pleasant land."—*Belfast Northern Whig*.

" Mr. Findlay's new book is a monumental work. Those who come to this book with open minds will find a light shone into many dark places."—*Kilmarnock Standard*.

"The author has accomplished a tremendous task and makes his plea with lucidity and skill. He is fearless in his exposition. On the historical side it is obvious there has been much research work."—*Public Opinion*.

"Mr. Findlay, in interesting and readable style, shows how so often the folly of ignoring events of the past has brought tragedy and misery to countless numbers of the human race. His work will repay most careful study and thought."—*Essex Weekly News*.

" Mr. Arthur Findlay has written a truly monumental history of mankind. Taking the widest sweep as a world citizen he traces the long story of man's upward climb and spot lights the mistakes that led to oppression and war through ignorance."— *East Anglican Daily Times*.